PUBLIC POLICY
Goals, Means, and Methods

PUBLIC POLICY

Goals, Means, and Methods

STUART S. NAGEL
University of Illinois

ST. MARTIN'S PRESS   NEW YORK

Library of Congress Catalog Card Number: 83-61613

Manufactured in the United States of America
87654
fedcba

For information, write St. Martin's Press, Inc.,
175 Fifth Avenue, New York, N.Y. 10010

cover design: Darby Downey

ISBN: 0-312-65558-4

Dedicated to Brenda and Robert
for taking the relay baton
of social service
and public interest law

PREFACE

The purpose of *Public Policy: Goals, Means, and Methods* is to unite numerous ideas that were developed over a number of years regarding public policy analysis. In analyzing public policy from an evaluation perspective, it is necessary to have in mind: (1) a goal or goals that one is seeking to achieve, (2) proposed means for achieving those goals, and (3) methods for analyzing the extent to which the proposed means achieve the goals and for deciding what to do with that information. Public policy analysis may be logically divided into three parts corresponding to goals, means, and methods, and that is how this book is basically organized.

The first part of the book deals with basic concepts in public policy analysis. The second part covers the general goals with which policy analysts are likely to be concerned, such as efficiency, effectiveness, equality, freedom, and fair procedure. The third part discusses general means for achieving those kinds of goals, such as using positive and negative incentives, decreasing discretionary abuses while preserving flexibility, balancing public and private sector implementation, and structuring government for greater goal achievement. The fourth part provides the methods for determining relations between means and goals, and for deciding which means or combination of means to adopt. The fifth part presents the public policy profession as a career for undergraduate students, graduate students, practitioners, and others.

The framework of goals, means, and methods may seem to correspond to substance, process, and techniques. But substance tends to emphasize specific policy problems like agriculture, crime, defense, economic regulation, education, energy, environment, foreign policy, health, housing, labor, minorities, population, poverty, science policy, and transportation. Goals, on the other hand, cut across specific policy problems, and include effectiveness, efficiency, equity, public participation, predictability, and procedural fairness. Similarly, process emphasizes the movement of a problem from the agenda-setting stage through the formation of a policy and on to its implementation. Discussion of the means for achieving given goals tends to be less descriptive than that and is oriented more toward improving the process, focusing on cross-cutting issues such as incentives, discretionary abuses, public versus private sector implementation, and structuring government for greater goal achievement. Techniques frequently deal with low-level matters such as the appropriate measures of statistical significance, correlation, measurement, and other aspects of developing specific research designs. Here the concern for methods is on a higher level of generality and emphasizes the deducing of policy change effects, the optimizing of alternative public policies, the simplifying of statistical analysis and decision science in light of nonmonetary and unknown variables, and the importance of an interdisciplinary perspective.

I am grateful to a number of former and present graduate students with whom I have worked in developing some of the chapters. They include Marian Neef (who helped develop Chapters 7 and 11), Robert Geraci and Kathleen Levy (who participated in the development of Chapter 8), and Bradley Malis, who helped develop many chapters in his role as research assistant. The following reviewers also made helpful suggestions: Dennis C. Pirages, University of Maryland; Robert T. Nakamura, Dartmouth College; Walter Rosenbaum, University of Florida; Jay A. Sigler, Rutgers University, Camden College of Arts and Sciences; Jeffrey R. Orenstein, Kent State University; William N. Dunn, Graduate School of Public and International Affairs, University of Pittsburgh. Thanks are also owed to various funding sources which helped cover the cost of data gathering, data processing, and manuscript drafting, such as the Public Policy Committee of the Ford Foundation, the National Institute of Justice, the Illinois Law Enforcement Commission, and the University of Illinois Research Board. Thanks are further owed to the people I have worked with over the years in drafting this book and related materials, such as Judy Conover, Kay Matthews, Charlotte Proemmel, Alexis Smith, Karen Vaughn, and Julienne Wade. Credit is especially given to Joyce Nagel, who has been helpful in numerous ways on this book and other previous books and articles, starting with the November 1957 issue of the *Northwestern Law Review*.

My hope is that future work may develop more applications of policy analysis methods to determine relations between means and goals. These applications are likely to result in improvements in methods, means, and goals to the benefit of the public policy field and society in general.

Stuart S. Nagel

SUMMARY
OF
CONTENTS

ix

CONTENTS

PUBLIC POLICY
Goals, Means, and Methods

PART ONE

General Matters

Part I discusses basic concepts in public policy analysis and indicates the sources of goals, policies, and relations between the policies and the goals. This discussion involves such basic concepts as:

1. *Public policy:* governmental decisions designed to deal with various matters such as those related to foreign policy, environmental protection, crime, unemployment, and numerous other social problems.
2. *Public policy analysis:* the determination of which of various alternative policies, decisions, or means are best for achieving a given set of goals in light of the relations between the alternative policies and the goals.
3. *Goals:* the objectives or criteria which a public policy is directed toward achieving.
4. *Means:* types of public policies which are means toward achieving societal goals.
5. *Methods:* the techniques or procedures for either (a) determining the relations between policies and goals or (b) drawing conclusions from goals, alternative policies, and relations, in regard to which policy or combination of policies is best under given constraints and conditions. It also refers to procedures for clarifying and measuring goals and policies.
6. *Relations:* the extent to which an increase in a policy results in an increase or a decrease in a goal, or the extent to which the presence of a policy results in the presence or absence of a goal.
7. *Public policy profession:* the combination of individuals, training programs, research centers, associations, journals, ethical codes, job opportunities, and other institutions involved in public policy analysis.

8. *Sources:* the origins of goals, policies, and relations, including (a) authority, (b) statistical and observational analysis, (c) deduction, and (d) sensitivity and guessing analysis.
9. *Authority:* persons, books, articles, or other entities that are considered reasonably reliable sources of information on the relevant goals, policies, or relations.
10. *Statistical or observational analysis:* the analyzing of specific instances in order to generalize what the goals, policies, or relations might be.
11. *Deduction:* the drawing of a conclusion from premises that have been established from authority, observation, and/or intuition.
12. *Sensitivity analysis:* the guessing of goals, policies, or relations, and the determination of what effect, if any, the guessed values have on the final decision regarding which policy is best.

CHAPTER 1

Basic Concepts in Public Policy Analysis

Chapter 1 provides a preview of the whole book. Like the book, it is organized in terms of fundamental ideas, public policy goals, means for achieving goals, methods of evaluation, and the public policy profession.

Fundamental Ideas

Public policy refers to governmental decisions designed to deal with various social problems, such as those related to foreign policy, environmental protection, crime, unemployment, and numerous other social problems. Public policy analysis generally refers to the determination of which of various alternative policies, decisions, or means are best for achieving a given set of goals in light of the relations between the alternative policies and the goals. In this context, *methods* refers to methods used in determining those relations and in drawing a conclusion as to which policy or combination of policies is best. This book discusses goals, policies, and relations on a general enough level so that the reader can apply the discussion to a great variety of policy problems. The discussion, however, involves numerous examples in order to make the general principles more concrete.[1]

In addition to an optimizing or prescriptive emphasis, policy analysis can also include the study of the nature of public policies. This approach divides the subject matter into foreign policy, environmental protection, crime, and so on, rather than into goals, means, and methods. Policy analysis can also include the study of the policy process. This approach usually divides the subject matter into stages, such as agenda setting, adoption, implementation, evaluation, and termination of policies. These are important subjects in political science and American government. Their importance is recognized throughout this book, especially in the section on means for achieving goals. The emphasis here, however, is on policy analysis as a subject more distinct than both the traditional political science emphasis on the political process and a quickly obsolete discussion of current events.[2]

When policy analysis is defined in terms of goals, policies, and relations, a question that is often raised is, Where do the goals, policies, and relations come from? The answer is in terms of four sources which are not mutually exclusive:

1. authority, or consulting one or more persons, books, articles, or other sources that are considered reliable.
2. statistical or observational analysis, or analyzing specific instances in order to generalize about what the goals, policies, or relations might be.
3. deduction, or drawing a conclusion from premises that have been established from authority, observation, and/or intuition.
4. sensitivity analysis, or guessing the goals, policies, or relations, and then determining what effect, if any, the guessed values have on the final decision regarding which policy is best.

These concepts are discussed in further detail in Chapter 2.

Some people object to the possibility of systematic policy analysis because it requires a degree of rationality which is impossible to achieve. The concept of rationality can be defined in three ways. *Rationality of intentions* refers to people trying to maximize benefits minus costs in whatever they do. This is a tautology, or an occurrence that is true by definition. *Benefits minus costs* is a synonym for net satisfaction, and *net satisfaction* refers in a circular way to that which people are trying to maximize. Although this kind of rationality is present by definition, it is still a useful concept in providing an initial premise at a high level of generality for many examples of policy analysis.

Rationality of consequences refers to being successful in maximizing benefits minus costs in reaching decisions. There are two reasons why it is not always possible to do this. One is that although often little information is needed to make optimizing decisions, sometimes even a minimum amount of accurate information is lacking with regard to goals, policies, and/or relations. The other is that many policy decisions are based on probabilities or averages that may not be present in a given situation. For example, a decision maker may go ahead with a project because it truly has a 0.90 probability of success. The decision maker, however, may be unlucky enough to hit that one-in-ten case in which the project fails, and he or she may not get ten chances or even one more chance to come out ahead.

The third sense in which rationality is used, which is what this book is all about, is *rationality of procedures*. It refers to developing a set of procedures that will maximize benefits minus costs if one has adequate information and average luck. These procedures in turn refer to such methods as (1) benefit-cost analysis, or choosing among discrete alternatives; (2) decision theory, or making decisions under conditions of risk; (3) optimum level analysis, or reaching decisions where doing too much or too little is undesirable; and (4) allocation theory, or deciding on an optimum mix of resources among activities, places, persons, or other entities. These concepts will be further clarified throughout the book, especially in the section on methods of evaluation.

Public Policy Goals

As for policy analysis goals, Chapter 3 deals with the relative importance of such basic concepts as efficiency (or benefits/costs); profitability (benefits minus costs); effectiveness (benefits regardless of costs); equity (the distribution of benefits or costs); detriments (negative social indicators like crime); and marginal rate of return (change-in-benefits/change-in-costs). Seeking to clarify these basic concepts raises some interesting questions. For example:

1. Which is better, a good benefit/cost ratio or a good benefits-costs difference?
2. Which is better, a one-unit increase in efficiency or a one-unit increase in effectiveness?
3. Which is more efficient, a city with 100 crimes and $50 in anticrime expenditures, or a city with 200 crimes and $25 in anticrime expenditures?
4. Which is better, a project with a good benefit/cost ratio, or a project with a good ratio of change-in-benefits to change-in-costs?

Chapter 4 goes into further detail on the matter of equity as a policy goal. It defines equity in terms of providing people, groups, and places with a minimum level of income, education, freedom from crime, or other things of value which a government or society can allocate. It is also concerned with measuring degrees of equity or inequity, using equity as a criterion for choosing among policies, and the problems of trade-offs between equity and other goals, such as efficiency or freedom.

Chapter 5 deals with supplementing the basic substantive goals with process goals. These emphasize public participation, predictability of decisions, and procedures that facilitate proving one is deserving of benefits or innocent of wrongdoing. These goals are referred to as the three *P*s—participation, predictability, and procedure. They are especially associated with political science in contrast to the three *E*s—effectiveness, efficiency, and equity—which are especially associated with economics. These process matters may often be goals in themselves; for example, society and policy makers are often willing to sacrifice some effectiveness, efficiency, and equity in order to provide for more participation, predictability, and procedural due process as ends in themselves. In this context, *equity* and *equality* are nearly synonyms, and *productivity* can refer to either effectiveness or efficiency. Likewise, *public participation* is a synonym for democracy or political freedom, which includes both majority rule and the right of minorities to try to convert the majority.

Chapter 6 emphasizes how goals of freedom of speech and religion, equality of treatment, fair criminal procedure, and basic economic security can be justified in terms of their social consequences. These consequences include higher standards of living, psychological well-being, and both effectiveness and efficiency in achieving general societal goals. The chapter also emphasizes that freedom can help secure equality for individuals who might otherwise be deprived, and that a satisfactory level of equality tends to generate an atmosphere that allows more freedom. Particularly important is the idea of justifying minority rights that relate to political freedom, equity, and fair procedure in terms of how they benefit the majority and the total society.[3]

Means for Achieving Goals

As for policy-analysis means, Part III is divided into four chapters. All four chapters discuss fundamental issues that relate to goal-achieving means. These issues consist of:

1. using positive and negative incentives.
2. decreasing discretionary abuses while preserving flexibility.
3. balancing public and private sector implementation.
4. structuring government for greater goal achievement.

This part of the book, like the goals part, is broadly applicable. We are not, for example, specifically interested in whether the energy shortage might be resolved better by emphasizing nuclear or solar energy. We are, however, concerned with the general problem of providing incentives, including incentives for encouraging energy conservation and innovation. We are also concerned with decreasing the abuses of discretionary power (including the power of energy regulators) by providing clear guidelines or other controls. In addition, we are concerned with the controversy of public versus private ownership, both in the energy field and in other fields. Likewise, energy policy is influenced by basic government structures, but so are all policy problems. There is less general agreement on goal-achieving means than on the goals themselves, but all four of the means chapters try to find aspects of the opposing arguments in which a compromise or agreement is more likely to be found. *Goal-achieving means* refers to both formation and implementation of policy, but with an emphasis on implementation.

An important means issue is the use of positive and negative incentives in order to encourage socially desired behavior, especially behavior that will increase societal productivity. In recent years there has been an increasing advocacy of the use of positive incentives. For example, liberals advocate decreasing criminal behavior by providing would-be burglars and muggers with the incentive of legitimate job opportunities. Such positive incentives probably keep middle-class people from committing crimes more than does the fear of serving time in jail. Likewise, conservatives recommend a system that provides business firms with tax incentives in order to encourage greater productivity and the hiring of unemployed minority workers, rather than a system that orders business firms to comply with various regulations. Both groups recognize that society probably can get better compliance through rewards than punishments.

When it comes to discretionary abuses, one often thinks of decision makers who have wide discretion for holding arrested persons in jail pending trial, or for holding defendants in prison after conviction. Both liberals and conservatives agree that such discretion is often abused and should be subjected to more effective control, although not necessarily for the same reasons. Liberals tend to believe that pretrial decision making results in too many people being held in jail, contrary to the presumption of innocence. Conservatives tend to think pretrial decision making results in too few people being held in jail, contrary to the desire to prevent crimes by those who are out on bail. When it comes to sentencing, liberals want the discretion of judges and parole boards decreased, because they believe the discretion is used discriminatorily. Conservatives often want to decrease such discretion, because they find it is used too leniently.

A controversial implementation issue is the extent to which various societal functions should be carried out by government or by private enterprise. Both sides, operating in a democratic context, tend to agree on such goals as the need for achieving more gross national product, freedom and popular control, opportunity, and security and initiative. However, they generally disagree on whether the public sector or the private sector is more capable of achieving these goals. The degree of disagreement may be lessening, however, as socialist advocates recognize the value of using the marketplace to aid in determining prices and production quantities, and the value of competitive income incentives to stimulate productivity and innovation. Likewise, the capitalist advocates recognize increasingly the value of more national economic planning, especially in dealing with inflation and unemployment and with taxation and subsidy incentives for productivity and innovation. There may be a trend toward more responsiveness of the economy to consumers and workers, regardless of whether the government-economy relation is socialistic or capitalistic.

How to structure government for greater goal achievement raises a particularly important set of issues for political science. These issues relate to fundamental governmental structures in terms of the relations between:

1. the national government and the states and provinces.
2. the chief executive and the legislature.
3. the courts as constitutional guardians and the executive-legislative branches of government.
4. the political parties vis-à-vis each other.
5. the government and the people in terms of majority rule and minority rights to try to convert the majority.

Among political and social scientists, there is increasing concern about how these structural issues relate to societal productivity. There is an increasing trend toward giving more power to the national government and the executive branch to cope with policy problems. At the same time, the courts have imposed new constraints on civil liberties, and have expanded majority rule by widening the franchise. Structural issues tend to be influenced by who is occupying the structure, but there is underlying agreement on many aspects of these issues among both liberals and conservatives.[4]

Methods of Evaluation

As for policy analysis methods, Part IV is divided into three sections. The first deals with two specific methods. One has to do with establishing relations between means or policies on the one hand and goals on the other. The other is concerned with using these relations as inputs into an analysis that begins with some normative premises about goals to be achieved and finishes with a prescription for action. Establishing relations between policies and goals can be done through deductive reasoning or through statistical induction. Deductive reasoning in this context may involve drawing upon an understanding of how decision making occurs within groups, between individuals, or by individuals. Prescriptive methodology (in contrast to causal or predictive analysis) may involve: (1) determining an optimum choice among discrete alternatives with or without contingent probabilities; (2) determining an optimum policy level where doing too much or too little is undesirable; or (3) determining an optimum mix across activities or places. Here we are more concerned with methods in the abstract than with applications of the methods (which is more of a concern in Part III, "Means for Achieving Goals").

The second methods section deals with simplifying procedures. This book takes a stand in favor of simplicity in measuring and weighting goals and policies and in relating policies to goals, especially in causal relations. Simplicity in these contexts may mean working with dichotomous policies or goals, using relative rather than absolute values, drawing small purposive samples, expressing relations in terms of direction without necessarily being precise on magnitude, and using introspective interviewing to obtain information on relations and values. Simplifying procedures is especially important in working with nonmonetary variables, in contrast to the more complex approach of trying to monetize these variables. Simplifying procedures in that context means handling nonmonetary variables mainly by converting the decisions into questions as to whether a given nonmonetary return is worth more or less than a given dollar cost, even though we do not know how many dollars the nonmonetary return is worth. Simplifying procedures is also important in working with unknown variables or missing information in contrast to the more complex approach of trying to find the missing information. Simplifying procedures in that context means handling unknown variables mainly by converting the decisions into questions as to whether a given benefit, cost, or success probability is more or less than a given figure, where that figure is the threshold above which the proposed project would be relatively profitable and below which it would be relatively unprofitable. The type of policy evaluation that especially needs simplifying is evaluation involving many goals (at least some of which are nonmonetary) and many policies. Chapter 16, "Multiple Goals and Policies," is especially oriented toward that problem. It discusses how simple percentages can be used to obtain many insights for deciding among mutually exclusive projects, combinations of policies, rank orders, or optimum mixes of resources among the policies. Three key objections to the possibility of doing systematic policy evaluation are (1) the subjectivity of working with nonmonetary variables, (2) missing information, and (3) the multiplicity of goals and policies. Those three objections are dealt with in Chapters 14 through 16.

The third section of Part IV deals with interdisciplinary perspectives including statistics, political science, economics, and sociology-psychology. As for statistical analysis, that methodology is especially useful for empirically validating the premises in deductive causal models. This applies to both the normative premises about the goals and the empirical premises about the relations between means and goals. Statistical analysis can include interviews with relevant people and correlation-regression analysis of available data. There is a need for a variety of disciplinary orientations in policy evaluation, including a political science emphasis on political and administrative feasibility, a sociological-psychological emphasis on using the pretest-posttest, experimental-control approach to analysis, and an economics emphasis on benefit-cost analysis.[5]

The Public Policy Profession

Part V is divided into three chapters dealing with the public policy profession. It attempts to explain how an analysis of public policy goals, means, and methods can be put together as a professional career activity. Chapter 18 is concerned with resolving ethical dilemmas that policy analysts or evaluators often face. Openness is important in the handling of such dilemmas, as is the need for the evaluators to take an affirmative position on such matters as optimizing, sensitivity analysis, representing special interests, unforeseen consequences, equity, research-cost saving, data sharing, research validity, and not putting people at undue risk.

Chapter 19 discusses the placing of political and social scientists in government positions, and getting political and social science used in government. Placement and utilization are improving as social scientists develop and apply more policy-relevant skills. These skills include methods for relating policies to goals and for recommending choices in light of those relations. They also encompass a creative ability to suggest policies or means for achieving goals, and a sensitivity about which goals are worth achieving. Chapter 19 is also concerned with factors that facilitate the utilization of policy evaluation research and discusses 13 factors relevant to research utilization by legislative, judicial, and administrative policy makers. These factors relate to opposition-support, policy goals, policy effects, efficient cost-saving, and communication methods. Each factor is illustrated by one or more successful or unsuccessful case studies.[6]

Uses of Public Policy Evaluation

Policy evaluation models that work with goals, policies, relations, and conclusions have four general uses: making decisions, influencing decisions, predicting decisions, and measuring decisional propensities.

For *making* decisions, the basic approach is: .

1. Determine the goals, policies, and relations between the goals and policies. In benefit-cost terms, this means determine the benefits and costs for each policy. The benefits and costs are the goals that are to be increased and decreased, respectively. The quantity of benefits or costs which a policy is predicted to achieve is a measure of the relations between the policies and the goals.
2. Draw a conclusion from this input data as to which policy or combination of policies should be adopted or decided upon for maximizing the goals or for maximizing benefits minus costs. This is the use emphasized in this book, with examples especially present in Chapter 12, "Optimum Choice, Risk, Level, Mix, and Timing."

For *influencing* decisions, the basic approach is:

1. Start out with a decision that is considered socially desirable or desirable from the perspective of whoever is seeking to influence decisions. This desired decision can be considered as the rightdoing decision, and its opposite is the wrongdoing decision.
2. Seek to change the reality and the perceptions of the benefits and the costs in order to encourage more rightdoing. This means drawing conclusions about how to increase the benefits of rightdoing, decrease the costs of rightdoing, increase the costs of wrongdoing, decrease the benefits of wrongdoing, and/or increase the probability that the benefits and costs will be received. The section on "Encouraging Socially Desired Behavior" in Chapter 7 provides concrete examples.

For *predicting* decisions, the basic approach is:

1. Determine what the relevant decision makers consider the benefits and costs to be, in contrast to what they might actually be. Also, determine how these input benefits and costs might change.
2. Draw conclusions about how the output decisions are likely to change in light of various changes in the benefits and costs of the alternative course of action, policies, or decisions. The section on "Deductions Based on a Bilateral Decision-Making Model" in Chapter 11 provides a concrete example.

For *measuring* decisional propensities, the basic approach is:

1. Determine a model that relates decisional outcomes to the perception of the benefits and costs of alternative courses of action. Ask people whose decisional propensities are being measured how they assess the various benefits and costs; do not ask them directly about their decisional propensities.
2. From data provided by their answers and from the model that relates decisions to benefits and costs, draw a conclusion about the decisional propensities of these individuals. The conclusion can be expressed in the form of a threshold probability above which they are likely to decide in one direction and below which they are likely to decide in the opposite direction. The conclusion might also be expressed in the form of a threshold benefit/cost ratio in which the questions deal mainly with perceptions about certain facts occurring, rather than with questions asking about values. The section on "Determining an Optimum Policy Choice" in Chapter 11 provides a concrete example.

All four of the preceding uses relate to improving public policy and to obtaining a better causal understanding of public policy matters. Public policy is clearly improved if (1) decisions can become more effective and efficient, (2) socially desired behavior can be better encouraged, (3) decisions of people can be better predicted so we can plan accordingly, and (4) decisional propensities, perceptions, and values can be better measured for testing various proposals. Causal understanding is also a part of all four uses because (1) in order to make more effective decisions, one is stimulated to learn more about cause-and-effect relations between policies and goals; (2) in order to more effectively influence decisions, one is stimulated to learn more about causal relations between changed behavior and changing the benefits and costs; (3) predicting decisions generally involves knowing about causal relations; and (4) an indirect propensity-measuring model is in effect a causal-predictive model.

Policy evaluation uses can also be classified in a variety of other ways, such as (1) explicit or implicit; (2) legislative, judicial, or administrative; (3) present or future; (4) reinforcing or mind-changing; (5) international, national, state, or local; (6) by subject matter, such as defense, energy, or education; and (7) public sector, private sector, nonprofit sector, or personal. Chapter 19, "Research Utilization," is especially concerned with factors that influence the adoption of policy evaluation findings in the decision making of policy makers. Utilization is important in policy evaluation in view of its practical orientation, but just as important is the concern of policy evaluation for seeking to achieve worthwhile public policy *goals*, using effective and efficient *means* for achieving these goals, and using effective and efficient *methods* for evaluating the alternative means. These concerns for goals, means, and methods are the essence of this book.

NOTES

---

1. On basic concepts in public policy analysis, see William Dunn, *Public Policy Analysis: An Introduction* (Prentice-Hall, 1981); Phillip Gregg (ed.), *Problems of Theory in Policy Analysis* (Lexington-Heath, 1976); and Austin Ranney (ed.), *Political Science and Public Policy* (Markham, 1968).
2. On the analysis of specific public policies, see Theodore Lowi and Alan Stone (eds.), *Nationalizing Government: Public Policies in America* (Sage, 1978); Clarke Cochran, et al., *American Public Policy: An Introduction* (St. Martin's Press, 1982); and S. Nagel (ed.), *Encyclopedia of Policy Studies* (Marcel Dekker, 1983). On a process approach to public policy, see James Anderson, *Public Policy-Making* (Holt, Rinehart & Winston, 1979); Charles Jones, *An Introduction to the Study of Public Policy* (Duxbury, 1977); and Garry Brewer and Peter deLeon, *The Foundations of Policy Analysis* (Dorsey, 1983).
3. On public policy goals, see Fred M. Frohock, *Public Policy: Scope and Logic* (Prentice-Hall, 1979); William Dunn (ed.), *Values, Ethics, and the Practice of Policy Analysis* (Lexington-Heath, 1983); and Frank Fischer, *Politics, Values, and Public Policy* (Westview, 1980).
4. On general means for achieving policy goals, see Robert Dahl and Charles Lindblom, *Politics, Economics, and Welfare* (Harper, 1953); Robert MacIver, *The Web of Government* (Macmillan, 1951); and Lawrence Friedman, *The Legal System: A Social Science Perspective* (Russell Sage, 1975).
5. On general methods of policy evaluation, see Duncan MacRae and James Wilde, *Policy Analysis for Public Decisions* (Duxbury, 1979); Edward Quade, *Analysis for Public Decisions* (North Holland, 1982); and S. Nagel, *Policy Evaluation: Making Optimum Decisions* (Praeger, 1982).
6. On the public policy profession, see Harold Lasswell, *A Pre-View of Policy Sciences* (Elsevier, 1971); Yehezkel Dror, *Design for Policy Sciences* (Elsevier, 1971); and S. Nagel, *The Policy-Studies Handbook* (Lexington-Heath, 1980).

QUESTIONS

The following questions are designed to obtain your initial reaction to various concepts. You are not expected to discuss them in depth at this point in your reading.

1. Define *public policy*, *public policy analysis*, a *prescriptive or optimizing approach to public policy*, a *substantive approach*, and a *process approach*.
2. With simple examples, explain *rationality of intentions, rationality of consequences*, and *rationality of procedures*.
3. Discuss briefly the similarities and differences between such basic goal concepts as *effectiveness, efficiency, equity, public participation, predictability*, and *procedural due process*.
4. Discuss briefly the consequences of a nation scoring high or low on such basic policy goals as *freedom of speech* (closely related to public participation); *equality of treatment* (closely related to equity);

safeguarding the innocent from conviction and harassment (closely related to procedural due process); and the *right to basic economic security.*

5. Define such basic means-concepts for achieving goals as *positive incentives, negative incentives,* the *desirable use of discretion,* and the *abuse of discretion.*

6. Define such basic economic and political structure concepts as *capitalism, socialism, federalism, separation of governmental powers, judicial review, political parties,* and *democracy.*

7. What is the meaning of *arriving at an optimum choice, level,* or *mix?*

8. Discuss the idea that policy evaluation does not require that every policy or combination be ranked or scored, but rather only that the evaluator determine the best policy or combination, or the one that can achieve a given goal or goals.

9. Give an example of an ethical dilemma that someone in government or university research might face in trying to decide which of two public policies is better.

10. Describe one factor that helps enable public policy evaluations to be adopted by public policy decision makers.

REFERENCES

Dahl, Robert, and Charles Lindblom, *Politics, Economics, and Welfare* (Harper, 1953).

Dunn, William, *Public Policy Analysis: An Introduction* (Prentice-Hall, 1981).

———(ed.), *Values, Ethics, and the Practice of Policy Analysis* (Lexington-Heath, 1983).

Frohock, Fred M., *Public Policy: Scope and Logic* (Prentice-Hall, 1979).

Lasswell, Harold, *A Pre-View of Policy Sciences* (Elsevier, 1971).

MacIver, Robert, *The Web of Government* (Macmillan, 1951).

MacRae, Duncan, and James Wilde, *Policy Analysis for Public Decisions* (Duxbury, 1979).

Nagel, S., *The Policy-Studies Handbook* (Lexington-Heath, 1980).

Quade, Edward, *Analysis for Public Decisions* (North Holland, 1982).

Ranney, Austin (ed.), *Political Science and Public Policy* (Markham, 1968).

CHAPTER 2

Sources of Goals, Policies, and Relations[3]

Public policy evaluation can be defined as the determination of which of various governmental policies or decisions is best for achieving a given set of goals in light of (1) the relations between the alternative policies and the goals and (2) various constraints and conditions. This definition emphasizes four key elements in public policy evaluation:

1. a set of goals to be achieved within various normative constraints.
2. a set of alternative policies or combinations of policies that could be relevant to achieving the goals.
3. a set of relations between the policies and the goals.
4. the drawing of a conclusion from those goals, policies, and relations as to which policy or combination is best.[1]

Where do these goals, policies, and relations come from? The answer includes four main possibilities:

1. authority; one or more persons, books, articles, or other reliable sources of information regarding the relevant goals, policies, or relations.
2. statistical or observational analysis; the analyzing of specific instances in order to generalize what the goals, policies, or relations might be.
3. deduction; the drawing of a conclusion from premises that have been established from authority, observation, and/or intuition.
4. sensitivity analysis; the guessing of the goals, policies, or relations, and the determination of what effect, if any, the guessed values have on the final decision regarding which policy is best.[2]

Table 2-1 shows the types of situations which illustrate the sources of goals, policies, and relations in policy evaluation. Since there are four basic sources of information and three basic elements in policy evaluation, there are 12 situations that need illustrative examples. This chapter is organized in terms of the four sources. Within each source, the three elements are discussed. The order of discussion, as indicated in Table 2-1, is from situations 1 through 12. Many of the examples come from the fields of criminal justice, poverty programs, and legislative redistricting, although one can easily reason by analogy to other subject matters.[3]

TABLE 2-1
Types of Situations to Illustrate the Sources of Goals, Policies,
and Relations in Policy Evaluation

Sources	AUTHORITY	STATISTICAL OR OBSERVATIONAL ANALYSIS	DEDUCTION	SENSITIVITY ANALYSIS
Elements	**1**	**4**	**7**	**10**
GOALS	Acquitting the innocent versus convicting the guilty	Police legality versus police morale	Probability of appearing versus probability of being held	The relative weight of respect for the law versus delay reduction
	2	**5**	**8**	**11**
POLICIES	Feasible legal aid policies	Allocating to places versus allocating to activities	Deducing a combination of volunteer and salaried attorney system	Checking a proposed redistricting against the last redistricting
	3	**6**	**9**	**12**
RELATIONS	Effect of police expenditures on crime reduction	Relating defendant characteristics to appearing in court	Relation between judge versus jury and discriminatory decision making	Relation between satisfaction and law reform versus case handling

The four basic sources can be subclassified in various ways. For example, authority can be meaningfully discussed in terms of expert authority and general public opinion. Authority could also be contemporary or historical. Observation can be impressionistic or systematic, including statistical. Deductive approaches can be based on intuitively accepted premises or based on empirically validated premises. Sensitivity analysis is threshold analysis in which we want to know the break-even point, above which we should take one course of action, and below which we should take another.

Consulting Authority as a Source

Consulting authorities, rather than establishing the goals, feasible policies, or relations in a policy evaluation with original data or reasoning, can be a big time-saver.[4] A good example of the use of authority as a source of *goals* can be found in the policy evaluations of the United States Supreme Court. For instance, in deciding the constitutionality of alleged violations of the First Amendment, the Supreme Court frequently seeks to clarify the intentions of the framers of the Constitution. In doing so, the Court generally refers to prior Supreme Court opinions as authority. These opinions often refer back to the writings or speeches of the framers of the Constitution, such as the *Federalist Papers*. In addition, the Court sometimes consults the writings of William Blackstone, John Locke, and Charles de Montesquieu, which influenced the framers.

A good example of systematic policy evaluation by the Supreme Court occurred in the case of *Ballew* v. *Georgia*, U.S. 223 (1977). The question was whether a state could allow juries to be as small as 5 people without violating the right to trial by jury stated in the Sixth Amendment. If juries decrease in size, then it is easier for prosecuters to get convictions because there are fewer people to convince of the guilt of the defendant. This means fewer cases of freeing the guilty, but an increase in cases of convicting the innocent. Deciding the optimum jury size, therefore, involved some notion of the relative importance of avoiding wrongful nonconvictions versus wrongful convictions. In his decision, Justice Harry Blackmun referred approvingly to William Blackstone, who considered convicting one innocent person to be ten times as bad as not convicting one guilty person. Blackmun also cited a study which concluded that the optimum jury size was between 6 and 8, based on Blackstone's ideas and some deductive calculations regarding the relationship between jury size and conviction rates. That analysis partly enabled Blackmun to decide that a jury could become smaller than 12, as previously decided, but should not be allowed to become smaller than 6. A key goal in the analysis was the 10-to-1 trade-off based on consulting an authority known to have influenced the framers of the Constitution.[5]

Consulting authority is often helpful in determining what policies are feasible to work with in a policy evaluation analysis to determine the optimum policy among the feasible ones. For example, in determining how to provide legal services to the poor in civil cases, there are many possible alternatives, as indicated by *The Delivery Systems Study* of the Legal Services Corporation. The conceptually possible alternatives are three: They consist of (1) volunteer attorneys, (2) attorneys who are salaried by the government to represent the poor, and (3) nongovernmental attorneys who represent the poor and are reimbursed by the government on a case-by-case basis. The third alternative, which is referred to as Judicare, is analogous to Medicare or Medicaid in the field of medical services for the poor. Judicare was recommended by President Ronald Reagan while campaigning for the presidency largely because it maximizes the use of the private marketplace in providing legal services for the poor. After being elected, however, Reagan rejected Judicare as being too expensive and endorsed the volunteer-attorney system. Liberals such as Edgar and Jean Cahn had already rejected Judicare because it did not provide lawyers who were specialists in poverty law or who were interested in actively broadening the legal rights of the poor. Thus, by consulting these prominent conservative and liberal authorities, one could rule out Judicare as a politically feasible possibility and concentrate instead on a systematic comparison between the volunteer and salaried systems of legal services.[6]

An example of the use of authority to establish relations can be taken from the field of anticrime allocation. A number of studies have been made of the effectiveness, efficiency, and equity of allocations of the Law Enforcement Assistance Administration (LEAA) across states and cities in the United States. One approach was to try to determine the extent to which the LEAA money was allocated in proportion to the marginal rates of return or the elasticity coefficients of different places. One way to establish the relationship between incremental anticrime dollars and crime reduction of different places is to do a statistical analysis with time series data. Such an analysis may not produce meaningful results, however, because of the problems of reciprocal causation, spurious causation, interaction, and invalid data in dealing with crime and anticrime expenditures. In this context, an alternative approach might be to consult with authorities who know police efficiency, court efficiency, and corrections efficiency across many places. For instance, representatives of the International Association of Police Chiefs might be able to position cities on a 1-to-10 efficiency scale better than a statistical analysis of crime and police expenditures could. Likewise, members of the American Judicature Society or the National Center for State Courts might be able to position state court systems on a 1-to-10 efficiency scale better than a statistical analysis of crime and court expenditures could. Traditional social science tends to downplay introspective information-gathering methods, in contrast to nonobtrusive methods. In policy evaluation, however, perhaps more consultation with insiders is needed in order to obtain more meaningful information about relationships than can be obtained from the limited and questionable data records that are available.[7]

Who constitutes an authority on goals, policies, or relations? The answer depends on the subject matter. The Supreme Court is an authority, for example, on what goals are legitimate in satisfying the right-to-counsel clause of the Sixth Amendment to the Constitution. The Court has said that saving money is not an appropriate goal, but that saving innocent persons from being convicted is. If, however, the issue is not *whether* right to counsel should be provided but rather *how* it should be provided, then saving money is an appropriate goal. For this issue, the goals of a county board would be relevant because it generally appropriates money to pay court-appointed lawyers to represent the poor. Such goals might include satisfying the local bar while minimizing expenditures. The board might, therefore, decide on a salaried public defender system, rather than on a less expensive but less politically feasible assigned counsel system or a less legally feasible volunteer system. For other policy problems, the key authorities might be legislative opinion, public opinion, the head of an administrative agency, or the like.

Statistics, Induction, or Observation as Sources

Statistical analysis is the most systematic form of inducing generalizations from many instances or observations. It is generally used for establishing relations, rather than for establishing goals or feasible policies.[8] Statistical analysis can, however, be useful in establishing goals or weights for the goals whenever the goals, rather than being ultimate, are instrumental for achieving higher objectives. For example, in the controversy over whether illegally seized evidence should be admissible in court, there is a goal-weighting problem: what is the importance of encouraging police adherence to legality in making searches relative to the importance of keeping police officers interested in obtaining evidence of guilt? Excluding illegally seized evidence may increase police adherence to the law, but it may unduly decrease police morale as it relates to making searches. In 1963, data were gathered in each of the 50 states from police chiefs, prosecuting attorneys, judges, defense attorneys, and American Civil Liberties Union (ACLU) officials concerning changes in police adherence, police morale, and other behaviors. The focus was on changes made since the 1961 Supreme Court decision requiring the adoption of the exclusionary rule by the 24 states which had not already done so. The analysis revealed a $+0.18$ relationship between new adoption of the exclusionary rule and increased police adherence, but a -0.37 relationship between new adoption and police morale. If police adherence has less than twice the value of police morale, then the exclusionary rule is doing more harm than good; however, if police adherence is valued at more than twice the value of police morale, then it does more good than harm. To determine the relative value of police adherence and police morale, one could try to relate statistically the changes in police adherence and police morale to such higher goals as crime reduction or respect for the legal system. The relational coefficients could be useful in deciding the relative weight of the goals of adherence and morale.[9]

In many policy evaluation problems, a basic question to resolve is what alternative policies need to be evaluated. For example, in allocation analysis, one may be interested in knowing the best way to allocate a budget across a set of places or across a set of activities. And, on a more fundamental level, one may want to know whether the allocation problem involves allocating to places or to activities. A statistical analysis could predict the goal achievement of allocating a budget across the activities in proportion to their marginal rates of return. A separate statistical analysis could predict the goal achievement of allocating the budget across the places in proportion to their marginal rates of return. If the activities allocation has higher predicted goal achievement than the places allocation, then the policy problem should be how to allocate best across the activities; otherwise, it should be how to allocate best across the places.

A related allocation problem is determining how the federal government should allocate money for education, environmental protection, anticrime, or other activities across places. A more fundamental question might be whether the policy variables should be states or cities. In this case, a statistical analysis can help clarify which policies should be analyzed by operating at a metapolicy level, just as a statistical analysis can be useful to help clarify how conflicting goals should be weighted by operating at a metagoal level.[10]

On the matter of relations between policies and goals, statistical analysis can be especially helpful or at least especially prevalent. A good example is the subject of pretrial release. The key goal is getting released defendants to appear in court for their court dates without being arrested while released. To determine the variables correlating with that kind of goal achievement, data can be obtained on 500 or so prior cases involving released defendants. Each case can be coded according to whether or not the defendant appeared in court without being arrested while released. Each case can also be coded in terms of the characteristics of the defendant, such as length of time living in the community and length of time holding his or her present job. One can then do a statistical analysis of the relationship between such characteristics and appearance in court. The analysis can provide relational coefficients which can be used in assigning points for determining who should be released and who should be held in jail pending a speedy trial.

One finding of such a statistical relation is that one may obtain better predictability from knowing how truthful a defendant is than can be obtained from knowing how long the defendant has been around. Thus, the defendant who admits to being a drifter may be a better risk to release than a defendant who has been in the community for two years, but who says he or she has been around for five years. One may also get better predictability from knowing whether a defendant was required to report periodically to a parole or probation officer while released than from knowing anything about the defendant's characteristics. These examples of statistical analysis may be especially useful in determining relations between policies and goals. Nevertheless, relations are sometimes determined better through authority, deduction, or sensitivity analysis.[11]

Accounting is a variation on statistical analysis. Like statistical analysis, it involves aggregating data, but accounting data is generally more precise than statistical analysis that is based on averages or the fitting of curves to scattered data points. A public opinion survey is not a variation on statistical analysis in the context of the typology of sources used in this chapter. Rather, it is a form of consulting authority in which the authority is the general public or a special segment of it. A statistical analysis (as a distinct source of information on goals, policies, or relations) involves a cross-tabulation, an analysis of the variation between averages, or a regression-equation analysis. These forms of statistical analysis involve determining a relation which is relevant to (1) weighting goals, (2) deciding which policies are feasible to choose among, or (3) relating a policy to a goal.

Deduction as a Source

Deduction involves arriving at a conclusion from premises that have been established by way of authority, empirical validation, prior deduction, or intuition. The more acceptable the premises are, the more acceptable the conclusions should be, assuming the conclusions have been validly deduced from the premises. Deduction is especially helpful where there is no authority and no empirical data for determining the information desired.[12]

For example, in determining an optimum set of bail bonds, it may be helpful to know the relative goal-weights for wrongly holding a defendant in jail who would have been a good risk to release versus wrongly releasing a defendant who turns out to be a bad risk. An optimum bond maximizes the weighted probability of a defendant appearing in court without having been arrested for committing a crime while released minus the weighted probability of the defendant being held in jail. Appearing in court is like income, while being held in jail is like an expense. Those optimum bonds thus seek to maximize income minus expenses or benefits minus costs. Although William Blackstone said that it is 10 times as bad to convict an innocent person as it is to acquit a guilty person, he never said anything about the relative undesirability of wrongful pretrial holding versus wrongful pretrial releasing. Knowing that Blackstone's trade-off is respected by the Supreme Court provides us with an initial premise. A second premise that should have virtually universal acceptance is that it is worse to wrongly convict someone than it is to wrongly hold someone in pretrial detention. From these two premises, one can deduce that it is less than 10 times as bad to wrongly hold a defendant in jail prior to trial than it is to wrongly release a defendant. That is, the trade-off is somewhere between 9 to 1 and 1 to 1. This statement assumes that wrongful holding is worse than wrongful releasing, as implied in state statutes and court precedents which say that the defendant must be given the benefit of the doubt. The 9-to-1 and 1-to-1 trade-off could enable us to arrive at a range of optimum bond levels for different crimes in which judges could legitimately operate. If they set a bond that exceeds that range, they could be required to give detailed justification.[13]

In discussing the use of deduction in arriving at feasible policies, we will use the example of providing legal services to the poor. One premise is that the Reagan administration will not endorse a salaried government-attorney program for providing legal services. A second premise is that Congress will not abandon the salaried legal program in favor of a volunteer program. A third premise is that there will be a confrontation at least once a year between the president and Congress unless a third policy can be developed which combines elements of both the salaried and volunteer programs. A major defect in volunteer programs is that they often involve well-meaning volunteers who do not have an adequate communication system to make their availability known to the poor, and vice versa. In addition, volunteer attorneys often lack competence in dealing with the specialized legal problems of the poor, which may involve public aid, public housing, consumer credit, and so on. One type of compromise would call for salaried attorneys to devote a minimum percentage of their resources to recruiting volunteers and making their availability known to the poor by way of legal services offices. The salaried attorneys could also devote a percentage of their resources to training volunteers so that they can provide better representation to the poor. It is important to note that deductively analyzing the preceding premises leads to an alternative policy that might be missed if one only relies on authority or statistical analysis. Authority is often not very creative in foreseeing problems, and statistical analysis is incapable of dealing with policies that have never been adopted.[14]

The use of deduction in establishing relations between policies and goals is often done in two ways. One might be referred to as the *single-analogy deduction*. It involves the following type of reasoning:

1. X_1 causes Y, where X_1 is one policy and Y is a goal.
2. X_2 is like X_1 on everything that is relevant.
3. Therefore, X_2 also causes Y.

A variation on the single analogy is:

1. X causes Y_1.
2. Y_2 is like Y_1 on everything that is relevant.
3. Therefore, X also causes Y_2.

A second general way that deduction is useful in relating policies to goals might be referred to as the *double-analogy deduction*. It involves reasoning of the form:

1. X_1 and X_3 cause Y, although in different ways.
2. X_2 is between X_1 and X_3 in its relevant characteristics.
3. Therefore, X_2 will cause Y in a way that is like X_1 or X_3, depending on how close X_2 is to each of them.

All these forms of deductive reasoning enable one to say something about the relationship between a policy and a goal where direct statistical, inductive, or observational data are lacking.

An example of a single-analogy deduction involves establishing the relationship between the dichotomous policy variable of judge-versus-jury decision making and the goal variable of reducing racial disparities in sentencing. We have no direct data in which judges and juries decide the same cases separately. Instead, we have judicial decisions in bench trials and jury decisions in jury trials. The two are not necessarily comparable; common knowledge tells us that jury trials generally involve more serious matters, and any differences between judicial and jury decision making may be due to differences in the cases and not in the decision makers. The University of Chicago Jury Project asked judges in jury trials what decisions they would have reached in the same cases on which both the judge and jury sat, but the analysis did not compare the treatment of black versus white defendants by judges and juries. American Bar Foundation data show a 15-percentage-point difference between black and white defendants with regard to being recommended for probation in federal assault cases in the early 1960s, but only a 6-point difference in judicial sentencing in the same cases. If one considers jurors to be more like probation officers than judges in their background and attitudes, then one can deduce that the treatment of blacks compared to that of whites in jury decision making would also be more biased than in judicial decision making. Thus, although juries may serve as a check on the undemocratic tendencies of judges, they do not serve as a check on possible racial disparities in judicial decision making.

An example of a double-analogy deduction involves establishing the relationship between jury size and conviction rates. It is impossible to obtain meaningful empirical data for determining this relationship. One cannot compare a 12-person-jury state with a 6-person-jury state because differences in their conviction rates can be readily attributed to differences in substantive law, procedural law, case facts, and especially the conviction propensities of different parts of the country. Nor can one compare conviction rates in a state before and after it shifts from a 12-person-jury system to a 6-person system; the cases are likely to change because defense attorneys will be less willing to bring their weak cases before the new 6-person juries. The cases tend to change toward ones in which the evidence presented favors the defense side. Showing a videotaped criminal case to numerous 12- and 6-person juries only provides a sample of one case. Working with a larger sample of videotapes may be too expensive and may not capture reality sufficiently.

Jury decision making resembles 12 coins being flipped simultaneously to see if all of them will come up heads. It is also like 12 bowling pins being hit or missed by the evidence/instructions ball, with the pins bumping into each other being analogous to the interaction among the jurors. Each of those models has different implications regarding the average juror's propensity to convict, given that the average total jury convicts at a 64 percent rate. The coin-flipping model implies that the individual juror has a 0.964 propensity because only 0.964 raised to the 12th power will equal 0.64. The bowling model implies that the individual juror has a 0.64 propensity because the model, in effect, arrives at a conviction rate that reflects how the average pin or juror behaves. We know from the University of Chicago jury data that individual jurors vote to convict 0.677 of the time. Therefore, the bowling model is much closer to reality than the coin-flipping model. By weighting the two models accordingly, we can determine what would happen if the exponent of 12 in the coin-flipping term were reduced to an exponent of 6. The answer is that the 64 percent conviction rate will increase to 66 percent. This assumes that everything else is held constant, particularly the propensities of individual jurors, regardless of whether they are serving with 11 or 5 other people.[15]

Another example of deducing relations is the more traditional syllogism which takes the form of $A = B$, $B = C$, and therefore $A = C$, or the form of A causes B, B causes C, and therefore A causes C. Following is a concrete example.

1. The voting behavior of judges from different congressional districts is like the voting behavior of members of Congress from those districts in labor-management matters.
2. The voting behavior of these members of Congress is like the attitude scores of public opinion from the same districts on various political controversies.
3. Therefore, the voting behavior of judges from different congressional districts is probably like the attitude scores of public opinion from the same districts on various political controversies, even though data is not available for judicial voting on cases other than labor-management cases.[15]

Sensitivity Analysis as a Source

In policy evaluation, sensitivity analysis is a useful source of information about goals, policies, and relations when authority, statistics, and deduction do not provide clear answers regarding them. Sensitivity or threshold analysis enables one to determine how much room for error there is in weighting the goals, listing out the policies, or measuring the relations. Often, the controversy over precision in these matters is wasted because, within the range in which the controversy occurs, the overall conclusion as to which policy or combination is best is still the same. Sensitivity analysis also enables the policy evaluator to convert difficult questions about goals, policies, and relations into relatively easy questions, such as, Is a given weight, policy, or relation above or below some threshold? rather than, What is the exact weight, policy score, or relation?[16]

How to dispose of criminal cases provides an example of applying sensitivity analysis when the goals and their relative weights are unclear. There are basically two ways to dispose of criminal cases, namely, through trials and guilty pleas. The main goals for deciding which type of disposition is better are (1) the respect for the legal system which each method generates and (2) the time consumption which each method incurs. If trials receive a score of 6 on a 1-to-10 respect scale in a public opinion survey and pleas receive a score of 2, then trials get a percentage score of 6/8, or 75 percent, and pleas get a score of 2/8, or 25 percent. If trials average 120 days and pleas average 30 days from complaint to disposition, then trials get a percentage score of 120/150, or 80 percent, and pleas get a score of 30/150, or 20 percent. If the two goals are weighted equally, then trials are the loser because they have a benefit score of 75 percent and a cost score of 80 percent, whereas pleas have a benefit score of 25 percent and a cost score of 20 percent. It is difficult to determine how much weight respect should be given relative to time consumption. However, one does not have to make that determination. All one has to do is note that the threshold equation in which the benefits minus the costs of trials equals the benefits minus the costs of pleas is $75\%(W) - 80\% = 25\%(W) - 20\%$, where W is the relative weight of respect versus time consumption. Solving for W yields a threshold value of $W^* = 1.20$. Therefore, if we can agree that respect is worth more than 1.20 times saving days, then trials are the better method of disposition; it is unnecessary to decide the relative value of their importance. One (or both) of the two scores on each of the two goals of 6, 2, 120, and 30 could also be converted into a letter in the threshold equation to be solved in order to determine its threshold value.[17]

In using sensitivity analysis to determine a set of feasible policies, we have to distinguish between a method that will provide a set of policies from which we can choose, rather than a method designed to arrive at an optimum policy. All four sources of information can be used to arrive at either feasible policies or an optimum policy. In the context of this chapter, however, we are referring to methods for determining the goals, policies, and relations from which an optimizing conclusion can be drawn. Legislative redistricting provides a good example of where a variation on sensitivity or threshold analysis can be used to narrow the policies, but not to arrive at an optimum policy. In the redistricting of a state legislature by grouping counties, precincts, or other units together, millions of policies are possible because every grouping or pattern is a different policy. A frequently used method for dealing with such a huge number of policies is to (1) start with the status quo districting, (2) move a unit out of the first district into the second district, and then (3) compare the new pattern with the original pattern. If the new pattern is an improvement over the previous pattern, then it becomes the new threshold above which the next pattern has to improve. After going through many rounds, the last pattern left can be declared the winner, even though it may not be the optimum. Sensitivity or threshold analysis is closely related to the concept of satisficing. This concept involves going through as many rounds of moving units from one district to another until we arrive at a pattern that satisfies whatever constraints we have to abide by.[18]

Sensitivity analysis can be used to help determine the relations between policies and goals. In many instances, the same conclusion will be reached as to the best policy, regardless of the magnitude of the relation between the policy and the goal, as long as the relation is known to be higher or lower than a given level. In 1970, for example, the 250 legal services programs of the Office of Economic Opportunity were evaluated by teams of lawyers and representatives of the poor. Each program was scored according to its overall satisfaction *(S)*. In addition, the percentage of time and money which each program spent on case handling and on law reform was determined. These percentages were then multiplied by the program budget and divided by the number of clients in order to obtain a figure for case-handling dollars per client *($C)* and law-reform dollars per client *($L)* for each program. With these data, the relation between *S* and *$C*, and then the relation between *S* and *$L* across the programs could be determined. The first relation is −0.03 by way of a linear regression analysis, and the second relation is +0.34. A linear relation was used contrary to the principle of diminishing returns because the feasible allocations were narrowly confined. The programs were expected to spend 80 to 90 percent on case handling and 10 to 20 percent on law reform. Within that range, substantial diminishing returns does not have an opportunity to occur. The analysis generates controversy over whether the case-handling relation is truly negative. For allocation purposes, however, it makes no difference. One would optimally allocate as much money as possible to law reform and as little as possible to case handling within the constraints, as long as the case-handling relation fell below +0.34—and even if it were +0.20 or +0.30.[19]

Intuition is closely related to sensitivity analysis as a source of goals, policies, and relations. Sensitivity analysis frequently involves determining how different guessed values affect the optimizing conclusions. Intuition is also a form of guessing or basing estimates on strong feelings. Goals are sometimes accepted intuitively rather than being justified in terms of authority, statistics, or higher premises. This is especially so if the goals are general or near-ultimate goals, rather than instrumental. Policies may often be suggested as a result of a flash of insight, which is the case with hypotheses in traditional social science research. Although it is not generally respectable in social or policy science to arrive at relations through intuition, one can repeatedly guess at a relation until the reasonable possibilities have been exhausted and then see how these guesses affect the optimizing conclusions. One may find that it is unnecessary to be any more scientific than that, since all the reasonable guessed values may yield the same conclusion as to which policy is best.

Ultimately all goals and relations depend on intuition. Goals can be justified by appeal to authority, statistics, or deduction. However, how does one justify (1) the authority, (2) the dependent or goal variable in a statistical analysis, and (3) the basic premises in a deductive analysis? One can likewise ask for a justification of these justifications. In policy evaluation, one usually has an overall goal that is accepted intuitively, such as promoting the greatest happinesss for the greatest number or satisfying the decision makers. Likewise, one can ask, why does policy X cause goal Y? The answer might be that there is a Z variable between X and Y which is caused or increased by X, and which in turn causes or increases Y. One can then ask, why does X cause Z and why does Z cause Y? At each stage of the causal regress, one tends to move further away from substantive policy and social science toward natural science and metaphysics. Ultimately, the question becomes, how do we know there is an X or a Y? That is, how do we know there is such a thing as a congressional statute or an American population that has social-indicator characteristics? In other words, on a philosophical level, we have to accept some empirical reality, such as the existence of the world. Fortunately for most policy evaluation, the goals in dispute are seldom ultimate goals, but rather instrumental goals that can be justified in terms of authority, statistics, or deduction. Similarly, the relations are seldom, if ever, metaphysical; rather, they can also be explained in a satisfactory, nonphilosophical way in terms of authority, statistics, and deduction.

Conclusion

We can conclude from this analysis of the sources of goals, policies, and relations in policy evaluation that there are a variety of sources that can be systematically classified. We can also conclude that perhaps policy evaluation should be making more use of the variety of sources available. Unfortunately, certain disciplines tend to overlook some sources at the expense of others. Law and political science seem to rely heavily on authority as a source, especially legal authority. Psychology and sociology may rely too heavily on statistical analysis, which tends to overemphasize variables that are easily measurable and policies that need to be adopted before they can be evaluated. Economics and engineering often rely too heavily on deduction, especially mathematical modeling, which sometimes involves unrealistic or incomplete premises. By working with a combination of authority, statistics, and deduction, one provides a form of triangulation which increases the likelihood of arriving at more meaningful goals-weights, policies, and relations.[20]

There is no need to argue over which source between authority, statistics, and deduction is the most desirable. Authority is clearly a big time-saver if an accessible and respected authority is involved. Deduction enables one to draw conclusions about goals, policies, and relations without having to gather original data, but instead by synthesizing already known information. Statistical analysis does constitute a more ultimate, but more difficult, form of proof. In any concrete policy evaluation situation, the best source depends on the subject matter and what is to be done with it. If the policy evaluation involves constitutional policy, an appeal to Supreme Court authority may be most relevant. If it involves the effects of a strike in the coal industry on another segment of the economy, a deductive input-output model may be the preferable type of analysis. If it concerns the trade-off problem of inflation and unemployment, a time-series statistical analysis may be especially appropriate in relating inflation and unemployment to suicide rates, to the percentage of the two-party vote that goes to the incumbent party, or to other social indicators.

We can also conclude that sensitivity and threshold analysis is a useful tool in policy evaluation because even with authority, statistics, and deduction, it may still not be possible to arrive at precision in weighting goals, measuring policies, or determining relations. Sensitivity analysis enables one to determine whether increased precision is needed. It is only needed if the range of unclearness on a goal-weight, a policy, or a relation happens to encompass a threshold value. Thus, if the range of unclearness on a goal-weight or a relation is between 20 and 30, but the threshold value of the goal-weight or the relation is 10, then one can forget about clarifying the unclearness if one is mainly concerned with determining which policy is best. If, however, the threshold value is 26, then one should seek additional information from authority, statistics, and/or deduction to determine whether the actual value is above or below 26.

The purpose of this chapter has been to discuss the sources of goals, policies, and relations in policy evaluation. The chapter represents a synthesis of reasonable common sense, at least as a matter of hindsight. That is what good policy evaluation should be, namely, codified common sense. For thousands of years, many human beings have been making effective and efficient decisions. What decision science and policy science should now try to do is to capture the essence of what these good decision makers have done implicitly. Less naturally competent decision makers can then improve their decision-making or policy-evaluating skills.[21]

NOTES

1. In addition to the present text, policy evaluation textbooks that view the key elements in policy evaluation as being goals, alternative policies, relations, and conclusions include Edward Quade, *Analysis for Public Decisions* (North-Holland, 1982) (especially Chapters 4, 6 through 9, and 12); Edith Stokey and Richard Zeckhauser, *A Primer for Policy Analysis* (Norton, 1978) (especially Chapter 15); and Duncan MacRae and James Wilde, *Policy Analysis for Public Decisions* (Duxbury, 1979) (especially Chapters 3 and 4). Other policy evaluation textbooks emphasize measuring relations (especially books associated with sociology-psychology evaluation-research), or else they emphasize models for drawing conclusions from goals, policies, and relations (especially books associated with operations-research management science).

This chapter does not deal with how to draw prescriptive conclusions from goals, policies, and relations. That is the subject of other literature, such as S. Nagel, *Policy Evaluation: Making Optimum Decisions* (Praeger, 1982); Christopher McKenna, *Quantitative Methods for Public Decision Making* (McGraw-Hill, 1980); and John Gohagan, *Quantitative Analysis for Public Policy* (McGraw-Hill, 1980). Drawing prescriptive conclusions from premises as to goals, policies, and relations is basically a deductive process. The nature of the deduction depends on whether the situation involves (1) optimum choice among discrete or continuum alternatives, (2) mutually exclusive choices or choices that allow combinations, (3) choices with relations that are or are not contingent on the occurrence of probabilistic events, (4) choices in which doing too much or too little is undesirable, and (5) the allocation of scarce resources among activities, places, or other objects.

2. On sources of information in general, especially relations among variables, see Dickinson McGaw and George Watson, *Political and Social Inquiry* (Wiley, 1976); Claire Selltiz, Marie Jahoda, Morton Deutsch, and Stuart Cook, *Research Methods and Social Relations* (Holt, Rinehart & Winston, 1976); and William Goode and Paul Hatt, *Methods in Social Research* (McGraw-Hill, 1962).

3. The policy evaluation books in note 1 do not deal systematically with sources of goals, policies, and relations, but tend to take them as givens, especially goals and policies. The social research and epistemology books in note 2 are not particularly concerned with goals, policies, or relations between goals and policies, as contrasted to more abstract or less policy-relevant matters. There is thus no substantial prior literature to cite that deals directly with the sources of goals, policies, and relations in policy evaluation on a general level.

4. On authority as a source of information relevant to policy evaluation, see Richard Merritt and Gloria Pyszka, *The Student Political Scientists' Handbook* (Schenkman/Harper & Row, 1969); E. E. Schattschneider, Victor Jones, and Stephen Bailey, *A Guide to the Study of Public Affairs* (Dryden, 1952); and Myron Jacobstein and Roy Mersky, *Fundamentals of Legal Research* (Foundation, 1977).

5. On the example of weighting the goals of acquitting the innocent and convicting the guilty in the context of finding an optimum jury size, see S. Nagel and Marian Neef, *Legal Policy Analysis: Finding an Optimum Level or Mix* (Lexington-Heath, 1977), 75–158.

6. On the example of determining what alternatives are available for providing legal services for the poor, see *The Delivery Systems Study* (Legal Services Corporation, 1980); and "Legal Services for the Poor" in Arthur Berney, Joseph Goldberg, John Dooley, and David Carroll (eds.), *Legal Problems of the Poor* (Little, Brown, 1975), 499–588.

7. On the example of allocating anticrime expenditures, see "Allocating Anti-Crime Dollars across Places and Activities" in S. Nagel, *Policy Evaluation: Making Optimum Decisions* (Praeger, 1982), 203–229.

8. On statistics, induction, and observation as sources of information relevant to policy evaluation, see Jerome Murphy, *Getting the Facts: A Fieldwork Guide for Evaluators and Policy Analysts* (Goodyear, 1980); Susan Welch and John Comer, *Quantitative Methods for Public Administration: Techniques and Applications* (Dorsey, 1983); and William Fairley and Frederick Mosteller (eds.), *Statistics and Public Policy* (Addison-Wesley, 1977).

9. On the example of systematically evaluating the effects of excluding illegally seized evidence, see "Choosing Among Alternative Legal Policies" in S. Nagel,

Improving the Legal Process: Effects of Alternatives (Lexington-Heath, 1975), 7−26; and Dallin Oaks, "Studying the Exclusionary Rule in Search and Seizure," 37 *University of Chicago Law Review* 665−757 (1970).

10. On the example of deciding whether the alternative policies are places or activities, see "Comparing Geographic Allocation with Activity and Functional Allocation" in S. Nagel and Marian Neef, *Legal Policy Analysis: Finding an Optimum Level or Mix* (Lexington-Heath, 1977), 250−254.

11. On the example of relating defendant characteristics to their probability of appearing in court, see Charles Ares, Anne Rankin, and Herbert Sturz, "The Manhattan Bail Project: An Interim Report on the Use of Pretrial Parole," 38 *New York University Law Review* 67−95 (1963); and J. Locke, *Compilation and Use of Criminal Court Data in Relation to Pre-Trial Release of Defendants* (National Bureau of Standards, 1970).

12. On deduction as a source of information relevant to policy evaluation, see Martin Greenberger, Matthew Crenson, and Brian Crissey, *Models in the Policy Process: Public Decision Making in the Computer Era* (Russell Sage, 1976); Saul Gass and Roger Sisson, *A Guide to Models in Governmental Planning and Operations* (Sauger Books, 1974); and Charles Lave and James March, *An Introduction to Models in the Social Sciences* (Harper & Row, 1975).

13. On the example of arriving at optimum bail-bond levels, including the problem of weighting the probability of appearing against the probability of being held, see "The Bond-Setting Decision Across Cases" in S. Nagel and Marian Neef, *Decision Theory and the Legal Process* (Lexington-Heath, 1979), 45−62; and John Goldkamp, Michael Gottfredson, and Susan Mitchell-Herzfeld, *Bail Decision-making: A Study of Policy Guidelines* (National Institute of Justice, 1981).

14. On the subject of finding compromise policies between public-sector implementation and private-sector implementation of various activities, see Dennis Thompson (ed.), *Policy Toward Public-Private Relations: A Symposium* (special issue of the *Policy Studies Journal*, 1983); and Burton Weisbrod, *The Voluntary Non-Profit Sector: An Analysis* (Lexington-Heath, 1977).

15. On the example of deducing the relation between (1) judicial versus jury decision making and (2) racial disparities in case outcomes, see "The Litigants: Disparities in Safeguards and Sentencing" in S. Nagel, *The Legal Process from a Behavioral Perspective* (Dorsey, 1969), 81−112. On the example of the relation between jury size and conviction rates, see "Impact of Jury Size on the Probability of Conviction" in S. Nagel and Marian Neef, *The Legal Process: Modeling the System* (Sage, 1977).

16. On sensitivity analysis as a source of information relevant to policy evaluation, see Carl Moore, *Profitable Applications of the Break-Even System* (Prentice-Hall, 1971); Thomas Gal, *Postoptimal Analysis, Parametric Programming, and Related Topics* (Wiley, 1980); "Policy Analysis with Unknown Variables" in S. Nagel, *Contemporary Public Policy Analysis* (University of Alabama Press, 1983); and "Sensitivity Analysis" in Bruce Baird, *Introduction to Decision Analysis* (Duxbury, 1978).

17. On the example of the relative weight of respect for the law versus delay reduction in deciding among alternative ways of disposing of criminal cases, see Donald Newman, *Conviction: The Determination of Guilt or Innocence without Trial* (Little, Brown, 1966); and Chapter 16 in this book.

18. On the example of using a variation on threshold analysis to determine feasible redistricting patterns, see "Simplified Bipartisan Computer Redistricting" in S. Nagel, *The Legal Process from a Behavioral Perspective* (Dorsey, 1969),

321–359; and Terry O'Rourke, *Reapportionment: Law, Politics, Computers* (American Enterprise Institute, 1972).

19. On the example of the relation between (1) law reform versus case handling and (2) the satisfaction of legal services evaluators, see "Minimizing Costs and Maximizing Benefits in Providing Legal Services to the Poor" in S. Nagel, *Improving the Legal Process: Effects of Alternatives* (Lexington-Heath, 1975), 271–310; and "The Volume Problem" in Eli Jarmel (ed.), *Problems in the Legal Representation of the Poor: Cases and Materials* (Matthew Bender, 1972), 3/1–3/19.

20. On the differing perspectives of the various social sciences toward the sources of goals, policies, and relations in policy evaluation, see George McCall and George Weber (eds.), *Social Sciences and Public Policy* (Kennikat Press, 1983); Duncan MacRae, *The Social Function of Social Science* (Yale University Press, 1976); and S. Nagel (ed.), *Policy Studies and the Social Sciences* (Transaction Books, 1976).

21. For greater detail on the perspective that good policy evaluation should be codified common sense, see Chapters 11 through 14.

QUESTIONS

1. How does one judge the meaningfulness of authority as a source of goals, policies, or relations?
2. How does one judge the meaningfulness of statistics, induction, and observation as a source of relevant knowledge?
3. How does one judge the meaningfulness of deduction as a source?
4. What are the advantages and disadvantages of the four sources—authority, statistics, deduction, and sensitivity analysis—relative to each other?
5. How does intuition relate to the main sources of policy-relevant knowledge?
6. To which policy evaluation element is each source especially relevant?
7. From your awareness of public policy matters, give an example of authority as a meaningful source of goals, policies, or relations other than the examples given in this chapter.
8. From your awareness of public policy matters, give an example of statistical analysis, deduction, and sensitivity analysis.
9. How do the basic social-science fields of political science, economics, and sociology-psychology tie in with the basic sources of authority, statistical analysis, and deduction?
10. With just one concrete policy-evaluation example, illustrate the use of authority, statistics, deduction, and sensitivity analysis to determine goals, policies, and relations. (This is in contrast to Table 2-1, in which 12 different examples are used to relate the four sources to the three elements.)

REFERENCES

Goode, William, and Paul Hatt, *Methods in Social Research* (McGraw-Hill, 1962).

Greenberger, Martin, Matthew Crenson, and Brian Crissey, *Models in the Policy Process: Public Decision Making in the Computer Era* (Russell Sage, 1976).

Hoaglin, David, Richard Light, Bucknam McPeek, Frederick Mosteller, and Michael Stoto, *Data for Decisions: Information Strategies for Policymakers* (Abt Associates, 1982).

McGaw, Dickinson, and George Watson, *Political and Social Inquiry* (Wiley, 1976).

Merritt, Richard, and Gloria Pyszka, *The Student Political Scientists' Handbook* (Schenkman/Harper & Row, 1969).

Moore, Carl, *Profitable Applications of the Break-Even System* (Prentice-Hall, 1971).

Murphy, Jerome, *Getting the Facts: A Fieldwork Guide for Evaluators and Policy Analysts* (Goodyear, 1980).

Selltiz, Claire, Marie Jahoda, Morton Deutsch, and Stuart Cook, *Research Methods and Social Relations* (Holt, Rinehart & Winston, 1976).

Welch, Susan, and John Comer, *Quantitative Methods for Public Administration: Techniques and Applications* (Dorsey, 1983).

PART TWO

Public
Policy Goals

The purpose of Part II is to discuss various goals that can be used as criteria for evaluating alternative public policies, including:

1. *Net benefits:* the quantity of benefits minus costs produced by each policy.
2. *Effectiveness:* the extent to which a policy achieves its intended goals, or the quantity of benefits which a policy achieves.
3. *Efficiency:* the ratio of benefits achieved to costs incurred.
4. *Equity:* the spread of the benefits and the costs among various groups or places in proportion to population, need, or other criteria of basic fairness.
5. *Equality:* the spread of benefits and costs among various groups and places so that they each have an equal share, which may not be equitable.
6. *Public participation:* the extent to which the majority of the affected public has a substantial impact on the policy, and the extent to which minority viewpoints are allowed to try to convert the majority.
7. *Freedom:* the freedom of minority viewpoints to try to convince the majority; the entrepreneurial freedom to make money without necessarily considering damage to labor, the environment, consumers, and so on.
8. *Predictability:* the extent to which a policy is objectively applied so that one can know in advance what the policy covers.
9. *Procedural fairness:* the application of a policy in a manner that allows those who are deserving to defend themselves against accusations of being undeserving. For example, procedural fairness is considered present in criminal cases if defendants have the right to trial by jury and a court-appointed counsel. In welfare terminations, however, procedural fairness is considered present if welfare recipients have the right to present evidence in their behalf and to cross-examine their accusers but do not have a right to a jury or a lawyer.

CHAPTER 3

Effectiveness and Efficiency

Efficiency is a term that is frequently used and sometimes misused in policy analysis. There seems to be general agreement as to what it means in verbal rather than in quantitative terms. It is the extent to which a policy, program, activity, agency, or place gets a lot of output for a little input. In somewhat more precise terms, *efficiency* is the ratio between output and input, the number of output units per unit of input, or the number of output units per dollar spent.

Problems often arise, however, when one attempts to quantify these concepts. For example:

1. How do output/input measures differ in interpretation from input/output measures and outputs minus inputs, including their relative importance?
2. How do measures of efficiency relate to measures of effectiveness and equity, including their relative importance?
3. How does one measure efficiency where the output involves a detriment like crimes rather than a benefit like convictions?
4. How does an output/input ratio relate to the ratio of change in output to change in input, both conceptually and in terms of importance?

These are some of the problems that this chapter will discuss.[1]

More specifically, the chapter seeks to answer such intriguing questions as these:

1. Which is better, a good benefit/cost ratio or a good benefit-cost difference?
2. Which is better, a one-unit increase in efficiency or a one-unit increase in effectiveness?
3. Which is more efficient, a city with 100 crimes and $50 in anticrime expenditures, or a city with 200 crimes and $25 in anticrime expenditures?
4. Which is better, a project with a good benefit/cost ratio, or a project with a good ratio of change-in-benefits to change-in-costs?

35

Ways of handling these problems will be illustrated mainly with examples from the criminal justice field, which involves such output measures as crimes, arrests, convictions, trials, and reversals. Some of its outputs are benefits, such as cases settled or cases decided; others are detriments, such as crimes or appellate reversals. Still others are benefits to some units within the system and detriments to others, such as conviction rates, which indicate good work by prosecutors, but not such good work by public defenders. It is a field for which illustrative data are available, and on which much has been written. It is thus a rich field for illustrating the problems of measuring efficiency, and one can easily reason from the criminal justice examples to examples in any policy field.[2]

This chapter will emphasize concrete illustrations, but it will also attempt to state principles in general terms. Doing so is sometimes facilitated by using the following symbols: B for benefits, D for detriments, C for expenditure costs, Y for effects or outputs regardless of whether they are benefits or detriments, X for inputs regardless of whether they are dollar costs or other inputs, B/C for benefits divided by costs, B-C for benefits minus costs, and C/B for costs divided by benefits.

B/C, B-C, and C/B

CLARIFYING AND RELATING MEASURES

Measuring and increasing efficiency in government operations or public policy problems can often benefit from using methods developed by management science for business operations and business policy problems. Sometimes, however, business measures are inapplicable. This is clearly so with regard to income minus expenses (or total profits) as the most important business goal. Concepts such as monetary income are inapplicable because government programs are not normally income-producing. Instead they are usually designed to produce nonmonetary benefits like safe highways or to reduce detriments like crime occurrence. Using the concepts of benefits and costs rather than income and expenses partly covers the government analogy. Governmental costs, however, normally cannot be subtracted from governmental benefits because they are not both measured in the same units. It thus makes no sense to subtract dollars spent from highways built or dollars spent from crimes.[3]

One can, however, talk meaningfully about the ratio between highway miles built and dollars spent. Doing so might involve noting that in one city or program a highway mile (5,280 feet) costs $1 million, while in a more efficient city or program a highway mile costs $900,000. An alternative way of expressing the same benefit/cost ratio would be to say that in the first city they can create 0.00528 feet of highway for $1.00, whereas in the second city they can create 0.005867 feet of highway for $1.00. Another way of expressing the relative efficiency of the two places or programs is simply to invert the benefit/cost ratio to calculate a cost/benefit ratio. Doing so for the first city indicates that it spends $189 for each highway foot, whereas the second, more efficient city only has to spend $170 for each foot. Either measure of efficiency can be translated into the other. However, most people prefer to talk about dollars per foot than about fractions of feet per dollar. The units can also be changed to dollars per mile, which might frighten taxpayers more than dollars per foot, although civil engineers may customarily talk in terms of dollars per mile.[4]

BENEFITS/COSTS AS A HIGHER GOAL

There may be times when the benefits and costs of government projects are both measured in a common unit such as dollars. Under those circumstances, the alternative projects should be judged by benefits minus costs rather than benefits/costs. This is so because an investment of $100 that yields a $200 return is preferable to an investment of $10 that yields a $30 return if the remaining $90 is going to remain idle. The first investment leaves one with $200 in assets at the end of the time period, whereas the second leaves only $120 in assets.[5] Either the $B-C$ or B/C criterion will give the same results in an analysis of which of the two investments or projects is more desirable, where both investments involve the same costs—that is, where both involve only $100 or only $10. In that sense, benefits minus costs is more important than benefits/costs.[6]

When benefits and costs cannot be measured in the same units, it may make more sense in terms of the values involved to judge projects not by looking to B/C but by looking for the alternative, with (1) the highest B, provided a maximum C is not exceeded; (2) the lowest C, provided a minimum B is reached; or (3) a compromise between those two projects. One might also want to satisfy a minimum equity constraint under either formulation. When the various benefits or costs are not measured in a common unit, one may still be able to add or subtract them meaningfully if one can arrive at reasonable multipliers that consider their relative importance and differences in measurement units.[7]

Some people might object to the statement that $B-C$ is the supergoal of policy analysis on the grounds that doing so does not adequately consider the minimum benefits needed or equity constraints. $B-C$ is a supergoal in that it is objectively more important than B/C or B alone when there is a conflict among these criteria. One can imagine situations in which the consequences would be a total loss unless a minimum benefits level is obtained. For example, suppose a candidate running for Congress in a 100-voter district has two choices. Choice 1 will yield 51 votes at a cost of $100,000, and choice 2 will yield 49 votes at a cost of $1. At first glance, it seems that although the preferred choice (1) has a smaller $B-C$ than the less preferred choice (2), it is preferred because a minimum benefits level is met. It seems that choice 2 scores higher on *B-C* because the costs are so much lower and the benefits are almost the same as in choice 1. At second glance, however, choice 1 probably scores higher on *B-C*, because the benefits increase drastically as one moves from 49 to 51 votes. In effect they move from almost no benefits at all if one is a loser, to an infinite percentage increase if one is a winner. Winning the election may be worth $300,000 to the candidate, whereas losing the election may be worth nothing. Thus, choice 1 yields a net profit of $200,000, and choice 2 yields a net loss of $1. Those who object to benefits minus costs as a supergoal may believe that such thinking is overly concerned with a monetary orientation. There is, however, no reason why the benefits and costs being considered cannot refer to highly nonmonetary values, such as civil liberties, aesthetics, and intangible benefits or costs to religious values.

The supergoal of *B-C* does not necessarily conflict with equity considerations, but rather provides a measure of the extent to which different groups are equally receiving or bearing benefits, costs, and benefits minus costs. One could object on philosophical grounds that using *B-C* as a criterion might lead to the adoption of a program that will increase *B-C* overall for a society, to the benefit of some individuals who become better off, but to the detriment of others who become worse off. Those who raise this kind of objection generally argue for a Pareto optimum supergoal in which nobody is worse off. One can answer this objection by stating that for the sake of discussion, we are talking about benefit/cost analysis from the perspective of an indivisible individual or government unit. One can also supplement the Pareto criterion by stating that an increase in total *B-C* is desirable, because individuals receiving substantial benefits can compensate those undergoing detriments to bring them back to the status quo, while those benefiting will still receive a net gain. Another approach is to think in terms of minimum constraints, such that an increase in *B-C* is desirable when (1) some people are made substantially better off, (2) other people are slightly worse off but still above a minimum constraint, and (3) there is a net gain for the total group. That thinking combines *B-C* with equitable constraints for a supergoal.

CHOOSING AMONG DISCRETE POLICIES

Why would anyone want to know the *B/C* ratio if we can measure both benefits and costs in terms of dollars and thus obtain a more useful *B-C* difference? The answer can be illustrated by considering two projects. In the first, $B = \$15.00$, $C = \$10.00$, and thus net benefits equal $5.00. In the second, $B = \$20.00$, $C = \$15.00$, and the net benefits also equal $5.00. However, the first project is more efficient because its *B/C* ratio is $1.50, whereas the second project's *B/C* ratio is only $1.33. What does the first project do that enables it to get $1.50 back for every $1.00 in cost? Knowing the answer might enable us to increase the efficiency of the second project so that it can also get $1.50 back on each $1.00, or $22.50 for its $15.00 in expenses. With that new efficiency, the new net benefits would be $7.50. This example illustrates that increased efficiency *(B/C)* generally means increased profit *(B-C)* and that knowing the efficiency scores of related projects can lead to increased profits or net benefits.

An increase in efficiency inherently brings an increase in profits only if the increase in efficiency occurs when benefits are held constant and costs decrease, or when costs are held constant and benefits increase. If efficiency increases as a result of a change in both benefits and costs, then profits may decrease. For example, suppose we initially have $B = \$10$ and $C = \$5$. That gives us an efficiency of 2 and profits of $5. If, however, the project changes so that $B = \$3$ and $C = \$1$, then efficiency increases to 3, but profits drop to $2. This example further illustrates that a project that is higher on *B-C* may not be higher on *B/C*, because the initial project had a *B-C* of $5 and a *B/C* of 2, whereas the subsequent project had a *B-C* of $2 and a *B/C* of 3. We were better off with the initial project in being able to take home an extra $5 rather than $2, assuming that the initial project satisfied the minimum constraints with regard to equity and benefits achieved, and that it did not exceed the maximum constraints with regard to costs, as compared to the subsequent project.[8]

Knowing the *B/C* ratio for each policy or project can be quite helpful in picking a subset of projects that will maximize total benefits minus costs. For example, in Table 3-1, we have benefit and cost information for five projects.[9] If the projects are mutually exclusive, project E would be the one to adopt because it has the best *B-C* difference. If the projects are not mutually exclusive and we have enough money for all of them, then all would be worth adopting because each one has a positive *B-C* difference. Suppose, howev-

---

TABLE 3-1
Data for Deciding on a Subset of Projects to Maximize Total Benefits Minus Costs

Project	Benefits	Rank	Costs	Rank	B-C	Rank	B/C	Rank
D	$ 4.20	5	$ 3.00	2	$ 1.20	5	1.40	4
E	13.50	1	10.00	5	3.50	1	1.35	5
F	3.50	4	2.00	1	1.50	4	1.75	1
G	9.00	2	6.00	4	3.00	2	1.50	3
H	6.40	3	4.00	3	2.40	3	1.60	2
Total	$36.60		$25.00		$11.60		7.60	
Average	$ 7.32		$ 5.00		$ 2.32		1.52	

$10 = Maximum Budget Available

Note that for $10, the most profitable combination of projects is G and H, even though they are individually not the most profitable, efficient, effective, or least expensive.

er, that they are not mutually exclusive and we only have $10 to spend. Then what is the best combination of projects on which to spend the $10? One's initial reaction might be to buy the first most profitable project, then the second, and so on, until the $10.00 is used up. In this example, that would mean buying project E, which would use up the $10.00. However, doing so would not be a wise decision because it would only produce a profit of $3.50. We can easily improve on that with our $10.00 by buying more than one less expensive project, each of which has less profit but which collectively equal greater total profit. We cannot buy the three most efficient projects, namely, F, G, and H, because that will cost $12.00. We can, however, drop relatively expensive project G (which ranks third on efficiency) and add less expensive project D (which ranks fourth). Doing so will generate a profit or a net return of $5.10, which is a substantial improvement over $3.50. The defect in that combination, however, is that it only uses $9.00 of our $10.00 budget, and thus $1.00 is idle when it could be yielding some return. Yet there is no combination that adds up to $10.00 that includes project F, the most efficient project. Thus, if we drop project F and substitute H for D, we will buy H and G and get $5.40 net return.

This analysis leads one to the following rules for deciding a subset of projects to maximize total *B-C*. Rule 1 is to spend the whole budget or as much of it as is possible to spend. Rule 2 is to spend it on the most efficient list of projects that can be included and still satisfy rule 1.[10] In this common situation, the overall criterion is still to maximize total *B-C*, even though it is not rational to suboptimize by buying the individual projects that have the highest *B-C* differences, rather than the highest *B/C* ratios. It might also be noted that the F, H, D combination, which has only $5.10 in net benefits, is more efficient than the G and H combination, which has $5.40 in net benefits. The F, H, D combination has a yield of 57 percent (that is, $5.10/$9.00), whereas the F and H combination has a less efficient yield of 54 percent (i.e., $5.40/$10.00). The better combination, however, is the one which yields the most profit, rather than the one that is most efficient.[11] It should be noted that the rules for optimally selecting a subset of projects apply even when benefits and costs are not measured in the same units.

To clarify what is involved in optimally choosing among a subset of lump-sum projects, Table 3-2 presents the alternative constraints under which we might operate and the optimum choices, given the data in Table 3-1. The first constraint involves whether the projects are mutually exclusive, or whether it is possible to adopt all of them if we have the budget to do so. A middling position would be that some of the projects are mutually exclusive and some are not—for example, we cannot adopt both D and E, but we can adopt any other combination of projects. The second constraint involves whether the total budget is enough or less than enough to buy all the projects. The total budget only has to be $25 to enable us to buy all the

TABLE 3-2
Optimum Decisions in Choosing a Subset of Lump-Sum Projects

	Mutually Exclusive Projects	*Not Mutually Exclusive Projects*
Unlimited Budget (i.e., $25)	Choice = E B-C = $3.50 B/C = 1.35	Choice = D, E, F, G, H B-C = $11.60 B/C = 1.46
Limited Budget (i.e., $10)	Choice = E B-C = $3.50 B/C = 1.35	Choice = G, H B-C = $5.40 B/C = 1.54

projects. There are a variety of less-than-enough possibilities, but we have chosen $10 for illustrative purposes. A third constraint implied in this analysis is that each of these projects is a lump-sum or indivisible project. Thus, if we spend less than $3.00 for project D, we do not get anything, and we cannot get 1.5 projects by spending $4.50. In other words, each project is like buying a $50-million dam at a given point in a river. It would be meaningless to buy half a dam; it would also be meaningless to have two dams, one behind the other. Later in this chapter we discuss allocating a budget across policies or projects that are divisible along a continuum of costs. We could also complicate matters by having some projects that are nondivisible, in which only certain costs can be expended, and other projects that are divisible, in which a continuum of costs can be expended. The classification of linear versus nonlinear relations between benefits and costs (or the type of nonlinear relations) is irrelevant to lump-sum projects in which no variation is allowed on the costs.[12]

Given these three constraints, Table 3-2 shows that if the projects are mutually exclusive, we go with the project that has the highest *B-C* score, provided that our budget will cover that project. If it will not, then we go with the project with the next-to-highest *B-C* score, and so on. If the projects are not mutually exclusive, we buy all those that have positive *B-C* scores, provided we have enough budget to cover them. If we do not, then we go with the projects in the order of their efficiency scores, while spending as much of the available budget as possible. The overall goal is always to find a combination of projects that will maximize total benefits minus costs rather than maximize benefits, maximize benefits/costs, or minimize costs, unless we are operating under political constraints that require shifting to one of these other goals or taking the distribution of the benefits and costs into consideration.

Efficiency, Effectiveness, and Equity

CLARIFYING AND RELATING MEASURES

Efficiency is normally defined in terms of output/input ratios, whereas effectiveness is normally defined in terms of quantity of output. Thus, the effectiveness or ineffectiveness of a criminal justice system might be measured in terms of the number of crimes that occur within the system. A more sophisticated measure would weight some crimes more heavily than others, possibly depending on the average sentence received for various crimes. A more sophisticated measure might also look to victimization surveys rather than just police reports. Efficiency within a criminal justice system might sometimes be measured by determining the number of crimes and the anticrime expenditures.[13] Thus, if one city has 100 crimes per capita and spends only $50 to fight crime, it is clearly more efficient than a city that has 100 crimes per capita and spends $75, at least when both cities are equally subjected to crime-causing stimuli.[14]

At first, one would think that an increase in effectiveness would mean an increase in efficiency, because effectiveness is benefits and efficiency is benefits/costs. Thus, if the numerator goes up, the value of the fraction goes up. This is true by definition if the other relevant variables are held constant. In reality, however, effectiveness and efficiency tend to have an inverse relationship. This is so because effectiveness or total benefits tend to increase only if there is an increase in costs. If, however, there is an increase in costs, there is likely to be a decrease in efficiency because efficiency varies inversely with costs. Given the principle of diminishing returns, benefits are not likely to increase proportionately with an increase in costs.

Equity is normally defined in terms of equality across groups. More specifically, equity refers to providing benefits or detriments equally to groups that are alike on whatever characteristics society defines as being relevant to one's worthiness in receiving benefits or detriments. In the criminal justice field, society tends to pay lip service to the idea that blacks should not be subjected to any more crime than whites are subjected to. In this context, equity would involve the extent to which crime rates are equal in both black and white neighborhoods. In other words, equity is mainly concerned with the extent to which effectiveness measures are equally distributed. Equity can also be concerned with the extent to which efficiency measures are equally distributed, which in this context would be the extent to which anticrime expenditures per crime occurrence are equal in both black and white neighborhoods. Equity is sometimes expressed in terms of a minimum B, B/C, or C for each activity or place regardless of the marginal rate of return of the activity or place.[15]

COMPARING MEASURES

Which is most important, efficiency, effectiveness, or equity? There is nothing to indicate inherently that a one-unit reduction in crime is worth more or less than a one-unit reduction in expenditures or crimes-expenditures. Which is worth more depends on how many dollars a crime is worth. That obviously depends on what the crime is and who the victim is. Murder is worth more than larceny. Theft of an individual's life savings may be more disruptive than a theft from a insured bank. We could assess a dollar value for property crimes in terms of the property stolen, but that would not allow for psychological or physical injury. We could use average damage awards in related civil cases to assess comparable crimes, such as assault and battery.

The problem becomes more difficult when we try to convert deviations from equity into dollar values. Small deviations from equity may be less disruptive than a big increase in crime, but big deviations from equity may be more disruptive. Likewise, we may be willing to incur large expenditures to reduce inequities, as well as to reduce crime. How to combine such goals as efficiency, effectiveness, and equity into a composite goal, or how to consider the trade-offs is the subject of other policy analysis research.[16] To compare the relative importance of efficiency *(B/C)* and effectiveness *(B)* may require having a higher goal than either of them, namely, the goal of net benefits *(B-C)*.[17]

If benefits and costs are measured in dollars, we can easily say whether a given quantity or increase in benefits is worth more or less than a given quantity or increase in costs by just looking to the effect on benefits minus costs. Thus, whether an increase in B is worth more than a decrease in C depends simply on which is larger. Likewise, if benefits and costs are both measured in dollars, we can determine whether various kinds of increases in effectiveness are worth more or less than various kinds of increases in efficiency. Table 3-3, for example, deals with the question of whether a 100 percent increase in effectiveness (and no change in efficiency) is worth more or less than a 100 percent increase in efficiency (and no change in effectiveness). The table answers that question by reducing the words to algebraic symbols so that one can more easily see the general relations. Table 3-3 also provides hypothetical numerical data to clarify the algebraic symbols. Before the increase, effectiveness equals B, efficiency equals B/C, and net benefits equal $B-C$ for both governmental programs. After the effectiveness increase in program 1, effectiveness doubles to $2B$; efficiency remains constant by doubling the cost; and net benefits therefore equal $2B - 2C$. After the efficiency increase in program 2, effectiveness remains constant at B; efficiency doubles to $B/0.5C$ by halving the cost; and net benefits therefore equal $B - 0.5C$.

Thus, the problem shown in Table 3-3 reduces to whether $2B - 2C$ is greater or less than $B - 0.5C$. That statement in turn simplifies to whether B is greater than $1.5C$ by getting all the Bs on one side of the relation and all the Cs on the other side as one does in solving an equation, although here we are simplifying an inequality. The answer to whether B is greater than $1.5C$ is generally no, because it would be an unusual government program that provides benefits at 1.5 times the cost. That would be the equivalent of a

TABLE 3-3
A Comparison of an Increase in Effectiveness with an Increase in Efficiency

	Before the Increase	After the Increase
Program 1 (Receives a 100% increase in effectiveness, but no change in efficiency)	Effectiveness Before: $10 (B) Efficiency Before: $10/$5 = 2 (B/C) Profit Before: $10 − $5 = $5 (B-C)	Effectiveness After: $20 (2B) Efficiency After: $20/$10 = 2 (2B/2C) Profit After: $20 − $10 = $10 (2B − 2C)
Program 2 (Receives a 100% increase in efficiency, but no change in effectiveness)	Effectiveness Before: $10 (B) Efficiency Before: $10/$5 = 2 (B/C) Profit Before: $10 − $5 = $5 (B-C)	Effectiveness After: $10 (B) Efficiency After: $10/$2.50 = 4 (B/0.5C) Profit After: $10 − $2.50 = $7.50 (B − 0.5C)

Note that the problem simplifies to whether $2B − 2C$ is greater or less than $B − 0.5C$, which further simplifies to whether B is greater than $1.5C$. The answer is generally no, since it would be an unusual government program that provided benefits valued at 1.5 times the cost.

50 percent return on an investment. Thus, a 100 percent increase in efficiency is normally worth more than a 100 percent increase in effectiveness. One can often determine whether B is worth more or less than $1.5C$, even though B and C are not measured in the same units. Through similar reasoning, any kind of increase in effectiveness can be compared with any kind of increase in efficiency.[18]

Working with Detriments Rather Than Benefits

THE PROBLEM

Many public policy problems involve reducing a detrimental social indicator rather than increasing a beneficial one. For example, we talk about reducing crime, pollution, discrimination, poverty, disease, and illiteracy more than we talk about increasing safety, clean air, equality, wealth, health, and education. We do so because the detrimental social indicators are usually easier to measure. These detrimental social indicators, like crime, can be meaningfully used as measures of effectiveness. Problems arise, however, when we attempt to interpret detriments/costs as a measure of efficiency, as in crimes/expenditures.

METHODS THAT DON'T WORK

Suppose we have two cities. City J has 100 crimes and spends $50 to fight crime. City K has 200 crimes, but spends only $25 to fight them. Which city is more efficient? The problem would be easy if city J were doing better on both crimes and dollars, or worse on both. Thus, city J's crime/cost ratio of 100/$50 is more efficient than city K's if city K spends $50 but has more than 100 crimes, or if city K has 100 crimes but spends more than $50. With city J's ratio of 100/$50 and city K's ratio of 200/$25, one might initially divide crimes by dollars in order to obtain a crimes-per-dollar figure. Doing so would produce a figure of 2/$1 for city J, and a figure of 8/$1 for city K. One could then conclude that city J is more efficient because it experiences only 2 crimes for a $1 expenditure, whereas city K experiences 8 crimes for $1. However, such division is meaningless because it implies that if we reduce out anticrime dollars from $50 to $1, we will somehow reduce our crimes from 100 crimes to 2. Common sense tells us that if we reduce our anticrime dollars, the 100 crimes should go up, not down.[19]

Thus, we may need a figure that (1) indicates how many crimes would occur in each city if each only spent $1, and (2) recognizes the inverse relationship between anticrime dollars and crime.[20] To do this with city J, we first state that the initial figure of 100/$50 implies 2 crimes for $1, and that for every $1 we reduce expenditures, there should be a 2-crime increase. Thus, if we reduce expenditures from $50 to $1, there should be a 98-crime increase, or a total of 198 crimes. City K's figure of 200/$25 implies 8 crimes for $1. Therefore, if it reduces its expenditures by $24 down to $1, city K should have an increase of 192 crimes (8 times 24), for a total of 392 crimes. We could then conclude that city J is more efficient because it reduces crime to only 198 crimes for $1.00 whereas city K has 392 crimes for $1.

This approach does not make sense because it implies a constant and arbitrary rate of change with regard to crime reduction for every dollar increase in anticrime dollars. For example, the logical implication of the analysis is that for city J to have 200 crimes, it would have to reduce its $50 expenditure by $100, at 2 crimes per $1. Therefore, it would have to spend −$50. One cannot spend less than nothing. The preceding analysis also implies that if city J spent $150, it could get crime down to zero. Moreover, if city J spent more than $150, it could get crime into the negative range, but a city cannot have fewer than zero crimes.[21]

As an alternative to the preceding attempts to manipulate crime and expenditure figures in order to obtain a measure of efficiency, we could try to convert the crime occurrence information into a measure of benefits rather than detriments. We could then meaningfully divide the benefits measure by expenditures to obtain an output/input measure of efficiency. In other words, we would like to have a measure such as "crimes prevented" for the numerator of our ratio.[22] One way to do that is to calculate the average quantity of crimes (or crimes per capita) for the set of cities which we are comparing. In the preceding example, the average quantity of crimes for the two cities is 150. Thus, city J could be considered as having prevented 50 crimes because it only had 100 crimes, or 50 less than might be predicted for city J. We could then divide the 50 crimes prevented by the $50 that city J spent, and conclude that it costs $1 for each crime prevented in that city. We could do the same with each city in our study in order to determine its relative efficiency. This approach, however, also makes no sense because about as many cities will have crime figures above the average crime figure as below. For example, with its 200 crimes, city K is 50 crimes above the average of 150. In a sense, therefore, its expenditures did not prevent any crimes. On the contrary, city K has a crime prevention score of −50, which has no more meaning than negative expenditures or negative crimes. Clearly, city K's expenditures are not causing crimes but preventing them, and thus city K should continue spending anticrime money.[23]

As a more sophisticated approach to obtaining a benefits numerator, one might determine the difference between the actual crime in a city and an appropriate amount of crime, considering the costs of both crime occurrence and crime prevention. Thus, one could obtain an appropriate or desired crime figure for a set of cities by determining for each city (1) how much crime occurred, (2) what damage costs were incurred, and (3) what the enforcement or anticrime costs were. With that information, one could plot a curve showing the relation between crime (on the horizontal axis) and damage costs (on the vertical axis). The curve would be positively sloped since damage costs increase as crime increases. One could also plot a curve showing the relation between crime and enforcement costs which would be negatively sloped because enforcement costs increase as crime decreases. Where the total cost curve bottoms out is the most appropriate crime level for the set of cities. If, for example, the bottom point for cities J and K was at 250 crimes, then city J would receive a crime improvement score of 150 since it has only 100 crimes, and city K would receive a score of 50 since it has only 200 crimes. Dividing the score of 150 for city J by its $50 gives an efficiency score of 3, whereas dividing city K's score of 50 by its $25 gives an efficiency score of only 2. This approach is not very meaningful or practical because (1) it is difficult to assess crime damage costs; (2) many cities have crime figures above the desired or optimum level, creating interpretation problems, such as being above the average; and (3) any deviation above or below the optimum seems like a bad rather than a good, and thus will not convert our detriments numerator into a benefits numerator.[24]

METHODS THAT WORK

One fairly simple approach that might work for converting crime detriments into a benefits measure of crimes prevented would involve obtaining data for each city at a second point in time.[25] Thus, if we know that city J has a 100/$50 figure for 1975 and an 80/$60 figure for 1970 (adjusting 1975 for inflation), we can draw a curve between these two data points on a graph like that shown in Figure 3-1. This curve can be expressed by the equation $Y = 13,335(X)^{-1.25}$. This equation follows from the fact that a diminishing-returns curve can be expressed by an equation of the form $Y = aX^b$, which

FIGURE 3-1
The Relation Between Crime and Expenditures in City J

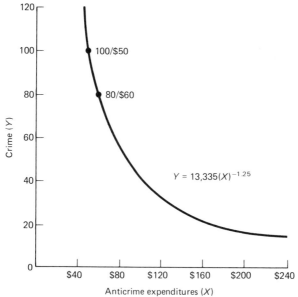

100/$50

80/$60

$Y = 13,335(X)^{-1.25}$

Crime (Y)

Anticrime expenditures (X)

*Note that for $1 or one expenditure unit, 13,335 crimes occur, and that for $50, one obtains 100 crimes. Thus, spending $50 rather than only $1 can be said to be associated with a reduction or prevention of 13, 235 crimes (13,355 − 100). That means a B/C ratio of 13,235/$50 or 265/$1.

is the equivalent of log Y = log a + b log X. The values of a and b can be determined with a scientific calculator after inserting the logarithms of the Y and X scores.[26] With the equation, we can now predict how many crimes will occur in city J if only $1 is spent to fight crime. The answer is 13,335. In other words, when we plug $1 or one cost unit into the equation for the X expenditures, Y becomes equal to the a scale coefficient because 1 raised to any exponent still equals 1.

The next logical step would be to determine how many crimes city J is preventing as a result of spending $50 rather than only $1. The answer is the difference between 13,335 crimes and 100 crimes, or 13,235 crimes prevented. We can then divide that crimes-prevented figure by $50 spent to obtain the figure of 265 crimes prevented per $1.[27] We can perform the same kind of analysis for city K if we can obtain data for an earlier point in time. We can then compare the efficiency of the two cities to determine which one can obtain more crime prevention for $1 in anticrime expenditures. The same approach can be used with other detriment measurements, such as units of pollution or discrimination, in order to obtain a measure of pollution prevented or discrimination prevented where one wants to use a benefit/cost or output/input measure of efficiency.[28]

Another approach is to argue that city J is the better city if we place a higher value on a 100-crime reduction than we do on saving $25, but that city K is the better city if we place a higher value on saving $25 than we do on a 100-crime reduction. However, this comparison is meaningless because it involves a false dichotomy, as if those were the only two choices available. If we spend $50 the way city J does, there will be 100 crimes. If we spend $50 the way city K does, we do not know how many crimes there will be, although presumably there will be less than 200 because city K gets its crimes down to 200 when it spends only $25. Perhaps spending $50 the way city K does might yield less than 100 crimes, making city K the more efficient city. In other words, we must be able to project how much crime city K would be likely to have if it had the same $50 to work with that city J has. Another way of stating the problem is that we would like to know by how much crime would increase in city J if the city had only $25 to work with, as city K does.

If we were dealing with benefits rather than detriments, we could assume that the second data point involves zero benefits for zero costs. We could then connect the two data points together in a linear equation of the form, $Y = 0 + (B/C)X$. In other words, when we are working with benefits rather than detriments, the B/C ratio can be treated as a linear slope. When we are working with detriments rather than benefits, more creativity and data are needed in order to make meaningful comparisons across cities, projects, or other alternatives.

There are three new methods whereby one can conclude which city is more efficient without having to obtain information for a second point in time for each city. The first method involves an incremental or decremental analysis whereby we seek to determine whether the decision makers would prefer the lowered crime figure which city A can provide or the lowered expense figure which city B can provide. In other words, if the relevant decision makers consider a reduction of 100 crimes to be preferred over a cost-saving of $25, then city A is the better project. If, however, they consider a cost-saving of $25 or 25 monetary units to be preferred over a reduction of 100 crimes, then city B is the better project since it provides the cost-saving.

	Crime	Part/ Whole (%)	Expenses	Part/ Whole (%)	Unweighted Sum (%)	Weighted Sum ($W_1 = 2$) (%)
City A	100	−33	$50	−67	−100	−133
City B	200	−67	$25	−33	−100	−167
Total	300	−100%	$75	−100%	−200%	−300%
Difference	100		$25			

The second method involves a percentaging analysis whereby we seek to convert the raw scores of crimes and dollars (which cannot be added together) into relative or pure numbers (which can be added together). Specifically, we convert the crime scores into part/whole percentages by noting that the sum of the crimes scores is 300. The part/whole percentage for city A is thus 33 percent, and it is 67 percent for city B. On dollar expenses, the sum is $75. The part/whole percentage for city A on dollars is thus 67 percent, and it is 33 percent for city B. The sum of those two percentages for city A is 100 percent, and it is also 100 percent for city B. We can consider all these percentages as being negative or multiplied by −1, because they represent detriments or costs rather than benefits. This analysis generates a tie between city A and city B. If, however, the relevant decision makers consider reducing one crime unit to be twice as important as reducing one monetary unit, then the weighted sum is more favorable to city A than to city B because −133 percent is less than −167 percent. In light of this, all city A has to do to be a winner is to have the weight of one crime reduction be worth anything more than the weight of one monetary-unit reduction.

The third method involves determining a threshold dollar value for a one-crime reduction. If the true value is above the threshold value, then city B would be the worse city because it has more crime. If the true value is below the threshold, then city A would be the worse city because it has less crime. To calculate the threshold dollar value, we must solve for V in the equation $100(V) + 50 = 200(V) + 25$. Doing so yields a threshold V of 0.25. At the threshold, city A and city B are incurring the same total costs. City A then has $25 in crime costs and $50 in anticrime expenses for a total cost of $75. If the decision makers decide that a one-crime reduction is worth more than 0.25 or one-fourth of a monetary unit, then city A is the better city. For example, if one crime reduction is worth $0.26, then city A has a total cost of $76, whereas city B has a higher total cost of $77. If, however, one crime reduction is worth $0.24, then city A has a total cost of $74, whereas city B has a lower total cost of $73. It is difficult to determine the actual cost of a one-crime reduction, but it is not so difficult to determine whether the cost is above or below a threshold.[29]

We can conclude that a project that is better on crime but worse on anticrime expenses cannot be meaningfully compared with a project that is worse on crime but better on anticrime expenses by such methods as (1) dividing crimes by dollars; (2) converting the basic data into a regression equation by dividing dollars by crimes (or the logarithm of dollars by the logarithm of crimes) and then multiplying by −1 to obtain the linear slope (or the nonlinear elasticity coefficient), since this assumes that when dollars equal 0, crimes equal 0, which is only true if crimes were a benefit; and (3) trying to convert crimes into a benefit by subtracting the actual crime from the average crime or optimum crime. We can, however, meaningfully compare two such projects by (1) obtaining data for a second point in time and then fitting a negative diminishing-returns curve to the two data points, or talking in terms of crime reduction over time as a benefit; (2) comparing the crime difference between the two cities with the expenditure difference; (3) converting the crime scores and expense scores into weighted part/whole percentages; or (4) determining whether the value of a crime is above or below the threshold value, which makes the two cities equal in crime-dollar cost plus anticrime-dollar cost. The fact that these three methods of incremental, percentaging, and threshold analysis were substantially developed during 1983 illustrates that the field of policy evaluation is indeed in an exciting state of ferment.[30]

Comparing Benefits/Costs with Marginal Rate of Return

CLARIFYING AND RELATING MEASURES

Why would one want to use a measure of efficiency to compare alternative policies, programs, activities, agencies, or places? The purpose of using such a measure is probably to evaluate how well, for example, a given policy is doing. We can then praise or reward those who are doing well and criticize or penalize those who are not.[31] When it comes to allocating funds in order to maximize benefits minus costs, however, we would not necessarily want to allocate in accordance with B/C ratios. It might be wasteful to give additional funds beyond its previous year's budget to a program that is doing well because it may be doing as well as it can, and the additional funds would just be wasted. Likewise, it may be profitable to give additional funds beyond its previous budget to a program that is inefficient or ineffective because it may be capable of showing a big improvement from a small additional expenditure. In other words, what we need for allocating additional funds is a measure of how much of an improvement would occur in each place as a result of an increase in expenditures.

Such a measure or marginal rate of return is easy to calculate with data from at least two points in time. One can use the preceding approach in fitting a line or curve to the crime and expenditure data points for city J. With a linear equation of the form $Y = a + bX$ for a city or program, the marginal rate of return is simply b or the linear slope. This quantity is also equal for two time points to $(Y_{75} - Y_{70})/(X_{75} - X_{70})$. In other words, it shows the ratio between a change in crime over a change in expenditures. With a nonlinear equation of the form $Y = aX^b$, the marginal rate of return is baX^{b-1}. This expression shows that the marginal rate of return or slope of a nonlinear curve varies depending on the level of expenditures. In other words, when diminishing returns occur, as they generally do, then as expenditures increase, good outputs (such as crime reduction) also increase, but at a diminishing rate. The expression baX^{b-1} is equal to the slope of a line drawn tangent to the curve at any point on the curve.[32]

Efficiency measures like benefits and costs can be translated into marginal rates of return if one is willing to make certain assumptions. In other words, a B/C ratio for a single point in time can be used to generate a line or curve by making assumptions that enable one to determine a second point. For example, if we assume a positive linear relation between inputs and outputs ($Y = a + bX$), the problem is fairly easy. To obtain a second data point, we can just assume that when there is no input there is no output; that is, when X equals zero, then Y equals zero. We then have two data points which can be connected, and the slope can be determined for the connecting lines. It will be B/C since $B - 0/C - 0$ equals B/C. If we assume a positive nonlinear relation ($Y = aX^b$), matters become somewhat more arbitrary. The positive nonlinear relation could involve diminishing returns, which would mean a b value that is positive but less than 1. One could assume a b value of 0.5, and then calculate the a value by solving for $(Y)/(X)^5$. The positive nonlinear equation could also involve increasing returns, which would mean a b value that is greater than 1. One could assume a b value of 2, and then calculate the a value by solving for $(Y)/(X)^2$. In these expressions, Y/X is the equivalent of B/C.

If we assume a negative linear or nonlinear relation between inputs and outputs, the problem of obtaining a second data point is not so easy. For example, if city L has 50 crimes and \$100 in expenditures and city K has 25 crimes and \$200 in expenditures, we could arrange for them to have equal or unequal marginal rates of return, depending on where we assume the line or curve like that in Figure 3-1 crosses the vertical axis. In order to establish a negative relation, the amount of crime when \$0 is spent has to be higher than either 50 or 25 crimes. If we assume that the anchor point or Y-intercept is 75 crimes for \$0, then crimes in city L went down by 25 (i.e., from 75 to 50) when expenditures increased \$100 (i.e., from \$0 to \$100). This yields a slope or marginal rate of return of -0.25. Likewise, crimes in city K decreased by 50 (i.e., from 75 to 25) when expenditures went up \$200 (i.e., from \$0 to \$200), also for a -0.25 slope. If however, we assume the anchor point is 100 crimes for \$0, then city L has a slope of -0.50 (50 less crimes when expenditures go up \$100), and city K has a slope of -0.375 (75 less crimes when expenditures go up \$200). Thus, the assumption determines the relative marginal rates of return, and no assumption about a negative-sloping anchor point is more reasonable than any other assumption, unlike the assumption of zero benefits for \$0 with a positive-sloping anchor point. The problem is not lessened by working with concave curved lines because we still have to make an assumption about where the negative curve crosses the vertical axis. If, however, we are working with a convex curve line like that shown in Figure 3-1, it might not be unreasonable to assume $a = -1$ for the exponent or elasticity coefficient in the equation $Y = aX^b$. One can then calculate the value of a by multiplying Y times X, or B times C. These assumption methods for converting a B/C efficiency measure to a marginal rate of return are, however, less meaningful than obtaining B/C information for at least two points in time, although the methods may be useful for arriving at rough allocation decisions in which only one-point-in-time data are available.[33]

ALLOCATING TO CONTINUUM POLICIES

When one has meaningful marginal rates of return for each policy, program, or place that is part of a set of allocation decisions, what does one do with this information? If linear or constant relations are involved, all of the budget should be allocated to the entity that has the highest slope or marginal rate of return after all the entities have been provided with any minimums to which they are entitled. If maximums are also involved, then after the first entity is allocated its maximum, the next highest entity is allocated to, and so on. If nonlinear relations are involved ($Y = aX^b$), then the budget should be allocated to all the entities that have favorable slopes in proportion to their elasticity coefficients *(b)* when they share a common scale coefficient *(a)*, after satisfying the minimum constraints. When they do not share a common scale coefficient, one can allocate funds in proportion to the products of their respective scale and elasticity coefficients.[34] Additional allocation rules apply for such variations as seeking to minimize expenditures within a minimum output, rather than maximize output within a maximum budget. It is important to remember that one does not normally allocate in accordance with efficiency measures *(B/C)*, effectiveness measures *(B)*, or cost measures *(C)*, but rather in terms of marginal rates of return (change in *B* / change in *C*).[35]

To illustrate some of these basic principles, suppose we have (1) the benefit and cost information for two programs, like those shown in Table 3-4, and (2) $10 to allocate to these programs in period 3. These data were chosen to illustrate marginal versus efficiency allocation, because one program (L) is highly efficient but has a low marginal rate of return, and another program (M) is relatively inefficient but has a better marginal rate of return. The top part of Table 3-4 shows that in both periods 1 and 2, program L was much more efficient. In moving from period 1 to period 2, however, an additional dollar given to program L only produced 1 additional benefit unit, whereas an additional dollar given to program M produced 3 additional benefit units. The middle of Table 3-4 shows four regression equations relating benefits to costs for each of the two programs, depending on whether we assume linear or diminishing returns relations and whether we allow for the possibility that an expenditure of $0 can produce some benefits. The nonlinear diminishing returns equations are generally more realistic and better fit actual data. Not allowing for some benefits when costs are $0 is also more realistic (as with a savings account), although in some policy situations (such as political campaigning), one can obtain benefits or votes without spending anything.[36] The bottom part of the table shows what the optimum allocations would be in light of the predictive equations from the middle part, as well as what the total benefits minus costs would be with those optimum allocations.[37]

TABLE 3-4
Two Governmental Programs to Illustrate Marginal Versus Efficiency
Allocation (Allocating $10 Between Two Programs)

Program	Period 1			Period 2			Changes		
	BENEFITS	COSTS	B/C	BENEFITS	COSTS	B/C	ΔB	ΔC	$\Delta B/\Delta C$
L	20	$2	10	21	$3	7	+1	+1	+1
M	3	$2	1½	6	$3	2	+3	+1	+3

Program	Linear Predictive Equations $(Y = a + bX)$		Nonlinear Predictive Equations $(Y = a + b \log X)$	
	$a \neq 0$	$a = 0$	$a \neq 0$	$a = 0$
L	$B = 18 + 1C$	$B = 8.20C$	$B = 18 + 6 \log C$	$B = 53 \log C$
M	$B = -3 + 3C$	$B = 1.80C$	$B = -2 + 17 \log C$	$B = 12 \log C$

Program	Linear Allocations		Nonlinear Allocations	
	$a \neq 0$	$a = 0$	$a \neq 0$	$a = 0$
L	$ 0	$10.00	$ 2.61 (6/23 × $10)	$ 8.15 (53/65 × $10)
M	$10.00	$ 0	$ 7.39 (17/23 × $10)	$ 1.85 (12/65 × $10)
Total Benefits ($C = $10)	45.00 (18.00 + 27.00)	82.00 (82.00 + 00)	33.27 (20.50 + 12.77)	51.50 (48.29 + 3.21)

Note that by more realistically predicting that when $C = $0, $B = 0$, one thereby allocates more to the more efficient program because then it has a higher marginal rate of return. Note also that by more realistically considering diminishing returns, one thereby allocates something to the less efficient program that is showing improvement, rather than the all-or-nothing linear allocations.

Note that the marginal allocation both opposes and reinforces the efficiency allocation, depending on the predictive equations we use. If we work with the equations that allow some benefits when no costs are spent, which is generally unrealistic, then we tend to allocate to the more inefficient program because it has a higher marginal rate of return. If, however, we work with the equations that do not allow for benefits when no costs are spent, then the recalculated marginal rates of return are higher for the more efficient program. This makes sense not only because it is in conformity with a more reasonable assumption, but also because one might logically expect a $10.00 investment in program L to produce about an $85.00 return and a $10.00 investment in program M to produce a return of only $17.50. This is so because program L returned 10 benefit units for every $1.00 spent in period 1, and 7 units for every $1.00 spent in period 2, averaging 8.50 units per dollar spent over the two periods, whereas program M averaged only 1.75 units per dollar. The contrary argument is that an extra $1.00 will generate 3 benefit units in program M, but only 1 benefit unit in program L. This argument is intuitively not as convincing as noting the greater efficiency of program L, especially when efficiency allocations are also supported by marginal analysis that is based on the reasonable assumption of a 0/$0, B/C point. (That is, when $0 is spent on costs, zero benefits are obtained.)[38] Working with the nonlinear equations is also desirable, not only because they more realistically take into consideration diminishing returns, but also because they result in allocations which give something rather than nothing to the less efficient program that is showing improvement.[39] The situation is like that of the parable of the prodigal son in the New Testament in which Jesus recommends rewarding those who show improvement, as well as those who maintain a continuing high level of goodness.

The importance of considering that no costs lead to no benefits can be illustrated by a program in which both the benefits and costs have been improved. For example, suppose that in period 1 a government agency generates 10 benefit units at $5 in costs. In period 2, which is a time of budget retrenchment, the agency works especially hard and generates 15 benefit units at only $3 in costs. Such an agency has a marginal rate of return of -2.5 and a regression equation of $B = 22.5 - 2.5C$. Under these circumstances, marginal analysis would indicate that this agency should receive less of an allocation than it would if it (or another agency) had held its costs constant and undergone a slight increase in benefits in order to produce a positive slope. Such an allocation does not make sense because this efficiency-increasing agency is in effect being punished (or at least not rewarded) relative to other agencies for increasing its benefits output while decreasing its costs. The paradox of punishing the efficient and rewarding the inefficient under marginal analysis can, however, be resolved by fitting a line or curve to these data which will go through the origin. Doing so produces a regression equation of $B = 3.5C$. The slope is now positive and is approximately equal to the average efficiency score between the 2 and 5 of periods 1 and 2.[40]

There is, however, no way for a regression equation (in which B is a function of C) to distinguish between an efficiency-increasing agency (in which $B = 10$ and $C = 5$ for period 1, and $B = 15$ and $C = 3$ for period 2) versus an efficiency-decreasing agency (in which $B = 15$ and $C = 3$ for period 1, and $B = 10$ and $C = 5$ for period 2) because both agencies would have the same pair of dots and lines on a regression graph. To distinguish between the two agencies so that the first one can be rewarded and the second one can be negatively sanctioned, information from outside the regression analysis must be brought in to take into consideration the sequence or time series of the data.[41] In other words, we need to know that the benefits went up from the first year to the second, and that the costs went down. An ordinary regression analysis would merely plot and connect two dots without indicating which dot occurred first in time. To consider both the relation between benefits and costs and the time sequence requires a preliminary decision rule. Such a rule might state, if the initial slope between benefits and costs is negative, do not automatically exclude the place from receiving an allocation. Instead, see whether it has recently improved in efficiency. Then give it an allocation in accordance with the approach shown in Table 3-4 for nonlinear allocations in which it is assumed zero costs yield zero benefits. Doing so will exclude the efficiency-decreasing agency, but not the efficiency-increasing agency, from receiving an allocation. The object in allocating is to receive a high marginal rate of return, to reward efficiency, and to thereby maximize total net benefits. Doing so has the effect of simultaneously considering multiple-policy analysis goals.

Conclusion

In light of the preceding analysis, we can offer some answers to the questions raised in the introduction to this chapter, namely:

1. It is more desirable to score high on a positive benefits-costs difference than to score high on a benefits/costs ratio, when a policy is capable of being scored on a benefits-costs difference.
2. When efficiency and effectiveness are measured in the same units, a percentage increase or an absolute increase in efficiency is generally more profitable than the same increase in effectiveness.
3. The efficiency of a city with 100 crimes and expenditures of $50 cannot be compared to that of a city with 200 crimes and expenditures of $25, unless a second pair of crimes and costs can be obtained for each city at another point in time. In other words, places and activities cannot be meaningfully compared on their detriments/costs ratios, but they can be compared on their detriments prevented and costs. One can also use the methods of incremental paired comparisons, percentaging analysis, and threshold analysis.
4. A project with a good benefit/cost ratio should be praised, rewarded, and studied as a model, but incremental funds should be allocated to those projects with good ratios of change-in-benefits to change-in-costs, provided that one considers both diminishing returns and the fact that zero costs generally produce zero benefits.

We can thus conclude that there is more to measuring and using concepts of efficiency in policy analysis than one might at first think. By "measuring," we have only been referring to measurement on a fairly high level of definitional generality corresponding to the various conflicting concepts. (By "high generality" we mean benefits and costs regardless of subject matter, in contrast to the benefits and costs associated, for example, with defense, education, or energy.) Once the basic distinctions are made among these concepts, the problem of measuring efficiency moves out of these general issues into issues that relate to the specific subject matter under consideration. The problem then becomes one of determining the benefits and costs of each specific policy, program, activity, agency, or place across which comparisons are being made. This involves first listing conceptually or verbally the relevant effects, regardless of whether they are benefits or costs. Whether an effect is called a benefit or cost may be a matter of semantics because, for example, the ranking of policies on expensiveness should be the same as their ranking on inexpensiveness, but with the order reversed. The process next involves indicating how the relevant effects can be quantified so that the alternative policies can at least be rank-ordered if not intervally measured. Quantifying benefits and costs in order to measure efficiency is closely connected with specific subject matters, such as crime, pollution, health, unemployment, and so on.[42] Each of these fields raises separate measurement problems. Nevertheless, they could all probably benefit from a greater awareness of the kind of efficiency measurement issues which this chapter has endeavored to clarify.

On a more general level, we can also conclude that substantial similarities and differences exist between policy analysis and business analysis. The most important similarities have to do with (1) trying to maximize benefits minus costs; (2) being concerned with the B/C or efficiency of alternative nondivisible projects as a means of choosing a subset of projects; and (3) being concerned with the changes in benefits and changes in costs as a means of allocating to alternative continuum projects.

The most important differences are (1) the greater difficulty of measuring benefits and costs in policy analysis, especially in the same units; (2) the greater concern in policy analysis for equity constraints and minimum benefits; (3) the frequent statement of policy analysis problems in terms of detriments and costs rather than benefits and costs; and (4) the more frequent allocation of budgets to people, in contrast to allocating budgets to manufacturing processes, alternative raw materials, or other matters that do not require as much concern for the psychology of rewarding continued high efficiency rather than rewarding improvement. These aforementioned similarities indicate that policy analysis has much to learn from business analysis; the differences, however, indicate that policy analysis is a different kind of analysis. This is so even at the abstract level of what constitutes efficiency and what one does with it, in contrast to the more concrete level of measuring benefits and costs, causally relating them, and the political processes of adopting and implementing policies.

NOTES

The author wishes to thank Wesley Skogan of Northwestern University, Eugene Bardach of the University of California, Berkeley, Robert Nagel of the University of Illinois, Mary Frances Miller of the University of Chicago, and Kay Daniel of

Urbana, Illinois, for their comments relevant to this research. Thanks are also owed to the Illinois Law Enforcement Commission for its financial aid relevant to the criminal justice research examples.

1. Previous literature dealing with general matters of measuring efficiency of public policies includes Ronald McKean, *Efficiency in Government Through Systems Analysis: With Emphasis on Water Resources Department* (Wiley, 1966); Werner Hirsch, *The Economics of State and Local Government* (Mc-Graw-Hill, 1970); Ezra J. Mishan, *Cost Benefit Analysis* (Praeger, 1976); and A. R. Prest and R. Turvey, "Cost-Benefit Analysis: A Survey," 75 *Economic Journal* 683–746 (1965). This literature, however, tends to emphasize the determination of benefits and costs rather than the more fundamental matter of distinguishing benefits divided by costs from related concepts with which efficiency is often confused. It also frequently emphasizes problems involved in discounting benefits and costs to consider the fact that the benefits and costs may take a while to be received or paid. For the sake of simplicity, this chapter assumes that the benefits and costs for each project discussed have been accurately measured (including the time discounting), or else it assumes the benefits and costs are immediately received and paid. Also, for the sake of simplicity this chapter assumes that researchers have established a predictable causal relation between the benefits received and the costs expended for each project or policy, although, like measuring benefits and costs, that is often quite difficult to do.

2. For further details on measuring efficiency and related concepts in the criminal justice field, see Lee McPheters and William Stronge (eds.), *The Economics of Crime and Law Enforcement* (Thomas, 1976); Leonard Oberlandar (ed.), *Quantitative Tools for Criminal Justice Plannning* (Law Enforcement Administration Agency, 1975); and S. Nagel (ed.), *Modeling the Criminal Justice System* (Sage, 1977).

3. Business problems involve both benefits and costs, which generally can be measured in dollars. Policy problems often involve costs which are measured in dollars, but benefits that are measured in terms of votes, highway miles, crimes, longevity, education levels, pollution, and so on. A typical business optimization problem involves determining the optimum quantity of goods to produce or price to charge in order to maximize profits. A typical policy optimization problem involves determining how much money to spend on a project in order to maximize benefits within a cost constraint.

4. For a discussion of the relationship of highway expenditures to miles of road serviced, see Eugene Bardach, "The Truth About the Spending-Service Cliché" (unpublished paper available from the author at the University of California, Berkeley, 1978). According to Bardach, there can be a great deal of inefficiency across states (that is, many states operating at a much higher C/B ratio than the most efficient states), while at the same time there is a highly positive or a highly negative correlation between highway expenditures and miles of road serviced. Thus, the extent to which benefits correlate with costs is not a good measure of efficiency. See note 27 for a discussion of the meaning of B/C versus C/B where a detriment like crime is involved, rather than a benefit like highway miles.

5. As a further illustration, one could compare projects E and F from Table 3-1. For project E, $B = \$13.50$, $C = \$10.00$, $B{-}C = \$3.50$, and $B/C = 1.35$. For project F, $B = \$3.50$, $C = \$2.00$, $B{-}C = \$1.50$ and $B/C = 1.75$. Thus, E is more profitable, and F is more efficient. If we invest in E, at the end of the time period we will have \$10.00 in principal, \$3.50 in interest, and no idle funds, for total assets of \$13.50. If we invest in F, we will have \$2.00 in principal, \$1.50 in

interest, and $8.00 in idle funds, for total assets of only $11.50. Or, if we buy one E, we will have $13.50 in benefits, whereas if we buy one F, we will have $3.50 in benefits and $8.00 in unspent money, for a total of only $11.50.

6. On justifying net benefits as a supergoal, see Edith Stokey and Richard Zeckhauser, *A Primer for Policy Analysis* (Norton, 1978), 134–158. In this context, *return* means benefits, and *investment* means costs. Thus, the net benefits or profits from the first investment is $100 (i.e., $200 − $100), and the *B-C* from the second investment is $20 (i.e., $30 − $10). The first investment is preferable because in effect we "take home" an extra $100, whereas in the second we only take home an extra $20. *Return* is sometimes used to refer to benefits minus costs, which is a net rather than a gross return. *Costs* is sometimes used to refer to expenses and other times to a capital investment. Normally this distinction makes no difference because if two alternatives are being compared, they usually both involve either alternative expenses or alternative investments. If one project involves an expense (e.g., labor expense) and a competing project involves an investment (e.g., purchasing a building), it is customary to translate the second project into expense language by talking in terms of depreciation costs rather than the cost of the initial investment. Likewise, *benefits* is sometimes used to refer to income and other times to the equivalent of principal plus interest. When *benefits* refers to income, *costs* refers to expenses. When *benefits* refers to principal plus interest (or investment plus profits), then *costs* refers to principal or what is invested.

   Stokey and Zeckhauser offer a second reason for preferring *B-C* to *B/C*, namely, the ambiguity of the concepts of positive cost and negative benefit. For example, building a pier may provide $4 in recreational benefits at a construction cost of $1. However, the pier may cause $2 in environmental damage. If one subtracts the $2 from the $4 to obtain a net benefits figure before subtracting the cost, then *B/C* is 2/1, whereas if one considers the situation as involving $4 in benefits and $3 in costs, then *B/C* is 4/3. By using *B-C*, this ambiguity is avoided; it could also be avoided simply by stating that all negative benefits should be treated as costs. The problem arises from the analogy to business accounting in which goods returned are considered negative income to be subtracted from gross sales before subtracting costs in arriving at profits.

7. For example, in minimizing errors of innocent defendants convicted (*E1*) and errors of guilty defendants acquitted (*E2*), it may be meaningful to talk in terms of minimizing $10(E1) + (E2)$. The weight of 10 reflects the fact that William Blackstone has said it is 10 times as bad to convict an innocent person as it is to acquit a guilty one. See S. Nagel and Marian Neef, "Deductive Modeling to Determine an Optimum Jury Size and Fraction Required to Convict," *Washington University Law Quarterly* 933–978 (1975).

8. A better way of comparing these two projects (i.e., $B = $10, C = 5, versus $B = $3, C = 1) is to note that if we have only $5 to invest between the two, we would be better off investing only in the first project. After such an expenditure, we would have $10, whereas after investing in the second project, we would have $3 in income plus $4 in unused funds, for a total of only $7. We would thus be better off investing in the more profitable—although less efficient—project when we do not have enough funds to invest in both.

9. This benefit and cost information comes from a related example given in Mark Thompson, "A Passage for Benefit Cost Analysis: Adapting to Changes and Challenges in Middle Age" (unpublished paper presented at the annual meeting of the Evaluation Research Society, 1978). Thompson uses his data to argue that the proper decision-making criterion is sometimes the *B/C* ratio, rather than the *B-C* difference. However, this is not so, as the present analysis shows.

The *B/C* ratios of the individual projects are only useful in finding the combination that maximizes the total *B-C* difference.

10. A less sophisticated approach would involve listing all the combinations of projects that one could buy for $10. These would include any one of the five projects alone, any pair of two projects except the pairs that would include project E, and the three-way combination of D, F, and H. For each of these twelve possibilities, one would determine the benefits minus costs, and then pick the possibility that provides the highest *B-C*. The approach that involves the two suggested rules enables one to obtain the solution more quickly. If, however, one were faced with a situation involving hundreds of possibilities, it might be helpful to write a simple computer program whereby a computer could quickly go through all the possibilities—or all the feasible ones—and arrive at the one with the highest *B-C*.

11. The better combination includes principal plus interest plus idle funds. Thus, for the F, H, D combination at the end of the year or other time period, we would take home $9.00 + $5.10 + $1.00, for a total of $15.10. For the G and H combination, we would take home $10.00 + $5.40, or $15.40. The concept of *yield* is closely related to the benefit/cost ratio. It can be defined as net benefits divided by costs, or *(B-C)/C*, which equals *(B/C)* − 1. Thus, the yield figures for projects D, E, F, G, and H are 0.40, 0.35, 0.75, 0.50, and 0.60. These figures are like interest rates.

One might argue that the most profitable way to spend $10 is to buy five F's. However, one cannot do this if the F's are lump-sum projects, which can neither be bought in multiples of a project or parts of a project. One might argue that one should buy one F for $2 and put the other $8 in a bank to draw interest. No bank though is likely to pay as much interest as the worst project on this list—namely, E—which provides an interest rate of 0.35, or 35 percent.

12. An example of a set of five lump-sum projects in the criminal justice field might be five different ways of notifying released defendants to appear in court. They could include (1) sending defendants postcards scheduled to arrive within a few days of their trial; (2) phoning them within that time period; (3) going to their homes; (4) having them report to the court within a few days of their trial; and (5) putting a general notice in the newspaper emphasizing that defendants who fail to appear for their court dates will be arrested. It would not be meaningful, however, to send each defendant three postcards or half a postcard, nor would it be meaningful to go to their homes twice or to only go halfway to their homes. Deliberately notifying or going to only half the homes might be unconstitutional, unequal treatment.

13. The concept of *productivity* is sometimes used as a synonym for *effectiveness* or *efficiency*. When one talks about the productivity of a policy, program, activity, agency, or place, one usually means the producing of many units of a given product (which is the same as effectiveness). When one talks about the productivity of a person or a worker, one generally refers to the quantity of units produced by an average person of a given type. In that context, the worker is considered to be a cost unit, and productivity then refers to the number of units produced per cost unit (which is efficiency).

14. On measuring effectiveness or benefits, see Robert Haveman and Burton Weisbrod, "Defining Benefits of Public Programs: Some Guidance for Policy Analysts," 1 *Policy Analysis* 169–196 (1975); Robert Dorfman, *Measuring Benefits in Government Investments* (Brookings, 1964); and David Alberts, *A Plan for Measuring the Performance of Social Programs* (Praeger, 1970). On measuring costs or expenditures, see Gene Fisher, *Cost Considerations in Systems Analysis* (Elsevier, 1971); Samuel Chase (ed.), *Problems in Public*

Expenditure Analysis (Brookings, 1978); and Jacob Birnberg and Natwar Gandhi, "How Accountants Can Help Policy-makers in Social Program Evaluation," 8 *Policy Sciences* 469–481 (1977). *Effectiveness* is sometimes used as a synonym for the objective function to be maximized or minimized and thus could refer to benefits, detriments, or benefits minus costs. This usage sometimes appears in the operations research literature, as in Samuel Richmond, *Operations Research for Management Decisions* (Ronald Press, 1968), 24 and 260.

There are many ways of classifying benefits and costs. The most useful might be in terms of total, average, and marginal costs. See note 30 and the corresponding text on pp. 49—50. Another useful classification is in terms of immediate, intermediate, and ultimate with regard to a hierarchical level of importance, or short run versus long run with regard to a temporal ordering. Still another useful classification is in terms of societal, group, and individual. For example, in legislative redistricting, the societal benefits to maximize might be equality among districts, proportional representation, and competitive districts. The group or political party benefits might be to maximize the number of districts one's party dominates. The individual officeholder benefits might emphasize having a legislative district that will maximize his or her percentage of the vote.

15. On measuring equity, see E. S. Savas, "On Equity in Providing Public Services," 24 *Management Science* 800–808 (1978); Arthur Okun, *Equality and Efficiency: The Big Tradeoff* (Brookings, 1975); and Edmund Phelps, *Economic Justice* (Penguin, 1973). In addition to the substantive goals of effectiveness, efficiency, and equity in public policies, there may also be procedural goals that relate to the nature of the decision making with regard to democratic participation, openness or visibility, predictability or objectivity, and procedural fairness or due process. See Chapter 5.

16. On combining goals in policy analysis, see Allan Easton, *Complex Managerial Decisions Involving Multiple Objectives* (Wiley, 1973); Ralph Keeney and Howard Raiffa, *Decisions with Multiple Objectives: Preferences and Value Tradeoffs* (Wiley, 1976); and S. Nagel and Marian Neef, *Policy Analysis: In Social Science Research* (Sage, 1979), 105–132.

17. In comparing efficiency with effectiveness, it is often customary to express *effectiveness* scores for cities in per capita terms, but not efficiency scores. Thus, it makes sense to divide by population in comparing crime figures across cities, because population is a large determinant of quantity of crime, regardless of how well the city is doing. Population, however, is not such a determinant of *efficiency*, nor is it a neutral variable in the sense that increased population causes increased crime and also increased anticrime expenditures.

18. If, for example, one wants to compare a 1-unit increase in effectiveness (and no change in efficiency) with a 1-unit increase in efficiency (and no change in effectiveness), the first program in the after-period must have effectiveness equal to $B + 1$; efficiency equal to $(B + 1)/[(B + 1)(C/B)]$, since this expression is equal to B/C; and net benefits equal to $(B + 1) - [(B + 1)(C/B)]$, since the first expression shows the new benefits, and the second expression shows the new costs with constant efficiency. This second expression comes from solving for X in the equation $(B + 1)/X = B/C$. Likewise, the second program in the after-period has unchanged effectiveness equal to B; a one-unit increase in efficiency equal to $(B)/[BC/(B + C)]$ since this expression is equal to $(B/C) + 1$; and net benefits equal to $(B) - [BC/(B + C)]$, since the first expression shows the constant benefits, and the second expression shows the new costs to get a one-unit increase in efficiency with constant benefits. This second

expression comes from solving for X in the equation $B/X = (B/C) + 1$. Thus, the problem becomes whether $(B + 1) - [(B + 1)(C/B)]$ is greater than $(B) - [BC/(B + C)]$. This inequality can be easily simplified to whether $B^2/(B + 1)$ is greater than C^2. If the answer is yes, a 1-unit increase in effectiveness is more profitable than a 1-unit increase in efficiency. If the answer is no, then a 1-unit increase in effectiveness is less profitable than a 1-unit increase in efficiency.

Applying this analysis to the data at the top of Table 3-3, where effectiveness increases 1 unit, $B + 1$ equals 11; B/C equals 11/5.50, which still equals 2; and profit equals $11 - 5.50$, which equals 5.50. Applying the analysis to the bottom of Table 3-3, where efficiency increases 1 unit, B equals 10; B/C equals 10/3.33, or 3; and profit equals $10 - 3.33$, which equals a greater 6.67. One could have predicted that a 1-unit increase in efficiency would be more profitable when $B = 10$ and $C = 5$ because $10^2/(10 + 1)$ is less than 5^2. Normally, a 1-unit increase in efficiency is more profitable unless the initial benefits are much larger than initial costs. Thus, if the initial benefits are $10.00, the initial costs have to be less than $3.02 to make it more profitable to increase effectiveness by 1 unit.

19. To avoid the problem of dividing crimes by expenditures as a measure of efficiency, one can define *efficiency* as arrests/expenditures, as in Wesley Skogan, "Efficiency and Effectiveness in Big-City Police Departments," 36 *Public Administration Review* 278–286 (1976). This makes sense when one is only concerned with the efficiency of the police, rather than the total criminal justice system. Skogan defines *effectiveness* as output per input, which is how *efficiency* is usually defined. In measuring effectiveness, he then considers crimes to be the input where arrests are the output, although, in measuring efficiency, he considers expenditures to be the input where arrests are the output. Arrests/crimes, or clearances, is an important output for measuring the quality of a police force. For measuring its efficiency, one would logically divide arrests/crimes by expenditures rather than or in addition to dividing arrests by expenditures. Contrary to the analysis in Eugene Bardach, "The Truth About the Spending-Service Cliché" (unpublished paper available from the author at the University of California, Berkeley, 1978), Skogan correlates inputs with outputs across cities as a measure of effectiveness.

20. At first glance, the problem sounds analogous to the following one: If 50 workers take 100 hours to do a job, then how long will it take one worker to do the job? One might initially answer 2 hours, thinking that somehow the 100 hours is divided into 2 hours per worker. One quickly realizes, though, that one worker would take a lot longer than 50 workers. Specifically, if 50 workers take 100 hours, then the total job takes 5,000 hours; thus, one worker working alone will have to put in 5,000 hours to complete the job. This reasoning, however, will not tell us how many crimes we will get for $1 if we get 100 crimes for $50. The workers are analogous to dollars, since both are input figures. The hours, though, are not analogous to crimes. Crimes are like outputs, which are analogous to the jobs which are the output of the workers. The hours are also input components since the total inputs are person-hours.

21. The problem is not resolved by converting crimes into dollars. If, for example, each crime causes $5 in harm, then the total cost for city J is $550, with $500 in crime-damage costs and $50 in anticrime costs. Such a figure is the equivalent of benefits minus costs, although here all the effects are costs and the object is to minimize losses rather than maximize profits. It would not be meaningful, however, to divide losses ($550) by costs ($50) as a measure of efficiency, nor would dividing crimes (100) by costs ($50).

22. Sometimes one can algebraically convert a bad into a good by simply multiplying both sides of an equation by -1 or noting that a double negative makes a positive. For example, it is equally meaningful in environmental policy analysis to say we want to (1) minimize pollution damage costs ($C1$) plus cleanup costs ($C2$); (2) maximize cleanup costs-saved ($B1$) plus damage costs-saved ($B2$); (3) maximize damage costs-saved ($B2$) minus cleanup costs ($C2$); or (4) maximize cleanup costs-saved ($B1$) minus damage costs ($C1$). It is, however, not meaningful simply to multiply crimes by -1 in order to obtain a benefits figure that can then be divided by expenditures. Likewise, multiplying both crimes and expenditures by -1 achieves nothing other than to get us back to what we started with, namely, a detriments-costs figure for which division is meaningless.

23. The idea of calculating a residual measure of efficiency or effectiveness is used by Wesley Skogan, "Efficiency and Effectiveness in Big-City Police Departments," 36 *Public Administration Review* 278–286 (1976). Skogan defines the relative effectiveness of police departments as the difference between actual and predicted clearance rates. Predicted clearance rates for each city are determined by creating a regression line in which arrests are predicted from crimes instead of using arrests-crimes as a dependent variable to be predicted from the demographic or other characteristics of the cities. A residual between predicted time consumption and actual time consumption of cases might be taken as a measure of unnecessary time consumption like a detriment to be minimized. See S. Nagel, "Measuring Unnecessary Delay in Administrative Proceedings: The Actual versus the Predicted," 3 *Policy Sciences* 81–96 (1972).

    One could use a residual approach to attempt to hold constant other variables when relating crime to anticrime expenditures. Doing so involves first relating crime (Y) to the demographic or other variables to be held constant (Z) in order to obtain a predicted crime figure (Y_p) for each city. The difference or residual (Y') between predicted crime and actual crime could be interpreted to represent crime that is explained by the demographic variables and not explained by anticrime expenditures. This residual figure for each city could then be used as the dependent variable in a regression equation, with anticrime expenditures as an independent variable and time points as the units of analysis. Doing so might obtain a marginal rate of return for each city with regard to the effect of additional expenditures on reducing unexplained crime. That method does not work, however, because there is so little left for anticrime expenditures to explain and because the influence of these expenditures are already considered by virtue of their relation with the demographic variables. See S. Nagel, "Allocating Anti-Crime Dollars across Places and Activities" in *Policy Evaluation: Making Optimum Decisions* (Praeger, 1982).

24. For an analysis of the concepts and methods relevant to the notion of an optimum crime level, see Llad Phillips and Harold Votey, "An Economic Basis for the Definition and Control of Crime" in S. Nagel (ed.), *Modeling the Criminal Justice System* (Sage, 1977); and Gary Becker, "Crime and Punishment: An Economic Approach" in Gary Becker and William Landes (eds.), *Essays in the Economics of Crime and Punishment* (Columbia University Press, 1974).

25. Merely knowing that a city had an increase or decrease in crime tells us nothing about its efficiency. For example, a city that has had an increase of 50 crimes may be more efficient than a city that has had a decrease of 50 crimes if the first city has a crimes-expenditures ratio of 200/\$100 and the second city has a ratio of 300/\$100, even though the first city formerly had a ratio of 150/\$100 and the second city formerly had a ratio of 350/\$100. Merely knowing change scores (i.e., change in crimes) also tells us nothing about the marginal rate of return of

the two cities. For example, a city that is having a 10-unit increase in crime may be a good anticrime investment opportunity if that increase was accompanied by a 100-unit decrease in anticrime expenditures. Likewise, a city that has a 10-unit decrease in crime may be a bad investment if to get that decrease it had to greatly increase its expenditures.

26. This equation was arrived at by obtaining the logarithms of the two crime figures and the two expenditure figures. We then divide the difference between the crime logs by the difference between the corresponding expenditure logs in order to obtain the exponent or elasticity coefficient of -1.25. We also solve for the multiplier or the scale coefficient of 13,335 by solving for a in the equation $Y_m = a(X_m)^b$, where Y_m is the mean of the Y scores and X_m is the mean of the X scores. For further details on using regression analysis to obtain the parameters for a diminishing returns curve such as that shown in Figure 3-1, see Edward Tufte, *Data Analysis for Politics and Policy* (Prentice-Hall, 1974), 108–131; Jacob Cohen and Patricia Cohen, *Applied Multiple Regression/Correlation Analysis for the Behavioral Sciences* (Wiley, 1975), 212–264; and S. Nagel and Marian Neef, *Legal Policy Analysis: Finding an Optimum Level or Mix* (Lexington-Heath, 1977), 297–298.

27. Dividing anticrime expenditures by crimes prevented (C/B rather than B/C) could be interpreted as a measure of how much it is worth to the community to avoid one crime. Suppose a community can prevent 0.05 of a crime for $1, which is a more realistic figure than 13,235 based on only 100 crimes for $50. By taking the reciprocal of 0.05/$1, we get $20/1, which is like $20 per unit of merchandise. This figure, however, does not tell us that avoiding one crime is worth only $20 to this community, because the community might be willing to spend more than $20 to avoid a crime, just as a consumer who buys a $20 product might be willing to spend more than $20 for it. The $20/1 figure can also be interpreted to mean that as crimes prevented go up by 1, the cost goes up $20, assuming a constant rate. Likewise, the 0.05/$1 figure can be interpreted to mean that as dollars go up $1, crimes prevented go up 0.05, assuming a constant rate.

28. The method of calculating B/C with crimes/costs information for two points in time should be distinguished from calculating a slope or marginal rate of return, which is discussed on pp. 50—55. The formula for calculating the B/C figure is $(a - Y)/X$, where a is the scale coefficient in the equation $Y = aX^b$, and where Y and X represent crimes and expenditures at the one known point. The formula for calculating a marginal rate of return is baX^{b-1}, with an equation of the form $Y = aX^b$, as mentioned on p. 46. With an equation of the form $Y = a + bX$, the slope or marginal rate of return is $(Y_2 - Y_1)/(X_2 - X_1)$, which is quite different from $(a - Y)/X$. In other words, putting together two points in time does not necessarily generate a slope. A further example is the concept of average efficiency, whereby one calculates an average from a series of B/C scores at different points in time in order to obtain a more accurate efficiency score for a place or program. A place or program can have high efficiency and a low marginal rate of return if it is operating at a point where additional money will not produce additional benefits. Likewise, a place or program can have low efficiency and a high marginal rate of return if it is operating at a point where additional money will produce substantial additional benefits. One might also note that the two dots can be connected by a curved line of the form $Y = a + b \log X$, rather than $Y = ax^b$. The log form has certain advantages, as discussed in note 39.

29. For further details on the method of incremental analysis, see S. Nagel, "Nonmonetary Variables in Benefit-Cost Evaluation," 7 *Evaluation Review* 37–64 (1983). On the method of percentaging analysis, see Chapter 16, "Multiple

Goals and Policies." On the method of threshold analysis, see S. Nagel, "Unknown Variables in Policy/Program Evaluation," 5 *Evaluation and Program Planning* (1983).

30. For further details on the problems involved in relating governmental expenditures to a negative social indicator (such as crime) for the purpose of evaluating programs or allocating budgets, see "Allocating Anti-Crime Dollars across Places and Activities" in S. Nagel, *Policy Evaluation: Making Optimum Decisions* (Praeger, 1982).

31. One could also use the B/C scores for a set of cities as a dependent variable in a regression or correlation analysis designed to determine why some cities are more efficient than others. In the criminal justice context, however, one would normally prefer to know why some cities have more crimes, crimes cleared, or other outputs, and why some cities spend more than others, rather than lump both benefits and costs together by dividing them to make a composite dependent variable. One could also use change in crimes cleared (or change in expenditures) as a dependent variable to be related to change scores on the independent variables.

32. For further details on calculating marginal rates of return or calculus derivatives, see Michael Brennan, *Preface to Econometrics: An Introduction to Quantitative Methods in Economics* (South-western, 1973), 111–167; and Samuel Richmond, *Operations Research for Management Decisions* (Ronald Press, 1968), 40–86. If a relation between outputs and inputs is of the common form $Y = aX^b$, then total benefits are aX^b for any given X; marginal benefits are baX^{b-1} as one goes from any given X to about $X + 1$; and average benefits are aX^b/X, which simplifies to aX^{b-1}. These expressions can be used to predict total detriments, marginal detriments, or average detriments where Y is a bad rather than a good, although the exponent is then likely to have a negative rather than a positive value. Average benefits are equal to B/C or efficiency, but average detriments cannot be interpreted as an efficiency measure. In the less common situation where the relation between outputs and inputs is of the linear form $Y = a + bX$, then total benefits are $a + bX$ for any given X; marginal benefits are b as one goes from any given X to $X + 1$; and average benefits are b if benefits are 0 when costs are 0 (i.e., if a equals 0). If, however, a does not equal 0, then average benefits or efficiency equals $(a + bX)/X$, which is the equivalent of $b + aX^{-1}$. These same expressions can be used to calculate total, marginal, and average detriments where Y is a bad, like crime. Within a narrow range on X or costs, these linear expressions may fit reality, although nonlinear diminishing returns are likely to appear over a wider range of costs. Total, average, and marginal benefits can also be defined in terms of the quantity rather than the cost of input units. In the linear context, the expressions would be $a + bQ$, $(a + bQ)/Q$, and b. In the nonlinear context, the expressions would be aQ^b, aQ^b/Q, and baQ^{b-1}. Talking in terms of benefits per dollar of input, however, normally makes more sense than talking in terms of benefits per quantity of input.

33. On using one-point-in-time B/C information and reasonable assumptions to deduce slopes or marginal rates of return, see S. Nagel and Marian Neef, "Allocating Resources Geographically for Optimum Results," 3 *Political Methodology* 383–404 (1976). Wesley Skogan, "Efficiency and Effectiveness in Big-City Police Departments," 36 *Public Administration Review* 278–286 (1976), provides an example of such use by using arrests/expenditures figures to determine marginal rates of return. He makes the reasonable assumption that if there were no police expenditures, there would probably be no arrests.

34. Proving that important principle simply involves solving two equations simultaneously. One equation says that the sum of what is spent for project 1 plus project 2 should add up to the total cost, that is, $X_1 + X_2 = TC$. The other equation says that the marginal rates of return of the two projects should be equalized so that nothing can be gained by switching funds from one to the other. If benefits relate to costs for a project by the formula, $Y = a + b \log X$, then the marginal rate of return is b/X by the rules of elementary calculus. Thus, equation 2 should read, $b_1/X_1 = b_2/X_2$. If one solves these two equations simultaneously, then $X_1 = [b_1/(b_1 + b_2)](TC)$, and $X_2 = [b_2/(b_1 + b_2)]$ (TC). This indicates that the values for X_1 and X_2 which will maximize total benefits at a given total cost require allocating the total cost to the two projects in proportion to their logarithmic regression coefficients or b values. This rule also logically follows from the fact that in a relation of the form $Y = a + b \log$ X, the slope (or marginal rate of return) of Y to X is determined solely by b since a is a constant.

35. For further details on optimally allocating scarce resources, see Philip Kotler, *Marketing Decision Making: A Model Building Approach* (Holt, Rinehart & Winston, 1971); David Montgomery and Glen Urban, *Management Science in Marketing* (Prentice-Hall, 1969); and S. Nagel, "Finding an Optimum Mix in Allocating Scarce Resources" in *Policy Evaluation: Making Optimum Decisions* (Praeger, 1982). Allocating in accordance with efficiency measures produces the same results as allocating in accordance with marginal measures only when (1) we are dealing with positive linear relations and (2) spending nothing produces no benefits. This is so because under these circumstances marginal benefits (i.e., change in benefits/change in costs) equal average benefits (i.e., B/C), since marginal benefits equal b, and average benefits then equal bX/X, which also equals b. With nonlinear relations, the only way baX^{b-1} (marginal benefits) could equal aX^b/X or aX^{b-1} (average benefits) would be if b equals 1, which would mean we have a linear relationship.

36. The easiest way to obtain the predictive equations for these data is with a calculator that is or can be programmed for linear and nonlinear semilog regression analysis. For program L, one simply inserts two pairs of data points, namely, 20/2 and 21/3, to determine the parameters for the linear equation which allow for a Y-intercept greater than zero. A programmable calculator is not needed for Table 3-4, which has only two data points. The values of all the slopes and intercepts in the table can be determined by simple arithmetic formulas. For a linear relation, $b = (Y_2 - Y_1)/(X_2 - Y_1)$, and $a = Y_2 - bX_2$. For a semilog nonlinear relation, $b = (Y_2 - Y_1)/(\log X_2 - \log X_1)$, and $a = Y_2 - b \log X_2$. If X changes and there is no change in Y, then the slope is zero. If Y changes and there is no change in X, then the slope is infinity. If there is no change in either variable, then the slope is undefined.

To determine the slope for the equation which sets the Y-intercept equal to zero, simply divide the average of the benefit scores by the average of the cost scores; that is, 20.5/2.5, which equals 8.20. This follows from $Y = a + bX$ and $a = \bar{Y} - b\bar{X}$, where $\bar{Y}$ and $\bar{X}$ are the averages of Y and X, respectively. Therefore, if $a = 0$, then $b = \bar{Y}/\bar{X}$. One can do likewise for program M. To determine the parameters for the semilog equation, insert the same data, except use the semilog routine that is generally given with programmable scientific calculators. To determine the slopes for the equations which set the Y-intercept equal to zero, divide the average of the benefit scores by the average of the logarithms of the cost scores. That is, $b = \bar{Y}/\overline{\log X}$, which follows from $a = \bar{Y} - b \log X$, with a log curve of the form $Y = a + b \log X$. When detriments (e.g., crime) are involved rather than benefits (e.g., highway miles), then it is meaningful to have a nonzero Y-intercept because one would not expect to have zero crime by spending zero dollars. The preceding method for determining the value of b when a is assumed to be zero is only a close approximation to the least-squares solution and works when there is only one independent variable. A more exact solution can be obtained by using the option now available in the Statistical Programs in the Social Sciences for fitting a least-squares line with the requirement that the Y-intercept be zero.

37. The optimum allocations with the linear equations are arrived at by simply giving all of the $10 to the program that has the better slope. The optimum allocations with the nonlinear equations are arrived at by allocating in proportion to the multipliers of the log values in the equations. Thus, with the third pair of equations, program L gets 6/23 of the $10, and program M gets 17/23. This allocation can be algebraically proved to be equal to solving a pair of simultaneous equations of the form $\$L + \$M = \$10$, and $b_L/\$L = b_M/\$M$, where $\$L$ and $\$M$ are the number of dollars to be allocated to programs L and M, respectively. The first equation says spend the whole $10. The second equation says set the marginal rate of return of program L equal to the marginal rate of return of program M, so that there is nothing to be gained by shifting any money from one program to the other when their marginal rates of return or nonlinear slopes have been equalized. If a benefit/cost relation is of the form $B = a + b \log C$, then the marginal rate of return or slope of B to C is b/C.

Instead of operationally defining the optimum allocation as the allocation that spends the total budget and equalizes the marginal rates of return of each project, we can define it as the allocation in which one maximizes profits (or $B-C$) or where incremental profits (or incremental benefits minus incremental costs) are zero, indicating that total profits have reached a peak. This alternative way of conceptualizing the optimum allocation provides little help, however, in arriving at the optimum allocations to each program.

If the benefit units in Table 3-4 were measured in dollars, we would obtain the same allocation results by using either $B-C$ or B as the dependent variable in the predictive equations shown in the table, although changing the dependent variable would change the predictive equations. The four equations for program L would then be $B-C = 18 + 0C$; $B-C = 7.20C$; $B - \log C = 18 + 5 \log C$; and $B - \log C = 52 \log C$. With these equations and the preceding allocation rules, identical allocation results occur. This is so because if one knows $B = a + bC$, then one can deduce the parameters for $B = C$ as a function of C, and vice versa. The slope simply changes by one unit, which can be algebraically proved and which can be seen by comparing the four equations with those in the middle of Table 3-4.

38. By forcing the value a to be zero in the predictive equations, we decrease the correlation coefficient, since the regression line or curve will no longer go through the two data points; however, the new regression is more realistic and results in a more meaningful allocation. The restricted regression also predicts higher total benefits (in that 85 is greater than 45, and 53 is greater than 33) because forcing the regression line through the origin normally results in a steeper line. The diminishing-returns fit of the nonlinear equations results in smaller predicted total benefits (in that 33 is less than 45, and 53 is less than 85), but the nonlinear regression is more realistic and results in a more meaningful allocation. Forcing the Y-intercept to be zero will always result in a positive slope. Under some circumstances, this may distort what would otherwise be a negative relation, although one would usually expect an increase in costs to produce an increase in benefits. This possible distortion can, however, be

avoided by using a nonlinear fit of the form $Y = aX^b$, since it automatically provides for a Y-intercept equal to zero while allowing for either a positive or negative relation.

39. The common alternative to a log function of the form $Y = a + b \log X$ is a power function of the form $Y = aX^b$. The log function, however, has a number of advantages over the power function when each entity or place being allocated to has a separate equation, in contrast to each entity or activity being represented by an independent variable in the same equation. The log function can show that when costs are very low, benefits can be equal to nothing, or they can be substantial as with a linear relation, whereas when costs are zero with a power function, benefits can be nothing other than zero. The log function always shows diminishing returns, regardless of whether positive benefits or negative detriments are involved, whereas the power function can unrealistically show increasing returns. The main advantage of a log function in this context, however, is the ease of allocating to the places in proportion to their b values, in contrast to the much more complicated (and often unsolvable) set of simultaneous equations when power functions are used (especially if there are many places), unless one uses approximation methods. The power function does have the advantages of a simpler interpretation of the b values, more flexibility in being able to show increasing returns or costs when they are applicable, the capability of being positive or negative when the Y-intercept is zero, the incapability of allowing crime or other negative goals to go below zero, and ease of allocating in proportion to the b values when the allocation entities or activities are all part of the same equation.

40. The only paper of which this author is aware that deals with the conflict between allocating on the basis of efficiency or merit or on the basis of marginal productivity is A. Wuffle, "Should Political Scientists Be Paid to Think?" (unpublished paper available from the author at the University of California, Irvine, 1979). Wuffle deals with the dilemma of a government research-funding agency that must decide between (1) funding research by meritorious, efficient researchers who would probably do the research without the funding, versus (2) funding research by possibly less meritorious researchers, who are likely to do the research only if they get the funding. Wuffle recommends the optimum strategy of funding projects which are likely to produce results even if not funded, but funding them only nominally so that the funding agency can get credit for sponsoring good research and also for increasing the quantity of research.

41. An equation of the form $B = a + b_1C + b_2t$ (where t represents the period number) will distinguish between these two agencies on b_2 but not b_1. Plotting B/C against time does not enable one to allocate to the high-efficiency program (e.g., program L) that is going slightly down rather than the low-efficiency program (e.g., program M) that is going slightly up. One cannot change this by forcing the trend line through the origin because doing so would distort the time trend, and there is no reason why at time zero, B/C should equal zero. If time zero is when there are neither benefits nor costs, then B/C is undefined since $0/0$ is undefined.

42. Case studies dealing with measuring benefits and costs with regard to specific policy problems can be found in Robert Haveman and Burton Weisbrod, *Public Expenditure and Policy Analysis* (Rand McNally, 1977); Llad Phillips and Harold Votey, "An Economic Basis for the Definition and Control of Crime" in S. Nagel (ed.), *Modeling the Criminal Justice System* (Sage, 1977); and Harley Hinrichs and Graeme Taylor, *Systematic Analysis: A Primer on Benefit-Cost Analysis and Program Evaluation* (Goodyear, 1972). Also see the annual volumes on *Benefit Cost and Policy Analysis: An Aldine Annual on Fore-*

casting, Decision-Making, and Evaluation, edited by Richard Zeckhauser (1974), Robert Haveman (1973), William Niskanen (1972), and Arnold Harberger (1971).

QUESTIONS

1. In evaluating alternative public policies, is the best policy the one that maximizes benefits minus costs, benefits divided by costs, or some other general criterion. Why?
2. Which project in Table 3-1 would be the best project if the benefits were cases solved rather than dollars? Why? Which combination of projects would be the best combination? Why?
3. Is it better to have a policy that improves on effectiveness or one that improves on efficiency? Why?
4. Is it better to have a policy that improves on equity or one that improves on effectiveness? Why? How about equity versus efficiency? Why?
5. Is it better to have a policy that produces low crime (or other detriments) but at high cost, or one that produces high crime but at low cost? Why?
6. Is it better to have a public policy that produces a good benefit/cost ratio, or one that produces a good ratio of change-in-benefits to change-in-costs? Why?

REFERENCES

Alberts, David, *A Plan for Measuring the Performance of Social Programs* (Praeger, 1970).

Dorfman, Robert, *Measuring Benefits in Government Investments* (Brookings, 1964).

Haveman, Robert, and Burton Weisbrod, "Defining Benefits of Public Programs: Some Guidance for Policy Analysts," 1 *Policy Analysis* 169–196 (1975).

Hirsch, Werner, *The Economics of State and Local Government* (McGraw-Hill, 1970).

McKean, Ronald, *Efficiency in Government Through Systems Analysis: With Emphasis on Water Resources Department* (Wiley, 1966).

Mishan, Ezra J., *Cost Benefit Analysis* (Praeger, 1976).

Prest, A. R., and R. Turvey, "Cost-Benefit Analysis: A Survey," 75 *Economic Journal* 683–746 (1965).

CHAPTER 4

Equity as a Policy Goal

The purpose of Chapter 4 is to analyze various aspects of equity as a policy goal. The chapter is divided into three main parts covering: (1) the meaning of equity, both conceptually and operationally; (2) the choice of alternative policies when equity or equality is a criterion; and (3) the possible conflicts or trade-offs between equity and goals such as efficiency and freedom.[1]

The Meaning of Equity

In order for an equity issue to be raised, one first has to have an allocation situation—that is, a situation in which something of value is to be allocated by a government, a society, the marketplace, or the like. The allocating must be to groups, persons, or places, not just to activities. Only people can be treated inequitably, not activities or inanimate objects. An allocation thus involves (1) something of value, (2) a decision-making mechanism, (3) people who are recipients of the valued benefit or the disvalued cost, and (4) some explicit or implicit criteria for determining who gets what. These criteria are especially important in discussing equity.

DEFINING EQUITY

Equity is not the same as equality, although they are related concepts. In a policy-analysis context, *equality* means that two or more places, groups, or people receive equal treatment. *Equity* generally means that they receive proportionate, not absolute, equality. Thus, if two places each receive $15 in federal anticrime money, we have equality between the two places, as is shown in Table 4-1, part I, column 1. We may not, however, have equity if their being treated equally is unfair. If one place has twice as many people as the other, then of the $30 available, perhaps $20 should go to the larger place and $10 to the smaller place. This would be equality in proportion to the population of the two places, as is shown in Table 4-1, part I, column 4. If the grand total is symbolized by G, then one kind of equitable allocation involves giving to each place an amount equal to G multiplied by the equity criterion score (S) divided by the sum of the scores (S).

There are situations in which equity and equality are identical, such as the redistricting of state legislatures. In this context, we are not allocating

69

TABLE 4-1
Allocating Anticrime Dollars to Clarify the Meaning of Equity

I. Allocating $30 to Two Places Equally and on the Basis of Population

	EQUAL ALLOCATION	PEOPLE SCORE ($S1$)	PERCENT ($P1$)	PROPORTIONATE ALLOCATION ($A1$)
Place J	15	80	67	20
Place K	15	40	33	10
Total	$30	120	100%	$30

II. Allocating $30 on the Basis of Population and Crime

	CRIME SCORE ($S2$)	PERCENT ($P2$)	ALLOCATION ($A2$)	COMPOSITE ALLOCATION ($A3$)	WEIGHTED COMPOSITE ALLOCATION ($A4$)
Place J	10	17	5	12.50	10
Place K	50	83	25	17.50	20
	60	100%	$30	$30.00	$30

III. Allocating With a Criterion That Needs to be Reversed

	WEALTH SCORE ($S3$)	PERCENT ($P3$)	REVERSED PERCENT	ALLOCATION ($A5$)
Place J	150	75	25	7.50
Place K	50	25	75	22.50
	200	100%	100%	$30.00

IV. Allocating on the Basis of Criminal Justice Efficiency

	POLICE EFFICIENCY ($S4$)	JUDICIAL EFFICIENCY ($S5$)	CORRECTIONS EFFICIENCY ($S6$)
Place J	70	60	40
Place K	50	30	80
	120	90	120

money or other resources to places, groups, or people. Rather, we are allocating people to legislative districts. However, this is the same as allocating legislative power to places or groups of people. For example, if one district has 6 people, and a second district has 4 people, then the first district has 20 percent more than the average population, and it is thus underrepresented in the legislature. The second district has 20 percent less than the average population, and it is thus overrepresented. The fair allocation of 10 people to two districts is to give each district 5 people, assuming that each district has one legislative representative. Given the one-person, one-vote principle, the equitable way to allocate people among single-member districts is to allocate them equally. Equitable allocation, however, in contrast to proportionate allocation, is rarely equal allocation.

Proportionate equality comes closer to equity if the criterion for apportioning benefits or costs seems fairer than absolute equality or an alternative apportionment. What constitutes fairness or distributive justice, however, is highly subjective. Perhaps it is fairer to allocate the $30.00 according to the amount of crime each place has. If the smaller place has five times as much crime as the larger place, then perhaps it should get $25.00, and the larger place should get $5.00, as is shown in Table 4-1, part II, column 3. Perhaps the most equitable allocation would simultaneously consider both population and crime. If so, then perhaps place J should receive an allocation halfway between $20.00 and $5.00, or $12.50. Likewise, if population and crime are equally important, place K should receive an allocation halfway between $10.00 and $25.00, or $17.50, as is shown in part II, column 4. The composite allocation ($A3$) is equal to the sum of the separate allocations (A) divided by the number of allocations (N), assuming each allocation criterion or score is considered equally important.

If need (as measured by crime occurrence) is considered twice as important as population, then we should calculate a weighted composite allocation, analogous to calculating a weighted grade-point average. We simply weight the crime allocation by 2 before we add the separate allocations (ΣWA), and then divide by the sum of the weights (ΣW). In this example, the weighted composite allocation ($A4$) for each place is equal to $A1$ plus twice $A2$, divided by a weight of 3. That means place J would have a weighted composite allocation equal to $20 plus $10 divided by 3, which equals $10, as is shown in Table 4-1, part II, column 5. The idea of a weighted composite allocation is important because we almost always want to allocate in accordance with more than one criterion, and we almost always weight the criteria differently.

Besides population and crimes, we could have an additional criterion that also gets at need, namely, the wealth of each place. This type of criterion should be reversed in order to be usable in our proportionate allocation system. It is a score like that in golf, in which a high score is undesirable. In this context, a high score makes a place less needy and therefore less entitled to an equitable or minimum allocation. The easiest way to reverse a criterion that is like a golf score is to first convert it into a set of part/whole percentages, and then obtain the complement of each percentage. These complements or reversed percentage scores are in effect poverty scores derived from the wealth scores. One can then allocate in proportion to these complements or reversed percentages. This is more meaningful than trying to reverse the raw scores by subtracting them from an arbitrary number that is larger than any of the raw scores. These steps are shown in Table 4-1, part III. The first column shows the wealth scores of the two places. The second column converts those scores into part/whole percentages. The third column determines the complements of these percentages. The fourth column allocates the $30 in proportion to those complements.

If one wanted to allocate to each place in proportion to the people, crime, and wealth with all three criteria weighted equally, a logical way to do so would be to give place J a composite score equal to 67% + 17% − 75%, which equals 9%. One would likewise give place K a composite score equal to 33% + 83% − 25%, which equals 91%. This tells us that place J should get 9 percent of the $30 and place K should get 91 percent. In other words, if one is allocating to a single, golflike criterion, then one should allocate in proportion to the complements of the part/whole percentages. If, however, it is one of a set of criteria, then calculate a composite score for each place or other object of the allocations. The composite score is the algebraic sum of the positive percentages and the negative percentages. Then allocate in proportion to these algebraic sums.

We can combine population and wealth into one criterion called *wealth per capita*. Likewise, we can combine population and crimes into one criterion called *crimes per capita*. Crimes per capita gets at the external aspect of need, and wealth per capita gets at the internal economic ability to deal with that need. We can further combine these two criteria into one criterion called *crimes per capita divided by wealth per capita*. If we do this, however, we get outside the realm of equity criteria and into efficiency criteria, because we are approaching an output/input measure. We would have such a measure if we used change-in-crimes-per-capita divided by change-in-wealth-per-capita. This would give us a marginal rate of return showing to what extent crimes are reduced by increasing the wealth of each place. If we allocate on the basis of such an efficiency criterion, then we are not allocating on the basis of an equity or needs criterion.

To further clarify the distinction between equity or needs criteria and efficiency criteria, part IV of Table 4-1 provides hypothetical data for each place on the efficiency of their police, judicial, and corrections systems. Such data could perhaps be obtained by asking knowledgeable police chiefs, state supreme court justices, prison wardens, and the like to rank-order each place on a 1-to-N scale, or to rate each place on a 0-to-100 scale. The scores can be treated arithmetically like the equity scores of population, crime, wealth, and poverty. If we allocate only in accordance with efficiency scores, we may get more crime reduction for our $30 than if we allocate in accordance with the equity scores. We may, however, be violating our sense of fairness that no place should receive less than a certain minimum allocation in view of its population, social problems, and poverty.

A compromise might be to weight the three equity allocations equally along with the three efficiency allocations. One can also use a differential weighting, as described previously. An alternative to allocating with equity and efficiency criteria simultaneously is to allocate to these criteria sequentially. Doing this involves deciding the amount that each place, group, or person needs in order to be at a minimum level of decency with regard to health, education, freedom from crime, or other societal benefits. If it is determined that place J needs a minimum of $4 beyond what it can afford and place K needs a minimum of $8 beyond what it can afford, the sequential method would allocate $12 to these two places and then allocate the remaining $18 in accordance with the efficiency criteria. The simultaneous method may be easier because it does not require determining a minimum constraint level for each place; however, it is less accurate in guaranteeing that each place will be at or above a minimum level of decency.

In light of the preceding analysis, we can define equity as allocating societal or governmental benefits or costs to places, groups, or people in such a way as to provide each of them with a minimum level of benefits and costs in light of their needs and resources. In this sense, equity is a minimum constraint regarding benefits that one should receive, such as income, or a maximum constraint on detriments, such as crime. It can also be considered a minimum constraint regarding costs one should be willing to bear, for example, taxes, or a maximum constraint on costs to which one should be subjected. In addition to being viewed as a constraint which is either met or not met, equity is often treated as a variable (1) in the sense of degrees of inequity and (2) even when all places, groups, or persons have met the appropriate constraint level. When one is referring to maximizing equity after the minimum constraint level, then the term *equality* might be better used. In this chapter, as in common usage, *equity* is used as both a constraint and as a variable; the context should make clear which type is being referred to.

Equity is often contrasted with efficiency, in which each place, group, or person receives benefits in accordance with its ability to put them to productive use. This means allocation in accordance with the marginal rate of return on a goal criterion, other than satisfying minimum needs. We should, however, point out that allocating in accordance with equity criteria may often be highly efficient. For example, allocating to the places that have the most crime may be efficient in the sense that it may be easier to lessen crime when there is a lot of it than when there is very little of it. Although equity and efficiency criteria can be conceptually distinguished, the places that are high on needs may also be high on efficiency because they need to be more efficient. Likewise, the places that are high on needs may not have such efficient, well-trained personnel. However, they may provide a high marginal rate of return despite their inefficient personnel because their problems respond so easily to relatively small incremental allocations.

The term *equity* is sometimes used as a synonym for *fairness*. The latter term, though, is broader in that it covers the question of how to allocate after the equity minimums have been met. An allocation can be unfair either because (1) the minimums have not been met or (2) they have been met, but the allocating above the minimum is not done in proportion to ability, need, worthiness, or some other criterion that is considered proper. Fairness is like equality, which is usually a variable, but unlike equity, which is usually a constraint. Discrimination is in some ways the opposite of fairness. Discrimination involves allocating things of value to individuals who are less able before allocating to those who are more able because of such irrelevant criteria as race and sex. Discrimination may be unfair and inefficient, but it is not inequitable if minimum needs of all the persons involved are satisfied.

It should be noted that equity is a result goal or a substance goal rather than a process. Some consider random selection an equitable way to allocate. It is also objective in that it involves no subjective criteria. However, random selection is not equitable if it produces inequitable results. For example, flipping a coin in order to allocate all the seats in a legislature to the Democrats or the Republicans is random and objective, but it is inequitable if either party is legitimately entitled to a minimum number of seats. An equitable process involves allowing a minimum amount of participation to all relevant groups. In other words, the concept of equity generally requires a minimum allocation level across groups, persons, or places.[2]

MEASURING EQUITY

Table 4-2 is designed to help clarify how one might go about determining the degree of equity that is present in various allocations. For the sake of simplicity, the table assumes a two-person society. The problem is to classify alternative ways of allocating the national income between the two people. Table 4-2 consists of a series of four-cell tables. Each row corresponds to person G or person H. The first column shows how the national income is actually allocated (A). The second column shows the minimum or equitable allocations (M). The column totals show the sum of the actual (ΣA) or minimum (ΣM) allocations.

Part I shows the three basic classifications of (1) an equitable society, wherein the minimum equitable allocations are met; (2) an inequitable but capable society, wherein the minimum allocations are not met, but there is enough national income to meet them; and (3) an inequitable and incapable society, wherein the minimums are not met and there is not enough national income to meet them. One could argue that only a capable society can be inequitable. This kind of reasoning emphasizes inequity as an intentional wrong, rather than as an objective occurrence regardless of intent or capability.

Part II provides examples of different kinds of equitable allocations. Society 4 is a poor society, barely capable of meeting the equity minimums, whereas societies 5 and 6 are rich, with national incomes more than double the sum of the minimum needs to be met. Society 6 provides equal allocations, whereas both 4 and 5 provide unequal allocations. Society 4 provides allocations proportionate to each person's needs, since persons G and H are receiving Q times his or her needs. Neither society 5 nor society 6 allocates income in proportion to needs. All three societies are, however, equitable in that they meet the minimum needs of all their people.

One is probably better off in a rich society that is unequal than in a poor

TABLE 4-2
Allocating National Income in a Two-Person Society to Clarify the
Measurement of Degrees of Equity

I. Basic Classifications

	1		2		3	
	A	M	A	M	A	M
PERSON G	≥6	6	G <6	6	G <6	6
	—and—		—or—		—or—	
PERSON H	≥3	3	H <3	3	H <3	3
	≥9	9	≥9	9	<9	9
	EQUITABLE		INEQUITABLE		INEQUITABLE	
			AND CAPABLE		AND INCAPABLE	

II. Examples of Equitable Allocations

	4		5		6	
	A	M	A	M	A	M
PERSON G	6	6	G 6	6	G 10	6
PERSON H	3	3	H 14	3	H 10	3
	9	9	20	9	20	9
	POOR SOCIETY		RICH SOCIETY		RICH SOCIETY	
	AND PROPORTIONATE		AND UNEQUAL		AND EQUAL	

III. Examples of Inequitable Allocations

	7				8				9			
	A	M	D	D^2	A	M	D	D^2	A	M	D	D^2
PERSON G	4	6	−2	4	G 5	6	−1	1	G 5	6	−1	1
PERSON H	5	3			H 2	3	−1	1	H 5	3		
	9	9	−2	4	7	9	−2	2	10	9	−1	1
	MORE				LESS				INEQUITABLE			
	INEQUITABLE				INEQUITABLE				BUT EQUAL			

IV. Other Kinds of Deviations

	10			11			12		
	A	E	D	A	P	D	A	D	D
PERSON G	18	15	+3	G 18	20	−2	G 18	8	+10
PERSON H	12	15	−3	H 12	10	+2	H 12	22	−10
	30	30		30	30		30	30	
	FROM			FROM			FROM		
	EQUALITY			PROPORTIONALITY			OPTIMALITY		

Allocation Symbols:
A = Actual E = Equal F = Efficient
M = Minimum or Equitable P = Proportionate O = Optimum $(M + F)$
D = Difference between $A - M$ or some other desired figure

society that is equal, or proportionate, or both. The odds may be good that those who are not so well-off in the rich society will succeed in redistributing some of the wealth in order to increase their standard of living, while not substantially decreasing the standards of those who are quite well-off. This is especially so if the transfer payments can be planned so that they provide incentives for individuals who are not so well-off to advance themselves and thus promote the collective good by increasing the total societal income and wealth.

Table 4-2, part III, provides examples of inequitable allocations. In all three societies at least some of the people do not have their minimum needs met. Society 9 illustrates that one can have an inequitable society in which all people are treated equally, but in which that treatment results in somebody being below the minimum-needs level. A crude way of measuring the degree of inequity is to determine what percentage of the people are not having their needs met. That percentaging measure would, however, make a two-person society look bad if both people deviate slightly from the minimum, as compared to a two-person society in which one person is at the minimum and the other person is way below.

It is more meaningful to determine how much each person, place, or group deviates below the minimum, and then to sum the deviations. According to Table 4-2, 50 percent of the people in societies 7 and 9 score below the minimum. However, society 7 is more inequitable, with the sum of its deviations equal to 2, rather than 1. Note that in calculating deviations from the equity minimums, we are only concerned with deviations below the minimum. This is so because we have defined an equitable allocation or an equitable society as one in which all persons, places, or groups are at or above a minimum level of decency for whatever is being allocated. Suppose that under one allocation, person G receives 8 units, and person H receives 3 units. Under a second allocation, person G receives only 4 units, and person H still receives 3 units. Under either allocation, the sum of the absolute deviations would be 2. However, the second allocation is obviously more inequitable because under it someone is below the minimum-needs level. Summing the deviations is also too crude because it would make societies 7 and 8 equally inequitable. Society 8 is, however, less inequitable because each person who is below the minimum is only slightly below. Society 7, on the other hand, has half its population substantially below the minimum-needs level.

To distinguish between the more inequitable society 7 and the more equitable society 8, the deviations must be squared in order to put more emphasis on the relatively extreme deviant cases. That way, society 7 receives an inequity score of 4, whereas society 8 receives an inequity score of only 2. If one is sensitive to extreme deviations, one could cube rather than square the deviations or even use a larger exponent; however, squaring is conventionally accepted and represents a compromise between working with the raw deviations and larger exponents. Even squaring and summing the deviations may not produce a sufficient measure of inequity, because the technique does not consider how many people there are in a society.

This disadvantage can be overcome by dividing the sum of the squared deviations by the number of people in order to produce an average squared deviation. This measure may be quite meaningful for comparisons across societies or allocations having different quantities of people, places, or groups. However, it may not be so meaningful in comparing allocations that involve different things of value, such as education, income, or freedom from crime.

In order to have such a comparative measure, the sum of the squared deviations must be normed so that perfect inequity will score 1.00 and perfect equity will score zero, or vice versa. To do that, we can divide the sum of the squared deviations by the sum of the maximum deviations. The maximum deviation for any person is the difference between receiving nothing and the minimum. Thus, the maximum deviation for person G in society 7 is zero minus 6, which equals -6. If we square that deviation, we get 36. Likewise, the maximum deviation for person H in society 7 is zero minus 3, which equals -3, which yields a squared deviation of 9. Therefore, the inequity score for society 7 is $4/(36 + 9) = 4/45 = 0.09$. If persons G and H had been allocated zero units, then the inequity score for society 7 would have been 45/45, or 1.00, which is perfect inequity. If person G had been allocated 5 units instead of 4, then the inequity score would have been 1/45, or 0.02, which is closer to perfect equity than a score of 0.09. A disadvantage of this inequity score (which is normed between zero and 1.00) is that we would prefer to have an equity score, rather than an inequity score.

If we subtract the inequity score from 1.00, we will have a score in which the higher it is, the more equity is present. That way, a score of 1.00 means perfect equity. A score of zero then means perfect inequity, in which every person, place, or group within the society is receiving nothing of what is being allocated and is thus maximally below the minimum needs. One can summarize these definitions and calculations by saying that

$$EQ = 1 - [\Sigma(A - M)^2/\Sigma(Z - M)^2]$$

where EQ = equity, A = actual allocation, M = minimum allocation, and Z = zero. This equation can be simplified to:

$$EQ = 1 - \Sigma D^2/\Sigma M^2$$

where D is the deviation of each actual allocation that is below the minimum allocation. The expression $(Z - M)^2$ simplifies to M^2. Table 4-3 summarizes what is involved in developing this equity formula.

Part IV of Table 4-2 provides examples of deviations other than those from equitable minimums. All three societies in part IV are assumed to have a national income of $30 to be allocated between two people. Allocation 10

TABLE 4-3
Measuring Equity

I. Symbols Used

A = actual allocation to a person, group, or place
M = minimum allocation
D = deviation between actual and minimum allocation
Z = zero allocation
EQ = equity

II. The Equity Formula

1. The formula simplified:

$$EQ = 1 - \Sigma D^2/\Sigma M^2$$

2. The formula expanded:

$$EQ = 1 - [\Sigma(A - M)^2/\Sigma(Z - M)^2]$$

III. Justification for the Elements of the Equity Formula

1. The *ratio* is subtracted from 1.00. Otherwise, the ratio would indicate the degree of inequity, rather than the degree of equity.
2. The *numerator* of the ratio shows the sum of the squared deviations between the actual allocation to each person, group, or place and the minimum decency allocation, where the actual allocation is below the minimum.
3. If an allocation is *above the minimum*, then $A - M$ is scored zero, since inequity only occurs when people are allowed to fall below a minimum decency level, although inequality may occur if people are allowed to rise too far above others.
4. The deviation between the actual allocation to a person, group, or place and the minimum is *squared*, rather than just using the absolute difference, because squaring accentuates extreme cases. Thus, a deviation of 1 for each of two people is not as bad as a deviation of 2 for one person, unless squaring is done.
5. The *denominator* of the ratio shows the sum of the squared deviations between the lowest possible allocation (which is zero) and the minimum decency level. This is the sum of the maximum possible deviations, since people cannot be allocated less than zero. By dividing by the maximum possible deviation, we obtain a part-whole ratio showing the percentage of actual inequity of the max-imum possible inequity.
6. $(Z - M)^2$ simplifies to M^2, and $(A - M)^2$ simplifies to D^2.

IV. Example of the Equity Formula Applied

A. The facts
   1. A society has 9 units to allocate between 2 people.
   2. One person should have a minimum of 6 units, but receives only 4.
   3. The second person should have a minimum of 3 units, but receives 5.

B. Calculating the equity measure
   1. The numerator of the ratio is:

$$(4 - 6)^2 + (5 - 3)^2 = (2)^2 + (0)^2 = 4 + 0 = 4$$

   2. The denominator of the ratio is:

$$(0 - 6)^2 + (0 - 3)^2 = (-6)^2 + (-3)^2 = 36 + 9 = 45$$

   3. The ratio is:

$$4/45 = 0.09$$

   4. The degree of equity is thus:

$$1 - 0.09 = 0.91$$

illustrates deviations from perfect equality, rather than from perfect equity. Allocation 11 illustrates deviations from proportionality in which person G is twice as large on family size, political power, ambition, or some other characteristic or combination that is considered relevant. Allocation 12 illustrates deviations from optimality—that is, a combination of equity and efficiency. Person G has a minimum need of 6 and an efficiency score of 2. Person H has a minimum need of 3 and an efficiency score of 19, measured in the same units. These scores could be converted into percentages, as was done in Table 4-1. That would give person G an optimality percentage of 8/30, or 27 percent, and person H an optimality percentage of 22/30, or 73 percent. It is important to note the conceptual and operational distinctions between deviations from optimality, proportionality, equality, and equity.

The most subjective and difficult aspect of measuring degrees of inequity is determining the minimum needs of the persons, groups, or places. The biological needs, such as determining how many calories a person needs to stay alive, are relatively easy. The matter becomes more subjective when we get into the economics. For instance, how many dollars must one have in order to buy the least expensive food that will provide the number of calories necessary to stay alive. The matter becomes still more subjective when we get into the philosophical aspects of what society or the government should provide in order to meet the minimum biological or economic needs. The answers to that decision vary over time and across places depending partly on what a society believes it can afford. The issue is more dramatic in the case of an individual who needs $100,000 a year for special medical treatment to stay alive. Under these circumstances, the biological and economic considerations have been calculated. For many policy analysts, there is also no philosophical problem, since they would argue that the government must pay for the medical treatment because enabling an individual to stay alive is the least the government can do. A counterargument, however, would be that spending $100,000 a year on one individual may mean that others will be kept from being at the minimum. Such decisions should be made by democratically chosen legislatures, when possible, or by those to whom they delegate decision-making authority, but with constitutional constraints to protect minority rights.

The availability of expensive medical equipment raises the issue of maximum equity constraints. Is it inequitable for only some people in a society to have access to high benefits? For example, is it inequitable that rich people can stay alive by purchasing a $100,000 dialysis machine to which poor people do not have access? One could argue that staying alive is not a high benefit, but rather a bare minimum. Attempting to establish maximum constraints can also be counterproductive because it decreases incentives for people to advance themselves and possibly to advance society in the process. Maximum constraints are often, in effect, established by available technology, economics, and societal custom. There is no question that people are harmed by being below minimum-benefit constraints, but the harm is less obvious when some people are especially well-off. The dialysis example is really more illustrative of some people falling below a minimum-benefit level than of some people being above a maximum level. Both of these aspects could theoretically be handled by denying dialysis machines to all people on the grounds that they are wasteful of society's scarce resources or by rationing them on the basis of criteria other than wealth. These solutions, however, may be incapable of being implemented efficiently in a market-place economy, in contrast to an economy which plans that there will be no dialysis machines. Regardless of the desirability of expensive equipment or services such as dialysis machines, the concept of equity applies more meaningfully to keeping people above minimum-benefit levels than to keeping them below maximum-benefit levels.[3]

The concept of equity implies that persons, groups, and places should receive a minimum quantity of benefits when allocations are made. The minimum wage law is an example of equity reasoning in legislation. Equity also implies that persons, groups, and places should not be subjected to more than a maximum quantity of costs. An example of this kind of equity is the maximum ceiling on social security taxes whereby no taxes are paid beyond a maximum cutoff. The concept of equity does not imply a ceiling on benefits. It is generally not considered inequitable for some people to be extremely rich, as long as no one is extremely poor. In fact, trying to bring down the rich may hurt the poor if bringing down the rich means decreasing potential employers of the poor. New technologies generally uplift both the poor and the rich by allowing for improved productivity and improved standards of living.

It should be noted that equality across groups does not necessarily guarantee equality across persons. For example, 100 blacks and 100 whites may both average 2-year sentences for the same crime, giving the appearance of nondiscrimination. On the individual level, though, 50 blacks whose victims were white may get 4-year sentences, and 50 blacks whose victims were black may get probation; 50 whites with white victims may get 4-year sentences, and 50 whites with black victims may get probation. This would indicate considerable discrimination at the individual case level. Moreover, whites could have a higher average sentence and yet receive sentencing favoritism, even when the crime is held constant. For example, if 99 of the 100 whites get 1-year sentences, and 1 big-time operator gets a sentence of 101 years, then the white average is 2 years. The 100 blacks may all get 1.5 years and thus average 1.5 years. The white average would be higher than the black average, and yet 99 percent of the whites would receive shorter sentences than the black average and shorter sentences than the black defendant who received the shortest of the black sentences. This points up the importance of talking about equity on both the group and individual level.

MEASURING EQUALITY AND PROPORTIONALITY

There are a variety of ways to measure equality. The simplest involves subtracting the lowest score from the highest score. Of course, this measure leaves out a lot of relevant information. Another relatively simple measure is the average deviation from the mean. It involves (1) determining the mean or average score for a set of persons, places, or groups; (2) determining by how much each entity deviates from the mean; and (3) then averaging the absolute values of these deviations. The average deviation from the mean uses all the information, and it has good commonsense imagery. Finally, there are more complicated measures that have more specialized purposes, such as the standard deviation, the Gini index, and the Schutz coefficient.

One defect in the average deviation from the mean is that it does not adequately consider extreme deviations, which are better considered by squaring the deviations, as was discussed previously. The average deviation from the mean also needs norming in order to improve its comparability across different subject matters. This leads to a measure of equality analogous to the previously developed measure of equity. An appropriate formula might thus be:

$$E = 1 - [\Sigma(A - M)^2/\Sigma(Z - M)^2]$$

This formula looks like the equity formula, but with the following differences:

1. E stands for equality, rather than equity.
2. M stands for mean score, rather than minimum allocation.
3. A stands for actual allocation, regardless of whether the actual allocation is above or below the mean. In calculating an equity score, a deviation is only considered to have occurred when the actual allocation is below the minimum.
4. Z stands for the worst possible actual score that each entity could have in light of the total sum to be allocated. It does not stand for zero because the denominator of the formula is supposed to show the worst possible allocation in terms of equality. Giving everybody nothing is the worst allocation in terms of *equity*. Giving one person everything and everybody else nothing is the worst allocation in terms of *equality*.

Suppose we have a two-person society; out of 10 units available to be distributed, one person receives 7 units and the other 3 units. If perfect equality were provided, they would each receive 5 units. The first person deviates by 2, and so does the second. The sum of the unsquared deviations is thus 4. The first squared deviation is 4, and so is the second. The sum of the squared deviations is 8, which is the numerator of the inequality ratio. The denominator is determined by randomly allocating all 10 units to one person and zero units to the other person. If the first person gets 10 units, that would mean a deviation of +5 and a squared deviation of 25. If the second person gets zero units, that would mean a deviation of -5 and a squared deviation also of 25. The sum of these squared deviations is 50. The ratio between 8 and 50 is 0.16. If we subtract 0.16 from 1.00, we get an equality score for this allocation of 0.84. This is a fairly high degree of equality since an allocation of 7 and 3 is close to 5 and 5, but quite different from 10 and zero. Table 4-4 summarizes what is involved in developing this equality formula.[4]

Through a similar analysis, one can develop a proportionality coefficient analogous to the equity and equality coefficients. The basic formula is:

$$\text{Proportionality} = 1 - [\Sigma(A - P)^2/\Sigma(Z - P^2)]$$

In this equation, A is the actual allocation to each person, place, or group. P is the proportionate allocation, or the allocation predicted from merit, or another score to which the allocations should be proportionate. Z refers to a zero allocation since this allocation is generally the furthest away from a proportionate allocation. Allocations cannot be negative. They cannot be much higher than P because they are constrained by G or the grand total available to be allocated. The P allocations sum to G, as do the A allocations. A simple way of calculating P for each person is to add the merit scores of each person, determine a part/whole percentage for each person, and then multiply the total available resources by each of those percentages to get the proportionate allocation. Thus, if two people have merit scores of 20 and 10, then their part/whole percentages are 20/30 = 67 percent and 10/30 = 33 percent, respectively. If the total resources are 9 units, the proportionate allocation is 6 and 3 units, respectively.

Suppose that instead of receiving a proportionate allocation of 6 and 3 units, the two people receive 4 and 5 units, respectively. Then the deviations from proportionality are 2 units for each of them, or 4 units apiece if the deviations are squared. The sum of the squared deviations is 8, which is the numerator of the proportionality ratio. The denominator involves assuming that each person gets zero and then summing the squares of 6 and 3. The figures of 6 and 3 are the maximum deviations possible from the proportional allocations, without having negative allocations and without exceeding the budget constraint of 9. Summing the squares of 6 and 3 yields a denominator of 36 + 9 = 45. The ratio of 8/45 is 0.18; that is, the proportionality score is 0.82, or 82 percent of perfect proportionality. Table 4-5 summarizes what is involved in developing this proportionality formula.

An alternative way of measuring proportionality is to determine how well one can predict allocations (such as salaries) from criteria (such as merit scores). Such a measure considers two allocations to be equal if they generate the same regression coefficient or slope. The method shown in Table 4-5, however, is sensitive to how close the data points are when they are not on a 45-degree line coming out of the origin. The regression approach, on the other hand, is only influenced by the slope of the connecting line. The regression approach thus ignores the degree of difficulty of putting the

TABLE 4-4
Measuring Equality

I. Symbols Used

A = actual allocation to a person, group, or place
M = mean or average allocation
D = deviation between actual and mean allocation
Z = worst possible allocation
E = equality

II. The Equality Formula

The formula:

$$E = 1 - [\Sigma(A - M)^2/\Sigma(Z - M)^2]$$

III. How the Equality Formula Differs From the Equity Formula

1. E stands for equality, rather than equity.
2. M stands for mean score, rather than minimum allocation.
3. A stands for actual allocation, regardless of whether the actual allocation is above or below the mean. In calculating an equity score, deviations are only considered as occurring when the actual allocation is below the minimum.
4. Z stands for the worst possible actual score that each entity could have in light of the total sum to be allocated. It does not stand for zero since the denominator of the formula is supposed to show the worst possible allocation in terms of equality. Giving everybody nothing is the worst allocation in terms of equity. Giving one person everything and everybody else nothing is the worst allocation in terms of equality.
5. The *numerator* of the ratio in the equality formula shows the sum of the squared deviations between the actual allocation to each person, group, or place, and the mean allocation as a measure of actual inequality.
6. The *denominator* of the ratio in the equality formula shows the sum of the squared deviations between the worst possible allocation and the mean allocation as a measure of maximum inequality. By dividing by the maximum possible inequality, we obtain a part-whole ratio showing the percentage of actual inequality of the maximum possible inequality.

IV. Example of the Equality Formula Applied

A. The facts
    1. A society has 9 units to allocate between two people.
    2. One person receives 4 units.
    3. The second person receives 5 units.

B. Calculating the equality measure
    1. The numerator of the ratio is:

$$(4 - 4.5)^2 + (5 - 4.5)^2 = (0.5)^2 + (0.5)^2 = 0.25 + 0.25 = 0.50$$

    2. The denominator of the ratio is:

$$(0 - 4.5)^2 + (9 - 4.5)^2 + (4.5)^2 + (4.5)^2 = 20.25 + 20.25 = 40.50$$

    3. The ratio is:
$$0.50/40.50 = 0.01$$

    4. The degree of equality is thus $1 - 0.01 = 0.99$. The equality is high because there are only two people, and they are very close to the mean. The equity is not so high in Table 4-3 because there is more deviation from the minimums than there is from the mean.

TABLE 4-5
Measuring Proportionality

I. Symbols Used

A = actual allocation to a person, group, or place
P = proportionate allocation
D = deviation between actual and proportionate allocation
Z = zero allocation
PR = proportionality

II. The Proportionality Formula

1. The formula simplified:

$$PR = 1 - \Sigma D^2 / \Sigma P^2$$

2. The formula expanded:

$$PR = 1 - [\Sigma(A - P)^2 / \Sigma(Z - P)^2]$$

3. The formula for P for any person, group, or place is:

$$G(X_i / \Sigma X),$$

where G is the grand total available to be allocated and X is each entity's score on merit or whatever the allocations should be proportionate to.

III. How the PR Formula Differs From the Equity Formula

1. The *numerator* of the ratio in the *PR* formula is the sum of the squared deviations between the actual allocations and the proportionate allocations, as a measure of actual disproportionality.
2. The *denominator* of the ratio in the *PR* formula is the sum of the squared deviations between zero allocations and proportionate allocations, as a measure of maximum disproportionality. Zero allocations are as far as one can get from proportionate allocations since one cannot allocate negative units to go any lower. We also cannot allocate units much higher than P because we are constrained by G.
3. By dividing the actual by the maximum, we obtain a *ratio* showing the percentage of actual to maximum. By subtracting that ratio from 1.00, we obtain the percentage of proportionality out of the maximum possible proportionality.

IV. Example of the PR Formula Applied

A. The facts
    1. A society has 9 units to allocate between two people.
    2. One person has a merit score of 20, and the second person has a merit score of 10.
    3. The first person receives 4 units, and the second person receives 5 units.
B. Calculating the *PR* Measure
    1. The P score for the first person is:

$$9(20/30) = 9(0.67) = 6$$

The P score for the second person is:

$$9(10/30) = 9(0.33) = 3$$

TABLE 4-5 (continued)
Measuring Proportionality

2. The numerator of the ratio is:

$$(4 - 6)^2 + (5 - 3)^2 = (2)^2 + (2)^2 = 4 + 4 = 8$$

3. The denominator of the ratio is:

$$(0 - 6)^2 + (0 - 3)^2 = (6)^2 + (3)^2 = 36 + 9 = 45$$

4. The ratio is:

$$8/45 = 0.18$$

5. The degree of proportionality is thus:

$$1 - 0.18 = 0.82$$

persons, groups, or places in their proportional positions. In geometric or graphing terms, it ignores how many notches each data point or dot has to be moved to the right, left, up, or down to bring about perfect proportionality.

In a practical context, proportionality problems frequently occur in employment discrimination cases, especially in controversies over whether workers are being discriminated against because of their sex or race. A related problem is whether the percentage of females or blacks in a given job category is low enough to be contrary to chance probability. In this context, one would be concerned with the deviation between the actual allocation of job positions and the allocation predicted by chance. The usual analysis involves determining the extent to which the deviation is readily or not readily attributable to chance. Closely related to deviations from proportionality are deviations from optimality. The optimal allocation to persons, groups, or places is often in proportion to their elasticity coefficients in a marginal rate-of-return analysis, or in proportion to their part/whole percentages in a multiattribute efficiency analysis. Thus, measuring the percentage of optimality achieved is mathematically like measuring the percentage of proportionality achieved.[5]

Although the words *equity*, *equality*, and *proportionality* may create favorable images, they are not inherently desirable. Equality may conflict with proportionality. In addition, the desirability of proportionality depends on what the proportionality criterion is. Allocating in proportion to racial purity may be very different from allocating in proportion to social contribution. Finally, equity may be inherently desirable in that people should not be allowed to fall below minimum decency levels, although it may be highly subjective as to what these levels are.

Using Equity as a Criterion for Choosing among Policies

Now that we have clarified the meaning of equity both conceptually and operationally, it seems logical to discuss how equity can be used as a criterion for choosing among policies. Two examples will be given. The first, which is quite general, involves allocating $10 between two policies, one of which scores better on efficiency and the other of which scores better on equity. The second example, which is more specific, involves choosing among alternative ways of sequencing court cases or other forms of governmental case processing. A discussion of general principles for choosing among alternative policies while taking into consideration benefits and costs, and how they are spread, is then presented.

WHY PROMOTE EQUITY?

Before discussing the use of equity as a criterion for choosing among policies, we will address the fundamental question of why it should be a criterion. Some analysts argue that equity (in the sense of bringing people up to a minimum-needs level) should be a goal constraint that is accepted intuitively, that is, without justification in terms of the consequences. In other words, the idea of an equitable society or an equitable allocation should be accepted because it is inherently wrong to allow people to have less than a minimum of decency in terms of income, education, health care, or other basic needs. One might argue, however, that there would be greater acceptance of the idea of an equitable society if it could be established that an inequitable society is highly unlikely to function smoothly.

Establishing this point is not difficult. One can accept intuitively that people who are below a minimum-needs level are likely to react antisocially if there is no socially acceptable way for them to rise above the minimum-needs level. It is not, however, necessary to accept this phenomenon intuitively. Numerous historical examples can be given, such as the French Revolution, the Russian Revolution, and the riots in American cities in the 1960s. Even if inequities do not lead to violence, it makes good political sense for government officeholders to be concerned with bringing people up to minimum levels in matters like employment, freedom from crime, and so on. Otherwise, in a democratic society, these officeholders may be elected out of office. Equity is also important for public-image reasons because governments are embarrassed internationally and domestically when certain groups are suffering to extremes.

Along related lines, one might ask, why promote efficiency as a criterion? This is an easier question than asking, why promote equity as a criterion? because efficiency is inherently better. The usual definition of *efficiency* is benefits divided by costs, or benefits minus costs, or sometimes, change-in-benefits divided by change-in-costs. All these definitions involve the concepts of benefits and costs. *Benefits* are occurrences or events that are desired by the values of the people with whom we are concerned. *Costs* are occurrences or events that the people want to minimize. Thus, a society wants to be efficient or productive because it wants more benefits and less costs. It is impossible to maximize benefits and minimize costs simultaneously because some costs have to be incurred in order to achieve benefits. We therefore talk in terms of maximizing benefits minus costs. Equity can be considered among the benefits, or as a basic constraint to be achieved even before maximizing benefits minus costs.

TWO PROJECTS THAT DIFFER IN EFFICIENCY AND EQUITY

Table 4-6 provides data to illustrate the use of equity as a criterion for choosing among policies. The table considers two policies. One involves spending $6 in ward L of a city, and the other involves spending $6 between wards M and N. If the first policy is adopted, it will generate benefits worth $10 for schools, highways, streets, crime reduction, or whatever the subject is. If the second policy is adopted, it will generate benefits worth only $9. The second policy, however, involves more equity because it covers two of the three wards, whereas the first policy only covers one. Which policy should be followed?

If only the efficiency criterion is followed, then policy L should be adopted because it scores higher on benefits minus costs, where the benefits refer to the substantive purpose of the two policies. If only the equity criterion is followed, then policy M&N should be adopted because it gives something to more places than does policy L. In deciding between the two policies, one must decide whether one would prefer (1) the satisfaction that comes from the extra dollar in net monetary benefits, or (2) the extra satisfaction that comes from covering wards M and N, rather than just ward L. If policy M&N provides no extra satisfaction, then policy L is clearly better. If covering wards M and N yields more satisfaction than covering ward L alone, then one must decide whether that satisfaction is worth more than the extra dollar to the general public, the city council, or the relevant decision maker. If the extra ward coverage is worth more, then policy M&N would have the highest net benefits score, where the net benefits equal $B1 + B2 - C$. This is true even though we do not know (1) the net benefits of either policy M&N or policy L; (2) how much better it is to cover M&N than to cover L; or (3) the monetary value of the two coverages. Likewise,

TABLE 4-6
The Use of Equity as a Criterion for Choosing Among Policies

Policy	Efficiency Benefits (B1)	Costs	B1 − C	Equity Benefits	B1 + B2 − C
L	$10	$6	$4	Ward L covered	?
M&N	$ 9	$6	$3	Ward M&N covered	?
Increment	$1	$0	$1	?	?

if the extra dollar is worth more than the extra ward coverage, then policy L would have the higher net benefits score, even though we do not know what it is.

The same analysis can apply if the efficiency benefits are nonmonetary, such as 10 lives saved from policy L versus 9 lives saved from policy M&N. The question then becomes, Which is preferred, the one life saved from policy L or the extra ward coverage of policy M&N? The same analysis also applies if the efficiency benefits are different types of nonmonetary benefits, such as 10 students trained versus 9 patients treated. The question then is, Which is preferred, the extra satisfaction from 10 students trained over 9 patients treated, or the extra ward coverage? If training 10 students does not produce more satisfaction than treating 9 patients, then policy M&N would dominate on both kinds of benefits and would be preferred over policy L. The same analysis can be applied if the costs are unequal or if they are nonmonetary. If one project costs $2 less than the other, this saving of $2 is considered a third benefit. The best of a set of multiple policies can be determined by comparing contending projects two at a time.

Equity does not have to be measured with quantitative precision in order to be used as a criterion for choosing among policies. All we need to know is whether the incremental equity is worth more or less than the incremental efficiency, where the two conflict. Equity can be considered as just another nonmonetary benefit. Likewise, so-called efficiency benefits may involve equity considerations that relate to minimum benefits with regard to lifesaving, education, health care, or other governmental or societal benefits. Thus, the problem becomes one of choosing among policies in light of conflicting benefits, some of which may be nonmonetary. The problem is not clarified by calling some of the benefits *equity benefits* and some *efficiency benefits.*[6]

THE EXAMPLE OF OPTIMUM SEQUENCING

Table 4-7 illustrates the use of equity as a criterion for choosing among alternative ways of sequencing the processing of cases by a governmental agency. The cases could be court cases, applications for zoning changes, requests for new trucking routes, or other kinds of governmental case processing. Part I of the table shows the results of processing the cases on a first come, first served basis, where the longer cases happen to arrive first, or at least not last. The total time for each case is equal to its waiting time plus its processing time. The waiting time in this simplified illustration is equal to the processing time of the preceding cases. The processing time for each case is taken as a roughly predictable given. By handling the cases on a first come, first served basis, the average total time is 28 days.

If we let the cases accumulate until the end of the day, however, and docket them for processing with the shortest cases first, a substantial amount of waiting time—and thus total time—can be saved. By pushing the longest

TABLE 4-7
The Use of Equity as a Criterion for Choosing Among Alternative Ways of Sequencing the Processing of Cases

I. First Come, First Served

CASE	WAITING TIME	+	PROCESSING TIME	=	TOTAL TIME
20	0		20		20
10	20		10		30
5	30		5		35
Total	50		35		85
Average	16		12		28

II. Shortest Cases First

CASE	WAITING TIME	+	PROCESSING TIME	=	TOTAL TIME	GAIN OR LOSS
5	0		5		5	+30
10	5		10		15	+15
20	15		20		35	−15
Total	20		35		55	+30
Average	6		12		18	+10

cases to the back, we minimize how often their processing times are figured into the waiting times of the other cases. Thus, the average waiting time is decreased from 16 days (rounded to the nearest even whole number) to 6 days. The average total time drops from 28 days to 18 days. This kind of delay reduction requires neither additional expenditures for court personnel nor a decrease in anyone's procedural rights, because each case receives the same personnel and processing as before. The system is administratively feasible given (1) the predictability of time consumption from case characteristics and (2) the fact that no one has to be physically removed from his or her place in line.

What about the equities? A key equity consideration is that no case should be allowed to have a waiting time greater than an equitable maximum. Thus, the longer cases should not be pushed back so that they never get heard. Rather, there should be an appropriate time limit (e.g., 90 days), and the cases should be docketed for processing, for example, at least once a week. These maximum constraints with an undesired allocation subject such as delay are the equivalent of minimum constraints with a desired allocation subject such as income, education, or health care. Even if there are maximum constraints, equity problems may still exist if some cases are taking relatively big losses under the new system of hearing the shortest cases first.

The last column in part II of Table 4-7 shows the gain or loss for each case in terms of days saved. The 5-day case gains 30 days; the 10-day case gains 15 days; and the 20-day case loses 15 days. The gains clearly outweigh the losses. To compensate the 20-day case for its 15-day loss, the shorter cases could be asked to pay higher filing fees. If, for example, one lost day is considered to be worth $1 or one monetary unit, then the two shorter cases could be asked to pay an extra $15 to compensate the 20-day case. The 5-day case could pay an extra $10, and the 10-day case could pay an extra $5 because the 5-day case saved twice as much time. This system of side payments, however, is unnecessary; the 20-day case is already receiving extra compensation because it is allowed to consume 20 days of the government's resources, which is substantially more than the shorter cases receive. Thus, asking the longer case to wait to be heard is offset by giving it more governmental service. The allocation of waiting time to the cases is made equitable, though, particularly by not allowing any case to exceed a minimum decency threshold.[7]

PRINCIPLES FOR CHOOSING AMONG POLICIES

The choice between the two alternative ways of processing cases can be analyzed in terms of four philosophical principles. Pareto optimality is one such principle. In its purest form, it specificies that no policy should be adopted if it results in anybody being worse off than he or she was formerly. Stated more positively, it says that all policies that are adopted should result in everyone either being better off—or at least as well off—as they were formerly. In a less pure form, Pareto optimality states that one policy is better than another if the first policy involves fewer people being worse off than they were before. It is a principle that emphasizes change before and after the adoption of a policy, rather than how many people are below a minimum-needs level. At first glance, a statement that nobody should be made worse off by a policy seems to be sensitive to not hurting people. The Pareto optimality principle, however, is insensitive to how many people are hurt by being below a minimum-needs level. It is especially insensitive to how many of them could be helped by a transferal of some income from individuals who are especially well-off and whose psychological loss would be more than offset by the psychological gain of those who would be brought up to a minimum-needs level.

If by societal rationality or productivity we mean maximizing societal benefits minus costs, then the Pareto optimality principle is irrational and counterproductive. This is demonstrated by Table 4-7. The pure Pareto optimality principle would reject the shortest-cases-first alternative because it would make the longest case worse off than it was formerly. As a result, the principle sacrifices the improved effectiveness and increased benefits of reducing a 28-day average delay to an 18-day average delay. It also sacrifices efficiency because both the benefits-costs difference and the benefits/costs ratio are improved, since the benefits go up with no substantial increase in cost. The principle gains nothing in terms of equity if the new system does not cause anyone to fall below a minimum-needs level of no more than a 90-day delay, and if no one suffers an excessive, unjustifiable loss in adopting the new policy. According to a less pure version of the Pareto optimality principle, it is all right for people to have losses as a result of policy changes, as long as they are compensated or could be compensated by the gainers. The "could be" qualifier, in effect, destroys the principle if there is no compensation in actuality.

The second relevant philosophical principle is the Rawlsian principle, which states that the better of two policies is the one that brings up those who are least well-off on whatever value is involved. This principle seems to be sensitive to the idea of bringing people up to a minimum level, but it is not. The Rawlsian principle favors a policy that brings person H up, possibly at the expense of person G, even if person H is already above a minimum-needs level, as long as person H is below person G. Like the Pareto principle, this may also be irrational and counterproductive because merely transferring income or wealth may do nothing to enable a society to have more income or more wealth. This is in contrast to transfers with strings attached that are designed to provide incentives toward greater societal productivity. Transfers from the rich to the not-so-rich may promote equality, but equality is generally not promoting equity where the transferees are already above a minimum-needs level.

The irrationality of the Rawlsian principle is demonstrated by Table 4-7. A typical policy problem comes closer to the more mundane values of reducing delay, crime, or pollution than to the redistribution of societal income or wealth. The Rawlsian principle applied to delay reduction would show sympathy to the case that is generally the worst off, namely, the case with the longest processing time. Doing so might make one sensitive to bringing up the longest or worst-off cases, which would lead to a procedure of the longest cases first within a 90-day (or other maximum) constraint. Following that kind of sensitivity would generally lead to an average total time that is even worse than processing the cases on the basis of first come, first served.

The third relevant philosophical principle is utilitarianism, which states that the best policy is the one that promotes the greatest happiness for the greatest number. It comes close to an intuitive commonsense notion that is consistent with choosing the shortest cases first. The term *happiness* creates a more hedonistic image than *benefits* in benefit-cost analysis. *Happiness* may also imply a gross happiness, regardless of the costs. *The greatest number* may imply an insensitivity to people below a minimum-needs level. Thus, utilitarianism can result in the choice of a policy that gives a lot of happiness to individuals above a minimum-needs level rather than one that enables a society to bring those below the level up to it. In case-processing, for example, the utilitarian principle would lead to the choice of the shortest cases first, unlike the Pareto or Rawlsian principles. However, the longer cases could be moved back indefinitely; doing so would result in more gains than losses, even though the longer cases might thereby exceed a minimum decency level.

Thus, the principle that seems to make the most sense in light of this example is the principle stating that the best policy is the one that maximizes societal benefits minus societal costs, while providing a minimum-needs level for all persons, groups, or places with regard to whatever benefits or costs are involved. By maximizing societal benefits minus costs, we maximize net gain, net benefits, or net profits, and thus produce a maximum increase in societal assets minus liabilities or societal net worth. This principle, in effect, combines the best of each of the other three principles. It emphasizes the idea of a net gain associated with utilitarianism and the Pareto variation that talks in terms of compensating the losers from the gains of the winners. It also emphasizes bringing up the bottom, which is associated with Rawlsianism, but only if the bottom is below a minimum-needs level. Thus, the principle of societal benefits-costs analysis combines (1) the efficiency of Pareto optimality, (2) the effectiveness of utilitarianism, and (3) the equity of Rawlsian sensitivity.[8]

Trade-offs Between Equity and Other Goals

The purpose of this section is to discuss, with examples and principles, some of the problems involved in the alleged conflicts or trade-offs between equity and the goals of efficiency and freedom. The illustrative examples involve the allocation of pretrial release across arrested defendants, the allocation of funds to libraries in rich and poor neighborhoods, and the making of decisions about societal development.

EQUITY AND EFFICIENCY

Optimum Bail-Bond Setting. The problem of arriving at optimum bail-bond figures is a good example of a situation in which the optimum policy in terms of efficiency is not the optimum policy in terms of equity. This problem can be contrasted with others in which the optimum policy is both efficient and equitable. Optimally efficient bail bonds are bonds that maximize the probability of released defendants appearing in court minus the probability of arrested defendants being held in jail. Released defendants appearing in court is like income. Arrested defendants being held in jail is a big expense. Thus, by maximizing the difference between these probabilities, we are in effect maximizing income minus expenses, or benefits minus costs.

To arrive at this kind of theoretically ideal bond, we could obtain data for many prior criminal cases in which we know (1) the crime for which the defendant was charged; (2) the amount of bond the defendant was asked to pay in order to be released; (3) whether the defendant was held or released; and (4) if released, whether the defendant appeared for trial without committing a crime during his or her release. With that kind of data for each case, we could plot a graph like that in Figure 4-1. The horizontal axis shows bond levels in dollars, and the vertical axis shows probabilities or percentages of a defendant's appearing for trial or being held without bail. The open circles indicate for each bond category the percentage of defendants who were held in jail pending trial. The black dots indicate for each bond category the percentage of released defendants in the category who appeared for trial without having been arrested during release.

We would logically expect the open circles in the figure to exhibit an S-shaped relation between bond category and the probability of being held. In other words, with low bond categories, we would expect only a small percentage of defendants to be held, and at high bond categories for nearly all the defendants to be held. Among the middle categories, there would be a positive slope like that shown in Figure 4-1. Likewise, one would expect the black dots to also exhibit an S-shaped relation between bond category and the probability of appearance. That is, with low bonds, defendants would not have much of an incentive to appear, especially if they believe that their case will be resolved as a simple bond forfeiture if they do not appear.

FIGURE 4-1
The Assumed Relations Between Bond Levels, Court Appearance, and Being Held in Jail

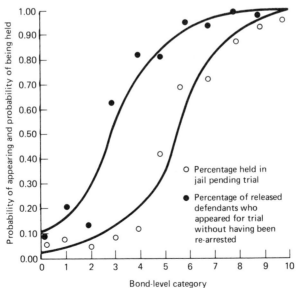

Bond-level category

Based on hypothetical data for the crime of disorderly conduct in medium-sized cities in the state of Illinois.

At higher bond levels, theoretically, the defendants would have more of an incentive to appear, because (1) they have more of a bond to recover and (2) they are likely to believe that nonappearance will result in a warrant for their arrest. With these assumptions as plotted in Figure 4-1, one can see that the optimum bond is in category 4. This category might be bonds from $500 to $1000.

The main defect in such a benefit-cost approach to nondiscretionary bond setting is that the bonds are likely to place an unnecessary and inequitable burden on low-income defendants. In other words, this is a good example of a solution that is efficient in the sense of maximizing benefits minus costs yet may be inequitable because (1) the benefits of being released are distributed disproportionately to nonindigent defendants and (2) the costs of being held are distributed disproportionately to the indigent defendants. The nonindigent often pay higher taxes to support pretrial jailing; however, this does not offset the often needless incarceration of indigent defendants who would be good risks to release, but who cannot meet the optimum or average bond for the crime with which they have been charged. New York City data show that in the bond category of $101 to $500 (which seems to be low), 57 percent of the defendants could not post bond and were held in jail pending trial. They were then (1) more vulnerable to needlessly pleading guilty, (2) less capable of preparing their defense, and (3) more susceptible to experiences that stimulate crime-committing reactions. The system could allow judges to consider special circumstances in setting bond, including ability to pay, but this might not be sufficient. The system could also allow release on recognizance for good risks who cannot meet the nondiscretionary bond, just as nondiscretionary sentencing systems allow for the possibility of probation.

Perhaps the system should provide that all defendants either be released on their own recognizance or not be released until after a speedy trial. To prevent abuses of discretion in making release-nonrelease decisions, judges could be required to follow a point-setting table similar to the one devised by the Vera Institute of New York City. It allocates points to such criteria as how long the defendant has lived in the community and how long the defendant has held his or her current job. Using such a system, judges can be informed of how many points each criterion is worth, based on previous statistical analysis of the relationship between various criteria or predictors and whether the released defendants appeared for trial without being re-arrested. Such a point system would amount to a set of quantitative guidelines for releasing defendants without requiring them to put up bond money; money bonds discriminate across economic classes even when the bond figures are low. The guidelines could also allow for adding or subtracting points for aggravating and mitigating circumstances, while still preserving the basic objectivity of the system. This type of solution is equitable because it is not biased against the poor, contrary to their probability of appearing in court. It may also be quite efficient because one can probably achieve a higher appearance rate through better screening of arrested defendants than by trying to manipulate the bond level to maximize benefits minus costs— which is how a monopolistic business firm tries to manipulate the price and quantities of its products to maximize income minus expenses. Better screening can also be supplemented by (1) requiring periodic reporting of released defendants to the courthouse; (2) reminding released defendants by postcard or other means that their court date is coming up; and (3) selectively prosecuting those who do not appear.[9]

The Allocation of Library Funds. Bond setting may be a good example of a situation in which efficiency and equity conflict, but there are many examples in which the most efficient policy is also the most equitable. Allocating funds to libraries in both rich neighborhoods and poor neighborhoods is such an example. The equitable approach would see that every neighborhood library has a minimum allocation. The efficient approach, at first glance, would seem to involve a big allocation to the library in the rich neighborhood, on the grounds that the average person in that neighborhood borrows more books than does the average person in the poor neighborhood.

Whether or not this is true is not as relevant in terms of efficient allocation as are the differences between the marginal rates of return in the two neighborhoods. In other words, perhaps an additional $1,000 spent in the poor neighborhood will have a bigger impact in terms of increased book borrowing than will $1,000 spent in the rich neighborhood. This may be so because the rich kids may be reading almost up to their capacity, but the poor kids may have more room for improvement and would be more responsive to expenditures for popular books, advertising, or whatever is available. The rich library might have more borrowing because it has traditionally had better facilities and publicizing of its services. The rich library may also be at a higher point on a diminishing-returns curve than the poor library, which means it has a higher benefit/cost ratio, or ratio of books borrowed to annual budget. Being at such a point, however, may indicate that the rich library has a lower ratio of change-in-benefits to change-in-costs, or a lower ratio of improvement in books borrowed to improvement in the annual budget. We want policies that will provide a high marginal rate of return on our investments, rather than a high benefit/cost ratio if these two criteria conflict. The rich library may have a generally steeper curve showing the relation between benefits and costs than has the poor library. We still would not want to give all of our resources or our incremental resources to the rich library because of the principle of diminishing returns and the plateauing of those curves showing the relationship between satisfaction and library dollars. Thus, it makes sense to switch some of the rich-library dollars to the poor library, because the poor library may have a steeper slope at low-dollar levels than the rich library has at high-dollar levels, even though the rich library would give a better return if both libraries were at the same budget levels.

This analysis can be applied to allocations for schools, police, parks, and other kinds of funding between rich and poor neighborhoods. The important point is that the equitable principle bringing the poor library, school, police district, or park up to a minimum level or higher may conform with the efficiency principle which says to allocate in proportion to the marginal rates of return of the alternative investments and thus maximize benefits for a given cost. In other words, because poorer places may show more of an increased output from an increased expenditure, one can often justify increased expenditures to poorer places on both efficiency and equity grounds. Numerous other examples can be given in which being equitable is efficient and being efficient is equitable, contrary to conventional wisdom which implies that equity and efficiency are inherently in conflict.[10]

Deciding Between Equity and Efficiency. Perhaps the conflict between equity and efficiency has been exaggerated, as the preceding examples indicate. Nevertheless, there are situations in which there is a conflict, at least in the sense that some policies score higher on efficiency but lower on equity than do others. In such a case, meeting the equity minimum constraints is preferred over increasing efficiency. This is true if we define *equity* in terms of the need to meet minimum constraints before maximizing or achieving other variables. If, by equity, we mean promoting equality after the minimum constraints have been met, then equity becomes just another benefit variable, as was discussed in the context of Table 4-4.

How might one handle the question, Which is better, a 1-unit increase in equity or a 1-unit increase in efficiency? Likewise, how might one handle the question, Which is better, a 100 percent increase in equity or a 100 percent increase in efficiency? These questions treat equity as a variable, rather than as a constraint. To avoid confusion, we should substitute the word *equality* for *equity* in these questions. Answering the questions requires one to develop a way of measuring equality so that one can talk more meaningfully about a 1-unit increase or a 100 percent increase.

With a measure of equality like that developed in Table 4-4, one can define a 1-unit increase in equality as a move from 0.01 to 0.02 or from any two-place decimal to the next highest two-place decimal. Likewise, a 100 percent increase in equality refers to a doubling of the equality score on that scale from a low of zero (i.e., as little equality as possible) to a high of 1.00 (i.e., as much equality as possible). To determine whether a 1-unit increase in equality or a 1-unit increase in efficiency is better, we could try to translate both equality and efficiency into dollars. This would probably be difficult. It would be easier and more meaningful simply to determine which of the alternatives gives more satisfaction in the context of exactly what the equality increase is, what the efficiency increase is, and whose satisfaction is relevant. In other words, there is no general rule to follow. The outcome depends on those substance-oriented matters, particularly when equality and efficiency are not defined in terms of each other. Substance-oriented matters are questions such as, which is better, an increase in the ratio of women's wages from 57 percent of men's wages to 65 percent, or a cost-saving of $10,000,000 in government expenditures?

This is unlike effectiveness and efficiency. Where effectiveness is benefits achieved and efficiency is benefits achieved divided by costs incurred, one goal is defined in terms of the other. Under certain circumstances, equality (or equity as a variable rather than a constraint) could be considered the only benefit. One could then deductively analyze the relationship between B and B/C. Doing so might provide some general insights with regard to benefit-cost analysis, but they would probably be too abstract for answering questions about the relative value of equality and efficiency.[11]

EQUITY-EQUALITY AND FREEDOM

Types of Equality, Freedom and Tension. Another alleged trade-off is that between equity-equality and freedom. Whether a conflict exists depends partly on the kinds of equity-equality and freedom being referred to. It also depends on the kind of society being examined: is it predeveloping, developing, or industrialized? If, by *equality*, one refers to equality of opportunity rather than of economic status, there seems to be less conflict with freedom. If, by *freedom*, one means political freedom—free speech, the right to vote, and due process in criminal proceedings—then there is also less conflict with equality than would be the case if the term referred to entrepreneurial freedom—the freedom to deal with employees, consumers, competitors, and stockholders as one wishes.

Figure 4-2 indicates the degree of tension that tends to exist between the two types of equality and the two types of freedom. Tension is relatively high along the entrepreneurial-freedom row. Complete entrepreneurial freedom may limit the freedom of employees, consumers, competitors, and stockholders by virtue of the tendency of unrestricted entrepreneurs to establish monopolistic or oligopolistic relations with the persons and groups with whom they deal. Tension also is relatively high along the equality-of-economic-status column with regard to wealth and income. This is so because economic equality may mean restricting entrepreneurial freedom and, to a lesser extent, the political freedom associated with the lobbying aspects of free speech and the campaign-contributions aspect of voting activities. The lowest degree of tension is between political freedom and equality of opportunity because (1) political freedom includes the opportunity to participate in political activities without racial, economic, or other arbitrary discrimination; and (2) equality of opportunity includes the opportunity to advance oneself in the political and leadership realm.

One could also discuss the possible reciprocal tensions between the two kinds of freedom and between the two kinds of equality, as indicated by the arrows in Figure 4-2. Entrepreneurial freedom is likely to seek to restrict

FIGURE 4-2
Types of Equality, Freedom, and Tension

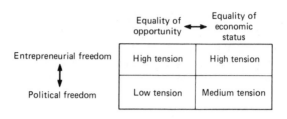

political freedom in a conservative direction because the exercise of political freedom via the people is likely to result in restrictions by government on business activities. On the other hand, equality of economic status almost by definition facilitates equality of opportunity, although the latter can lead to inequality of economic status. Thus, the reciprocal relations between the two types of freedom and between the two types of equality produce less clear relations than those between equality and freedom.

It is also interesting to analyze the effect of government and law on both equality and freedom. A strong government may be necessary in order to provide near-equality of economic status or wealth, as well as equality of opportunity, because government has the potential for being a counter-acting force against private entrepreneurial interests which would otherwise produce greater inequalities of both economic status and opportunity. On the other hand, a weak government would facilitate entrepreneurial and political freedom, since powerful government is often restrictive regarding business, free speech, meaningful voting rights, and due process to protect the innocent from conviction and harassment.

Stages of Societal Development. Individuals who emphasize tensions between equality and freedom often refer to the situation in a developing country in which the citizens or their leaders want to establish a fast equality while raising the gross national product instead of merely redistributing it. Under such circumstances, some writers perceive a need for restricting certain freedoms (especially entrepreneurial economic, but sometimes po-litical, freedom) in order to comply with a national economic plan. Develop-ing countries may not only seek quick internal equality at a higher standard of living, but also external equality with more developed countries in order to overcome an international sense of relative deprivation.

The tensions between equality and freedom in developing countries, however, may only be short-run tensions that exist in a postrevolutionary era in which some political freedom and much economic freedom are often sacrificed to produce equality and higher standards of living. In the long run, the increased affluence that comes with industrialization and urbanization may bring increased equality and higher standards of living because of technological facilitators, pressure from below to share in the new wealth, and increased willingness to make concessions from above. (Pressure from below refers to protest behavior on the part of disadvantaged groups within a society, and concessions from above refers to the more advantaged groups changing the opportunity-distribution rules.) At the same time, increased affluence may also bring increased freedom (at least political freedom) because of the increased education to handle the new technology, the increased security from want, and the increased tolerance of deviant behavior that goes with the anonymity of urbanization. Thus, freedom and equality may be long-run effects of material developments that may be inherent in the accumulation of knowledge and technology.

Perhaps the history of industrial development involves an inverted U-shaped relation with regard to equality-freedom tensions and stage of societal development, as shown in Figure 4-3. In predeveloping feudalistic societies, there is little freedom or equality. Moreover, there is little tension between the two because they are both negative effects of a low-technology society in which survival may depend on the surrender of one's freedom to a feudalistic protector who generally lives with his retainers in relative luxury. In modern developing societies, tension is more likely to exist because of the striving for upward equality while freedom is restricted. The tensions are probably again lessened in industrialized, urbanized societies, for which a

FIGURE 4-3
The Possible Average Relation Between Societal Development and the Tension Between Equality and Freedom

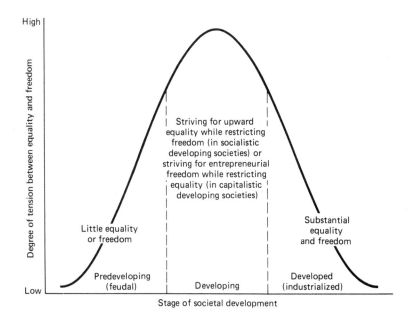

diamond-shaped class structure with a dominant educated middle class replaces a pyramid-shaped antagonistic caste system. This reduced tension, at least in the long run, is at a substantial level of both equality and freedom. In other words, developed industrialized societies generally combine low tension between equality and freedom with a high degree of both equality and freedom.

There are a number of indicators of increased equality and political freedom in industrialized, urbanized societies. The increased equality is manifested in the fact that the average deviation from the average income is substantially less than it was formerly. The rich may be richer because they can buy much more with money than in preindustrial times, but the poor also often have material possessions that were unavailable to medieval kings—for example, vaccines, electricity, plumbing, radio and television, automobiles, and farm machinery. If the average deviation from the average income is now smaller than it once was, there is probably more equality of opportunity because income does make for opportunities for oneself and one's children. Opportunity, however, also manifests itself in more free public schools, lessened racial and sexual discrimination, and greater geographical mobility. Indicators of increased political freedom include the expansion of the voting franchise to nonpropertied persons, freed serfs and slaves, women, and younger adults. Increased political freedom has also manifested itself in the United States and other industrial, urbanized countries in the right to speak against the prevailing government or norms without risking a jail sentence. Nevertheless, such freedom tends to rise and fall over short periods despite long-run upward trends. Entrepreneurial freedom, however, seems to be undergoing a long-run decline because of the increase of socialistic governments and also government regulation within the context of mixed economies. The latter phenomenon refers to government controls on business enterprise in economies that involve both socialistic and capitalistic elements. Since equality and political freedom are often effects of an increasingly educated middle class and the other previously mentioned factors, both equality and political freedom are likely to increase together as long as those underlying causes are increasing.[12]

Resolving the Tensions Between Equality and Freedom. We turn now to the normative question of which goal is preferable, and why. The consensus seems to be that in a capitalistic developing society, much equality is sacrificed (and some say ought to be sacrificed) in order to allow entrepreneurial freedom to bring about the equality and political-freedom benefits of industrialization. On the other hand, the consensus seems to be that in a socialistic developing society, much freedom is sacrificed (and some say ought to be sacrificed) in order to allow nationalization and economic planning to bring about the equality of comfort and middle-class freedoms that are associated with industrialization.

An interesting problem involves industrialized societies in which one cannot use the need to industrialize as an excuse for sacrificing either equality or freedom. One way to conceptualize this problem is to think in terms of a trade-off like that shown in Figure 4-4. There, a two-person society is used for the purpose of allocating degrees of equality and freedom. The analysis could just as easily apply to a two-class society of rich and poor or to a multiperson society, although it is impossible to represent more than three dimensions geometrically.

Figure 4-4 shows that there is a minimum level of freedom and equality that nearly all writers on the subject would provide for each member of society. The area encompassed by the minimum constraints represents a feasible allocation region, such that any allocation point within it would satisfy all the minimum constraints. The optimum point within that feasible region is logically the one where the total satisfaction of the two persons in the society, Joe and Bob, is at a maximum. This may involve taking something from Bob to give to Joe, or vice versa. Although this is contrary to the notion of Pareto optimality, it is within the Benthamite notion of maximizing the greatest happiness for the greatest number, subject to the Rawlsian notion of a minimum level of benefits for all.

FIGURE 4-4
**Allocating Between Equality and Freedom among Different Segments of a Society:
An Allocation-Box Approach**

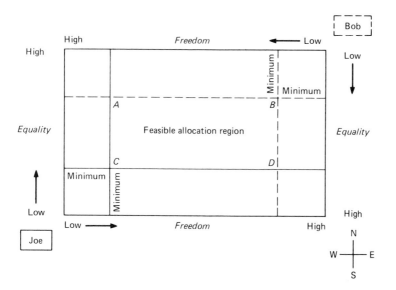

In general, if a trade-off must be made between equality and freedom, the feeling among Anglo-American writers is that people should prefer political freedom to equality; there is less of a consensus about economic freedom. Political freedom seems to be the preferred goal because, through it, one can communicate the allegedly undesirable social effects of inequality, thereby encouraging society to overcome these effects with regard to inequality. In the marketplace of communication, more effective remedies for the problems of inequality are likely to develop than would be the case without such a free marketplace. On the other hand, equality is less likely to lead to political freedom than political freedom is likely to lead to equality.

Concrete examples of situations in industrialized societies in which trade-offs between equality and freedom may be necessary include:

1. producing greater equality of economic status and opportunity by restricting the quality of schools to which wealthier parents can send their children
2. producing more freedom for individuals to be able to receive welfare payments without seeking work, although this may involve unequal treatment relative to the working poor
3. producing conflicts between the individual's freedom to advance and aggressive affirmative-action programs designed to produce more racial equality

Perhaps some or all of these are false dilemmas, so that we can have both freedom and equality in some or all three situations by pursuing a compromise or an unmentioned alternative.

The allocation box, or Edgeworth box, presented in Figure 4-4, is useful for the following purposes:

1. It helps to clarify the notion of minimum or equitable constraints on equality and freedom and the related notion of a feasible allocation region.
2. It helps to clarify situations in which giving one person or group more freedom takes away from another person or group. This is true of many laws which increase one person's freedom from being treated in a certain way, but thereby decrease someone else's freedom to treat the first person in that way. The treatment could involve personal injuries, property rights, contract rights, criminal behavior, and other relations among people.
3. It helps to clarify situations in which upgrading a person who was below the average on an allocation dimension means downgrading either a person who had been above the average or another below-average person.
4. It indicates that for any given individual or group, there can be a simultaneous expansion in both equality and freedom. This is what happens to Joe when the allocation between Joe and Bob on equality and freedom moves toward the northeast.

5. It indicates that point B is the optimum allocation if Joe gets more happiness out of both equality and freedom than Bob does, assuming a linear relation between happiness and incremental equality or freedom. Point C is the optimum allocation if Bob gets more happiness from additional equality and freedom than Joe does.
6. Point A is the optimum allocation if Joe gets more happiness from additional equality, but less happiness from additional freedom, than Bob does. Point D is the optimum allocation if Bob gets more happiness from additional equality, but less happiness from additional freedom, than Joe does. These optimum allocations assume that society is trying to maximize the sum of the happiness of its members.
7. It encourages attempts to measure equality and freedom, especially on a 0-to-100 scale, and also to measure minimum equality and minimum freedom.

An allocation box like Figure 4-4 may, however, do more harm than good in discussing general relations between equality and freedom for the following reasons:

1. It is virtually useless in dealing with more than two persons or groups.
2. The corner points are not optimums in the real world of diminishing incremental returns. Thus, it makes sense to give Joe less than the maximum freedom, even if he values freedom more highly than Bob. The hundredth unit of freedom given to Joe is not likely to produce as much incremental happiness as is the first unit beyond the minimum constraint given to Bob. Each incremental unit of freedom, like almost any good, is likely to produce diminishing incremental satisfaction, even though the additional satisfaction is positive.
3. Its big defect is that it forces one to wrongly think of allocating freedom and equality among societal groups as being analogous to allocating dollars or two kinds of tangible goods. If a $100 budget is being allocated, then if Bob gets $80, Joe can only get $20. If 10 bottles of beer and 50 pretzels are being allocated and Bob gets 6 bottles and 20 pretzels, then Joe can only get 4 bottles and 30 pretzels. However, in allocating freedom measured on a 0-to-100 scale, it is possible for both Bob and Joe to each get the maximum, or 100 percent. Figure 4-4, however, does not allow for this possibility.
4. It also implies that there may be a conflict between equality and freedom for Joe because of the indifference curve toward the southwest corner of the figure. Moving along such a curve involves tradeoffs between equality and freedom, which also may not conform to the empirical reality shown in Figure 4-3.

In light of these considerations, perhaps Figure 4-5 is a better way to depict all that is involved in allocating equality and freedom among different persons or segments of a society. Using an input-output approach, rather than an allocation-box approach, the figure consists of a series of nonlinear graphs in which the input variable (i.e., equality or freedom) is on the horizontal axis and the output variable (i.e., happiness) is on the vertical axis. This approach, which can be used with any number of persons or groups, also considers diminishing returns. It is capable of showing that Bob's equality does not inherently have anything to do with Bob's or Joe's freedom, and that Bob's inputs do not inherently have anything to do with Joe's inputs.

Figure 4-5, however, still has a defect: it treats equality and freedom as allocation problems in that it implies an optimum degree of equality and freedom for each societal segment, where increased equality and freedom both bring increased happiness with diminishing incremental returns, but not diminishing absolute returns. In other words, maybe the curves in Figure 4-5 have to reach a peak at some point and then turn down. As an alternative, one could thus treat equality as an optimum-level problem, arguing

FIGURE 4-5
Allocating Equality and Freedom among Different Segments of the Society: An Input-Output Approach

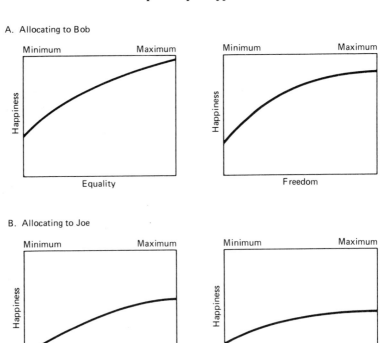

that too much equality removes the availability of economic incentives to stimulate greater productivity. Too little equality can result in societally destructive resentment. Likewise, too much freedom can make for chaos if it includes no rules governing interactive behavior. On the other hand, too little freedom can stifle creativity.

Another way of viewing both equality and freedom is as on-off constraints, rather than as a continuum of degrees. In that sense, *equality* would mean the same as *equity*, or meeting minimum constraints. These constraints are either met or not met, although there can be degrees of deviation from equity. Likewise, freedom in the political sense could refer to the absence of restrictions on the freedom to peacefully criticize the government. In this sense, freedom either exists or it does not, although there can be degrees of deviation from it. The constraint idea emphasizes that equity and political freedom in a society are not variables subject to being traded off for more beer and pretzels. They are basically minimum constraints that have to be met before one can maximize or minimize other variables.[13]

Conclusion

One can conclude that *equity* mainly refers to allocating benefits in various policy fields in such a way as to provide groups, persons, and places with at least a minimum level of benefits to satisfy basic needs. This general definition can refer to such examples as allocating anticrime dollars, legislative seats, national income, city services, speed in case processing, pretrial release, funds for neighborhood libraries, and freedom and equality across people. Measuring equity, in contrast to defining it, involves determining the sum of the squared deviations between the actual and the minimum allocations for each person, place, or group and then dividing by the sum of the minimum allocations squared. This provides a measure of the proportion of the maximum *inequity* that has been obtained. By subtracting this measure from 1.00, one has a measure of the proportion of the maximum *equity* that has been obtained. Determining the minimum benefit levels is subjective, but generally feasible.

On using equity as a criterion for choosing among policies, one can conclude that equity is worth promoting, at least for the purpose of preventing antisocial or antiestablishment reactions from those who are treated inequitably. By definition, equity as a minimum constraint has to be met before other goals can be maximized or achieved. *Equity* as a synonym for *equality after minimum constraints have been met* can be dealt with as a nonmonetary benefit. One must ask whether the increased efficiency benefits are worth more or less than the decreased equity benefits, where one policy is better on efficiency, but worse on equity, than another policy. The best way to process cases so that the average waiting time plus processing time per case is minimized is to process the shortest cases first, with the longer cases being subject to a maximum time constraint. This approach is consistent with maximizing benefits minus costs subject to minimum-benefit constraints. It is not consistent with conventional criteria such as (1) Pareto optimality, which says no case should be worsened as a result of a new policy; (2) Rawlsian justice, which says do whatever can be done to bring up the worst-off or longest case; and (3) Benthamite utilitarianism, which says maximize benefits minus costs, but shows no sensitivity to those cases that fall below a minimum decency level in terms of speedy processing.

On trade-offs between equity and other goals, one can conclude that equity and efficiency are sometimes in conflict. One example is the setting of bail bonds so as to maximize the probability of a defendant appearing in court without having committed a crime during release minus the probability of being held in jail, even though such efficient bail bonds may greatly decrease the allocation of pretrial release to the poor. Equity and efficiency may, however, go together. One example is the allocation of substantially greater funds to poor neighborhoods than to rich neighborhoods, because poor neighborhoods have a higher marginal rate of return; they are able to increase their output substantially for a relatively small incremental allocation. One can also conclude that equity and freedom are sometimes in conflict, as in a socialistic developing society in which freedom is restricted while striving for upward equality, or in a capitalistic developing society in which equality is restricted while striving for entrepreneurial freedom. In an industrial, urban, and educated society, substantial equality and freedom usually prevail, with relatively low tension between the two.

This chapter has not resolved the controversial issues that could be raised concerning equity as a policy goal, especially in specific substantive areas. It is hoped, however, that the organization of the ideas and the issues raised will stimulate insights into what might be appropriate approaches for finding the answers to the empirical and normative issues concerning (1) the meaning of equity, (2) the use of equity as a criterion for choosing among policies, and (3) the trade-offs between equity and other goals.

NOTES

1. On equity in general, see Edmund Phelps (ed.), *Economic Justice: Selected Readings* (Penguin Books, 1973); Robert Lineberry, *Equality and Urban Policy* (Sage, 1977); Douglas Rae, Douglas Yates, Jennifer Hochschild, Joseph Morone, and Carol Fessler, *Equalities* (Harvard University Press, 1981); and Roland Pennock and John Chapman (eds.), *Equality: Nomos IX* (Atherton, 1962).

2. On the example of allocating anticrime dollars to places in an equitable and efficient manner, see S. Nagel, "Allocating Anti-crime Dollars across Places and Activities" in *Policy Evaluation: Making Optimum Decisions* (Praeger, 1982),

203–229. On the example of allocating legislative representatives to places so as to provide minimum equity, plus other goals including equality and partisan proportionality, see S. Nagel, "Computers and the Law and Politics of Redistricting" in *Improving the Legal Process: Effects of Alternatives* (Lexington-Heath, 1975).

3. On the problems involved in measuring equity, see Philip Coulter, "Measuring the Inequity of Urban Public Services: A Methodological Discussion with Applications," 8 *Policy Studies Journal* 683–698 (1980); Rein Taagepera, "Inequality, Concentration, Imbalance," 6 *Political Methodology* 275–291 (1979); and James Ray and David Singer, "Measuring the Concentration of Power in the International System," 1 *Sociological Methods and Research* 403–437 (1973). Thanks are owed to Philip Coulter for helping to clarify the problems of measuring equity. He sees equity as being in accordance with appropriate proportionality, so that being above or below it is considered equally undesirable.

4. On the measurement of inequality, see Hayward Alker, "Measuring Inequality" in *Mathematics and Politics* (Macmillan, 1965); and Paul Allison, "Measures of Inequality," 40 *American Sociological Review* 865–880 (1978).

5. On measuring deviations from proportionality and optimality, see the references cited in note 2. Also see David Baldus and J. Cole, *Statistical Proof of Discrimination* (McGraw-Hill, 1980); M. Hallock, "The Numbers Game: The Use and Misuse of Statistics in Civil Rights Litigation," 23 *Villanova Law Review* 5 (1977); and Mack Player, "Equal Pay Act" in *Federal Law of Employment Discrimination in a Nutshell* (West, 1976). The proportionality measure was developed along with Brad Malis and Linda Simmons, students at the University of Illinois.

6. On the problems involved in choosing among alternative policies in which nonmonetary benefits are involved, see Mark Thompson, *Benefit-Cost Analysis for Program Evaluation* (Sage, 1980); Edward Gramlich, *Benefit-Cost Analysis of Government Programs* (Prentice-Hall, 1981); and S. Nagel, "Dealing with Non-Monetary Variables in Policy Analysis" in *Contemporary Public Policy Analysis* (University of Alabama Press, 1983).

7. On the example of alternative ways of sequencing the processing of cases, see Jack Byrd, *Operations Research Models in Public Administration* (Lexington-Heath, 1975), 139–156; Richard Conway, William Maxwell, and Louis Miller, *Theory of Scheduling* (Addison-Wesley, 1967); and S. Nagel, "Dynamic Programming or Optimum Sequencing" in *Policy Evaluation: Making Optimum Decisions* (Praeger, 1982).

8. On Pareto optimality, see William Baumol, "General Equilibrium and Welfare Economics" in *Economic Theory and Operations Analysis* (Prentice-Hall, 1965), 355–385. On Rawlsian equity, see John Rawls, *A Theory of Justice* (Harvard University Press, 1971); and Norman Daniels (ed.), *Reading Rawls* (Basic Books, 1974). On Benthamite utilitarianism, see Jeremy Bentham, *Principles of Morals and Legislation* (Oxford University Press, 1948); and D. Baumgardt, *Bentham and the Ethics of Today* (Princeton University Press, 1952).

9. On the example of optimum bond-setting, see S. Nagel and Marian Neef, "The Bond-Setting Decision Across Cases" in *Decision Theory and the Legal Process* (Lexington-Heath, 1979); and Andrew Schaffer, "Bail and Parole Jumping in Manhattan in 1967" (Vera Institute, 1967).

10. On the example of allocating to libraries and related neighborhood institutions, see Frank Levy, Arnold Meltsner, and Aaron Wildavsky, *Urban Outcomes*

(University of California Press, 1974); and William Lucy, "Equity and Planning for Local Services," 47 *Journal of American Planning Association* 447–457 (1981).

11. On the conflict and overlap between equity and efficiency, see Arthur Okun, *Equality and Efficiency: The Big Tradeoff* (Brookings, 1975); Robert Buchele and Howard Cohen, *Equity and Efficiency in Public Policy* (Policy Studies Associates, 1978); and Chapter 3. On the measurement of inequality, see Hayward Alker, "Measuring Inequality" in *Mathematics and Politics* (Macmillan, 1965) and Paul Allison, "Measures of Inequality," 40 *American Sociological Review* 865–880 (1978).

12. See Daniel Nelson, "Worker-Party Conflict and the Dialectics of Developed Socialism" (paper presented at the annual meeting of the American Political Science Association, 1981), for an analysis of the idea that as socialistic countries industrialize and develop more educated workers, the workers demand a more responsive government and are less willing to sacrifice and to do as they are told. Socialist economies thus emphasize equality first and freedom second, whereas capitalist economies emphasize freedom first and equality second; even so, both tend to wind up in about the same place.

13. On the conflict and overlap between equity and freedom, see Harry V. Jaffa, *Equality and Liberty* (Oxford University Press, 1965); Albert Lauterbach, *Economic Security and Individual Freedom: Can We Have Both?* (Cornell University Press, 1948); and Muriel Jaeger, *Liberty vs. Equality* (Nelson, 1943).

QUESTIONS

1. What elements must be considered in order to define equity in verbal terms and in quantitative terms?
2. What justifications are there for providing minimum levels of health care, education, welfare, and other societal or governmental benefits to all persons, groups, or places within a society?
3. How can one quantitatively take equity criteria into consideration in choosing among alternative policies?
4. What are some of the major philosophical principles used for deciding among alternative ways of allocating scarce resources to persons, groups, or places?
5. Give examples of situations in which equitable policies might not be efficient and situations in which equitable policies are likely to be efficient.
6. Under what circumstances is there likely to be relatively high or low tension between the goals of equality and freedom?

REFERENCES

Alker, Hayward, "Measuring Inequality" in *Mathematics and Politics* (Macmillan, 1965).

Baldus, David, and J. Cole, *Statistical Proof of Discrimination* (McGraw-Hill, 1980).

Jaffa, Harry V., *Equality and Liberty* (Oxford University Press, 1965).
Lineberry, Robert, *Equality and Urban Policy* (Sage, 1977).
Okun, Arthur, *Equality and Efficiency: The Big Tradeoff* (Brookings, 1975).
Pennock, Roland, and John Chapman (eds.), *Equality: Nomos IX* (Atherton, 1962).
Phelps, Edmund (ed.), *Economic Justice: Selected Readings* (Penguin Books, 1973).
Rae, Douglas, Douglas Yates, Jennifer Hochschild, Joseph Morone, and Carol Fessler, *Equalities* (Harvard University Press, 1981).

CHAPTER 5

Participation, Predictability, and Procedural Due Process

A fundamental aspect of policy evaluation is deciding which criteria to use in evaluating alternative public policies. The literature in the field generally emphasizes the goals of effectiveness, efficiency, and equity. In this literature, the administrative process is usually considered as a means to achieving these goals. The purpose of this brief chapter is to discuss how the administrative process for achieving these goals may be a goal in itself.[1]

The Means as a Goal

LEGAL SERVICES FOR THE POOR: AN EXAMPLE

To clarify what is meant by "the means as a goal," we should explain the concepts of *effectiveness*, *efficiency*, and *equity*. We can do so in the context of the Legal Services Program of the Office of Economic Opportunity. The program's effectiveness can be measured in terms of the number of units of service it provides. These units may be cases opened, cases won, or clients serviced in various fields of law at various levels of the judicial system. The efficiency of the program can be measured in terms of the costs per unit of service. Such a measure might simply be the total number of cases for the whole program divided by the total budget in a given year, or a similar measure for each office or individual legal services agency. Finally, the program's equity refers to how equally the units of service are distributed across the 50 states, between urban and rural areas, among poor people of different racial or ethnic groups, or among other classifications of potential recipients. One could also measure how much equity the program produces by determining the extent to which the program reduces the inequality of access to the legal system between poor people in general and people who are not poor.

It may not be enough, however, for the program to be effective, efficient, and equitable. We may be willing to sacrifice some achievement of these three goals in order to have a more desirable delivery process. In other words, how the legal services are provided may in itself be important, and not important just because one delivery system is more effective, efficient, or equitable than another. When we refer to a desirable administrative process, we usually mean one or more of the following criteria:

1. participation in the decision making by the target group, the general public, relevant interest groups, or certain types of decision makers whose involvement appeals to our desires to use democratic procedures for achieving given goals.
2. a predictability in the decision making by way of following objective criteria in making decisions.
3. a procedural fairness in the decision making that enables those who feel they have been unfairly treated to have (a) a notice of rejection or wrongdoing, (b) a right to present evidence, (c) a right to confront their accusers, (d) a decision maker who is not also an accuser, and (e) an opportunity for at least one appeal.[2]

In the context of the Legal Services Program, the extent to which the three process-type goals are being achieved can be roughly measured by:

1. the extent to which representatives of the poor, the bar, and the general community participate in the general decision making of each legal services agency, as well as the extent to which each agency establishes a client advisory group.
2. objective family income criteria for determining who is eligible for free legal services, such that different decision makers are less likely to arrive at different conclusions on eligibility or how the cases should be processed.
3. a procedure whereby people who are denied free legal services can object in at least an informal proceeding with a right to appeal to someone at a higher level in the program.[3]

SOME GENERAL MATTERS

How can one measure participation, predictability, and procedural fairness? All three concepts can be measured subjectively with regard to the perceptions of relevant persons. For example, participation can be measured by the percent who respond yes when asked whether they believe they have adequate representation and opportunities to be heard. Predictability can be measured by the extent to which the respondents agree on what will happen under various circumstances. And procedural fairness can be measured by the frequency with which respondents perceive, out of 100 typical cases, the number of type 1 errors of treating the innocent as if they were guilty, plus the number of type 2 errors of treating the guilty as if they were innocent. An alternative measurement system would investigate the structures designed to facilitate participation, predictability, and procedural fairness. The most valid measurement system would examine how much participation actually occurs, how accurately cases are predicted, and how many errors of each kind are made, although these measures are generally difficult to obtain.

We sometimes talk about the three Es of *effectiveness, efficiency*, and *equity* and the three Ps of *public participation, predictability*, and *procedural fairness*. The three Es are usually associated with an economics approach to policy analysis, although they can be at least partly measured in nonmonetary terms. The three Ps are generally associated with a political science approach, although they can be at least partly measured in monetary terms. We can also discuss participation, predictability, and procedural fairness as effectiveness measures for some policies, and in terms of how efficiently and equitably they are provided. If, however, the procedural goals are merged with the substantive goals, the procedural ones are likely to be neglected more than if they are treated separately.

By "the means may be a goal" is meant that certain procedures may be ends in themselves rather than means to higher goals. We are thus talking about ultimate, rather than instrumental, values. It can be argued that the substantive and procedural goals are all instrumental values designed to achieve an ultimate goal of happiness, utility, or satisfaction. These "higher" concepts are so general that any policy which can only be justified in terms of them can be considered an ultimate goal having value in itself. All three "happiness" concepts are at least partly tautologous, circular, or valid. Satisfaction, for example, can be defined as that which people seek to maximize. Thus, satisfaction becomes the ultimate goal of all value systems. Being equal to "goal" makes satisfaction no goal at all in terms of its being a meaningful criterion. In other words, if "satisfaction" means the same as goal, then it is not a concept that clarifies what goals, objectives, or criteria we should be seeking.

There are basically two ways one can justify ultimate goals like effectiveness, efficiency, equity, participation, predictability, and procedural fairness. The first is a traditional philosophical approach that talks in terms of the inherent nature of human beings, divine authority, intuitive obviousness, and the like. The second approach is associated with social science and survey research. It defines an ultimate value as something which people do seek, or at least advocate, as an end in itself, rather than as a means to a higher end. In light of this definition, one might determine whether participation, predictability, and procedural fairness are ultimate goals by analyzing various public policy controversies to determine the justifications given by people, including highly knowledgeable, articulate people. There are many policy controversies to which that kind of analysis could be applied. Some controversies that have been highly divisive in recent history include national independence, socialism versus capitalism, dispute resolution through negotiation rather than the adversary system, constitutional interpretation, and what to do with convicted criminals. These examples are discussed in the following section.

The Means as a Goal: Further Examples

A number of examples can be given of situations in which it is clear that the people involved would not be satisified if a policy were only capable of achieving a high degree of effectiveness, efficiency, and equity, but did not satisfy the process considerations mentioned previously. If effectiveness were great enough, however, some process desirability could possibly be sacrificed, because these process considerations are often goals capable of being traded off, rather than minimum binding constraints. Nevertheless, effectiveness is not usually enough to cause a complete ignoring of process considerations.

PUBLIC PARTICIPATION

The Israelis may accurately say that they can provide a government for the West Bank Arabs that will be more effective, efficient, and equitable than Arab self-government. By this, the Israelis mean that they can provide a higher total income for the population as a measure of effectiveness, a better ratio of total income to taxes as a measure of efficiency, and a more equal distribution across people than Arab societies have traditionally provided. Nevertheless, the Arabs of the West Bank would probably be willing to sacrifice some of these measures in order to have more democratic participation in controlling their own government and economy. Predictability and fair procedures are relatively unimportant in this situation, in which self-determination is the key controversial consideration. Advocates of independence for nations controlled by a colonial power or a minority ethnic group often emphasize that independence will mean a higher standard of living at lower cost and more equal treatment. Such a standard may be achieved by keeping the profits from natural resources and manufacturing in the hands of the subjugated group, rather than in the control of the dominant group which the advocates seek to overthrow. Independence advocates often recognize, however, that there may be a substantial short-run or even long-run drop in the standard of living due to the disruption of the economy. Even so, they still advocate independence because there is value in self-determination and popular control, regardless of the economic benefits and costs.[4]

Another example in which process considerations may be a key criterion is the socialism-versus-capitalism controversy, a broad policy problem with wide implications. Both sides agree that effectiveness and efficiency are important. Effectiveness in this context is the ability to produce a high gross national product (GNP), and efficiency is the GNP divided by the costs necessary to produce it. How to measure these costs may be highly subjective. If one just looks to government expenditures, one would expect them to be greater in a socialistic economy than in a capitalist one. However, if one looks to all social costs, including pollution, on-the-job injuries, unemployment, crime, ill health, energy shortages, and unsafe products, then a capitalistic economy may not fare as well as a planned socialist one. On the matter of equity, there is more likely to be equality across groups under a socialist economy, but capitalists would argue that this kind of equality destroys incentives. Also, both sides, if we are referring to American social-ists and American capitalists, would probably wish to talk about popular participation. The socialist might emphasize popular participation by way of the ballot box and point out that wealthy individuals can influence more votes than poor people can. The capitalist might emphasize the free market-place on both the consumer-demand and producer-supply side, especially the freedom of business entrepreneurs to influence the market with their decisions. The important point is not whose definition of costs, desirable equity, or popular participation is right, but rather that merely talking in terms of effectiveness, efficiency, and equity does not adequately cover the socialism-capitalism controversy. In discussing this controversy as well as narrower policy problems, an important evaluative criterion is the means or process for achieving those substantive goals, including democratic participation.[5]

PREDICTABILITY

An example in which predictability may be a key process consideration for many observers is in the decision making of the United States Supreme Court. If all we were concerned with was effectiveness, efficiency, and equity, then we would want the Supreme Court to reach results in accor-dance with our substantive goals as quickly as possible and to do so equally in all cases. For a liberal, these results might be automatic decisions favoring such interests as the poor, minority groups, political and religious dissidents, economic regulation, and people accused of crimes. For a conservative, they might be automatic decisions favoring the well-off, the majority ethnic group, establishment ideas in politics and religion, business freedom, or the prosecution point of view. However, neither liberals nor conserva-tives might want such automatic decisions. These groups will probably recognize that favorable decisions are more likely to be respected if they are principled—that is, based on prior court-expressed principles or prece-dents. Both liberals and conservatives are probably willing to lose a few cases in order to have the Supreme Court operate in accordance with principled decision making, acknowledging that otherwise their victories would not have much meaning. Some predictability in court decisions for which one is willing to trade some favorable results is also desirable; without predictabili-ty, a favorable pattern might be unpredictably reversed, contrary to one's expectations and activities in reliance on the prior decisional pattern.[6] In other words, business firms, nonprofit entities, individuals, government agencies, and others may become overly cautious in doing desirable things for fear that these activities may be declared illegal even though prior decisions have declared them to be legal.

PROCEDURAL FAIRNESS

The substitution of plea bargaining for jury trials is a good example of a case in which procedural fairness may be especially important. Individuals argue that in order to avoid time-consuming and expensive jury trials, it would be desirable if more criminal cases could be resolved by the prosecutor getting the defendant to plead guilty to the original or a lesser charge. Thus, a system of encouraging defendants to plead guilty in return for a lighter sentence than they would have received if convicted is quite effective in achieving the main goal of a judicial system, namely, resolving cases. It is also quite efficient, because resolving cases by negotiation is far less expensive than bench or jury trials. One can also argue that the system is equitable because both the poor and the rich can plead not guilty and ask for a jury trial that will slow down the system in order to get concessions out of a prosecutor.

Despite its apparent effectiveness, efficiency, and equity, plea bargaining may result in considerable procedural unfairness—that is, in acquitting the innocent and convicting the guilty. Plea bargaining, however, may convict the innocent and free the guilty, especially when it is combined with pretrial detention. Defendants who are detained pending trial because they cannot meet the bail-bond requirements for release are often vulnerable to prosecution offers designed to encourage them to plead guilty. A defendant sitting in jail awaiting trial may be informed that by pleading guilty, he or she can go home immediately; the prosecutor will then recommend probation or a sentence equal to the time already served in jail. If the defendant claims to be innocent and demands a trial, he or she may be truthfully informed that:

1. in view of the trial backlog, the defendant will have to wait a substantial time period before the case can be heard.
2. when the trial is heard, the witnesses the defendant is relying upon may not prove to be so reliable.
3. if the defendant is convicted, he or she may receive additional time in jail.

Under these circumstances, the typical defendant may find a prosecution offer of immediate freedom to be difficult to refuse, regardless of the defendant's innocence or the inability of the prosecutor to prove the defendant's guilt. This is particularly true for defendants who already have a criminal record; an additional guilty plea does not do as much incremental harm to their résumés.

Defendants awaiting trial out of jail who can afford counsel may be able, in effect, to threaten to be very time-consuming for the prosecutor. As a result, they may get the prosecutor to reduce the charges in return for a plea of guilty, even though they may be guilty of the original charges. Such a charge reduction may amount to the acquittal of an individual who is guilty of serious charges. In recognition of the effects of plea bargaining, the President's Crime Commission (1973) has advocated its abolition, regardless of its effectiveness, efficiency, and equity. Abolition may be impossible, however, unless prosecutors and defendants are provided with the resources, knowledge, and legal rules that they need in order to take all cases to trial if necessary.[7]

DETERMINATE SENTENCING AND PROCEDURAL GOALS

In criminal sentencing, effectiveness can be measured by the extent to which different sentencing methods reduce crime. Efficiency involves the costs of administering alternative sentencing methods, especially the incarceration costs. Equity means that, in sentencing, there should be no substantial difference across defendants or judges, unless the difference reflects how damaging the crime is and the defendant's prior criminal record. In other words, when crime damage and prior record are held constant, an equality of sentencing should exist across economic class, race, and other background characteristics. Because traditional sentencing allows a great deal of discretion by judges, it lacks equity-equality, as statistical studies have shown and as criminal defendants have perceived. This perception, which generates substantial antisocial bitterness, may be an important crime-producing factor. As a result, it adversely affects the effectiveness and the equity of traditional discretionary sentencing.

Contemporary determinate-sentencing reform emphasizes the need for improving the three substance considerations of equity, effectiveness, and efficiency and the three process considerations of predictability, procedural fairness, and participation. To achieve such improvement, sentencing must be made more a matter of legislative than judicial discretion. The sentencing system that reduces judicial discretion the most involves legislation specifying which sentence will be given to a defendant upon conviction for a certain crime when he or she has a given prior record. It also includes no more than 10 percent leeway in either direction for considering aggravating or mitigating circumstances and guidelines as to what those circumstances are. The determinate sentencing system provides improved predictability, and it advances procedural fairness, because appeals for a change in a sentence are more meaningful when there is more openness about how the sentence was decided and what objective criteria were used to review it. The process involves more democratic participation in emphasizing popularly elected legislators, rather than appointed or less meaningfully elected judges. By improving the process in these ways, the substance goals may also benefit, especially with regard to equity-equality. In addition, substance goals may benefit with regard to effectiveness if the legislative decisions reflect social science studies of the relation between sentence length and reduction of crime and if the system lessens the criminogenic bitterness of the present system. Whatever improves effectiveness indirectly improves efficiency, because efficiency is effectiveness units divided by monetary costs. The process considerations in this example are partly a means to achieving greater equity, effectiveness, and efficiency; they are also desirable in themselves because we would probably be willing to sacrifice some of these substance goals in order to have more predictability, procedural fairness, and democratic participation in the important sentencing aspects of our criminal justice system.

Determinate sentencing can be advocated not only for its relevance to the three *E*s and the three *P*s, but also for its relevance to the goal of openness in decision making. Determinate sentencing involves openness in that one can determine how the judge arrived at the sentence and what the justifications were, although the legislative justifications may not be as clear. In addition, a statement can be required from the judge in each case, explaining his or her use of limited discretion concerning aggravating or mitigating circumstances. Under one variation of determinate sentencing, the judge must confer with two colleagues if he or she deviates from the legislated sentence by more than a certain percentage. This adds some openness, or visibility, to the decision-making process. Openness may be desirable, but it is not an end in itself. Rather, it is a means for increasing the achievement of the procedural goals. The public can more meaningfully participate or criticize if it knows what is going on. Likewise, one can predict better if records are available as a basis for prediction. In addition, procedural fairness can be better promoted if unfairness is more out in the open.[8]

Other Policy Analysis Ideas

Saying that the process for achieving certain goals may be a goal in itself is related to but different from other policy analysis ideas. For example, the idea that the end justifies the means can have at least two meanings. One not-so-controversial meaning is that one evaluates two different policies by how well they achieve their intended and unintended consequences. A second meaning, which is more controversial, is that highly desirable goals can justify any procedures for achieving them. These ideas often come up in discussions about the desirability of violent, rather than parliamentary, means for achieving revolutionary goals. Virtually all revolutionaries would prefer to use nonviolent means if such means could bring about the desired goals, rather than to say that it makes no difference which means are used, or worse, that violence is preferable. The idea that the end justifies the means is almost the opposite of saying that the means may be a goal. The first idea indicates that the means are of little or no importance in themselves, whereas the second idea makes them a goal jointly with other goals, although not necessarily of equal value. Saying that the end justifies the means implies that the process has some adverse unintended consequences, but that the desirable intended consequences can offset the unintended ones. Saying that the means may be a goal implies that the process has some less-than-maximum intended consequences, which we are willing to settle for because the nature of the process provides some offsetting side benefits.[9]

The idea of the means as a goal is also related to the policy analysis controversy between rationalism and incrementalism. In this context, *rationalism* refers to the attempt to find policies that will maximize goals all at once, whereas *incrementalism* emphasizes that policies tend to get adopted piecemeal, which is desirable. Piecemeal adoption facilitates learning from experience and abandoning a project or making midcourse corrections before one gets too deeply involved. It also has greater feasibility and public acceptance, although it has the disadvantage of delaying benefits that could otherwise be obtained. Incrementalists are thus saying that an incremental process is desirable, even if an optimum policy could be developed all at once. They do not, however, consider incrementalism desirable in itself, but rather for the trial-and-error benefits and public acceptance which it provides. These goals are not the same as the process goals of participation, openness, predictability, and fair procedure. They are more closely related to achieving the substance goals of effectiveness, efficiency, and equity. In other words, both the incrementalists and rationalists tend to argue that their approaches are desirable, not so much in themselves, but because in the long run, over many situations, they are more effective, efficient, and equitable.[10]

Along related lines is the idea of political and administrative feasibility. This concept is more a policy constraint than a policy goal. All policy proposers would like their policies to be feasible—that is, capable of being adopted and implemented. In order to assess the probability of a proposal being adopted and implemented, one must understand the political and administrative process. For example, taxes to reduce pollution may be an excellent idea from the perspective of internalizing into business-firm decisions the external costs of business pollution, thereby shifting the burden from the general public to the business firms responsible for pollution. However, such a policy may reflect a lack of understanding of the power and motivation of business firms to defeat such burdensome legislation. Likewise, a program of homeownership for the poor is likely to become involved in destructive scandal if administered by private-sector real-estate operators rather than government employees. Advocating a greater awareness of the political and administrative process as part of a feasibility assessment within a policy analysis is related to the idea of being sensitive to the political process. It is not, however, the same as saying that policy goals often include by implication, or should include, such process goals as public participation, openness, predictability, and fair procedure.[11]

An important aspect of policy analysis is the notion of trade-offs among conflicting goals. This idea is as applicable to process goals as it is to substance goals. One can easily offer examples of situations that involve conflicting process goals or conflicts between process and substance goals. A good example is the free-press, fair-trial problem. Free press is a process goal which states that public participation in trials by reading and commenting on newspaper reports is socially desirable. Fair trial is a process goal which states that defendants should have the right to cross-examine adverse witnesses, but this is virtually impossible for them to do if the adverse evidence consists of unidentified statements made in newspaper articles which may be read by the decision-making jurors. A good example of substance conflicting with process is any policy problem that requires speed and technical competence such that public participation and openness might prevent the substance goals from being achieved within the limited time available. The same concern for how to weight conflicting goals applies in these situations, as with the classic substantive conflicts between guns and butter, energy and environment, or labor and capital.[12]

The idea of process as a goal should also be seen in the context of the role of social values and public policy in general. Social values enter policy analysis in various ways. On the most basic level is the issue of being value-free in policy analysis research, whereby one avoids value judgments, in contrast to empirical statements about what is rather than what ought to be. Policy analysis is concerned with maximizing values, but policy analysts can go out of their way to avoid letting their biases affect their empirical findings. Higher-level values sometimes play a role in justifying the immediate goals which a policy analyst is seeking to maximize, but often that linkage is not explicit. Sensitivity analysis is an important part of policy analysis in which one shows how prescriptive conclusions would be affected by changing the values to be maximized or their relative weights. Policy analysts are sometimes faced with the dilemma of being asked to maximize goals that are not legal or in the public interest; however, this is not so likely in a democratic society. The most important aspect of the relationship between social values and public policy is probably the need for policy analysts to be constantly conscious of what goals they are seeking to maximize or achieve, including both substance and process goals.[13]

Conclusion

This chapter does not express revolutionary ideas with regard to policy goals, although some of the civil libertarian ideas may be considered revolutionary under certain present and past political systems. The chapter mainly brings together a series of examples and ideas designed to emphasize the importance of the means or process for achieving goals as a goal or series of goals in itself. These considerations may be implicit in most policy analyses, but sometimes they must be made more explicit. This need may be even greater as policy analysis becomes more quantitative because process goals may be more difficult to quantify than substance goals, which increases the likelihood of their being given less explicit emphasis. This need may also be greater as policy analysis becomes more concerned with outputs and impact, rather than with determinants and process.

The notion of effectiveness, efficiency, and equity covering the relevant goals of policy analysis is too narrow in light of the preceding examples and ideas. To these substantive goals should be added the process goals of participation, predictability, and procedural fairness. Doing so will help recommended policies to achieve optimality in the sense of maximizing the kind of values at least implicitly present in utilitarian, transcendental, Marxist, and most other widely accepted political philosophies. In light of all this, the means may indeed be a goal.

NOTES

The author gratefully thanks William Dunn of the University of Pittsburgh for his helpful comments concerning this chapter, and also the people who participated on the panel or in the audience of the workshop of the Policy Studies Organization on "Social Values and Public Policy" at the 1980 American Political Science Association meeting.

1. The concern for effectiveness, efficiency, and equity in policy analysis is expressed in such places as Edward Quade, *Analysis for Public Decisions* (Elsevier, 1975), 83–115; Werner Hirsch, *The Economics of State and Local Government* (McGraw-Hill, 1970), 147–198; and E. S. Savas, "On Equity in Providing Public Services," 24 *Management Science* 800–808 (1978). On measuring and comparing effectiveness, efficiency, equity, and related concepts, see Chapter 3, "Effectiveness and Efficiency."

   A concern for process as a goal (and not just as a means for achieving effectiveness, efficiency, and equity) is not as clearly expressed in the policy analysis literature, although some items come close to giving procedure the importance of a goal—for example, Edith Stokey and Richard Zeckhauser, *A Primer for Policy Analysis* (Norton, 1978), 283–285; and Duncan MacRae, Jr., and James Wilde, *Policy Analysis for Public Decisions* (Duxbury, 1979), 45–77.

2. On the importance of considering public participation, predictability, and procedural fairness, see J. Roland Pennock, *Liberal Democracy: Its Merits and Prospects* (Rinehart, 1950); David Fellman, *The Defendant's Rights Today* (University of Wisconsin Press, 1976); and Chapter 6, "Societal Consequences of Basic Human Rights."

3. On the goals of the Office of Economic Opportunity's (OEO) Legal Services Program, see Harry Stumpf, *Lawyers and the Poor* (Sage, 1973); Eli Jarmel, *Legal Representation of the Poor* (Matthew Bender, 1972), Chapter 3, 1–19; and Herbert Semmel, *Social Justice Through Law* (Foundation Press, 1970), 56–69.

4. On the importance of popular participation in resolving the Arab refugee problem, see Don Peretz, *Israel and the Palestine Arabs* (Middle East Institute, 1958); and Rony Gabbay, *A Political Study of the Arab-Jewish Conflict: The Arab Refugee Problem* (E. Droz, 1959). On the psychological value of self-determination regardless of the benefit-cost results, see Franz Fanon, *Wretched of the Earth* (Grove Press, 1965).

5. On the importance of popular participation in the socialism-capitalism controversy, see John Putnam, *The Modern Case for Socialism* (Meador, 1946); David McCord Wright, *Capitalism* (McGraw-Hill, 1951); and Paul Sweezy, *Socialism* (McGraw-Hill, 1949).

6. On the importance of principled predictability in the Supreme Court and other appellate court decisions, see Herbert Wechsler, *Principles, Politics, and Fundamental Law* (Harvard University Press, 1961); and Karl Llewellyn, *The Common Law Tradition: Deciding Appeals* (Little, Brown, 1960).

7. On the importance of procedural fairness in deciding whether to have more jury trials replaced by negotiated settlements, see Suzanne Buckle and Leonard Buckle, *Bargaining for Justice: Case Disposition and Reform in the Criminal Courts* (Praeger, 1977); Arthur Rossett and Donald Cressey, *Justice by Consent: Plea Bargains in the American Courthouse* (Lippincott, 1976); and Donald Newman, *Conviction: The Determination of Guilt or Innocence Without Trial* (Little, Brown, 1966).

8. On criminal sentencing reform, see Don Gottfredson, Leslie Wilkins, and Peter Hoffman, *Guidelines for Parole and Sentencing: A Policy Control Method* (Lexington, 1978); and Alan Dershowitz, *Fair and Certain Punishment* (McGraw-Hill, 1976).

9. On the end justifying the means, see Harold Titus, *Ethics for Today* (American Book, 1947), 197–210.

10. On the rationalism-incrementalism controversy, see Yehezkel Dror, *Public Policymaking Reexamined* (Chandler, 1968); David Braybrooke and Charles Lindblom, *A Strategy for Decision* (Free Press, 1963); and Amitai Etzioni, "Mixed Scanning: A Third Approach to Decision-Making," 27 *Public Administration Review* 385–402 (1967).

11. On political and administrative feasibility, see Giandomenico Majone, "On the Notion of Political Feasibility," 3 *European Journal of Political Research* 259–274 (1975); and Arnold Meltsner, "Political Feasibility and Policy Analysis," 32 *Public Administration Review* 859–867 (1972).

12. On weighting conflicting goals, see Allan Easton, *Complex Managerial Decisions Involving Multiple Objectives* (Wiley, 1973); Ralph Keeney and Howard Raiffa, *Decisions with Multiple Objectives: Preferences and Value Tradeoffs* (Wiley, 1975); and S. Nagel and Marian Neef, *Policy Analysis: In Social Science Research* (Sage, 1979), 105–132.

13. On social values and public policy in general, see Duncan MacRae, Jr., *The Social Function of Social Science* (Yale University Press, 1976); Phillip Gregg, *Problems of Theory in Policy Analysis* (Lexington, 1976); Wayne Leys, *Ethics for Policy Decisions: The Art of Asking Deliberate Questions* (Prentice-Hall, 1952); and Joel Fleishman and Bruce Payne, "Ethical Dilemmas and the Education of Policymakers" in Daniel Callahan and Sissela Bok (eds.), *Ethics Teaching in Higher Education* (Hastings Center, 1980).

QUESTIONS

1. In what sense are public participation, predictability, and procedural fairness ends in themselves, rather than means to achieving greater effectiveness, efficiency, and equity? Why?

2. Give an example of a situation in which decision makers were (or are) willing to sacrifice some policy effectiveness in order to have greater public participation.

3. Give an example of a situation in which decision makers were (or are) willing to sacrifice some policy effectiveness and efficiency in order to have greater predictability.

4. Give an example of a situation in which decision makers were (or are) willing to sacrifice some policy effectiveness and efficiency in order to have greater procedural fairness.
5. How does the idea of "the means as a goal" differ from related ideas, such as "the ends justify the means" or "rationalism versus incrementalism"?
6. How does the idea of "the means as a goal" differ from related ideas, such as political feasibility, administrative feasibility, or trade-offs among conflicting goals?

REFERENCES

Fellman, David, *The Defendant's Rights Today* (University of Wisconsin Press, 1976).
Gregg, Phillip, *Problems of Theory in Policy Analysis* (Lexington-Heath, 1976).
Leys, Wayne, *Ethics for Policy Decisions: The Art of Asking Deliberate Questions* (Prentice-Hall, 1952).
MacRae, Duncan, Jr., *The Social Function of Social Science* (Yale University Press, 1976).
National Advisory Commission on Criminal Justice Standards and Goals, *Courts* (U.S. Government Printing Office, 1973).
Pennock, J. Roland, *Liberal Democracy: Its Merits and Prospects* (Rinehart, 1950).
Wechsler, Herbert, *Principles, Politics, and Fundamental Law* (Harvard University Press, 1961).

CHAPTER 6

Societal Consequences
of Basic
Human Rights

Basic Concepts

This chapter describes some of the consequences of providing various controversial basic legal rights to a society. A *right* can be defined as: (1) a behavior which a society tolerates without subjecting a person who engages in it to an injunction or penalty for doing so, or (2) a benefit which a society confers upon a person that cannot be withdrawn unless the society's rules change. Rights can thus be *tolerated rights*, which a society allows, or *affirmative rights*, which a society grants.

Rights can also be controversial or noncontroversial, depending on whether their exercise arouses much or little dissension within the society. The tolerated right to breathe is generally noncontroversial, but the tolerated right to advocate radical ideas is often controversial. Likewise, the affirmative right to receive mail from the post office is generally noncontroversial, but the affirmative right to receive a minimum income as provided for in welfare legislation is often controversial.

There are both legal and human rights. Legal rights, promulgated by the government, specify how people (including government officials) ought to behave toward each other or else be subject to sanctions. These proclamations are in constitutions, statutes, judicial precedents, or in administrative regulations or adjudications. Human rights are similar to legal rights but are found in religious literature, in the inherent nature of man, or in an inductive analysis of the legal rights present in a variety of societies. This chapter deals explicitly with the consequences of legal rights, although it is applicable to human rights to the extent the two overlap.

Legal rights are either basic or nonbasic. Basic legal rights are embodied in a society's governmental constitution or in statutes that can be supplemented, although they are unlikely to be repealed. This chapter emphasizes the consequences of controversial basic legal American rights, although the information is generally applicable to other societies as well.[1] Those particularly discussed rights relate to: (1) freedom of speech and religion, (2) equality of treatment, (3) safeguarding the innocent from conviction and harassment, and (4) the right to basic economic security. The consequences discussed do not concentrate on the effects on the individuals who exercise these rights, but rather on the effects on the total society. Behavioral science studies or empirical research relating to these effects will be cited wherever appropriate.[2]

Freedom of Speech and Religion

The right of free speech in America can be defined as allowing both popular and unpopular viewpoints to be advocated or communicated without penalty in any medium of communication, provided the communication does not involve hard-core pornography, untruthful defamation, obtaining money under false pretenses, invasion of privacy, or the likely promotion of bodily injury. In the United States this is a tolerated rather than an affirmative right because it does not include providing free access to the communications media, with the exception of the narrow Federal Communications Commission (FCC) equal-time rules.

What are the effects on society of providing the right of free speech? Philosophers emphasize three basic effects.[3] First, in empirical science, free speech improves the chance that truth will be accepted. The suppression of Galileo's observation that the earth revolves around the sun rather than vice versa is a case in point.

Second, in matters of normative policy, free speech ensures the most effective means toward given ends will have a better chance of being accepted. For example, suppression of the slavery abolitionists delayed the improved labor productivity per labor expense and the improved capital equipment which free labor promoted.

Third, free speech provides a check on corrupt and inefficient leadership and administrative personnel. Even dictatorships recognize the value of encouraging critics of administrate inefficiency, even though criticism of top national officials or fundamental government policy is not encouraged.

Free speech is indirectly responsible for higher standards of living to the extent that it promotes scientific discovery and dissemination, more effective means of achieving given societal goals, and more efficient governmental personnel. This partly explains why Table 6-1 shows a positive correlation between the level of free-speech permissiveness and the level of modernity in the 84-country sample used.[4] Some of the positive correlation is also due to the reciprocal fact that higher standards of living create a more tolerant middle class, which allows still more freedom of speech.

Some critics argue that free speech leads to political instability and revolution. The empirical data shows the opposite relation. Table 6-2 displays a positive correlation between countries with a permissive free-speech policy and countries with a high degree of stability. This relation is partly

TABLE 6-1

Relationship Between Permissiveness and Modernity in 84 Countries, 1948–1960

Level of Modernity	Level of Permissiveness			
	COERCIVE	MIDLEVEL PERMISSIVE	PERMISSIVE	TOTAL
Modern	Argentina East Germany Czechoslovakia USSR **(4)**	Austria France **(2)**	Australia Netherlands Canada New Zealand Belgium Norway Denmark Sweden Finland Switzerland Iceland United Kingdom Ireland United States Israel Uruguay Luxembourg West Germany **(18)**	24
Transitional	Albania Paraguay Bulgaria Poland Cuba Portugal Dominican Rep. Romania Egypt Spain Hungary Union S. Africa Korea Venezuela Nicaragua Yugoslavia **(16)**	Brazil Honduras Ceylon Japan Chile Lebanon Colombia Panama Cyprus Peru Ecuador Syria El Salvador Thailand Guatemala Turkey Greece Tunisia **(18)**	Costa Rica Italy Mexico **(3)**	37
Traditional	Afghanistan China Ethiopia Haiti Morocco Saudi Arabia Taiwan **(7)**	Bolivia Jordan Burma Laos Cambodia Liberia Ghana Libya Indonesia Malaya India Pakistan Iran Philippines Iraq Sudan **(16)**	**(0)**	23
Total	27	36	21	84

TABLE 6-2
Relationship Between Permissiveness and Political Stability, 1955–1961

Degree of Political Stability	Level of Permissiveness			TOTAL
	COERCIVE	MIDLEVEL PERMISSIVE	PERMISSIVE	
Stability	Czechoslovakia, East Germany, Ethiopia, Portugal, Romania, Saudi Arabia, Taiwan **(7)**	Austria, Cambodia, Libya, Philippines, Tunisia **(5)**	Australia, Canada, Costa Rica, Denmark, Finland, Iceland, Ireland, Israel, Luxembourg, Netherlands, New Zealand, Norway, Sweden, Switzerland, United Kingdom, United States, Uruguay, West Germany **(18)**	30
Midlevel Instability	Afghanistan, Albania, Bulgaria, China, Dominican Rep., Egypt, Haiti, Morocco, Nicaragua, Paraguay, Poland, Spain, Union S. Africa, USSR, Yugoslavia **(15)**	Burma, Ceylon, Chile, Ecuador, El Salvador, France, Ghana, Greece, Iran, Japan, Liberia, Malaya, Pakistan, Panama, Jordan, Sudan, Thailand **(17)**	Belgium, Italy, Mexico **(3)**	35
Instability	Argentina, Cuba, Hungary, Korea, Venezuela **(5)**	Bolivia, Brazil, Colombia, Cyprus, Guatemala, Honduras, Indonesia, India, Iraq, Laos, Lebanon, Peru, Syria, Turkey **(14)**	**(0)**	19
Total	27	36	21	84

attributable to the fact that free speech facilitates nonviolent change. It provides peaceful outlets through which potential revolutionaries can make themselves heard and win converts without resorting to revolution. The positive relation between free speech and nonviolent change is also partly attributable to the fact that free speech and nonviolent change are partly coeffects of having a large, tolerant middle class. The correlation between permissiveness and stability is, however, not as high as the correlation between permissiveness and modernity.

Freedom of religion is a legal right with two aspects. One aspect disallows governmental interference with religion and the other bans governmental aid to religion. The American version allows exceptions to the no-interference principle for dangerous religious practices like rattlesnake ceremonies, and exceptions to the no-aid principle for indirect or minor aid like bus-fare reimbursement to parochial school children.[5]

The effects of the no-interference right are similar to those of the free-speech right since religious activity is a form of communication. With religious speech, it is especially important to allow all viewpoints to be heard since truth and effectiveness are so difficult to determine. Religion also tends to be a highly emotional area, and small interferences can lead to strong resentments and to severe social conflict, especially in a religiously heterogeneous society. Indeed, the Thirty Years' War of the Protestant Reformation represented a greater per capita loss of life to the nations involved than any political war in European history.

Violations of the right prohibiting the government to give aid to religion can produce many effects that even members of the aided or dominant religion might consider socially detrimental. First, aid can lead to interference toward the religion aided. The Catholic hierarchy had opposed federal aid to parochial schools for fear that it would lead to restrictions on religious teaching. Second, aid can easily lead to real or perceived favoritism, since it is almost impossible to allocate aid equally among religions, partly because of disagreement about how equality should be measured. Third, government aid can decrease church and home initiatives, as John F. Kennedy noted in supporting the Supreme Court's ban on school prayers. Fourth, in a country having many religious denominations, being a member of the safe majority in one location does not guarantee that one will be in the safe majority in another place. Thus, what may be beneficial aid to religion in one part of the country may be viewed by the same religion as detrimental in other places. Fifth, aid, like interference, can generate strong resentments and severe social conflicts, as exemplified by the repeated anticlerical conflict in France over government aid to the Catholic Church.

Equality of Treatment

Equal treatment under American law mainly relates to prohibitions on ethnic group discrimination, particularly discrimination against blacks. Discrimination refers to denying someone because of his or her race various opportunities for which the person would otherwise be qualified. Discrimination can take many forms, including: (1) governmental discrimination with regard to criminal procedure, school access, and voting, or (2) private discrimination with regard to housing, public accommodations, and employment.[6] Discrimination exists when the dominant group forces segregation or involuntary separation on the minority group, but not when minority group members voluntarily choose to live together or to be distinctive. What are the effects of discrimination on the total society, particularly on the dominant racial group (not just on the group discriminated against)?[7]

Discrimination probably substantially decreases the gross national product by failing to fully use the actual and potential skills that blacks and other minorities have. Long established discrimination by the building trade unions is a good example. Similarly, housing discrimination may prevent qualified blacks from living near suburban job openings to which they may otherwise lack access. Past school discrimination and inferior school facilities may prevent blacks from becoming lawyers or doctors or greatly lessen the chances that black lawyers or doctors will achieve their potential.

Another societal economic effect results from segregated school and housing facilities. Segregated school systems may incur duplicative costs, as in the case of the Texas black law school and the Tennessee black medical school which were established to avoid integrating the universities of Texas and Tennessee. Segregated housing patterns combined with employment discrimination can lead to ghetto slums with their disproportionately high costs for police, fire protection, and welfare recipients.

Discrimination against a minority frequently depresses the weaker members of the majority. Thus, when blacks and whites are employed in the same jobs and blacks receive low wages, whites' wages are held down too. Black strike-breaking labor can also deter more aggressiveness on the part of white unions. Likewise, depressed standards of police behavior in dealing with blacks are sometimes hard to change when the police encounter whites, especially poor whites.

Psychologically speaking, discrimination against blacks creates a false sense of superiority for some whites. This may partly account for many white southerners' lack of educational and occupational ambition; they fall back on their race to compensate for their lack of education and job status. Discrimination can also cause whites to feel guilt and anxiety, especially if their behavior and attitudes toward blacks conflict with the democratic ideals preached in their society, thereby creating the American dilemma. Discrimination can, of course, have severe, psychologically disturbing effects on blacks, but this impact analysis emphasizes the effects on the total society in general and on the majority whites in particular.

Concerning American foreign and military policy, domestic discrimination decreases the United States' ability to influence Africa, Asia, and Latin America. Domestic discrimination also decreases the morale of blacks in the armed forces, especially in a war against non-Caucasians, and it also increases interracial friction within the armed forces, as indicated by numerous clashes in the late 1960s.

Discrimination generates antagonism and hatred on the part of blacks toward whites, which can spark intraghetto riots and possibly interneighborhood riots. Discrimination also divides whites between those who advocate faster removal of discriminatory barriers and those who advocate retention or slower removal. This intrawhite hostility sometimes manifests itself in student and other youthful protest activities.

Miscellaneous effects of discrimination include the loss of new manufacturing developments by discriminatory communities which business executives consider to be undesirable environments for raising their families. By reducing black income, discrimination can also reduce black consumer purchasing power, thereby hurting white business concerns. Finally, discrimination often deters nondiscriminatory behavior on the part of whites who do not want to discriminate, but who feel compelled to comply with what they perceive to be the dominant viewpoint, unless it is outlawed by antidiscrimination legislation.

In addition to mentioning various phenomena that behavioral scientists usually agree are effects of discrimination, some alleged effects that have no scientific acceptance should also be mentioned. For example, the absence of discrimination may indeed lead to increased intermarriage, but no accepted biological study has shown that the children of a racially mixed marriage are in any sense biologically defective. In fact, by lessening the "purity" of the races, friction between the races may decrease. In addition, the children of a racially mixed marriage are likely to have access to more societal opportunities than black children.

It is alleged that by integrating schools, the learning level of white students will be lowered without necessarily raising the level of black students. The Coleman Report (1966), however, showed that economic class integration or racial integration along class lines (that is, poor blacks with middle-class whites, poor whites with middle-class blacks, poor blacks with middle-class blacks, or poor whites with middle-class whites) does not generally lower the learning level of middle-class children, but does raise the learning level of the poorer children.

Some whites, in more frank moments, allege correctly that their jobs would be in jeopardy if discrimination barriers were dropped. Dropping discrimination against blacks is like dropping tariff discrimination against foreign products. It might mean a temporary relocation of marginal, less efficient persons, but the total national economy would benefit from lowered consumer prices and from more efficient use of labor. Likewise, in the long run, by removing inefficiencies caused by racial discrimination, the gross national product can be raised, governmental costs attributable to slums and duplicative facilities can be decreased, depressed wages can be increased, and there can be more efficient geographical allocation of industry and increased consumer purchasing power, as has been previously mentioned.

Safeguarding the Innocent from Conviction and Harassment

In America, approximately 10 different rights safeguard the innocent from conviction and harassment. They relate to all the stages of criminal procedure, from the legislative process passing criminal laws through arrest, trial, and sentencing. They include the right to:

1. no retroactive or vague criminal statutes, or statutes declaring named persons to be guilty of wrongdoing.
2. no arrest or search unless there is substantial likelihood of guilt.
3. no involuntary confessions or self-incrimination.
4. release pending speedy trial.
5. hired or provided counsel before and at trial.
6. formal notice of charges.
7. unanimous decision by a group of one's peers.
8. questioning adverse witnesses and calling one's own witnesses.
9. no excessive punishment.
10. no repeated prosecution for the same matter[8].

The effect of these rights is to lessen the likelihood that an innocent person will be convicted or harassed. This effect can be easily supported by people who are unlikely to commit crimes, but who recognize the possibility that they or other innocent people might find themselves in a situation or business practice in which they could be falsely suspected or accused of wrongdoing. These rights also decrease the likelihood that a guilty person will be convicted of a greater crime than he or she has committed, or that such a person will receive punishment or treatment disproportionate to his or her crime. This effect can also be easily supported by people who recognize that if the guilty are overconvicted or oversentenced, unnecessary bitterness and general disrespect for the law are bred, rather than rehabilitation or deterrence. While these rights make it more difficult to convict the guilty, people recognize that it is more detrimental to their self-interest and the orderly functioning of society for one innocent person to be convicted than for one or even a few guilty persons to go unpunished for a specific crime.

The specific right to a hired or provided lawyer is probably the most important one for preventing wrongful convictions and harassment.[9] Having a lawyer aids investigation of the facts, negotiation with the prosecutor, examination of witnesses, presentation of legal and factual arguments to the judge and jury, and preparation of an appeal. A lawyer also provides the defendant with psychological support and an air of objectivity, which the defendant himself could not provide. All the other procedural rights become less meaningful without an attorney to inform the defendant of his or her rights and to call violations to the attention of the courts, including violations that occur at the police interrogation stage. Of all basic legal rights, only free speech may be more important, because without it, violations of rights could not be readily called to the public's attention.

Right to counsel has some important effects on the legal system besides protecting the innocent or preventing excessive punishment of the guilty. The American adversary system presumes that both sides will be vigorously represented so that the neutral judge can arrive at the truth, which probably lies somewhere between the adverse positions. If only one side is represented, the system may not function effectively. If the poor generally lack lawyers in prosecutions, evictions, repossessions, or other cases, their respect for the law will decrease, although right to counsel currently extends only to criminal, not civil, cases. Counsel for the poor and other alienated groups also contributes to orderly reform of the law as an alternative to disorderly or violent change. In addition, widespread availability of counsel educates those who otherwise would be without counsel, and such education may prevent them from encountering legal trouble with creditors, landlords, and others.

While it is generally agreed that brutal or random arrests, searches, and confession-obtaining techniques have adverse social effects (by creating an unduly fearful population and disrespect for the police), some controversy has arisen over how to deter such police tactics. One cannot expect the prosecutor to vigorously prosecute police who have zealously tried to help him or her. Likewise, private damage suits are costly, time-consuming, embarrassing to the plaintiff, unlikely to result in victory because of police discretion and generally unsympathetic juries, and if victorious, are unlikely to result in a deterring damage judgment because of the officer's lack of money, the difficulty of assessing damages, and a tendency of the city to pay the judgment. Internal police administration in these matters is more protective than disciplinary. As a result of the lack of more effective alternatives, the courts have excluded illegally obtained evidence from the courtroom in hopes that the police will be encouraged to operate more within the law when making arrests or searches and when obtaining confessions. Behavioral studies have shown that this exclusionary rule has changed some police behavior.[10]

Important behavioral research has recently shown that regardless of the nature of the crime or the defendant's prior record, he or she is more likely to be convicted if not released pending trial.[11] The defendant's conviction chances are increased because (1) being in jail awaiting trial decreases his or her ability to investigate and prepare a defense and (2) the defendant makes a relatively bad impression on the judge and jury when brought for each trial session from the prisoners' lockup area, rather than appearing on his or her own through the regular courtroom entrance. Denying pretrial release for lack of bail also discriminates against the poor, increasing jail costs, promoting loss of jobs, and increasing the likelihood that the innocent will spend time in jail and that the guilty will spend more time than their sentence or the law provides. Studies have shown that careful screening of defendants to determine their roots in the community, followed by reminders of their court dates, produces a higher percentage of pretrial releases and a lower percentage of failures to appear in court than the traditional money bond system does.[12] Other behavioral studies have provided useful information on reducing court congestion so that both released and jailed defendants can be tried and convicted or acquitted sooner.[13]

There has been more behavioral research on the consequences of criminal procedure rights than on any other basic legal right. The effects of criminal jury trials rather than bench trials has been well researched, revealing that juries are more likely to acquit in 17 percent of the cases, although there is agreement in 75 percent, and the judge is more likely to acquit in 2 percent, with the jury being undecided in 6 percent.[14] The unanimity requirement, the multiple decision makers, and the less upper-class composition of juries probably account for their lesser propensity to convict compared to judges. Studies have also been conducted on the effects of various punishments, especially capital punishment, although the right to be free from capital punishment has not been established in American legal rights.[15]

Although there has been no behavioral research on some of the other procedural rights, the effects of their presence or absence can be readily hypothesized. Vague or retroactive criminal statutes obviously cannot have a meaningful deterrent effect if the statute does not clearly refer to future behavior. Likewise, if a prosecutor could repeatedly prosecute a defendant for the same matter, he or she might eventually convict an innocent person or overconvict a guilty person, to say nothing of the obvious harassment involved. Lacking both clear notice of the pending charges and the right to call his or her own witnesses and to question opposition witnesses, an innocent defendant would clearly have more difficulty establishing innocence.

Due process safeguards for the innocent are designed to separate the innocent from the guilty, not to reduce crime. Nevertheless, along with other civil liberties, due process safeguards can reduce crime in the following ways:

1. Separating the innocent from the guilty increases respect for the law.
2. Higher due process standards promote higher educational levels, improved training, and closer supervision of police officers, all of which increase the effectiveness of the police.

3. Crime by police officers can manifest itself in wrongful police violence. This is less likely to occur with better qualified, trained, and supervised police.
4. Decreased discrimination by the criminal justice system promotes respect for the law by minorities.
5. Decreased discrimination by society provides minorities with more meaningful alternatives to criminal activity.

The Right to Basic Economic Security

The right to basic economic security is a relatively modern right in America. It is embodied in statutes rather than in the Constitution. To the extent provided however, constitutionally, no arbitrary classifications of recipients are allowed or the equal-treatment right will be violated. Likewise, a person cannot be deprived of government economic benefits unless the recipient is provided with due process to give him or her an opportunity to show the illegality of the deprivation.

Relevant statutes in American law include: (1) the National Labor Relations Act of 1935, which provides the right to join labor unions which can aid in providing economic security; (2) the Fair Labor Standards Act of 1938, which provides for the rights to a minimum wage, maximum hours, and safe working conditions, and prohibits child labor; (3) the Social Security Act of 1935, which provides for aid to the aged, disabled, unemployed, and dependent children; and (4) the Employment Act of 1946, which declares that Americans have the right to expect the federal government to provide maximum employment, production, and purchasing power.[16]

Sometimes, critics discuss the conflict between freedom and economic security. To the contrary, freedom of speech was important in revealing the harm that befell society by the absence of these economic rights. By the same token, basic economic security is necessary to make freedom of speech meaningful, because those lacking economic security can not generally take advantage of expensive forms of communication. Moreover, economic insecurity makes one less tolerant of deviant ideas and less adaptable to social change, except change that will mean personal economic benefits. A close relationship exists between economic security and equal treatment with regard to race relations, since: (1) being black and being poor are positively correlated, (2) those who discriminate often do so out of economic insecurity, and (3) being poor makes one more subject to discrimination.

An important general effect of increased economic security is to lessen workers' economic anxieties. Such anxieties interfere with morale and efficiency and thereby lower the gross national product. Too much security, however, might cause workers to lessen attempts to improve themselves.

All three of the key New Deal statutes plus the 1946 act have influenced American society, just as related statutes have in other countries. Statistics show a substantial increase in union membership subsequent to the passage of the National Labor Relations Act, and a substantial decrease in strikes for union recognition, in contrast to strikes for more favorable contract terms. Other studies have indicated that unions produce higher wages, shorter hours, and safer conditions, at least for union members. For non-union members, the Fair Labor Standards Act has provided similar, although lower benefits. These economic effects have directly benefited a large segment of the population and indirectly benefited the total economy. This is evident by (1) the more efficient use of capital and labor which raising the price of labor has encouraged and (2) the economic stimulus stemming from increased purchasing power to the extent that wages have increased more than prices. Politically, strengthening unions has increased the likelihood that legislation favoring union interests will be passed.

The Social Security Act has encouraged earlier retirement for the aged and therefore earlier advancement for the young. The aid to dependent children provisions have spawned a tremendous bureaucratic apparatus that may eventually be replaced by legislation that provides for income supplements by way of Internal Revenue Service payments. The Employment Act has not eliminated unemployment or price inflation, but by encouraging greater government spending and lower taxes in time of unemployment, and the reverse in time of inflation (combined with other governmental regulatory devices), the business cycle has dampened somewhat. Provisions in the Social Security Act that provide for payments to the unemployed, dependent children, and the retired also help level business cycles because they increase in times of recession and decrease in times of prosperity.

In summary, this chapter has described and footnoted some of the broad consequences of providing various basic legal rights. Additional behavioral research on the impact of rights is needed to supplement the more philosophical discussion of the definitions, justifications, identifications, and relations of both human rights and legal rights. Such social science research will also help further bridge philosophy and the behavioral sciences. Ideally, this chapter has joined some of the relevant ideas and literature for others to build upon.

NOTES

1. For empirical studies of basic legal rights in a non-American context see D. Bayley, *Public Liberties in the New States* (Rand McNally, 1964); and references under "Constitutional Law" in C. Szladits, *A Bibliography on Foreign and Comparative Law Books and Articles in English* (Oceana Publishers, 1955 to present).
2. Behavioral materials that deal with the social consequences of general legal rights include S. Wasby, *The Impact of the United States Supreme Court: Some Perspectives* (Dorsey Press, 1970); T. Becker, *The Impact of Supreme Court*

Decisions: Empirical Studies (Oxford, 1969); and J. Levine, "Methodological Concerns in Studying Supreme Court Efficacy," 4 *Law and Society Review* 583–611 (1970).

3. For the philosophical, historical, legal, nonbehavioral aspects of free speech, see Norman Dorsen, Paul Bender, Burt Neuborne (eds.), *Emerson, Haber, and Dorsen's Political and Civil Rights in the United States*, 1–28 (Little, Brown, 1976).

4. The free speech, modernity, and political stability data come from I. Feierband and R. Feierband, "The Relationship of Systematic Frustration, Political Coercion, International Tension, and Political Instability: A Cross-National Study" (paper presented at the annual meeting of the American Psychological Association, 1966). See their paper for further details on the criteria for categorizing the countries. Other empirical studies in the free speech area include J. Levine, "The Bookseller and the Law of Obscenity: Toward an Empirical Theory of Free Expression" (Northwestern University Ph.D. dissertation, 1967) and S. Stouffer, *Communism, Conformity, and Civil Liberties* (Doubleday, 1955).

5. Studies dealing with the impact of decreasing government aid to and interference with religion as manifested in prayers in the public schools include W. Muir, *Prayer in the Public Schools: Law and Attitude Change* (University of Chicago Press, 1967) and R. Johnson, *The Dynamics of Compliance: Supreme Court Decision-Making from a New Perspective* (Northwestern University Press, 1967).

6. A detailed description of the right to be free of discrimination is provided in Norman Dorsen, Paul Bender, Burt Neuborne (eds.), *Emerson, Haber, and Dorsen's Political and Civil Rights in the United States* (Little, Brown, 1976).

7. For behavioral science approaches to the effects of racial discrimination, see "The Effects of Segregation and the Consequences of Desegregation," 37 *Minnesota Law Review* 427 (1953), and G. Grier and E. Grier, *Equality and Beyond* (Quadrangle, 1966). For the effects of antidiscrimination legislation, see M. Berger, *Equality by Statute* (Doubleday, 1967), and L. Mayhew, *Law and Equal Opportunity* (Harvard University Press, 1967). For the effects of school integration, see J. Coleman, *Equality of Education Opportunity* (Office of Education, 1966), (also known as the Coleman Report); on housing integration, see Wilner, *Human Relations in Interracial Housing* (University of Minnesota Press, 1955).

8. A description of the nature of the safeguards to protect the innocent from conviction and harassment is given in D. Fellman, *The Defendant's Rights* (Rinehart, 1958) and W. Lockhart, Yale Kamisar, and Jesse Choper, *Constitutional Rights and Liberties* (West, 1970).

9. Behavioral studies of the consequences of having counsel include L. Silverstein, *Defense of the Poor* (Little, Brown, 1966); N. Lefstein and V. Stapleton, *Counsel in Juvenile Courts* (National Council of Juvenile Court Judges, 1967); and D. Wenger and C. Fletcher, "The Effect of Legal Counsel on Admissions to a State Mental Hospital: A Confrontation of Professions" (paper presented at the annual meeting of the American Sociological Association, 1967).

10. Empirical research on protecting the right to be free from unreasonable arrests, searches, and interrogation techniques includes R. Medalie, L. Zeitz, and P. Alexander, "Custodial Police Interrogation in Our Nation's Capital: The Attempt to Implement Miranda," 66 *Michigan Law Review* 1347–1422 (1968); S. Nagel, "Testing the Effects of Excluding Illegally Seized Evidence," *Wisconsin Law Review* 283–310 (1965); and E. Green, "Race, Social Status, and Criminal Arrest," 35 *American Sociological Review* 476–90 (1970).

11. A. Rankin, "The Effect of Pretrial Detention," 39 *New York University Law Review* 641–55 (1964).
12. C. Ares, A. Rankin, and H. Sturz, "The Manhattan Bail Project: An Interim Report on the Use of Pretrial Parole," 38 *New York University Law Review* 67–95 (1963).
13. H. Zeisel, H. Kalven, and B. Buccholz, *Delay in the Court* (Little, Brown, 1959); and J. Navarro and J. Taylor, *Data Analysis and Simulation of a Court System for the Processing of Criminal Cases* (Institute for Defense Analysis, 1967).
14. H. Kalven and H. Zeisel, *The American Jury* (Little, Brown, 1966), 56.
15. H. Bedau, *The Death Penalty in America* (Doubleday/Anchor, 1967).
16. Empirical studies of the statutes relating to the right to basic economic security are described in H. Koontz and R. Gable, *Public Control of Economic Enterprise* (McGraw-Hill, 1956), 487–590, 758–94; G. Bloom and H. Northrup, *Economics of Labor Relations* (Irwin, 1954); M. Lee, *Economic Fluctuations* (Irwin, 1955), 421–538; and G. Steiner, *Social Insecurity: The Politics of Welfare* (Rand McNally, 1966).

QUESTIONS

1. How can one justify freedom of speech and religion for antisocial advocacy?
2. How can one justify separation of church and state from the perspective of a religious person?
3. How can one justify to members of the majority that minority groups should have equal treatment under the law?
4. How can one justify criminal justice procedures that clearly make obtaining arrests and convictions more difficult?
5. What useful purposes are served by providing a right to hire an attorney to defend oneself in a criminal case or a right to a court-provided attorney if one cannot afford to hire an attorney?
6. How can one justify providing greater economic security if doing so is likely to decrease initiative, ambition, and providing for oneself?

REFERENCES

Bayley, D., *Public Liberties in the New States* (Rand McNally, 1964).
Becker, T., *The Impact of Supreme Court Decisions: Empirical Studies* (Oxford, 1969).
Emerson, Thomas, *The System of Freedom of Expression* (Random House, 1970).
Johnson, R., *The Dynamics of Compliance: Supreme Court Decision-Making from a New Perspective* (Northwestern University Press, 1967).
Levine, James, Michael Musheno, and Dennis Palumbo, *Criminal Justice: A Public Policy Approach* (Harcourt, Brace Jovanovich, 1980).
Lockard, Duane, *Toward Equal Opportunity: A Study of State and Local Antidiscrimination Laws* (Macmillan, 1968).

Muir, W., *Prayer in the Public Schools: Law and Attitude Change* (University of Chicago Press, 1967).

Rodgers, Harrell, *The Cost of Human Neglect: America's Welfare Failure* (Sharpe, 1982).

————, and Charles Bullock, *Law and Social Change: Civil Rights Laws and Their Consequences* (McGraw-Hill, 1972).

Schauer, Frederick, *Free Speech: A Philosophical Enquiry* (Cambridge University Press, 1982).

Stouffer, S., *Communism, Conformity, and Civil Liberties* (Doubleday, 1955).

Wasby, S., *The Impact of the United States Supreme Court: Some Perspectives* (Dorsey Press, 1970).

PART THREE

Means for Achieving Goals

This section discusses various general means that can be used for achieving given goals. These means or policies on a high level of generality include:

1. *Incentives:* the manipulation of perceived benefits and costs to encourage socially desired behavior.
2. *Productivity:* maximizing or increasing societal benefits minus societal costs, or societal benefits divided by societal costs, including nonmonetary benefits and costs.
3. *Discretion:* the extent to which decision makers are allowed a latitude of choice within a range of legal bounds.
4. *Implementation:* the process whereby a policy is converted into benefits for those to whom the policy is directed; an important issue is whether implementation should be accomplished by the government or the private sector.
5. *Government structures:* how governments are positioned on (a) the relation between the national and state governments, (b) the legislative and executive branches of government, (c) the power of the courts to declare legislative and executive acts unconstitutional, (d) the two-party system, and (e) democratic provision for majority rule and for minority rights to try to convert the majority.

CHAPTER 7

Using
Positive and Negative
Incentives

This chapter discusses positive and negative incentives as especially important goal-achieving means. The first half of the chapter covers traditional criminal behavior, business wrongdoing, and noncomplying public officials. The second half deals with stimulating increased societal productivity, whereby society improves its societal benefits while it reduces societal costs.

Encouraging Socially Desired Behavior

This part of the chapter presents the usefulness of a benefit-cost perspective to generate ideas for encouraging socially desired behavior in a variety of different situations. The illustrated situations emphasize traditional criminal behavior, business wrongdoing, and public officials who do not comply with relevant rules.

To maintain a benefit-cost perspective, view individuals as being motivated by a desire to maximize their benefits minus costs. These benefits and costs may be nonmonetary as well as monetary. They may depend on the occurrence or nonoccurrence of some key event such as escaping detection when engaged in wrongdoing.

A regulatory perspective, on the other hand, is one in which socially desired behavior is mandated by government orders, emphasizing administrative agencies and courts for enforcement, rather than manipulating incentives that prompt people to comply. The perspective can be contrasted with a rehabilitative one, which emphasizes changing wrongdoers' values rather than convincing them that they are acting contrary to their values, or better yet, changing the situation so that their values cause them to behave in a socially desired manner.

Using a benefit-cost perspective to encourage desired behavior for an individual, group, or society would mean: (1) increasing the benefits of doing the right thing, (2) decreasing those costs, (3) decreasing the benefits of doing the wrong thing, (4) increasing those costs, (5) increasing the probability of being detected and negatively sanctioned if one does the wrong thing, and (6) increasing the probability of being discovered and positively rewarded if one does the right thing.

By thinking in these terms, one can often generate relevant ideas that might otherwise be overlooked, thought of less quickly, or thought of in a less organized way. One can also avoid ideas that may not be so relevant in the sense of not substantially affecting relevant benefits and costs.

There are a variety of ways to classify the applications of benefit-cost analysis to encourage socially desired behavior. The first, in terms of the subject matter, includes criminal behavior, business wrongdoing, and non-complying government officials. A second, in terms of the purpose, includes having a deterrence problem for which suggested approaches are needed, or having suggested approaches for which a discussion of their effectiveness is needed. The third classification involves situations in which the benefits and costs of "rightdoing" are independent, rather than merely the complements of the benefits and costs of wrongdoing. A situation would be complementary if the benefits of rightdoing mainly involve avoiding the costs of unsuccessful wrongdoing, and the costs of rightdoing basically mean missing out on the benefits of successful wrongdoing.

TRADITIONAL CRIMINAL BEHAVIOR

Traditional criminal behavior provides a good example of using the benefit-cost general scheme to suggest and organize approaches for encouraging rightdoing. Since the benefits and costs of rightdoing are complementary to those of wrongdoing, there are basically three, rather than six, approaches. One can: (1) increase the probability of being arrested, convicted, and imprisoned; (2) decrease the benefits from successful wrongdoing; or (3) increase the costs of unsuccessful wrongdoing. Each general approach generates two sets of specific approaches, a relatively conservative or prosecution-oriented set and a relatively liberal or defendant-oriented set.

Regarding increasing the probability of being arrested, convicted, and imprisoned, a conservative orientation would emphasize reducing due process restrictions. Thus, one might argue in favor of making arrests, stops, or searches easier—that is, making them permissible on the basis of mere suspicion rather than the stricter standard of probable cause of wrongdoing. Similarly, convictions could be made easier by allowing evidence based on an illegal seizure, a confession without warnings, or questionable hearsay. Imprisonment upon conviction could be guaranteed by abolishing probation, suspended sentences, and community-based corrections. On the other hand, a more liberal orientation would emphasize increasing the probability of arrest, conviction, and imprisonment by developing a higher standard of professionalism on the part of police, prosecutors, and other criminal justice personnel. That might include automatic suspensions of police officers on the first occasion they engage in illegal searches and automatic dismissals on the second occasion, especially if illegally seized evidence tends to decrease the chances of obtaining convictions.

Regarding decreasing the benefits of successful wrongdoing, a conservative orientation was reflected in the policies of the Law Enforcement Assistance Administration (LEAA) under Richard Velde during Gerald Ford's administration. It emphasized what is sometimes referred to as hardening the targets. In store robberies, this might mean developing systems of computerized credit via pushbutton telephones which would minimize the amount of cash carried in the cash register or by customers. It could also entail building bulletproof glass walls through which salespeople would transact business with customers to decrease a would-be robber's access to the cash register.

A more liberal orientation, although not necessarily mutually exclusive of target hardening, might decrease the peer-recognition benefits enjoyed by many successful store robbers. More specifically, the typical robber or mugger is between age 15 and 25 and engages in such behavior partly because he gains a kind of prestige among fellow teenage gang members. Thus, what may decrease the benefits of successfully knocking over a gas station or a mom-and-pop grocery store is to somehow change the way prestige is obtained among these people. The Office of Economic Opportunity Community Action Program attempted to do this among the Black Peacestone Rangers on Chicago's south side in the 1960s by redirecting their aggressiveness into rent strikes, consumer boycotts, election campaigns, and picketing government agencies. This type of antipoverty gang work was stopped, however, largely as a result of the negative reaction of Senator McClellan's investigating committee. Some people interpreted this community behavior to be more bothersome than the robbing and mugging it may have decreased.

Vis-à-vis increasing the costs of unsuccessful wrongdoing, a conservative orientation might suggest longer prison sentences, greater use of the death penalty, and more severe prison conditions. Liberals, on the other hand, might equally recognize the need for increasing the costs of noncompliance, but they would propose increasing the opportunity costs suffered from being arrested, convicted, and/or imprisoned.

Middle-class business executives do not rob stores or mug people in parks. They probably do not refrain from doing so because they fear lengthy and severe imprisonment, since they would likely receive probation if it were a first offense. A more important reason for their restraint is their fear of losing the opportunities available to them in the middle-class business world. What may be needed is to provide would-be store robbers with more alternative opportunities that they would risk losing if they were arrested for any crimes.

To make these alternative opportunities more meaningful would require changing our educational institutions, neighborhood housing patterns, hiring procedures, and other socioeconomic institutions. If the teen-age gang member had more employment opportunities, he would not only suffer greater opportunity costs from getting arrested, but he would also receive less incremental benefits from money obtained from a robbery, and he would require less antisocial peer recognition. Clearly, however, this approach to increasing the cost of noncompliance is a much larger social undertaking than the approach emphasizing longer and more severe sentences.

One can see from the previous example that a benefit-cost model can suggest ideas that might otherwise be overlooked, less emphasized, or be less clearly organized. Two caveats are necessary, however. First, the model is no substitute for thinking or for understanding the subject matter, since the model only provides general categories into which the specific approaches can be placed. Second, the general categories are logically deduced from the model, but the specific approaches reflect value judgments and empirical facts, not deductive logic. In other words, it follows logically that criminal behavior can be reduced by decreasing its benefits and increasing its costs, but target hardening and more severe sentences are not logically more meaningful than changing peer group values and emphasizing social opportunity costs.[1]

BUSINESS WRONGDOING

Business wrongdoing illustrates use of the general scheme to solve a deterrence problem by starting with a set of suggested solutions and then analyzing their effectiveness in light of the model. The subfield of business pollution especially lends itself to this approach. A number of incentives have been unsystematically proposed for encouraging compliance with environmental standards. They include pollution taxes, injunctions, civil penalties, fines and jail sentences, tax rewards and subsidies, selective government buying, publicizing polluters, and conference persuasion.

A pollution tax is often cited as an especially effective incentive. It would be effective because it would increase the cost of noncompliance. The tax would be proportionate to the amount of pollution produced by the business taxpayer. A common formula for arriving at a water pollution fine involves determining the total cost of maintaining a river segment at a given level of water quality, and then assessing each business on that river segment a portion of the total cost equal to the ratio between the firm's pollution and the total pollution in the river segment. By reducing its pollution, each firm thereby lowers its tax assessment, and that lowered assessment represents an increased benefit of compliance. The effectiveness of pollution taxes is also enhanced by virtue of automatic monitoring systems which are often a part of such proposals. These systems increase the probability of the above costs and benefits occurring by making the assessment and collection of the tax or fee relatively automatic, as compared to proposals that require more active judicial action for enforcement.

Proposed judicial action against polluters falls into three categories: injunctions, civil penalties, and criminal sanctions. Like pollution taxes, the effectiveness of each depends on how it influences the costs of noncompliance (and the complementary benefits of compliance) and on the probability of those benefits and costs occurring. Injunctions to cease or suspend operating are the most costly to the polluting business firm, but they have the lowest probability of occurring. If an injunction is requested by a government agency, a private group, or an individual, then a judge would normally be quite reluctant to order a steel mill or other manufacturing establishment to shut down in view of the economic damage such a decision might mean to the employees, consumers, stockholders, and the community of the business.

Civil damages are normally easier to obtain, especially if they are brought under a legal procedure that limits defenses available, such as in workers' compensation actions. Civil damages, however, are normally less costly to the business firm than injunctions, unless a large class action decreases the probability of success.

Criminal pollution penalties are almost exclusively fines, rather than jail sentences. Such fines are easier to obtain than injunctions since they are not as economically disruptive to third parties, but they are more difficult to obtain than civil damages since they involve the more stringent due process standards associated with criminal law. Such fines lie in between injunctions and individual damages regarding costs to the polluting firm, although fines can range from low, easily absorbed business expenses to assessments comparable to pollution taxes, on up to the unlikely possibility of highly punitive fines.

Other proposals emphasize decreasing the money saved by noncompliance while decreasing the cost of compliance, rather than increasing the cost of noncompliance. Such proposals include tax rewards and subsidies. For example, installing equipment to decrease air, water, and other forms of pollution is normally an expensive compliance cost. Government policy can ease that cost by providing accelerated business deductions or credits for doing so, or the government can provide outright grants or no-interest, long-term loans to further reduce the cost of compliance. These benefits would likely occur if such government programs were instituted. In other words, businesses are likely to change if the government makes these alterations cost-free or combines a cost-reducing program with a program that enforces penalties for noncompliance. Large government subsidies to private industry, however, are unlikely to pass the legislative process because of opposition from those who feel business should be more independent. In the same vein, pollution taxes are not likely to pass the legislative process because of opposition from those who believe they are too burdensome to business.

Other proposals will be less effective than those mentioned because they do not influence the key benefits, costs, and probabilities of the benefits and costs occurring. For example, the government sometimes goes out of its way to buy from sellers who have good records as nonpolluters. Such selective government buying power in theory rewards nonpolluters for complying (a benefit of compliance) and punishes polluters with an opportunity cost (a cost of noncompliance). In practice, however, too many polluting firms are not greatly affected by government purchases. Legislators and government purchasing agents also find it difficult to sacrifice to pollution criteria relating to the cost and quality of the products purchased. Similarly, if the government publicized polluters' names so private consumers could buy selectively, the probability of the benefits and opportunity costs occurring would also be low, especially if the product was not a name brand or not bought by ultimate consumers. Conference persuasion is an especially ineffective approach, although prior to 1972 it was a major part of anti-water-pollution enforcement. Merely trying to convince business polluters that they are inflicting social harm will not encourage any legally desired behavior since the costs of noncompliance are not increased and the benefits of noncompliance are not decreased. Furthermore, the probability of either these costs or benefits occurring goes unchanged.

The model can also be applied to other forms of business regulation, such as consumer fraud, worker safety, product safety, antitrust practices, unfair management or union practices, stock manipulation, and landlord abuses.[2]

NONCOMPLYING PUBLIC OFFICIALS

Noncompliance by public officials can take a variety of forms to which the model can be applied to suggest ideas for encouraging legally desired behavior. A good example, including all six elements in the model, is encouraging criminal court personnel (especially prosecutors and assistant state's attorneys) to make time-saving decisions that conclude trials quickly, rather than time-lengthening decisions that involve postponements and delay. To increase the benefits of reducing the average time consumption per case, the system can reward assistant state's attorneys with salary increases and promotions. To decrease the costs, one could establish a computerized system that informs assistant state's attorneys about which cases are running behind schedule, thus minimizing the attorneys' keeping track of time. They could also be provided with more investigative and preparation resources.

To decrease the benefits of improper behavior, the system can release more defendants from jail prior to trial. When many defendants are in jail awaiting trial, the prosecutor benefits by delay, since it increases the defendants' willingness to plead guilty in return for probation or a sentence equal to the time they have already served awaiting trial, rather than to wait for a trial. To increase the costs for wrongdoing, speedy trial rules can be adopted. They would provide for the absolute discharge of defendants whose cases extend beyond the time limits through no fault of their own. An absolute discharge is a heavier cost than merely releasing the defendant from pretrial detention because the defendant cannot be tried for the incident at a later date.

To increase the probability of being detected and negatively sanctioned for delaying cases, the speedy trial rules can allow fewer exceptions, such as suspending their application "for good cause" or "exceptional circumstances." These exceptions decrease the probability that the penalty costs will be imposed. To increase the probability of being discovered and positively rewarded, the aforementioned computerized system can also inform the head prosecutor which assistants are doing an especially good job so they can receive salary increases and promotions.

On a more general level, compliance of governmental administrators to judicial precedents and legislative statutes could be increased by: (1) increasing the probability of being caught and sanctioned, (2) increasing the severity of the sanctions, and (3) decreasing the benefits of continuing the former noncomplying behavior. The probability of being caught and sanctioned can be increased by encouraging citizen suits, as seen in the fields of environmental protection and equal employment, partly as a check on government agencies in those fields. Whistle-blowers reporting wrongdoing within government can be protected by civil service rules. More wrongdoers would be caught if wrongdoing were clearly defined, as has occurred in the field of school desegregation by way of guidelines from the Department of Education.

To obtain administrative compliance, the severity of the sanctions can range from reprimands (which may not be a significant cost to the average administrator, but can be significant when directed by a court toward an agency lawyer) to stiffer penalties, such as decreasing or blocking appropriations, as courts have used when dealing with racially discriminatory police examination procedures or public housing site selection. An especially severe sanction might hold an administrator in contempt of court subject to a jail sentence, as has occurred with public aid administrators who do not comply with maximum waiting periods for processing public aid cases. Such contempt sanctions, though, are less effective against government union officials who lead strikes contrary to federal or state law.

Decreasing the benefits of continuing the former noncomplying behavior may require changing the constituents' approval of the noncomplying public official. For example, if the official refuses to comply with desegregation orders because he or she perceives the constitutents are in favor of it, the noncomplying benefits can be decreased by convincing local business interests how detrimental such noncompliance is to local business expansion. Likewise, if an official refuses to comply because he or she perceives noncompliance is demanded by the immediate superior or peers, the system should sway those supportive elements. An example is when the Supreme Court or the Department of Justice communicates with police chiefs in order to change police behavior with regard to interrogations and searches.

A key benefit from noncompliance is the satisfaction received from doing things in a customary way. Courts and legislatures should, therefore, adopt successive incremental changes, as has been accomplished by increasingly providing counsel for the poor in criminal cases, starting with capital punishment cases in the 1930s, some felony cases in the 1940s and 1950s, the rest of the felony cases in the 1960s, and misdemeanor cases in the 1970s.

Numerous other applications of the model could be applied to noncomplying public officials in the judicial, administrative, or legislative realm. For example, judges could be encouraged to be more sensitive to avoiding errors such as holding in jail defendants who would appear for trial if released, rather than releasing defendants who might not appear. A similar sensitivity problem may exist: (1) at the police arrest stage, (2) with the decision to incarcerate a convicted defendant or rely on community-based probation, and (3) with the decision to release on parole. It can be applied to discussing how to obtain greater compliance on the part of administrators such as school board officials, with regard to school desegregation, school prayers, and disciplinary procedures. The model can also be applied to discourage legislators from corruption. This application may involve a combination of proposals directed simultaneously at legislators, businesses, and bribe-offering individuals, thereby combining all three applications discussed in this section.[3]

LIMITING ONE'S OPTIONS

The previous analysis contains useful ideas for using positive and negative incentives to encourage individuals to make the right decision when considering either socially desired or socially undesired behavior. This analysis should, however, be carried an important step further by limiting the options for would-be wrongdoers so such choice is unavailable.

As a specific example, let's examine bottle and can littering. We can try to discourage littering by placing penalties on doing so. This does not seem to be very effective because neither the wrongdoers nor the rule enforcers take littering very seriously. A $100 fine is therefore unlikely to be a deterrent and is seldom enforced. Special enforcement units, in which promotions and other rewards were allocated for antilittering enforcement, could be started up. This is contrasted to enforcement by regular police who are likely to consider antilittering to be almost beneath their dignity in comparison with more serious crimes. Special enforcement units, though, are not likely to be adopted because neither do policy makers take littering seriously. The individual littering case is not a serious matter. The sum total of all littering, however, costs the public millions of dollars to clean up.

Another tack could offer rewards for returning used bottles and cans. As is often the case with rewards, they are probably more effective than punishments. One problem, however, is that the reward would have to be substantial to make the program fully effective. This might require a large deposit on each bottle, which could be the equivalent of an undesirable regressive tax on lower-income people. Trying to pass legislation requiring large deposits can also be politically unpopular. Bottle manufacturers often defeat such legislation because of the burden the deposits might impose on the public. An alternative would be to require manufacturers to offer rewards for returned bottles and cans, without a deposit. This proposal would be fought less strenuously if the rewards came out of taxes, but it would possibly be even more politically unpopular than deposits.

A third alternative to the littering problem could simply prohibit the manufacturing of certain nonbiodegradable containers that are especially responsible for littering expenses. If such a solution were technologically and politically possible, it would solve this littering problem. The would-be wrongdoer would no longer be faced with the choices of throwing the bottle by the roadside, putting it in a wastebasket, or returning it to the grocery store if the bottle didn't exist. It is conceivable that beer bottles, for example, could be replaced by biodegradable plastic containers similar to milk cartons. Development of such a container would be encouraged by offering government subsidies or by prohibiting the present containers. The new containers would most likely be adopted if they were less expensive to manufacture than the old containers. In encouraging socially desired behavior, the important point is that a technologically and politically meaningful way of eliminating a wrongdoing-rightdoing choice should be adopted in lieu of the punishments-rewards or incentives approach, although they are not mutually exclusive for different aspects of the same problem.

Another good example of the options-limiting approach versus the incentives approach to encourage socially desired behavior is in gun control. Gun control advocates claim its adoption will reduce serious crimes. They generally do not link gun control to a rewards-punishments framework. One could, however, counter that without access to a gun, less crime benefits will be achievable in a robbery. Bank robbers normally have guns, and bank robbery probably has the most amount of money at stake. Muggers are less likely to have guns, and mugging probably reaps the least amount of money. Even a mugger is more likely to be successful with a gun than with a knife, club, or other weapon. Gun control will most likely be effective in crime reduction by decreasing the options of would-be criminals who would not engage in certain kinds of crime without a gun. It must substantially decrease the availability of guns to would-be criminals. Another argument in favor of gun control is that it eliminates the decision-choice of whether or not to shoot one's spouse, friend, or other antagonist in an emotional dispute. The choice may then be whether or not to punch the person, generally a much less serious crime.

Limiting the options of would-be wrongdoers can be approached in two ways. One way is to make the wrongdoing decision physically impossible, or quite difficult. This is the case when no beer bottles are available or when guns are not readily obtainable. A second way is to make the wrongdoing decision psychologically impossible or quite difficult to conceive. The main reason the average person refrains from shooting anybody is not because guns are unavailable. Rather, the average person has been socialized against deliberately killing someone, other than in self-defense, and thus doing so is virtually an unthinkable alternative. This analysis stresses the importance of a well-socialized conscience. Many people dismiss the idea of a conscience by saying that every person has a price for which he or she would kill someone. If, however, the right price is totally unfeasible, like $10 million, then for all practical purposes, it is an unthinkable alternative.

ENCOURAGING SOCIALLY DESIRED BEHAVIOR: CONCLUSION

From the analysis in the last section, one can see that a benefit-cost perspective may help to generate, organize, and analyze ideas for encouraging socially desired behavior. Individuals, in this perspective, are motivated by a desire to maximize their benefits minus costs both monetarily and non-monetarily, while considering the probability of the occurrence of events on which these benefits and costs depend. Thus, people will change their behavior if the perceived expected benefits minus costs become greater for a new behavior. If society or public policy makers want to encourage socially desired behavior, they should arrange for it to have a higher perceived expected value than the undesired behavior. Additional researchers and practitioners are necessary to apply this perspective to a variety of undesirable behaviors, in order to encourage more socially desired behavior.

In conclusion, think of the process of encouraging socially desired behavior as an obstacle course where society barricades people against making wrong choices and facilitates their making the right choices. From this analysis three general kinds of barriers-facilitators emerge. First, children must be socialized into treating various wrongdoing as so unthinkable that no matter whether the wrongdoing was physically possible or no matter what the immediate rewards and punishments were, the wrongdoing would not occur. Second, the physical possibility of wrongdoing should be decreased to deter those who have not previously been well socialized. Third, punishments for wrongdoing and rewards for rightdoing should be provided for those decisions which have not already been well handled by the socialization process or the structuring of the environment so as to limit the options. In a society that knows what kind of wrongdoing it wants to discourage and what kind of rightdoing it wants to encourage, in time, these three approaches should achieve their goals when meaningfully implemented.[4]

The New Productivity

Socioeconomic reforms can be readily adopted when they are supported by both liberals and conservatives, although not for the same reasons. Let's examine some aspects of the criminal justice system to illustrate the point. In the last few years, there has been a substantial countrywide trend toward decreasing criminal sentencing discretion. Liberals perceive the previous discretion resulted in sentences that were discriminatory along class, race, sex, and other lines. Conservatives believe it resulted in sentences that were unduly lenient. As a result, one finds liberals like Edward Kennedy joining with conservatives like Strom Thurmond to support decreased sentencing discretion in the federal courts.

DEFINITIONS AND HISTORICAL CONTEXT

The field of productivity serves as an even better example. Liberals and conservatives agree that the nation would benefit by being more productive. Virtually everyone would endorse the idea of producing 20 units of output with only 5 units of effort instead of 10 units of effort. Likewise, most people would endorse the idea of being able to get as much as 30 output units, rather than 20, for 10 units of effort. This concept of increased productivity and creativity for the United States may have been the main appeal of the 1980 Reagan campaign. The 1980 Carter campaign probably erred by over-emphasizing the traditional Democratic-party concern for equalizing the pie at a time when Americans were more concerned with having a bigger pie to equalize.

American history alternates between periods of growth and equalization. We were in a period of industrial and geographical development from the end of the equalizing Reconstruction Era to the administrations of Theodore Roosevelt and Woodrow Wilson. Both presidencies favored the progressive income tax and consumer oriented economic regulation. The 1920s resumed business growth, and the Depression and World War II also focused more on growth than equality. The 1960s was a period of equalizing with regard to poverty, civil rights, women, gays, the handicapped, the aged, children, and even animals, although further equal opportunity reforms are necessary. This period extended until about 1980. We are now reentering an era emphasizing bipartisan growth and productivity. The periods of growth are not necessarily Republican dominated, and the periods of equalization are not necessarily Democratic periods. The growth in the late 1800s was promoted by both Cleveland and McKinley. The equality of the early 1900s was associated with both Theodore Roosevelt and Woodrow Wilson. The renewed emphasis on growth from 1920 to 1960 involved both Republican and Democrat presidents, as did the equalization period from 1960 to 1980.

In inflationary times, when prices are rising without any corresponding increase in the quantity or quality of products, there is a heightened concern for productivity. Wage and price increases are justifiable and acceptable if they are based on increased productivity. If a worker who was formerly being paid $3 an hour now produces twice as much in an hour, he or she should receive $6 an hour, although deductions for the cost of buying and maintaining the capital equipment which made possible that increased productivity may be called for. Similarly, if a $1 head of lettuce spoils in a week, and new technology is developed which enables lettuce to stay fresh for a month, the seller should be entitled to charge more than $1. The price increase is justified because of the additional costs and because the better product will increase demand.

A strong concern for productivity also occurs in time of recession or depression when so many potentially productive people are not producing in accordance with their skills. Keynesian fiscal policy and Friedman's monetary policy may be relevant when dealing with inflation and unemployment, but these policies are too broad when specifically focusing on improving productivity.

The forthcoming era of new productivity might also be called the era of new incentives. The concept of "incentives," however, emphasizes the main means for bringing about the new productivity, rather than the goals toward which those means are directed. These incentives are government policies designed to reward various segments of the population for increasing productivity rather than regulations that emphasize controls and penalties. Tax incentives are the main incentives that government has available for stimulating the new productivity. While the federal government in particular makes this available, with its control over corporate and individual income taxes, state and local governments also use tax incentives, given their control over property taxes. Tax foregoing is also more politically feasible than outright cash grants since taxpayers are more willing to support government policies that do not involve explicit government expenditures. Tax foregoing also enables the recipients of the incentives to preserve their self-respect more than if they were receiving an outright cash grant, just as farmers prefer indirect price supports over the direct subsidies associated with the Brannan Plan. (During the Truman administration, Secretary of Agriculture Brannan proposed giving farmers who were below the poverty level a direct subsidy designed to bring them up to a minimum annual income.)

SPECIFIC MEANS AND GOALS

The federal government can develop a list of business activities which will increase national productivity and that business firms might otherwise not engage in. The participating business firms could be entitled to various types of tax breaks, including depreciation or expense allowances, tax credits, or even tax exemption under special circumstances. A good example of such an activity might be to hire willing and able people who are otherwise unemployed. Many welfare recipients, including those receiving aid for the aged, disabled, or unemployed, or those caring for dependent children, could be hired. If, through a tax subsidy, a business could be encouraged to hire such people, then society would benefit in two ways. First, the individual would add to the gross national product (GNP), which aids society's benefits. Second, the subsidy would probably cost society less than the welfare payments, which reduces the societal cost.

That example clarifies the concept of increased productivity. Generally, it means increasing societal benefits or income, while holding constant or decreasing societal costs. It can also mean holding constant societal benefits, while decreasing societal costs. In both situations, the positive difference between societal benefits and societal costs increases. Productivity also refers to increased benefits, regardless of costs, or benefits divided by costs, but benefits minus costs is the preferred criterion. Society would favor a situation in which $100 in benefits and $60 in costs yielded a net gain of $40, rather than one in which $10 in benefits and $3 in costs resulted in a net gain of only $7, even though the latter situation involves a 10-to-3 benefit/cost ratio and the former a 10-to-6 ratio. Additional terms refer to improving benefits minus costs, such as *profitability*, *net benefits*, *efficiency*, or *effectiveness*, but *productivity* has the semantic advantage of arousing more positive connotations than the other concepts, and is more commonly understood.

Other business activities that can stimulate productivity through tax subsidies include:

1. Developing and implementing new technologies. When a new technology enables workers to produce more with less labor, the quantity and possibly the quality of the products produced is raised, while the cost per item produced decreases.
2. Locating plants and job opportunities in high unemployment areas. This is like putting welfare recipients to work. The marginal rate of return is higher when moving someone from unemployment to employment than when moving someone from one form of employment to another. Stimulating business firms to locate in such areas can be aided by local property-tax exemption, as well as federal income tax incentives.
3. Subsidizing business firms to engage in programs designed to upgrade the work of traditionally discriminated against groups in obtaining jobs that are commensurate with their skills. Such groups include blacks, the handicapped, and the aged. Subsidies would cover advertising available jobs in media likely to reach these groups. The subsidies might also be designed to facilitate transportation and housing patterns to bring discriminated, underemployed, and unemployed people closer to the job opportunities.
4. Expanding business operations because technological developments enable price reductions, so that larger quantities could be sold, in contrast to expanding through the increased revenue from advertising.
5. Developing training programs to upgrade workers' skills and thereby make them more productive. The cost of training is generally substantially less than the cost of the product which the workers are able to produce.

The above business activities cluster around two kinds of activities. One relates to technological development as emphasized in points 1 and 4. The other refers to more productive hiring and training, as illustrated in points 2, 3, and 5, and the point about welfare recipients. To make the hiring and training opportunities more meaningful, business must be stimulated to make them available, and the potential worker participants must be stimulated to take advantage of those opportunities. For welfare recipients, this may mean permitting them to keep both the first $60 or so earned each month, and about $1 out of every $2 earned until a welfare cutoff figure is reached. This kind of system clearly makes more sense than deducting every dollar that a welfare recipient earns from the welfare payment (as was done prior to the late 1960s), or exempting substantially less than about $60 or $1 out of every $2 earned (which is the current system). The Nixon-Moynihan family assistance plan in the early 1970s originally proposed such incentives for encouraging productive work for welfare recipients, but the plan never passed due partly to Watergate distractions. Also, it was not combined with a business incentives program to provide jobs for welfare recipients and other unemployed and underemployed people.

For technological incentives to be more meaningful, basic research in the universities must be stimulated. Businesses have the capability of implementing new technologies, especially when tax subsidies cover the costs. However, they do not do so well in running departments of physics, genetics, psychology, or other fields of knowledge which are the province of universities. American universities have been quite effective in producing basic research and teaching, as indicated by the Nobel prize winners and foreign students' choice of schools. Unfortunately, American industry has not taken sufficient advantage of the creative American academic research. It is ironic that Japanese industry is more computerized than American industry, when much of the basic computer technology was developed in American universities. Persuading American business to implement new research ideas can be partly accomplished through tax subsidies, but further stimulation of basic research, especially in these times of tight academic budgets, is imperative.

Tax exemption for American universities, though, is not the answer since they are already tax-exempt. What can be done, however, is to allow tax credits to people who contribute to universities. Under the present system, a person earning $10.00 who contributes $1.00 to a university receives an itemized deduction, reducing the person's taxable income to $9.00. If the tax rate is 20 percent, the tax in this hypothetical situation is $1.80. If, however, the government were to provide a $1.00 tax credit in addition to the $1.00 deduction, then the tax payable would only be $0.80. This kind of tax credit could provide a strong incentive for private individuals and business firms to contribute much needed funding to American universities. The tax law could also specify that the contributions must be earmarked for research purposes rather than athletic, dormitory, or other university activities.

The previous analysis emphasizes the role of business, welfare recipients, and universities in the new productivity. What, however, is the role of the great mass of middle-class people who are not business executives, welfare recipients, or professors? Their role is mainly to be the beneficiaries of the increased GNP, at a lower cost than had these incentives not been instituted. The increased GNP becomes widely spread, partly because the middle class usually works for the businesses that benefit from these subsidies by using them to increase their productivity and their workers' income. Both large and small businesses can improve their hiring practices and adopt improved technologies with subsidies. Most of the American population could benefit from the new productivity by virtue of having a reduced workweek, if the new productivity resulted in producing as much or more with a 30-to-35-hour workweek as we were formerly producing with a 40-hour workweek. More jobs could be distributed if each person could work less but be just as productive and, therefore, earn the same or additional salary. Middle-class people could also take advantage of the tax subsidies by investing their money in activities that would entitle them to tax deductions or tax credits. At present, the middle class may be overinvested in real estate because of real estate tax breaks. Money tied up in real estate may represent lost opportunities to society because it is unavailable for investment in more productive technological development.

ALTERNATIVES

It is important to distinguish the already mentioned incentives-productivity program from related programs that emphasize governmental tax cuts. The key distinction is that the former are granted to the taxpayers in return for their contribution to national productivity. The Reagan administration's tax-cut legislation involved a 30 percent tax cut across the board without strings attached. Such legislation may represent a missed opportunity to use tremendous potential rewards, if no productivity strings are attached to the tax cut. The saved taxes may go into savings or consumption, which would stimulate the economy. However, if the increased consumption was not adequately met by increased production, it would prove inflationary. Much of the saved taxes could result in increased dividends, real estate purchases, and other purchases which in themselves contribute little, if anything, toward increased productivity. The increased property-tax reductions and restrictions resulting from California's Proposition 13 do little to increase productivity. Unless strings are attached to these tax savings, whereby propertyholders must do something in return for the tax reductions, the system won't be worthwhile. That something might include changing the insulation or the heating system of their property to conserve energy and reduce society's energy costs. The property tax reductions could also be more selective to encourage property development in depressed areas, or residential development in areas with job opportunities but without adequate housing for a local labor force.

There are basically two alternatives to the aforementioned incentives program for seeking increased societal productivity. One is to accomplish goals through controls and penalties for lack of productivity. This is not very viable. Socially desired behavior can generally be better encouraged through rewards than punishments. This concept may even be applicable to traditional criminal law. As was pointed out in an earlier chapter, the main reason the middle class does not commit robberies is not because they fear jail penalties (which they may not receive for a first offense anyhow). Instead, the main deterrent may be lost available career opportunities. Because poor teenage blacks and whites are not so rewarded for good behavior, mugging may often be a wise entrepreneurial decision, given the alternative incentives available. While penalties like jail and fines are meaningful in the traditional criminal context, they are not effective in the realm of economic matters like occupational safety, environmental protection, and increased productivity. They are especially ineffective when expensive, time-consuming, and difficult litigation is required to enforce them.

The second alternative is to leave the matter to the marketplace, which is also ineffective with regard to improved technology or improved hiring practices. The new technologies often require massive investment which takes years to pay off. American business, and possibly business in general, does not want to wait that long for a large capital investment to become profitable. Moreover, even large businesses may lack the capital for developing and implementing large-scale modern technologies. As a result, government, with its financial resources, could facilitate the development and implementation of new technologies, especially through the indirect approach of tax breaks, rather than through outright government expenditures.

Regarding hiring practices, business firms have no incentive to hire welfare recipients, locate in high unemployment areas, or develop outreach programs to attract previously discriminated groups. A government subsidy could provide this. Engaging in these hiring practices may be beneficial to society, but not to the individual business firm. Businesses are oriented toward profitability, not toward idealism. In other words, hiring a welfare recipient produces an external, rather than an internal, benefit minus cost. If society wants the external benefits minus costs, it should pay for them in the form of tax reductions, especially if a relatively small tax reduction can produce a relatively large increase in output as well as a reduction in other societal costs like welfare payments. An effect of marketplace competition is it stimulates American business to request tariff protection from foreign competition. Sheltering American businesses from foreign businesses that have adopted new technologies runs contrary to a government policy of stimulating new technology for increased productivity. All nations would eventually benefit by initiating incentive programs that stimulated their respective national productivities. Each country would then concentrate on whatever it does best relative to other countries.

POLICY ANALYSIS AND PARTNERSHIP

To effectively implement the new productivity ideas, the government must select the beneficiaries of the tax reductions, be they governmental programs in housing, transportation, poverty, economic regulation, or criminal justice, etc. Development and implementation of improved methods for evaluating alternative programs and policies regarding their ability to effectively and efficiently achieve their goals would be necessary. These methods are being increasingly developed in interdisciplinary policy analysis programs and social science departments at American universities. Government budget cutbacks have recently stimulated their development, since they often necessitate evaluating existing programs to determine which ones should be cut. Unfortunately, budget cutbacks have a negative connotation. The public sector should emphasize the need to get more government output from those reduced budgets. A reduced budget can be viewed like a half-empty bottle, or a half-full bottle. You can see cutbacks on what can be accomplished or you can see opportunities to maximize whatever can be accomplished.

In conclusion, we may indeed be entering an era of new productivity involving a partnership between: (1) the public sector of government agencies, using tax reduction incentives to encourage productive behavior; (2) the private sector of business, taking advantage of those incentives to increase their productivity; and (3) the not-for-profit sector, including the academic world, seeking to develop new knowledge relative to improved technologies, industrial psychology, public administration, and other relevant fields. Productive partnership can increase societal benefits and reduce societal costs, which in turn can greatly expand the cornucopia of societal goodies, and lead to the next cycles of equalization and growth of American political history.[5]

NOTES

1. On manipulating benefits and costs to decrease traditional criminal behavior, see Alfred Blumstein (ed.), *Deterrence and Incapacitation: Estimating the Effects of Criminal Sanctions on Crime Rates* (National Academy of Sciences, 1978); Franklin Zimring and Gordon Hawkins, *Deterrence: The Legal Threat in Crime Control* (University of Chicago Press, 1973); Jack Gibbs, *Crime, Punishment, and Deterrence* (Elsevier, 1975); and Gary Becker and William Landes (eds.), *Essays in the Economics of Crime and Punishment* (Columbia University Press, 1974). One should note that many anticrime activities cannot be meaningfully

categorized as liberal or conservative. For example, both ideological orientations endorse the idea of increased public participation to reduce crime occurrence, especially with regard to people being encouraged to report crimes, although not in a reckless manner in which noncrimes are frequently reported or people are falsely accused of wrongdoing.

2. On manipulating benefits and costs to decrease business wrongdoing, see Frank Grad, George Rathjens, and Albert Rosenthal, *Environmental Control: Priorities, Policies, and the Law* (Columbia University Press, 1971); William Baumol and Wallace Oates, *The Theory of Environmental Policy* (Prentice-Hall, 1975); and Richard Posner, *Economic Analysis of Law* (Little, Brown, 1977).

3. On manipulating benefits and costs to decrease noncomplying public officials, see Harrell Rodgers and Charles Bullock, *Law and Social Change: Civil Rights Laws and Their Consequences* (McGraw-Hill, 1972); Samuel Krislov and Malcolm Feeley, *Compliance and the Law* (Sage, 1970); and S. Nagel and Marian Neef, *Decision Theory and the Legal Process* (Lexington-Heath, 1979).

4. A leading exponent of the general theory of making wrongdoing physically difficult is C. Ray Jeffrey, *Crime Prevention Through Environmental Design* (Sage, 1977), although he is also concerned with reduction in crime benefits by hardening the targets of criminal behavior. Leading exponents of the general theory of socialization of legal norms are June Tapp and Felice Levine (eds.), *Law, Justice, and the Individual in Society: Psychological and Legal Issues* (Holt, Rinehart & Winston, 1977).

5. For further detail on the new productivity, especially governmental use of positive and negative incentives to encourage societal productivity, see A. Dogramaci, *Productivity Analysis: A Range of Perspectives* (Martinua Nijhoff, 1981); Barry Mitnick, *The Political Economy of Regulation* (Columbia University Press, 1980); Jacob Schmookler, *Invention and Economic Growth* (Harvard University Press, 1966); Gail Garfield Schwartz and Pat Choate, *Being Number One: Rebuilding the U.S. Economy* (Lexington Books, 1980); Lester Thurow, *The Zero-Sum Society: Distribution and the Possibilities for Economic Change* (Penguin Books, 1980); and Louis Tornatzky, E. O. Fergus, J. W. Avellar, and G. W. Fairweather, *Innovation and Social Process: A National Experiment in Implementing Social Technology* (Pergamon Press, 1980).

QUESTIONS

1. In general, what key variables can society attempt to influence in order to encourage socially desired behavior, and how can it influence them, especially with regard to traditional criminal behavior?

2. What are the pros and cons of getting business to comply with economic regulations by offering economic incentives for "right-doing," versus a system of legal action for wrongdoing, as in the environmental field?

3. Clarify the idea that certainty of punishment may or may not be more important than severity of punishment in terms of the individual would-be wrongdoer, and in terms of the allocation of societal resources.

4. How can society encourage socially desired behavior by limiting the options available to would-be wrongdoers?

5. How can tax incentives and subsidies be most effectively used to encourage productivity?
6. Give some examples illustrating how better decision-making systems can increase productivity, possibly even more than better worker motivation or better technology.
7. How does an incentives-productivity program differ from a tax-cut program to encourage productivity?
8. How does an incentives-productivity program compare with a productivity program based on controls-penalties or reliance on the marketplace?

REFERENCES

Blumstein, Alfred (ed.), *Deterrence and Incapacitation: Estimating the Effects of Criminal Sanctions on Crime Rates* (National Academy of Sciences, 1978).

Dogramaci, A., *Productivity Analysis: A Range of Perspectives* (Martinua Nijhoff, 1981).

Grad, Frank, George Rathjens, and Albert Rosenthal, *Environmental Control: Priorities, Policies, and the Law* (Columbia University Press, 1971).

Greiner, John, Harry Hatry, Margo Koss, Annie Mitlar, and Jane Woodward, *Productivity and Motivation: A Review of State and Local Government Initiatives* (Urban Institute, 1981).

Mitnick, Barry, *The Political Economy of Regulation* (Columbia University Press, 1980).

Rodgers, Harrell, and Charles Bullock, *Law and Social Change: Civil Rights Laws and Their Consequences* (McGraw-Hill, 1972).

Zimring, Franklin, and Gordon Hawkins, *Deterrence: The Legal Threat in Crime Control* (University of Chicago Press, 1973).

CHAPTER 8

Dealing with Discretion

This chapter presents the results of a series of quantitative social science studies dealing with discretion in the criminal justice system. The studies are concerned with:

1. the occurrence of disparities based on the demographic characteristics of defendants and judges
2. the development of internalized incentives to channel criminal justice discretion along lines that are in conformity with the law
3. the rational reduction of discretion
4. the external controlling of discretion to reduce the disparities rather than the discretion

These concerns correspond to analyzing, channeling, reducing, and controlling discretion.[1]

Analyzing Discretion across Defendants and Judges

The simplest way to analyze discretion is to obtain a set of criminal cases dealing with the same charge, such as felonious assault or larceny, and then determine the extent of variation among defendants or judges regarding pretrial release, delay, sentencing, or other matters. For example, three assault cases could differ greatly with regard to the amount of bail bond, the length of time from arrest to disposition, and/or the sentence imposed upon conviction. To measure the amount of variation, determine the average bond, delay, or sentence, and then determine the average amount by which each case deviates from the average. The greater the average deviation, the more discretion is present on those matters, or at least the more discretion is being exercised.

One can also calculate the average discretion exercised by a given judge. One can then calculate an overall average for a set of judges and then determine each judge's deviation. The greater the average deviation among either the judges or among the cases, the more discretion is being exercised.

In dealing with a dichotomous or binary variable like convict versus acquit, one can: (1) calculate a conviction percentage for each judge, (2) determine the average conviction percentage for the set of judges, and (3) determine each judge's deviation from the average. The average deviation becomes a measure of the degree of discretion being exercised.[2]

Studies of the average deviations revealed wide variations across judges and across cases. Even more interesting, the deviations have a systematic relationship with the demographic characteristics of either the defendants or the judges. For example, not every convicted defendant is imprisoned for larceny, and not every convicted defendant gets probation. A nationwide sample of American larceny-case data shows that 56 percent of all the convicted defendants received a prison sentence rather than a suspended sentence or probation. This is a great variation, as compared to 100 percent receiving either a prison sentence or probation. More noteworthy, 74 percent of the black defendants and only 49 percent of the white defendants received a prison sentence. In view of the large sample sizes, the 25 percent difference cannot be readily attributed to chance.[3] Similar differences are evidenced in the same nationwide sample with regard to blacks, low-income defendants, and less educated defendants receiving harsher treatment at other stages in the criminal justice process. Males and adults (as contrasted to women and juveniles) receive harsher treatment with regard to being held in jail before or after conviction, but they are more likely to receive such safeguards for the innocent as a preliminary hearing, an attorney, and a jury trial. Table 8-1 summarizes many of these results.[4]

In a nationwide sample of state supreme court criminal cases, 42 percent of the judges were above the average of their respective courts with regard to deciding in favor of the defense. Interestingly, of that figure, 55 percent of the democratic judges were above the average of their respective courts, whereas only 31 percent of the republican judges were, for a difference of 24 percentage points. This disparity too cannot be readily attributed to chance.[5] In the same nationwide sample, similar differences arise with regard to ex-prosecutors, Protestant judges, and judges with conservative off-the-bench attitudes being more likely to decide in the prosecution's favor than judges without prosecution experience, Catholic judges, or judges with liberal off-the-bench attitudes. Table 8-2 summarizes many of these results.[6]

Perhaps more interesting than either showing variation across cases or judges, or relating variation to the backgrounds of defendants or judges, are studies on channeling, reducing, and/or controlling discretion, to which we now turn. These studies reflect a contemporary policy analysis perspective toward criminal justice research, whereby researchers are concerned with testing the effects of alternative policies for increasing the effectiveness, efficiency, or equity of the criminal justice system. Reducing discretion abuses by channeling, reducing, or controlling discretion can be justified in terms of making the system: (1) more effective by reducing the crime-

TABLE 8-1
Disparities Across Defendants in Larceny Cases

Fraction in Sample	Criminal Procedure Treatment	Class		Sex		Race		Age		Education		Urbanism		Region	
		INDI-GENT	NON	MALE	FEM.	BLACK	WHITE	UNDER 21	21 & OVER	ELEM.	HIGH	URBAN	RURAL	NORTH	SOUTH
$\frac{300}{676}$	% who received *no* preliminary hearing	48 + 40		45 + 43		35 – 43		42 + 41		57 ⊕ 43		42 – 50		55 ⊕ 35	
$\frac{415}{874}$	% who were *not* released on bail	73 ⊕ 31		50 ⊕ 24		58 ⊕ 45		55 + 47		62 ⊕ 50		46 – 53		49 + 45	
$\frac{109}{879}$	% who had *no* lawyer	2 ⊖ 14		13 + 10		10 – 17		16 + 12		24 ⊕ 9		8 ⊖ 25		12 – 17	
$\frac{80}{245}$	% who had over two months delay from arrest to disposition or trial while in jail	37 + 29		33 – 40		22 ⊖ 35		46 ⊕ 29		50 + 48		31 – 36		38 ⊕ 24	
$\frac{167}{243}$	% of those tried who had *no jury* trial	73 + 66		69 ⊕ 53		68 – 70		60 – 70		57 – 67		72 ⊕ 58		53 ⊖ 78	
$\frac{820}{958}$	% who pleaded or were found guilty	91 + 87		87 ⊕ 76		91 + 88		91 91		93 – 100		87 + 82		90 + 83	
$\frac{414}{735}$	% who received a prison sentence rather than a suspended sentence or probation	65 ⊕ 45		57 ⊕ 36		74 ⊕ 49		49 ⊖ 60		67 ⊕ 48		56 56		51 – 60	
$\frac{148}{266}$	% of those imprisoned who received over one-year prison terms	45 ⊖ 58		55 ⊖ 67		46 – 53		46 – 49		38 ⊕ 19		54 – 61		34 ⊖ 66	
1,103	Number in sample	337	465	967	77	197	397	159	379	42	120	810	293	490	463

Based on 1,103 grand larceny cases from a nationwide sample of United States cases in 1962.
+ = the group on the left has a percent greater than the group on the right.
– = the group on the left has a percent less than the group on the right.
The sign is circled where the difference is greater than 10 percentage points.

TABLE 8-2
Disparities Across Judges in Criminal Cases

Group 1 (Hypothesized to be Less Defense Minded)	Group 2 (Hypothesized to be More Defense Minded)	Number of Judges Involved in Each Group		% of Group 1 Above Their Court Average on the Decision Score*	% of Group 2 Above Their Court Average on the Decision Score*	Difference	Probability of the Positive Difference Being Due to Chance
		(1)	(2)				
PARTY							
Republicans	Democrats	45	40	31%	55%	+24	Less than 0.05
PRESSURE GROUPS							
Members of a business group	Did not indicate such membership	15	71	47	52	+5	0.20 to 0.50
Members of ABA	Did not indicate such membership	105	88	37	52	+15	Less than 0.05
Members of a nativist group	Did not indicate such membership	11	33	36	48	+12	0.20 to 0.50
OCCUPATIONS							
Former businesspeople	Did not indicate such occupation	22	71	32	40	+8	0.05 to 0.20
Former prosecutors	Did not indicate such occupation	81	105	36	50	+14	Less than 0.05
EDUCATION							
Attended high tuition law school	Attended low tuition law school	24	22	54	59	+5	0.20 to 0.50
AGE							
Over age 65	Under age 60	67	66	43	42	−1	Negligible difference
GEOGRAPHY							
Practiced initially in small town	Practiced initially in large city	31	37	35	35	0	Negligible difference
RELIGION AND ANCESTRAL NATIONALITY							
Protestants	Catholics	39	18	31	56	+25	Less than 0.05
High-income Prot. denomination	Low-income Prot. denomination	54	54	41	50	+9	0.05 to 0.20
Only British ancestry	Part non-British ancestry	96	97	38	47	+9	0.05 to 0.20
ATTITUDES							
Low general liberalism score	High general liberalism score	22	23	27	57	+30	Less than 0.05
Low criminal liberalism score	High criminal liberalism score	26	17	27	59	+32	Less than 0.05

Based on the nonunanimous cases of the United States state and federal supreme courts of 1955 on which both groups being compared are present.
*Decision score = proportion of times voting for the defense in criminal cases.

causing bitterness generated by perceived disparities, (2) more efficient by reducing the numerous administrative complaints, lawsuits, and case issues which are generated by perceived disparities, and (3) more equitable by reducing the unfairness whereby the burden of the disparities is disproportionately incurred by certain more vulnerable demographic groups.[7]

Channeling Discretion

To channel and control discretion, the original discretion, as indicated by the statutory power granted to judges or other decision makers, must be retained. *Channeling* discretion involves developing internalized incentives for encouraging the socially desired exercise of that power. *Controlling* discretion requires developing external devices for monitoring and possibly reversing abuses of discretion.

ENCOURAGING PRETRIAL RELEASE WHEN IN DOUBT

The American legal system prides itself on being governed by laws rather than by people, despite the highly subjective nature of fact finding and law applying. The legal system is also proud of presuming innocence until guilt is proven. Yet the system simultaneously makes it more costly for decision makers to follow that presumption of innocence when in doubt, rather than a presumption of guilt. For example, when a pretrial judge is undecided about whether or not to hold a defendant in jail pending trial, the judge should release, rather than hold, the defendant. In reality, however, a judge stands to lose more by releasing a pretrial defendant who fails to appear for trial or who commits a crime while released, than by holding a defendant who would have appeared without committing a crime if released. The releasing error embarrasses the judge, because it is visible; but the holding error does not, because it is totally invisible.

This concept also applies to the police officer who is unsure whether to arrest a suspect and bring him to the station, or to release him with a summons to appear in court on a certain day. The police officer suffers embarrassment or frustration if the released defendant fails to appear. Likewise, a sentencing judge or a parole-board member who grants probation or parole may be embarrassed if the convicted defendant commits a crime shortly after being released, but may not be embarrassed if the convicted defendant is jailed or continued in jail, even though the defendant would not have committed a crime if released. The actual workings of the legal system make it more profitable to presume wrongdoing (guilt) rather than "rightdoing" (innocence) when in doubt, contrary to the legal norms that supposedly prevail.

The legal system must make it more profitable to presume rightdoing, as the law requires. Merely declaring such a fiat, though, will not change human behavior, unless the perceptions of the costs of a releasing error versus the costs of a holding error change. This could occur by publicizing each judge's or other decision maker's: (1) holding rate, (2) appearance rate, and (3) crime-committing rate for released defendants in every judicial or police district. The decision makers with high holding rates are then likely to decrease, partly from the embarrassment of their deviant behavior, where uniformity should be the norm with like sets of cases. They may also change from failure to pinpoint reasons to justify their relatively high holding rate. Publicizing only the holding rates would not alter anyone's behavior, since the high holders could claim it reduces the rate of nonappearance and crime committing.

For example, suppose there are three judges on a given court. Judge Brown holds 70 percent of all the defendants involved in his pretrial release decisions; Judge Green holds 40 percent; and Judge Smith holds 20 percent. Judge Brown may have about 95 percent of his released defendants appearing in court without being rearrested; Judge Green, about 92 percent; and Judge Smith, about 90 percent. Publicizing these figures among judges, lawyers, and possibly the public, would probably cause Judge Brown to lower his holding rate, especially if the high cost of holding relative to the cost of releasing were also publicized. Holding costs include jail maintenance, lost gross national product, welfare costs for families whose breadwinners are jailed, and bitterness about being jailed largely for lacking bond money rather than for being a bad risk. Releasing costs include the cost of rearresting the relatively few defendants who fail to appear, and the crime-committing costs of those relatively few defendants who commit crimes while released. Even though we do not know whether Judge Brown has ever wrongfully held a defendant, he is obviously amiss if he has virtually no better appearance rate or crime-committing rate than Judge Green, who holds only 40 percent of her defendants. Preliminary data from various cities tend to show great variation among judges and police on holding rates, but relatively little variation on appearance rates and crime-committing rates of those released. This indicates the strong possibility that holding rates could come down substantially without affecting appearance rates and crime-committing rates.[8]

The same kind of publicity can be used to influence police and parole-board members to better conform to the law. The basic assumption is that decision makers with relatively expensive holding rates will come down if their high holding cannot be justified with better effectiveness rates. The author is designing before-and-after field experiments to be conducted in various court districts to see the extent to which publicity can influence decision-making behavior in the criminal justice system. The publicizing will take different forms in different districts, such as providing information so that each judge can only identify himself or herself, or identifying all the judges, but providing the information only to the judges, or also to the local lawyers, or also to the local press, in order to see the relative effects of different information methods. This research may well exemplify how governmental decision makers' behavior can be channeled in accordance with social norms by compiling and publicizing relevant research information.

In addition to publicizing the fact that high-holding judges generally do not have any better appearance rates or crime-committing rates than the low-holding judges, one can also use other means to channel pretrial release decisions in the direction of releasing, rather than holding, when in doubt. Table 8-3 summarizes many of the possibilities. They can be classified as involving: (1) raising and clarifying the probability of appearance, (2) making more visible the type 1 errors and costs of holding defendants who would have appeared, and (3) decreasing the costs of the type 2 errors of releasing defendants who fail to appear.[9] In Table 8-3, the release-hold decision is one in which the decision maker implicitly tries to select the alternative that will have the higher expected value. Expected value means expected benefits (i.e., benefits discounted by the probability of their occurring) minus expected costs (i.e., costs discounted by the probability of their occurring). In terms of political feasibility, it may be easier to raise the probability of appearance (by screening, reporting in, notifying, and prosecuting) and to decrease the costs of nonappearance (by reducing the time from arrest to trial) than it is to arrange for a system publicizing individual pretrial release rates and appearance rates. Judges who do not want their performances quantified or publicized are likely to oppose performance publicizing. And performance publicizing could backfire if it causes low-holding judges to increase their holding because of public pressure which concentrates only on the holding scores regardless of the appearance rates.[10]

ENCOURAGING TIME-SAVING DECISIONS

Optimum choice analysis operates on the assumption that when individuals choose one activity over another, they are implying that the expected benefits minus costs of the chosen activity are greater than the expected benefits minus costs of the rejected activity. Table 8-4 applies optimum choice analysis to the problem of convincing prosecutors and assistant state's attorneys to decide to accelerate the slow and difficult cases so that they do not exceed a maximum time threshold. This could entail: (1) increasing the benefits and decreasing the costs of making time-saving decisions, (2) decreasing the benefits and increasing the costs of making time-lengthening decisions, and (3) increasing or decreasing the probabilities of relevant contingent events. To encourage favorable time-consumption decisions, assistant state's attorneys can be rewarded with money (to increase the benefits) and work-saving resources (to decrease the costs). To discourage unfavorable time-consumption decisions, state's attorneys can be punished by providing for an absolute discharge, not subject to reprosecution, of excessively delayed defendants. They can also be deprived of the plea bargaining benefits of lengthy pretrial incarceration by providing more release on recognizance. If primarily concerned with time-saving, optimum

TABLE 8-3
Channeling Discretion to Encourage Pretrial Release in Doubtful Cases

Probability of Appearance

		WOULD APPEAR *(P)*	WOULD FAIL TO APPEAR *(1 − P)*	*Expected Values*
Alternative decisions available	RELEASE VIA ROR OR LOW BOND	$+A$	type 2 error $-B$	$EV_R = (+A)(P) +$ $(+B)(1 - P)$
	HOLD VIA NO OR HIGH BOND	type 1 error $-A$	$+B$	$EV_H = (-A)(P) +$ $(+B)(1 - P)$

There are three general approaches to widening the positive difference between EV_R and EV_H:

1. Raise and clarify the probability of appearance (i.e., increase P).

Raise P through better screening and notification.
Clarify P through statistical studies of what percentage of various types of released defendants appear in court.
More vigorously prosecute those who fail to appear.

2. Make more visible the type 1 errors and costs of holding defendants who would appear (i.e., increase A).

Publicize for each judge the percentage of defendants he/she holds and the appearance percentage he/she attains. (Judges vary widely on percentage held, but appearance percentages tend to be about 90.)
Make more visible how much it costs to hold defendants in jail.
a. Jail maintenance
b. Lost income
c. Bitterness from case dismissed after lengthy wait
d. Families on welfare
e. Increased conviction probability
f. Jail riots from overcrowding

3. Decrease the costs of type 2 errors of releasing defendants who fail to appear (i.e., decrease B).

Make rearrest easier through pretrial supervision.
Decrease the time from arrest to trial.
a. More personnel, more diversion, and shorter trial stage.
b. Better sequencing of cases.
c. Shorter path from arrest to trial.
Decrease pretrial crime committing.
a. Increase probability of being arrested, convicted, and jailed.
b. Decrease benefits of successful crime committing.
c. Increase costs of unsuccessful crime committing.

TABLE 8-4
Channeling Discretion to Encourage Time-saving Decisions

Alternative occurrences

	BEING PENALIZED FOR LENGTHENING TIME (P)	NOT BEING PENALIZED FOR LENGTHENING TIME ($1 - P$)
Alternative decisions TIME-SAVING DECISION (S)	B_S Benefits from S	C_S Costs from S
TIME-LENGTHENING DECISION (L)	C_L Costs from L	B_L Benefits from S

Benefits minus costs equals profits.

The object of this optimum choice analysis is to make time-saving decisions more profitable than time-lengthening decisions. (In the equation, P represents the probability that the prosecutor will be penalized.)

$$B_S - C_S > (B_L)\,(1 - P) - (C_L)\,(P)$$

How can we encourage prosecutors to make time-saving decisions?

1. *Increase the benefits from making time-saving decision (increase B_S).*
   For example, reward assistant state's attorneys with salary increases and promotions for reducing the average time per case.

2. *Decrease the costs of making time-saving decisions (decrease C_S).*
   For example, establish a computerized system to inform assistant state's attorneys about actual and predicted times at various stages for all cases to minimize the trouble of keeping track of cases. Provide more investigative and preparation resources.

3. *Increase the costs of making time-lengthening decisions (increase C_L).*
   For example, provide under the speedy-trial rules for absolute discharge of the defendant whose case extends beyond the time limit rather than just release on recognizance.

4. *Decrease the benefits from making time-lengthening decisions (decrease B_L).*
   For example, increase release on recognizance so that lengthening the pretrial time will not make the jailed defendant more vulnerable to pleading guilty.

5. *Raise the probability of the decision maker being penalized for lengthening time (increase P).*
   For example, allow fewer exceptions to the speedy-trial rules such as suspending their application "for good cause" or "exceptional circumstances."

choice analysis can stimulate one's thinking regarding how decision makers can be influenced to make time-saving decisions.

A similar analysis could be applied to public defenders' or private defense attorneys' decisions. However, suggestions for encouraging time-saving by defense attorneys may conflict with suggestions for encouraging time-saving by prosecutors. For example, one might recommend more pretrial release to decrease the benefit the prosecutor receives from the increased willingness on the part of defendants held in jail to plead guilty. On the other hand, one might recommend less pretrial release to cause the defendant, and indirectly, his or her attorney, additional suffering from delaying the case. In such conflicts one must either decide which side is more responsible for the delay, or decide on the basis of another criteria.

Additionally, this analysis provides benefit-cost suggestions applicable to the defense side that do not conflict with those suggestions applicable to the prosecution. For example, providing monetary rewards and more resources to assistant public defenders does not conflict with the prosecutor's suggestions, unless one assumes there is a fixed quantity of resources available to the criminal justice system, and whatever the prosecutor receives must be deducted from the public defender or other parts of the system.

Another optimum choice analysis is applicable to judicial decisions affecting delay. For example, judges currently incur virtually no personal costs from granting repeated continuances or making other delaying decisions. If, however, records publicized each judge's average time for processing various types of cases, the visibility might prompt especially slow judges to move faster. Such a publicizing system (even among the judges themselves rather than the general public) would increase the costs of time-lengthening decisions. This record-keeping method can also be used for comparing either assistant state's attorneys and assistant public defenders in a given court system or court systems, if separate averages are calculated for cases of different severity and expected time consumptions. Encouraging time-saving decisions is closely related to encouraging pretrial release. One reason judges are reluctant to release defendants prior to trial is the long time span that often occurs between release and trial. That freedom facilitates the defendant's disappearance and provides more opportunities for him or her to commit crimes. Were the time interval shorter, both the defendants, sitting in jail awaiting trial, and the general public, concerned about the defendants out of jail awaiting trial, would suffer less harm.[11]

Reducing Discretion

REDUCING SENTENCING DISCRETION
Table 8-1 shows a 13 percentage point difference between the indigent and the nonindigent defendants convicted of larceny who received prison sen-

tences of more than one year. Column 1 of Table 8-1 reveals that 45 percent of the indigent defendants convicted of larceny received sentences of more than one year, whereas 58 percent of the nonindigent defendants convicted of larceny received sentences of more than one year. What would be the effect on that difference of reducing judicial sentencing discretion?

Table 8-5 helps answer that question with regard to larceny cases. Column 4 of Table 8-5 shows that if we work with cases from all the states, we get a 13 percentage point difference in the direction of longer sentences for nonindigent defendants.[12] This difference may be due to the probable fact that nonindigent convicted defendants steal larger sums of money, and thus deserve longer sentences than indigent defendants. If, however, we separate out the cases from the high discretion states, then we observe that the 13 percentage point difference increases to a 27 percentage point difference. Likewise, if we separate out the cases from the low discretion states, we observe that the difference decreases to only 7 percentage points. By the term *high discretion states*, we mean states that were above the national average regarding the ratio between: (1) the range in years within which a judge is allowed to sentence in larceny cases, and (2) the minimum number of years a judge must give when there is no probation. *Low discretion states* are those that were below the national average. From the analysis of the relation between judicial sentencing discretion and economic class disparities in larceny sentencing, one can conclude that reducing discretion reduces the sentencing disparity that otherwise exists between indigent and nonindigent defendants, regardless of whether or not those disparities are deserved. A similar conclusion is reached if one analyzes the effect of reducing judicial sentencing discretion of the disparities between black-white, southern-northern, and rural-urban defendants.[13]

The greatest corrections policy controversy is currently the extent to which judges and parole boards should have discretion in sentencing convicted defendants. This controversy is being resolved in the direction of lessening their discretion.[14] Conservatives often support this trend because they perceive discretionary sentencing results in unduly lenient sentences. Liberals often support it too because they believe it results in unduly arbitrary sentences. A key question, if the legislature is to determine the new, relatively fixed sentences, is how that determination should be made. What is the optimum sentence level for a given crime and prior record, in recognition of the fact that sentences which are either too long or too short may be socially undesirable?

One approach to answering this question might be to gather data for many former convicts, showing for each one:

1. the crime for which the defendant was convicted
2. the number of months which the defendant actually served in prison (symbolized *L* for length)

3. the number of months the defendant previously served in prison (R for prior record)
4. the number of months the defendant subsequently served in prison, as part of a follow-up study (S for subsequent sentence)
5. the number of months the defendant delayed committing the crime for which he was subsequently convicted (D for delay)

After that data is gathered, we might like to know the relation between length and subsequent criminal behavior, discounted by how long the misbehavior is delayed, while holding the prior record constant. We would use the following regression equation: $S^2/D = a(L)^{b1}(R)^{b2}$. We tentatively square S to indicate we consider severity to be twice as important as delay. The regression analysis is nonlinear in recognition that length may reduce subsequent misbehavior, but at diminishing returns, rather than in proportion to the length of sentence. Likewise, prior record may predict subsequent misbehavior, but also with diminishing returns, rather than in proportion to the prior record. The model thus hypothesizes that b_1 will be negative, and b_2 will be positive.[15]

If we plot that hypothesized curve, it should be negative convex and will clarify how the releasing cost (in months) relates to sentence length. We can then easily draw a holding cost curve, which would be a positive straight line originating from the origin of the graph, relating holding cost (in months) to sentence length. The holding cost would be positive linear, since holding a defendant in prison for 10 months costs twice as much as doing so for five months, adjusting for inflation. The object is then to determine the total cost curve, which is simply the sum of the releasing and holding cost curves. By observing where the total cost curve bottoms out, we learn the optimum sentence length for a given crime and prior record, which minimizes the sum of the costs. Figure 8-1 summarizes these relations. One defect in this analysis, however, is that sentence length does not consistently relate negatively to the severity of subsequent misbehavior. The longer a defendant is sentenced, the worse his or her subsequent behavior often is, regardless of the alleged effects of maturing, deterrence, or rehabilitiation, or whether we control for additional variables besides prior record, such as age and prior job duration.

A possibly meaningful alternative to such a rationalist benefit-cost approach is an incrementalist approach, which involves determining the average sentence currently served for each type of crime and prior record, and then allowing small increments about 25 percent above or below those prevailing averages for aggravating or mitigating circumstances. Such an averaging approach recognizes that existing sentences by individual judges in individual cases may be too high or too low relative to (1) society's values and (2) the empirical facts concerning the relations between sentence length and the goals of sentencing. These goals include deterrence of the defen-

TABLE 8-5
Effects of Reducing Sentencing Discretion in Larceny Cases

Defendants / *States*	RURAL VS. URBAN	SOUTH VS. NORTH	BLACK VS. WHITE	POOR VS. NONPOOR
All states	+0.07(~0) (263)	+0.32 (214)	+0.07(~0) (148)	-0.13 (175)
High discretion states	+0.18 (100)	+0.29 (83)	00(~0) (76)	-0.27 (76)
Low discretion states	-0.02(~0) (163)	+0.24 (131)	-0.12 (72)	-0.07(~0) (99)
Difference in disparity	+0.20	+0.05	+0.12	-0.20
Effect of reducing discretion	Reduces disparity against rural defendants	Reduces disparity against southern defendants	Reduces favoritism for white defendants	Interferes with giving longer sentences to bigger thieves

The -0.13 in the upper right-hand corner means there were 13 percentage points separating the percentage of indigent defendants who received more than a year in prison (45%) from the percentage of nonindigent defendants who received more than a year in prison (58%), with the group on the left receiving the shorter sentences. The same interpretation can be given to all the numbers in the first three rows of the above table.

FIGURE 8-1
The Assumed Relations Between Sentence Lengths and Releasing-Holding Costs to Arrive at a Nondiscretionary Sentence Length

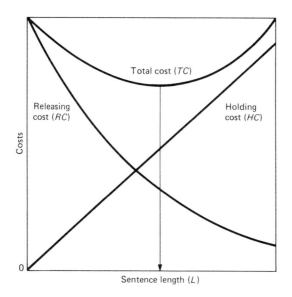

dant, general deterrence of others, incapacitation, maturation, and rehabilitation. Such an approach, however, implies that by averaging the results of judges and cases, one thereby obtains the collective wisdom on these normative and factual matters and that collectively, judges have reasonably representative normative values and reasonably accurate perceptions of reality. By averaging the sentences actually served, one is also in effect including the collective wisdom of the legislators who set the sentencing constraints within which the judges operate, and the collective wisdom of the prison administrators and parole officials who generally have the authority to modify these judicial sentences. Such an incrementalist approach to arriving at an optimum or recommended policy makes sense where one cannot accurately assess the benefits and costs of alternative policies, and where the values of the individual decision makers are not as likely to conflict with relevant societal values.[16]

REDUCING PRETRIAL RELEASE DISCRETION

Just as one can discuss optimum nondiscretionary sentencing, one can also talk about optimum nondiscretionary bond setting. The object would be to arrive at a set of bond levels which would minimize the sum of pretrial holding and releasing costs. The key variable determining the holding cost is the percentage of defendants held in jail prior to trial. Optimally, bonds should minimize that percentage. Having no bond or other criteria as a prerequisite to release will reduce the percentage held to zero, but the releasing costs will be too high in terms of nonappearance and crime committing while released. The key variable determining the releasing cost is the percentage of defendants appearing for trial who have not committed crimes while released. Bonds should maximize that percentage. Bonds which are infinitely high will raise the percentage to 100 percent, but the holding costs will be too high in terms of holding everybody, including those who are good risks to release. An ideal bond for a given crime might maximize the percentage of defendants who appear for trial without committing a crime minus the percentage of defendants who are held in jail for being unable to meet the bond set. This kind of bond is analogous to arriving at a price or quantity for a product that will maximize income minus expenses, since a defendant appearing for trial is likened to income, and a defendant being held is clearly an expense.

Optimum bail-bond setting was discussed in Chapter 3 regarding the relationship between equity and efficiency. The analysis showed that we could have more efficient bonds which would maximize the probability of appearing in court minus the probability of being held in jail. The analysis, however, also demonstrated that such a bail-bond system would likely be inequitable, because the burden would be on the poor, who are disproportionately unlikely to afford meeting even efficiently set bonds. The alternative proposal would be to be released on one's own recognizance or promise to appear. Determining who would be released could be based on a point system with limited judicial discretion. Those who are held would be guaranteed a speedy trial.

This system could effectively promote appearance, providing the point system is meaningful and backed with periodic reporting to the courthouse by released defendants along with a realistic threat of prosecution for failure to appear. Such a system would be efficient in saving jail-maintenance costs if it substantially reduces pretrial detention. It would also be equitable if the allocation of points is based strictly on the probability of appearing and possibly on the probability of not committing a crime while released, rather than on factors that are unduly oriented toward economic class, race, or other legally irrelevant characteristics.

The point system could be based on a systematic analysis of the variables that correlate with appearing in court, such as years in the community, length of present job, and truthfulness in reporting such information. Such a point system makes more sense than averaging prior bonds, because they tend to: (1) involve amounts that are too high for poor defendants to pay, (2) reflect a strong sensitivity on the part of judges to avoiding releasing errors, although the law says to be more sensitive to avoiding holding errors, and (3) be less effective in separating the good risks from the bad than a methodologically feasible point system.[17]

CONTROLLING DISCRETION

To prevent abuses of discretion, the legal system can *channel* discretion along desired directions. It can also *reduce* discretion where properly channeling it may be too difficult. A third approach is to *control* discretion by developing devices external to the decision makers, such as controls represented by appellate courts, juries, judicial colleagues, and attorneys for the state and the defense. Appellate control is difficult to achieve because so few cases are appealed. In those rare instances of appeal, it is difficult for the appellate court to second-guess the trial judge on such factual matters as whether the defendant's demeanor merits a more or less severe sentence. Some states provide for automatic appellate review in capital punishment cases, but this does not control more routine sentencing or nonsentencing matters. Abuses of pretrial-release discretion are especially difficult to control through the appellate process since defendants whose pretrial detention has been unduly prolonged are likely to be out of pretrial detention long before a meaningful appeal can occur.

The jury is a frequently mentioned check on conviction errors and on abuses of judicial discretion. The jury often performs the latter function when the law lags public opinion, as in personal injury cases. Personal injury law generally provides that plaintiffs shall be barred from collecting damages if they have failed to exercise due care, regardless of how negligent the defendants may have been. Juries often award damages to plaintiffs, but they lower the damages in consideration of the relative extent to which the plaintiff has contributed to the accident. This control over judges, who are more likely to follow the legal rules, could be considered an abuse of discretion by juries, rather than a control on the discretion of judges. In criminal justice, juries operate only in the stage at which guilt is determined, although in the past, some states' juries have participated in capital and noncapital sentencing matters. An analysis of the data presented in Table 8-5 shows that discriminatory patterns are less obvious in determining guilt than in determining a sentence. When the cases are divided between jury trials and bench trials, stronger differences exist between the percentage of blacks versus whites found guilty with jury trials than with bench trials. This difference may arise because more juries act in accordance with popular stereotypes of defendants than judges act in accordance with the law and the facts.[18] This difference was also found between probation officer recommendations and judicial decisions in the same cases. There is, however, no way to subject judges and juries to the same cases using the data from Table 8-1. The jury cases usually involve more serious matters. If juries are more like probation officers than judges in their decision making, the pattern would run contrary to the idea that jury trials might mean less disparity than bench trials.[19]

Judicial colleagues can exert meaningful control on some aspects of judicial discretion through the experimental system used in Denver's federal district court. In brief, the district court judges were instructed not to sentence given crimes that would deviate by more than about 25 percent from the previous averages unless they consulted with two of their judicial colleagues. The consultation was a mere discussion and not a three-person vote. Nevertheless, the requirement substantially brought the sentences closer to the average than they were before the experiment. This experiment, however, has not been continued, and it has not been repeated elsewhere. Judges resist that kind of control over their decisions. The system is also time-consuming, especially when judges are needed for processing large backlogs rather than for formally consulting on deviant sentences.[20]

Having attorneys represent both parties in criminal and civil cases may substantially reduce abuses of judicial discretion without reducing the needed discretion itself. Table 8-6 shows how the attorneys' presence at the preliminary hearing stage of criminal cases reduces racial disparities. The data is derived from the same 50-state sample of larceny cases as the data in Tables 8-1 and 8-5. Only racial disparities are noted because: (1) the sample sizes are too small to talk about females, juveniles, or defendants known to have gone only to elementary school, (2) too much overlap exists between being labeled indigent and having a court-appointed attorney for discussing indigents versus nonindigents, and (3) the presence of attorneys is not especially relevant to reducing rural-urban or south-north differences.

The sentencing stage is not used because an attorney may help effect a lower sentence. However, defendants who hire attorneys tend to be involved in more serious crimes, which may more than offset the effect of having an attorney. Nonetheless, there is no way of controlling the degree of larceny in the Table 8-6 cases. Likewise, having an attorney may correlate with long delay while in jail awaiting trial because these more serious cases may take longer to prepare for trial.

Other stages are not usable because: (1) other stages may not have enough cases for systematic comparisons such as the jury-trial stage, which is relatively rare; (2) they involve no substantial disparities to be reduced as with the determination of guilt, and (3) they involve issues over which attorneys have less control, such as the defendants' ability to meet the bail-bond requested.

TABLE 8-6
Effects of Having Attorneys on Reducing Racial Disparities

	No Attorney (%)		Had Attorney (%)	
	BLACK	WHITE	BLACK	WHITE
Had preliminary hearing	33	50	68	58
No preliminary hearing	67	50	32	42
Total	100	100	100	100
(Sample size)	(9)	(34)	(118)	(209)

In Table 8-6 we find that if comparisons are made only between white defendants without attorneys and black defendants without attorneys, there's a substantial disparity (17 percentage points) in favor of the white defendants. If, however, we compare the white defendants to the black defendants, both having attorneys, the figure drops below zero, to −0.10. One might also note that 62 percent of the defendants with attorneys received preliminary hearings, but only 46 percent of the defendants without them did so. Thus, attorneys have two effects: (1) reducing discrimination or equalizing differences between demographic groups which otherwise show substantial disparities, and (2) increasing the extent to which proper legal procedure is complied with. Although exact data is not available, one could reason by analogy that providing attorneys would reduce disparities in: (1) economic class differences, (2) civil cases, and (3) non-American cases where court-appointed attorneys are not readily available.[21]

The data also reveals some differences between types of attorneys. For example, by using the comparisons between indigent and nonindigent defendants with attorneys, we are in effect comparing court-provided counsel with hired counsel. We find that preliminary hearings occur in 63 percent of the cases with hired counsel, 52 percent of the cases with court-provided counsel, and 38 percent of the cases with no counsel. Thus, hired counsel seems more effective in guaranteeing the legal rights of defendants, although the percentage for court-provided counsel is closer to hired counsel than to no counsel. Moreover, the more favorable treatment of the defendants with hired counsel may be due to the fact that they have non-indigent characteristics, not that they have hired, as opposed to court-provided, counsel. The data does not divide court-provided counsel into volunteer, salaried, and reimbursed attorneys. One might, however, expect reimbursed private attorneys to be more effective, but more expensive than volunteer attorneys. Salaried public defenders may be skilled defense attorneys, but given their heavy caseloads, they often lack the time and resources to vigorously pursue the rights of defendants concerning such matters as receiving a preliminary hearing, jury trial, or appeal. They may, however, represent a meaningful compromise between relatively inexperienced and unavailable attorneys, and expensive reimbursed attorneys.[22] Reimbursed attorneys are paid for their expenses and hourly fees by the counties in state cases and by the federal government in federal cases.

Conclusion

An analysis of a given set of cases in which all the defendants have been charged with the same crime is likely to reveal substantial differences among individual defendants and across demographic types of defendants regarding: (1) safeguards for the innocent, such as preliminary hearings and trial by jury, (2) pretrial release, and (3) postconviction sentencing. Also, an analysis of a given set of judges who have heard the same type of criminal cases on the same state supreme courts shows substantial differences among individual judges and across demographic types of judges regarding: (1) political party affiliation, (2) prior occupation, (3) ethnic group membership, and (4) liberalism attitudes.

One method to decrease these differences is to internalize a common set of desired values among criminal justice personnel, especially when values may conflict with what is legally desired. For example, one can convince judges that it is more costly to hold a defendant wrongly prior to trial than to release a defendant wrongly, even though they might consider a releasing error to be more costly, since holding errors go undetected. One can also have prosecutors, public defenders, and judges make time-shortening rather than time-lengthening decisions when faced with those alternatives, even though the longer method might be easier.

Another way to combat these disparities is to reduce the discretion. This decreases undesirable exercises of discretion, such as those reflecting stereotyped notions of the relative seriousness of black-on-white crimes versus black-on-black crimes. However, it may also decrease desirable exercises in discretion, such as those involving penalizing more severe criminal behavior. The best way for a legislature to arrive at nondiscretionary sentences is to average past sentences (of cases and judges) for a given crime and type of prior record, rather than to determine the benefits and costs for various sentence lengths. The most advantageous method of arriving at nondiscretionary pretrial release, however, is to establish a point system for predicting good risks, and applying it when considering release-nonrelease decisions, instead of relying on bail bonds to encourage court appearances.

The best way to deal with discretionary disparities is to perhaps concentrate on controlling and reducing the abuses, rather than on reducing the discretion. Appeals could be made easier by requiring collegial decisions and explicit justifications for deviant decisions. Juries can reduce conviction errors, but not necessarily the undesirable disparities across demographic groups. The best control might be access to attorneys by all defendants. This would reduce abuses by police, prosecutors, judges, and other criminal justice personnel by decreasing disparities and increasing compliance with the law.

NOTES

The author gratefully thanks the law faculty of the University of Natal in Durban, South Africa, for inviting him to present a variation on this chapter at their 1981 conference on "Discretion and Criminal Justice." Special thanks are owed to Professors Olmesdahl, McQuoid-Mason, Cassim, Steytler, Matthews, Patel, and Wilde for their hospitality and inspiration. Thanks are also owed to Professors van Zyl Smit and Dugard of the University of the Witwatersrand.

1. On the subject of discretion and criminal justice in general, see Burton Atkins and Mark Pogrebin (eds.), *The Invisible Justice System: Discretion and the Law* (Anderson, 1978); Keith Bottomley, *Decisions in the Penal Process* (Rothman, 1973); Kenneth Davis, *Discretionary Justice: A Preliminary Inquiry* (Louisiana State University Press, 1969); Kenneth Davis, *Discretionary Justice in Europe and America* (University of Illinois Press, 1979); Margaret Evans (ed.), *Discretion and Control* (Sage, 1978); Mortimer Kadish and Sanford Kadish, *Discretion to Disobey: A Study of Lawful Departures from Legal Rules* (Stanford University Press, 1973); Thomas Lee and Ben Overton, *Judicial Discretion* (National College of the State Judiciary, 1972); and James Vorenberg, "Narrowing the Discretion of Criminal Justice Officials," 1976 *Duke Law Journal* 651–97 (1976).

2. On the extent to which there are substantial variations in sentencing across cases involving the same crime or across judges, see Robert Dawson, *Sentencing: The Decision as to Type, Length, and Conditions of Sentence* (Little, Brown, 1969); Marvin Frankel, *Criminal Sentences: Law without Order* (Basic Books, 1973); and W. Gaylin, *Partial Justice: A Study of Bias in Sentencing* (Random House, 1974). Variations across cases and other stages of the criminal justice process are discussed in Arnold Trebach, *The Rationing of Justice: Constitutional Rights and Criminal Process* (Rutgers University Press, 1964), and the books in note 1 by Bottomley and by Atkins and Pogrebin.

3. More specifically, the sample size is about 398 for the relation between race of convicted larceny defendants and receiving a prison sentence, rather than a suspended sentence or probation. The 398 was arrived at by noting that the number of defendants for which we have racial information is 594 (i.e., 197 blacks and 397 whites). We also note that of the total sample of 1,103 defendants, only 735 were convicted and could be positioned on whether they received a prison sentence (i.e., 67 percent of the total). If we multiply 594 by 0.67, we get a sample size of 398 defendants. We could have also arrived at the same result by noting that the number of defendants for which we have sentencing information is 735, and that we only have racial information for 54 percent of the defendants (i.e., 594 out of 1,103). If we multiply 735 by 0.54, we also get about 398 defendants in our sample. To determine the probability of obtaining a difference as large as 0.25 (i.e., 74 percent minus 49 percent), we multiply the square of 0.25 by the sample size of 398 and obtain a product of 25. We then take that product to the first row of what is known as a χ-square probability table. From that row, we read off that a product of 25 in this context corresponds to a chance probability of less than 0.001. It is customary among social scientists to assume that any relation which has a chance probability less than 0.05 is a real relation and not a chance occurrence. For further details on calculating chance probabilities or statistical significance, see Hubert Blalock, Jr., *Social Statistics* (McGraw-Hill, 1972).

4. On the extent to which variations in sentencing and other aspects of criminal justice treatment vary with the demographic characteristics of defendants, see Jon Hagan, "Extra-Legal Attributes and Criminal Sentencing: An Assessment of a Sociological Viewpoint," 8 *Law and Society Review* 357–83 (1974); Elton Long, James Long, Wilmer Leon, and Paul Weston (eds.), *American Minorities: The Justice Issue* (Prentice-Hall, 1975); Charles Owens and Jimmy Bell (eds.), *Blacks and Criminal Justice* (Heath, 1977); and Charles Reasons and

Jack Kuykendall (eds.), *Race, Crime, and Justice* (Goodyear, 1972). For more detail on Table 8-1, see "The Litigants: Disparities in Safeguards and Sentencing" in S. Nagel, *The Legal Process from a Behavioral Perspective* (Dorsey, 1969), and S. Nagel and Marian Neef, "The Racial Disparity that Supposedly Wasn't There: Some Pitfalls to Watch for in Analyzing Court Statistics on Sentencing and Other Matters" in *The Legal Process: Modeling the System* (Sage, 1977).

5. See note 3 above. For this relation, the sample size is 85 (i.e., 45 Republicans and 40 Democrats). The difference between the two percentages is 0.24 (i.e., 55 percent minus 31 percent. Thus the product to take to a χ-square probability table is 0.24 squared times 85, which is 5. The corresponding probability is between 0.05 and 0.02 according to the first row of the table, which is less than 0.05.

6. On the extent to which variations in sentencing and other aspects of criminal justice treatment vary with the demographic characteristics of judges, see Sheldon Goldman and Austin Sarat (eds.), *American Court Systems: Readings in Judicial Process and Behavior* (Freeman, 1978), 372–416; Joel Grossman, "Social Backgrounds in Judicial Decision-Making," 79 *Harvard Law Review* 1551 (1966); and John Hogarth, *Sentencing as a Human Process* (University of Toronto Press, 1971). For more detail on Table 8-2, see "The Policymakers and the Policy Appliers" in S. Nagel, *The Legal Process from a Behavioral Perspective* (Dorsey, 1969), and "Improving Judicial Personnel" in S. Nagel, *Improving the Legal Process: Effects of Alternatives* (Lexington-Heath, 1975).

7. For an analysis of the bitterness generated by perceived disparities in the criminal justice system, see Jonathan Casper, *American Criminal Justice: The Defendant's Perspective* (Prentice-Hall, 1972) and *Criminal Courts: The Defendant's Perspective* (Law Enforcement Administration Agency, 1976).

8. Variations among the judges in holding rates is partly indicated by substantial variations in holding rates across cities. See William Thomas, *Bail Reform in America* (University of California Press, 1976), and S. Nagel, Paul Wice, and Marian Neef, *Too Much or Too Little Policy: The Example of Pretrial Release* (Sage, 1977). Lower variations among judges on appearance rates and crime-committing rates is indicated partly by the lower variation in those rates across cities. (See Thomas, and Nagel, Wice, and Neef cited above.) The Thomas study showed that when felony holding rates dropped from 52 percent in 1962 to 33 percent in 1971, and misdemeanor holding rates dropped from 40 percent in 1962 to 28 percent in 1971, the appearance rates of the increasingly large number of defendants released only dropped from 94 to 91 percent.

9. In this context, the term *type 1 error* refers to wrongly holding a defendant who should have been released contrary to the presumption of innocence and in favor of releasing defendants. A *type 2 error* refers to wrongly releasing a defendant who should have been held, although one is then acting in accordance with the presumption of innocence and in favor of releasing defendants. On a more general level, type 1 errors refer to making mistakes contrary to a presumption or hypothesis, and type 2 errors refer to making mistakes while acting in accordance with a presumption or hypothesis.

10. On encouraging criminal justice decision makers to comply with the law, see David Aaronson, Thomas Dienes, and Michael Musheno, "Improving Police Discretion Rationality in Handling Public Inebriates," 29 and 30, *Administrative Law Review*, 447–85, 93–132 (1977–1978); Samuel Krislov and Melcolm Feeley, *Compliance and the Law* (Sage, 1970); James Levine, "Implementing Legal Policies Through Operant Conditioning: The Case of Police Practice," 6 *Law and Society Review* 195–222 (1971); and Robert Stover and Don Brown,

"Reducing Rule Violations by Police, Judges, and Corrections Officials" in
S. Nagel (ed.), *Modeling the Criminal Justice System* (Sage, 1977). For more
detail on Table 8-3 see "The Bond-Setting Decision in Individual Cases" in S.
Nagel and Marian Neef, *Decision Theory and the Legal Process* (Lexington-
Heath, 1979). Judges might have a greater tendency to comply with the law if
they were specially trained to be judges, as is done in the French civil service
system. The American counterpart is to suggest that appellate court judges
should have prior judicial experience. That might result in judges who are more
precedent oriented, but might also result in judges who are older and more
ideologically conservative.

11. On encouraging criminal justice decision makers to make more efficient and
    time-saving decisions, see Thomas Church, Kenneth Chantry, and Larry Sipes,
    Pretrial Delay: A Review and Bibliography (National Center for State Courts,
    1978); Burke Fort, et al., *Speedy Trial* (Law Enforcement Assistance Adminis-
    tration, 1978); and National Center for State Courts, *Justice Delayed: The Pace
    of Litigation in Urban Trial Courts* (NCSC, 1978). For more detail on Table 8-4,
    see "Reaching Decisions that Optimize Time" in S. Nagel, *Policy Evaluation:
    Making Optimum Decisions* (Praeger, 1982).

12. It is possible that indigent larceny defendants steal larger sums of money than
    nonindigent, but that they spend their loot faster. It is also possible that
    nonindigent larceny defendants have more nontheft sources of income. It does,
    however, seem more logical that nonindigent larceny defendants are more
    successful thieves than the indigent larceny defendants and thus deserve more
    severe sentences.

13. On the predicted effects of reducing judicial sentencing discretion see Jack
    Foster, *Definite Sentencing: An Examination of Proposals in Four States*
    (Council of State Governments, 1976); Law Enforcement Assistance Admin-
    istration, *Determinate Sentencing: Reform or Regression?* (Government Print-
    ing Office, 1978); and Richard Singer, *Just Deserts: Sentencing Based on
    Equality and Desert* (Ballinger, 1979).

14. The trend is toward a lessening of judicial sentencing discretion, as described in
    Alan Dershowitz, *Fair and Certain Punishment* (Twentieth Century Fund,
    1976); P. O'Donnell, M. Churgin, and D. Curtis, *Toward a Just and Effective
    Sentencing System: Agenda for Legislative Reform* (Praeger, 1977); and
    Richard Singer, *Just Deserts: Sentencing Based on Equality and Desert* (Bal-
    linger, 1979).

15. For more detail on working with this kind of equation to relate subsequent
    sentence (discounted by delay) to the length of the main sentence (while holding
    constant prior record), see S. Nagel and Kathleen Levy, "The Average May Be
    the Optimum in Determinate Sentencing," 42 *Pittsburgh Law Review* 583–636
    (1981).

16. On arriving systematically at nondiscretionary sentences, see Peter Aranson,
    "The Simple Analytics of Sentencing" in Gordon Tullock and Richard Wagner
    (eds.), *Policy Analysis and Deductive Reasoning* (Lexington-Heath, 1978);
    Brian Forst, William Rhodes, and Charles Wellford, "Sentencing and Social
    Science Research for the Formulation of Federal Sentencing Guidelines," 7
    Hofstra Law Review 355–78 (1979); and Don Gottfredson, Leslie Wilkins,
    and Peter Hoffman, *Guidelines for Parole and Sentencing: A Policy Control
    Method* (Lexington-Heath, 1978). For more detail on Figure 8-1, see S. Nagel
    and Kathleen Levy, cited in note 15 above. Other ways to reduce judicial
    discretion without adopting nondiscretionary sentencing include having: (1)
    more statutory law and less case law, (2) clearer, more detailed statutes, and (3)
    nonmandatory guidelines.

17. The data is included in an unpublished paper entitled "Bail and Parole Jumping in Manhattan in 1967" by Andrew Shaffer of the New York Vera Institute of Justice. For a description of the Vera Institute's point system, see Charles Ares, Anne Rankin, and Herbert Sturz, "The Manhattan Bail Project: An Interim Report on the Use of Pretrial Release" 38 *New York University Law Review* 67 (1963). On pretrial release reform in general, see Daniel Freed and Patricia Wald, *Bail in the United States* (United States Department of Justice, 1964); Barry Mahoney, *An Evaluation of Policy Related Research on the Effectiveness of Pretrial Release Programs* (National Center for State Courts, 1975); William Thomas, *A Decade of Bail Reform* (University of California Press, 1976); and Paul Wice, *Freedom for Sale: A National Study of Pretrial Release* (Lexington-Heath, 1974).

18. For a study of differences between judges and juries in sentencing as contrasted to determining guilt or innocence, see Betts, "Jury Sentencing" 2 *National Probation and Parole Association* (1975), and Eckert and Ekstrand, "The Impact of Sentencing Reform: A Comparison of Judge and Jury Sentencing Systems" (paper presented at the annual meeting of the Law and Society Association, 1982).

19. Judges convict at a higher rate than juries hearing the same cases, as shown in Hans Zeisel and Harry Kalven, *The American Jury* (Little, Brown, 1965). Thus, pushing for jury trials provides a control on the greater propensity of judges to convict, but a negative influence on racially discriminatory abuses of judicial discretion. There is thus a trade-off or cost in having the jury as a prodefense safeguard for the innocent, since it results in greater differences between the treatment of blacks and whites. Working with the same data-set used to generate Tables 8-1 and 8-5, one finds that in the larceny cases, the bench trials resulted in an approximately 90 percent conviction rate, and the jury trials in only a 70 percent conviction rate. The conviction rate was approximately the same, 90 percent for both black and white defendants in the bench trials, but approximately 80 percent for black defendants in the jury trials and 60 percent for white defendants in the jury trials. The author thanks Mark Beeman of the University of Illinois for his help in analyzing these differences between bench and jury disparities.

20. The Denver experiment also required judges to write opinions justifying their sentencing decisions when those decisions deviated by more than about 25 percent from the previous averages. Writing opinions facilitates external control by revealing to appellate courts, judicial colleagues, lawyers, the press, and others what a judge claims to be a justification for unusually severe or lenient sentences.

21. Some of the differences between cases with and without attorneys may possibly be attributed to the fact that cases with attorneys are usually more serious cases, having more formal safeguards (like preliminary hearings) even without attorneys. At the time of writing, data are being obtained from the prosecution management information system for Washington, D.C., which contains information for criminal cases on the presence of an attorney, the race of the defendant, the treatment of the defendant at various stages of the criminal justice process, the charges, and the seriousness of the crime as indicated by the amount stolen or the degree of injury caused. These data should generate further insights concerning the effects of having an attorney, having a jury trial, and other such procedures on the reduction of discriminatory patterns. Having attorneys may be relevant to reducing the kind of disparities across defendants shown in Table 8-5, but not as relevant to the disparities across judges shown in

Table 8-6. Only appellate court cases are included in Table 8-6, and these tend to involve attorneys. Suggestions for reducing disparities across appellate judges have included requiring prior judicial experience, not wearing robes, and requiring scholarly qualifications. See S. Nagel, "The Litigants: Disparities in Safeguards and Sentencing" in *The Legal Process from a Behavioral Perspective*, (Dorsey, 1969). Having judges subject to election and reelection provides an external control. Such a control may, however, not be desirable if it pushes judges in a majoritarian direction which is less sensitive to minority rights, nondiscrimination, and safeguards for the innocent than judges otherwise would be. See "Comparing Elected and Appointed Judicial Systems" in S. Nagel, *Improving the Legal Process: Effects of Alternatives* (Lexington-Heath, 1975).

22. On devices to control sentencing disparities, including appeals, juries, colleagues, and opinion writing, see the references cited in Walter Carr and Vincent Connelly, *Sentencing Patterns and Problems: An Annotated Bibliography* (American Judicature Society, 1973); John Ferry and Marjorie Kravitz, *Issues in Sentencing: A Selected Bibliography* (Law Enforcement Assistance Administration, 1978); and "Sentencing" in Franklin Zimring and Richard Frase (eds.), *The Criminal Justice System: Materials on the Administration and Reform of the Criminal Law* (Little, Brown, 1980). For further details on the importance of legal representation to reduce abuses in criminal cases, see Jonathan Casper, *American Criminal Justice: The Defendant's Perspective* (Harper & Row, 1972); A. S. Matthews (ed.), *Legal Aid in South Africa* (University of Natal Press, 1974); Dallin Oaks and Warren Lehman, *A Criminal Justice System and the Indigent: A Study of Chicago and Cook County* (University of Chicago Press, 1968); and Lee Silverstein, *Defense of the Poor in Criminal Cases in American State Courts* (Little, Brown, 1965).

QUESTIONS

1. To what extent are disparities present in the criminal justice system across different types of defendants or different types of judges? Why?
2. How can the criminal justice system encourage judges to make more law-conforming decisions, when judges have a tendency to promote their own interests, which may conflict with the law, as in pretrial release?
3. How can the criminal justice system encourage prosecutors and defense attorneys to make time-saving decisions when they have a tendency to put off matters unduly?
4. To what extent are disparities across defendants lessened or changed by reducing judicial sentencing discretion?
5. What is the most meaningful way of developing nondiscretionary sentences and bond levels for judges to follow?
6. To what extent are disparities across defendants lessened or changed by using juries or attorneys as a check on abuses by judges?

REFERENCES

Atkins, Burton, and Mark Pogrebin (eds.), *The Invisible Justice System: Discretion and the Law* (Anderson, 1978).

Davis, Kenneth, *Discretionary Justice: A Preliminary Inquiry* (Louisiana State University Press, 1969).

Frankel, Marvin, *Criminal Sentences: Law without Order* (Basic Books, 1973).

Gaylin, W., *Partial Justice: A Study of Bias in Sentencing* (Random House, 1974).

Kadish, Mortimer, and Sanford Kadish, *Discretion to Disobey: A Study of Lawful Departures from Legal Rules* (Stanford University Press, 1973).

Long, Elton, James Long, Wilmer Leon, and Paul Weston (eds.), *American Minorities: The Justice Issue* (Prentice-Hall, 1975).

Stover, Robert, and Don Brown, "Reducing Rule Violations by Police, Judges, and Corrections Officials," in S. Nagel (ed.), *Modeling the Criminal Justice System* (Sage, 1977).

Trebach, Arnold, *The Rationing of Justice: Constitutional Rights and Criminal Process* (Rutgers University Press, 1964).

CHAPTER 9

Balancing
Public and Private
Sector Implementation

This chapter discusses the policy-relevant arguments in favor of socialism and capitalism in the 1980s and concentrates on the United States. These more modern arguments contrast with the more traditional arguments of classical Marxist-socialist literature or the classical laissez-faire capitalist literature. Relevant literature is cited, but arguments emphasize common sense rather than an appeal to authority.[1]

Basic Concepts and Criteria

Socialism is generally defined in terms of the following two key elements: (1) government ownership or collective ownership of the major means of production and distribution, and (2) government encouragement of equality of income and wealth, particularly through progressive income taxes and inheritance taxes, accompanied by government subsidies to aid the needy. Capitalism is generally defined as private ownership of the major means of production and distribution, with a minimum of government regulation. In a capitalistic system, the government doesn't advocate equality of income and wealth.

Socialism is basically either democratic or dictatorial, as is capitalism. Democracy is also generally defined by two key elements: (1) majority rule, whereby virtually all segments of the adult population can legally participate in choosing national leaders in the legislative branch of government and at least indirectly in the executive branch of government, and (2) permission for minority viewpoints to try to convert the majority, including the right to organize interest groups and to support candidates for office who are sympathetic to those viewpoints. A dictatorship lacks both majority rule and minority rights to convert the majority. Socialism and capitalism can also be defined in industrial or nonindustrial terms. To be *industrial* is to have a high percentage of the labor force involved in manufacturing goods or providing services, rather than in producing food.

Democratic capitalism versus democratic socialism is discussed in this chapter because they are the only seriously considered alternatives in the United States, where basic elements of democracy are generally taken for granted. The American population is, however, divided over the extent to which socialistic rather than capitalistic institutions are advocated. Regarding socialism versus capitalism, emphasis is on industrialized socialism and capitalism, rather than on forms from other technological systems, such as hunting and fishing, agricultural, or commercial societies before the nineteenth century. The chapter also concentrates on late twentieth-century technology, which moves away from relying on small factories using steam- and coal-driven machinery toward large factories using oil and nuclear fuels, with a concurrent trend away from large factory-labor forces toward more electronics and robotization.

To evaluate the conflicting arguments, it is helpful to establish a set of criteria general enough so both socialists and capitalists can agree that the criteria are worth achieving. We set forth four:

1. The production of a high gross national product. Both sides would agree that societal productivity, as measured by the GNP, is desirable.
2. Concepts of freedom and popular control, although they might be defined differently by socialists and capitalists. Socialists define freedom in terms of civil liberties or the United States Bill of Rights, whereas capitalists emphasize freedom of property and profit. Socialists define popular control in terms of voting power, but capitalists focus on consumer sovereignty in the marketplace.
3. The concept of opportunity. Socialists stress equality of opportunity, while capitalists concentrate on the quality of opportunity or how far one can advance.
4. The balance between security and initiative. Socialists lean toward security and capitalists toward initiative.[2]

Achieving More Gross National Product

Both socialists and capitalists agree that an economy which produces 100 units of goods is better than one which produces only 80 units, all other things held constant. They may both frown upon including in the gross national product income which is received from antisocial activities, although opinions about what is antisocial may differ. We will assume that the example consists of socially useful products.

Some socialists and capitalists believe that "small is beautiful," including small economies. They are unusual people who are expressing a nostalgic longing for a primitive communal socialism or individual entrepreneurship. These advocates are generally unwilling to forego the benefits of large-scale economies of operations, such as relatively inexpensive medicines, food products, housing, clothing, and other commonly accepted necessities. In view of the large and expanding populations of the world, they may, in effect, be advocating disease, starvation, and lack of basic necessities for most countries. A larger gross national product may even be desirable for industrialized countries like the United States. It can mean the production of goods and services that can raise the living standards for the world's poor as well as for the middle class.

SOCIALIST ARGUMENTS

To compare socialist and capitalist arguments concerning national productivity, think of the economy as involving a set of activities that relate to business, labor, government, consumption, and investment. Regarding *business* activities, socialists claim that government-owned business firms are more productive because they:

1. Eliminate duplicative services and facilities, such as one gas station on each of the four corners of an intersection.
2. Obtain the maximum benefits from large-scale operations which cannot be achieved if many small, competing firms exist.
3. Obtain maximum benefits from standardization while maintaining sufficient variety.
4. Eliminate seasonal and cyclical fluctuations in production through governmental economic planning of the nationalized industries, governmental control over monetary and fiscal policy, and some direct control over nonnationalized industries. Abolition of stock exchanges will also reduce the psychological cause of business cycles, and greater equality of income will reduce the underconsumption cause.
5. Eliminate the wasteful exploitation of natural resources.

Regarding *labor* activities, socialists believe that government ownership will improve productivity due to:

1. Employing human resources on the basis of competency, barring discrimination.
2. Providing security, free education, medical, and other services which will keep the labor force in good physical and mental condition.
3. Provide wages and psychological incentives in direct proportion to output and social contribution.
4. Eliminate exploitation of labor, such as excessive hours, undesirable working conditions, and lower wages.
5. Ban labor-union featherbedding and wage rigidities by eliminating fear of unemployment and by basing wages on supply and demand rather than on a desire to maximize income. Labor unions would, however, maintain or acquire important activities, such as bargaining, lobbying, management, grievance handling, social security administration, worker stimulation, education, and recreation.

Regarding *government* waste, socialists advocate that government:

1. Reduce economic imperialism and extreme nationalism, thus reducing war.

2. Reduce crime due to:
   a. less wealth extremes, unemployment, poverty, and slums.
   b. less economic frustration and thus less aggressive violence.
   c. less discrimination.
   d. government encouragement of constructive ways to spend leisure time.
   e. reduction of acquisitive greed.
   f. more professional and modern police, courts, and corrections.
3. Ban expensive government controls over private industry that are ineffective in eliminating capitalistic waste, but which decrease personal freedom and increase friction.
4. Bar protective tariffs and discriminatory immigration laws that prevent the maximization of benefits from comparative costs and that prevent optimum population distribution. Self-selected immigrants may be particularly ambitious.
5. Eliminate agricultural subsidies by promoting greater consumption and employing incentives for unneeded farmers to take city jobs.
6. Simplify the tax structure to equalize the tax burden; almost all taxes should arise from graduated wage deductions.

As for *consumer* waste, socialists desire to:

1. Eliminate exploitation of the consumer through high prices, defective merchandise, and misinformation.
2. Eliminate much selling and advertising cost.
3. Price goods to more accurately measure the relative intensities of human desires for them, in a system with greater equality of income.
4. Promote satisfaction from improving the national income by taking a dollar from the rich and giving it to the poor.
5. Eliminate restrictions on foreign trade, which prevents the standard of living from being maximized.

Regarding *investment* waste, socialists claim they can:

1. Eliminate exploitation of the investor as a consumer of stocks and bonds.
2. Step up investment in scientific research and other socially desirable projects.
3. Eliminate stock market speculation by closing the stock market. Speculating could not be a source of wealth or a temptation to lose one's savings. Speculators distort the price structure by buying when prices are already too high and selling when they are already too low.
4. Make investments that will not pay off for a long time. The government is better able to delay gratification than are corporate executives who are pressured to announce dividends and annual profits.
5. Amass enough capital to develop projects which are too large for individual entrepreneurs. For example, only the government seemed able to bring together enough capital to develop such projects as the

initial implementation of nuclear energy, synthetic fuels that involve creating oil-like fuels from organic materials, and the proposed large-scale development of solar energy, which may require microwave structures in the sky.

CAPITALIST ARGUMENTS

Monopolistic Business Firms. To improve the gross national product, capitalists downplay the notion of competitive wastes and emphasize that competition stimulates productivity. In the past, capitalist economies involved small competitive firms that could not take advantage of modern economies of large-scale production. They are currently dominated by large monopolistic or semimonopolistic businesses that use modern technology. If an efficient firm produces 1,000 units, and if there is a market for 2,000 units, then there will only be room for two efficient firms in that industry. As technology develops, there may be room for only one optimally efficient firm. The issue thus becomes whether the large, monopolistic business should be government-owned or privately owned, not whether it should be competitive or monopolistic.

For example, with monopolistic electric companies that already enjoy economies of large-scale operations, the main arguments favoring government ownership are as follows:

1. Government can borrow money less expensively and, if necessary, can raise money through taxation.
2. Government will be more sensitive to environmental protection.
3. Government might be more sensitive to safety and service quality.
4. Government might have better relations with workers and consumers.
5. Less friction would exist between government and the government-owned electric company, and there would be fewer attempts to corrupt politicians.

The counterarguments for preserving a natural monopoly in private hands include:

1. Government agencies' budgets are often strained; thus, they cannot raise capital for expansion any more easily than private industry can.
2. Managers of government-owned electric companies or factories have no more incentive to reduce pollution than managers of privately owned companies, unless the government establishes a rewards and penalties system for doing so. In the absence of such an incentive system, a good factory manager (both public and private) will try to produce as much output for as little cost as possible (including antipollution costs).
3. The quality of service provided by municipally owned enterprises, such as electricity, water, and transportation, surpasses that of privately owned counterparts only if the former are heavily subsidized to raise the quality. This has been especially true in instances when en-

terprises have been taken over by the government because they are not privately profitable.

4. Worker and consumer relations may be worse under government ownership if workers are not allowed to strike and if the enterprises are not responsive to consumer demands. The key issue may not be government ownership versus private ownership, but the extent to which workers and consumers participate (either directly or indirectly) in the decision making of the enterprises.

5. Relations between the government and the firms might improve if the government were to take over these natural monopolies. The question is whether those benefits would justify the friction costs that would be created. Socialists might consider it more important to improve the responsiveness of the firms to consumers, workers, and the community, than to opt for a nominal change in ownership which would not affect responsiveness.

Competitive Business Firms. Competition may be undesirable when it requires a natural monopoly to be broken into separate firms, as in providing telephone, electricity, water, natural gas, or railroad services. There seems to be no place in the United States where one has a choice of companies from which one can buy these products. It would be wasteful to have a duplicate set of telephone poles, underground electric cables, water mains, gas supply facilities, or railroad tracks. Competition, however, stimulates better consumer service and technological developments in the airline and trucking services, and in automobile manufacturing. If such competition is desirable, only private enterprise will provide it, because competition between government-owned firms is not productive.

Competition stimulates productivity, not only among firms, but also among individuals vying for Nobel Prizes, promotions, and praise from their colleagues. While this type of competition does not necessitate private ownership, it may flourish in this environment. Competition to earn the most money may be frowned upon by socialists who believe it fosters antisocial behavior. However, competition motivated by the desire to make the greatest social contribution is desirable by definition of social contribution. This spirit may be more inherent in a capitalist economy that emphasizes individualism than in a socialist economy that emphasizes collectivism.

Some 1900s Changes in Socialism and Capitalism. A major capitalistic argument used in the past against socialistic productivity has been that a planned economy could not work because it is too difficult to decide on prices and quantities by planning. Rather, the marketplace should determine prices. Some of its validity has been lost because socialist economies have proved themselves capable of functioning. They do so, however, by relying heavily on the marketplace and supply and demand factors to determine prices and quantities, although the business firms are government-owned rather than privately owned.

Many of the socialist arguments about exploitation and wastes involving business, labor, government, consumers, and investment have been deflated in capitalist societies since the Depression, due to a variety of regulations. Laws relating to union recognition, minimum wages, maximum hours, child labor, safe working conditions, union abuses, tariff reduction, elimination of agricultural subsidies, and consumer protection have been passed and enforced. In more recent years, legislation to abolish racial and sexual discrimination and pollution, and to provide increased equalizing benefits for the poor has been adopted and enforced. These occurrences raise the question, does a capitalist economy cease to be capitalist when there is so much regulation and public-aid activity? Thus, one more controversy has arisen between socialism and regulated capitalism, rather than between socialism and unregulated capitalism.

In a modern context, at least two general kinds of regulation exist. The more traditional regulation involves penalties and is associated with illegal practices relating to union-management relations, consumer protection, stock-market trading, environmental protection, and antitrust matters. The more recent regulation focuses on incentives such as tax reductions, subsidies, and the lessening of restrictions to encourage socially desired business behavior. This is endorsed by capitalist thinkers who advocate enterprise zones to relieve unemployment in inner-city areas by attracting businesses with these incentives. It is also endorsed by socialist thinkers who advocate that pollution taxes be funneled to government-owned or private businesses that adopt antipollution devices. Positive incentives may generate more socially desired behavior, but they may be more expensive, difficult to adopt, and not sufficiently effective where highly dangerous practices are involved.[3]

Achieving More Freedom and Popular Control

SOCIALIST ARGUMENTS

Both socialists and capitalists endorse freedom and popular control. By freedom, we mean the right of minorities to try to convert the majority. By popular control, we mean majority rule in the sense of voting rights for all adults, with one person, one vote. These concepts may, however, be defined and applied differently by socialists and capitalists. Socialists emphasize the *freedom* associated with the Bill of Rights or with Roosevelt's four freedoms, namely: freedom from want, freedom of religion, freedom of speech, and freedom from fear. Socialists claim they can provide greater freedom:

1. From poverty or want by way of more power to workers and consumers through prolabor and proconsumer legislation as well as government antipoverty programs.

2. Of religion through reduction in business control over church policy, as well as separation of church and state.
3. Of speech through the reduction of big business control over the media of communication, especially the press, radio, and movies. Under a socialist system, these media might be run by private organizations such as unions, cooperatives, and clubs, as well as by a theoretically representative government.

Regarding *popular control* and democracy, socialists claim that their system provides:

1. Greater popular control of a nation's economic structure through the legislature, political parties, and electoral process.
2. Greater worker control through employee representation, strong unions, and producer cooperatives, especially in agriculture.
3. Greater consumer control through consumer representation, strong consumer lobbies, and the encouragement of consumer cooperatives, especially in retailing.
4. Greater equality of political influence through reductions in unequal wealth, although inequalities, based on competence and interest in politics, will continue; the lessening of inequality in wealth will also mean greater equality of legal and judicial influence.
5. More leisure time and better education so that people can participate in politics and political discussion, although these may be related more to industrialization than to the nature of the economy.

CAPITALIST ARGUMENTS

When capitalists speak about freedom, they emphasize *freedom* of profit and property. The definition of freedom differs under both systems. Regulated capitalism restricts methods of profitmaking, particularly those designed to protect consumers, workers, stockholders, and the environment from being unduly exploited. Regulated capitalism also restricts freedom of property, at least by way of zoning laws and building codes. These laws, though, are often supported by capitalist property owners who are fearful that in the absence of such laws, other property owners will use their property to decrease the value of the neighborhood.

A stronger argument supporting capitalism with regard to freedom might be based on the recognition that government ownership can lead to a concentration of power which can be highly restrictive of freedom. Under a capitalist system, a difference exists between the government and private enterprise. The two serve as a partial system of checks and balances on each other. If the two are merged, the system wouldn't exist, and the government could become more restrictive of freedom than big business was formerly capable of becoming. This may be particularly true if the government outlaws strikes which were legal before industries were nationalized. The extent to which a powerful socialist government abuses its power depends on the presence of a strong two-party or multiparty system, counterbalancing interest groups, and on a democratic culture. In the absence of these factors, a move from capitalism to socialism could mean an undesirable move away from democracy, even as defined by democratic socialists.

With *popular control*, capitalists stress control over the marketplace rather than control over politicians. In a competitive industry, consumers can vote with their pocketbooks by buying the products whose benefits and costs they prefer. This is impossible when all the firms or production units in an industry are owned by the government, and thus are not competing with each other. In the past, socialists have argued that consumer sovereignty was a myth, by virtue of the monopolistic and near monopolistic nature of most major American industries. In recent years, however, that situation has changed substantially as a result of foreign competition. American business firms must now be more sensitive to their consumers in view of the competition from Japan, West Germany, Scandinavia, and other countries in autos, steel, textiles, and other basic products. One could argue that desirable international competition would be as prevalent if those industries were government owned. However, the government's incentive and ability to restrict desirable foreign competition might be stronger than that of privately owned industry.[4]

Achieving More Opportunity

SOCIALIST ARGUMENTS

Regarding opportunity, socialists emphasize equality while capitalists stress the possibility of unlimited opportunities. Equality of opportunity in society is certainly preferable to one that arbitrarily discriminates on the basis of race, sex, and other demographic characteristics, rather than on individual ability. The former type of discrimination can be logically opposed on the following grounds, among others (all of which were discussed in more detail in Chapter 4, "Equity as a Policy Goal"):

1. Manpower is wasted when people are not allowed to apply their skills or can apply them only if they overcome discriminatory barriers.
2. Talent is wasted when people with the potential to develop skills are deterred from doing so by a lack of available opportunities due to racial, sexual, or related discrimination.
3. Discrimination can depress the working conditions of the dominant group whose militant workers can be threatened with replacement by the group that is discriminated against.
4. Discrimination can have a depressing effect on how decision makers relate to members of the dominant group when they are accustomed to treating others poorly.
5. When discrimination means segregation, duplicative facilities can be highly expensive.

6. Segregation breeds depressed areas that suffer with high costs for police, fire, public aid, and other services.
7. Discrimination can adversely affect a nation's ability to win friends
   and influence people in the international realm.
8. Discrimination can weaken a nation's defense effort due to racial
   friction within the military.
9. Discrimination can breed a false sense of superiority among members
   of the dominant group and thus be a disincentive to ambition.
10. Discrimination can breed distressing guilt feelings among the domi-
    nant group.
11. Discrimination can generate hatred and even violence by the group
    that is discriminated against toward the dominant group.
12. Discrimination prevents members of the dominant group from being
    able to refrain from discriminating because they fear ostracism.
13. Discrimination creates opportunity costs for manufacturing firms
    that are unwilling to locate in certain areas where discrimination is
    strong.
14. Discrimination may mean lost consumer purchasing power that
    would be detrimental to the economy.
15. Discrimination may divide members of the dominant group, in-
    cluding older and younger members, and parents and their children.

Socialists argue that socialism will create (or enjoys) more equality of
opportunity because:

1. Job hiring and promotion will be based on applied ability since:
   a. advantages stemming from the inheritance of wealth and power
      will be reduced.
   b. merit examinations will be administered for positions in govern-
      ment-owned industry.
   c. evaluation procedures for job promotions will be more objective.
2. Discrimination based on the following will be prohibited: economic
   class background; race, religion, or ancestral nationality; regionalism
   and rural-urban distinctions; sex and sexual preference; age; and political beliefs. Socialists attribute much of the existing discrimination to
   economic frustration, a desire to lessen competition, economic scape-
   goating, a desire to exploit, and economic symbolism. These factors
   will supposedly be lessened under a socialist economy.
3. Free developmental services will be provided, freeing individuals to
   develop themselves and maximize their social contributions. Services
   would include: education, medical care, social casework counseling,
   recreational facilities, and rehabilitation programs for those mentally,
   physically, or emotionally incapacitated so that they can resume, if
   possible, a productive role in life.

CAPITALIST ARGUMENTS

Capitalists declare that equality of opportunity is meaningless if few opportunities exist. People may be better off in an unequal society where the

median family income is $20,000 than in an equal society where it is $2,000. This argument, however, partly assumes that capitalism can provide greater opportunities than socialism, which returns to the question of who can provide the higher GNP. Even if socialism could provide a higher GNP, capitalism can allow some individuals to prosper more than they could under more egalitarian socialism. This inequality may be an important stimulus for encouraging ambition and innovation. Just as capitalists are no longer opposed to virtually all government regulation, socialists no longer favor equality based solely on need. They recognize increasingly that some income, wealth, and other differentials may facilitate productivity and economic growth.

Capitalists also maintain that capitalism's unequal distribution of income and wealth does not necessarily create unequal opportunity. In a just, capitalist society, or one that is subject to equal-opportunity regulation, members of formerly discriminated against groups can advance themselves on the basis of their individual talents and can become rich if they work hard enough. Capitalists do not defend arbitrary discrimination, and they do not consider it inherent in a capitalist society; it may be inherent in an insecure society, but not a reasonably affluent one. To some extent, the antidiscrimination laws that were passed in the United States in the 1960s reflect affluent capitalists' willingness to make concessions. They also reflect the demands of those who had been discriminated against to share in an affluent society.

Discrimination does not necessarily disappear or even decrease with government ownership. If the Republic of South Africa were to nationalize some of its industries, discrimination might increase. Some of these private industries are influenced by American and British stockholders who would like to see less discrimination. And a society with a tradition of corrupt governmental favoritism (such as, to some extent, the Philippines and Latin America), may be better off keeping industry in private hands because factory owners would have a profit incentive to hire the most competent people. The effect of government ownership on equality of opportunity may, therefore, depend on societal traditions of fairness more than on ownership of the major means of production and distribution. These traditions were also cited as key factors influencing the possible effects of government ownership on freedom and popular control.[5]

Better Balance Between Security and Initiative

Both socialists and capitalists favor some degree of security within a society. Nobody wants an especially unstable society. They both also encourage initiative and new ideas. Nobody craves a society with the security of a well-managed prison at the expense of initiative being stifled. Security, however, requires some planning, whereas initiative involves spontaneity and taking chances. These two goals may thus be in conflict. A key goal, therefore, is to obtain an optimum balance between security and initiative.

SOCIALIST ARGUMENTS

Socialists decry an economy in which people are insecure about their continued future income. They believe that their system will provide greater economic security by:

1. Reducing unemployment through economic planning of the nationalized industries, government employment agencies, fiscal policy (as to government spending and taxing), monetary policy (as to government controls over the money supply), and some direct controls over wages and prices
2. Reducing fear of wage loss due to accident or sickness through factory safety programs, free medical care, adequate compensation laws, rehabilitation programs, and disability insurance
3. Reducing poverty and dependence in old age through retraining programs, tax-based pension systems, and jobs for all who can qualify
4. Guaranteeing economic security for those who are truly unable to work, such as dependent children, the totally and permanently disabled, and the unemployable aged

Socialists and capitalists also recognize other forms of insecurity. Many people lack the security associated with being a member of a stable family, neighborhood, or support group. Socialists more than capitalists find ways in which the government can provide each kind of mentioned security. Doing so may mean providing: (1) counseling to hold families together, (2) community facilities to create a feeling of belonging to a neighborhood, and (3) opportunities to join clubs and organizations.

Another noneconomic form of insecurity is the fear of being subjected to criminal violence and theft. Socialists feel that crime will be reduced when the economic causes of crime are reduced, but that relates to other issues associated with producing a high gross national product and providing for equality of opportunity. Having worthwhile noncriminal opportunities available that can be lost by engaging in criminal activities may deter criminal behavior more than the threat of substantial prison sentences.

A more modern socialist posture on security and initiative recognizes that contemporary capitalism is highly regulated, which may produce less managerial *initiative* than either unregulated capitalism or government ownership. A highly regulated industry may provide for a fixed rate of return on the capital invested, which may be a disincentive for developing new ideas, since a profit-making goal is absent. Under government ownership, factory managers could be encouraged to develop new ideas through the rewards of promotions, increased salaries, and societal recognition. Regulation can definitely be stifling, but the more meaningful alternative to it may be government ownership instead of unregulated private ownership.

Also on the matter of initiative, socialists aver that if an underdeveloped country wants to develop new industries, it can do so faster through government-raised capital and government planning than by relying on private capital. This may be especially true if private capital is lacking and foreign capital has too many strings attached, in terms of possible exploitation and political corruption. An example of socialist development is the Soviet Union. It was almost feudalistic in 1917, yet by 1958 had entered the space age ahead of the United States. Capitalists, however, point out how rapidly the United States was developed in the late 1800s under the influence of capitalist incentives. The truth is that an underdeveloped country can be rapidly industrialized under either socialism or capitalism, but the costs are high. Rapid socialistic development may severely restrict freedom to oppose the socialistic plans. Rapid capitalistic development may severely exploit workers, consumers, and even some investors, as occurred during the robber baron era of American development and the earlier era of the British Industrial Revolution. Arguments relating to how to industrialize a country are no longer applicable when discussing socialism versus capitalism in the already industrialized United States.

CAPITALIST ARGUMENTS

Traditionally, capitalists have fostered entrepreneurial *initiative*. To some extent, big business discouraged this phenomenon in the late 1900s, as new ideas resulted from government research or the research and development departments of large firms. However, as late as 1960–1980, many important new initiatives began with small businesses. These initiatives have especially occurred in the computer and electronics industry with the development of input, output, storage, and other auxiliary devices. If these small businesses had been eliminated in a government program to assume their previous functions, their replacements might not have exhibited that kind of creativity. Granting monopolistic patent rights can also stimulate small business creativity.

Being part of a large bureaucratic structure is stifling due to the numerous rules necessary to maintain organization, regardless of whether it is a government bureaucracy or a big business bureaucracy. Having small government agencies analogous to small businesses is no more beneficial than having government-owned business firms competing with each other. Many small businesses are inefficient and go bankrupt, but enough develop new, highly useful ideas to warrant preserving this type of economic entity. Even when economies of scale are not so great, the benefits of small business may outweigh the costs, just as competition may have both stimulus-benefits and duplication-costs.

On the matter of *security*, capitalists no longer concede that socialistic planning is capable of leveling the business cycle. A key aspect of socialistic planning in western societies has been to eliminate periods of unemployment by decreasing taxes, increasing government spending, and increasing the money supply, and then to eliminate periods of inflation by increasing taxes, decreasing government spending, and decreasing the money supply. This seemingly logical approach no longer works, partly because unemployment and inflation now tend to occur simultaneously. Even though unemployment may be up and business sales may be down, wages and prices do not fall because of the reduced competitive forces that might have formerly brought wages and prices down. Wages tend to be subject to control by labor unions, and prices are subject to control by near-monopolistic firms, rather than by the competitive forces of the marketplace.

Not even government ownership would guarantee full employment without inflation. Government-owned industries can only guarantee jobs if they are producing products for which there is a demand. Demand may fall off, however, due to international economic factors over which a socialist country has no control. The American automobile industry would probably be in as much trouble competing with Japan and West Germany if it were government owned. Inflation plagued socialist Poland in the early eighties because prices were driven up by product shortages as well as lack of productivity. This lack of productivity may owe itself to a failure to utilize modern methods of coal mining, shipbuilding, steel making, and other technologies, rather than because of its socialist economy. In fact, any industry with a captive market of consumers will lack incentive to adopt new, improved technologies, regardless of whether it is U.S. Steel or its Polish equivalent.

Even if socialism could provide the security of full employment without inflation, the cost might be prohibitive. Artificially low prices that would not meaningfully ration scarce resources would be required. For example, the rising price of gasoline was a key factor responsible for inflation in the late 1970s in the United States. Attempts to artificially depress gasoline prices by conserving gasoline consumption may be an undesirable disincentive to develop energy independence. Similarly, a socialist economy could secure full employment by employing people in artificially created jobs, rather than by creating jobs through the marketplace of supply and demand. Doing so, however, might be undesirably wasteful if those people are producing unneeded products and are not using their skills in a meaningful manner.[6]

Trends and the Future of Socialism versus Capitalism

PAST TRENDS

In examining trends from 1850 to 1950, one is struck by how much of what was considered socialistic in 1850 has been accepted without controversy in the United States since 1950. A dramatic illustration is to note the ten points

Karl Marx advocated in the Communist Manifesto of 1848 and the extent to which they are now part of American government and economy:

1. "Abolition of property in land and application of all rents of land to public purposes." People can still own land, but we now have zoning laws, building codes, and rent control.
2. "A heavy progressive or graduated income tax." Income taxes are now the main source of revenue for the American government.
3. "Abolition of all right of inheritance." People still inherit, but there are federal and state inheritance and estate taxes.
4. "Confiscation of property of all emigrants and rebels." The United States has had no violent socialist revolution in which that might have occurred. The property of emigrants was often confiscated after the American Revolution, and so was the property of southern rebels after the Civil War.
5. "Centralization of credit in the hands of the State." We have had a Bank of the United States since the early 1800s and a Federal Reserve System since the early 1900s.
6. "Centralization of the means of communication and transport in the hands of the State." We have had agencies regulating interstate communication, interstate commerce, civil aeronautics, and maritime shipping for some time. Now the government owns passenger railroads, municipal transportation, airports, and highways.
7. "Extension of factories and instruments of production owned by the state." The Tennessee Valley Authority and municipal utilities are an example of that.
8. "Equal liability of all to labor." Wartime and peacetime conscription exemplifies this point as do the work-incentive rules for public aid.
9. "Combination of agriculture with manufacturing." The United States has long had industrialized agriculture, with farms now more accessible by highways, telephones, and radio-TV.
10. "Free education and abolition of children's factory labor." The United States pioneered free public schools and state universities. Child labor has been illegal nationwide since the 1930s.

With respect to trends from 1850 to 1950, the government has grown tremendously in terms of the number of people who work for it, the size of the budget, and the nature of its activities. This growth has outdistanced that of the United States in terms of population and territory at federal, state, and local levels, although mainly at the federal level. This growth is due partly to socioeconomic forces—*pushing factors*—relating to:

1. growth of big business, accompanied by the loss of face-to-face consumer-manufacturer relations and the growth of monopoly power
2. growth of big labor and other pressure groups promoting government activities
3. increasing severity of war and defense needs
4. increasing severity of periods of depression and inflation
5. urbanization and the resulting loss of self-sufficiency
6. ideological competition with socialist systems

This growth is also partly due to the following *enabling factors*:

1. expanded sources of government revenue needed for conducting increased government programs
2. improved managerial techniques for handling large-scale government operations
3. changing constitutional interpretations

In addition to these pushing and enabling factors, there has also been the pulling or goal factor of a shift from a prevailing attitude that the best government is the government that governs the least to an attitude that the government has many positive responsibilities.

THE FUTURE

These enumerated past trends might lead one to predict that socialism is the wave of the future, but this is not necessarily so. The abovementioned forces are still continuing and will probably result in further governmental growth and activities, but not necessarily an increase in government ownership or in government-induced equality of income and wealth. To the contrary, socialists have lessened their call for increased government ownership. The French Socialist Party nationalized some additional firms when it assumed power in 1981, but not nearly as much as that advocated by the French Socialist Party in the 1930s. Western socialists are now more concerned with the issue of control of industry by workers, consumers, and the public than with the issue of ownership. It is being increasingly recognized that government ownership does not equal popular control, and that popular control is more important than ownership of a business. In West Germany and Japan, a key issue is the extent to which workers should participate in management decision making. This is also important to the Polish labor movement, which is advocating increased worker input into the decision-making processes rather than denationalization. Capitalists are more willing to concede some control than to concede outright ownership, which bodes well for partially reconciling socialists and capitalists. Also note that as of 1980, conservatives had a much more positive attitude toward the role of government in stimulating the economy. This manifests itself in the Reagan administration program to stimulate the economy through tax breaks, rather than to rely solely on the marketplace. These tax breaks may not be sufficiently focused or require enough of a quid pro quo, but they represent affirmative governmental planning by a conservative administration.

A middle ground is also being reached with equality of income and wealth. Socialists are no longer so strongly advocating redistribution of wealth or property. They are insisting upon better employment opportunities for the poor. In the United States, that partly means prohibition of employment discrimination along racial and ethnic lines (since the poor tend to be disproportionately black and Hispanic) and along sexual and age lines (since the poor tend to be disproportionately female-headed families, old people, or both). Providing more employment opportunities also means stimulating the private sector through subsidies to seek out the unemployed and underemployed. Educational subsidies are also advocated for the poor to obtain training that will qualify them for available and better jobs. Since the 1980s emphasis has been placed on increasing productivity and the gross national product, in contrast to the previous drive for equalization. Both socialists and capitalists would like to enable poor people and people in general to be more productive. The new emphasis on productivity and equality of opportunity also bodes well for a partial reconciliation of socialist and capitalist differences.

Those differences, though, will not disappear. Socialists will probably always demand more popular control and equality of opportunity than capitalists are willing to relinquish. The battle lines have shifted away from government ownership (irrespective of control), and away from equality (irrespective of the size of the pie to be equally divided). However, the intensity of these differences is likely to lessen because we have been moving away from a pyramidal economic class structure where a large mass of have-nots are at the bottom demanding more, and a small segment of haves are at the top resisting change. We have been moving toward a diamond-shaped economic-class structure, with a high percentage of the population being white-collar, middle-class people, rather than factory workers or factory owners. The socialist and capitalist advocates thus come from basically the same economic class, which mitigates antagonisms and facilitates a reasonably calm analysis of socialism versus capitalism. It is hoped that this chapter has contributed to this analysis.

NOTES

Thanks are owed to Belden Fields of the University of Illinois for his insightful comments concerning this chapter on socialism versus capitalism in a modern context.

1. The classic socialist literature includes Karl Marx, *Capital* (Kerr, 1906–1909) (originally published between 1865 and 1895); and Vladimir Lenin, *The State and Revolution* (International, 1932) (originally published in 1917). The classic capitalist literature includes Adam Smith, *The Wealth of Nations* (Methuen, 1930) (originally published in 1776); Alfred Marshall, *Principles of Economics* (Cambridge University Press, 1890). By *classic*, in this context, is meant highly influential works that were originally published between the late 1700s and the early 1900s up until about 1945. On the history of capitalism-socialism in theory and practice, see Edward Burns, *Ideas in Conflict: The Political Theories of the Contemporary World* (Norton, 1960); Harry Laidler, *Social-Economic Movements* (Crowell, 1946); and George Soule, *Ideas of the Great Economists* (Viking, 1952).

2. On the general aspects of socialism versus capitalism, see Ralph Blodgett, *Comparative Economic Systems* (Macmillan, 1956); William Ebenstein, *Modern Political Thought: The Great Issues* (Rinehart, 1954); William Loucks and William Whitney, *Comparative Economic Systems* (Harper & Row, 1973); Joseph Schumpeter, *Capitalism, Socialism, and Democracy* (Harper, 1942); and Earl Shaw (ed.), *Modern Competing Ideologies* (Heath, 1973). Modern defenses of socialism include Michael Harrington, *Why We Need Socialism in America* (Dissent, 1971); Robert Heilbroner, *Marxism: For and Against* (Norton, 1980); John Putnam, *The Modern Case for Socialism* (Meador, 1946); and Paul Sweezy, *Socialism* (McGraw-Hill, 1949). Modern defenses of capitalism include Milton Friedman, *Capitalism and Freedom* (University of Chicago Press, 1963); George Gilder, *Wealth and Poverty* (Basic Books, 1980); Frederick Hayek, *The Road to Serfdom* (University of Chicago Press, 1945); and Irving Kristol, *Two Cheers for Capitalism* (Basic Books, 1978). On regulated capitalism as a system between pure socialism and pure capitalism, see James Anderson (ed.), *Economic Regulatory Policies* (Lexington-Heath, 1976); Barry Mitnick, *The Political Economy of Regulation* (Columbia University Press, 1980); and James Q. Wilson, *The Politics of Regulation* (Basic Books, 1980).

3. On achieving a greater gross national product, see Kevin Allen (ed.), *Balanced National Growth* (Lexington-Heath, 1979); Ali Dogramaci (ed.), *Productivity Analysis: A Range of Perspectives* (Nijhoff, 1981); Walter Rostow, *The World Economy: History and Prospect* (University of Texas Press, 1978); Gail Schwartz and Pat Choate, *Being Number One: Rebuilding the U.S. Economy* (Lexington, 1980); George Sternlieb and David Listokin (eds.), *New Tools for Economic Development: The Enterprise Zone, Development Bank, and RFC* (Rutgers University Press, 1981); and Lester Thurow, *The Zero-Sum Society: Distribution and the Possibilities for Economic Change* (Penguin Books, 1980). On the economics of socialism in a modern Anglo-American context see Burnham Beckwith, *The Economic Theory of a Socialist Economy* (Stanford University Press, 1952); G. D. H. Cole, *Socialist Economics* (Gollancz, 1950); Ludwig Von Mises, *Socialism* (Yale University Press, 1951); and J. Wilczynski, *The Economics of Socialism* (Aldine, 1970). On the economics of capitalism, see Stuart Brandes, *American Welfare Capitalism* (University of Chicago Press, 1976); Stanley Lebergott, *The American Economy* (Princeton University Press, 1976); Andrew Shonfield, *Modern Capitalism* (Oxford University Press, 1965); Paul Sweezy, *The Theory of Capitalist Development* (Monthly Review Press, 1964); Jude Wanniski, *The Way the World Works* (Basic Books, 1978); and David Wright, *Capitalism* (McGraw-Hill, 1962).

4. On popular control and freedom, see Maurice Cranston, *What Are Human Rights?* (Basic Books, 1962); Norman Dorsen et al., *Political and Civil Rights in the United States* (Little, Brown, 1976); Ivo Duchacek, *Rights and Liberties in the World Today: Constitutional Promise and Reality* (ABC-Clio, 1973); Alexander Meiklejohn, *Political Freedom* (Harper, 1960); and Roland Pennock, *Liberal Democracy: Its Merits and Prospects* (Rinehart, 1950). On the politics of democratic socialism, see Richard Crossman, *The Politics of Socialism* (Atheneum, 1965); and E. Durbin, *The Politics of Democratic Socialism* (Routledge & Kegan Paul, 1965). On the politics of democratic capitalism, see Harold Chase and Paul Dolan, *The Case for Democratic Capitalism* (Crowell, 1964); Allen Guttmann, *The Conservative Tradition in America* (Oxford University Press, 1967); and Clinton Rossiter, *Conservatism in America* (Vintage, 1962).

5. On equality of opportunity, see Marian Palley and Michael Preston (eds.), *Race, Sex, and Policy Problems* (Lexington-Heath, 1979); and Harrell Rodgers (ed.), *Racism and Inequality: The Policy Alternatives* (Freeman, 1975). On the relations between socialism and capitalism and the interaction of economic

classes, ethnic groups, and the sexes, see Bernard Barber, *Social Stratification: A Comparative Analysis of Structure and Process* (Harcourt Brace, 1957); Milton Barron, *Minorities in a Changing World* (Knopf, 1967); Jerome Davis, *Capitalism and Its Culture* (Farrar and Rinehart, 1935); Raymond Mack, *Race, Class, and Power* (Northwestern University Press, 1968); and Wilbert Moore, "Sociological Aspects of American Socialist Theory and Practice" in Donald Egbert and Stow Persons (eds.), *Socialism and American Life* (Princeton University Press, 1952).

6. On the problems of obtaining economic security, see Milton Friedman, Philip Gagan, John Klein, Eugene Lerner, and Richard Selden, *Studies in the Quantity Theory of Money* (University of Chicago Press, 1956); John Maynard Keynes, *The General Theory of Employment, Interest, and Money* (Harcourt, Brace & World, 1964); Leon Keyserling, *Full Employment without Inflation* (Conference on Economic Progress, 1975); Maurice Lee, *Economic Fluctuations: An Analysis of Business Cycles and Other Economic Fluctuations* (Irwin, 1955); and Thomas Sowell, *Say's Law: An Historical Analysis* (Princeton University Press, 1972). On the problems of encouraging initiative and innovation, see Catherine Burke, *Innovation and Public Policy: The Case of Personal Rapid Transit* (Lexington-Heath, 1979); Office of Policy Development and Research, *Factors Involved in the Transfer of Innovations: A Summary and Organization of the Literature* (U.S. Department of Housing and Urban Development, 1976); Office of Technology Assessment, *Government Involvement in the Innovation Process* (Government Printing Office, 1978); Alex Osborn, *Applied Imagination: Principles and Procedures of Creative Problem-Solving* (Scribner, 1963); Simon Ramo, *America's Technology Slip* (Wiley, 1980); Jacob Schmookler, *Invention and Economic Growth* (Harvard University Press, 1966); Calvin Taylor and Frank Barron (eds.), *Scientific Creativity: Its Recognition and Development* (Wiley, 1963); and Louis Tornatzky, E. O. Fergus, J. W. Avellar, and G. W. Fairweather, *Innovation and Social Process: A National Experiment in Implementing Social Technology* (Pergamon, 1980). On the relations between socialism and capitalism and psychological attitudes such as security and initiative, see E. W. Bakke, *The Unemployed Man* (Nisbet, 1983); George Hartmann, "The Psychology of American Socialism" in Donald Egbert and Stow Persons (eds.), *Socialism and American Life* (Princeton University Press, 1952); Armand Mauss (ed.), *The New Left and the Old* (special issue of *Journal of Social Issues*, 1975); and "Economic Factors" in Ross Stagner, *Psychology of Personality* (McGraw-Hill, 1948).

QUESTIONS

1. Define socialism and capitalism. What criteria might be appropriate for comparing them? Why?
2. What are the socialists' arguments that socialism is capable of achieving a higher gross national product than capitalism? What are the capitalists' counterarguments?
3. What are the socialist arguments as to how socialism facilitates freedom and popular control? What are the capitalist counterarguments?
4. What are the arguments in favor of equality of opportunity, and what arguments do socialists use to show that socialism can achieve more opportunity than capitalism? What are the capitalist counterarguments?

5. What are the socialist assertions relative to improved security and initiative? What are the capitalist counterassertions?
6. What are the trends in the overall controversy between socialism and capitalism?

REFERENCES

Burns, Edward, *Ideas in Conflict: The Political Theories of the Contemporary World* (Norton, 1960).
Friedman, Milton, *Capitalism and Freedom* (University of Chicago Press, 1963).
Gilder, George, *Wealth and Poverty* (Basic Books, 1980).
Harrington, Michael, *Why We Need Socialism in America* (Dissent, 1971).
Heilbroner, Robert, *Marxism: For and Against* (Norton, 1980).
Kristol, Irving, *Two Cheers for Capitalism* (Basic Books, 1978).
Putnam, John, *The Modern Case for Socialism* (Meador, 1946).
Schumpeter, Joseph, *Capitalism, Socialism, and Democracy* (Harper, 1942).
Sweezy, Paul, *Socialism* (McGraw-Hill, 1949).

CHAPTER 10

Structuring Government for Greater Goal Achievement

This chapter discusses the relevance of basic governmental structures to effective public policy outputs. Examples are drawn mainly from American government, but there are references to other nations as well. The chapter is divided into the following four parts:

1. The main controversial issues in structuring governments
2. The relations among alternative government structures
3. The mutual effects of government structures on domestic and foreign policy
4. The effects of American government structures on societal productivity[1]

Controversial Issues in Structuring Government

The five basic dimensions that are especially relevant in discussing governmental structures relate to:

1. The national government to the state or provincial governments
2. The chief executive to the legislature
3. The courts to the executive-legislative branches of government
4. The political parties to each other
5. The government to the people

FEDERALISM

On national-provincial relations, there are basically three alternatives. They consist of:

1. A unitary form of government, in which all power goes to the national government to delegate to the states, as it sees fit
2. A confederate form of government, in which all power goes to the states to delegate to the national government, as they see fit
3. A federal form of government, in which a constitution specifies that some powers go to the national government and some powers to the state governments

Unitary government, the prevailing form in the world, is well exemplified by England. Examples of confederate governments include the American Articles of Confederation in the 1780s and the Southern Confederacy in the 1860s. The contemporary United States is a good example of the federal form of government. The United States, as of 1980, however, is more nearly unitary than it was as of 1880 or 1800, although the long-term trend has its ups and downs. Increased national government has resulted from socioeconomic forces such as increases in:

1. Severity of wars.
2. Interstate and international business.
3. Big labor and other pressure groups that seek aid and require regulation.
4. Urbanization and resulting loss of self-sufficiency.
5. Severity of periods of inflation and recession.
6. Competition with foreign ideologies.

It has also resulted from such enabling factors as:

1. Expanded sources of national government revenue for carrying on increased government programs.
2. Improved managerial techniques for handling large-scale government operations.
3. Changing constitutional interpretations.

The growth has also resulted from an ideological or attitudinal shift from favoring minimal government toward believing a government has many positive responsibilities. The increased national government represents absolute growth and growth relative to the states, but state government activities have also increased.[2]

SEPARATION OF POWERS

Apropos to executive-legislative relations, the basic alternatives are these:

1. A parliamentary form of government, whereby the legislature chooses the chief executive.
2. A monarchic or autocratic form of government, whereby the chief executive either selects the legislature or advisory body, or has none.
3. A presidential form of government, whereby the people choose the chief executive and the legislature independently of each other.

Parliamentary government is the prevailing form, and is exemplifed by England. Examples of monarchic autocracy include Saudi Arabia and the feudal versions of western European countries. The contemporary United States is a good example of the presidential form of government. The United States as of the early 1980s, however, allows more power to the chief executive relative to the legislature than it did in 1880 or 1800, although the long-term trend has vacillated. Increased chief executive power has resulted from the same socioeconomic forces, enabling factors, and ideological shift as the increase in national government power. Increased power of chief executives over legislatures represents absolute growth, but this is relative, because the power of legislatures has also increased.[3]

JUDICIAL POWER

Regarding judicial power, there are basically two alternatives:

1. A system of concurrent review, whereby the legislature, the chief executive, and the courts have equal responsibility for upholding the constitution.
2. A system of judicial review, whereby the courts (particularly the highest national court) are authorized to declare legislative and executive acts unconstitutional.

England exemplifies concurrent review. The United States represents judicial review, although this has changed. Prior to the 1930s, judicial review declared economic regulation unconstitutional, but showed little sensitivity to civil liberties. Since the 1930s, judicial review has left economic regulation to legislative discretion, and has declared much legislation in violation of civil liberties unconstitutional. The retreat from declaring economic regulation unconstitutional is largely due to the social forces mentioned previously that are responsible for the increased power of the national government and of the executive branch. The more aggressive position on protecting civil liberties is due to: (1) the growth of a more educated population which adapts to change and recognizes the value of minority viewpoints, (2) middle-class tolerance as contrasted to the greater anxieties of the rich in an unbalanced society, especially the newly rich, and to the poor, who cannot afford to be so tolerant of minority competition, (3) the pressure of interest groups like the American Civil Liberties Union (ACLU) and the National Association for the Advancement of Colored People (NAACP), (4) urbanism and its accompanying greater tolerance of deviant behavior, and (5) the growth of greater diversity in the American population.[4]

POLITICAL PARTIES

Political parties work together in groups to help elect their members to political office. The basic political party choices are:

1. A one-party system, in which opposition parties are virtually nonexistent, although the party may have factions.
2. A multiple-party system, although the parties may be grouped into coalitions.
3. A two-party system, wherein minor parties and factions within the two major parties may exist.

The Soviet Union is an example of a one-party system, as are many developing countries. France and Italy have multiple-party systems. Both England and the United States have basically two-party systems. Interest groups and associations and direct public participation supplement the political party system by converting portions of the public will into governmental policy makers or policy.

British and American parties differ to the degree that ideological difference between the political parties exist. The alternatives are:

1. A relatively strong ideological difference, generally over matters of socialism versus capitalism.
2. A relatively weak ideological difference, generally over the ins versus the outs, although with a different sensitivity to less well-off groups within the society.

The American party system has always been oriented toward two parties, although there have been changes in the party names, the influence of third parties, and the degree of factionalism. Ideological differences become greater in times of domestic crises, although the long-run trend is toward more liberalism by both parties for reasons that relate to the growth of economic regulation and civil liberties.[5]

DEMOCRACY

On the relation between the government and the people, there are two basic alternatives:

1. A dictatorial system, in which:
   a. the general public has relatively little impact on the government, and/or
   b. minority viewpoints are repressed.
2. A democratic system in which:
   a. the adult public has voting rights for determining officeholders,
   b. holders of minority viewpoints are allowed to try to convert the majority.

The Soviet Union qualifies as a dictatorial system, although it may be less dictatorial since Stalin's death. The United States is a democracy. Voting rights in the United States, though, were restricted until the twentieth century with regard to race, sex, and age. Free speech rights have also increased under twentieth-century Supreme Court interpretations, for reasons mentioned in the judicial power section.[6]

Relations among the Government Structures

This chapter treats American government structures as policies in three different ways: (1) how they affect each other, (2) as basic structural policies which affect domestic and foreign functional policies, and (3) as basic policies that facilitate and sometimes hinder societal productivity. As for the relations among government structures, there are five structures, which means 20 relations, as shown in Figure 10-1. In that figure, relation 1 deals with the impact of separation of powers on federalism, and relation 2 displays the impact of federalism on separation of powers. Thus, each relation corresponds to the impact of the column category on the row category. The order of the relations is the order in which they are discussed in the text.

The first pair of those 20 relations is the mutual impact of separation of powers on federalism. The separation between the national legislature and the chief executive weakens the national government, which may result in states exercising more power than would be the case with a more cohesive national government. In the other direction, the divisiveness of 50 states weakens the total American government, and may thereby create a semi-vacuum into which the president and the executive branch step to fill the need for more national leadership. The president, by his national constituency, represents national unity more than Congress, which reflects federalism by having two senators from each state.

The second pair of relations is judicial review and federalism. Judicial

FIGURE 10-1
Relations Among the Government Structures

	Federalism	Separation of powers	Judicial review	Two-party system	Democracy
Federalism		1	3	5	7
Separation of powers	2		9	11	13
Judicial review	4	10		15	17
Two-party system	6	12	16		19
Democracy	8	14	18	20	

review has restricted the power of the states. From 1880 to 1935, the Supreme Court declared many state statutes unconstitutional, arguing that they interfered with interstate commerce, violated substantive due process, or impaired the obligation of contracts. From 1935 on, the Supreme Court has declared many state statutes unconstitutional on the grounds that they violated the equal protection clause, due process, or the First Amendment. The Supreme Court has been more willing to declare state legislation unconstitutional than congressional legislation.

In the other direction, federalism has effected judicial review by generating the existence of state supreme courts which, in turn, also exercise the power of judicial review over legislation, although mainly on state legislation and constitutions. Until 1970, these state supreme courts were generally more conservative than the United States Supreme Court, especially on civil liberties matters. Since 1970, however, some state supreme courts have become more liberal than the United States Supreme Court. For example, some states have declared both capital punishment and the inequalities in educational funding across schools in different parts of a state unconstitutional.

The two-party system influences federalism by providing a connecting link between the states and the national government. Thus, the division between a state and the White House or Congress is lessened if they are controlled by the same political party, as they tend to be. In another direction, federalism affects the two-party system by encouraging the development of more decentralized political parties than would otherwise be the case. Some states, in effect, have both a national party organization and a state and local party organization, especially in those instances where there are differences between national and state Democrats or Republicans.

Democracy affects federalism by providing elections at both levels of government. This has a partially unifying effect, although there are attempts in some states to keep the elections at separate times. Also, federalism has adversely affected democracy by allowing for undemocratic states, such as when Mississippi, Alabama, Georgia, and South Carolina sought to disenfranchise blacks and poor whites prior to the civil rights period of the 1960s.

Judicial review had decreased the power of quasi-legislative regulatory agencies from 1880 to 1935, but it now readily allows such regulation. Separation of powers influences judicial review; that is, when Congress and the president are split between the two major political parties, they are less likely to interfere with judicial review by court-curbing legislation than when they are united by one party. This is especially true if the Supreme Court is dominated by the opposition party.

The two-party system decreases the separation of powers when the same party controls both the White House and Congress and increases it when opposite political parties control each branch. Separation influences the two-party system by creating presidential and congressional political parties the way federalism encourages state political parties that are separate from the national parties.

Democracy affects separation of powers since the voters demand participation in selecting both the President and Congress. Separation of powers, however, has adversely affected democracy by allowing less democratic parts of the country to unduly influence Congress. This happened for many years when southern senators and representatives from one-party areas blocked civil rights legislation by virtue of their seniority, committee chairmanships, and filibustering.

The two-party system stimulates judicial review when there is a party split between Congress and the Supreme Court, especially if congressional legislation is passed along party lines. Court-curbing activities most often occur when the dominant party in Congress disagrees with the judicial review of the Supreme Court. As for the impact of judicial review on the two-party system, it has prompted significant Supreme Court decisions, such as redistricting, the rights of minority parties to get on the ballot, the constitutionality of election financing laws, prohibiting white primaries, and decisions on residence or other requirements for voting.

Democracy may have an impact on judicial review to the extent that the Supreme Court is influenced by election returns. In 1936, the overwhelming victory of the Democrats may have been partly responsible for changing the Supreme Court's voting behavior. Presidential election returns are also influential because the president chooses members of the Supreme Court. Moreover, judicial review has furthered democracy through Supreme Court decisions which have protected minority-rights. On the other hand, the majority rule in judicial review is undemocratic when exercised by non-elected judges with long tenure. It is, however, democratic when exercised to allow minority viewpoints to try to convert the majority.

Democracy and the two-party system are partly related by definition. Democracy requires that minority viewpoints be allowed, which implies an opposition political party. Democracy is thus incompatible with a one-party system. Allowing minority viewpoints also allows for a healthy opposition party. The two-party system preserves democracy since the dominant party favors majority rule and the out-party supports minority rights.

Mutual Effects of American Government Structures on Public Policy

Public policy can be classified in a variety of ways. One classification is in terms of domestic and foreign policy. The most controversial issues in American domestic policy over the last generation have related to government regulation and the provision of public goods. Government regulation has included both economic and noneconomic regulation. The traditional economic matters concern inflation and unemployment, union-management relations, and consumer and antitrust matters. Noneconomic regulation involves nondiscrimination and environmental protection. Providing public goods includes public education, public health, and public aid. Foreign policy issues are divided into regions of the world, but for the past generation, most of these issues have related to competition between the United States and the Soviet Union, or to competition between American democratic capitalism and Soviet dictatorial communism.

Figure 10-2 displays ten relations between the five governmental structures and the two functional policy areas. Five of them treat the impact of the structures on the policies, and five cover the impact of the policies on the structures. There are thus 20 relations; 10 relate to domestic policy and 10 to foreign policy.

The figure clarifies that socioeconomic forces also influence governmental policies and structures. For example, the growth of large-scale economic units has been a key force in shaping domestic policy. Intimate contact between workers and employers and between consumers and producers has been lost. Likewise, the growth of nuclear missile warfare has played a major role in shaping foreign policy. It has generated a partial stalemate of military power between the United States and the Soviet

FIGURE 10-2
Mutual Effects of American Government Structures on Public Policy

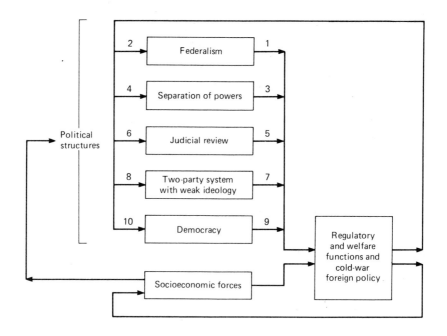

Union. Domestic and foreign policy can in turn influence socioeconomic forces, such as the growth of large multinational businesses. Socioeconomic forces also affect the structural variables, both directly (as, for example, when the Supreme Court responds to the historical context in which it operates) and indirectly, by their effect on domestic regulation and foreign policy, which in turn influences government structures.[7]

DOMESTIC POLICY

Federalism has influenced governmental regulation by making it more decentralized than it would otherwise be (e.g., telephone company regulation). It has provided: (1) testing grounds for new forms of government regulation in particular states (e.g., workers' compensation in Wisconsin); and (2) a less uniform regulatory program than a unitary governmental system would, with accompanying possibilities of intergovernmental conflict (e.g., trucking regulation) and intergovernmental vacuums (e.g., union-management regulation). Government regulation also has a feedback effect on federalism whereby the responsibility has increased the power of both federal and state governments. Relatively speaking, the increase has been substantially greater at the federal level, because many regulatory programs require interstate regulation to be effective (e.g., programs designed to prevent depression and inflation).

Just as federalism has produced relatively uncoordinated regulatory programs in intergovernmental relations, separation of powers has fostered relatively uncoordinated regulatory programs in interbranch relations. Separation of powers enables Congress and the administration to be controlled by opposed political parties or opposed ideologies, which leads to at least temporary inaction (e.g., the lack of a vigorous relief and recovery program between 1930 and 1932). On the other hand, increased government regulation has weakened the separation of powers by concentrating more quasi-legislative and quasi-judicial power in the hands of administrative agencies, where quicker and more expert action can generally be taken than in Congress or the courts (e.g., on transportation rate setting or adjudicating stock brokerage violations).

Judicial review has slowed the increase in governmental regulation (e.g., child labor cases), but has not prevented it. On the other side of the picture, government regulation has grown so large that this phenomenon, along with personnel and social changes, has probably contributed to the withdrawal of the federal courts from nullifying economic regulatory legislation since 1937.

The check and balance provided by the two-party system has made regulatory programs operate more efficiently then they otherwise would have done. The out-party is constantly trying to expose examples of waste, corruption, and unresponsiveness on the part of the in-party to the public. However, with the two-party system, regulatory program planning is more short-term oriented than a one-party system would be. Federal economic programs, for instance, generally cannot be planned for more than one administration period because of the possibility of a change in the political party occupying the White House. The relatively weak ideological split in the American party system, however, has meant that when the out-party assumes control, it will not drastically change all the former in-party's economic programs. Additionally, campaign disputes over regulatory issues are generally fought along pragmatic, rather than along ideological, lines of socialism versus capitalism. On the other hand, increased government regulation and regulatory issues have probably sharpened the differences between Democrats and Republicans. In the early 1960s for instance, the keenest interparty disputes were over Keynesian fiscal policy, Medicare for the aged, and President Johnson's antipoverty program. Upsurges in economic regulation during the Wilson and Roosevelt administrations clearly accentuated interparty differences.

The democratic platform for universal adult suffrage combined with relative freedom for unpopular viewpoints has enabled substantial economic reforms to be introduced without violent revolution. In both England and the United States, socialist-reformist philosophies were accepted without generating reactionary repression. Probably the most controversial relation shown in Figure 10-2 is that of economic regulation on democracy. If a democracy includes the right to operate a business for profit as the owner sees fit, without being subject to government regulation, then government regulation by definition has decreased democracy. If, on the other hand, one defines democracy in terms of universal adult suffrage combined with freedom to gain recognition of unpopular viewpoints, then most regulatory programs of the twentieth century have directly or indirectly increased American democracy. Surely, universal adult suffrage can be more effectively exercised by workers who have the time to familiarize themselves with politics than by those who have been working long hours since early childhood at a bare subsistence wage. Maximum hour, minimum wage, and child labor laws have freed workers to increase their political familiarity. Business regulation legislation has helped (along with the mass media and increased education) decrease the undue power that businesses exercised over state and federal legislatures in the past.

FOREIGN POLICY

In some ways, the mutual relations between governmental structure and American foreign policy are similar to those between structure and domestic functions. Federalism, for instance, has affected American foreign policy by making it more provincial and isolationist than it would be if state governments exerted less influence on the national government. When state or local governments act contrary to American foreign policy, federalism embarrasses the national government. Such occasions include the Little

Rock school desegregation riots, New York's attempt to disrupt the American acceptance of Czarist bank deposits in New York banks in payment of Russian debts in the 1930s, and the New Orleans lynching of Mafia-associated Italians in the 1900s. The national government, however, has been greatly strengthened by the cold war and increased American international activity because only it, and not the states, conducts diplomatic relations and provides for a common defense.

Separation of legislative and executive powers has hampered presidential foreign policy making in comparison with such countries as Great Britain, where the chief executive is always the leader of the dominant legislative party. A classic example of the lack of coordination is the post-World War I period when Congress and the president could not agree on the role the United States should play in the Versailles Treaty and the League of Nations. The cold war, however, has enhanced the president's importance by virtue of his access to secret diplomatic and intelligence information, his ability to make relatively quick decisions (combined with the increased need for such decisions), his power to recognize revolutionary governments, and his status (along with the vice president) as the only elected official with a national constituency.

Judicial review has hardly, if at all, affected American foreign policy. The Supreme Court has ruled that American treaties and foreign policy actions must conform to the Constitution, but the Supreme Court has never proclaimed a treaty to be unconstitutional. On the other hand, treaty making has affected judicial power because as the law of the land, a treaty empowers the courts to declare contrary state laws illegal. This power could become more important if the United States signs the United Nations Declaration on Human Rights, although practically all its provisions have already been incorporated explicitly or by interpretation into the federal Constitution or federal statutes.

The American two-party system divides a united front that the United States might otherwise counterpose against the one-party, communist system. This interparty friction, to the extent it exists, could have been a factor in Nazi Germany's conviction that the United States could be defeated. On the other hand, the cold war has promoted a substantial bipartisanship in Congress that might otherwise be absent.

America's democratic government influences its foreign policy by partially determining with whom and against whom the United States is allied. It also indirectly shapes American foreign policy by emphasizing debate and consensus. On the opposite side of the coin, the cold war and an intense foreign policy in general reduce aspects of democracy relating to the freedom to disagree. Tolerance of political nonconformists diminishes, particularly for nonconformists whose ideology leans in the same direction as the enemy's. Nevertheless, the cold war has strengthened American democracy by encouraging the political and economic upgrading of depressed economic and ethnic groups in order to unify the country and improve the national image. Some aspects of the New Deal—providing for the right to join unions and to set up social insurance programs—were probably motivated partly by ideological competition with the Soviet Union. Likewise, the cold war provided incentives to pass civil rights laws, which have broadened the base of American democracy.

RELATING POLICIES TO STRUCTURES

Substantive public policies can be grouped together by the government structures with which they are especially associated. For example:

1. Some policy fields, such as civil liberties, personal liability, and contractural rights, mainly involve policy making by judicial decision makers. Other policy fields involve presidential decision making, such as foreign and defense policy. For taxing and spending policy, Congress, state legislatures, and city councils are all important.
2. Local government has jurisdiction on policy matters of zoning, sanitation, police, fire, and schools, although these are often financed with federal money. The state controls criminal justice, property rights, and family relations. Foreign policy and defense, unemployment and inflation, and civil liberties policy are considered at the national level.
3. Relatively little citizen participation in policy making exists in policy fields at the national level. There is relatively much more in local fields, such as public housing, public schools, and public parks. Interest groups tend to be more important in fields where citizen participation is less important, such as economic regulation, including antitrust, consumer protection, and union management relations.
4. Private exercise of public functions constitute another grouping. This occurs primarily in local matters like hospitals, transportation, and communication, and less so in national matters like foreign defense and postal policy.

American Government Structures and Societal Productivity

Societal productivity means maximizing societal benefits minus societal costs through effective, efficient, and equitable public policies. American government structures both facilitate and hinder the achievement of this general goal. By discussing the productivity effects of these structures, the advantages and disadvantages of the structural alternatives are clarified in a more modern context than by referring to Montesquieu, Locke, Hobbes, Rousseau, and other political thinkers who were frequently mentioned when the American Constitution was adopted. The previous section emphasized how American government structures influence the substance and process of American domestic and foreign policy. This section illustrates how those structures influence the productivity of these policies and thus of society, although similar examples can sometimes be used for both matters.[8]

FEDERALISM

One way that federalism facilitates productivity is by providing a testing ground for new ideas, such as the contrived experiments of the 1970s, including the housing experiments conducted by the Department of Housing and Urban Development (HUD). In one such experiment, HUD arranged for rent supplements for the poor in a number of communities. In some of the communities, HUD specified maximum rents landlords could charge to protect poor people and the taxpayers from being overcharged. In other communities, landlords were not informed about what the maximum charge should be. In accordance with true experimentation, the communities were randomly allocated to each of these two alternative policies. Interestingly, the communities which, in effect, had rent control standards tended to charge higher rents under the rent supplement program than communities without rent control standards. The explanation was that the landlords interpreted the standards as allowing or even encouraging them to raise their rents to the maximum without risking loss of any rent-supplement tenants. In the other communities, landlords were reluctant to raise their rents for fear they would lose tenants who paid the rent reliably as a result of the rent supplements and who tended to take reasonably good care of the property as a result of the selection criteria for determining who received rent supplements.

Another example of how federalism aids productivity includes the attempts by the Law Enforcement Assistance Administration (LEAA) to fund special pretrial release projects in various communities and then compare them with one another or with communities having no projects at all. Federalism is not essential for the occurrence of such interplace experiments, since unitary governments can also conduct them in their diverse cities. A federal form of government, however, encourages diversity and an experimental bent across both states and cities more than a unitary government is likely to.

Federalism provides multiple policy-formation places for generating new ideas. In the United States there are 50 state governors and 50 state legislatures. They are more likely to introduce innovations on public policy than if they were, instead, employees in 50 field offices of a national government department. The semiautonomy of the 50 states generates independence which leads to innovation. Innovation, in turn, leads to increased productivity, although only a small portion of innovative ideas may be productivity successes. Examples include new technological and management science developments in dealing with crime, fire fighting, pollution, transportation, and other urban policy problems. State highway departments, for example, sometimes develop ideas relevant to road building, and state universities are certainly a source of innovations. However, state government agencies, in contrast to state universities, have not developed as many new technologies as private contractors have. This may reflect a lack of adequate incentives in state bureaucracies, but they are more likely to be innovative under a federal system than under a unitary system. State government agencies have generally not been as innovative as private business firms (with the exception of state universities versus private universities), but they are probably more innovative than federal field offices.

One of the main ways in which federalism encourages societal productivity is by creating a healthy competition among the states to attract businesses and population. While competition is healthy when it affords improved governmental services, it is not so healthy if it allows firms to operate with child labor, racially discriminatory practices, or unsafe working conditions. These socially undesirable forms of competition, though, are eliminated or lessened by federal legislation. To a considerable extent, people move from one state to another for reasons of economic opportunities, educational opportunities, and climate or scenery. State governments influence educational opportunities by deciding how much money to allocate to schools. They influence economic opportunities by offering tax breaks to businesses that locate in their respective states, especially when they have mutually beneficial interests. States can even influence the scenery factor by allocating money to improve their recreational environment.

On the other hand, federalism interferes with societal productivity by generating wasteful duplicative effort and conflicting governmental regulations. Maintenance of 50 state governments may not involve much incremental cost beyond what it would be if there were 50 or even 10 national government regions or subregions. More important, the costs of excessive duplication may be substantially less than the costs of missing the opportunities for innovation that derive from 50 government seats rather than one. As for conflicting interstate regulations, the Supreme Court declares them in violation of the free flow of interstate commerce. When businesses object to so-called conflicting state regulations, they generally oppose being subject to economic regulation, regardless of whether it is uniform or nonuniform regulation.

SEPARATION OF POWERS

Just as 50 state governments plus one national government are more likely to lead to innovative ideas than only one national government (with or without 50 regional offices), there would be more opportunities for innovation by having independent executive and legislative branches of government each separately seeking to appeal to voters. Separation of powers was originally defended as a conservative check-and-balance idea. It could also be defended as a method to increase innovation. However, by requiring that new ideas be adopted by two branches of government and two legislative houses, implementation of new ideas can be delayed.

A healthy competition between federal executive agencies and Congress clearly exists to develop technically competent units that can evaluate and propose new policies for achieving given goals. During the 1970s, four congressional agencies greatly improved their competence, namely, the General Accounting Office, the Congressional Budget Office, the Office of Technology Assessment, and the Congressional Research Service. The congressional staffs' competence in policy analysis also improved. The executive side, the Office of Management and Budget, the White House Domestic Staff, and specialized evaluation units within the Department of Housing and Urban Development, Health and Human Services, the Departments of Energy, Labor, and Defense, etc., were doing more systematic policy evaluation. These developments are partly attributable to executive agencies taking the lead and Congress feeling the need to keep up by improving its own policy evaluation competence. If the chief executive were an extension of the legislature by way of being a parliamentary prime minister, these developments, which are conducive to better governmental policies and societal productivity, would less likely occur.

Many recent examples illustrating this concept are apparent between Congress and the White House. For example, since 1965 substantial differences concerning foreign policy in Vietnam and in Latin America existed between the branches of government. There have also been substantial differences on methods forwarded to handle energy problems, inflation and unemployment, and social welfare matters. These differences have occurred no matter what party the incumbents were—when Congress was dominated by a different political party than the president was, as in the Nixon and Ford administrations; when Democrats controlled both branches of government, as in the Johnson and Carter administrations; and in the Reagan administration, with the White House and the Senate under Republican control, and the House of Representatives under democratic control. The key question is whether the productivity benefit of multiple sources of ideas outweighs the productivity detriment of slowness in adopting the new ideas. The system, in effect, compromises between innovation and stability, with innovation especially apparent during domestic crises, such as depression or recession or a period of upheaval in the demands of relatively worse-off groups within society, as indicated by the innovative policy periods of the 1930s and the 1960s.

JUDICIAL REVIEW AND JUDICIAL POWER

Whether or not judicial review has been conducive to societal productivity is a controversial issue. Judicial review suppressed workers' and consumers' rights from about 1800 to 1935, and it furthered minorities' rights from 1935 to the present. Thus, the value of judicial review to societal productivity depends partly on whether one considers the expanded rights of workers, consumers, and minorities to be productive or counterproductive. The matter of minorities is explored under the heading "Democracy." This section discusses worker and consumer rights, although it is partly an issue of socialism versus capitalism, which was discussed in the previous chapters.

Judicial review or judicial power can be discussed as an abstract structural matter (as was done with federalism and separation of powers) or as the substance of its exercise. As an abstraction, it seems neither productive nor unproductive, unlike federalism or separation of powers. Its productivity is more meaningfully judged by evaluating the substantive policies it has eventually allowed or even endorsed.

By increasing the rights of workers, the Supreme Court and the judicial process have advocated adopting labor-saving technology, which has thereby increased the productivity of labor and of society. The same concept can be applied to workers' rights with respect to child labor, minimum wages, maximum hours, unionization, occupational health and safety, and workers' compensation. Many of these rights have derived from legislation, but the Supreme Court has played an important role in nullifying or legitimizing the legislation, and the courts in general have often developed rights through their interpretation of statutes and/or common law principles.

On the other hand, one can argue that productivity increased most in the United States during the 1800s when the courts gave business largely a free hand in dealing with workers and consumers. A counterargument is that when one starts with such a low base, large percentage increases are easy to achieve. Further, in the 1800s, the geographical frontier and the new immigration facilitated productivity increases. Moreover, the 1800s represented a stage in knowledge development when inventions were relatively easy. They may be even easier now, however, given our greater knowledge base.

By increasing consumers' rights, the courts have encouraged the development of better-quality products. This has increased societal productivity in terms of societal benefits minus societal costs. Areas that have been influenced include: consumer rights (concerning labeling of products), product safety, rights to sue for negligent manufacturing, and rights to sue for breach of implied warranties. On the other hand, the best way to improve the quality of products is through the marketplace, by having people vote with their dollars. Yet, consumer sovereignty is meaningless in a relatively noncompetitive economy. Consumers can also exercise their dollar voting more effectively if informative labeling is required.

By increasing worker rights, workers' morale is lifted, their work attitude is better, and they are thus likely to be more productive. The question remains, is management happier when workers have more rights? Management's incentives to develop new technologies may be tempered, since the court decisions cause an enterpreneurial business to be less profitable than it otherwise would be.

Freeing capital from its obligations to workers and consumers does not guarantee it will be invested in improved technology. The freed capital may just generate bigger profits, bigger executive salaries, and more corporate waste. By freeing capital, however, business can earmark at least some of it for new technology development. One must be willing to incur some waste in order to get productive new technologies. Much of the potential technology money may go to profits and salaries, but if it goes to workers, it may be equally or even more unproductive.

THE TWO-PARTY SYSTEM

Democracy and the two-party system are interrelated, as mentioned in the section on the relations among the governmental structures. Majority rule would not be very meaningful unless political parties served as intermediaries between the people and the government. Political parties provide candidates for government representatives whom the majority will elect. Likewise, minority rights imply the right to form an opposition party for systematically expressing minority viewpoints and for attempting to convert the majority. In view of these relations, the following section on the productivity of both the majority-rule and minority-rights aspects of democracy is a main part of the discussion on productivity aspects of the two-party system.

Some aspects of the system should be mentioned separately from the democracy discussion. The two-party system stimulates more innovation than a one-party system, although maybe less than a multiparty system. The two-party system, however, functions more effectively and has more stability to carry out the dominant party's program than a multiple-party system. However, it may do this less effectively than a one-party system. In other words, the two-party system represents a compromise between (1) the greater innovation but lesser efficiency of the multiple-party system and (2) the lesser innovation but greater efficiency of the one-party system.

The lack of relatively sharp ideological differences between the American parties allows new ideas to be developed and applied without fearing that a change in the political parties will eradicate everything accomplished. On the other hand, the lack of ideological differences means less competition and thus less choice for the voters, although choices across individuals remain. Thus, American ideological differences provide more competition and choice than a one-party system or a system of nonideological parties, but not enough contrast to jeopardize desirable continuity when there is a change in parties.

DEMOCRACY

Democracy, as previously defined, includes both majority rule and minority rights to try to convert the majority to minority viewpoints. As for majority rule, the following points show how it is conducive to societal productivity:

1. People, by nature, desire to exert control over their destinies. Democracy provides them with the feeling that they play some part in controlling the government. Democracy thereby tends to make people feel happier in that regard, assuming all other things are held constant.

2. The more people who participate in government and politics, the greater the leadership pool and the innovation potential. Thus, if an adult with valuable ideas and leadership qualities is a member of a disenfranchised group, that person's abilities may not be well utilized.
3. A democratic form of government is more efficient because it can be more easily voted out of office. A government that is not subject to being removed by majority rule may be less likely to improve itself. It may change by shifting officeholders (the equivalent of a palace revolution), but not by altering basic principles.
4. A democratic government learns quickly about complaints, and can thus remedy the situation more readily. By doing so, the government will obtain more popular support and society will likely have a more productive population than if people feel antagonistic toward the government and society.
5. Democratic governments rely on an educated citizenry to function well, but they also encourage citizens to become more politically enlightened by providing them with learning experiences like participation in governmental activities, especially on the local level.
6. Democracies are criticized because of their inability to make fast decisions by virtue of their governmental structures, which require more approval by representatives of the people than other forms of government do. Such delays may, however, be more than justified if the decisions reached are more effective and efficient than they otherwise would be.
7. Democracies are also criticized because majority rule bestows much authority on those who lack an expert's knowledge, a favorable orientation toward new ideas, or an attitude toward being especially productive. This may be largely irrelevant though, if the leadership is reasonably knowledgeable, receptive to innovation, and oriented toward societal productivity.

As for the minority-rights element of democracy, the following points show how it is conducive to societal productivity:

1. In matters of science, the free circulation of popular, unpopular, and extremely unpopular ideas allows the truth a better chance of getting accepted. A dramatic example in which a dictatorial society was severely hurt by restricting freedom of scientific speech was Nazi Germany, with regard to the development of nuclear weapons. In the 1930s Einsteinian physics was viewed by Hitler as Jewish physics and was not encouraged. As a result, Nazi Germany lost time developing nuclear energy and weapons. In the meantime, Einstein helped convince President Roosevelt to develop the atomic weapons which helped the United States win World War II. A dramatic example in which a dictatorial socialistic society was severely hurt by restricting freedom of scientific speech was communist Russia, with regard to the development of hybrid grains. In the 1950s, Mendelian genetics was looked upon by Stalin as Catholic biology and was

discouraged. As a result, the Soviet Union provided a good environment rather than good genes for growing crops. Environmentalism conformed with Stalin's interpretation of Marxism. Those were the years in which the Soviet Union fell from being a breadbasket of Europe to an importer of foreign grains, to the substantial detriment of its economy and its international trade, from which it still may have not fully recovered.

2. In matters of policy, freedom of speech allows the most effective means for achieving given ends, which thus have a better chance of getting adopted. A dramatic example of this from within the United States is the prohibition on advocating the abolition of slavery, which existed in the South in the 1800s prior to the Civil War. Restrictions on this minority viewpoint may have delayed the conversion of the South from a slave economy to a free economy, which may have, in turn, facilitated the Civil War. More important, slavery's legacy was probably a key factor in holding back the South for years after the Civil War. Even now, it may be responsible for at least some of the race relations problems of the United States. Slavery is highly correlated with a relatively unproductive, inefficient economy that provides little incentive for introducing the modern labor-saving technology which can greatly raise standards of living. The poorest parts of the world practice slavery, serfdom, peonage, and related forms of human bondage, and generally restrict advocating alternative economic systems.

3. Freedom of speech checks corrupt, inefficient leadership that does not comply with the legal system. The United States Supreme Court has recognized (in some of its opinions) that freedom of speech may be the most important right in the Bill of Rights. The other rights are less meaningful if one cannot inform others that those rights are being violated. At the height of the Stalin era, even the dictatorial Soviet Union encouraged people to speak out against corrupt and inefficient leadership, at least at the lower and middle leadership levels, so long as the basic principles of communism were not attacked. The government has provided a subsidized periodical, *Krokodile*, which critizes bureaucrats who are not properly carrying out five-year plans and other Soviet policies.

4. Freedom of speech raises standards of living by way of points 1, 2, and 3 with regard to developing better science, public policy, and the implementation of science and public policy. Some of free speech's effects on higher standards of living are indirect, as it leads to increased industrialization and education, which in turn lead to higher standards of living. Cross-national studies which classify countries in terms of being permissive, middling, or repressive with regard to free speech, show that the more permissive societies enjoy the most industrialization and the highest standards of living, as shown in Tables 6-1 and 6-2.

5. An argument against freedom of speech is that it creates an unstable society by encouraging agitation and possibly even violent change. The realities, however, are just the opposite. The same cross-national

studies indicate that the more permissive societies are the most stable and effect change through peaceful means. The explanation is partly that free speech provides a safety valve which decreases the likelihood of resorting to violence. Free speech is also highly correlated with having a large, educated middle class, which in turn demands majority rule, which tends to facilitate nonviolent change. In the absence of majority rule, entrenched minorities sometimes have to be dislodged by means other than voting them out of office. Examples from history include the French Revolution, the Russian Revolution, and any revolution which occurred under circumstances that did not allow for substantial social change through electoral means.

Conclusion

EVALUATING GOVERNMENTAL STRUCTURES IN HISTORICAL TERMS

On the basis of this analysis, one can conclude that the American government structures may be desirable from the perspective of promoting societal productivity, but they are not necessarily transportable to other nations. In other words, these structures may be quite productive to the United States in light of its historical development, but they might not benefit another country, such as England or the Soviet Union, in light of its historical development. For example, federalism is more meaningful to the United States than to England because the United States is larger and more diverse and would be more difficult to govern as a unitary country. It also came into existence by building on 13 separate nations that formed a confederacy. For the country, a federal form of government was as big a step as it would have been likely to take, given its background.

Likewise, the absence of separation of powers in England reflects the fact that Parliament developed as a manifestation of middle-class opposition to a feudal monarchy. The prime minister was originally spokesperson for Parliament or the dominant party in Parliament. As the power of the monarchy receded, the prime minister became the chief executive, but his or her election by the Parliament, rather than by the people, was retained. The United States, on the other hand, elected its chief executive because it needed one, and a democratic procedure was more appropriate to the principles of the Declaration of Independence and the American Revolution than establishment of an American monarchy.

Judicial review is also more meaningful to America than to England. One cannot have a meaningful system of judicial review (whereby the courts determine whether the constitution is being violated by the executive or legislative branches of government) unless the constitution is embodied in a reasonably clear and integrated document. This is true of the American constitution. The British constitution (in the sense of the fundamental principles of British government) is scattered among a variety of documents and traditions. American judicial review also owes its existence to the coincidental presence of Chief Justice John Marshall in the formative years of American government, in view of his establishment of the principle in the case of *Marbury* v. *Madison*. This case allowed John Marshall to declare unconstitutional an act of the previous Federalist Congress which provided for judicial appointments that President Jefferson did not want to make.

The United States party system does not have as sharp an ideological split as the English party system, largely because the American population is not as sharply divided along class lines (in view of the greater upward mobility in the United States). To have a labor party, it is important for the working class to identify itself as a working class. In the United States, however, people have traditionally considered themselves only temporarily in the working class until they or their children could, through hard work and education, become management people or professionals. If the ideological differences are extremely sharp and antagonistic, a one-party system is likely to develop because the party in power may find it difficult to tolerate the opposition party, given a history of antagonism. This phenomenon helps explain the one-party system of the Soviet Union, where intense hatreds between the conflicting ideologies developed prior to 1917. This kind of conflict also leads to a tradition of not tolerating vigorous advocacy of minority viewpoints. As less developed countries become better educated, however, the people tend to demand more popular input and more tolerance of ideological differences.

EVALUATING STRUCTURES IN MORE GENERAL TERMS

In general, the position that a nation takes on each of the five basic dimensions reinforces the other positions. For example, federalism, separation of powers, judicial review, the two-party system, and democracy in the United States are supportive of each other, as indicated by the analysis of the relations among the government structures in Figure 8-1. Likewise, in England, the unitary system, parliamentary government, concurrent review, the two-party system, and democracy are internally consistent, given England's smallness, homogeneity, and history. Within the Soviet Union, the nominal federal system, parliamentary system, concurrent review, the one-party system, and the absence of democracy are also internally consistent, given its largeness, heterogeneity, and history. If these structures were to operate inconsistently within a country, they would likely undergo change, regardless of whether the inconsistency is among the structures or is between the structures and the society or the economy.

Within America, England, or Russia, the structures influence policy decisions. In the United States, they tend to make for more decentralization, less coordination, more constitutional constraint, more stabilized political competition, and more popular support than would be the case if the United States chose opposite positions on those five dimensions. English and Russian policy, on the other hand, are more centralized, more coordinated, and less constrained by constitutionalism. English policy, however, differs from Russian policy partly because of the two-party competition in England and the greater influence of the public and minority viewpoints.

Although the structures that a policy system adopts and maintains are likely to be internally consistent and to influence public policy, not all structures are equally productive in terms of facilitating policy choices that will maximize or achieve societal benefits minus societal costs. A political climate more conducive to the development of innovative ideas is produced by federalism, separation of legislative and executive powers, judge-made laws, two or more political parties, and democratic tolerance of minority viewpoints. Innovation may be the key to large-scale productivity improvement on the theory that operating with the previous pool of ideas may stagnate a society no matter how well those ideas are applied.

Implementation, however, is also important. Japan implements ideas obtained from elsewhere well, but it has not been one of the world's innovators. The United States has been highly innovative in its universities, small businesses, and some aspects of government research, but it has recently been slow to implement new ideas, especially when doing so requires adoption by so many governmental entities. What may be needed are a set of governmental structures that allow for multiple policy-formation foci, but at the same time provide for governmental institutions specifically oriented toward the implementation of new ideas for increasing societal productivity.

POLICY IMPLICATIONS FOR IMPROVING GOVERNMENTAL STRUCTURES

In 1982, the countries that are progressing fastest in terms of productivity improvement include Japan, West Germany, and Sweden. Their governmental structures do not differ greatly from the United States. All four countries are democracies with two-party or two-bloc systems. West Germany is a federal government, whereas the other two are unitary. Sweden has no judicial review, whereas the other two have some aspects of judicial review, partly imposed by the United States after the end of World War II. All three have parliamentary forms of government that may facilitate coordination, which the United States lacks, and which are helpful in implementing new ideas. However, the United States' reluctance to implement new ideas in the private and public sector may be attributable to the following factors:

1. American business' traditional captive domestic markets provide a disincentive to implement new ideas. Other countries have been more accustomed to international competition.

2. American business and American public opinion seek profits within a short time frame, which interferes with implementing expensive new ideas with long payback periods.
3. American business may be less respectful of American academics' new ideas than businesspeople in Japan, West Germany, and Sweden are of their academics' ideas.
4. American business has had less incentive to restart because it wasn't destroyed by bombs, as West Germany and Japan were.
5. Long-term expensive investment may have to be government-funded, but American business may be more resistant to governmental activity in business decisions.
6. American labor may be more resistant to implementing new ideas because it is more insecure than Japanese labor.
7. The United States spends a larger dollar amount and percentage of the budget for defense than any of these countries. These expenditures can seriously interfere with the United States' ability to implement expensive new ideas.

If the above factors are restraining America's implementation of new ideas for increasing societal productivity, how can the government lessen its adverse influence? Relevant policies corresponding to the previous seven factors include:

1. The American government can stimulate international competition by refraining from adopting tariffs or other restrictions on foreign trade. International competition will stimulate American business, as well as benefit American consumers.
2. Government must play a greater role in societal investment decisions in partnership with business and labor, as the Japanese government does. The government does not have to report yearly profits to stockholders, like corporate officers do. A long-term and more national perspective can thus be facilitated.
3. American government should improve relations between business and academe by subsidizing exchanges of personnel through visiting professorships and visiting executiveships, as well as through subsidized conferences, midcareer training, and better information systems.
4. Government can pay for the dismantling and replacement of obsolete equipment in industry.
5. American government should use more positive incentives to persuade business to engage in socially desired activities instead of relying on regulation, litigation, and negative sanctions, which inevitably generate negative relations between business and government.
6. American government policy should endorse job security, retraining, and loans to start new businesses and provide jobs, to calm the anxieties of American workers who feel threatened by the implementation of new ideas.

7. American government needs to pursue more actively an arms control agreement with the Soviet Union in order to free billions of dollars for implementing new ideas.

None of these suggestions require that the United States abandon its presidential form of government for a better-coordinated parliamentary form of government in order to implement desirable new ideas more easily. Perhaps a parliamentary form of government would produce greater societal productivity, if all the other variables were constant. The benefits of a parliamentary government, however, seem relatively trivial in comparison to the more important governmental activities mentioned above; so too in comparison to the productivity benefits of federalism, having two or more major political parties, and allowing popular minority viewpoints to have an opportunity to try to convert the majority. One also needs to be politically realistic and recognize that there is virtually no chance of changing from a presidential to a parliamentary form of government, given how well entrenched the presidential form is, and given its consistency with the democratic desire of the people to elect the president.

In conclusion, the United States' political structures are reasonably conducive to societal productivity. These structures do not require change, as they are constantly evolving to fit changing times. Rather government's policy makers must recognize that the American government is responsible for stimulating societal productivity. These positive responsibilities may manifest themselves as tax breaks for big business when a conservative administration is in power, or as expansion of the public sector when a liberal administration is in power. The important development in the 1980s is the recognition by both sides that societal productivity is too important to be left to society and the economy alone. The help of meaningful public policy making is necessary.

NOTES

1. There seem to be no books, book chapters, or articles that deal systematically with the relations between governmental structures and public policy. In American government, three kinds of textbooks are somewhat relevant. They include: (a) Textbooks that devote the first half to government structures and the second half to government policies, or at least have a lot of policy-substance chapters. An example is John Ferguson and Dean McHenry, *The American System of Government* (McGraw-Hill, 1977). Earlier editions, though, contained more policy chapters before it became popular to have separate policy-substance books. Also see John Straayer and Robert Wrinkle, *Introduction to American Government and Policy* (Merrill, 1975). (b) Textbooks that discuss government structures from a public choice perspective which emphasizes the use of deductive models for explaining the behavior of government officials, but occasionally talk in terms of the behavior or structures that will maximize given goals. Examples are Peter Aranson, *American Government: Strategy and Choice* (Winthrop, 1981), and

Wayne Frances, *American Politics: Analysis of Choice* (Goodyear, 1976). (c) Textbooks that are highly evaluative of government structures in an ideological sense. They tend to be explicitly liberal-Marxist-socialist or sometimes conservative-capitalist. Examples would be Edward Greenberg, *The American Political System: A Radical Approach* (Winthrop, 1977), Duane Lockard, *The Perverted Priorities of American Politics* (Macmillan, 1971), and Richard Saeger, *American Government and Politics: A Neoconservative Approach* (Scott, Foresman, 1982).

2. Discussions of federalism include Daniel Elazar, *American Federalism* (Crowell, 1972); William Riker, *Federalism: Origin, Operation, Significance* (Little, Brown, 1964); and Kenneth Wheare, *Federal Government* (Oxford University Press, 1963).

3. Discussions of.separation of powers include Peter Odegard and Victor Rosenblum (eds.), *The Power to Govern: An Examination of the Separation of Powers in the American System of Government* (Fund for Adult Education, 1957); Howard Ball, *Constitutional Powers: Cases on the Separation of Powers and Federalism* (West, 1980); and Alexander Hamilton, James Madison, and John Jay, *The Federalist Papers* (New American Library,1961).

4. Discussions of judicial review and judicial power include Alexander Bickel, *The Supreme Court and the Idea of Progress* (Harper & Row, 1970); Richard Funston, *A Vital National Seminar: The Supreme Court in American Political Life* (Mayfield, 1978); and Donald Horowitz, *The Courts and Social Policy* (Brookings, 1977).

5. Discussions of party systems include James Sundquist, *Dynamics of the Party System: Alignment and Realignment of Political Parties in the United States* (Brookings, 1973); William Chambers and Walter Burnham (eds.), *The American Party Systems* (Oxford University Press, 1975); and Everett Ladd and Charles Hadley, *Transformations of the American Party System* (Norton, 1978).

6. Discussions of democracy include Roland Pennock, *Liberal Democracy: Its Merits and Prospects* (Rinehart, 1950); Henry Kariel, *Frontiers of Democratic Theory* (Random House, 1970); and Henry Mayo, *An Introduction to Democratic Theory* (Oxford University Press, 1960).

7. On the relations between societal structures and societal functions, see Don Martindale (ed.), *Functionalism in the Social Sciences: The Strength and Limits of Functionalism in Anthropology, Economics, Political Science, and Sociology* (American Academy of Political and Social Science, 1965); and James Charlesworth (ed.), *Contemporary Political Analysis* (Free Press, 1967), 72–107.

8. An analysis of the effects of government structures on societal productivity is partly related to an analysis of the advantages and disadvantages of alternative government structures, although such analyses use a variety of criteria other than societal productivity. See Herbert Levine, *Political Issues Debated: An Introduction to Politics* (Prentice-Hall, 1982); Charles Dunn, *American Democracy Debated* (Scott, Foresman, 1982); Neal Riemer (ed.), *Problems of American Government* (McGraw-Hill, 1952); and Leslie Lipson, *The Great Issues of Politics* (Prentice-Hall, 1981).

QUESTIONS

1. What is the optimum way to relate a national government to the state and local governments in order to maximize national goals with minimum costs and minimum inequities?

2. What is the optimum way to relate the chief executive and the executive branch to the legislature in order to maximize governmental goals?
3. What is the optimum way to relate the courts to the executive and legislative branches with regard to interpreting and making law, including constitutional law?
4. What is the optimum way to relate political parties to each other in terms of their number and ideological differences?
5. Clarify the meaning of the following terms: *federalism, separation of powers, judicial review, political parties,* and *democracy.* Give examples, trends, and causes for the trends.
6. What are the relations among the five key dimensions for structuring a government?
7. How do government structures influence public policy choices and vice versa?
8. What are the benefits and costs of *federalism, separation of powers, judicial review,* the *two-party system,* and especially *democracy,* with regard to both majority rule and minority rights?

REFERENCES

Aranson, Peter, *American Governent: Strategy and Choice* (Winthrop, 1981).
Dunn, Charles, *American Democracy Debated* (Scott, Foresman, 1982).
Ferguson, John, and Dean McHenry, *The American System of Government* (McGraw-Hill, 1977).
Frances, Wayne, *American Politics: Analysis of Choice* (Goodyear, 1976).
Greenberg, Edward, *The American Political System: A Radical Approach* (Winthrop, 1977).
Levine, Herbert, *Political Issues Debated: An Introduction to Politics* (Prentice-Hall, 1982).
Lipson, Leslie, *The Great Issues of Politics* (Prentice-Hall, 1981).
Saeger, Richard, *American Government and Politics: A Neoconservative Approach* (Scott, Foresman, 1982).
Straayer, John, and Robert Wrinkle, *Introduction to American Government and Policy* (Merrill, 1975).

PART FOUR

Methods
of Evaluation

This section discusses various general methods for evaluating alternative policies for achieving given goals. These methods include:

1. *Deductive causal analysis:* deducing the effects of policies from premises that are empirically validated or intuitively accepted.
2. *Optimum choice analysis:* choosing among alternative public policies in which each is a discrete policy that does not allow for partial or multiple adoptions.
3. *Decision theory:* choosing among alternative policies in which the benefits or costs of each policy have to be discounted by the probability of those benefits or costs occurring.
4. *Optimum level analysis:* choosing along a continuum of alternatives where doing too much or too little is undesirable.
5. *Optimum mix analysis or allocation theory:* allocating a budget or other scarce resources among people, activities, places, or other units to maximize goal achievement subject to a budget constraint, or to minimize costs subject to a minimum satisfaction level.
6. *Threshold analysis:* resolving policy evaluation problems by reducing them to questions which ask whether one alternative is better than another without determining their rank order or the degree to which one is better than another.
7. *Percentaging analysis:* handling multiple goals and multiple policies by giving each policy a part/whole percentage on each goal and then calculating a weighted average percentage for each policy to determine which one or combination is best or how to allocate scarce resources among the policies.

8. *Statistical causal analysis:* generalizing about the effects of certain policies by gathering data on numerous past instances.

9. *Interdisciplinary analysis:* using the methods, goals, or means associated with political science, economics, or sociology and psychology, or their applied counterparts of public administration, business administration, or social work and education, or occasionally other fields of knowledge.

CHAPTER 11

Impact
and
Optimizing

All fields of scientific knowledge, especially the social sciences, are increasingly concerned about being relevant to important governmental policy problems. This increased concern has manifested itself in articles, books, journals, book series, convention papers, organizations, courses, curricula, grants, job openings, and other indicators of academic activity.

This trend began in the late 1960s as part of the general public's concern for civil rights, the war on poverty, peace, women's liberation, environmental protection, and other social problems. Its implementation was facilitated by the development and widespread application of computer software, statistical and mathematical methods, and interdisciplinary relations. The government's relative attractiveness as an employer and sponsor also increased as the role of universities in employment and research funding decreased.

Policy analysis or policy studies can be broadly defined as the study of the nature, causes, and effects of alternative public policies. Policy analysis is sometimes more specifically defined to refer to the methods used in analyzing public policies. The main methods, however, are no different from those associated with social science and the scientific method in general, except that they are applied to variables and subject matters involving relations among policies, policy causes, and policy effects. In that sense, policy analysis is not new methodologically. However, at least two relatively new and exciting developments are becoming increasingly associated with policy analysis.

One new development deduces the effects of alternative public policies before they are adopted, as contrasted to the more usual approach of quantitatively or nonquantitatively evaluating policies before and after they have been adopted. Deductive modeling involves drawing conclusions about the effects of policies from empirically tested premises, although the conclusions have not necessarily been empirically tested.

A second new development determines an optimum policy or combination of policies for achieving a given goal or set of goals. This evaluative approach can be contrasted with the more common situation in which policies are givens and the researcher determines the extent to which they are achieving their desired effects.

This chapter presents general principles concerning these new developments in deducing public policy effects and in optimizing public policy alternatives. Illustrative examples are drawn mainly from the criminal justice field, but the basic methods are applicable to a great variety of public policies.

Deducing the Effects of Policy Changes

GENERAL MATTERS

The main scientific alternative to deducing the effects of various public policies involves comparing people or places that have not experienced a certain policy, with people or places that have experienced it. This approach contains many methodological and normative defects. On a methodological level, none or not enough places may have adopted the policy. For example, currently, a leading criminal justice controversy is whether legislatures should specify a flat sentence to convicted defendants where judges would have no substantial discretion to deviate from these sentences. As of the late 1970s, we could not use a purely empirical or observational approach to evaluate this policy proposal because almost none of the states had adopted it. However, about ten states had done so by 1983.

Comparing places which have and have not adopted a policy may also be impossible because places without the policy do not exist, or all the relevant places adopted the policy simultaneously. For example, in the controversial *Miranda* decision, the Supreme Court required all states simultaneously to exclude the results of police interrogations in which indigent defendants were not provided with requested counsel. No state had previously adopted that rule, and after the rule was adopted, no control group existed for comparison purposes.

Along related lines, policies have been adopted by some states or places and not others, but the adoption involved nonrandom self-selection, which makes comparisons virtually meaningless. Random adoption means by pure chance. Nonrandom adoption can occur in various ways, such as being imposed from the outside on a selective basis. In American states, new policies tend to be adopted through self-selection, with each state deciding on its own what it will adopt subject to Constitutional constraints. For example, it may not be meaningful to compare murder rates in states that have capital punishment with those that do not, since so many other social characteristics relate to murder rates besides capital punishment, which may also relate to why some states have adopted capital punishment and others have not. One such social characteristic may be the existence of a relatively violent culture which causes both a high murder rate and a greater likelihood of adopting capital punishment as a means of dealing with murderers.

Another defect in the purely empirical approach is that the policy may have been adopted too recently for long-term evaluation. For example, the New Deal rural development program of the 1930s involved government purchase of bankrupt plantations and large farms in order to redistribute parcels to small farmers under long-term, low-interest mortagages. The program was judged a failure because so many of the small farmers were unable to maintain the payments and lost their land. However, 30 years later, in the 1960s, it was observed that the leaders of the voting rights movement in the Mississippi Delta were often older black farmers who had been among the recipients of the New Deal land redistribution, rather than young black militants. The older land-owning farmers fought for voting rights because they had more at stake in government programs and because they had less to fear with regard to losing their jobs. It took more than 30 years, though, to observe this effect, and most academics are unwilling to wait that long to publish the results of a before-and-after evaluation.

Another methodological defect in this system is that data may only be documented for the "before" period in people's memories, which may not be sufficient or reliable. For example, in a study of the effects of the Supreme Court's 1961 decision requiring the exclusion from state criminal courtrooms of illegally seized evidence, questionnaires were sent to police chiefs, prosecutors, judges, defense attorneys, and officials of the American Civil Liberties Union (ACLU), asking before-and-after questions. One interesting finding was that police chiefs in states that had adopted the exclusionary rule prior to the Supreme Court's ruling often thought it was imposed upon them by the Supreme Court. On the other hand, ACLU officials in states that had not adopted the exclusionary rule before the Supreme Court's ruling often thought their states had always had the rule. They could not imagine their states could be so insensitive to fair procedure that illegally obtained evidence would be admissible in court.

The approach of making comparisons across places or over time also has important normative or socially harmful defects, even if the methodology could accurately determine the effects of alternative public policies. One undesirable aspect of social experimentation is that once the policy is adopted, it is difficult to withdraw, even if the policy is ineffective or it produces undesirable consequences. This is exemplified by some aspects of the Law Enforcement Assistance Administration (LEAA). Although it has repeatedly been evaluated as being a relative waste of money in terms of crime reduction and other social indicators, it continues to operate with little change in its methods, mainly because vested interests have been established by federal, state, and local bureaucrats and grant recipients. The same reasoning may be applicable to farm programs which subsidize types of

farming that other governmental evaluators have found to be socially undesirable, such as tobacco farming or farming that is dependent on cheap
migrant labor.

Even when a governmental policy found to be harmful is terminated,
considerable damage could have been done while the policy existed. For
example, changing from a 12-person jury to a 6-person jury may substantially increase the conviction rate. If the change were implemented before
this was discovered, more innocent people would probably have been convicted. The damage from those wrongful convictions could not be alleviated
merely by terminating the 6-person jury policy.

To avoid these methodological and normative defects of the traditional
cross-sectional or time series analysis of policies or treatments, one can
attempt to deduce the effects of policies from empirically tested premises.
This kind of deductive modeling generally is based on one of three forms of
decision making: group, bilateral, or individual. A simple illustration of
each kind of deductive modeling applied to policy analysis research follows.

DEDUCTIONS BASED ON A GROUP DECISION-MAKING MODEL

A good illustration of this type of deductive modeling involves attempting to
determine the effects on conviction rates when juries are changed from
12 persons to 6 persons. At first, one might think this relation would be
simply determined by comparing the conviction rates in a state that uses
12-person juries with a state that uses 6-person juries. This approach is likely
to be meaningless because differences in conviction rates may result from
differences other than jury size, such as the characteristics of the law, the
people, or the cases in the two states or two sets of states.

As an alternative, one might do before-and-after comparisons in a
single state or set of states to control those characteristics which do not
generally change over short time periods. If the conviction rate was 64
percent with 12-person juries, the conviction rate with 6-person juries might
be substantially lower (although most criminal attorneys would predict a
higher conviction rate with 6-person juries). The conviction rate might fall
by virtue of the fact that if defense attorneys predict that 6-person juries are
more likely to convict, they would be more likely to plea bargain their clients
and to bring only their especially prodefendant cases before the 6-person
juries. Thus the nature of the new cases, not the change in jury size, would
cause at least a temporary drop in the conviction rate, and there would be no
way to hold constant the type of cases heard by the new 6-person juries.

As another alternative, one might suggest working with experimental
juries, all of whom would hear exactly the same case. Half the juries would
be six-person juries and half would be twelve-person juries. This experimental analysis is defective because its sample involves only one case, no matter
how many juries are used. Differences or nondifferences may be peculiar to
that one case, such as being proprosecution, prodefense, highly divisive, or

simply unrealistic, and the results may thus not be generalizable. For this method to work, it would be necessary to have about 100 different trial cases on audio- or videotape, selected in such a way that 64 percent of them have resulted in unanimous convictions before twelve-person juries and 36 percent in acquittals or hung juries as tends to occur in real jury trials. It would, however, be too expensive a research design to obtain and play so many trials before a large set of 12-person juries and the same trials before a large set of six-person juries, especially if the experiment lacks representative realism.

As an alternative to the cross-sectional, the before-and-after, and the simulation approaches, we could try a deductive approach to determine the impact of jury size on the probability of conviction. Table 11-1 shows, in a syllogistic form, how such a deduction might be made. The basic premise is that 12-person juries tend to convict 64 percent of the time, and individual jurors on 12-person juries tend to vote to convict 67.7 percent of the time. If jury decision making involved an independent probability model like coin flipping, individual jurors would vote to convict 96.4 percent of the time in order for 12-person juries to convict 64 percent of the time. If, on the other hand, jury decision making involved an averaging model analogous to bowling, where the 12 pins tend to stand or fall depending on what happens to the average pin, individual jurors would vote to convict 64.0 percent of the time in order for 12-person juries to convict 64 percent of the time. Since individual jurors actually vote to convict 67.7 percent of the time, jury decision making is much more similar to the bowling model than to the coin-flipping model. To be more exact, it is about 1.00 to 0.13, or 8.0 to 1.0, more like the bowling model. This information and some simple calculations analogous to calculating a weighted average between the two models enable us to deduce (as Table 11-1 shows) that if we switch from a 12-person jury to a six-person jury and everything else remains constant, the conviction rate should rise from 64 percent to 66 percent.

The conviction rate rises so slightly when jury size is reduced from 12 to six because jury decision making is more like the bowling or averaging model than it is like the independent probability or coin-flipping model. The reason the conviction rate goes up at all is probably because nonconvicting hung juries decrease with a 6-person jury since holdouts are less likely to have a fellow holdout for reinforcement. The number of reinforcing supporters is more important in maintaining a holdout than the number of opponents within the six-to-12 range. Knowing the relation between jury size and conviction rates can be relevant information as input into the empirical premises of an optimizing model designed to arrive at an optimum jury size that minimizes the weighted sum of type 1 errors (convicting the innocent) plus type 2 errors (not convicting the guilty). This, however, is a separate optimizing problem rather than a problem of deducing the effects of alternative policies.

TABLE 11-1
The Impact of Jury Size on the Probability of Conviction

I. Basic Symbols   ·

PAC = probability of an average defendant before an average jury being convicted (empirically equals 0.64 for a 12-person jury shown to two decimal places).

pac = probability of an average defendant receiving from an average juror a vote for conviction (empirically equals 0.677 for a juror shown to three decimal places).

II. Implications of the Coin-Flipping Analogy
(Independent Probability Model)

$PAC = (pac)^{NJ}$.

$0.64 = (pac)^{12}$, which deductively means the coin-flipping pac is 0.964.

III. Implications of the Bowling Analogy (Averaging Model)

$PAC = pac$.

$0.64 = pac$, which deductively means the bowling pac is 0.640.

IV. Weighting and Combining the Two Analogies

Actual pac $= [weight \ (coin\text{-}flipping \ pac) + (bowling \ pac)] \ / \ (weight \ + \ 1)$

$0.677 = [weight \ (0.964) + (0.640)] \ / \ (weight + 1)$, which deductively means that the relative weight of the coin-flipping analogy to the bowling analogy is 0.13.

V. Applying the Above to a Six-Person Jury

$PAC = [weight \ (coin\text{-}flipping \ PAC) + (bowling \ PAC)] \ / \ (weight + 1)$

$PAC = [0.13 \ (0.964)^6 + (0.64)] \ / \ 1.13$, which deductively means PAC with a 6-person jury is 0.66.

VI. Applying the Above to a Decision Rule Allowing Two of Twelve Dissenters for a Conviction

$PAC = [weight \ (coin\text{-}flipping \ PAC) + (bowling \ PAC)] \ / \ (weight + 1)$

$PAC = [0.13 \ (0.99) + (0.64)] \ / \ 1.13$, which deductively means that PAC with a 10/12 rule is 0.68.

DEDUCTIONS BASED ON A BILATERAL DECISION-MAKING MODEL

A good illustration of deductive modeling based on a two-sided, decision-making model involves attempting to determine the effect of increasing the pretrial release rate on the pretrial jail population. One might jump to the conclusion that if pretrial release rates increase, then, of course, the pretrial jail population will decrease. This, however, is not necessarily so, as is shown in Figure 11-1. This figure shows that an increase in pretrial release decreases guilty pleas by lowering a key cost—sitting in jail awaiting trial—

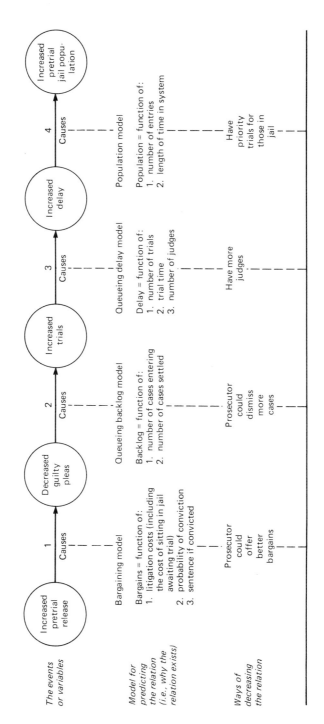

FIGURE 11-1
The Impact of Pretrial Release on the Pretrial Jail Population

that defendants otherwise often have to pay when they refuse to plead guilty. If more defendants are released prior to trial, they are less vulnerable to a prosecutor's promise to recommend a sentence equal to the time already served waiting in jail in return for a plea of guilty, or to recommend probation, which also means the defendant can be immediately released from jail. Thus, plea bargains will less likely be struck since the probability of arriving at a bargain is partly a function of the costs to the litigants of not reaching an agreement or, in this context, of forcing a trial.

If there is a decrease in guilty pleas, an increase in trials is likely. If trials increase, delay in the system will likely increase, since queueing models and common sense indicate that more trials mean more delay for those awaiting trial, in jail or out. If those awaiting trial in jail must wait longer, the jail population will increase since it is a function of (1) the number of people going to jail, which has gone down as a result of increased pretrial release, and (2) how long they remain there, which has gone up because of the increased pretrial release and its intervening effects. This increased jail time may more than offset the decrease in jail entries, thereby increasing, rather than decreasing, the pretrial jail population—all because of an increase in pretrial release.

It is interesting to note how each of the four relations of causal arrows at the top of Figure 11-1 is explained by a deductive model summarized in the middle of the figure. The first relation is explained by bargaining models which show that plea bargains are a function of litigation costs and the probability of conviction, and the sentence, if a conviction occurs, as perceived by the defendant and the prosecutor. One of the defendant's most important litigation costs is the cost of possibly having to sit in jail awaiting trial if a trial is demanded. By lowering this cost, the defendant's upper time limit is likely to be lowered, reducing the possibility that it will be higher than the prosecutor's lower limit, and thereby reducing the possibility of a settlement.

The second relation is explained by the queueing model for determining backlog sizes, and the third relation is explained by the queueing model for determining the amount of delay or time consumption per case. The fourth relation involves a population model like that which says the world's population is a function of the number of births and how long people live. Likewise, the jail population is a function of (1) the number of people entering the jail by not being released prior to trial, which has decreased; and (2) the length of time the average detained defendant lives in the jail, which has risen.

Interestingly, each model not only predicts and explains the chain of relations from pretrial release to the size of the jail population, but also suggests meaningful ways of lessening the extent to which these undesired relations occur, as is indicated at the bottom of Figure 11-1. The bargaining model suggests that the prosecutor could hold the percentage of guilty pleas constant, even in the face of an increased pretrial release rate, by making better offers to those who are released. The better offers might consist of shorter sentences and more probation than the expected value of the sentence if convicted, discounted by the probability of being convicted. Even if the guilty plea rate goes down, the prosecutor can hold the quantity of trials constant by dismissing more cases since he or she is under no obligation to prosecute just because the defendant pleads not guilty. Even if cases increase, delay can be held constant by providing for additional judges and other court personnel. If delays increase, the length of time spent in jail awaiting trial need not increase if the prosecutor provides priority trials for those who are in jail. Their cases could be tried before those of defendants who are out of jail.

DEDUCTIONS BASED ON AN INDIVIDUAL DECISION-MAKING MODEL

A good illustration of deductive modeling based on an individual decision-making model involves attempting to determine the effect on judicial behavior of publicizing judicial propensities. More specifically, the law provides that when in doubt, a judge should release rather than hold a defendant in jail prior to trial. In reality, however, as we discussed earlier, a judge stands to lose more by releasing a defendant who fails to appear for his or her court date or who commits a crime while released, than by holding a defendant who would appear without committing a crime while released. Thus, the rational judge, when in doubt, may tend to hold rather than to release because his or her expected cost of holding is less than the cost of releasing. The deductive modeling problem involves determining the effect on judicial behavior of publicizing the holding rates of judges in light of this decision-making model.

It is unlikely that publicizing the holding rates of the judges serving in a given area will lower these holding rates because this information will not increase the judge's costs of holding. Similarly, publicizing the holding rates for each individual judge on the court is not likely to lower the holding rates of the high holders because they can justify that their high holding is needed to decrease nonappearances and crime committing by defendants released prior to trial. If, however, the holding rates of individual judges are publicized along with the appearance rates and non-crime-committing rates they achieve among the defendants they release, the high holders might come down.

Empirical studies show that holding rates vary greatly across judges, but appearance and non-crime-committing rates tend to be almost uniformly high among both high-holding and low-holding judges. Thus, Judge Jones, who holds 80 percent of all defendants, may look bad in comparison with his fellow judge, Judge Smith, who holds only 30 percent of all defendants. Each is likely to have about a 90 to 95 percent appearance rate and non-crime-committing rate for those defendants they release. Judge Jones seems to be holding 50 percent more defendants than necessary to have a 90 to 95 percent appearance and non-crime-committing rate, even though we cannot determine whether Judge Jones has made any holding errors. This kind of publicizing increases Judge Jones' expected cost of holding and is likely to cause him to decrease his holding, if everything else remains constant. This effect can be further accentuated by also publicizing the undesirable effects and high social costs incurred by holding defendants in jail, such as jail maintenance, lost gross national product, increased number of families on welfare, jail congestion, and the frequency of held defendants being found not guilty, or only guilty of crimes involving sentences shorter than the jail time already served while awaiting trial.

The same individual decision-making model can be used to deduce other changes' effects on decreasing the decision to hold. The expected cost of holding relative to releasing is likely to decline if one decreases the costs of releasing by such means as making rearrests more easy through pretrial supervision or decreasing the time from arrest to trial, leaving the defendant with less time to disappear or commit crimes. The expected cost of releasing also decreases if the probability of appearance and non-crime-committing can be increased by improved screening and notification methods and by vigorously prosecuting those who fail to appear.

Optimizing Alternative Public Policies

GENERAL MATTERS

The main scientific alternative to optimizing alternative public policies is to accept policies as givens and then to determine their effects. This is often referred to as impact analysis or evaluation research. With an optimizing perspective, on the other hand, goals are givens and then policies that will maximize those goals are determined.

In general, the optimum policy (or set of policies) maximizes benefits minus costs, subject to economic, legal, political, or other constraints. Models for optimizing alternative public policies are classified in terms of whether they involve finding (1) an optimum policy level where doing too much or too little may be undesirable; (2) an optimum policy mix where scarce resources require allocation; or (3) an optimum policy choice among discrete alternatives, especially under uncertain conditions.

In optimum level problems, one needs to relate adoption costs and nonadoption costs to various policy levels. The optimum policy level is the level or degree of adoption that minimizes the sum of the adoption costs plus the nonadoption costs. In optimum mix problems, the relative slopes or marginal rates of return of each of the places or activities under consideration must be determined. If there are linear relations, the optimum mix allocates the entire budget to the most productive places or activities subject to the constraints. If diminishing returns are assumed, the optimum mix allocates the budget in such a way that the marginal rates of return are equalized across the places or activities so nothing can be gained by re-distributing the budget. In optimum choice problems, the benefits and costs of each choice must be determined. The optimum choice has the highest benefits minus costs, with the benefits and costs being discounted by the probability of their being received.

These general concepts and principles are greatly clarified by the following illustration of the three major types of optimizing models.

DETERMINING AN OPTIMUM POLICY LEVEL

A good example of finding an optimum policy level is the problem of determining the optimum size jury. Many states which have either lowered or are contemplating lowering their jury size from 12 to six or even five, to economize on the time and money spent on selecting 12-person juries, are facing this problem. The United States Supreme Court has heard a number of cases in which defendants have questioned the constitutionality of juries smaller than 12 persons. In the 1978 case of *Ballew* v. *Georgia*, the Supreme Court referred favorably to some of the policy analysis literature which has analyzed both the effects on conviction rates of changing jury sizes, and what the optimum jury size might be.

The relation between jury size and conviction rates can be the input into the empirical premises of an optimizing model designed to arrive at an optimum jury size that minimizes the weighted sum of type 1 errors of convicting the innocent, plus type 2 errors of not convicting the guilty. Figure 11-2 summarizes what this kind of analysis involves. The curve of "weighted errors of innocent convicted" was determined by using the analysis in Table 11-1, operating on the tentative assumption that a 12-person jury would likely convict an innocent person only about 40 percent of the time rather than 64 percent, and that about five out of 100 defendants tried by juries may be innocent. The curve of "errors of guilty not convicted" was determined with the tentative assumption that a 12-person jury would likely convict a guilty person about 70 percent of the time rather than 64 percent, and that about 95 out of 100 defendants tried by juries are guilty.

The "weighted sum of errors" curve was calculated by summing the other two curves (after multiplying the points on the first curve by 10 to indicate that convicting the innocent is traditionally considered 10 times as bad as not convicting the guilty). Using these tentative assumptions and this analysis, the weighted sum of errors bottoms out at jury sizes between 6 and 8. Justice Blackmun referred favorably to this analysis when he announced the Court's decision that it was meaningful for juries to be smaller than 12 but no smaller than six.

Justice Blackmun indicated agreement with the analysis in Table 11-1 and the 10-to-1 trade-off weight. The model, however, is not particularly sensitive to this trade-off weight because it can be reasonably varied and the

FIGURE 11-2
Graphing the Number of Errors for Various Jury Sizes

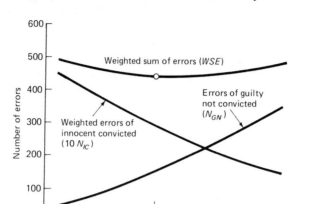

weighted errors curve will still bottom out at about 7. The model, however, is particularly sensitive to the assumption that prosecutors operate at a 0.95 level of confidence in deciding whether a defendant is guilty such that he or she can be brought to trial. If prosecutors are operating substantially below a 0.95 level, larger juries would be needed to protect additional innocent defendants from being convicted. If prosecutors are operating substantially above a 0.95 level, smaller juries could increase the probability of convicting these additional guilty defendants.

Thus, the optimum size jury mainly depends on one's assumption regarding how many jury-tried defendants out of each 100 are guilty. People favoring 12-person juries probably perceive the number of innocent jury-tried defendants as being greater than the number perceived by those favoring 6-person juries. Thus, the optimum jury size ultimately depends on normative values, rather than observed relations or relations deduced from empirical premises. Nevertheless, the combination of the predictive model of Table 11-1 and the optimizing model of Figure 11-1 enable us to better comprehend the factors involved in choosing among alternative jury sizes. The same analysis can be applied to choosing among alternative fractions required to convict, such as unanimity, a 10-to-12 rule, or a 9-to-12 rule.

DETERMINING AN OPTIMUM POLICY MIX

To illustrate finding an optimum policy mix, we will use the problem of determining what the optimum allocation is between law-reform activities and routine case handling in the legal services agencies funded by the Office of Economic Opportunity (OEO). The average legal services agency in 1971 had $67 to spend per client. Of that amount, not less than 10 percent could be spent on law-reform activities, and not less than 80 percent could be spent on routine case handling, according to the general policies of the national office. The question, thus, is how to allocate the $67 per client to maximize the program evaluators' satisfaction, or how to minimize expenditures while providing a minimum level of satisfaction.

To obtain the optimum mix, one could determine for each of a number of legal services agencies: (1) the overall satisfaction score it received in the 1971 evaluations; (2) the number of dollars it spent per client on law-reform activities; and (3) the number of dollars it spent per client on case-handling activities. One could then compute this data through a linear regression analysis. This equation tells us the relation between satisfaction on the one hand and law reform and case handling on the other, especially if other variables that might influence satisfaction were held constant. Such an equation indicates that law reform has a higher slope or marginal rate of return than case handling. With this finding, one can say the optimum mix for maximizing satisfaction is to allocate the minimum constraint to case handling and the rest of the per-client budget to law reform. Also, the optimum mix for minimizing expenditures is to allow the minimum constraint for case handling and the remainder to law reform, up to the point that a satisfaction score of 7 is obtained, since that score represents the minimum satisfaction level.

The actual average allocation was substantially less efficient than either of the above optimums because many conservative legal services agencies felt the emphasis on law reform would cause trouble with the national office. Many liberal legal services agencies that were dominated by a client orientation felt that individual clients did not desire law reform. The evaluators, on the other hand, were prominent lawyers who highly regarded the technical competence required to do such law reform work as appellate case argument, but they disdained the relative lack of competence necessary to do much routine case handling, like default divorce cases, regardless of whether the lawyers had conservative or liberal backgrounds. If the evaluators had included more low-income clients than lawyers, the slope of law reform may have become lower than the slope of case handling in the regression equation developed from the agency-by-agency data. The optimum mix, however, would still be the same if the law-reform slope were decreased but still higher than the case-handling slope, given the linear nature of the data for the somewhat narrow range of discretionary allocation.

DETERMINING AN OPTIMUM POLICY CHOICE

To illustrate how to determine an optimum policy choice, examine the problems of how a juror should decide whether to convict or acquit a given defendant, and how jurors should be instructed to maximize objectivity and conformity with the principle that convictions should occur only if the defendant is guilty beyond a reasonable doubt.

A rational juror should vote to convict or acquit, depending on which choice will give him or her the highest expected value, although these are calculated implicitly rather than explicitly. The expected value of each choice equals the perceived benefits minus costs, discounted by the probability of their being received. The probability in this context is that of the defendant actually being guilty. To obtain the highest expected value, a juror should vote to acquit if the perceived probability of guilt is below a threshold probability, and vote to convict if the perceived probability of guilt is above a threshold probability. The threshold probability can be determined by knowing the relative value a juror places on avoiding the conviction of an innocent defendant versus the acquittal of a guilty one.

To stimulate jurors to have a common threshold probability and a high threshold probability in the 0.90s in accordance with the law, jurors can be instructed that it is considered 10 times as undesirable to convict an innocent defendant than it is to acquit a guilty one (i.e., the 10-to-1 trade-off instruction). Merely instructing them that the standard of guilt is "beyond a reasonable doubt" or that a conviction requires a 0.90 probability does not generate a common or high threshold of probability. For example, male and female students at the University of Illinois were given diverse instructions on how to decide criminal cases, and then their threshold probabilities in rape cases were determined by asking them questions about their relative satisfaction or dissatisfaction from convicting a guilty defendant, convicting an innocent defendant, acquitting a guilty defendant, or acquitting an innocent defendant. The results were roughly as follows:

Type of Jury Instruction	Threshold Probability (in rape cases)	
	MALE	FEMALE
No instruction	0.65	0.45
Beyond a reasonable doubt	0.75	0.60
0.90 probability	0.85	0.75
10-to-1 trade-off	0.90	0.90

With no instruction, there is considerable divergence between the two groups and both groups are substantially below the desired 0.90 threshold probability. A verbal instruction increases both objectivity and conformity with the law, but not enough. A quantitative instruction makes for an improvement, but not as much as the 10-to-1 trade-off instruction.

Although the optimum choice seems to be the 10-to-1 instruction, the empirical reality is that, in general, no instruction is given. The difference between the empirical and the optimum may possibly be caused by judges being aware that a 10-to-1, a 0.90, or a verbal instruction will make convictions more difficult to obtain, which they oppose doing. We assume that judges have decided to go the no-instruction route because they perceive that convictions will be more difficult to obtain by giving the recommended instructions. We thereby deduce that their values must generally be oriented toward bolstering the conviction rate, since no other deduced value position seems capable of reconciling the decision reached with the assumed factual perception. This illustrates how optimizing analysis can often relate to making deductions about decision-making behavior, just as deductions about decision-making behavior can often be the premises for an optimizing model.

Conclusion

These aforementioned dimensions of deducing policy change effects and optimizing alternative public policies represent two of the newest and most interesting aspects of policy analysis research. Although newly conceived, they are rooted in a traditional social philosophy concerned with the logical and normative analysis, prevalent in the writings of such classical social philosophers as Aristotle, Saint Thomas Aquinas, and other pre-twentieth-century thinkers. They also acknowledge behavioral science's concern for quantifying relationships, prevalent in the post-World War II social science literature. Thus, policy analysis research synthesizes classical social philosophy and modern behavioral science as applied to important policy problems.

Policy analysis also synthesizes the interdisciplinary methodological and conceptual contributions from such disciplines as economics, business administration, industrial engineering, and social psychology. Political science and public administration contribute an added perspective that emphasizes the need to consider problems of policy adoption, implementation, and political philosophy. The examples we have presented are drawn from the substance of legal policy problems, but they can be easily analogous to policy problems from a broad variety of substantive fields. Both deductive modeling and optimization have wide potential applicability. We need even more researchers for developing this applicability for its theoretical and practical usefulness.

QUESTIONS

1. How does one deduce the effects on conviction rates of changing the size of juries from 12 to six?
2. How does one deduce the effects of judicial system changes on the likelihood and level of out-of-court settlements?
3. How does one deduce the effects of various changes on increasing the likelihood that judges will release more defendants prior to trial, rather than hold them in jail?

4. Provide examples of deducing the effects of alternative policies from: (a) an individual decision-making model, (b) a bilateral decision-making model, and (c) a group decision-making model, other than the main examples given in the chapter.
5. How does optimizing differ from determining or deducing the effects of alternative public policies?
6. How do the basic optimizing procedures differ with regard to optimum choice, risk, level, and mix analysis?

REFERENCES

Gass, Saul, and Roger Sisson, *A Guide to Models in Governmental Planning and Operations* (Environmental Protection Agency, 1974).

Greenberger, Martin, Matthew Crenson, and Brian Crissey, *Models in the Policy Process: Public Decision Making in the Computer Era* (Russell Sage Foundation, 1976).

Grumm, John, and Stephen Wasby (eds.), *The Analysis of Policy Impact* (Lexington-Heath, 1981).

Nagel, S., *Policy Evaluation: Making Optimum Decisions* (Praeger, 1982).

Quade, Edward, *Analysis for Public Decisions* (Elsevier, 1975).

Stokey, Elizabeth, and Richard Zeckhauser, *A Primer for Policy Analysis* (Norton, 1978).

White, Michael, Ross Clayton, Robert Myrtle, Gilbert Siegel, and Aaron Rose, *Managing Public Systems: Analytic Techniques for Public Administration* (Duxbury, 1980).

CHAPTER 12

Optimum Choice, Risk, Level, Mix, and Timing

Policy evaluation methods can be defined as the set of skills for determining which alternative public policies will maximize benefits minus costs in achieving a given set of goals.

Policy evaluation combines the fields of policy analysis and program evaluation. Policy analysis is characterized by its association with:

1. Political science and economics
2. Foreign policy, civil liberties, inflation and unemployment, and economic regulation, since these problems are emphasized in political science and economics
3. Policies across places and times
4. Taking goals as givens and determining the policies which will maximize or achieve them
5. Evaluating policies before they are adopted

Program evaluation is characterized by its association with:

1. Psychology and sociology
2. Health, education, and welfare problems
3. Policies as of a given time and place
4. Taking policies as givens and determining their effects
5. Evaluating policies after they have been adopted

Policy evaluation combines policy analysis and program evaluation across these five dimensions. The field of crime and criminal justice transverses both political science and economics and psychology and sociology. Examples will frequently be drawn from this field.

Maximizing benefits minus costs is the overall criterion for judging alternative public policies because it maximizes the favorable change in society's net worth or its assets minus its liabilities. Other criteria include:

1. Efficiency (benefits/costs or costs/benefits)
2. Effectiveness (benefits achieved)
3. Cost saving (costs incurred)

4. Equity (fair distribution of benefits and costs across groups)
5. Elasticity or percentage slope (percentage change in benefits divided by percentage change in costs)
6. Marginal rate of return or absolute slope (change in benefits divided by changes in costs)
7. Detriments/costs
8. Public participation
9. Predictability
10. Procedural due process

Policy evaluation methods fall into the following five categories:

1. Benefit-cost analysis (optimum choice among discrete alternatives without probabilities)
2. Decision theory (optimum choice with contingent probabilities)
3. Optimum level analysis (finding an optimum policy where doing too much or too little is undesirable)
4. Allocation theory (optimum mix analysis)
5. Time optimization models (optimum choice, level, or mix applied to time minimization)

This chapter is organized in five sections, corresponding to these five sets of skills or methods. Within each section, at least one illustrative example is presented, interspersed with and followed by relevant general principles.[1]

Choosing among Discrete Alternatives

The simplest kind of policy evaluation involves a set of discrete alternatives with no inherent order. This occurs when choosing among alternative legislative redistricting patterns, when choosing among alternative ways of providing legal counsel to the poor, and in deciding whether or not to adopt a policy of excluding illegally seized evidence from criminal proceedings.

DELIVERING LEGAL COUNSEL TO THE POOR

How to provide legal counsel to the poor is a good example of optimum choice without probabilities. There are basically three alternative policies through which the poor can be serviced:

1. Volunteer attorneys
2. Attorneys who provide services to the poor by way of a government salary
3. A Judicare system whereby poor people select private attorneys who will be reimbursed by the government

There are basically four criteria for evaluating the policies. The selected policy should be:

1. Relatively inexpensive
2. Visible and accessible

3. Politically feasible
4. Staffed by attorneys who have specialized competence and aggressive representation

Policy evaluation in this context involves determining:

1. The relevant policies
2. The relevant goals
3. The relations between the policies and the goals
4. The best policy in light of these relations

For each goal, we can indicate the policy alternative that is relatively more positive, meaning the alternative that best achieves the goal. These relations are summarized in Table 12-1. On being inexpensive, the volunteer system receives a plus, while the salaried attorney and especially the Judicare system receive relative minuses. On being visible and accessible, the salaried attorney scores a relative plus, and Judicare and especially the volunteer attorney system, relative minuses. On being politically feasible, neither the volunteer nor the Judicare system creates any substantial political problems; thus, they might be scored pluses, but the salaried attorney system has encountered political problems, which gives it a minus. The salaried attorney system, though, results in specialized competence and more aggressive representation, which gives it a plus, with minuses going to the volunteer and Judicare systems on that goal.

With this information, the volunteer and salaried systems are tied, with

TABLE 12-1
Evaluating Alternative Programs for Delivering Legal Counsel to the Poor

		Policies and Relations		
		VOLUNTEER	SALARIED	JUDICARE
Goal	*Weight*	(X_1)	(X_2)	(X_3)
Ya. Inexpensive	Less (0)	+	−	−
Yb. Visible and accessible	More (1)	−	+	−
Yc. Politically feasible	Less (0)	+	−	+
Yd. Specialized competence and aggressive representation	More (1)	−	+	−
Unweighted sum of pluses		2	2	1
Weighted sum of pluses		2−	2+	1−

+ = yes, relative to the other alternative policies (or 1).
− = no, relative to the other alternative policies (or 0).

two pluses apiece. The volunteer system scores well on being inexpensive and politically feasible, whereas the salaried system scores well on being visible and accessible, and being specialized and aggressive. To resolve this tie, these goals need relative weights. A conservative evaluator or policy maker would probably place relatively more weight on being inexpensive and politically feasible, and would thus favor a volunteer system. A liberal evaluator would emphasize being visible and accessible and specialized and aggressive, and would thus favor the government salaried system. As in most policy analysis, no conclusions can be reached without specifying the relative weights of the goals, even if goals are agreed upon. The policy analyst can, however, clarify the best policy in light of given goals and value weights. It is important to note that insights about which policy is best can be obtained by working with relations between policies and goals that are expressed only in terms of relative direction.

This right-to-counsel problem can be tackled by determining which policy scores highest on benefits minus costs, or which scores highest by summing algebraically the weighted positive or negative effects of each policy. Each effect can be expressed as a quantity multiplied by the price relative to each goal. Each quantity is either a 1 or a 0. For example, on being inexpensive, the volunteer system gets a 1 and the other two policies get 0s. Each value or price is also marked by a 1 or a 0. Thus, the value of being inexpensive gets liberals a relative 0, and conservatives a 1. Therefore, each of the three policies $(X_1, X_2,$ and $X_3)$ can be given a total score equal to $(QP)_a + (QP)_b + (QP)_c + (QP)_d$, which shows the benefits or costs which the policy achieves on each of the four goals. The policy having the highest total score is the best, assuming the Q scores are accurate and that one accepts the value of the P scores. One could probably move without difficulty from a binary 0 and 1 scoring to a rank-order scoring. The Q scores can then receive ranks of 1, 2, or 3, depending on how well each policy scores relative to the other two policies. The P scores can then receive ranks of 1, 2, 3, or 4, depending on how well each goal scores relative to the other three goals.

INCREASING POLICE ADHERENCE TO LEGALITY IN SEARCHES

The right-to-counsel problem is especially easy to solve, since the relations are each expressed as ones and zeros (or relatively low versus relatively high) and the weights for each goal are also expressed as ones and zeros (or relatively less or more). Whether to exclude illegally seized evidence from the courtroom exemplifies an optimum choice problem in which the relations can take a greater variety of positions. In 1961, the Supreme Court, in the case of *Mapp* v. *Ohio*, declared that the Fourth Amendment required illegally seized evidence to be inadmissible in criminal cases, at least when objected to by defense counsel.

In 1963, a questionnaire was mailed to one randomly selected police chief, prosecuting attorney, judge, defense attorney, and American Civil Liberties Union (ACLU) official in each of the 50 states to determine, among other things, their perceptions of changes in police behavior before and after *Mapp* v. *Ohio*. The experiment was aided by the fact that 24 states had adopted the exclusionary rule before *Mapp* v. *Ohio*. These respondents thus served as a control group. Twenty-three states were forced to adopt the rule at that time, and these respondents thus served as an experimental group. Three states had partially adopted it, and they were not used in the analysis.

Figure 12-1 shows that 57 percent of the respondents from the control group reported an increase in police adherence to legality in making searches since 1961, whereas 75 percent of the respondents from the experimental group reported an increase. (In 1961, the Supreme Court forced the newly adopting states to adopt the exclusionary rule.) This 18 percentage point difference cannot be readily attributed to a fluke in the sample of respondents since the probability is less than 5 out of 100 that one could

FIGURE 12-1

Evaluating Alternative Policies for Increasing Police Adherence to the Legality of Making Searches: *a*, The Relation Between Adopting the Exclusionary Rule and Increased Police Adherence to Legality in Making Searches; *b*, Alternative Policies and Goals Involved in Increasing Police Adherence to Legality in Making Searches.

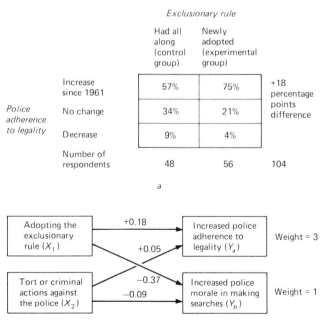

distribute 104 respondents over the six cells in Figure 12-1 purely by chance and end with a +0.18 relation. This +0.18 relation cannot be readily attributable to a misperception of reality on the part of the respondents, since agreement on the empirical question of police adherence to legality was so high among the different kinds of respondents from the same state or type of states, even though there was great disagreement on the normative question of the desirability of the exclusionary rule. The +0.18 relation between newly adopting the exclusionary rule and increased police adherence to legality in searches is largely attributable to the fact that the states that newly adopted the exclusionary rule also reported a disproportionate increase in programs designed to educate the police as to search-and-seizure law, which in turn correlates highly with increased police adherence to legality. States that had the exclusionary rule also often increased their police adherence to legality, possibly because the cases's publicity stimulated it and because long-term public opinion trends demanded higher standards of police behavior.

Figure 12-1b shows the relation between alternative policies and alternative goals involved in increasing police adherence to legality in making searches. The top part of Figure 12-1 shows that the exclusionary rule (X_1) should be adopted if increased police adherence to legality (Y_a) is one's only goal, since there is a positive relation between X_1 and Y_a. Many judges and others (including Felix Frankfurter in his dissenting opinion in *Mapp* v. *Ohio*) have argued that damages and criminal actions against the police are more effective than adopting the exclusionary rule in increasing police adherence to legality. The questionnare asked the respondents how often damages or criminal actions had occurred against the police in their communities for making illegal searches. If one divides the respondents into the relatively few who said there had been at least one such action in recent years versus those who said there had been none, there is only a +0.05 relation between the occurrence of such actions and increased police adherence to legality. The low relation and the low occurrence of such actions may be attributable to the fact that prosecutors are reluctant to prosecute the police who have been aiding them, and searched individuals are reluctant to sue because of the time, cost, embarrassment, unsympathetic juries, police discretion, and difficulty of assessing collectible damages. Thus, the exclusionary rule (X_1) should be preferred over damages or criminal actions (X_2), if increased adherence to legality (Y_a) is one's only goal, and if the decision maker cannot adopt both policies. This is so because there is a greater positive relation between X_1 and Y_a than there is between X_2 and Y_a.

An additional goal for handling the problem of increasing police adherence to legality in making searches is to simultaneously increase police morale, or at least not to decrease it. The questionnaire asked about changes in police morale before and after *Mapp* v. *Ohio*. The relation between respondents from a state that had newly adopted the exclusionary rule (X_1) and reporting increased police morale in making searches (Y_b) was a -0.37. The negative relation may be attributable to the fact that when evidence that the police have worked hard to obtain through what they considered a lawful search is thrown out, it demoralizes them and dampens their enthusiasm for making future searches. If the relation between X_1 and Y_b had been positive, like the relation between X_1 and Y_a, then it would be easy to decide in favor of adopting X_1. However, since the relation between X_1 and Y_b is negative, one must decide whether that negative relation offsets the positive relation between X_1 and Y_a. The matter is not resolved simply by noting that the X_1 and Y_b relation is greater than the X_1 and Y_a relation, because it is unlikely that one would weight Y_a and Y_b equally. If the Y_a goal has a weight of three times or more than the Y_b goal, then the -0.37 relation would not be enough to offset the $+0.18$ relation in view of the fact that three times 0.18 is greater than one times 0.37. On the other hand, if the Y_a goal has a weight of two times or less than the Y_b goal, then the -0.37 relation would be enough to offset the $+0.18$ relation. In other words, if the relation between X_1 and Y_a (times the weight of Y_a) plus the relation between X_1 and Y_b (times the weight of Y_b) is greater than zero, then X_1 should be adopted if Y_a and Y_b are one's only goals.

The most complicated situation involves both multiple policies and multiple goals, but even this problem is conceptually simple to resolve. Suppose the weight of Y_a is three times greater than the weight of Y_b, as determined by a survey of public, legislative, or judicial opinions. Note also that the relation between the occasional occurrence of damages or criminal actions against the police and increased police morale was a -0.09. Thus, the exclusionary rule (X_1) should be preferred over damages or criminal actions (X_2), if increased adherence to legality (Y_a) and increased police morale (Y_b) are one's only goals, and if the decision maker cannot adopt both policies. This is so because in Figure 12-1, the $+0.18 \times 3$ plus -0.37×1 is greater than $+0.05 \times 3$ plus -0.09×1. In other words, 0.54 plus -0.37 is greater than $+0.15$ plus -0.09.

The weight of each goal can be considered a price. The regression coefficients between each policy and each goal can be interpreted as a marginal rate of return, or a quantity of goal units to be achieved as a result of a one-unit increase in the policy. Thus, the total revenue from policy X_1 is equal to P times Q on goal Y_a, and the total cost from policy X_1 is equal to P times Q on goal Y_b. The relation between X_1 and Y_a is a benefit since the marginal rate of return or Q is positive, but it is a cost on Y_b since the marginal rate of return or Q there is negative. To compare X_1 with X_2, one logically compares the benefits minus costs which each policy produces. Instead of talking in terms of benefits and costs, one could simply talk in terms of effects. Policy X_1 has some positive effects and some negative effects. One can determine the algebraic sum of the positive effects ($P \times Q$

for Y_a) and the negative effects ($P \times Q$ for Y_b). One can do likewise for X_2, and then compare the net effects of X_1 and X_2 to determine which is better if they are mutually exclusive, or which is profitable if they can both be adopted.

One can determine the relative value of one goal versus another by surveying the relevant segments of the public or the government, or by performing a content analysis of relevant commentators. One can also relate each goal to a higher goal and use these relational coefficients to indicate the relative value of the intermediate goals. Additionally, one can use the values of the researcher, supplemented by a sensitivity analysis to show how the conclusions would change with other values.[2]

Making Decisions under Conditions of Risk

Sometimes one cannot decide among alternative policies by simply selecting the one that scores best on the benefits minus costs test because the benefits and/or the costs could be contingent on the occurrence of some event. The benefits and/or the costs must then be discounted or multiplied by the probability that the event will occur. This may occur when an administrative agency decides whether or not to gather certain data for future reference.

DATA GATHERING AS AN EXAMPLE

Virtually everyone is opposed to excessive data gathering by federal agencies. The key issue, however, is what is "excessive"? This example should give this concept some operational meaning. "Expected" benefits and costs refer to the benefits and costs of using (or not using) the data, discounted by the probability of its being used (or not being used). In other words, we have a decision problem under conditions of risk or uncertainty. As such, we can gain substantial insights by analyzing the problem in terms of a simple decision theory table.

Table 12-2 provides a decision theory table for analyzing a data-gathering problem. There are basically two alternatives available. One either gathers the data or a certain amount, or one does not gather the data. We could, however, complicate matters by talking in terms of gathering multiple quantities or percentages of data, and thus have many rows on our table. Such an extension can logically be made after clarifying the simpler choice between two alternatives. Likewise, there are basically two outcome possibilities. Either the data gets used in a certain way, or it does not get used at all. Again, we could further complicate the problem by talking in terms of multiple uses, with a separate expected benefit for each use.

With two alternative decisions and two alternative occurrences, there are four possible outcomes. Two are clearly undesirable or costly, namely, to gather the data and not have it used (cell C_g), or to not gather the data when it would have been used if it had been gathered (cell C_n). Two

TABLE 12-2
Deciding Whether to Gather Data That May or May Not Be Used

	DATA WOULD NOT BE USED $(1 - P)$	DATA WOULD BE USED (P)	EXPECTED BENEFITS AND COSTS
GATHER THE DATA (g)	C_g -10 Costs of gathering unused data	B_g $+100$ Benefits of gathering used data	$(B_g)(P) + (C_g)$ $(+100)(0.60) + (-10) = +5$
DO NOT GATHER THE DATA (n)	B_n $+10$ Costs saved by not gathering unused data	C_n -100 Benefits missed by not gathering used data	$(B_n) + (C_n)(P)$ $(+10) + (-100)(0.60) = -5$

Alternative Decisions

Rules for Applying the Above Figure:

1. Determine the alternative decisions (i.e., what is the data to be gathered or not gathered?). One can have multiple rows.
2. Determine the alternative occurrences (i.e., what is the potential use that will occur or not occur?). One can have multiple tables.
3. Determine the ratio of the costs of gathering the data to the benefits of gathering the data, but ignore the positive and negative signs.
4. If P is greater than that ratio, then gather the data. If less, don't gather the data.

Alternatives to Rules 3 and 4:

3. Determine the probability that the data will be used.
4. If the cost/benefit ratio is greater than that probability, then gather the data. If less, don't gather the data.

P = probability of use. B = benefits. C = costs. g = gathering the data. n = not gathering the data.

outcomes are clearly desirable or beneficial, namely, to gather data which subsequently gets used (cell B_g), and not to gather data which would not have been used if it had been gathered (cell B_n). Of the two undesirable outcomes, it is normally worse not to gather data that would have been used, although sometimes the other undesirable outcome may be worse.

If cell C_n is the least desirable of the two costs, then for convenience we can anchor it at a value of -100. For consistency, we could then also anchor cell B_n at $+100$ as the better of the two beneficial outcomes. Now all we have to do is determine how many times worse a cell C_n outcome is compared to cell C_g. If failing to gather needed data in a given situation would be 10 times as bad or as costly as gathering the data and not having it used, then the value of cell C_g on our -100 to $+100$ scale would be -10. Similarly, for consistency, the value of cell B_n would be $+10$. In this context, many people would find it simpler to work with the benefit/cost ratio of 100 to 10, or 10 to 1. And, instead of talking in terms of a scale of 0 to 100, or 1 to 10, one could substitute dollar amounts (or other units) for the benefits and the costs.

Armed with this information for our hypothetical situation, we can determine the expected values of gathering or not gathering the data. The expected value of gathering the data equals $(+100)(P) + (-10)$, where P is the probability that the data will be used. In other words, the expected value of gathering the data equals the benefits and the costs of the gathering, discounted by the probabilities of the benefits and costs occurring. Likewise, the expected value of not gathering the data equals $(+10) + (-100)(P)$, which equals the benefits and the costs of not gathering, discounted by their respective probabilities. Note that the cost of gathering the data is not discounted by any probability, since we must bear this cost when the data is gathered regardless of whether it is used. Similarly, we save this cost when we do not gather the data regardless of whether the data would have been used. We could take into consideration an embarrassment cost, which would have to be discounted by $1 - P$ since it is incurred only if the data is not used.

Logically, what we do now is determine how high P has to be before the expected value of gathering the data will exceed the expected value of not gathering the data. To do this, we have to set these two expected values equal to each other and solve for P. This will give us the threshold probability above which we should gather the data and below which we should not gather it. One can show algebraically that the threshold value of P (or P^*) equals C_g/B_g, ignoring the plus and minus signs. This means the data's threshold probability is 10 to 100, or 0.10. In other words, if there is better than a 0.10 probability that the data will be used, then we should gather it. Otherwise, it's not worth the trouble.

The above analysis can be applied without the users translating costs or benefits into dollars, satisfaction units, or any kind of absolute units. The users only have to determine which of the two undesirable outcomes is the more undesirable, and to determine the rough ratio of the undesirability of the more undesirable outcome to the less undesirable outcome, taking the specific situation into consideration. The users can then apply the simple formulas of C_g/B_g or the cost/benefit ratio to determine the threshold probability. They should then ask whether the actual or perceived probability in this specific situation is greater or less than the threshold probability. If it is greater, gather the data; if it is less, don't gather the data.

VARIATIONS ON THE BASIC EXAMPLE

If the cost of gathering the data is greater than the benefits, even before the benefits are discounted by the probability of their occurring, then we would not, of course, want to gather the data, no matter how high the probability that the data will be used.

This type of analysis could also be used to determine what the cost/benefit ratio must be in order to justify gathering the data. Suppose we know that the data has a 0.60 probability of being used. We have previously determined that the threshold probability is equal to the cost/benefit ratio. Therefore, if P equals 0.60, then the cost/benefit ratio must be less than 0.60 to justify gathering the data. If the cost/benefit ratio is greater than 0.60 and there is only a 0.60 probability of the data being used, the data should not be gathered.

This alternative type of analysis provides us with an alternative definition of excessive data gathering. It is excessive or nonrational to gather data when the opportunity cost of not gathering data that would be used is less than R^* times as great as the cost of gathering unused data. In this definition, R^* is the threshold ratio between the C_g and B_g costs when we know (or think we know) what the probability is of the data being used.

This type of analysis can also be used to make data gathering more rational, by concentrating on doing one of three things. First, increase the probability (P) that the data will be used, possibly by increasing its visibility. Second, decrease the relative cost of gathering data (C_g), possibly by providing for more automatic data-gathering routines. Third, increase the benefits of gathering the data when the data would have been used (B_g), possibly by providing more opportunities or ways in which data can serve as inputs into governmental decision making.

This type of analysis might help us better appreciate the value of data gathering. This purpose is harder to justify than the aforementioned purposes, which follow from the simple logic of the decision theory table. Saying the table is supportive of data gathering is based on a feeling that if the analysis is applied, one will generally discover that the threshold probability (P^*) need not be very h· ⅰ (relative to reality) to justify most data gathering, given the relative costs of the cell C_g and B_g outcomes. Also, the threshold ratio (R^*) of cell C_g to B_g probably need not be very high (relative to what it is likely to be in most factual situations) to justify gathering the data in question, given the probability of the data being used.

OTHER PURPOSES AND EXAMPLES

This type of analysis can be applied to a variety of administrative and policy problems involving decision making under conditions of risk. The problems can be classified in various ways. One classification emphasizes the purpose of the analysis, although this classification could be applied to other policy evaluation methods. One purpose is to aid decision making, which is illustrated by the example given about whether or not to gather data for future reference. A second purpose is to influence decisions, which can be illustrated by applying the last analysis to a would-be wrongdoer who is trying to decide whether to violate an administrative regulation in light of the probability of being detected, adjudicated as a wrongdoer, and negatively sanctioned (P), the error costs of committing the violation and being negatively sanctioned (A), and the error costs of not committing the violation when one could have gotten away with it (B). This analysis tells us that if we want to reduce violations of administrative regulations, we should increase P and A, and decrease B. If we can numerically evaluate P, A, and B, then we can calculate a threshold probability (P^*) and a threshold trade-off ratio (R^*) between A and B.

A third purpose is to make predictions rather than to make or influence decisions. This purpose can be illustrated by the example of trying to predict nonhearing settlements of worker's compensation cases or other kinds of claims. The claimant is likely to settle if the defendant offers more than the claimant's perception of the expected value of going through a hearing. This expected value equals the perceived award (A_1), discounted by the probability of the claimant winning the hearing on the liability issue (P_1), plus a discount which the claimant is willing to take off to avoid the expense of a hearing (X_1). Similarly, the defendant is likely to settle if the plaintiff is willing to accept less than the defendant's perception of the expected value of going to a hearing. This expected value equals the defendant's perception of the award (A_2), discounted by the probability of the claimant winning (P_2), plus a bonus which the defendant is willing to add on to avoid the expense of a hearing (X_2). One can predict the effect of system changes on the direction and possibly the magnitude of the likelihood and level of a settlement by knowing how these system changes influence A_1, P_1, X_1, A_2, P_2, and/or X_2.[3]

Making Decisions When Doing Too Much
or Too Little Is Undesirable

A common public policy problem involves deciding the extent to which a policy should be adopted when doing too much or too little may be undesirable. This optimum level analysis can be illustrated with the problems of arriving at an optimum level of delay in administrative or judicial proceedings.

MEASURING DELAY COSTS IN FINDING AN OPTIMUM DELAY LEVEL

Delay is a common problem in public administration, including judicial adminstration. Delay can sometimes be reduced through better allocation of resources, more careful sequencing of the way in which cases are heard, the use of a decision theory perspective to influence decision makers to make time-saving rather than time-lengthening decisions, and other management science methods. Before deciding how to reduce delay, determine the level of delay one should seek to achieve. One approach to figuring this is to determine how quickly it is possible to process whatever is being processed. This approach is referred to as *capability analysis*, because it emphasizes what one is capable of doing, regardless of the benefits or costs. One can determine how fast the cases could be processed by researching historical data, by seeing how fast they have been processed by other agencies, or by setting an average time that each case should take after adjusting for some measures of complexity.

Optimum level analysis represents an alternative approach. It recognizes that the speed-up costs may occasionally be greater than the delay costs, such that we may benefit by having some delay. Optimum level analysis in the context of optimum time consumption is designed to determine the optimum level of delay in the sense of minimizing the sum of the delay costs (Y_1) and the speed-up costs (Y_2). Figure 12-2 shows the factors involved in an optimum level analysis for a hypothetical metropolitan court system. To apply the analysis, we must develop an equation showing the relation between delay costs and time consumed. A survey and an accounting analysis might reveal that each extra day that completion of a criminal case is delayed costs the system about $7 per jailed defendant. This money represents waste in holding the defendants in jail who will receive an acquittal, dismissal, or probation when their case is tried. Of that $7, about $2 represents wasted jail maintenance costs, and $5 represents lost gross national product. The $2 is calculated by noting that it costs $6 per day to maintain a defendant in jail, and one-third of defendants receive nonjail dispositions upon trial, meaning $2 per day is wasted by delaying the nonjail disposition. The $5 is arrived at through knowing that defendants can earn about $15 a day if they are not in jail, and that about one-third of them would not be in jail if their acquitted or dismissed cases came up sooner, meaning an additional $5 per day is wasted by delay.

About $3.00 per day might be wasted per released defendant through waste in releasing the defendants who will be jailed when they are eventually tried and convicted, but who, during the delay commit a crime or have to be rearrested for failure to appear in court. This $3.00 is determined by calcu-

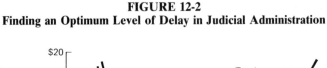

FIGURE 12-2
Finding an Optimum Level of Delay in Judicial Administration

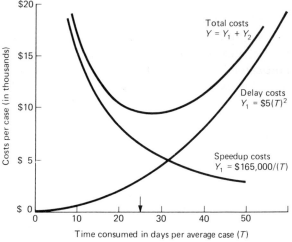

lating (1) the crime-committing cost or the rearresting cost for the average released defendant, (2) multiplying it by the low probability of the occurrence of crime committing or rearresting, (3) multiplying this figure by the middling probability of being convicted and jailed if the case were to come to disposition, and (4) dividing this number by the number of days released. If we assume half the arrested defendants are jailed and half are released, then the $7.00 delay cost per day per jailed defendant becomes $3.50, and the $3.00 delay cost per day per released defendant becomes $1.50. Thus, the total cost per day per case would be $5.00 (or $3.50 plus $1.50). If the $5.00 per day were a constant figure, we could say delay costs (Y_1) equal $5.00 times T days, or $Y_1 = \$5.00(T)$.

Since the likelihood of crime committing and the need for rearresting increase as delay increases, the relation between Y_1 and T might be better expressed by an equation, $Y_1 = \$5(T)^2$. This equation tells us that when T is 1 day, Y_1 is $5; but when T is X days, Y_1 is not $5 times X, but rather Y_1 increases at an increasing rate. More specifically, as T goes up 1 percent, Y_1 goes up 2 percent. The values of the multiplier of T and the exponent of T can be determined by performing a log-linear regression analysis if one has the following data for a set of cases: (1) the length of time each case lasted, (2) each case's rough cost in terms of jail maintenance and lost gross national product for those held, and crime-committing and rearresting costs for those released, and (3) the proportion or probability of cases in which nonjail sentences were handed down and the proportion of crime committing and rearresting of released defendants.

MEASURING SPEEDUP COSTS IN FINDING
AN OPTIMUM DELAY LEVEL

The more time consumed, the higher the delay costs become at a possibly increasing rate. However, the more cases are rushed to a disposition, the greater the speedup costs might be. These costs mainly include the monetary cost of hiring additional personnel or introducing new facilities or procedures. Suppose, either through deductive queueing theory or through the compilation of empirical data, we find that with only 20 judges, cases average 75 days per case; with 40 judges, 38 days; with 60 judges, 25 days; with 80 judges, 19 days. We can assume that with no judges, the number of days would rise to infinity, and to decrease the number of days to zero, we would need an infinite number of judges.

The speedup costs curve shown in Figure 12-2 incorporates this data and these assumptions. This kind of curve can be expressed by the equation $J = a/T$, where J stands for the number of judges, and T stands for time in days per average case. If $J = a/T$, then $T = a/J$. The a in the $J = a/T$ equation is the number of judges needed to reduce the time to one day per case (i.e., $T = 1$), and the a in the $T = a/J$ equation is the number of days consumed when there is only one judge (i.e., $J = 1$), if the relationships are carried out to their logical extremes, even though at the extremes the empirical data does not apply. From the above data and a computerized regression analysis, we can determine that $a = 1,500$. This means, according to our data, that $J = 1,500/T$ and $T = 1,500/J$.

Instead of discussing the relation between the number of judges and the number of days consumed, we should be noting the cost of judges and the number of days consumed. If one judge costs $40,000 a year, the per day cost would be $110, based on a 365-day year. Thus, the equation $J = 1,500/T$ should be changed to $Y_2 = \$165,000/T$. The Y_2 is the speedup costs or the additional judge costs, and the $165,000 is simply $110 times the previous a (also called the scale coefficient) of 1,500 to show we have increased the scale by $110 per judge per day. Our equation of $Y_2 = \$165,000/T$ is algebraically the equivalent of the equation shown in Figure 12-2 of $Y_2 = \$165,000(T)^{-1}$.

MINIMIZING THE SUM OF THE COSTS

Given the relationship between delay costs and time consumed of $Y_2 = \$5(T)^2$ and the relation between speedup costs and time consumed of $Y_1 = \$165,000(T)^{-1}$, the relation between total costs (Y) and time consumed is logically $Y = \$5(T)^2 + \$165,000(T)^{-1}$. We are now ready to calculate the optimum level of time consumed, which is graphically the value of T where the total costs curve hits bottom. Doing so involves recognizing that the total cost curve has a negative slope before it hits bottom, a positive slope after it hits bottom, and a zero slope when it bottoms out. Therefore, we must know what the slope of Y to T is. We can then set that slope equal to zero and solve for T. In elementary calculus, one learns that in an equation of the form $Y = aX^b$, the slope of Y to X is baX^{b-1}. Therefore, in our total cost equation, the slope of Y to T is $(2)(\$5)(T)^{2-1} + (-1)(\$165,000)$ $(T)^{1-1}$. If we set this expression equal to zero and solve for T, we get $10(T) - \$165,000/(T)^2 = 0$, or $T = (\$16,500)^{0.33}$, which means $T = 25$ days where the total costs hit bottom.

This means that 25 days, or about one month, is the optimum level of time consumption to minimize the sum of the delay costs and the speedup costs. We could also say that the optimum number of judges is 60, since $J = 1,500/T$, or $60 = 1,500/25$. This means that our court system would minimize its total costs if we had about 60 full-time judges. We could make this optimum level analysis more accurate by taking into consideration that speedup costs, (Y_2), may only be accurately indicated as a combination of the cost of judges, prosecutors, public defenders, other personnel, courtrooms, and other costs, rather than only judges. The methodology, however, is basically the same as we've already done. We must: (1) obtain empirical equations relating speedup costs to time and delay costs to time, (2) find the slope of the sum of these two equations, (3) set that slope equal to zero and solve for T to determine the optimum number of days per average case for minimizing total costs, and (4) thereby indirectly determine the optimum number of judges, prosecutors, public defenders, other personnel, courtrooms, and other costs.

OTHER EXAMPLES

Optimum level analysis can be applied to a variety of administrative problems in which too much or too little action is undesirable. The same general model and methods can be used to understand how much due process should be provided in administrative proceedings. By due process we mean safeguards for the innocent, such as rights to have an attorney, present witnesses, cross-examine one's accusers, receive reasons for the decisions reached, to take an appeal, and other such rights. If too much due process is provided, establishing wrongdoing may become too difficult when wrongdoing has occurred. If, however, too little due process is provided, establishing wrongdoing when wrongdoing has not occurred may become too simple.

Along related lines, optimum level analysis has been applied to determining an optimum jury size. With large juries, prosecutors may obtain unanimous convictions of too many truly guilty defendants, whereas with small juries, prosecutors may possibly obtain unanimous convictions of too many truly innocent defendants.

This general model and these methods can be applied to understanding how much enforcement should be applied in administrative regulation. By enforcement, we mean how much money might be spent to secure compliance with administrative regulations, how severe the negative sanctions, fines, or jail sentences might be, or how high the standards of compliance might be set. If too much compliance is demanded, the enforcement costs may exceed the benefits. If too little compliance is demanded, much inflicted damage could have been prevented. For example, let's examine the field of environmental regulation. Demanding zero water pollution with regard to biodegradable wastes may be extremely expensive; moreover, the small amounts of such pollution would cause little harm. On the other hand, by permitting the same extent of water pollution allowed prior to 1970, public health, commercial fishing, water recreation, industrial water uses, and other water uses could all be jeopardized. Furthermore, a small effort could have made a big difference. Optimum water pollution is, thus, somewhere between no pollution and 100 percent pollution. Likewise, the optimum jail sentence length for wrongdoers lies between no time and life imprisonment. Excessively long sentences involve high holding costs of defendants who may no longer be dangerous and may no longer be a deterrent example. Excessively short sentences incur high releasing costs of defendants who may still be quite dangerous and who, if released early, can represent a missed opportunity to deter others.

The a and b parameters in the equations of the form $Y = aX^b$ are determined by statistical regression analysis, surveying knowledgeable people, deducing from accepted premises, or making reasonable assumptions. If knowledgeable people are surveyed, questions such as the following should be relatively easy to answer: If there is a 100 percent increase on X (i.e., a doubling of X), then by what percent do you think Y would increase or decrease? Likewise, one can ask, If X were only one unit, then how much of Y do you think there would be? The first question aids in arriving at a value for b, and the second question helps determine a value for a. If assumed values are used, then show for various values of b or a how X^* would change.[4]

Allocating Scarce Resources

Another common policy problem involves allocating a budget of dollars or effort across various activities or places. We can illustrate this optimizing analysis by allocating the budget of the Legal Services Program of the Office of Economic Opportunity to various activities, or by allocating the budget of the Law Enforcement Assistance Administration to various places.

ALLOCATING LEGAL SERVICES DOLLARS TO ACTIVITIES

In 1970, the Auerbach Corporation, a management consulting firm, was contracted to evaluate the approximately 200 Office of Economic Opportunity (OEO) legal services programs across the country. Each program was evaluated on 113 different dimensions. The 114th dimension referred to overall satisfaction of the evaluators. This dimension was scored on a scale of 1 to 12, with 1 being the worst case, 12 being the best case, and 7 being acceptable. A key controversy in providing legal services to the poor has been how to allocate time, effort, and money between routine case handling and law-reform work. Law reform mainly involves taking appeals designed to establish new precedents with regard to enforcing the legal rights of the poor. The percentage of the budget devoted to law reform was determined for each legal services program, with the remainder devoted to routine case handling. These percentages were translated into dollars per client, and a statistical analysis determined the relation between satisfaction and expenditures for law reform and case handling.

The average legal service agency spent $68.34 per client, of which $6.16 was allocated to law reform and $62.18 to case handling. The average agency also received a satisfaction score of only 6.51, just below the acceptable level. We can plot a dot for each legal service agency on a three-dimensional surface showing: (1) its satisfaction score, (2) its law reform expenditures per client, and (3) its case-handling expenditures per client. We can then fit a line or a plane to those dots to minimize the squared distances from the dots to the line. The results are in Figure 12-3. The top left shows that as law reform expenditures increase, satisfaction also increases. When there is an increase of $1.00 for law reform per client in the average legal services agency, satisfaction scores increase by one-third or 0.34 of a unit. On the other hand, there is virtually no relation between an increase in case-handling dollars and an increase in satisfaction. The top right of the figure shows that as case-handling expenditures increase by $1.00, satisfaction declines by 0.03 of a unit, which amounts to almost no change.

Given this information, how would one logically allocate the $68 budget of the average legal services agency between these two activities? If there were no minimum or maximum constraints on law reform or case handling, one would allocate the entire $68 to law reform, since it has a higher marginal rate of return than case handling does in producing additional satisfaction per incremental dollar. The Office of Economic Opportunity in Washington, however, issued evaluation guidelines that implied legal service agencies should spend no more than about 20 percent and no less than 10 percent of their budget on law reform. Expenditures for case handling should be no more than 90 percent of an agency budget, and no less than 80 percent. If these constraints are imposed upon the two graphs in the upper part of Figure 12-3, one can readily see that the optimum allocation to law-reform dollars would be 20 percent of the $68 budget, and the optimum allocation to case-handling dollars would be 80 percent of the $68 budget. In other words, when one assumes linear relations between policy inputs and goals for different activities, one should allocate the entire budget to the activity with the best slope or marginal rate of return, up to whatever maximum constraint must be recognized, and then switch to the next best activity, and so on. Before making these allocations, however, one should give each activity whatever the minimum constraints provide for.

FIGURE 12-3
Allocating Legal Service Dollars across Activities: *a,* **Linear Relations:** $S = 6.29 + 0.34(\$L) - 0.03(\$C)$; *b,* **Nonlinear Relations:** $S = 14(\$L)^{0.33} (\$C)^{-0.33}$

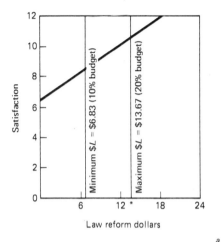
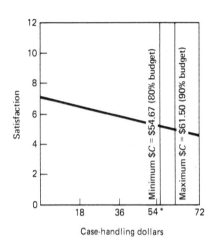

a

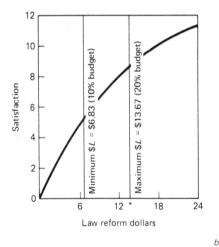
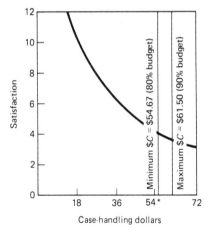

b

Note: Not drawn to scale
  * = Optimum allocations.
  S = Satisfaction score of each legal services agency as determined by a team of evaluators.
  $\$L$ = Dollars allocated to law-reform activities, as determined by multiplying the total agency budget by the percent spent on law reform and dividing by the number of clients.
  $\$C$ = Dollars allocated to routine case-handling activities, as determined by multiplying the total agency budget by the percent spent on case handling and dividing by the number of clients.

The lower part of Figure 12-3 fits curves to data more realistically. It recognizes that as one increases the policy inputs, satisfaction may increase, but probably at a diminishing rate of increase (rather than a constant rate), as is shown in the lower left. Additionally, the lower right part of the figure recognizes that as one increases an input that lowers satisfaction, the decrease is also likely to occur at a diminishing or plateauing rate, rather than a constant rate. The numerical parameters for the nonlinear equation can be obtained through the same kind of statistical analysis that we used to obtain the linear equation's numerical parameters, except the computer is instructed to locate a best-fitting curve instead of a straight line. Recognizing these diminishing returns does not affect the optimum allocation because case handling has a slightly negative marginal rate of return, and law reform has a positive marginal rate of return. Thus, one would allocate the maximum amount to law reform and the minimum to case handling, regardless of whether the relations are linear or nonlinear.

If, however, case handling would have produced a positive-shaped curve, like that in the lower left corner but not rising as high, the optimum allocation might have allocated less than the maximum to law reform and more than the minimum to case handling. If we give the maximum to law reform, money will be wasted as we approach the maximum, at which point the law-reform curve flattens, relative to the beginning part of the case-handling curve or the part just above the case-handling minimum. Although the law-reform curve may be steeper at any given dollar figure than the case-handling curve, the law-reform curve may not be steeper at its maximum constraint than the case-handling curve is at its minimum constraint. Under these circumstances, the optimum allocation would involve giving each activity its minimum allocation ($6.83 for law reform and $54.67 for case handling, for a total of $61.50). The remaining $6.84 would be allocated to the two activities in proportion to their elasticity coefficients. This means that when the relation between satisfaction, law reform, and case handling is $S = a(\$L)^b(\$C)^B$, law reform should receive $b/(b + B)$ part of $6.84, and case handling should receive $B/(b + B)$. One can prove algebraically that when both nonlinear relations are positive (i.e., have positive exponents), the optimum allocation involves allocating in proportion to those exponents after satisfying the minimum and maximum constraints.

ALLOCATING ANTICRIME DOLLARS TO PLACES

Suppose the state of Wisconsin had 20 crimes in 1970 and 10 crimes in 1972, and it spent $15 in 1970 and $35 in 1972. Let's also say that Illinois had 100 crimes in 1970, and 60 in 1972, and it spent $25 in 1970 and $75 in 1972. How could this information be used to develop an optimum allocation of a $10 budget between these two places? One might propose more money be given to Wisconsin because crime was reduced by half between 1970 and 1972. One could also suggest more money be given to Illinois because its crime problem is worse. One might also, however, give more to Illinois because the state is making more of an effort to fight crime in view of its anticrime expenditures tripling. Another alternative would be to give Wisconsin more money because it has less to spend.

Figure 12-4 graphically illustrates how this information can be used to determine an optimum allocation between Illinois and Wisconsin. The left side of the figure works with linear relations. It shows that as Illinois increased its allocation by $50 between the two years, crime decreased by 40 units. Each $1 increase in anticrime expenditures in Illinois produces a 0.80 reduction in crime, assuming other variables are statistically controlled for. Wisconsin, on the other hand, raised its expenditure by $20 in those two years and dropped 10 crime units. Each $1 increase in anticrime expenditures in Wisconsin produces a 0.50 reduction in crime. Therefore, it is better to invest an anticrime dollar in Illinois than in Wisconsin if one is trying to minimize total crime across both states, as might a federal agency such as the Law Enforcement Assistance Administration (LEAA). Thus, the entire $10 budget would be given to Illinois, unless there are some minimum constraints over how much should be allocated to each state. We can assume that this $10 represents discretionary money after the minimum constraints have been satisfied. The left side of the figure also shows that if nothing is given to Wisconsin, there will be 28 crimes there (or a prediction of 28 crimes) in light of the data which, in effect, extrapolates from the two data points of 10 crimes with $35 and 20 crimes with $15. Likewise, if zero dollars were given to Illinois, the extrapolation or projection of a line through its two data points indicates 120 crimes will occur. With the equations for these two lines, one can optimally allocate between the two places, and also arrive at a predicted crime score for each state in light of these optimum allocations.

The right side of Figure 12-4 uses the same two data points, but a curved line rather than a straight line is fitted to the Illinois and Wisconsin pair of data points, respectively. The numerical parameters for these curves can be determined with a hand calculator that provides for nonlinear curve fitting or with a statistical analysis program available at virtually all computing centers. The equation for the Illinois data is $Y = 437(X)^{-0.46}$, which means an increase of 1 percent in Illinois' expenditures will mean a crime decrease of 0.46. For Wisconsin, a 1 percent increase in expenditures will mean a crime decrease of 0.83. For a given number of dollars, Illinois is the better recipient for the investment because it operates at a higher level of crime, as indicated by the multiplier of 437. This multiplier indicates that if only $1 were spent, there would be 437 crimes as contrasted to 191 in Wisconsin. In other words, a 10 percent reduction in a state that has 1,000 crimes is much better than a 20 percent reduction in a state that has only 100 crimes. We do not, however, want to give the entire $10 to Illinois because the extra dollar expenditure between $9 and $10 doesn't produce much

FIGURE 12-4
Allocating Anticrime Dollars Across Places

	Crime Occurrence (Y)			Anticrime Dollars (X)		
State	1972	1970	CHANGE	1972	1970	CHANGE
Wisconsin	10	20	−10	$35	$15	$20
Illinois	60	100	−40	$75	$25	$50

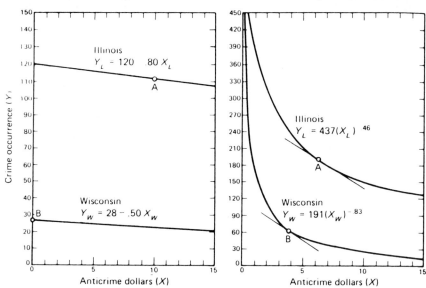

a. Constant Returns Relations: b. Diminishing Returns Relations:

Point A is the point of optimum allocation to Illinois.

At that point in the linear graph:

$X = \$10$, $Y = 112$ crimes, slope $= -.8$.

At that point in the nonlinear graph:

$X = \$6.21$, $Y = 189$ crimes, slope $= -14$.
Tangent line is $Y_L = 276 - 14X_L$.

Point B is the point of optimum allocation to Wisconsin.

At that point in the linear graph:

$X = \$0$, $Y = 28$ crimes, slope $= -.5$.

At that point in the nonlinear graph:

$X = \$3.79$, $Y = 63$ crimes, slope $= -14$.
Tangent line is $Y_W = 116 - 14X_W$.

added benefit. The tenth dollar would be better spent as the first dollar for
Wisconsin, where there is a relatively big crime drop when $1 as opposed to
no dollar is spent.

We will be in a state of equilibrium or optimum allocation when we
divide the $10 between Illinois and Wisconsin to satisfy simultaneously the

equations, $X_L + X_W = \$10$ and $ba(X_2)^{b-1} = BA(X_W)^{B-1}$. The second equation says the marginal rates of return of both states should be equal to each other when we are in an optimum position so that nothing can be gained by switching dollars from one state to the other. It recognizes that with a relation of the form $Y = aX^b$, the marginal rate of return or slope of Y to X is baX^{b-1}. The slope of Y to X is thus influenced by the value of X. Solving for X_L and X_W in this pair of equations informs us that the optimum allocation between Illinois and Wisconsin, when one works with more realistic diminishing-returns relations, is \$6.21 to Illinois and \$3.79 to Wisconsin. One can logically apply this analysis to any number of places. Note that each location has its own output-input equation. With activities, however, the output is shown on the left side of the equation, and the activities are depicted as interacting variables on the right side of the equation.[5]

Time-Oriented Optimizing Models

A frequent kind of policy optimization, especially in the realm of public administration, involves choosing among alternative policies to minimize the occurrence of unnecesssary delay. Such choice often involves finding an optimum choice, level, or mix among alternative policies, which means the methods we previously discussed will be used although time minimization is a goal. Time optimization or minimization models may also involve special methods other than finding an optimum choice, level, or mix. These methods include variations on: (1) queueing theory to predict the effects of system changes on backlog and delay, (2) optimum sequencing to reduce the amount of waiting time, and (3) critical path theory to determine where delay reduction efforts should be concentrated.

To illustrate how queueing theory can help us see things more clearly, we might look at the corrections problem of overcrowded jails. To reduce such overcrowding, one might recommend increased pretrial release. The opposite result, however, might occur (as illustrated in Figure 12-2) because increased pretrial release decreases the vulnerability of many defendants to the prosecutor's offer to reduce the sentence to time served or probation in return for a guilty plea. If increased pretrial release thereby decreases guilty pleas, then the queueing backlog model tells us to expect increased trials, assuming other variables remain constant. Likewise, the queueing delay model tells us to expect increased delay from the increased trials. If delay increases, then defendants sitting in jail awaiting trial will probably be there longer. This, in turn, means the pretrial jail population may increase, even though fewer defendants are being sent to jail to await trial.

Queueing theory and other models not only provide a better understanding of the causal relations, but they also indicate ways of decreasing the occurrence of these relations. Thus, increased pretrial release need not result in decreased guilty pleas if the prosecutor offers better bargains (such as probation) to defendants out of jail who otherwise would receive jail sentences. Even when there are decreased guilty pleas, they need not result in increased trials if the prosecutor dismisses more cases to offset the decrease in cases settled. Likewise, increased trials need not result in increased delay if the system offsets the increased trials with more judges. Finally, increased delay does not necessarily increase the pretrial jail population if priority trials are provided for those defendants who are in jail, even though this could mean even greater delay for defendants out of jail.

Optimum sequencing models can be illustrated by noting that if one has two cases to process and one case takes 20 days to process and the other takes 15 days to process, then the average amount of waiting time plus processing time will be affected by the order in which they are heard. If the 20-day case is heard first, it will have zero waiting time, plus 20 days processing time, for a total of 20 days. The 15-day case will then have 20 days waiting time and 15 days processing time, for a total of 35 days. The sum of these two total amounts for the two cases is 55 days, or about 28 days per case. On the other hand, if the 15-day case is heard first, it will have zero waiting time, plus 15 days processing time, for a total of 15 days. The 20-day case will then have 15 days waiting time and 20 days processing time, for a total of 35 days. The sum of these two total amounts is 50 days, or about 25 days per case. That is three days less than the original order, which might be the first-come, first-served order. The difference would be even greater with more cases and more variety among the cases. This simple example leads to the general rule that by reordering the cases to hear the shorter ones first, the average total time per case will be minimized, although one may have to comply with a constraint that sets a maximum on the waiting time to which a case can be subject.

Critical path analysis can be illustrated in administrative proceedings that involve the government regulating private business firms or the government being sued by private parties. Suppose the government spends six weeks in preparation, from the filing of the complaint initiating the proceeding through the administrative hearing, and the private parties average four weeks for the same preparation. The path from filing to hearing along the government route is then the critical path on which to concentrate one's time-reduction efforts. Case-processing time will not be reduced if private parties reduce their average from four weeks downward, if the government continues to use six weeks for preparation.[6]

Trends, Benefits, and Costs of Policy Evaluation

Between 1973 and 1983, there were a number of trends in the development of policy evaluation methods including more:

1. Building on business analysis
2. Seeking optimizing solutions rather than only determining effects

3. Questioning the goals to be achieved
4. Doing analysis prior to the adoption of policies
5. Increasing interdisciplinary interaction
6. Considering political and administrative feasibility
7. Simplifying procedures
8. Utilizing evaluation results
9. Developing training programs, research centers, funding sources, publishing outlets, scholarly associations, and other policy evaluation institutions

These trends have made the field of policy evaluation exciting to be in, particularly in these formative years. We need more public administrators who can apply and understand the policy evaluation methods discussed in this chapter. The chapter frequently mentions maximizing benefits minus costs. What, however, are some of the benefits and the costs of applying policy evaluation methods to public administration problems? They include:

1. Arriving at more effective and efficient decisions
2. Acquiring insights that might enable one to make recommendations for more favorably influencing the decision making of others
3. Predicting what decisions are likely to be reached by knowing how system changes influence perceptions of benefits and costs
4. Understanding better why actual decisions differ from the alleged optimum decisions, and then either attempting to change the actual decisions or adjusting one's criteria as to what constitutes optimum decisions

The costs of applying policy evaluation methods include hard work in gathering and processing data, and hard thinking in deciding what data to gather and how to process it. Although a number of applications of policy evaluation methods have been and can be given, the field remains almost virgin territory. With such a low level of development, a minimum effort may produce a high marginal rate of return before the occurrence of substantial diminishing returns. We hope that this chapter stimulates further effort to apply policy evaluation methods to public administration problems.

NOTES

1. On policy evaluation methods in general, see Michael White, Ross Clayton, Robert Myrtle, Gilbert Siegel, and Aaron Rose, *Managing Public Systems: Analytic Techniques for Public Administration* (Duxbury, 1980); Edith Stokey and Richard Zeckhauser, *A Primer for Policy Analysis* (Norton, 1978); William Dunn, *Public Policy Analysis: An Introduction* (Prentice-Hall, 1981); Edward Quade, *Analysis for Public Decisions* (Elsevier, 1975); and S. Nagel, *Policy Evaluation: Making Optimum Decisions* (Praeger, 1982).
2. On choosing among discrete alternatives, see Mark Thompson, *Benefit-Cost Analysis for Program Evaluation* (Sage, 1980); John Gohagan, *Quantitative*

Analysis for Public Policy (McGraw-Hill, 1980); and Guy Black, *The Application of Systems Analysis to Government Operations* (Praeger, 1968). On choosing among alternative programs for providing legal services to the poor, see Legal Services Corporation, *The Delivery Systems Study* (LSC, 1980); and S. Nagel, "How to Provide Legal Counsel for the Poor: Decision Theory" in Dorothy James (ed.), *Analyzing Poverty Policy* (Lexington-Heath, 1975). On choosing among alternative policies for increasing police adherence to legality in searches, see Dallin Oaks, "Determining the Effects of the Exclusionary Rule," 37 *University of Chicago Law Review* (1970); and S. Nagel, "Choosing Among Alternative Public Policies" in Kenneth Dolbeare (ed.), *Public Policy Evaluation* (Sage, 1975).

3. On making decisions under conditions of risk, see Ruth Mack, *Planning on Uncertainty: Decision Making in Business and Government Administration* (Wiley, 1971); Wayne Lee, *Decision Theory and Human Behavior* (Wiley, 1971); Charles Holloway, *Decision Making Under Uncertainty: Models and Choices* (Prentice-Hall, 1979); and S. Nagel and Marian Neef, *Decision Theory and the Legal Process* (Lexington-Heath, 1979). On deciding whether to gather data that may be unused, see General Accounting Office, *Data Collected from Non-Federal Sources: Statistical and Paperwork Implications* (GAO, 1978); and S. Nagel, "Determining When Data is Worth Gathering," 16 *Society*, 20–3 (1978) (Symposium on "Paperwork Control").

4. On making decisions where doing too much or too little is undesirable, see Michael Brennan, *Preface to Econometrics: An Introduction to Quantitative Methods in Economics* (South-Western, 1973); James Shockley, *The Brief Calculus: With Applications in the Social Sciences* (Holt, Rinehart & Winston, 1971); Martin Starr and D. Miller, *Inventory Control: Theory and Practice* (Prentice-Hall, 1962); and S. Nagel and Marian Neef, *Legal Policy Analysis: Finding an Optimum Level or Mix* (Lexington-Heath, 1977). On finding an optimum level of delay in judicial administration, see S. Nagel and Marian Neef, "Time-Oriented Models and the Legal Process: Reducing Delay and Forecasting the Future," *Washington University Law Quarterly* 467–528 (1978), especially 490–94, 520–21, and 525.

5. On allocating scarce resources in general, see Philip Kotler, *Marketing Decision Making: A Model Building Approach* (Holt, Rinehart & Winston, 1971); Sang Lee, *Linear Optimization in Management* (Petrocelli/Charter, 1976); and Claude McMillen, Jr., *Mathematical Programming: An Introduction to the Design and Applications of Optimal Decision Machines* (Wiley, 1970). On allocating to legal services activities, see "Minimizing Costs and Maximizing Benefits in Providing Legal Services to the Poor" in S. Nagel, *Improving the Legal Process: Effects of Alternatives* (Lexington-Heath, 1975). On allocating anticrime dollars to places, see "Allocating Anti-Crime Dollars Across Places and Activities" in S. Nagel, *Policy Evaluation: Making Optimum Decisions* (Praeger, 1982).

6. On time-oriented optimizing models, see Haig Bohigian, *The Foundations and Mathematical Models of Operations Research with Extensions to the Criminal Justice System* (Gazette, 1971); Jack Byrd, Jr., *Operations Research Models for Public Administration* (Lexington-Heath, 1975); Kenneth Baker, *Introduction to Sequencing and Scheduling* (Wiley, 1974); and Donald Gross and Carl Harris, *Fundamentals of Queuing Theory* (Wiley, 1974). On the use of queueing backlog and queueing delay models in governmental case processing, see "Time Optimization Models" in S. Nagel, *Policy Evaluation and the Legal Process* (Kennikat Press, 1984).

QUESTIONS

1. What is an appropriate set of rules for choosing among mutually exclusive or at least discrete policy alternatives?
2. What is an appropriate set of rules for making optimum decisions when the benefits and costs are contingent on the occurrence of one or more events?
3. What is an appropriate set of rules for making decisions in those instances in which doing too much or too little is undesirable?
4. What is an appropriate set of rules for allocating scarce resources across activities or places to maximize benefits for given costs, or to minimize costs at a given benefits level?
5. What is meant by queueing theory, optimum sequencing, and critical-path theory in time-oriented optimizing models?
6. What are the benefits and the costs of applying policy evaluation methods to public administration problems?

EXERCISES

Develop your own hypothetical data for drafting a three-to-five-page memo that involves applying the principles for each of the four main types of optimizing analysis. The four main types relate to benefit-cost, decision theory, optimum level analysis, and allocation theory. They are also referred to as optimum choice, risk, level, and mix analysis. Choose any subject matters that are of interest to you. Each of the four memos should involve a concrete problem, rather than the manipulation of algebraic symbols or graphs. Create illustrative data that reasonably conform to empirical reality. An appropriate organization for a policy evaluation memo might involve the following parts:

1. Identify the policy problem. This mainly involves indicating what goal or goals are to be achieved.
2. Indicate what program, policy, or project alternatives will be considered.
3. Discuss how you might obtain information for a set of relevant persons, places, or things, and show how they score on goal variables and policy variables.
4. Discuss how you would use this information to establish statistical, accounting, or other relations between the goals and the programs.
5. Discuss how you would use these relations to conclude which programs would be best under various constraints and conditions.

REFERENCES

Bohigian, Haig, *The Foundations and Mathematical Models of Operations Research with Extensions to the Criminal Justice System* (Gazette, 1971).
Byrd, Jack, Jr., *Operations Research Models for Public Administration* (Lexington-Heath, 1975).
Dunn, William, *Public Policy Analysis: An Introduction* (Prentice-Hall, 1981).
Gohagan, John, *Quantitative Analysis for Public Policy* (McGraw-Hill, 1980).
Mack, Ruth, *Planning on Uncertainty: Decision Making in Business and Government Administration* (Wiley, 1971).
McMillen, Claude, Jr., *Mathematical Programming: An Introduction to the Design and Applications of Optimal Decision Machines* (Wiley, 1970).
Nagel, S., *Policy Evaluation: Making Optimum Decisions* (Praeger, 1982).
Quade, Edward, *Analysis for Public Decisions* (Elsevier, 1975).
Stokey, Edith, and Richard Zeckhauser, *A Primer for Policy Analysis* (Norton, 1978).
Thompson, Mark, *Benefit-Cost Analysis for Program Evaluation* (Sage, 1980).
White, Michael, Ross Clayton, Robert Myrtle, Gilbert Siegel, and Aaron Rose, *Managing Public Systems: Analytic Techniques for Public Administration* (Duxbury, 1980).

CHAPTER 13

Simplifying
Basic
Methods

This chapter discusses the idea that simple data analysis is often all that is needed to decide among alternative public policies, because the results do not change with more complex measures. Policy analysis conclusions tend to be less sensitive or more robust to changes in the inputs than ordinary social science research. One key explanation is that the object of policy analysis is to select the best policy, and not necessarily to determine the extent to which this policy surpasses the second best policy. In ordinary social science research which attempts to explain variation on a dependent variable, the concern is to measure exactly how much more important one independent variable is than another. This chapter does not encourage sloppy data analysis; rather, it promotes forward momentum on important policy research without being paralyzed by an often undue concern for precise measurement, weighting, sampling, prediction, and causal analysis.

Relevant literature discusses sensitivity analysis or postoptimizing analysis, which appears in the literature of operations research and management science. This literature discusses how one determines the effects on conclusions when the goals, constraints, or empirical inputs are changed. It does not posit that prescriptive conclusions are less sensitive to such changes than descriptive conclusions.[1] Other relevant literature includes discussions of robust measures in statistical analysis. A good example is the median as a measure of central tendency because the only change in data it is influenced by is the score of the middle case. This literature concentrates on the relative insensitivity or robustness of alternative measures of central tendency, dispersion, correlation, regression, statistical significance, and other statistical measures. It does not, however, compare policy analysis statistics with ordinary social science statistics.[2]

Policy analysis or policy evaluation is basically a five-step process, corresponding to the five parts of this chapter. These steps are:

1. Determine the goals one is seeking to achieve or maximize and the policies available for doing so

2. Determine the goals, relative importance, since some policies may be better suited for some goals than others
3. Decide the persons, places, or things to which the proposed policies are going to apply
4. Determine the relations between the goals (as dependent variables) and the policies (as independent variables), at least with regard to the direction of the relations, but preferably with regard to the magnitude and general shape as well
5. Adjust these relations to reflect the extent to which the policies have a causal influence on achieving the goals, and not just a relation of correlation or prediction

With this information, one should be able to conclude which policies can best achieve the goals under various circumstances. These five steps correspond to a concern for precision or simplicity in *measuring* policies and goals, determining the relative *weights* of the goals, drawing a *sample*, *relating* polices to goals, and determining *causation*.[3]

Simplicity in Measuring Policy and Goals

The simplest measurement is a dichotomy like yes-no, high-low, or more-less. Adding additional categories or providing for a continuum of measurement (i.e., from 0 to 100 percent) may increase complexity without proportionately increasing insights generated and without changing the results.

A good example might be the policy problem of determining how judges should be selected and for what terms. There are, thus, two policy dimensions: (1) method of selection, which can be meaningfully dichotomized into selection by the electoral process or selection by gubernatorial appointment; and (2) length of term before reelection or reappointment, which can be dichotomized into above and below a national average. One might have many goals in this context, but two may be especially important—the liberalism or conservatism of judicial decisions in economic policy matters and liberalism or conservation in civil liberties matters.

To determine how elected judges differ from appointed judges, compare elected judges with interim appointed judges serving on the same state supreme courts and hearing the same cases. One can, also, determine how relatively long-term judges differ from relatively short-term judges by finding state supreme courts in which both types of judges are serving simultaneously. If more than two categories were used for method of selection or for length of term, then it would be difficult to find appropriate state supreme courts in which these multiple categories were represented. Comparing judges who are not sitting on the same cases would not be as meaningful, since any differences among them might be due to differences in the cases rather than in method of selection or length of term.

This type of analysis reveals that elected judges are more liberal than appointed judges on economic matters, but they do not differ substantially on civil liberties matters. This finding applies even when comparing elected and appointed judges within the same political party. The explanation might be that elected judges are more likely to come from lower income backgrounds and rise through the party ranks, whereas appointed judges are more likely to be plucked from prominent law firms, partly for their monetary contributions. The analysis also shows that long-term judges are more liberal than short-term judges on civil liberties matters, but they do not differ substantially on economic matters. Perhaps long-term judges are less sensitive to majoritarian pressures, which may run contrary to freedom of speech, equal treatment for minorities, and criminal procedure safeguards.

In conclusion, the best method of determining selection and length of term depends on one's preferences with regard to liberalism and conservatism in economic and civil liberties matters. More specifically, if one prefers liberal results on both dimensions, the best judges would be elected and long termers. If conservative results are preferred, the best judges would be appointed short termers. If one prefers judges who are likely to be liberal on economic matters but conservative on civil liberties matters, the best judges might be elected short termers. And, if one prefers conservatives on economic matters but liberals on civil liberties matters, then appointing judges for long terms may be the best solution. These relations are summarized in Figure 13-1. An important point from a policy analysis perspective is that meaningful deductions can be made about the important issues of how judges should be selected and for what terms, by using a measurement perspective that is no more complex than a simple dichotomy on each of the policy variables and a simple dichotomy on each of the goal variables. A more detailed measurement is often not worth the extra costs, as a small sensitivity analysis can often reveal.

With dichotomous variables scored 1 and 2, one can even express diminishing returns in a relationship between a Y goal and an X policy by working with the logarithms of the Y scores and the X scores. The result is the equation, $Y = aX^b$. If the regression analysis produces a value of b that is positive but less than 1, then there are diminishing returns. If b is greater than 1, then there are increasing returns. If b equals 1, then there is a linear or constant relation. If b is negative, then a convex curve will result, with Y going down at a diminishing rate as X goes up. One can even force a hill-shaped or valley-shaped curve on a relation between a goal and a policy when both are dichotomously measured. One can do so by fitting an equation to the data which has the form $Y = a + b_1X + b_2X^2$. Doing so means inputting Y or a dependent variable and both X and X^2 as independent variables. If b_2 is positive, a hill-shaped relation is present. If b_2 is negative, a valley-shaped relation is present. One can convey the same idea by wording the policy variable to combine the extremes into one category. This might

FIGURE 13-1
Illustrating Simplicity in Measuring Policies and Goals: *a*, Relations Between Sel-ection/Tenure and Direction of Judicial Decisions; *b*, Optimum Policy Choices for Achieving Given Types of Decisional Goals.

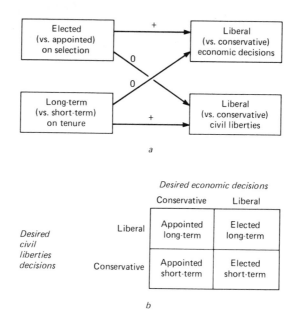

a

b

mean scoring X as a 1 when X is very large or very small, and scoring X as a 2 when X is in the middle. Such nonlinear or linear relations can be more precisely expressed if the X policy and Y goal are scored on continuum scales, rather than as dichotomies. This kind of interval measurement may, however, often be unavailable, interfere with clarity, and be unnecessary.[4]

Simplicity in Determining the Relative Weights of the Goals

A frequent problem in policy analysis, and one that causes substantial anguish, is how to determine the desirability of various goals, since one policy may be especially effective in achieving one of two goals, and another mutually exclusive policy may be especially effective in achieving the other goal. It never seems to be necessary in a practical problem to be able to measure desirability in absolute terms like satisfaction or utility units. Merely being able to say that one goal is W times as desirable or weighty than another goal is sufficient for meaningfully evaluating policy.

A good example might be the policy problem of whether or not to adopt the judicial rule that says evidence illegally obtained by the police or other government officials must not be admissible in criminal cases. Two key goals are: (1) increasing police adherence to the rules governing what constitutes a legal search and seizure, and (2) increasing, or at least not unduly decreasing, police morale in making legitimate searches and seizures. A research project designed to relate the exclusionary policy to these two goals involved sending questionnaires to police chiefs, prosecutors, judges, defense attorneys, and American Civil Liberties Union (ACLU) officials three years after the United States Supreme Court required all 50 states to adopt the exclusionary rule. The recipients were asked whether there had been an increase, no change, or a decrease in police adherence and police morale over the previous five years. About half the respondents came from states that were newly required to adopt the exclusionary rule (the experimental group on the policy), and about half came from states that already had the rule (the control group).

About 75 percent of the experimental group reported an increase in police adherence, whereas only 57 percent of the control group reported an increase, for a difference of 18 percentage points. That $+0.18$ approximates the marginal rate of return, such that when one goes from 0 to 1 on the policy variable, one goes from 0.57 to 0.75 on the goal variable, with the above three change categories numercially scored 0, 0.5, and 1.0. About 66 percent of the experimental group, however, reported a decrease in police morale, whereas only 28 percent of the control group did, for a difference of 38 percentage points. That -0.38 approximates the marginal rate of return on police morale, when one moves from 0 to 1 on the policy variable.

Using this information, one can now say whether the exclusionary rule is desirable or undesirable, providing that one can say something about the relative value of police adherence to legality versus police morale in making searches. If these are the only two goals and they are of equal value or normative weight, then the exclusionary policy does more harm than good. If police adherence is worth about twice as much as police morale, then the exclusionary policy is a toss-up as to whether it is worth adopting. If, however, police adherence is at least three times as beneficial as police morale, then the exclusionary rule should be adopted. One can be more precise by talking in terms of decimal weights rather than integer weights, but this may be unduly complicated, given the greater ease people have in expressing themselves in terms of integer relations like equal, twice as much, and three times as much. There is no need to know how many times more than three times as much police adherence might be valued over police morale, since the solution would be the same if the numerical value of W were any number above 3. One could determine the threshold value of W by simply solving for W in the equation, $18W = 38$.

The problem does not become substantially more difficult by adding a second alternative policy, such as the use of tort damages and criminal actions against the police. In the same survey, the recipients were asked the extent to which these policies were adopted in their communities. Relating these responses to their other responses concerning increased police adherence to legality (Y_a) and increased police morale in making searches (Y_b) indicated a $+0.05$ relation with the first goal and a -0.09 relation with the second goal. This information tells us that as long as the normative value of Y_a relative to Y_b was greater than 9 to 5, these policy activities would produce more benefits than costs. The benefits are $(5)(W)$, where the 5 represents the quantity of Y_a benefit units for a one-unit change in X_1, and the W represents the relative value per Y_a unit. The costs are $(9)(1)$ since we have anchored the relative value of Y_b at 1. Benefits minus costs are $5W - 9$. To compare policy X_1 with policy X_2, we would calculate the benefits minus costs for each policy to see which scores best on that criterion. We should also perform this type of algebraic summing with a policy that produces only beneficial effects or only harmful effects. These relations are summarized in Figure 12-2 in the previous chapter.

The problem would also not become substantially more difficult when we add additional goals. If the given problem had a third goal, we would simply express the normative weight of the least valued goal as 1, and then express the relative values of the other goals in relation to it. The weights of the three goals might thus be $W_1 = 4$, $W_2 = 2$, and $W_3 = 1$. To determine which of the two policies is better, we would then calculate for each policy a sum equal to $B_1W_1 + B_2W_2 + B_3W_3$. In this sum, B_1 is the standardized slope of the relation between policy i and the first goal, and B_2 is the slope of the relation between policy i and the second goal. Each of the two policies has an opportunity to be policy i, or the policy for which a summation score is being calculated. The policy that has the highest summation score is the better policy if there are two policies, and it is the best policy if there are more than two policies. One tricky problem, though, is to avoid overlap between the goals. If, for example, goals 2 and 3 are alike, then whatever they have in common will be unduly considered. Overlap can be partly avoided in how the goals are expressed. It can also be avoided by having the weights consider that there are other goals. Thus, goal 2 might receive a heavier weight than a weight of 2 in the absence of goal 3, and a lighter weight when goal 3 is included in the analysis.

Taking a step backward, one might ask where goal weights originate, as contrasted to what one does with them after they have been obtained. A frequent source is the policy researcher's suggestions. This does not mean the policy researcher is substituting his or her values for those of the policy maker's. Good policy research should clearly indicate how the results would change with alternative value weights. In other words, one should show what W_1, for example, has to be in order to shift from policy 1 to policy 2, given certain values for the slopes and the other weights. One can then do the same sensitivity analysis with W_2 and W_3. A more complicated source for obtaining goal weights would be to survey policy makers, the general public, or whatever people are considered relevant in the context of the policy problem. Goal weights can sometimes be determined by obtaining a higher value than goals 1, 2, and 3. The goal weights can then be the three slopes showing the relations between each of these subgoals and the higher goal. A fourth source of goal weights is deductive analysis. For example, suppose we accept that: (1) it is ten times as bad to convict an innocent person as it is to acquit a guilty person, and (2) it is less bad to wrongly hold in jail prior to trial someone who would appear for trial if released than it is to wrongly convict an innocent person. We can therefore deduce that (3) it is generally less than ten times as bad to make pretrial holding errors as it is to make pretrial releasing errors.[5]

Simplicity in Drawing a Sample

Would-be policy analysts can become paralyzed when confronting problems of measurement, goal weighting, drawing a sample of relevant persons or places, and the extent to which one can generalize beyond the sample drawn. In many situations, changing the sample will not influence the relation between a policy and a goal. Often the goal is a composite involving summing two subgoals, and a sample change will not offset effects on those two subgoals; thus the optimum policy or policy level remains constant.

A good example of this is the policy problem of determining the percentage of arrested defendants who should be held in jail prior to trial. One can obtain data from a set of cities which shows for each city: (1) its percentage of arrested defendants held in jail, or $\%H$, as the key policy variable, (2) its holding costs or HC, including estimates regarding jail maintenance and lost gross national product, and (3) its releasing costs or RC, including estimates regarding the cost of rearresting no-shows and the cost of crimes committed by released defendants. With this information, one can determine the relation between $\%H$ and HC (which tends to be positive convex) and between $\%H$ and RC (which tends to be negative convex). Using these two relations, one can calculate the relation between $\%H$ and total costs (which tends to be a valley-shaped curve). The point at which the curve bottoms out is the optimum percentage of defendants to hold in jail prior to trial.

One might feel the sample of cities on which these relations are based is too urban or too rural. One can test the effects of having a more urban or rural sample by splitting the cities into a relatively urban group and a relatively rural group, and then do the calculations. This method will likely find the same optimum percentage to hold for the urban group, the rural group, and the total group. As urbanism increases, so do the holding costs because urban jails are more expensive to maintain and urban defendants lose more income than rural defendants while held in jail. An offsetting factor is the fact that as urbanism increases, so do the releasing costs. No-shows and crime committing while released are higher in urban areas than rural areas because delay between arrest and trial is longer. This also increases holding costs. If the holding costs rise, then the optimum percent to hold declines, because holding is then more expensive. If, however, the releasing costs also go up, then the optimum percent to hold goes up because releasing becomes more expensive. Thus, if as a result of working with a more urban sample, both *HC* and *RC* go up about the same amount, then the optimum percentage to hold will remain about constant. The optimum holding policy is thus rather insensitive to this frequent kind of sampling error, as is the case with many other policies. This does not mean that the study involved a disproportionately large fraction of urban or rural communities. It only means that the optimum pretrial release level is not affected by city size. These relations are summarized in Figure 13-2.

In policy analysis, one can often work with smaller samples than might be acceptable in ordinary social science, for various reasons. Policy analysis often involves drawing samples that are not random. Rather, the samples are highly purposeful as they are deliberately selected to be representative of certain categories, such as northern rural, northern urban, southern rural, or southern urban. Policy analysis may often involve states as sampling units, which means samples larger than 50 may be impossible to gather. Using states at earlier points in time may be irrelevant, because the historical context may be too different. The optimum size of a sample in sampling theory is usually determined by a formula that assumes one is operating at a 0.05 or 0.01 level of statistical significance. In policy analysis, however, a higher level may be quite meaningful because a type 2 error may be just as costly as a type 1 error, or at least not 19 times or 99 times as costly. It may be much more expensive to collect units of analysis firsthand that are measured by countries or places rather than by individuals, because the latter can generally be surveyed less expensively. The cost of an experiment with 100 freshmen psychology students is probably much less than the cost of observing the court systems of 10 different countries. The latter, however, may reveal more about the effects of alternative judicial policies than a sample of 100 freshmen psychology students can reveal about psychology.[6]

FIGURE 13-2
Illustrating Simplicity in Drawing a Sample

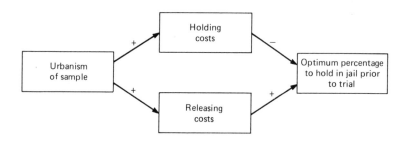

Simplicity in Relating Policies to Goals

The simplest way to express a relation between a policy and a goal is to express its direction; that is, whether the relation is positive or negative, or relatively positive or negative. The next higher degree of sophistication is to express the magnitude of the relation, possibly on a standardized scale ranging from -1 to $+1$, or better yet, in terms of a slope which shows how many units Y changes for a 1-unit change in X at a given point on X. At a still higher degree of sophistication, we can talk in terms of the shape of the relation between Y and X as being convex, concave, valley-shaped, hill-shaped, S-shaped, cyclical, or having other more exotic shapes.

The policy problem of how to provide counsel to the poor in civil cases will illustrate how one can gain insight even when relations are expressed only in terms of direction rather than magnitude or shape. This example was given in Chapter 12 to illustrate general principals in choosing among discrete alternative policies in which the relations between the policies and goals have been established. In this instance, we will use the example to illustrate simplicity in relating policies to goals. Three alternatives for providing counsel to the poor in civil cases are: (1) a volunteer list of free attorneys to be available when poor people have legal problems, (2) attorneys salaried by a government agency, like the Legal Services Corporation, to represent poor people, generally on a full-time basis, and (3) attorneys who are reimbursed for representing poor people by the government as part of a Judicare system analogous to Medicare. Four basic goals might be considered in comparing these three policy alternatives, namely, that they are (1) inexpensive, (2) visible and accessible, (3) politically feasible, and (4) offering specialized competence plus reasonably aggressive representation.

For each goal, we can indicate the policy alternative that is relatively more positive, meaning the alternative that best achieves the goal. On being inexpensive, the volunteer system gets a plus, with the salaried attorney and especially the Judicare system receiving relative minuses. On being visible and accessible, the salaried attorney scores a relative plus, with Judicare and especially the volunteer attorney system getting relative minuses. On being politically feasible, neither the volunteer or Judicare systems create any substantial political problems (particularly the volunteer system) and might thus be scored pluses, but the salaried attorney system has had political problems, which gives it a minus. The salaried attorney system, though, results in specialized competence and more aggressive representation, which gives it a plus, with minuses to the volunteer and Judicare systems on this goal.

The volunteer and salaried systems seem to be tied with two pluses apiece. The volunteer system scores well on being inexpensive and politically feasible, whereas the salaried system scores well on being visible and accessible and being specialized and aggressive. To resolve this tie, these goals need relative weights. A conservative evaluator or policy maker would probably place relatively more weight on being inexpensive and politically feasible, and would thus tend to favor a volunteer system. A liberal evaluator would emphasize being visible and accessible and specialized and aggressive, and thus would favor the government salaried system. As in most policy analysis, no conclusions can be reached without specifying the relative weights of the goals, even if there is agreement on what the goals are. The policy analyst can, however, clarify the best policy in light of given goals and value weights. Insights into which policy is best can sometimes be obtained by working with relations between policies and goals that are expressed in terms of relative direction without specifying the exact magnitude of the relations. Substantively speaking, this analysis shows that a compromise between the volunteer system and the salaried system may be necessary. Such a compromise might involve salaried attorneys who have as one of their main jobs the recruiting and coordinating of volunteer attorneys in order to make them more visible and accessible and in order to provide them with training that will improve their specialized competence and aggressive representation. The data for this example was presented as part of Figure 13-1.

To determine the direction, magnitude, or shape of the relations between policies and goals, one does not necessarily have to do a statistical regression analysis (which would require complicated data gathering and computerized data analysis). Often the parameters for functional relations or regression equations between goals and policies can be obtained more simply and meaningfully by seeking knowledgeable people's perceptions. For example, one could ask knowledgeable people such questions as this: If X is zero, what do you think the value of Y would tend to be for determining a in $Y = a + bX$?; or, If X increases by one unit, then by how many units do you think Y would increase or decrease for determining b? One could also ask such questions as this: If X is one unit, what do you think the value of Y would tend to be for determining a in $Y = aX^b$?; or, for determining b, If X increases by 1 percent, then by how much of a percent do you think Y would increase or decrease? A deductive approach to determine the numerical parameters might involve knowing the relation between X and Z and the relation between Z and Y, and then deducing the relation between X and Y. One can also sometimes determine the parameters by making assumptions that are more meaningful than the parameters produced by empirical data analysis. For example, we can make the important assumption that the value of a will be zero in the relation $Y = a + bX$, where Y is a benefit, X is a cost, and we recognize that there are generally no benefits without costs.[7]

Simplicity in Determining Causation

In policy analysis, we are unwilling to adopt policy X in order to achieve goal Y unless we know that there is a causal connection between the two, although the connection may involve an intervening Z variable which X causes and which then in turn causes Y. In other words, we don't adopt a policy X just because there may be a chance correlation with goal Y that has no causal basis. Policy analysis may be simpler than ordinary social science when it comes to causation because in policy analysis, we only want to know the extent to which policy X_1 causes goal Y as compared to other policies. It is not necessary to know the causal influence of various nonpolicy variables.

A good example might be the policy problem of how to allocate the budget of the Law Enforcement Assistance Administration (LEAA) across a set of cities to minimize crime. For each city, we could attempt to determine the marginal rate of return for each additional anticrime dollar by obtaining data at various points in time showing (1) the amount of crime occurring, and (2) the amount of anticrime dollars spent. For each city, we would then calculate the numerical parameters for the equation, $Y = aX^b$ when Y is crime and X is anticrime dollars. The marginal rate of return is then baX^{b-1}, which means that if X goes up 1 unit, Y will go up baX^{b-1} units. Common sense tells us that b should be negative; thus when anticrime dollars increase, crime should go down. The exponent or elasticity coefficient is likely to be positive because (1) the occurrence of crime has more of a positive influence on increasing anticrime dollars than the negative influence of anticrime dollars on crime, and (2) both crime and anticrime dollars are coeffects or correlates of other variables, such as urbanism, which cause them to vary positively together.

To control for the reciprocal causation, social scientists might use a complicated two-stage least-squares approach, which would determine how much causation goes in each direction. In policy analysis, however, we may only want to know one direction; that is, from X to Y. To control for the influence of other variables, social scientists might use a complicated multivariate regression analysis with many additional variables that influence both crime and anticrime dollars. In policy analysis, however, we may only want to control collectively, rather than to learn the causal influence of each of those variables individually.

For policy analysis purposes, the b coefficient can be almost consistently negative by working with the following equation: $Y_t = a(X_{t-1})^{b_1} (Y_{t-1})^{b_2}$. When we control for a crime at a prior point in time, we are indirectly controlling for all the variables that influence prior crime without knowing exactly what they are. By lagging anticrime dollars, we are decreasing the possibility that the elasticity coefficient (i.e., b_1) will be influenced by the impact of crime on anticrime dollars, since crime at time t cannot influence anticrime dollars at time $t - 1$. We can thus determine a meaningful marginal rate of return for each city by working with a single bivariate relation of crime and anticrime dollars, and we need not work with a series of simultaneous reciprocal multivariate equations. Figure 13-3 summarizes the relations among the relevant variables, and Table 13-1 shows the alternative

FIGURE 13-3
Illustrating Simplicity in Determining Causation: *a*, Relations Between Crime, Anticrime Dollars, and Other Crime Causes.

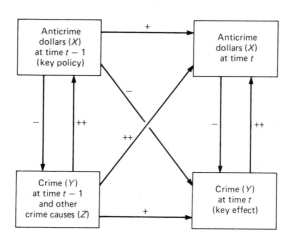

TABLE 13-1
Determining the Negative Relation Between Crime and Anticrime Dollars

Regression Equation	Direction of b_1	Direction of b_2
$Y_t = a(X_t)^{b_1}$	+	
$Y_t = a(X_t)^{b_1}(Z_t)^{b_2}$	+	+
$Y_t = a(X_{t-1})^{b_1}(Z_{t-1})^{b_2}$	+	+
$Y_t = a(X_{t-1})^{b_1}(Y_{t-1})^{b_2}$	−	+

regression equations for expressing the relation between crime and anticrime dollars.

Often in policy analysis, it is unnecessary to determine causation to prescribe effective policies. This is analogous to a psychiatrist who prescribes an antidepressant to provide psychological uplift. The goal is to buoy the patient long enough for a spontaneous recovery, the way cold capsules relieve cold symptoms while one recovers from a cold. It is not necessary to know exactly how antidepressants work, or what caused the psychological depression. An example in the legal process field would be adopting the policy of compulsory retirement of judges to lessen conservatism on the bench. One can feel reasonably confident such a retirement policy will generally help achieve that goal without knowing whether older judges are more conservative than younger judges because (1) there is something about the aging process that makes people become more conservative as they grow older, or (2) older judges are actually more liberal than they were when they were younger, but they are less liberal than younger judges because they were socialized at a more conservative time period. The latter explanation seems to be more accurate, but for prescriptive purposes, compulsory retirement might be prescribed or opposed regardless of the relative validity of explanation one or two.[8]

To further simplify statistically oriented causal analysis, policy-analysis students and professionals should purchase an inexpensive hand calculator that can do regression analysis. As of January 1983, they were available for less than $30. To use such a calculator, one generally follows a set of steps like these:

1. input an X and a Y value for the first person, place, or other unit of analysis
2. do likewise for the second unit and so on until a sample of about 30 units has been covered
3. hit the b button to read out the regression coefficient or slope
4. hit the a button for the Y-intercept or constant
5. hit the r button for the correlation coefficient

These basic steps can be varied by doing such things as: (1) hitting the log button after each X and/or Y value to obtain nonlinear regression coefficients, and (2) inputting many $X = 0$ and $Y = 0$ pairs to force the relation to show that a zero policy generates zero goal achievement. If there are more than 30 units of analysis, one can work with a random sample of the data and the results will almost perfectly reflect what the total data set would yield. If the number of independent variables is greater than one, then either (1) redefine the X or Y variable to be more of a composite, (2) determine the relations between Y and X_1, Y and X_2, and X_1 and X_2 and use these relations to determine the coefficients for the multivariate equation of Y as a function of X_1 and X_2, or (3) resort to a microcomputer if the essential number of X variables becomes unwieldy for a hand calculator.

Simplicity in Finding an Optimum Level

Would-be policy analysts are often frightened by the alleged need to learn and use calculus to find an optimum policy level (where doing too much or too little is undesirable) or to find an optimum policy mix (where allocations are made so as to equalize marginal rates of return). A good optimum-level example is the previously mentioned problem of determining the percent of defendants who should be held in jail prior to trial.

Suppose we know from a statistical analysis of data for a set of cities that the relation between holding costs (HC) and the percent held ($\%H$) is of the form $HC = a(\%H)^b$, where b is positive but less than 1. This equation shows that as $\%H$ goes up, holding costs go up at an increasingly steep rate. Suppose we also know from the same statistical analysis that the relation between releasing costs (RC) and the percent held ($\%H$) is of the form $RC = A(\%H)^B$, where B is a negative number. This equation shows that as

$\%H$ goes up, releasing costs go down but at a diminishing rate. Using this information, find the optimum policy level or percent to hold.

The calculus approach to solving this problem is to: (1) find the derivative of HC relative to $\%H$, (2) find the derivative of RC relative to $\%H$, (3) sum these two derivatives, (4) set the sum equal to zero, and (5) solve for $\%H$. Solving for $\%H$ involves summing $ba(\%H)^{b-1}$ and $BA(\%H)^{B-1}$, and then solving for $\%H$ in terms of these numerical parameters, which tells us that $\%H^*$ (or the optimum $\%H$) equals $-ab/AB$ raised to the power $1/(B - b)$. To simplify this analysis (at least semantically), talk in terms of slopes rather than derivatives. The increasing holding cost curve has an infinite number of slopes in the sense of straight lines drawn tangent to the curve. They are close to horizontal at first (when $\%H$ is close to zero), then become more diagonal, and finally become almost vertical (when $\%H$ is close to 100%). The slope at any point is equal to $ba(\%H)^{b-1}$. One can easily remember that when $Y = aX^b$, then a change in Y relative to a change in X at any point equals baX^{b-1}, which shows the slope depends on the value of X. This rule of slopes or calculus is sufficient information to enable one to perform many optimizing analyses. You need not understand the theory behind the rule or any other complicated calculus rules.

One can, however, avoid even this bit of complexity by thinking of all optimum level problems as involving discrete policies rather than an infinite continuum of policies. Thus, to solve the above problem, all one really needs is a hand calculator that can handle exponents. One then simply determines the value of the expression $a(\%H)^b + A(\%H)^B$ for various values of $\%H$. One is thereby determining the total costs for various levels of $\%H$. In doing so, one will quickly find that total costs go down when moving from zero to $\%H^*$, and then they go up. If the optimum is 4 percent, total costs decrease prior to 4 percent, and they increase subsequent to 4 percent. In a few minutes of trying alternative values for $\%H$, one can quickly find the bottom point on total costs to any number of decimal places one desires, although percentages are usually expressed in terms of two-place decimals. One can reach the convergence point even faster with a programmable calculator, which makes it unnecessary to reinsert the numerical values of a, b, A, and B every time one tries a new tentative value for $\%H$.[9]

Simplicity in Finding an Optimum Mix

A good optimum mix problem to illustrate the ease of avoiding calculus is the previously mentioned problem of allocating the budget of the Law Enforcement Assistance Administration (LEAA) across a set of cities to minimize crime. Suppose we know from a statistical analysis that the relation between crime at a given time (Y_t) and anticrime dollars at a prior time (X_{t-1}) takes the form $Y_t = a(X_{t-1})^{b_1}(Y_{t-1})^{b_2}$. Using an equation like that for each city, find the optimum mix of a given total budget across the cities.

A calculus approach to solving this problem involves: (1) finding the derivative of Y_t relative to X_{t-1} for each city, (2) setting these derivatives equal to each other which involves one equation if there are only two cities and an $N - 1$ chain of equations if there are N cities, (3) adding an equation that shows all the Xs summing to G or the grand total available to be distributed, and (4) solving this set of equations simultaneously by using laborious successive substitution or some other complicated method. This approach can be drastically simplified by changing the curve-fitting equations to the form $Y_t = a + b_1(\log X_{t-1}) + b_2(Y_{t-1})$. One can then prove with calculus and algebra that allocating to each city in proportion to its b_1 coefficient will provide an optimum mix. This means that X_i^* equals $(b_i/\Sigma b)G$. In other words, each city should receive a fraction of G equal to the ratio between (1) its semilog regression coefficient, and (2) the sum of the regression coefficients for all the cities that have coefficients going in the right direction.

To further simplify matters, one could score each city on a series of dimensions that indicate how efficiently the city spends its anticrime money. One dimension might include a merit system for hiring criminal justice personnel on a 1-to-10 scale. Another dimension might involve scoring each city according to its crime rate, and thus determining how much additional funds are needed. One could develop a set of meaningful unweighted or weighted dimensions and compute them the same way gymnasts or decathlon athletes are scored. One would then arrive at an overall score for each city and allocate the total budget in proportion to these overall scores after providing each city with a certain equitable minumum and possibly limiting each city to a certain equitable maximum. One would not want to allocate the entire budget to the best city, since this would probably be wasteful. Giving the 100th dollar to the best city may produce less crime reduction than giving the 1st dollar to the worst city. By allocating proportionately, the overall scores are used in the same way as the allocation coefficients. They are not identical, but they may be simpler to understand.[10]

Conclusion

One can summarize the preceding analysis in terms of five general principles as follows:

1. In measuring policies and goals, simple dichotomies or trichotomies can often be meaningful and provide insights in choosing among alternative policies for achieving given goals.
2. In deciding among alternative policies, the relative value of the goals to be achieved, but not their absolute value, generally must be determined. If three goals are being simultaneously considered, one needs to know how many times more valuable each goal is relative to the least valuable one, but seldom is anything more complicated than this necessary to know.

3. Policy analysis often works with small nonrandom samples because (a) the solutions are not very sensitive to sampling differences, (b) the sensitivity can be determined by partitioning the sample, (c) the samples are often purposively representative or cover a universe of legal jurisdiction, (d) the lack of place units can be partly offset by having many time points, as in a quasi-experimental policy-interrupted time series, and (e) the lack of sample size can be offset by in-depth analysis of the places studied.

4. In relating policies to goals, insights can often be obtained by merely expressing (a) the relative direction of the relations, (b) a rough range concerning the magnitude of the relations, and (c) their general shape. This information can sometimes be obtained more easily and meaningfully by surveying knowledgeable people, deducing it from known relations, or by making assumptions, than by performing a complicated statistical regression analysis.

5. Policy analysis generally does not require complete causal models. It only needs those portions that deal with the causal relations between the goals sought and the policies available. The causal relations among other related variables is generally irrelevant for making policy decisions, although possibly relevant for a complete understanding of what accounts for variation on a dependent variable.

6. When determining an optimum policy level at which either too much or too little action is undesirable, try many alternative numerical values for the policy until one arrives at the value that produces the lowest total costs, the highest total benefits, or the highest benefits minus costs, depending on how the goal to be maximized is phrased.

7. When determining an optimum mix in allocating scarce resources across activities or places, allocate the total budget in proportion to the nonlinear regression coefficients, or in proportion to overall scores that have been assigned each place or activity with regard to their relative efficiency on various dimensions.

In closing, note the simplicity of the data analysis in what may be the two most important criminal justice research projects in the last 25 years, namely, the Pretrial Release Project of the Vera Institute and the Jury Project of the University of Chicago. The Pretrial Release Project showed that a criminal justice system can substantially increase pretrial release, and not increase the nonappearance rate if screening and notification are used. This policy research was responsible for bail reform projects throughout the country, and yet the methodology for predicting whether a defendant was a good risk to release was quite crude. No regression, discriminant, probit, log-linear, or other sophisticated predictive tools were used, but percentages and crude integer weights as part of a predictive point system were used. The University of Chicago's Jury Project has had a substantial impact in generating numerous ideas for (1) reducing delay in the court without abolishing jury trials, (2) showing and explaining differences between outcomes in jury and bench trials, and (3) testing the effects of alternative jury instructions on evidence, insanity, and other matters. The main Jury Project books and articles (by Hans Zeisel and Harry Kalven) generally contain statistics no more complicated than percentages, bar graphs, and simple counting.[11]

Gilbert and Sullivan wrote that every child is destined to become a liberal or a conservative. In social science research, the analog is classifying researchers in terms of whether they have a can-do, optimistic attitude, or a can't-do, pessimistic one. Social science research can lead to two kinds of errors. One error is the failure to be accurate and precise in one's findings. The other error, for which there is less concern, is the opportunity-cost error of failing to plunge ahead with relatively crude tools for fear of being inaccurate, thereby missing the opportunity of developing a valuable project. An undue concern for precision may not only restrain research, but when it is completed the results may be too complex to communicate to policy makers and policy appliers. In policy analysis, including criminal justice policy analysis, more sensitivity to avoiding such opportunity errors, while preserving a reasonable concern for precision, is necessary. Policy analysis is too important to be hung up by overconcern for precision in measurement, weighting, sampling, prediction, and causal analysis. Policy researchers who use simple data analysis should be proud of doing so. We would be happy if their numbers multiplied.

NOTES

1. On sensitivity and postoptimizing analysis, see Harvey Wagner, *Principles of Operations Research: With Applications to Managerial Decisions* (Prentice-Hall, 1969), 129–64; David Anderson, David Sweeney, and Thomas Williams, *An Introduction to Management Science: Quantitative Approaches to Decision Making* (West, 1976), 143–70; and Hamdy Taha, *Operations Research: An Introduction* (Macmillan, 1971), 94–109.
2. On robustness in statistical analysis, see Sanford Labovitz, "Statistical Usage in Sociology: Sacred Cows and Ritual," 1 *Sociological Methods and Research* 13–37 (1972); Sanford Labovitz, "Some Observations on Measurement and Statistics," 46 *Social Forces* 151–60 (1967); and George Bohrnstedt and T. Michael Carter, "Robustness in Regression Analysis" in Howard Costner (ed.), *Sociological Methodology* (Jossey-Bass, 1971). Nonparametric statistics, which are relatively assumption free, are usually more robust than parametric statistics. See Sidney Siegel, *Nonparametric Statistics for the Behavioral Sciences* (McGraw-Hill, 1956). Statisticians are also increasingly advocating exploratory data analysis with relatively crude data and analytic methods. See John Tukey, *Exploratory Data Analysis* (Addison-Wesley, 1977). Unfortunately, statistical software packages like SPSS often encourage needless complexity by facilitating use of such methods as factor analysis to reduce the number of variables, rather than by encouraging thought on which variables are most important to use as

goals or as policies in light of the purposes of the analysis. By emphasizing purposes, policy analysis often presents clear questions that need answers. Quantitative social science, by generating products like a 100 by 100 correlation matrix, offers thousands of answers to which worthwhile questions should be applied.

3. On policy analysis as the social scientific method applied to evaluating alternative public policies, see David Nachmias, *Public Policy Evaluation: Approaches and Methods* (St. Martin's Press, 1979); Theodore Poister, *Public Program Analysis: Applied Research Methods* (University Park Press, 1978); and S. Nagel and Marian Neef, *Policy Analysis: In Social Science Research* (Sage, 1979). On policy analysis specifically in a criminal justice context, see Malcolm Klein and Kathie Teilmann (eds.), *Handbook of Criminal Justice Evaluation* (Sage, 1980); Daniel Glaser, *Routinizing Evaluation: Getting Feedback on Effectiveness of Crime and Delinquency Programs* (National Institute of Mental Health, 1973); and Suzette Talarico (ed.), *Criminal Justice Research: Approaches, Problems, and Policy* (Anderson, 1980).

4. On the example of choosing between an elected and an appointed judiciary, see S. Nagel, "Comparing Elected and Appointed Judicial Systems" in *Improving the Legal Process: Effects of Alternatives* (Lexington-Heath, 1975). On working with dichotomous measurement, see M. Dutta, "Dummy Variables" in *Econometric Methods* (South-Western, 1975).

5. On the example of deciding whether to adopt the rule excluding illegally seized evidence, see S. Nagel, "Choosing among Alternative Public Policies" in Kenneth Dolbeare (ed.), *Public Policy Evaluation* (Sage, 1975); and S. Nagel, "Effects of Excluding Illegally Seized Evidence" in *The Legal Process from a Behavioral Perspective* (Dorsey, 1969). On simple systems for weighting goals, see Allan Easton, *Complex Managerial Decisions Involving Multiple Objectives* (Wiley, 1973).

6. On the example of determining an optimum percent of defendants to hold in jail prior to trial, see S. Nagel and Marian Neef, "The Policy Problem of Doing Too Much or Too Little: Pretrial Release as a Case in Point" in *Legal Policy Analysis: Finding an Optimum Level or Mix* (Lexington-Heath, 1977). On alternatives to random sampling for drawing inferences in a policy analysis context, see Thomas Cook and Donald Campbell, *Quasi-Experimentation: Design and Analysis Issues for Field Settings* (Rand McNally, 1979).

7. On the example of choosing among alternative ways of providing lawyers to the poor, see S. Nagel and Marian Neef, "Reaching a Decision on How to Provide Legal Counsel for the Poor" in *The Legal Process: Modeling the System* (Sage, 1977). For further discussions of regression analysis applied to policy data, see Edward Tufte, *Data Analysis for Politics and Policy* (Prentice-Hall, 1974).

8. On the example of determining the impact of anticrime dollars on crime, see S. Nagel and Marian Neef, "Allocating Anti-Crime Dollars Across Places and Activities" in *Policy Evaluation: Making Optimum Decisions* (Praeger, 1982). On simple causal analysis with policy examples, see Hans Zeisel, *Say It With Figures* (Harper & Row, 1968); and Hubert Blalock, *Causal Inferences in Nonexperimental Research* (University of North Carolina Press, 1964).

9. On simple optimum level analysis, see Michael White, Ross Clayton, Robert Myrtle, Gilbert Siegel, and Aaron Rose, *Managing Public Systems: Analytic Techniques for Public Administration* (Duxbury, 1980), especially Chapters 10 and 16, and S. Nagel, *Policy Evaluation: Making Optimum Decisions* (Praeger, 1982), especially Chapters 6 through 9.

10. On simple optimum mix analysis, see Michael White, *ibid.*, note 9, especially Chapters 12 and 14; and S. Nagel, *ibid.*, note 9, especially Chapters 10 through 13.

11. The main Vera Institute report on the Pretrial Release Project is: Charles Ares, Anne Rankin, and Herbert Sturz, "The Manhattan Bail Project: An Interim Report on the Use of Pre-Trial Parole," 38 *New York University Law Review* 67–95 (1963). The main reports on the University of Chicago jury project are: Harry Kalven and Hans Zeisel, *The American Jury* (Little, Brown, 1966); and Hans Zeisel, Harry Kalven, and Bernard Buchholz, *Delay in the Court* (Little, Brown, 1959).

QUESTIONS

1. Give an example in which simple dichotomies for measuring policies or goals may be sufficient for reducing policy-evaluation decisions.
2. How might one determine the relative weight of policy goals in terms of a threshold value, rather than an exact value?
3. In policy analysis, why can one often work with smaller samples than might be acceptable in traditional social science?
4. In relating policies to goals, what methods might be quite meaningful other than scoring a number of persons, places, or things on both the policies and goals and then doing a cross-tabulation or regression analysis?
5. How can one separate the influence of goal achievement on policy level from the influence of policy level on goal achievement?
6. In finding an optimum policy level, how can one avoid the use of calculus by using reiterative guessing until one achieves convergence with a programmable calculator?
7. In finding an optimum policy mix or allocation, how can one avoid marginal analysis by allocating in proportion to elasticity coefficients or semilog regression coefficients?

REFERENCES

Bohrnstedt, George, and T. Michael Carter, "Robustness in Regression Analysis" in Howard Costner (ed.), *Sociological Methodology* (Jossey-Bass, 1971).

Labovitz, Sanford, "Statistical Usage in Sociology: Sacred Cows and Ritual," 1 *Sociological Methods and Research* 13–37 (1972).

Labovitz, Sanford, "Some Observations on Measurement and Statistics," 46 *Social Forces* 151–60 (1967).

Moore, C., *Profitable Applications of the Break-Even System* (Prentice-Hall, 1971).

Nagel, S., and Marian Neef, *Policy Analysis: In Social Science Research* (Sage, 1979).

Siegel, Sidney, *Nonparametric Statistics for the Behavioral Sciences* (McGraw-Hill, 1956).

Tukey, John, *Exploratory Data Analysis* (Addison-Wesley, 1977).

Zeisel, Hans, *Say It With Figures* (Harper & Row, 1968).

CHAPTER 14

Nonmonetary Variables

Benefit-cost analysis can be defined as choosing among alternative decisions by picking the decision that has the highest score on a combination of benefits and costs. A leading objection to the feasibility of such an approach is that one cannot combine benefits and costs meaningfully when the costs of various decisions are in dollars and the benefits are in nonmonetary units, especially units that relate to different kinds of outputs, such as cases processed and highway miles built. This chapter discusses some new but simple methods for applying benefit-cost analysis when the variables are nonmonetary. In essence, the approach involves handling nonmonetary variables by converting the problems into questions as to whether a given nonmonetary return is worth more or less than a given dollar cost, even though we do not know how many dollars the nonmonetary return is worth.[1]

Table 3-1 provides hypothetical data for illustrating benefit-cost analysis with nonmonetary variables. The data consists of information on the predicted benefits and costs of five projects which are referred to as projects D, E, F, G, and H. The letters A, B, and C are avoided because B and C refer to benefits and costs. The data is general enough to be applicable to any specific subject matter. Table 3-1 also shows each project's net benefits (or profits) and its benefit/cost ratio (or efficiency score). The rank order of each project on all four measures is also shown.[2]

Figure 14-1 clarifies that we will use the data from the table to answer eight types of problems that are common in benefit-cost analysis. These problems can be classified in terms of whether the goal is to maximize benefits subject to a cost constraint or to minimize costs subject to a benefit constraint. They can then be subclassified by whether they involve monetary or nonmonetary benefits. Those with nonmonetary benefits involve either one output (like varying degrees of cases processed) or different kinds of outputs (like cases processed, highway miles built, and so on). The problems can also be classified by whether the projects are mutually exclusive, or whether the problems allow for combinations of projects.[3]

FIGURE 14-1
Problems Illustrating Benefit-Cost Analysis with Nonmonetary Variables

Maximize benefits minus costs   *Minimize costs*

Monetary benefits   *Nonmonetary benefits*

	One output	Different kinds of outputs		
Mutually exclusive projects	1	3	5	7
Allowing combinations of projects	2	4	6	8

Monetary Benefits, Mutually Exclusive Projects

Suppose we have $10.00 available which will enable us to buy any one of the five projects. Which one should we buy? At first glance one might say project F is the most efficient because it has the highest benefit/cost ratio. The benefit/cost ratio is equal to the interest rate if we subtract 1.00 from the B/C ratio. Thus the 1.75 B/C ratio for project F is the equivalent of an interest rate of 0.75. An alternative way to arrive at 0.75 is to think of the $2.00 cost as being principal, the $1.50 net benefits as being interest, and the $3.50 as being principal plus interest. The ratio of interest to principal is thus $1.50/$2.00, or 0.75, which is a better interest rate than any of the other investments offer. Project E offers a benefit/cost ratio of 1.35, or an interest rate of 0.35.[4]

Nonetheless, it is most advantageous to invest our $10.00 in project E because it will increase our net worth more than project F or the other three projects would. If we invest our $10.00 principal in project E, we will have $3.50 in interest, $10.00 in principal, and $0.00 in unspent funds, for a total of $13.50 at the end of the one-year time period. If we invest our $10.00 principal in project F, we will have $1.50 in interest, $2.00 in principal, and $8.00 in unspent funds, for a total of only $11.50 at the end of the year. Our net worth would thus be $2.00 lower than with Project E. In other words, it is best to choose the project that maximizes benefits minus costs, rather than the project that maximizes benefits divided by costs.

An alternative way of viewing this problem is to liken the decision maker to a consumer rather than to an investor. Under these circumstances, if we consume our $10.00 by buying project E, we will receive the satisfaction that $13.50 buys, with no unspent funds, for a total satisfaction worth $13.50. If we consume our $10.00 by buying project F, we will receive $3.50 in satisfaction, with $8.00 in unspent funds, for a total satisfaction equal to

$11.50. Thus, either from the investor or the consumer analogy, it would be better to use our $10.00 budget to buy project E (with the higher B-C score) than to buy project F (with the higher B/C score). The project with the higher B-C score also usually has the higher B/C score because the costs are usually held constant. The two scores do not necessarily go together when the costs are not held constant. These ideas are summarized in Table 14-1, which compares two projects with monetary benefits.[5]

One might argue that the best alternative is to buy five project Fs for our $10.00 at $2.00 apiece. This alternative, however, is not available with the hypothetical data of Table 14-1. We only have a choice among D, E, F, G, or H with mutually exclusive projects, or among combinations of D, E, F, G, and H when we are allowing for combinations.[6] If they are mutually exclusive projects, they are like building five different dams on a given river segment. It would be wasteful to build more than one dam since only one dam is needed to hold back the water. It would be meaningless to build two copies of dam F next to each other or on top of each other. It would also be meaningless to build half of a dam. If we think of these projects as being noncontinuum and nondivisible projects that allow for combinations, then they are like buying neckties. One would not buy five copies of the same necktie; similarly, one would not buy half or any other fraction of a necktie. One could, however, meaningfully buy all five neckties.[7]

One might posit that buying F with our $10.00 budget would be more advantageous than buying E because we would have $8.00 remaining to spend elsewhere. There is, however, no elsewhere if these are mutually exclusive projects, according to the hypothetical (but frequently occurring) problem. If, however, the $8.00 could be spent on another project, what would the interest and interest rate have to be for that other project to make the combination of project F and the other project a better purchase than project E? The interest would have to be $2.01 to raise the total interest

---

TABLE 14-1
Comparing Two Projects with Monetary Benefits (relevant to problem 1)

Using an Investor Analogy

PROJECT	INTEREST		PRINCIPAL		UNSPENT FUNDS		TOTAL ASSETS
E	$3.50	+	$10.00	+	$0.00	=	$13.50
F	1.50	+	2.00	+	8.00	=	11.50

Using a Consumer Analogy

PROJECT	CONSUMER SATISFACTION		POTENTIAL SATISFACTION		TOTAL SATISFACTION
E	$13.50	+	$0.00	=	$13.50
F	3.50	+	8.00	=	11.50

Threshold interest = $13.50 − $11.50 = $2.00.
Threshold interest rate = $2.00/$8.00 = 0.25 = 25%.

above the $3.50 of project E. In other words, the threshold interest is the profit of the first-place project minus the profit of the second-place project. Exceeding the threshold interest means earning $0.01 more than $2.00. The threshold interest rate would have to be 0.25, or $2.00 divided by $8.00. If there is no such new project or if the $8.00 cannot be spent on it, then project E is the best alternative. Even if there is a project on which the $8.00 can be spent that crosses the threshold interest, we would favor project F plus that other project only because the combination produces a higher B-C score than the B-C score of project E alone. In other words, benefits minus costs is always the general criterion.[8]

An alternative way of comparing project E and project F is by part/whole percentaging. This involves converting the raw scores for each project into part/whole percentages and then calculating the average unweighted or weighted percentage for each project. More specifically, if E has 13.50 benefits and F has 3.50 benefits, then E has 79 percent of the total benefits and F has 21 percent. Likewise, if E has $10 in costs and F has $2 in costs, then E has 83 percent of the costs and F has 17 percent. We should work with the complements of these cost percentages since high costs are undesirable. This gives E a 17 percent score on the costs variable and F an 83 percent score. Project E thus has an average percentage score of 48 percent; that is, $(70\% + 17\%)/2$. Project F has an average percentage score of 52 percent; that is, $(21\% + 83\%)/2$. If we give a relative weight of 2 to the benefit units over the dollar costs, then project E has a weighted average of 58 percent; that is, $(70\% + 70\% + 17\%)/3$. With this weighting, project F's weighted average is 42 percent; that is, $(21\% + 21\% + 83\%)/3$. One can easily determine that the threshold weight which enables project E to move ahead of project F is 1.14. This is determined by solving for W in the break-even equation, $(70W + 17) = (21W + 83)$. A part/whole percentaging approach is especially useful if there are many different kinds of benefits and many different projects.

Monetary Benefits, Allowing Combinations

If we could buy any combination of projects with our $10.00, which would be the best combination? At first, one might say project E. It provides us with the highest score on benefits minus costs for any of the projects, and we want to maximize benefits minus costs. This, however, would be an unwise use of our $10.00 because other uses would yield higher net benefits than project E. For example, D and G only cost $9.00 and will yield $4.20 in net benefits. Likewise, the combinations of D-H, F-H, and F-H all cost $10.00 or less and produce more than $3.50 in net profit.

One might, therefore, buy as many projects as possible rather than buy the one project that by itself yields the highest net benefits. This approach would probably lead us to buy projects D, F, and H, since they would cost us only $9.00 and yield $5.10 in net benefits. This, however, would also be an unwise use of our $10.00 because it would not yield as much profit, and thus not as much net gain at the end of the time period as buying projects G and H. The superior nature of G and H can be seen by noting that if we invest in this pair of projects, we will have $5.40 in interest, $10.00 in principal, and $0.00 in unspent funds, for a net worth or total assets of $15.40 at the end of the time period. If, however, we buy projects D, F, and H, then we will have $5.10 in interest, $9.00 in principal, and $1.00 in unspent funds, for a total net worth of only $15.10.[9]

One irony of G and H as an optimum choice is that it involves two projects, rather than three. Another irony is that these two projects taken separately are ranked mediocre on every individual criterion. They have a middling score on benefits produced, costs saved, net benefits, and on their respective benefit/cost ratios. They are, thus, separately not very effective, inexpensive, profitable, or efficient projects. What counts, though, is that the G-H combination collectively produces the most total profit for an available budget of $10, given the hypothetical, but realistic data of Table 3-1. This is an example in which suboptimizing each individual project does not produce an overall optimum with regard to maximizing total benefits minus costs.

The next logical question is, How does one determine that the G-H combination is the best choice? The G-H combination maximizes total benefits minus costs. When dealing with a set of discrete or lump-sum projects, the most meaningful procedure is probably to list all the feasible combinations when the total number is manageable, as it usually is. There are five one-project possibilities here, namely, D, E, F, G, and H. There are 10 two-project possibilities, as shown in the costs-combinations matrix of Figure 14-2. Only costs are shown above the main diagonal, since the cells below the main diagonal duplicate those above it, and since cells on the main diagonal involve impermissibly combining a project with itself. This matrix shows: (1) there are 10 possible combinations with five projects taken two at a time, (2) what these 10 combinations are, and (3) how much each combination costs. We can immediately eliminate four of these 10 combinations since they cost more than $10. The remaining six combinations are shown in parentheses to add to our previous five one-project combinations, thereby yielding 11 combinations thus far. We can then look for combinations that involve three or more projects. By looking at Figure 14-2, we can see that the D-F combination could have H added to it without exceeding $10. Likewise, the D-H combination could have F added to it, and the F-H combination could have D added to it. Nothing can be added to the D-G, F-G, or G-H combinations. Thus there is only one three-project combination that is economically feasible, namely, D-F-H. We have thus quickly determined that there are 12 feasible combinations.

FIGURE 14-2
A Costs-Combinations Matrix for the Data from Table 3-1 (relevant to problem 2)

	D	E	F	G	H
D		13.00	(5.00)	(9.00)	(7.00)
E			12.00	16.00	14.00
F				(8.00)	(6.00)
G					(10.00)
H					

The next logical thing to do is to determine the profitability of each one of these 12 combinations. For the five one-project combinations we can look to column 2 of Table 3-1 and see that project E is the most profitable, with a profit of $3.50. Out of the 10 two-project combinations, only six are feasible. Figure 14-3 provides us with a profits-combinations matrix for the data from Table 3-1. The six economically feasible combinations are shown in parentheses. We can quickly see that the G-H combination is the most profitable of that set, with a $5.40 profit. It is more profitable than E or the D-F-H combination, yielding $3.50 and $5.10, respectively.

Listing the feasible possibilities and their profits may not be mathematically elegant, but it is generally a more meaningful approach than any formula or decision rule based on looking at the B/C ratios of each project. For example, some authorities recommend starting with the most efficient project for spending part of the budget, then moving to the next most efficient, and so on until we spend our available budget. If we followed this suggestion, we would first plug in project F, since it is the most efficient with a 1.75 B/C ratio. We would then move on to project H, since it is the next most efficient. We would then have spent only $6, and we would be ready for the next project. If we then buy G, we will have exceeded our $10 budget by $2. We can, therefore, forget about G, and move on to D as next in efficiency. This is economically feasible since the D-F-H combination costs only $9. We would, however, then get stuck with the D-F-H combination, which we have shown is inferior to the G-H combination. One could modify the rule about choosing the projects in the order of their B/C ratios by generally requiring in problem 2 that all of the available $10 budget be spent to maximize total benefits minus costs. This approach, however, is more complicated than simply listing the feasible combinations and noting their respective profits.[10]

FIGURE 14-3
**A Profits-Combinations Matrix for the Data from Table 3-1 (also relevant
to problem 2)**

	D	E	F	G	H
D		4.70	(2.70)	(4.20)	(3.60)
E			5.00	6.50	5.90
F				(4.50)	(3.90)
G					(5.40)
H					

Nonmonetary Benefits, One Output, Mutually Exclusive Projects

A key purpose of this chapter is to discuss benefit-cost analysis with non-monetary benefits, which is what benefits in public policy problems usually are. By first understanding the dynamics of handling B-C problems with monetary benefits, we better understand how they can be handled with nonmonetary benefits. Instead of considering the benefits column of the hypothetical data in terms of dollars, think that the 4.20 now represents 4.20 in benefit units for whatever type of subject matter one is interested in. For illustrating problems 3 and 4, consider the benefits as being 4.20 cases processed, 13.50 cases processed, and so on. Under these circumstances, which is the best project?

We cannot answer that question simply by subtracting the dollar costs from the nondollar benefits. It is meaningless to talk about 4.20 cases minus $3.00, and it is often too difficult to convert 4.20 benefit units into dollars. Instead, we must successively compare one project with another. If, for example, there were a project K that involved 4.60 cases for $2.50, that project would obviously be superior to project D, since D provides both less benefits (4.20 cases) and more costs ($3.00). None of the projects in Table 14-1, though, dominate any other project. There are five projects. This means 10 paired comparisons since five times four divided by two is 10. We multiply by four rather than five since we are not interested in comparing any project with itself. We divide by two since a comparison between D and E is the same as one between E and D. We must actually make only four paired comparisons to determine the best project. We can compare D with E. The winner is then compared with F. The winner of the second comparison is compared with G, with the winner of this third comparison being compared with H. The winner of this comparison is then declared the best project, since the last one left will beat any of the other four projects given the nature of the simple arithmetic involved.[11] How, though, does one conduct each comparison?

Suppose we want to compare projects E and F (remember that in problem 1, E had the best B-C score, and F had the best B/C score). Table 14-2 is helpful in clarifying the nature of the comparison. It shows that if we go from the less beneficial project (F) to the more beneficial project (E), we gain 10 cases or benefit units, but we lose $8.00. The comparison thus simplifies to the question of, Which would we rather have, $8.00 more or 10 more cases? One might find the question more comfortable if it is phrased as follows: Which is better, $0.80 or one case? This phrasing recognizes that $8.00 divided by 10 cases is $0.80 per case. It does not mean that we can buy one case since neither project allows for that. Neither does it mean that as we increase our expenditures by $0.80, we automatically increase the cases by one, since this may not be so in view of diminishing returns. If, however, we would rather have $0.80 (or $8.00) than one case (or 10 cases), we should choose project F. If we would rather have the cases than the money, we should choose project E. If both the costs and the benefits were measured in dollars, we would have no trouble choosing between projects E and F. Project E would be better since it provides an additional $10.00 in benefits for only $8.00 in costs, whereas project F saves $8.00 but loses $10.00. If the 10 benefit units are not $10.00, then it is not clear which project is better, unless we know that 10 benefit units are more desirable than $8.00. Important to note is that to decide between projects E and F, we need not know how much one case is worth in terms of dollars. All we must know is whether

TABLE 14-2
Comparing Two Projects or Combinations with Nonmonetary Benefits, One Output

Mutually Exclusive Projects (relevant to problem 2)

PROJECT	BENEFITS	COSTS	B-C
E	13.50 cases	$10.00	Unknown
F	3.50	2.00	Unknown
Increment	+10.00 cases	+$8.00	

Which is better or preferred: 10 cases gained from E, or $8.00 saved from F?

Allowing Combinations of Projects (relevant to problem 4)

PROJECT	BENEFITS	COSTS	B-C
G-H	15.40 cases	$10.00	Unknown
D-F-H	14.10	9.00	Unknown
Increment	+1.30 cases	+$1.00	

Which is better or preferred: 1.30 cases gained from G-H, or $1.00 saved from D-F-H?

one case is worth more or less than $0.80. If we can answer this question by saying "more," it does not make any difference whether one case is worth $1,000.00, $100.00, $10.00, or $1.00, so long as we feel confident that one case is worth more than $0.80.[12]

Technically speaking, the key question is not simply whether 10 cases gained from project E are preferred over $8 saved from project F. However, this is probably a more meaningful question than whether 1 case is preferred over $0.80 because the choice is not 1 case versus $0.80, but 10 cases versus $8. What is lacking in the comparison between 10 cases and $8, however, is a sensitivity to the base from which 10 cases is an increment and the base from which $8 is an increment. Thus, if one already has 500 cases, an additional 10 cases do not produce the same incremental satisfaction that they provide if one has none to begin with. Therefore, when stated more completely, the preference question should be, Which is better or preferred, 10 cases gained over a base of 3.5 cases, or $8 saved? This provides a better picture of the choice to be made. If there were no diminishing returns in the range between 3.50 and 13.50 cases, then it would not be necessary to be so technical in expressing the choice to be made. This is often the case when dealing with the narrow range of alternatives in public policy evaluation.

Through this analysis, we can see project E will be preferred to project F if one case is worth even $0.81. Project F will, however, be rejected in favor of project E if one case is only worth as much as $0.79. If one case happens to be worth exactly $0.80, then projects E and F would be equally worthwhile. Assuming one case is worth more than $0.80, and project E is thus superior to project F, one can then compare project E with any one of the other projects. The winner of this second comparison is compared with a project that has not yet competed. The winner of this comparison gets compared with the only remaining project, which would then complete the analysis. Note that the overall winner will not necessarily be project E just because it won when the benefit units were monetary. The winner with nonmonetary benefit units could be any of the five projects, depending on how many dollars a case is worth (although one does not need to know how many dollars a case is worth to determine the winner). More importantly, if we follow the analysis shown in Table 14-2 for choosing between projects E and F, then we will be choosing the project that scores best on benefits minus costs, even though we cannot calculate the B-C score for either project. This, however, is all right. We do not really care what the B-C score is for each project. We want to know which is the better project, using a B-C criterion.

Throughout this chapter, when we talk about nonmonetary variables we refer to nonmonetary benefits, since benefits are more likely to be nonmonetary than costs are. Any principles developed for nonmonetary benefits, however, would be applicable to nonmonetary costs. For example, if we were to drop the dollar sign from the costs column in Table 14-2, it would simply change the key question from which is worth more, $8 or 10 cases, to which is worth more, eight cost units or 10 benefit units? In the context of cases processed, nonmonetary costs might refer to a drop of eight percentage points in favorable attitudes toward the legal system. The question would then be, Which is worth more—(1) processing an additional 10 cases over a given time period or (2) having an additional eight percentage points in favorable attitudes toward the legal system (e.g., between 70 and 78 percent)? This problem is no more difficult to solve than 10 cases versus $8. Measuring dollar costs, though, might be easier than measuring nondollar costs. Exact, or even approximate measurement, however, may not be necessary, as will be discussed in the section on unknown variables.

When dealing with nonmonetary benefits, most benefit-cost textbooks or textbook chapters advocate either monetizing the benefits or maximizing the benefits subject to a cost constraint. Assigning a monetary value to the benefit units is obviously more difficult than merely stating whether one benefit unit is worth more or less than a threshold value, which can be easily determined by finding the ratio of the incremental benefits to the incremental costs, as in Table 14-2. The cost-effectiveness approach whereby benefits are maximized subject to a cost constraint is inappropriate in many situations. For example, suppose we add a project I to our five projects which provides 10 benefit units for $6 in costs. If we follow the rule of maximizing benefits subject to our $10 cost constraint, then we would spend our $10 on project E, since it provides the most benefits. This might be a mistake because it would provide 13.50 in benefit units and no unspent dollars. On the other hand, buying project I would provide 10 benefit units and $4 in unspent cash. If $1 is worth one benefit unit, then buying project I will give us more satisfaction or more total assets than buying project E, even though buying E maximizes our benefit units subject to our $10 cost constraint.[13] In other words, we do not necessarily want to maximize B subject to a maximum C. What we want to do is to maximize total B minus total C (although this might sometimes conflict with maximizing B subject to a maximum C).[14]

Nonmonetary Benefits, One Output, Allowing Combinations

The situation does not change substantially when we move from problem 3 to problem 4. With problem 3, we had five alternatives to choose from, namely, D, E, F, G, and H. With problem 4, we had 12 alternatives, namely, the five from problem 3, plus the six feasible two-project combinations shown in Figure 14-1 and the one feasible three-project combination. With 12 combinations, we should make 11 paired comparisons to determine which combination is best. Actually, there would be only seven comparisons if we had already made four as part of problem 3. The winner of that series of one-project combinations would then be pitted against any one of the two-project combinations for the fifth comparison. Its winner would then be compared to the next combination, and so on, until only one combination, the winner, remained after the 11 comparisons. The order in which the combinations are arranged should not influence results.

As an example of a comparison in problem 4, suppose we compare the D-F-H combination with the G-H combination. The G-H combination costs $1.00 more ($10.00 versus $9.00), but it results in 1.30 more cases solved (15.40 versus 14.10). If we divide $1.00 by 1.30, we obtain a ratio of $0.77 for one case. This is the ratio of the incremental costs to the incremental benefits. It can be referred to as a threshold-value ratio, because if a case is worth exactly this value, then the two combinations are equally profitable. If a case is worth more than $0.77, then the combination that gives more cases is more profitable. If a case is worth less than $0.77, then the combination that saves more money is more profitable. The question to be answered in making this comparison is, thus, which is better, one case or $0.77? If the answer is one case, then the G-H combination is more desirable. If the answer is $0.77, then the D-F-H combination is more desirable.

Which combination is more desirable does not depend on their relative efficiency. In that regard, the D-F-H combination is slightly more efficient, since its efficiency score or B/C ratio is 14.10 benefit units divided by $9.00, which yields a ratio of 1.57. The G-H combination has a B/C score of 15.40 benefit units divided by $10.00 for a ratio of 1.54. The D-F-H combination, though, will lose the comparison if one case is worth more than $0.77. Likewise, the B-C score in this context is irrelevant. The G-H combination has a higher B-C score of 5.40 compared to the D-F-H score of 5.10. Nevertheless, the D-F-H combination is more desirable if one case is worth less than $0.77. These ideas are summarized in Table 14-2, which compares two combinations of projects having nonmonetary benefits.[15]

Nonmonetary Benefits, Different Outputs, Mutually Exclusive Projects

As previously mentioned, benefit-cost analysis is often considered particularly inapplicable when nonmonetary benefits are involved with multiple kinds of outputs. We can illustrate how this type of problem can be handled with our hypothetical data simply by considering the benefits column as involving:

D. 4.20 cases processed (at $3)
E. 13.50 highway miles built (at $10)
F. 3.50 unemployment percentage points reduced (at $2)
G. 9.00 students trained (at $6)
H. 6.40 patients treated (at $4)

One can substitute any public-sector benefit measures. Also, to make the alternative projects more competitive, consider 4.20 as meaning 4.20 sets of cases processed, rather than individual cases, and consider each set as 10,000 cases. Also assume we know who benefits on each of these five outputs and the quality of the benefits. In other words, we are assuming we know what kinds of cases have been processed and how, where the highway miles have been built and how, whose unemployment has been reduced and how, and so on. With this kind of hypothetical data, which is the one best project to buy with our $10 or 10 monetary units?

Actually, the logical question to ask in this context is not which is the best project, but what is the best procedure for finding the best project? The best procedure will lead us to the best project without consuming undue mental or monetary resources and without providing us with unneeded information. In light of this criterion, the best procedure is a paired-comparisons elimination contest. This contest involves starting with the first project and comparing it with the second. The loser is eliminated, and the winner is paired with the third project. One continues through the five projects, which means there will be only four paired comparisons. Whichever project remains is the best project. How, though, does one conduct each comparison?

For example, suppose we compare E and F again. This time, however, the benefit units, rather than being cases for both, are miles for E and points for F. Thus, we cannot subtract 3.5 points from 13.5 miles, or vice versa, since they are different units of measurement. We can, however, subtract the $2 which project F costs from the $10 which project E costs. As a result, the comparison question becomes, Is the incremental satisfaction in going from 3.5 points to 13.5 miles worth the incremental $8? If there is no incremental satisfaction, then project F is clearly better, since it fares better on both dollars saved and satisfaction gained. If incremental satisfaction is derived from using the more costly E, then E is better if that incremental satisfaction is worth more than the incremental $8. If, however, that incremental satisfaction from F to E is worth less than the incremental $8, then less costly F is better.

Instead of asking whether the incremental satisfaction from F to E is preferred over the incremental $8, one could avoid talking about incremental satisfaction altogether. Suppose project E generates 13.50 patients treated, and project F generates 3.50 students trained. The preference question could then be phrased in terms of whether the 13.50 patients treated are preferred over 3.50 students trained plus an extra $8. In other words, the left side of the preference inequality shows the increment or increments of the first project, and the right side shows the increment or increments of the second project. Instead of talking about benefits as one goal and costs as a second, it is as if we have three separate goals.

If F wins, we can compare F and D. Suppose D wins. We might then compare D and G. Suppose D wins again, and also wins against H; D would then be declared the overall winner. Important to note is that this system does not necessarily tell us anything about which project is second best, or how far from first it is. All that we know from the example is that D is better than all the other projects. We also know that F is better than E. We do not know whether F, G, or H is second to D. So we cannot rank the projects, let alone position them on some kind of 0-to-100 scale. These tasks are generally not worth the extra effort. Usually, all we need to know is which project is best, and that is a relatively easy question to answer even with nonmonetary benefits and different kinds of outputs. If we do want to know which project is second best, we can simply compare F with G, and then the winner with H. We can then determine what the threshold interest, benefits, costs, or other threshold figure would have to be for the second-place project to win over project D and thus become the first-place project.[16]

Working with different outputs is not substantially more complicated if there are different outputs within a given project, as well as across projects. Suppose, for example, project D involved four cases processed and two defendants convicted. We would then want to know which is better between (1) four cases processed plus two defendants convicted at $3, and (2) 13.5 highway miles built at $10. This comparison involves an increment of $7. The question then becomes, Is the incremental satisfaction of 13.5 miles over four cases with two convictions and two acquittals worth more or less than the incremental $7? Important to this situation is that one need not find some way of adding cases processed to defendants convicted, or of subtracting that sum from highway miles built, or vice versa. It is enough to determine which is better. The decision making is simplified, however, by: (1) comparing only two projects at a time, (2) making only the minimum number of comparisons necessary to determine which project or combination is best, (3) deciding whether the incremental costs are justified by the incremental benefits, and (4) calculating the incremental costs.

The ability to work with different outputs for a given project enables the threshold-analysis system to take equity benefits as well as effectiveness benefits into consideration. Up to this point, we have said nothing about how the benefits or costs for each project are distributed, by implying this is an irrelevant consideration. In practical policy analysis, however, distributional equity may be a relevant consideration. Turning back to Table 14-2, for example, one might add a benefits column covering the spread or distribution of each of the two alternative combinations. The threshold question in Table 14-2 was originally, Which is better or preferred, an additional 1.30 cases or an additional $1? The threshold question might now be, Which is better, (1) an additional 1.30 cases, or (2) an additional $1 plus the coverage of an additional place or activity which is provided for by the D-F-H combination over the G-H combination? Saving an additional $1 may not be sufficient to make D-F-H a winner, but the added benefit of possibly more equitable coverage might do so. This approach to adding equity considerations is obviously more meaningful than ignoring these considerations and more meaningful than trying to monetize them as well as the effectiveness benefits of cases processed.

Nonmonetary Benefits, Different Outputs, Allowing Combinations

Neither does the situation become substantially more difficult when we allow for combinations. Assume we are still operating with the hypothetical data from Table 3-1, but the benefits column represents cases processed, highway miles built, and so on, and we are continuing with our $10 budget. Under these circumstances, there are 12 possible combinations, just as there were in problems 2 and 4. The 12 combinations include the five one-project combinations, the six feasible two-project combinations (which are shown in the costs-combination matrix of Figure 14-2), and the one three-project combination.

Problem 6 is reduced to a series of 11 paired comparisons, since N combinations generate $N - 1$ paired comparisons. It takes a little longer to go through 11 paired comparisons than four, but 11 is not so difficult for an average person to handle. If every possible pairing had to be made, there would then be $(12)(11)/2$ paired comparisons, or 66 pairings, which might involve too much work. If we calculate all 66 pairings, we can subject these results to a further analysis which will enable us to rank-order the 12 possible combinations along an interval scale from 0 to 100. This would require substantial data processing as well as mental strain. If all we want to learn is which combination is best, then 11 pairings should be adequate because whichever project remains at the end will defeat any of the other projects. If the remaining project in the elimination contest is only involved in the last pairing, we can assume it would defeat the winner or the loser in the first pairing. Thus, if the twelfth combination wins over the second combination, and the second combination wins over the first, then the twelfth would also win over the first.

Table 14-3 summarizes the analysis that relates to problems 5 and 6. Problem 5 reduces to the question of whether the incremental $8 is worth more or less than the incremental satisfaction of going from a reduction of 3.50 points in the unemployment percentage to 13.50 highway miles built, assuming this increments satisfaction. Problem 6 reduces to the question of whether the incremental $1 is worth more or less than the incremental satisfaction of going from 4.20 cases, 3.50 points, and 6.40 patients to 9.00 students and 6.40 patients, assuming this increments satisfaction.

Minimizing Costs, Mutually Exclusive Projects

In times of especially scarce resources or budget cutting, the goal of benefit-cost analysis may not be to find the project that will maximize benefits subject to a given cost constraint. Instead, the goal may be to discover the project that will minimize costs subject to obtaining a minimum benefit level.[17] This type of benefit-cost analysis can be illustrated with the data from Table 3-1, using either monetary or nonmonetary benefits. The most

TABLE 14-3
Comparing Two Projects or Combinations with Nonmonetary Benefits, Multiple Output

Mutually Exclusive Projects (relevant to problem 5)

PROJECT	BENEFITS	COSTS	B-C
E	13.50 miles	$10.00	Unknown
F	3.50 points	2.00	Unknown
Increment	? satisfaction	$8.00	

Which is better or preferred: the satisfaction gained from E, or the $8 saved from F?

Allowing Combinations of Projects (relevant to problem 6)

PROJECT	BENEFITS	COSTS	B-C
G-H	9.00 students	$10.00	
	(6.40 patients)		Unknown
D-F-H	4.20 cases	9.00	
	3.50 points		
	(6.40 patients)		Unknown
Increment	? satisfaction	$1.00	

Which is better or preferred: the satisfaction gained from G-H, or the $1 saved from D-F-H?

useful illustration might involve working with one nonmonetary output. One can then see how the method can be applied to monetary benefits or to a variety of nonmonetary outputs. Suppose the minimum benefit level is to have seven cases processed. Which project would best minimize costs and meet the minimum benefits constraint?

Obviously project D would be eliminated because it processes only 4.20 cases. Project E is feasible as it results in at least seven cases processed. We should, however, satisfy the minimum benefit constraint without having to spend the $10 that project E requires. Project F is the least expensive, but it will not meet the minimum benefit constraint. Through the process of elimination, project G is the best, since it is the least expensive project that will meet the minimum benefit constraint. Actually, only projects E and G will result in at least seven cases processed. G is better at minimizing costs. Project E, however, may be better on the goal of maximizing benefits minus costs because it provides an extra 4.5 benefit units, although at an extra $4 in costs. If we would rather have 4.5 benefit units than $4, then project E is better. If, however, our goal is to minimize costs, then we are implying that we would rather have the $4, so long as the minimum benefit constraint of seven cases processed has been met.

If we retain the mutual exclusivity requirement and go to five different outputs, then we might have a minimum benefit constraint for each output, such as seven cases processed, 10 highway miles built, 4 unemployment percentage points reduced, eight students trained, and nine patients treated. With this problem, no one project will meet the minimum constraints. Thus, this problem has no feasible solution. If we have to buy one project and we want to minimize costs, then we could buy the least expensive project. This solution would be unrealistic because no concern would be shown for the benefits obtained. If a goal was to solely minimize costs, the logical solution would be to buy no projects. If only one of the five outputs has a minimum benefit constraint which has to be met, such as seven cases processed, then we would buy the one project that has cases processed as its output, which would be project D. Buying this project, however, would result in only 4.20 cases processed. We would, thus, not achieve the minimum benefit constraint, but we would have chosen the best option possible.

Minimizing Costs, Allowing Combinations

Situations frequently call for deciding in favor of combinations of projects, programs, or policies. The problem then becomes, which combination will best minimize costs and satisfy a minimum of seven cases processed? As with problems 2, 4, and 6, there are five possible one-project combinations. There are also 10 possible two-project combinations. Only six of these 10 possible two-project combinations involve spending $10 or less. The minimum cost constraint, however, does not apply to problem 8, where we are concerned with meeting a minimum benefit constraint while minimizing costs. The problem can then be further restated as follows: Which of these 15 possible combinations can result in at least seven cases processed at a minimum cost?

On initial consideration, one might think the answer is project G, since it results in at least seven cases processed and only costs $6. This choice may be based on the fallacy that we save money by buying only one project. This is similar to the reverse fallacy of problem 2 where one wrongly thinks that buying as many projects as our budget allows will maximize benefits.

Buying project G may be wasteful if a combination of two other projects can meet the minimum benefit constraint and cost less than the $6 of project G. To aid in determining if such a combination exists, it is helpful to generate a benefits-combinations matrix like that shown in Figure 14-4. The cell in the upper left-hand corner that corresponds to the D-E combination shows these two projects together result in 17.70 cases processed. Likewise, the other cells in the matrix show the total benefits for their respective combinations. All the combinations in Figure 14-4 are feasible since they all result in at least seven cases processed. To determine which combination may be more beneficial than merely adopting project G, one must refer to Figure 14-2.

Figure 14-2 shows us that the F-H combination costs as little as project G alone. The F-H combination, however, improves on project G since for

FIGURE 14-4
A Benefits-Combinations Matrix for the Data from Table 3-1 (relevant to problems 7 and 8)

	D	E	F	G	H
D		17.70	7.70	13.20	10.60
E			17.00	22.50	19.90
F				12.50	9.90
G					15.40
H					

7 cases = Minimum satisfaction required.

the same $6, it provides 9.90 cases processed rather than just 9.00 cases processed. The D-F combination is even more of an improvement. It results in 7.70 cases processed, which satisfies the minimum constraint. It does so, however, at a cost of only $5, as contrasted to the $6 of project G. Project G processes more cases than D-F (9.00 versus 7.70), but D-F best satisfies the goal of minimizing costs while meeting the 7.00 minimum benefit level.

If we were dealing with monetary benefits, the solution would be the same as with nonmonetary benefits based on only one output. Thus, the best combination would still be D-F if the minimum benefit level were expressed as $7, rather than seven cases processed. If we were dealing with non-monetary benefits and multiple outputs, we would avoid the complications mentioned in discussing problem 7. If every output had a minimum benefits level, we would buy every project. This would enable us to come as close as possible to meeting these minimum benefits levels. If only some of the outputs had minimum benefit levels, then we would buy only these projects, since we are trying to minimize our costs in problems 7 and 8, as contrasted to trying to maximize our benefits in problems 1 through 6.

Conclusion

The simple logic for considering nonmonetary variables in benefit-cost analysis is summarized in the following basic rules:

1. The overall goal is to select the project or combination of projects that gives the highest score on benefits minus costs. If only one project is involved, it should give a positive score on benefits minus costs.
2. If one is trying to find the most beneficial combination of projects subject to a maximum cost constraint, prepare a matrix showing the total costs for each combination and a matrix showing the benefits minus costs for each combination.

3. If one compares two projects or combinations with nonmonetary benefits, with each having the same kind of output, the winning project produces more benefits at lower costs. If one project produces more benefits at higher costs, determine whether the increment in the benefits is worth more or less than the increment in the costs.

4. If one is comparing a set of projects or combinations that have nonmonetary benefits and different kinds of outputs, then compare the first one with the second to see which is better. The winner is compared with the third project or combination, and so on. The remaining project or combination wins.

5. If one is looking for the least expensive combination of projects subject to a minimum benefit constraint, prepare a matrix showing the total benefits for each combination. One can then pick the combination that satisfies the minimum benefit constraint while providing the lowest possible costs, as indicated on the previously prepared costs-combinations matrix.

In conclusion, one need not avoid applying benefit-cost analysis to a given situation just because the situation involves nonmonetary benefits, multiple competing projects, multiple kinds of outputs, or other variations on these basic concepts. The principles tend to represent reasonable commonsense logic, as contrasted to more technical mathematical principles. Benefit-cost analysis can be a highly useful tool for making decisions as well as for accounting or measuring purposes, or as a rationalization for preconceived adoptions or rejections. By using the tool well, decision makers in the public sector can increase the productivity of their governments and their societies, especially if productivity is defined as societal benefits minus societal costs.[18]

NOTES

Thanks are owed to the Management Sciences Training Center at the U.S. Office of Personnel Management and particularly to Ed Schroer, Frank Ponti, and Cathy McCarthy for providing an opportunity to present this chapter and Chapter 15 as part of a cost/benefit workshop. Thanks are also owed to the University of Alabama for including these chapters as part of the 37th Annual Lectureship in Public Administration, particularly Coleman Ransone and Philip Coulter. These chapters were also presented at the Conference on Operations Research Applied to State and Local Government at Sangamon State University with thanks to Rassule Hadidi and John Collins, and at the 1982 meeting of the International Political Science Association, with thanks to David Nachmias. Helpful comments were also made by such University of Illinois students as Francis Carpenter, Beth Shanfield, and others.

1. On benefit-cost analysis in general, see Mark Thompson, *Benefit-Cost Analysis for Program Evaluation* (Sage, 1980); Edward Gramlich, *Benefit-Cost Analysis of Government Programs* (Prentice-Hall, 1981); Robert Sugden and Alan Williams, *The Principles of Practical Cost-Benefit Analysis* (Oxford University Press,

1978); Ezra Mishan, *Cost-Benefit Analysis* (Praeger, 1976); and Peter Sassone and William Schaffer, *Cost-Benefit Analysis: A Handbook* (Academic Press, 1978). In dealing with nonmonetary variables, these books emphasize converting nonmonetary units into money. As an alternative, they recommend working with benefit/cost ratios or maximizing benefits subject to a cost constraint, rather than maximizing benefits minus costs.

Standard policy analysis textbooks generally include at least one chapter on benefit-cost analysis, although without much depth. See Michael White, Ross Clayton, Robert Myrtle, Gilbert Siegel, and Aaron Rose, *Managing Public Systems: Analytic Techniques for Public Administration* (Duxbury, 1980), 291 – 318; Edith Stokey and Richard Zeckhauser, *A Primer for Policy Analysis* (Norton, 1978), 134 – 58; Christopher McKenna, *Quantitative Methods for Public Decision Making* (McGraw-Hill, 1980), 127 – 63; and John Gohagan, *Quantitative Analysis for Public Policy* (McGraw-Hill, 1980), 181 – 266. Operations research and decision science textbooks include relevant material on decision theory, but generally only as applied to private sector problems, emphasizing decisions under conditions of probabilistic risk. See Samuel Richmond, *Operations Research for Management Decisions* (Ronald, 1968), 527 – 62; and Sang Lee and Laurence Moore, *Introduction to Decision Science* (Petrocelli/Charter, 1975), 41 – 89. The OR-DS textbooks have the advantage of treating benefit-cost analysis from a perspective that is more comfortable with nonmonetary benefits, whereas the textbooks by economists emphasize using cumbersome variations on supply and demand theory to attach prices to nonmonetary benefits.

2. This simplified data assumes (a) the benefits for adopting any of these projects occur at about the time the projects are adopted, (b) the time lags are about the same for all the projects, or (c) the time lags are different for all the projects, but the benefits column has already discounted these time differences. None of the principles in this article is affected by the problems of time discounting. In discussing unknown variables, the chapter does discuss the effects of discounting for the probabilistic occurrence of contingent events, since these probabilities are often relatively unknown. This simplified data also assumes that each individual project is operating as efficiently as possible. Thus, we assume for the sake of discussion that for the $3 invested in project D, the benefits could not be more than 4.20 or, for that matter, less than 4.20. We likewise assume that for 4.20 benefit units, we could not reduce the cost below $3. Later, in the portion of this analysis dealing with unknown variables, we do take into consideration that the 4.20, the $3, or both may be unknown, changeable, or subject to measurement error.

This data was used in Chapter 3 in discussing policy evaluation goals, rather than methods. It was used there mainly to show the importance of the B-C criterion over the B/C criterion, and to show the significance of having to operate within a budget constraint. Here, the data is used to show how one can meaningfully deal with nonmonetary benefits when making discrete choices among projects that do not allow for partial or multiple versions of a project.

3. Although this chapter talks in terms of maximizing benefits minus costs, it is equivalent to saying: (a) minimizing costs when the benefits are held constant across projects, (b) maximizing benefits when the costs are held constant, (c) maximizing benefits when all the effects are stated positively, such as talking in terms of dollars saved, rather than dollars spent, (d) minimizing costs when all the effects are stated negatively, such as talking in terms of cases not yet processed, rather than cases processed, and (e) maximizing benefits minus costs

where the usually negative effects are stated positively and the usually positive effects are stated negatively, such as talking in terms of dollars saved minus cases not processed.

4. The interest rate equals the B/C rate minus 1.00. Thus, there is no need to show both these rates in Table 3-1. One can prove that B/C equals the interest rate by noting that such a rate or yield equals $(B-C)/C$, or profit divided by cost, or interest divided by principal. The expression $(B-C)/C$ simplifies to $(B/C) - (C/C)$, which equals $(B/C)-1$.

5. Perhaps Table 3-1 should have included a project I, which produces $10.00 in benefits for $6.00 in costs. It thus has a B-C score of $4.00 and a B/C score of 1.67. It therefore has more profits but less benefits than project E. Which project is better? Applying the investor analogy, project I at the end of the year will have $6.00 in principal, $4.00 in interest, and $4.00 in unspent funds from an initial budget of $10.00. It will, thus, have total assets of $14.00, whereas project E will have total assets of only $13.50. This shows that it is better to buy a project with a higher B-C score (project I) than one with a higher B score (project E). Likewise, it is better to buy a project with a higher B-C score than one with a lower C score since all the other projects have a lower C score than project E.

To provide further varieties of experience, Table 3-1 could have also shown a project J, which produces $12.50 in benefits for $9.00 in costs. In other words, it has the same B-C score as project E. Which project is better? The answer is, they are equally good. Project E provides $10.00 in principal, $3.50 in interest, and no unspent funds, for a total of $13.50. Project J provides $9.00 in principal, $3.50 in interest, and $1.00 in unspent funds, also for a total of $13.50. The next logical question is, what to do? The answer with lump-sum projects is to flip a coin, because (a) both projects are equally good on B-C, (b) only one can be adopted, (c) they are not internally divisible to allow for buying half of one and half of the other, and (d) we are assuming there is no supplementary project where the $1.00 in unspent funds could be invested to earn more than the threshold interest, although in this case the threshold interest is $0.00, meaning that $0.01 exceeds it.

6. Even if we could buy five project Fs, it would still not change the rule that B-C is the guiding criterion (merely because F has the best B/C ratio). We would be buying five Fs with our $10.00 because doing so would give us $17.50 in benefits, which means a total B-C of $7.50. This is the best B-C one can obtain if we allow for buying multiples or parts of a given project.

7. Instead of buying five neckties to illustrate lump-sum projects that are not mutually exclusive, we could use five different ways of notifying or reminding defendants to appear in court. These methods could include (a) sending defendants postcards, scheduled to arrive within a few days before their trials, (b) phoning them within that time period, (c) going to their homes, (d) having them report to the court within that time period, and/or (e) placing a general notice in the newspaper emphasizing that people who fail to appear for their court dates will be arrested. It would *not* be meaningful, for example, to send each defendant three postcards or half a postcard. Nor would it be meaningful to go to their homes twice in that time, or to only go half way to their homes. Deliberately notifying or going to only half the homes might be unconstitutional, unequal treatment.

8. Most of the benefit-cost literature ignores the problem of choosing between a project that is high on B-C and one that is high on B/C by assuming that such a conflict seldom occurs since the costs are generally held constant. When the problem is addressed, some of the literature indicates that either criterion could

be used. See, for example, Henry Levin, "Cost Analysis" in Nick Smith (ed.), *New Techniques for Evaluation* (Sage, 1981), 19–23. Stokey and Zeckhauser, however, clearly advocate B-C as the fundamental criterion in *A Primer for Policy Analysis* (Norton, 1978), 137–46.

9. This analysis assumes that there are no interaction relations among these projects. By the absence of interaction relations is meant that if project G alone produces $9.00 in benefits, and project H alone produces $6.40 in benefits, then when the two together are adopted, there will be $15.40 in benefits. An interaction relation might involve the sum of the two projects producing less than $15.40 if there are diminishing returns or interferences as a result of adopting both projects. Interaction could produce more than $15.40 if there are increasing returns or a catalytic synergism as a result of adopting both projects.

10. The hypothetical data shown in columns 1 and 2 is based on data that was used by Mark Thompson of the Harvard School of Public Health in a paper entitled, "A Passage for Benefit-Cost Analysis: Adapting to Changes and Challenges in Middle Age," presented at the 1978 annual meeting of the Evaluation Research Society. This data was not used to illustrate working with nonmonetary or unknown variables, but rather to attempt to show that the proper decision-making criterion is sometimes the B/C ratio, rather than the B-C difference, in the sense of picking the projects on the basis of their B/C ratios. The overall goal, however, is to pick a set of projects that will maximize benefits minus costs.

11. Preference with a single decision maker is a transitive relation. Such a relation means that if a decision maker prefers D over E, and F over D, then F would have to be preferred over E. A double greater-than symbol can be used to show preferences as in $F >> D >> E$. With multiple decision makers, transitive relations often break down. For example, John may prefer the company of Mary, and Mary may prefer the company of Bill, but that does not mean John prefers the company of Bill. When we have multiple decision makers, we are likely to be adding conflicting criteria, whereas a single decision maker tends to be internally consistent. Conflicting dimensions are also present in sports play-offs. Thus if team A beats team B, and team B beats team C, that does not mean team A will beat team C, because who wins depends on inconsistent combinations of variables that relate to elements of one's offense and defense. Sports contests also occur at different times, creating inconsistencies over time which do not occur when one determines one's preferences at one point in time. With multiple decision makers, their preferences can be aggregated meaningfully by simply determining for each of N projects what percentage of the decision makers favored it over each of $N - 1$ other projects. For each project, one then averages these $N - 1$ percentages to get an overall preference score. One might also note that there is no reason to determine why a decision maker prefers one project over another in order to draw conclusions as to which project or combination in a set is best.

12. The C/B ratio is preferred in expressing the relation between dollars and benefits, because it talks in terms of decimal dollars to one benefit unit. The B/C ratio talks in terms of decimal benefit units to one dollar. Most people are more comfortable thinking of a benefit unit or a can of beans only as an integer, but they can easily handle decimal parts of dollars. In Table 3-1, B/C ratios are shown because in comparing governmental projects (as contrasted to buying court cases or cans of beans), we often want to know how efficient the projects are. The B/C ratio is the same as the efficiency score, or the ratio of outputs to inputs.

13. In terms of the analysis in Table 14-2, as one moves from the less beneficial project I to the more beneficial project E, one goes up 3.50 in benefit units (from 10.00 to 13.50), but one also goes up $4.00 in costs (from $6.00 to $10.00). The C/B ratio for the incremental costs divided by the incremental benefits is 1.14. Thus, to justify the extra expense of project E, one would have to show the incremental cases on the average are worth at least $1.14 apiece. They may or may not be worth $1.14. The important point is that we do not resolve the question of which project is better by saying, maximize benefits subject to a $10.00 budget constraint.

14. Cost-effectiveness analysis for dealing with nonmonetary variables is advocated in Mark Thompson, *Benefit-Cost Analysis for Program Evaluation* (Sage, 1980), 221−48; T. A. Goldman (ed.), *Cost-Effectiveness Analysis: New Approaches in Decision Making* (Praeger, 1967); and J. N. Wolfe (ed.), *Cost Benefit and Cost Effectiveness: Studies and Analysis* (George Allen & Unwin, 1973). Henry Levin defines cost-effectiveness analysis as having nonmonetary benefits and monetary costs, and then choosing the project that is the lowest on the C/B ratio or the highest on the B/C ratio. See Levin's "Cost Analysis" in Nick Smith (ed.), *New Techniques for Evaluation* (Sage, 1981), 23−30. This approach may not make sense since it ignores the relative value of a benefit unit to a dollar. He also makes the point that there is no meaningful way of comparing projects that have nonmonetary benefits and different kinds of outputs.

15. By now, one can see that allowing combinations is a form of decision making that is also mutually exclusive, since only one of the combinations can be chosen. So-called optimum level problems can also be considered as mutually exclusive choice problems. For example, deciding the optimum percent of defendants to hold in jail prior to trial to minimize holding costs plus releasing costs involves choosing among 101 alternative categories from 0 percent, 1 percent, on up to 100 percent. This assumes it is meaningful to treat the percentages as integers, as it often is. Likewise, so-called optimum mix problems are also mutually exclusive choice problems. For example, deciding how to allocate $100 between police and courts in fighting crime involves choosing among 101 alternative categories from $0 for police and $100 for courts, $1 for police and $99 for courts, and so on up to $100 for police and $0 for courts. If there are more than two activities or places to be allocated to, or a wider range on each activity than $0 to $100, then a computer can check which of the thousands of mutually exclusive alternatives scores highest on benefits minus costs, or highest on benefits if costs are held constant.

16. To convert a set of paired comparisons into a rank-order scale, it is necessary to pair each project with every other project. With five projects, there would be 10 paired comparisons (since 5 times 4 divided by 2 is 10), rather than only four paired comparisons. An alternative would be to have the decision maker rank order the projects from the beginning, but rank ordering five or more projects may be more difficult than comparing them two at a time.

To position the projects on a 0-to-100 scale, the decision maker can be asked to do so directly. An especially appropriate alternative when there is more than one decision maker is to have each of them go through the 10 paired comparisons. A preferences matrix would then be prepared with the five projects along the top and along the side. In each cell would be shown the decimal proportion of times that the project on the top was preferred to the project on the side. The average score in each column is the preference score for each project. It can be used as an interval scale value for each project.

One can also position the projects on a scale which has an absolute zero of indifference so that projects with a positive score are liked, and projects with a negative score are disliked. To position the projects on this type of scale requires asking each of the decision makers not only to go through the 10 paired comparisons, but also to indicate whether each is liked or disliked. The answers to this question enable us to determine what decimal proportion of the decision makers like each project. We can relate these two scores together to produce one score on a scale ranging from negative to positive infinity, with a neutral zero in between. For further details on scaling (although it is generally unnecessary), see J. P. Guilford, *Psychometric Methods* (McGraw-Hill, 1954), 154–222, especially 154–77.

If we have multiple decision makers, we should not simply ask them which project is best or even to do a paired-comparisons elimination contest. This could lead to a project receiving the most votes when it is only preferred by a plurality of the decision makers and disliked by the others who may be split among various projects. To remedy this situation, we can have each decision maker go through all 10 possible pairs for the five projects. The winning project is then the one that has the highest preference score as defined above.

17. Operating in accordance with a goal of minimizing costs subject to a safety net (or a minimum benefits level) may be irrational in terms of the goal of maximizing benefits minus costs (or maximizing net worth). For example, suppose one is faced with (1) project A, which costs $30 and produces $50 in benefits (or 50 benefit units), and (2) project B, which costs $40 and produces $500,000 (or 500,000 benefit units). Suppose further that the minimum benefits level is $45 (or 45 benefit units). Then either project would be feasible by virtue of satisfying this minimum constraint. Project A would have to be chosen if our goal were to minimize costs. Doing so, however, would mean missing the opportunity of making a huge profit by adopting project B. A businessperson would find a way to obtain the extra $10 in order to adopt project B. A government agency should also be capable of finding a way of obtaining or borrowing the extra $10. The Central American situation may be a concrete example of missed opportunities encouraged by seeking to minimize costs. Project A may be like gunboat diplomacy, which is relatively inexpensive but relatively ineffective. Project B may be like Marshall Plan diplomacy, which is relatively expensive but possibly highly profitable. Operating in accordance with a goal of maximizing benefits subject to a maximum cost constraint may likewise result in missed opportunities. Suppose one were faced with project A and project B. Suppose further that the object is to maximize benefits subject to a $35 maximum cost constraint. This goal framework would also lead to adopting project A over project B, contrary to common sense, business sense, and the goal of maximizing benefits minus costs or maximizing net worth.

18. On the relation between benefit-cost analysis and societal productivity, see Catherine Lovell, *Productivity Improvement and Measurement: An Administrative Perspective* (University of California, Riverside Graduate School of Administration, 1981), and S. Nagel, "Productivity Improvement, Management Science, and Policy Evaluation" (unpublished paper presented at the annual meeting of the American Society for Public Administration, 1982).

QUESTIONS

1. In choosing among alternative projects, is the best project the one with the highest score on benefits minus costs, benefits divided by

costs, benefits achieved, costs saved, or some other criterion? Why?
2. In deciding among alternative combinations of monetary projects, what is the best procedure to use to arrive at the optimum combination?
3. How can one choose among alternative projects in which the benefits are nonmonetary (like cases solved) for each project?
4. How can one choose among alternative projects in which the benefits are nonmonetary and there are different kinds of benefits for different projects, such as students trained, patients treated, highway-miles built, and so on?
5. In deciding among alternative combinations of nonmonetary projects, what is the best procedure to use to arrive at an optimum combination with a minimum of effort?
6. How can one arrive at a best project or combination when the goal is to minimize costs at a minimum benefit level, rather than to maximize benefits minus costs?

REFERENCES

Goldman, T. A. (ed.), *Cost-Effectiveness Analysis: New Approaches in Decision-Making* (Praeger, 1967).
Gramlich, Edward, *Benefit-Cost Analysis of Government Programs* (Prentice-Hall, 1981).
Guilford, J. P., *Psychometric Methods* (McGraw-Hill, 1954).
Mishan, Ezra, *Cost-Benefit Analysis* (Praeger, 1976).
Sassone, Peter, and William Schaffer, *Cost-Benefit Analysis: A Handbook* (Academic Press, 1978).
Smith, Nick (ed.), *New Techniques for Evaluation* (Sage, 1981).
Stokey, Edith, and Richard Zeckhauser, *A Primer for Policy Analysis* (Norton, 1978).
Sugden, Robert, and Alan Williams, *The Principles of Practical Cost-Benefit Analysis* (Oxford University Press, 1978).
Thompson, Mark, *Benefit-Cost Analysis for Program Evaluation* (Sage, 1980).
Wolfe, J. N. (ed.), *Cost Benefit and Cost Effectiveness: Studies and Analysis* (George Allen & Unwin, 1973).

APPENDIX TO CHAPTER 14
Monetizing Nonmonetary Benefits by Using Paired Comparisons

Another approach to dealing with nonmonetary variables is to convert them into dollar values. Suppose, for example, we want to compare two different affirmative action projects for recruiting black medical students. One project will result in 30 students trained and 10 patients treated. The second project will result in only 20 students trained, but 18 patients treated. If we could assign a dollar value to students trained and patients treated, we could then sum the dollar values for these two nonmonetary benefits for each project, and thereby determine which project has the higher dollar value.

This task is normally quite difficult. Economists tend to monetize by looking for relevant prices in the marketplace, reasoning by analogy to the marketplace, or creating artificial/imaginary markets. One could try to determine students trained by seeing how much it costs to train a student; however, this would not tell us the value or benefits from training a student. We would only learn the cost. Likewise, seeing how much it costs to treat a patient does not tell us the value of the benefits of treating a patient.

One could see how much more an individual with the student training is capable of earning than an individual without the training. This approaches some of the benefits of training, but many of the benefits may be nonmonetary, such as the prestige of the new position or the satisfaction derived from the creativity associated with the new position. Similarly, learning how much more a rehabilitated patient can earn does not equate to the satisfaction earned from overcoming a handicap.

Traditional monetizing thus ignores benefits that are important but difficult to assign a dollar value to. It also overly emphasizes the values manifested in the marketplace, rather than the values of the relevant decision makers who may price student training or patient treating at a higher or lower value than the marketplace does. We need a method of monetizing that reflects the values of the relevant decision makers or stakeholders, including their most subjective values, a difficult and often impossible concept to monetize.

A method of monetizing that meets these criteria is the method of paired comparisons between benefits and dollars. It involves presenting the decision makers with a series of questions like the following:

1. Which would you rather have, $1,000 or 10 students trained?
2. If the decision maker says 10 students trained, then in the next question, decrease the number of students trained and increase the number of dollars. For example, ask, which would you rather have, $2,000 or seven students trained?
3. If the decision maker still says seven students trained, then try another reduction in students trained and another increase in dollars. For example, ask, which would you rather have, $6,000 or two students trained?
4. If the decision maker now says $6,000 is more valuable, then one can deduce that his or her turning point is somewhere between $6,000 and $2,000 and between seven and two students. The interpolated midpoints between these boundaries are $4,000 and 4.5 students.
5. If the decision maker had said saving $1,000 is worth more than 10 students trained, decrease the number of dollars and increase the number of students trained. Continue on this track until a turning point is reached.
6. One could ask more questions after step 4 to further narrow the boundaries between $6,000 and $2,000 and between seven students and two students.
7. One could repeat these six steps using patients instead of students. We could start by asking, which would you rather have, $1,000 or 10 patients treated? When we get through step 4, we may find that the midpoints between the boundaries within which there was a turning point are $5,000 and six patients.

8. In most policy evaluation problems, there are multiple decision makers or many people whose values count. A sample of them could be asked a series of questions like these. Their midpoints could then be averaged to obtain an average turning-point equation among the decision makers for students trained and patients treated.

No matter what the decision maker's turning-point equation is, we do not know why he or she places any given amount of value on an amount of students. The decision maker may be the dean of a medical school and policies A and B may be two different affirmative action programs. The decision maker may be thinking in terms of the need to please the affirmative action requirements of the Department of Health and Human Services. He or she may want to provide more black role models for black undergraduates and high school students or may be thinking of the need to provide medical service in the black community. He or she may also be thinking about how much these students will contribute to the medical school as alumni. He or she may also be thinking about how many black medical students the school already has enrolled. For decision making purposes, as contrasted to motivational analysis, these reasons are unimportant. What is important is (1) that we have asked the right decision maker, namely one whose values count in determining what action will be taken, and (2) that we have asked the right questions so we are getting meaningful answers. The paired comparison approach satisfies these criteria better than a more direct approach of asking, What is the dollar value to you of a student trained? It also seems to be more meaningful than more subtle approaches involving artificial lotteries, which most people find difficult to grasp.

What does one do with the above data? The turning-point or threshold equation is, $4,000 equals 4.5 students. One could theoretically divide both sides of this equation by 4.5 to deduce that one student trained is worth $889. This kind of analysis, however, is the equivalent of saying that the relation between dollars and students trained is $Y = \$889(Z_1)$. This linear regression equation assumes that each incremental student produces $889 worth of satisfaction to society. If we prefer to think in terms of $1,000 units for simplicity, then the regression equation becomes $Y = .89(X)$, but it would be contrary to the virtually universal principles of diminishing returns. If these are medical students, a society or a community would obtain more benefit from the first one trained than from the 100th medical student trained. Likewise, there is more satisfaction as a result of a breakthrough in patients being treated than there is when the treatment becomes rather commonplace.

We must somehow convert the threshold equation or turning-point equation, $4,000 equals 4.5 students, into an equation that shows reasonable diminishing returns. A simple and meaningful way to do this is to divide the logarithm of $4 by the logarithm of 4.5 students. This quotient then becomes the exponent in a nonlinear regression equation of the form $Y = a(X)^b$, where $a = 1$. With these facts, the equation is, $Y = (X)^{.92}$ because Log 4/Log 4.5 = .60/.65 = .92. These calculations can be performed with a $10 calculator that is capable of determining logarithms and dividing. To prove that this translation equation makes sense, insert 4.5 in place of X in the equation, raise it to the power .92, and observe that the result is a Y of $4. Similarly, if we insert 0 in place of X in the equation, the result is a Y of 0, which also makes sense.

This approach works because it is a shortcut for a regression analysis with a statistical software system (like the SPSS system) or with a hand calculator that can do linear regression analysis. We are in effect working with two data points. One data point says when X = 4.5, then Y = 4. The other data point says when X = 0, then Y = 0. The double-log slope, elasticity coefficient, or exponent is equal to Δ Log Y/Δ Log X, or change in the logarithm of Y divided by change in the logarithm of X. This slope is equal to $(\text{Log } Y_1 - \text{Log } Y_2)/(\text{Log } X_1 - \text{Log } X_2)$. Substituting numbers, we have (Log 4 − Log 0)/(Log 4.5 − Log 0). It is customary and makes sense to substitute the log of 1 for the log of 0, partly because the log of 0 is undefined. The log of 1 is 0, which changes the expression to (Log 4 − 0)/(Log 4.5 − 0), which equals Log 4/Log 4.5, or .60/.65, or .92. The value of the scale coefficient (or the "a") in $Y = a(X)^b$ will always be 1 when the second data point involves X = 0 and Y = 0, and the 0s are converted into 1s before taking the logs of the Xs and the Ys.

We can now compare policy A with policy B to see which one generates the most monetary value. Policy A generates a monetary value of $Y = (30)^{.92}$ or $22.85 (i.e., 22.85 monetary units or $22,850) for students trained. Policy A generates a monetary value of $Y = (10)^{.90}$ or $7.94 for patients treated. This is a total for policy A of $30.79. Policy B generates a monetary value of $Y = (20)^{.92}$ or $15.74 for students trained, and a monetary value of $Y = (18)^{.90}$ or $13.48 for patients treated. This is a total for policy B of $29.22. Policy A thus generates more monetary value than policy B. The key subjective element in this analysis is where the turning-point or threshold equation is.

This method of using paired comparisons to monetize nonmonetary benefits works better and is more understandable if one bears in mind the following decision rules with regard to converting the turning-point equation (of the form, Y monetary units = X nonmonetary units) into a translation equation (of the form, $Y = aX^b$):

1. Reject a linear translation equation because it will not show diminishing returns.
2. Reject a semilog translation where one only logs the nonmonetary units because this causes the diminishing returns to be too great.
3. In the turning-point equation, express the dollar amounts in monetary units so the number of monetary units is less than the number of nonmonetary units. Otherwise, the double-log approach results in a translation that shows increasing returns, rather than diminishing returns.
4. In the turning-point equation, express the monetary units so they are greater than one monetary unit, and do likewise with the nonmonetary units. Otherwise, the double-log approach can result in translations in which Y = 1, Y = X, or in which there is a negative exponent.

These decision rules are easy to follow. They simply mean doing such things as expressing $10,000 as 10 monetary units worth $1,000 apiece, or five monetary units worth $2,000 apiece, and remembering these expressions in translating back from monetary units to dollars. By following the above procedures for arriving at a turning-point equation and then converting the turning-point equation into a translation equation, one can thereby meaningfully monetize nonmonetary variables, provided one has the cooperation of the relevant decision makers.

CHAPTER 15

Unknown
Variables

Benefit-cost analysis involves making a choice from among a number of possible decisions by picking the one that has the highest score on a combination of benefits and costs. However, one often cannot know what the benefits or the costs are likely to be for a given decision. This chapter discusses some new but simple methods for applying benefit-cost analysis in situations in which key variables are unknown, such as the benefits, costs, or success probabilities of alternative policies, programs, or projects. The essence of the approach handles unknown variables by converting the problem into questions as to whether a given benefit-cost or success probability is more or less than a threshold above which the proposed project would be relatively profitable and below which it would be relatively unprofitable.[1]

Figure 15-1 clarifies the types of problems useful in illustrating benefit-cost analysis with unknown variables. The seven problems are divided into those involving monetary benefits or nonmonetary benefits. Within this major division, the problems are then subdivided into those with zero, one, two, or three unknowns. The problem of whether or not to adopt a project that has monetary benefits and zero unknowns is treated as a nonproblem for the purposes of this chapter. Because it does not involve nonmonetary benefits or unknown variables, it is too simple and noncontroversial to merit being called a problem. The other seven problems all have interesting elements, partly because they seem unsolvable or at least difficult to solve.

An attorney who is deciding whether to accept a personal injury client is a good example of decision making where one weighs the costs of an action against the benefits discounted by the risky probability of those benefits being received. The benefits are the predicted damages awarded if the case is won. The amount of damages can be predicted partly from the potential client's medical expenses and lost wages. The success probability is the probability of the case being won since no damages are awarded unless the client wins. This probability can be predicted partly from knowing the type of accident involved. This probability should be multiplied by 0.33 because the attorney receives one-third of the damages awarded. The costs are

FIGURE 15-1
Types of Problems to Illustrate Benefit-Cost Analysis with Unknown Variables

Number of unknowns

	Zero	One	Two	Three
Monetary benefits	X	1	2	3
Nonmonetary benefits	4	5	6	7

mainly the attorney's time, expressed in dollars, which equals the predicted number of hours multiplied by the attorney's rate per hour. Of the three variables in this context, the one most likely to be unknown is the success probability, followed by the amount of benefits or the damages awarded. The costs generally tend to be known, although it is sometimes difficult to predict the number of hours worked, or to decide what the hourly rate should be.

On a more momentous level of decision making involving a governmental program, one might use the example of President Roosevelt deciding whether or not to authorize the development of an atomic bomb as of 1942. Like the decision to accept a personal injury client, this was basically a go/no-go decision, rather than a decision between conflicting choices, such as delivery by airplanes versus submarines versus guided missiles. Also, like the client-acceptance decision, the bomb-development decision involves balancing risky benefits against costs. Here, however, the probability of success, the benefits, and the costs were all almost virtually unknown.

The main benefits of developing an atomic bomb were perceived as the number of American and other lives that would be saved by shortening the war. However, it was quite unclear how many lives would be saved. Even more unclear was the probability that an atomic bomb could be developed before the war ended. By 1942, it was felt that the United States would be able to win the war by at least the late 1940s. If the bomb were not successfully developed until after that time, then these large but unclear benefits would never be obtained, although the bomb and its peaceful applications might contribute other benefits at a later time. Also unclear was the cost of a successful bomb development.

The following examples emphasize a high level of general applicability. Readers, however, can substitute any probabilities, benefits, and costs in the examples that relate to bomb development, client selection, or other decisions to adopt or reject a program that could produce benefits which are contingent on the occurrence of an event involving probabilistic risks. The same principles can be applied to policy or program evaluation such as developing an atomic bomb, or to more personal decisions such as whether a lawyer, a clinical psychologist, or some other human services worker should accept clients.

Later, we refer to decisions on conflicting choices. The decision maker would choose the client he or she believed would be more profitable. A decision maker would also decide between two bomb-delivery systems by determining which had the greater benefits minus costs, with the benefits discounted by the probability of their being received. There are likely to be different risks, benefits, and costs involved in relying on missiles, air-planes, and/or submarines. Any set of two or more conflicting choices can be reduced to a set of paired comparisons. One can also do a threshold analysis to determine the scores which the second-place project needs (to become the first-place project) on these variables when the scores are virtually unknown. The examples and applications are virtually unlimited, although there are only about eight generic problems and a manageable number of simple and useful rules for decision making.[2]

Monetary Benefits, One Unknown

Suppose a project that costs $10.00 will produce $50.00 in benefits if it is successful. Should the project be adopted? Initially, one might be tempted to say *yes*, since the benefits seem to outweigh the costs. However, one might realize that if the probability of success is only 0.02, then the expected benefits will only be $1.00. The expected profits would then be a negative $9.00 or a loss of $9.00, and the project would be rightfully rejected. One might then ask, what is the threshold value for the probability of success, above which it is profitable to adopt the project, and below which it is unprofitable?

To calculate the threshold probability, we simply recognize that the expected profits are equal to $PB - C$. At the threshold point, $PB - C$ equals zero, or PB equals C. Thus if we want to know the value of P at the threshold, we simply solve for P in the equation $PB = C$. Doing so means getting P to stand by itself on the left side of the equation and having all the other variables on the right side of the equation. This makes P equal to C/B at the threshold. Since we know C is $10.00 and B is $50.00, then the threshold value of P is $10/$50, or 0.20. This means if we believe the probability of success is greater than 0.20, we should adopt the project; otherwise, we should reject it. We have reduced the problem of determining the exact probability of success down to a relatively simple problem of determining whether the probability is more or less than a threshold figure. A decision maker might be quite unsure whether P is 0.60, 0.70, or 0.80, but feel quite confident it is more than 0.20. The answer to the question of whether the project should be adopted is *yes* if P is greater than 0.20, and *no* if P is less than 0.20. The concept of a threshold point with P being the unknown is summarized in row 1a of Figure 15-2.

FIGURE 15-2
The Data and the Solutions to the Monetary Problems with Unknown Variables

	Problem	$B	$C	P	Solutions — Adopt if symbols	Solutions — Adopt if numbers	Equation For graphing
Zero	(X)	$50	$10	0.60	$0 < PB - C$ $1 < PB/C$	$0 < \$20$ $1 < 3$	
One	(1a)	$50	$10	?	$P > C/B$	$P > 0.20$	
	(1b)	?	$10	0.60	$B > C/P$	$B > \$16.67$	
	(1c)	$50	?	0.60	$C < PB$	$C < \$30$	
Two	(2a)	?	$10	?	$PB > C$	$PB > \$10$	$P = C/B$ $P = 10/(B)$
	(2b)	$50	?	?	$C/P < B$	$C/P < \$50$	$P = C/B$ $B = 0.02(C)$
	(2c)	?	?	0.60	$C/B < P$	$C/B < 0.60$	$B = C/P$ $B = 1.67(C)$
Three	(3)	?	?	?	$PB - C > 0$ $PB/C > 1$	$PB - C > 0$ $PB/C > 1$	$P = C/B$, or $B = C/P$

Number of unknowns

Note: All the formulas are derived from the goal of maximizing $PB - C$ or at least having a positive $PB - C$. In each inequality, the unknowns are on the left, and the knowns are on the right.

For another example of monetary benefits with one unknown, suppose a project costs $10.00 and the probability of success is 0.60. Should the project be adopted? The answer depends on how much the benefits are, but say we do not know what the benefits are. The answer, then, is that the project should be adopted if the benefits exceed a threshold level, but otherwise it should be rejected. How does one determine the threshold level? Recognize that at the threshold, PB equals C, and then solve for B. This means B equals C/P at the threshold, and further, threshold B equals $10/0.60$ in this example, or 16.67. Thus, if the benefits are less than 16.67, we should not adopt the project even though the probability of success is high. If, however, we feel confident the benefits will likely exceed 16.67, this would be a profitable project to adopt, as indicated in row 1b of Figure 15-2.

We could also create a hypothetical situation in which B and P are known and C is unknown. We would then solve for C in the basic equation, such that at the threshold, $C = PB$. If, for example, P is known to be about 0.60, and B is known to be about $50, then the threshold costs are $30. This means the project should be adopted if one is confident that the costs will be less than $30, but the project should be rejected otherwise, as indicated in row 1c of Figure 15-2. If we feel that the costs will be exactly $30 in situation 1c or exactly at the threshold in any of the situations, then flip a coin to decide whether to adopt or reject. An optimist might recommend adoption to avoid missing unknown benefits; a pessimist might recommend rejection to avoid suffering unknown costs. A neutral decision maker should flip a coin, although projects are seldom exactly at the threshold of probability. Optimists and pessimists also differ on how they perceive the values of B, C, and P, but we are assuming the values given in the data columns of Figure 15-2 are accurate for the sake of discussion.[3]

Monetary Benefits, Two Unknowns

Suppose a project costs $10 and we do not know the probability of success or the benefits. Should we adopt the project? This appears to be an impossible question because it seems like there is one equation with two unknowns, given our basic equation of $PB - C = 0$. It is, however, possible to answer. Perhaps the best way to make the question more manageable is to graph what is involved, as in Figure 15-3. Often the human mind can work better with pictures than with words, algebraic symbols, or numbers. An appropriate graph might show the range of probabilities along the vertical axis. We know the probability of success cannot be less than zero or greater than 1.00. The range of possible benefits might be indicated along the horizontal axis. We know it also cannot be less than zero. We might also know that the benefits are not likely to be greater than $200, although we do not know exactly where they will fall between $0 and $200. Any point on this graph represents a possible combination of P and B. The graph clarifies which combinations are profitable or unprofitable. Any combinations in the upper right-hand corner of the graph are profitable and should be adopted. Conversely, combinations in the lower left-hand corner of the graph are unprofitable and should be rejected. The graph also clarifies which combinations are especially likely to occur.

To use the graph, think in terms of a threshold line or curve rather than a threshold point. A threshold curve is a combination of P and B above which the project should be adopted and below which it should be rejected. To determine the shape of the threshold curve, we express P in terms of C and B. This means converting the basic threshold equation of $PB = C$ into an equation of the form $P = C/B$. Since we know that C is $10, the equation can be expressed as $P = \$10/B$. We next substitute any value for B, such as $20, and then solve for P. Doing so gives P a value of 0.50 when B equals $20 at the threshold. The · in Figure 15-3a is the point where B is $20 and P is 0.50. We next substitute another value for B, such as $40, and solve for P, which would then be 0.25. The . in Figure 15-3a is the point where B is $40 and P is 0.25. We can continue finding additional threshold points, although three should be sufficient. Then we connect these points and we

FIGURE 15-3
Threshold Curves for Determining Whether to Adopt a Project

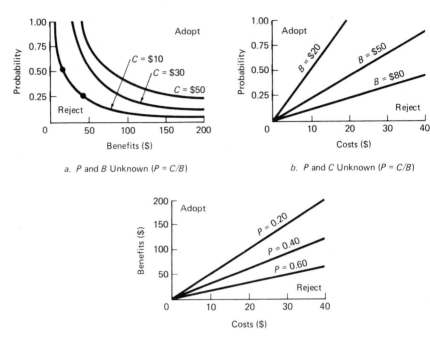

a. P and B Unknown (P = C/B)   *b.* P and C Unknown (P = C/B)

c. B and C Unknown (B = C/P)
Note: All the equations come from the basic threshold equation of $PB - C = 0$.

have a threshold curve at a $10 cost. Now all we have to do is decide whether the expected benefits, or the *PB* combination, are likely to be above or below this threshold curve. This is much easier to determine than the exact probability, the exact benefits, or the exact combination of *P* and *B*. The results of the calculations prompt us to adopt the project if *PB* is greater than $10, and to reject it if *PB* is less than $10, as indicated in row 2a of Figure 15-2. The graph helps to clarify these relations and to position the *PB* combination.

Figure 15-3a would be easier to use if we showed only the one threshold cost curve at $10. The other two threshold cost curves will be referred to when we deal with three unknowns. The figure would be still easier to use if we divided it into four quadrants. The upper-left quadrant involves a high probability with low benefits. The upper-right quadrant involves a high probability with high benefits. The lower-left quadrant involves a low probability with low benefits, and the lower right involves a low probability with high benefits. In light of this breakdown, the user simply decides the rough location of the expected value (or the combination of probability and benefits) in terms of the four quadrants. If the location is mainly quadrant 1, 2, or 4, then adopt it. If the location is mainly quadrant 3, then decide whether the location is basically above or below the threshold curve within that quadrant, given the data from situation 2a in Figure 15-2 on which the threshold curve is based.

For another example of monetary benefits with two unknowns, we can assume we know what the benefits will be, but C and P are unknown. If the known benefits are $50, this becomes the threshold number in the equation $PB = C$, or $(P)(\$50) = C$, or $P = C/\$50$, or $P = (0.02)(C)$. We can easily graph a threshold curve for this relation, with P on the vertical axis and C on the horizontal axis. We would then substitute some values for C such as $10, $20, and so on, and solve for P to find a few combinations of P and C that are consistent with benefits of $50 at the threshold. These combinations can be plotted on the graph to arrive at a threshold curve. This time, however, the threshold curve would be a positively sloped straight line, as in Figure 15-3b, rather than a negatively sloped curve as in Figure 15-3a. Also, the adopt region would be in the upper left-hand corner of the graph, where the probability of success is high, and the costs are low. The reject region would be in the lower right-hand corner, where the probability of success is low, and the costs are high. If we are confident that the combination of P and C is above the $50 benefits threshold line, then we would adopt the project. Otherwise, we would reject it. This is like saying we should adopt the project if the C/P ratio is less than B as is indicated on row 2b of Figure 15-2. A C/P or a C/B ratio should be as low as possible for a project, just as a P/C or B/C ratio should be as high as possible. The threshold number, when only one of the three variables is known, is the numerical value of the one known variable.

In light of this analysis, one can easily see how we would handle the third possible situation in which there are two unknowns, namely, when B and C are unknown and P is known. This situation is illustrated by Figure 15-3c. The vertical axis shows we know the benefits cannot be lower than $0 or higher than about $200. The horizontal axis shows that we know the costs cannot be lower than $0 or higher than approximately $40. In accordance with situation 2c in Figure 15-2, we know the probability of success is 0.60. Therefore, we can plot all the feasible B and C combinations just by inserting any feasible values for B and C into the equation $B = C/0.60$. Doing so generates a positively sloped straight line like that shown in Figure 15-3c. This figure is also like Figure 15-3b in that the adopt region is in the upper left, and the reject region is in the lower right. Thus, if we believe that the combination of B and C is a point above the 0.60 probability line, then we should adopt the project. If, however, we think it is below the 0.60 probability line, we should reject it. This is the same as saying we should adopt the project if the cost/benefit ratio is less than the probability of the benefits being received since: (1) P is the threshold value, (2) both C and B are unknowns, and (3) if we transpose the terms in the basic inequality $PB > C$, we then get $C/B < P$, as indicated in row 2c of Figure 15-2.[4]

Even with two unknowns, one can easily decide whether to adopt or reject a project without doing any graphing by determining whether any of the following situations describes the project:

1. If the benefits upon success would be less than the costs, then reject it no matter what the probability of success is.
2. If the costs are zero, then accept it no matter how low the benefits are or how low the probability of success is.
3. If the probability of success is zero, then reject it if there are any costs greater than zero, regardless of the benefits.
4. If the benefits are zero, then reject it if there are any costs greater than zero, regardless of the probability.

Monetary Benefits, Three Unknowns

The ultimate situation with unknown variables is to have all the variables unknown. This seems to be an impossible situation because we are, in effect, asking whether or not to adopt the project when we do not know the benefits, the costs, or the probability that the benefits will be received. We are also asking to solve for three unknowns in one equation of the form $PB - C = 0$. The best way to approach this problem is through graphing, rather than through the algebra of benefit-cost analysis. Any of the three graphs in Figure 15-3 can be used. For example, if we *do* know the cost is $10, but we do not know the benefits or the probability of receiving them, we would use Figure 15-3a. If, however, we also lack information about the costs, we can still use Figure 15-3a. Doing so involves drawing a family of cost curves, each one showing the possible P and B combinations at various cost levels. Thus, if C is $30, then all possible P and B combinations must be on the $30 threshold curve. Likewise, if C is $50, then the possible P and B combinations must be on the $50 threshold curve. Notice that as the costs increase, the adopt region narrows. To use Figure 15-3a when there are three unknowns involves drawing a circle or some other shape that defines an area on Figure 15-3a in which we feel confident the true combination of P and B will likely be. If this area is mainly above the highest possible or most likely cost curve, then we should adopt the project. If the area is mainly below the highest possible or most likely cost curve, we should reject the project. Emphasizing the highest possible cost curve is a pessimistic perspective, whereas emphasizing the lowest possible cost curve is an optimistic perspective. A compromise solution is to split the difference or to emphasize the most likely cost curve. One can also think of the area between the maximum cost curve and the minimum cost curve as being a threshold band. If the probability and benefits combination lies primarily above this band, then adopt the project. If the combination rests primarily below it, then reject.

When dealing with three unknowns and you feel that B is more capable of being positioned than P or C, then use Figure 15-3b. Notice that as the benefits decrease in Figure 15-3b, the adopt region decreases. As with Figure 15-3a, one needs to be able to draw a circle or other shape into which the possible P and C combinations are likely to occur. If the circle is mainly above the most likely B, then adopt the project; it should be rejected if the circle lies mainly below the most likely B.

In the third alternative, we have three unknowns, but the probability of the benefits being received is easier to position than the benefits or the costs. Notice that as P goes down, the adopt region decreases in Figure 15-3c. In using this figure, we need to draw a rough circle showing approximately where the combination of B and C lies. If this circle is mainly above the most likely P, we adopt. Otherwise, we reject.

These graphing approaches are the algebraic equivalents of saying adopt the project when $PB - C$ is greater than 0, or when PB/C is greater than 1. These formulas, however, are no help when one is deciding whether to adopt a project because they only define a profitable project. They do not stimulate us to generate perceptions of the approximate values of P, B, and C, as graphs do. In other words, even when all three variables are unknown, we may actually have enough information to make a meaningful decision. We always know: (1) P is between 0 and 1.00, (2) B is greater than \$0, and (3) C is greater than \$0. This information already makes the problem more manageable. We also are likely to know roughly the maximum B and the maximum C, so we can indicate the outer boundaries on a B or C axis. In addition, even if all three variables are unknown, they are not likely to be equally unknown. If we can decide that C is in some sense less unknown, then we can operate with Figure 15-3a. If B is less unknown, we use Figure 15-3b, and if P is less unknown than B or C, we can use Figure 15-3c to aid in making more meaningful decisions.

This kind of analysis can be applied to a great variety of benefit-cost problems, not just to those in which the net benefits are defined as $PB - C$. For example, one could readily see how Figure 15-1 and Figure 15-3 could be changed if the net benefits were defined as $B - PC$. In this type of situation, the costs (rather than the benefits) are dependent on the probability of some event occurring. One could also have a situation in which the net benefits are equal to $(P_1B) - (P_2C)$, which means both the benefits and the costs depend on the probability of some event occurring. In this situation, there are four variables, but we can still talk about what to do with zero, one, two, three, or four unknowns analogous to Figure 15-1. The best way to show four unknowns in Figure 15-3 would be to have a family of graphs in Figure 15-3a, just as we have a family of cost curves. In other words, there would be separate graphs for P_2 with values of 0.30, 0.60, and 0.90 if these are the three values of P_2 in which we are most likely to be interested. One can also have multiple benefits (i.e., B_1, B_2, etc.) and multiple costs (i.e., C_1, C_2, etc.), with any combination of unknowns and knowns. We simply follow the basic algebraic principle shown in Figure 15-1 of putting all the unknowns on the left side of a threshold inequality and all the knowns on the right side. We supplement the algebraic approach with a graphing approach when there are two or more unknowns.

Nonmonetary Benefits, Zero Unknowns

We will now discuss nonmonetary benefits with one or more unknowns. We must first clarify how nonmonetary benefits can be handled when we are operating under conditions of risk and when the benefits depend on the probability of some event occurring.

Suppose we have a project that costs $10.00. If the project succeeds, it will result in 50 cases processed, and the project has a 0.60 probability of succeeding. Should the project be adopted? Simplify the problem by reducing it to a question of which is worth more, 30 cases or $10.00. To answer this question, it is not necessary to know how many dollars we would be willing to spend to have one case processed. We would adopt the project if we consider three cases to be more valuable than $1.00 or one case to be more valuable than $0.33, or multiples of those numbers. In other words, we do not need to know whether the threshold or evenly balanced trade-off is four cases for $1.00 or six cases, as long as it is more than three cases. A simpler answer is to adopt the project if 30 cases are *preferred to* $10.00, and to reject the project if 30 cases are not preferable to $10.00. We cannot say that 30 cases are *greater or less than* $10.00 since cases and dollars are two different units of measurement.

Nonmonetary Benefits, One Unknown

Suppose, as in problem 5a, a proposed budget costs $10.00. If it succeeds, it will result in fifty cases, but we do not know the probability of success. Should we adopt the project? This problem simplifies to deciding whether we prefer having P times 50 cases or having $10.00? We cannot answer this question unless we know the value of P. Another question should lead us to answer the main question, whether or not we should adopt the project. This question is, How many cases would we have to process to be willing to give up $10? Suppose the answer is 20 cases. This number could have been arrived at by asking a single decision maker or averaging across decision makers.[5]

Once R has been determined, problems 5, 6, and 7 become relatively easy. If 20 cases is the answer, then we have also determined how much one case is worth in terms of dollars, or how much one dollar is worth in terms of cases. Considering 20 cases and $10.00 to be an even balance generally means two cases for $1.00. It also means $1.00 for two cases, or $0.50 for one case. We can use the symbol R to refer to the ratio of cases to $1.00, and the symbol Q to refer to the quotient of dollars to one case. Thus, R with this data is 2, and Q is 0.50. From here on, however, we will talk in terms of R, although the principles presented could be stated in terms of Q. In this context, R is easier to work with because it is an integer, whereas Q is a decimal (although in other contexts Q might be more comfortable to work with).[6]

One way to determine how much a case is worth is to ask (1) those who decide whether a project should be adopted or rejected, or (2) the beneficiaries of the project. They can be asked, or they can ask themselves, how many dollars their agency or they would be willing to give up to process an average case. One might also note how many cases the agency processed the previous year, and then divide by the total number of dollars the agency spent processing cases. If, however, one wants to know the marginal value of a case where one assumes diminishing returns, then (1) determine how many cases were processed in each of the last two years, (2) determine how many dollars were spent in each of the last two years, and (3) divide the change in the logarithms of the number of cases by the change in the logarithms of the number of dollars. One might object to this procedure because the calculations tell us the cost of a case, not the monetary benefits received from a case. The two figures are, however, likely to be roughly equal, or the monetary benefits might slightly outweigh the monetary costs. Otherwise, we would probably not spend dollars to process cases. These figures can be used as a starting point in asking or determining how many dollars one benefit unit is worth. More complicated methods involve applying principles of lotteries or of supply and demand to arrive at imaginary market prices.

Once we have determined the value of R, it is easy to determine the threshold value of P. We know that at the threshold, $PB - C = 0$ when the benefits are monetary. When the benefits are nonmonetary, we cannot subtract dollar costs from nonmonetary benefits. We can, however, convert these dollar costs into their cases' equivalent by multiplying C by R or 2. Thus, at the threshold, $PB - RC = 0$. Therefore, if we want to determine a threshold value of P, we put all the known variables on the right side of the equation and leave P on the left side. Doing so gives us $PB = RC$, and $P = RC/B$. Numerically speaking, $P = (2)(10)/50$, which reduces to $P = 20/50$, or $P = 0.40$ at the threshold. For the project to be profitable, P must be higher than the threshold of 0.40, as indicated on row 5a of Figure 15-4.[7]

If one prefers to talk about the quantity (Q) of dollars per one case, then the threshold rule on row 5a of Figure 15-4 would be $P > C/QB$. If Q equals 0.50, then P must be greater than 0.40 for the project to be adopted. One can, likewise, substitute other algebraic solutions for column 4 of Figure 15-4 by transposing the basic inequality of $PQB > C$ to show the unknown variables on the left side and the known numerical values on the right side.

Once we have established how to find the threshold P with nonmonetary benefits, we can easily find threshold B or threshold C, when the other two variables are known. For example, given the basic threshold equation of

FIGURE 15-4
The Data and the Solutions to the Nonmonetary Problems
with Unknown Variables

		Data			Solutions		Equations
	Problem	B cases	$C	P	Adopt if symbols	Adopt if numbers	For graphing
Zero	(4)	50	$10	0.60	$0 < PB - RC$ $0 < PQB - C$ $0 < PB - W$ $0 < PV - C$	$0 < 10$	
One	(5a)	50	$10	?	$P > RC/B$	$P > 0.40$	
	(5b)	?	$10	0.60	$B > RC/P$	$B > 33.33$ cases	
	(5c)	50	?	0.60	$C < PC/R$	$C < \$15$	
Two	(6a)	?	$10	?	$PB > RC$	$PB > 20$ cases	$P = 2C/B$ $P = 20/(B)$
	(6b)	50	?	?	$C/P < B/R$	$C/P < \$25$	$P = 2C/B$ $P = 0.04(C)$
	(6c)	?	?	0.60	$C/B < P/R$	$C/B < 0.30$	$B = 2C/P$ $B = 3.33(C)$
Three	(7)	?	?	?	$PB/C > R$	$PB/C > 2$	$P = 2C/B$, or $B = 2C/P$

Number of unknowns (vertical label on left spanning Zero through Three)

R = ratio or rate of cases per $1. Assume R = 2 cases.
Q = quotient or quantity of dollars per 1 case. Assume Q = $0.50.
W = worth of $C in terms of cases. Assume W = 20 cases if C = $10.
V = value of B in terms of dollars. Assume V = $25 if B = 50 cases.

$PB = RC$, the threshold value of B is RC/P. Given the numerical values for the variables on the right side, the threshold value of B is $(2)(10)/0.60$, or $20/0.60$, or 33.33. This means the benefits must be higher than 33.33 cases to justify adopting this project, as indicated on row 5b. Likewise, since $PB = RC$ is the basic threshold equation, it follows that at the threshold, $C = PB/R$. When substituting numbers, threshold C is $(0.60)(50)/2$, or $30/2$, or $15. The costs must be less than $15 to justify adopting the project, given the data on row 5c and the R of 2.[8]

One might say that considering 20 cases and $10 to be an even balance does not necessarily lead to considering two cases and $1 to be an even balance. The latter translation may not follow from the former because of the frequent occurrence of diminishing returns. In other words, if we are willing to spend $1 for two cases, it does not follow that we would be willing to spend $2.00 for four cases. We might only be willing to spend $1.50 for four cases because the incremental two cases do not provide as much satisfaction as the first two cases. Thus, for 20 cases, we might be willing to spend only $5.00 rather than $10.00. One could argue that it is often safe to assume linear or proportionate returns in most benefit-cost analyses, because the range in which we are operating on the cost variable tends to be relatively narrow. Within this narrow range the relation between costs and benefits may be virtually linear, even though the relation is nonlinear over a wider range.[9] If, however, the diminishing returns within our feasible range are substantial, we need not convert 20 cases for $10.00 into two cases for $1.00. Instead, we can create another translation concept (called W) to use instead of R or Q. The symbol W can be defined as the worth of C in terms of cases, or benefit units. If we assume that W is 20 cases when C is $10.00, then substitute W wherever RC is shown in the symbols column of Figure 15-4. Threshold P would then be defined in situation 5a as the value of P which is equal to W/B. This value is 0.40 if W equals 20 cases, or if R equals two cases. The W concept, though, is no help in situation 13c, since we want to know the threshold value of C (which is $15.00 if R equals 2), not the threshold value of W (which is 30 cases). The W concept is thus useful in situations 4, 5a, 5b, and 6a for avoiding R, but R is a more useful concept in situations 5c, 6b, 6c, and 7, when C is unknown.[10]

Table 15-1 clarifies the handling of nonmonetary benefits with one unknown. Table 15-1a shows that costs of $10 are the equivalent of 20 cases. This means P times 50 cases is equal to 20 cases at the threshold. Therefore, threshold P (or P^*) must be 0.40, since 0.40 times 50 is 20. In Table 15-1b, 0.60 times B is equal to 20 cases. Therefore, threshold B (or B^*) must be 33.33 cases, since 20 divided by 0.60 is 33.33. In Table 15-1c, the expected benefits are 0.60 times 50 cases, which is the equivalent of 30 cases. Likewise, 30 cases is the equivalent of $15. This means costs threshold C (or C^*) is $15 when P equals 0.60, B equals 50 cases, and Q equals $0.50.

Nonmonetary Benefits, Two Unknowns

As with the monetary problems in Figure 15-2, the nonmonetary problems of Figure 15-4 are more easily solved with graphs than with algebraic equations. The graphs are virtually identical to those in Figure 15-3 and need not be redrawn. The only difference is that the curves and straight lines move up as a result of doubling the costs in each of the equations on which the graphs are based. Thus, in Figure 15-3a the curve that corresponds to a C of $10 for situation 14a would be positioned where the $20 curve would be for situation 10a. The horizontal axis would also show benefits in cases, not in dollars. More important than these slight changes is the fact that the procedure for deciding whether to adopt or reject project 6a is virtually identical to that of project 2a. We would try to determine the location on the graph of the likely combination of the benefits and the success probability. If this combination is above the curve showing a C of $10, then we adopt it. Otherwise, we reject it.

The procedures for problems 6b and 6c are virtually identical to the

---

TABLE 15-1
Clarifying the Handling of Nonmonetary Benefits, One Unknown

---

a. Probability Unknown

$$\begin{array}{c} \text{(Probability)} \times \text{(Benefits)} = \text{(Costs)} \\ \boxed{\quad ? \quad \times \quad 50 \text{ cases} \quad} = \quad \$10 \\ 20 \text{ cases} = W \\ \therefore \ (?)(50) = 20 \\ \therefore \ P^* = 0.40 \end{array}$$

---

b. Benefits Unknown

$$\begin{array}{c} \text{(Probability)} \times \text{(Benefits)} = \text{(Costs)} \\ \boxed{\quad 0.60 \quad \times \quad ? \quad} = \quad \$10 \\ 20 \text{ cases} = W \\ \therefore \ (0.60)(?) = 20 \\ \therefore \ B^* = 33.33 \end{array}$$

---

c. Costs Unknown

$$\begin{array}{c} \text{(Probability)} \times \text{(Benefits)} = \text{(Costs)} \\ 0.60 \quad \times \quad 50 \text{ cases} \ = \quad ? \\ 30 \text{ cases} \ = \ \$15 \\ \therefore \ \$C^* = \$15 \end{array}$$

Note: To solve situations *a* and *b*, one only needs to know how many cases are the equivalent of \$10. One does not need to know the full relation between cases and dollars. Likewise, to solve situation *c*, one only needs to know how many dollars are the equivalent of 30 cases, not the full relation between dollars and cases. Knowing *R, Q, W,* or *V* will not necessarily tell us how many dollars 30 cases is worth in view of the diminishing relation between cases as a benefit and dollars as a measure of satisfaction. Incremental cases may not produce proportionately increasing satisfaction, since we may want to spend less incremental dollars for each additional case.

procedures for problems 2b and 2c. For problem 6, one can use a graph like Figure 15-3b, with the benefits expressed in terms of cases rather than dollars. The equation which is plotted is $P = 2C/B$, or $P = 2C/50$, or $P = 0.04(C)$, instead of $P = C/B$, or $P = C/50$, or $P = 0.02(C)$. This procedure results in a family of positively sloped straight lines that have steeper slopes than they would otherwise have by virtue of the multiplier of 2. If the likely combination of *C* and *P* is mainly above the line (showing *B* equals 50 cases), then adopt the project. Otherwise, reject it. In situation 6c, one uses a graph like Figure 15-3c and adopts the project only if the likely *B* and *C* combination is mainly above the line showing *P* equals 0.60.[11]

Nonmonetary Benefits, Three Unknowns

With three unknowns, the nonmonetary problem is also like the monetary one in the sense that graphing it similarly to Figures 15-3a, b, and c can help determine whether the project should be adopted or rejected. If one decides that narrowing the range on C is easier than B or P, then use Figure 15-3a. Doing so involves applying the equation $P = 2C/B$ to create a set of cost curves. One then attempts to determine the approximate area in which the combination of P and B is likely to occur. If this combination lies mainly above the most likely cost curve, then adopt; otherwise reject. If it is easier to position the predicted benefits, use a graph like Figure 15-3b which involves a set of benefit curves plotted via the equation $P = 2C/B$. If the approximate area of the P and C combination is mainly above the most likely benefit curve, then adopt; otherwise, reject. If it is easier to position the probability of success, then use a graph like Figure 15-3c with a set of positively sloped straight lines, and determine whether the area of the B and C combination is mainly above the most likely P line. Even a project with nonmonetary benefits and three key unknown variables can be systematically analyzed to conclude whether one should adopt or reject the project.

Unknown Variables and Multiple Projects

The last analysis emphasized a situation in which the main issue is whether or not a single project should be adopted. When multiple projects are involved, one can apply the same kind of threshold analysis for dealing with unknown variables. Suppose, for example, that we are faced with two possible projects. One produces $10 in benefits for $6 in costs (project A), and the second produces $8 in benefits for $5 in costs (project B). Suppose we only have $6 available; we can buy either project, but not both. Also assume that the benefits and the costs are not contingent on the probability of some event occurring. We would prefer project A, since it provides us with $4 in net benefits, while project B provides us with only $3. Project A in effect gives us $6 in principal and $4 in interest on our investment, for a net worth at the end of the time period of $10. Project B yields $5 in principal, $3 in interest, and $1 in unspent funds, for a net worth of only $9.

Suppose we consider any one of those four variables to be unknown, including the $10, the $6, the $8, or the $5. Under these circumstances, which is the better project? More specifically, suppose we do not know the benefits from project A. We are asking, what is the threshold value for this variable? Answering this question involves setting $B = C$ for project A equal to $B = C$ for project B, and then solving for the one unknown variable. This means $(B - \$6) = (\$8 - \$5)$, or $B = \$3 + \$6$, or $B^* = \$9$. In other words, if the benefits of project A are perceived as being greater than $9, then project A is a better investment than project B. If the benefits are perceived as being less than $9, then project B is the better investment.

Suppose we have three projects, rather than two. One should then determine which is the best project among those for which we have complete information. Then each project for which we have incomplete information can be analyzed to determine the threshold value for its unknown variable. A questionable project would be best if (1) the true value of an unknown benefit variable is perceived to be higher than its threshold, or (2) the true value of an unknown cost variable is perceived to be lower than its threshold. The threshold value is calculated by setting the benefits minus costs of the project in question equal to the benefits minus costs of the leading project.

Suppose we have more than one unknown variable for a given project. We can still set its benefits minus costs equal to the benefits minus costs of the leading project, but use symbols rather than numbers for the unknown variables. We can then put the symbols on the left side of the equation and the numbers on the right side. Doing the arithmetic on the right side reveals the threshold value for the combination of symbols on the left side. We can then plot the relation between the unknown variables, as was done in Figure 15-3. This will provide a useful visual aid for deciding whether the combination of unknown variables is above or below a threshold curve or family of curves.

The problem of unknown variables or missing information can take numerous forms. An additional form is missing information in survey research that is to be the basis for a go/no-go decision. For example, suppose we plan an attitudinal survey and we will adopt a proposal if it is endorsed by more than 51 percent of the 1,000 population, not just 51 percent of those participating in the survey. Suppose further, we receive 800 responses with 60 percent (or 480) saying yes and 40 percent (or 320) saying no. We could do an expensive follow-up to determine the attitudes of the missing 200. On the other hand, we might note that in order for the yeses to cease to be in the majority, 181 (or more than 90 percent) of the 200 nonrespondents would have to say no. If it seems unreasonable that 90 percent of the nonrespondents would say no when only 40 percent of the respondents said no, then we can go ahead with the proposal feeling confident that it would have been endorsed by a majority if all 1,000 had responded.

Conclusion

The simple logic this chapter proposes for dealing with unknown variables in benefit-cost analysis can be summarized by a few basic rules as follows:

1. If one is trying to decide whether to adopt or reject a project that has costs, benefits, and a success probability, and one or more of these variables is unknown, then one should put the numerical values of the known variables on the right side of an equation of the form $PB = C$, and put the algebraic symbols for the unknown variables on the left side. This equation will then indicate the threshold

value of the unknown variables, such that they must be either more or less than this value for the project to be profitable.

2. If there are two or more unknown variables, graphing the relation between one unknown and a second unknown while the known or partially known variables are held constant can further clarify the problem. With this two-dimensional graph or set of graphs, indicate the adopt corner and the reject corner within each graph. Also indicate, with a circle or other shape, approximately where the combination of the unknown variables is likely to be. Adopt the project if the combination is mainly in the adopt region; otherwise, reject it.

3. Principles 1 and 2 also apply when nonmonetary benefits are involved, provided that one modifies the basic equation of $PB = C$ to read $PB = RC$. The R concept is the number of benefit units which the relevant persons would be willing to forego in return for one monetary unit.

4. If two or more projects are being compared, then set the benefits minus costs of the questionable project equal to the benefits minus costs of the leading project. Then put the numerical values on the right side of the equation and the symbols for the unknown variables on the left side of the equation to indicate what their combined threshold value is. Also graph the relation between the unknown variables to provide a useful visual aid for deciding whether the combination of unknown variables is above or below a threshold curve or a family of curves.

In conclusion, it is not necessary to avoid applying benefit-cost analysis to a given situation just because it involves unknown variables, nonmonetary benefits, probabilities, or other variations on these basic concepts. The principles represent reasonable commonsense logic, as contrasted to more technical mathematical principles. Benefit-cost analysis is a highly useful tool for making decisions. It should not be relegated to only accounting or measurement purposes, or as a rationalization for preconceived adoptions or rejections. By using the tool well, decision makers in the public sector can increase the productivity of their governments and their societies, especially if productivity is defined as societal benefits minus societal costs.[12]

NOTES

1. See note 1 of Chapter 14 for books dealing with benefit-cost analysis. None of the books, however, deals systematically with the problems of missing information when one does not know the benefits, the costs, or the relevant probabilities.

2. For further details concerning the use of threshold analysis in the decision making of lawyers, judges, legal policy makers, and others associated with the legal process, see S. Nagel, "Lawyer Decisionmaking and Threshold Analysis," 37 *University of Miami Law Review* (1983). For further details concerning the

Roosevelt decision to develop the atomic bomb, see Henry Smyth, *Atomic Energy for Military Purposes: The Official Report on the Development of the Atomic Bomb* (Princeton University Press, 1947); Arthur Compton, *Atomic Quest* (Oxford University Press, 1956); and Ronald Clark, *The Birth of the Bomb* (Horizon, 1961).

3. In this context, optimists can be defined as those who perceive ties and the values of *B, C,* and *P* as being relatively favorable for adoption, whereas pessimists perceive them as being relatively unfavorable. Risk preferers are those who decide to adopt even though they perceive $PB-C$ to be negative, as when $PB - C$ is 0.10(50)−10. The risk preferers are saying that they are willing to risk that next time the 1-in-10 benefits will occur. Risk-adverse people decide to reject even though they perceive $PB - C$ to be positive, as when $PB - C$ is 0.60(50)−10. Risk-adverse people are unwilling to take a chance that next time the 6-in-10 benefits will occur. Most people are probably risk neutral, and act in accordance with the expected values. Regardless of how most people actually act, rational decision making acts in accordance with the expected values, since this will maximize benefits minus costs in the long run, or over an average set of situations.

4. The inequality $C/B < P$ logically follows from $P/B > C$ by the following steps:
   $PB > C$
   $PB/C > 1$ (dividing both sides by *C*)
   $B/C > 1/P$ (dividing both sides by *P*)
   $C/B < P$ (inverting both sides and reversing the sense of the inequality)

5. There is no need to know the dollar value of a benefit unit except when dealing with situations that involve both nonmonetary benefits and unknown variables. If we are dealing with nonmonetary benefits but no unknown variables, then monetization is unnecessary, as shown in situation 4. If we are dealing with monetary benefits, there is no need to monetize regardless of whether the variables are all known or partly unknown, as shown in situations 2 and 3. Only situations 5, 6, and 7 involve monetizing. One objective is to make the monetizing as simple as possible, partly by talking in terms of the worth of C in terms of cases (*W*), and the value of *B* in terms of dollars (*V*), rather than the rate of cases per $1 (*R*), or the quantity of dollars per 1 case (*Q*). We can avoid monetizing in situations 5, 6, and 7 by converting the unknown variables into known variables. One way to do this is to insert the average *P, B,* or *C* score for the missing information. Other methods for solving for missing information are discussed in Jacob Cohen and Patricia Cohen, *Applied Multiple Regression/Correlation for the Behavioral Sciences* (Erlbaum, 1975), 265−90; and S. Nagel and Marian Neef, *Policy Analysis: In Social Science Research* (Sage, 1979), 227−30. To meaningfully deal with missing information in statistical analysis, substitute a predicted score for the missing scores. The predicted score can be the mean score on the variable or it can be determined by doing a regression analysis. To successfully handle missing variables (rather than missing information on known variables), control for them indirectly. One example is doing a time series analysis between crime and anticrime expenditures, holding constant prior crime. By doing so, we indirectly hold constant whatever variables cause crime (besides variation in anticrime expenditures), even though we do not know exactly what variables cause crime.

6. See William Baumol, *Economic Theory and Operations Analysis* (Prentice-Hall, 1977), 420−36; Edward Gramlich, *Benefit-Cost Analysis of Government Programs* (Prentice-Hall, 1981), 53−87; and Ezra Mishan, *Cost-Benefit Analysis* (Praeger, 1976), 24− 164. One can also use the methods of the psycho-

metricians, rather than the econometricians, to put benefit units and dollars on the same numerical or verbal scales. See J. P. Guilford, *Psychometric Methods* (McGraw-Hill, 1954).

7. If one prefers to talk about the quantity (Q) of dollars per one case, then the threshold rule on row 5a of Figure 15-4 would be $P > C/QB$. If Q equals 0.50, then P has to be greater than 0.40 for the project to be adopted. One can likewise substitute other algebraic solutions for column 4 of Figure 15-4 by transposing the basic inequality of $PQB > C$ to show the unknown variables on the left side and the known numerical values on the right side.

8. None of the benefit-cost literature discusses the problems of dealing with benefits, costs, or probabilities that are unknown as contrasted to discussing how to measure or monetize these variables. The situation is analogous to statistics textbooks assuming that one has data for all the variables and entities in a statistical analysis. Few statistics textbooks include the concept of missing information in their indexes, but see note 5. Dealing with missing information in benefit-cost analysis is closely related to sensitivity analysis. See Thomas Gal, *Postoptimal Analysis, Parametric Programming, and Related Topics* (Wiley, 1980); and Harvey Wagner, *Principles of Operations Research: With Applications to Managerial Decisions* (Prentice-Hall, 1969).

9. When we make a linear assumption, we are creating an equation between benefits and costs of the form $B = 0 + (B/C)C$, or $B = RC$. If we substitute numbers, then we are saying $B = (20/10)C$, or $B = 2C$. In other words, we are fitting a linear regression equation to two points. One point has the coordinates of 20 and 10. The second assumed point has the coordinates of 0 and 0, where spending nothing produces no benefits. If we wanted to show a nonlinear diminishing returns relation, we could fit a curve to the point that has the coordinates of the logarithms of 20 and 10 and a second assumed point with the logarithms of 1 and 1. We cannot use an assumed point of 0 and 0 since there is no logarithm of the number 0.

10. One might feel more comfortable answering the question of how many dollars one would be willing to give up in return for 50 cases processed (V for value), rather than the question of how many cases would have to be processed in order to give up \$10 (W for worth). In this case, all the algebraic solutions in column 3 could be expressed as variations on the basic threshold equation, $PV - C = 0$, and the basic inequality of $PV > C$. This procedure, for example, means that the inequality for a situation 13c would be $C < PV$, or $C < \$15$, where V equals \$25.

11. The equations for problems 2a and 6a are algebraically equivalent to $P = 10(B)^{-1}$, and $P = 20(B)^{-1}$. The doubling of the scale coefficient pushes the newly plotted curves upward in a northeast direction. The equations for 2b and 4b are algebraically equivalent to $P = 0.02(C)$, and $P = 0.04(C)$. This doubling of the regression coefficient causes the newly plotted curves to be steeper, but they still begin at the origin of the graph. The equations for 2c and 6c are equivalent to $B = 1.67(C)$, and $B = 3.33(C)$. This also involves a doubling of the slope in recognition of our hypothetical data, whereby two cases are the equivalent of \$1 in satisfaction produced.

12. On the relation between benefit-cost analysis and societal productivity, see Catherine Lovell, *Productivity Improvement and Measurement: An Administrative Perspective* (University of California, Riverside Graduate School of Administration, 1981), and S. Nagel, "Productivity Improvement, Management Science, and Policy Evaluation" (unpublished paper presented at the annual meeting of the American Society for Public Administration, 1982).

QUESTIONS

1. How can one reach a decision to adopt or reject a project if one does not know one of the following variables—the benefits, the costs, or the probability of success for the proposed project—but one does know the other two variables?
2. How can one deal with decision making in a benefit-cost analysis in which two or more key elements cannot be measured?
3. How can one approach decision making when one is faced with the problems of nonmonetary benefits and missing information?
4. Discuss how to handle unknown variables through threshold analysis when there are conflicting-choice decisions, rather than go/no-go decisions.
5. Discuss the concept of the optimist and pessimist and risk-preferring and risk-adverse person in the context of unknown variables.
6. What are various ways of determining how much a nonmonetary benefit is worth in terms of dollars?

REFERENCES

Cohen, Jacob, and Patricia Cohen, *Applied Multiple Regression/Correlation for the Behavioral Sciences* (Erlbaum, 1975), 265–90.

Gal, Thomas, *Postoptimal Analysis, Parametric Programming, and Related Topics* (Wiley, 1980).

Harris, Clifford, *The Break-Even Handbook* (Prentice-Hall, 1978).

Kenny, David, "Unmeasured Variables," in *Correlation and Causality* (Wiley, 1979), 110–83.

Kmietowicz, Z. W., and A. D. Pearlman, *Decision Theory and Incomplete Knowledge* (Gower, 1981).

Moore, C., *Profitable Applications of the Break-Even System* (Prentice-Hall, 1971).

Nagel, S., and Marian Neef, "Methods for Handling Missing Data" in *Policy Analysis: In Social Science Research* (Sage, 1979), 227–30.

Richmond, Samuel, "Decision Making Under Complete Ignorance" in *Operations Research for Management Decisions* (Ronald Press, 1968), 535–40.

Seigle, David, "Some Aids in the Handling of Missing Data," 6 *Social Science Information* 133–50 (1967).

CHAPTER 16

Multiple Goals
and
Policies

One of the more difficult aspects of evaluating alternative public policies, or allocating a budget to various activities, has been that the criteria for evaluating may relate to dollars, days, percentages, ranks, lives, or other diverse units of measurement. When this happens, figuring out a way of giving each alternative policy an overall score poses a problem. One simple way to do this is to use percentaging analysis. This involves converting the scores into part/whole percentages, and then summing the unweighted or weighted percentages. This chapter discusses the implications of percentaging analysis. This method can be used to choose among or to allocate funds to alternative governmental activities.

The Problem

Suppose we must decide whether a criminal justice system should resolve criminal cases by emphasizing trials or plea bargaining. This is not inherently mutually exclusive since court systems use them both. However, only one alternative can be chosen, since we are asking which alternative should be emphasized or given more importance. We could add such alternatives as diverting cases to nonjudicial tribunals or dismissing cases, or combinations of alternatives. The analysis, however, is easier to follow with only two alternatives, although one can easily extend it to more alternatives.

Appropriate criteria, goals, or attributes to use for evaluating these two policy alternatives might include time consumption and respect for the law. Table 16-1 provides relevant hypothetical data for analyzing the problem. It shows that the average trial in our hypothetical court system consumes 120 days from arrest to disposition. The average plea bargaining consumes only 30 days, assuming that we have controlled for the type of criminal charge and the severity of the case. If time consumption were our only criterion for judging trials versus pleas, then pleas would win. It would also be impossible to sum the criteria measured in different units since there would only be one

TABLE 16-1
Data Illustrating Percentaging Analysis

	Criteria (Goals)				Overall Scores		
	TIME CONSUMPTION (WEIGHT = 1)		RESPECT FOR LAW (WEIGHT = 3)		FOR CHOOSING		FOR ALLOCATING
	Raw Score (Days)	Part/Whole Percent	Raw Score (1–10)	Part/Whole Percent	Unweighted Sum	Weighted Sum	Part/Whole Percent
Alternatives Trials	120	−80	6	75	−5%	+145%	+72
(Policies) Pleas	30	−20	2	25	+5%	+55%	+28
Totals	150	100%	8	100%	0%	200%	100%

The above percentaging analysis can be applied to any number of goals and alternatives. It can be used to choose:

1. The one best alternative where the alternatives are mutually exclusive. It is the one which has the highest weighted percentage.
2. The best combination of alternatives. Determine the sum of the weighted percentages for each possible or feasible combination. Pick the combination that has the highest weighted sum of percentages. Sometimes it might be meaningful to rank-order the alternatives in terms of their weighted percentages and then pick the better ones until the budget runs out.
3. The best alternative where doing too much or too little is undesirable. The alternatives are arranged on a continuum for doing a little to doing a lot. The one best alternative is the one where the weighted percentages reach a peak if the goals are positively stated, or reach a bottom if the goals are all negatively stated.
4. The best mix across alternatives. Multiply the weighted percentages in the last column by the total available budget after allocating minimums to each alternative.

criterion. If, however, we add respect for the law as a second criterion, which is measured on a 1-to-10 scale, then we do have a summing problem. We cannot add days as a raw score to 1-to-10 scale units as a second raw score.

A 1-to-10 scale means that the respondents can choose among 10 ordered verbal categories. The verbal categories could be: (10) extremely high respect, (8) substantial respect, (6) mild respect, (5) neutral between respect and disrespect, (4) mild disrespect, (2) substantial disrespect, and (0) extremely high disrespect. Numerical scales should be accompanied by words to be meaningful to respondents and those who will interpret the responses. This chapter, however, does not analyze how to measure goal achievement, but it does explore what to do with goal measures that are reasonably valid, reliable, and understandable so they can be useful in arriving at decisions with multiple goals and multiple alternatives.

The raw scores can be expressed on any dimension with which one is comfortable, such as days, dollars, students trained, unemployment percentages, change in unemployment percentages, and so on. Normally, there are multiple nonmonetary benefit-dimensions and at least one monetary cost-dimension. The raw scores do need to be expressed in terms of numbers and not just words. This is so because we will be adding the raw scores for a given goal in order to obtain a total or a whole score for the purpose of calculating part/whole percentages. Words like *more* and *less* should not be converted into the numbers 1 and 0 because they then sum to 1 and generate part/whole percentages of 100 and 0 percent, which are not likely to fit what the scorer has in mind. Instead, the scorer should indicate roughly how many times the alternative scored more is valued or disvalued over the alternative scored less. If the alternative scored more is twice as high on the dimension, then the proper numbers to use in place of the words would be 2 and 1, which sum to 3 and generate part/whole percentages of 67 and 33 percent.

Converting the Raw Scores

A simple way out of the problem of trying to add days to 1-to-10 scale units is to convert each set of raw scores into part/whole percentages by summing the raw scores on a given criterion and then determining its percentage of the sum for each raw score. Thus, on time consumption the sum of the raw scores is 150. The part/whole percentage for trials is then 120/150 or 80 percent, and the part/whole percentage for pleas is 30/150 or 20 percent. One might propose an alternative of calculating part/maximum percentages. There is, however, no meaningful maximum number of days, although 10 is the maximum on the 1-to-10 scale of respect for the law. On promoting respect for the law, trials receives a score of 6, and pleas receives a score of 2. If respect for the law were the only criterion, trials would win. Converting these raw scores into part/whole percentages gives trials a percent score of

6/8 or 75 percent on respect for the law, and plea bargaining receives a percent score of 2/8 or 25 percent.

The most objective way of making the percentage conversions is to use part/whole percentages. One can always objectively determine the "whole" since it is simply the sum of the raw scores. One cannot always objectively determine an absolute maximum. One can, however, objectively determine the highest score that is present, and then calculate part/highest percentages. Doing so may be objective, but not so meaningful. Calculating part/whole percentages is analogous to optimally allocating resources among alternative activities or places when one works with elasticity coefficients. These coefficients show how much the goal criterion changes for a 1 percent change on the activity or place variable. In this type of allocation, one allocates to the activities or places by determining the ratio between the elasticity coefficient for each activity or place and the sum of the elasticity coefficients.[1] Calculating part/whole percentages depends on the scores included in the set. Thus, the percentage scores are relative to each other. This is desirable since we want to determine the best policy relative to the other available policies.

Sometimes it may be more meaningful to calculate part/maximum percentages if there is a true maximum to work with, as when one is allocating resources to persons on the basis of their test scores. It would not work to use a part/maximum percentage for one criterion, a part/whole percentage for another criterion, and then to average the two. This is equivalent to adding apples and oranges, or days and attitudes. In Table 16-1, the 20 percent in column 3 on the time dimension does not have the same meaning as a 20 percent in column 5 would have if one converted the raw score of 2 into a part/maximum score of 2/10 or 20 percent, rather than a part/whole score of 2/8 or 25 percent. Although they are conceptually different, part/whole percentages and part/maximum percentages do not generally produce substantially different results, partly or completely, especially when we want to know which alternative is best or which set of alternatives is relatively high among the alternatives on the goals we are seeking.

Closely related to converting the raw scores is the problem of how to deal simultaneously with part/whole percentages for a goal such as time consumption on which low scores are desirable and a goal such as respect for the law on which high scores are desirable. Many methods of inverting the raw scores will reverse the order of the scoring, but these methods either distort the absolute differences or the ratios among the raw scores, or else they are meaningless in dealing with zeros, low scores, ties, or near ties. These methods include those inverting methods which: (1) subtract each score from the highest score, (2) divide each score into the highest score, (3) divide each score into the whole, (4) multiply each score by −1, (5) divide each score into 1, or (6) physically flip the raw scores by giving the highest score to the item that has the lowest score and giving the next to the highest score to the item that has the next to the lowest score, and so on. They also include inverting methods which work on the part/whole percentages rather than the raw scores, such as: (1) taking the complements and dividing by $N - 1$ items, (2) subtracting each percentage from the highest percentage, (3) dividing each percentage into the highest percentage, (4) dividing each percentage into the whole, (5) dividing each percentage into 1 or 100, or (6) physically flipping the percentages. The only method that preserves the differences and the ratios and has no trouble dealing with low scores or near ties is to multiply the percentages by -1 and then add, which is the same as subtracting each percentage for the cost-goals from the benefit-goals.

How meaningful is working with scores as of one point in time, rather than working with change scores, especially the ratio between a change in benefits and a change in costs? The object in any policy analysis is to pick the alternative that will provide the most benefits minus costs, not the alternative that has the highest linear or nonlinear slope, or change in benefits divided by change in costs. These slopes can sometimes be useful in arriving at the alternative that will maximize benefits minus costs, but the slopes are only the means to finding that optimum alternative. Table 16-1 in effect says that trials will give us benefits minus costs equal to 145 relative units, and pleas will give us benefits minus costs equal to only 55 units. We therefore choose trials as the most profitable alternative.

Calculating Summation Scores

If we add the negative part/whole percentages for each alternative on time consumption to the positive part/whole percentages for each alternative on respect for law, we obtain a -5 percent for trials and a $+5$ percent for pleas. This is roughly equivalent to subtracting costs from benefits. The sum of these net benefit figures will add to 0 percent since we are subtracting a 100 percent column from another 100 percent column. With only two alternatives, the net benefits of one alternative will equal the net benefits of the other alternative, although opposite in sign. If we consider respect for law to be three times as important as time consumption, then we should multiply by 3 the part/whole percentages under respect for law before doing the adding. For the trials, we would be adding 225 percent to -80 percent, which equals a 145 percent weighted summation score. For the pleas alternative, we would add 75 percent to -20 percent, which equals a 55 percent weighted summation score. The sum of these two scores is 200 percent, because we are subtracting a 100 percent column from a 300 percent column. It is interesting to note that pleas win on the unweighted summation scores, but trials win on the weighted summation scores. If both goals had been positive, then the best alternative policy would be the one having the highest sum of the weighted benefit percentages. If both goals had been negative, then the best policy would have the lowest negative sum of the weighted cost percentages.

The most subjective part of the analysis is deciding on the relative weights of the goals. To reach this decision, it is helpful to determine a numerical value for the threshold weight. The threshold weight is the numerical value of a goal which will cause the weighted summation scores of the two alternative policies to be tied. The two policies are generally in first and second place. To calculate the exact threshold weight for the data in Table 16-1, one must solve for W in an equation in which the weighted benefits minus costs of the first alternative are set equal to the weighted benefits minus costs of the second alternative. Doing so involves working with the following equation: $W(0.75) - 0.80 = W(0.25) - 0.20$. Solving for W in this equation yields a W^* or threshold weight of 1.20. If respect for the law is worth more than 1.20 times saving days, then trials is the better of the two alternatives. The weighting problem becomes easier because we may have no difficulty saying that respect for law is worth more than 1.20 times the value of saving time in days, although we might have some difficulty determining whether respect for law is worth, for example, two or three times as much as time consumption.

In addition to a threshold weight, we can talk about a threshold value for any of the elements which determine the winning alternative. A general threshold equation would be: $Wa - b = W(1 - a) - (1 - b)$, where $a =$ the part/whole decimal of the first alternative on the benefit goal and $b =$ the part/whole decimal of the first alternative on the cost goal. To use this equation, insert numbers for two of the three variables and then solve for the third. On an even more general level, the subtraction could be converted to addition if we think in terms of adding to determine the algebraic sum of the part/whole percentages regardless of whether they are positive or negative.

If there were more than two alternative policies, we would want to know the threshold weight between the two policies that are competing for first place. We could, however, determine a threshold weight between every pair of policies. If there were more than two goals, we would assign a weight of 1 to the goal that is the least valued. We would then give relative weights to the other goals that are easy to value. Then, we would use the threshold equation or a set of threshold equations to solve for the threshold weight of the goal that is the most difficult to value. We could have multiple threshold weights, depending on the pairs of policies that were being compared. We could also allow each goal to take a turn at being the most difficult to value.

Usefulness of Percentaging

Table 16-1 illustrates how one can use a percentaging approach for choosing the best alternative policy among those that are mutually exclusive. The table can be used to find the best combination of alternatives when they are not mutually exclusive. It can also illustrate how the percentaging approach enables one to rank the policies. They can be ranked according to their weighted percentage scores. A percentaging table can also clarify which alternative is best when doing too much or too little is undesirable. In addition, with percentaging, there is no problem in dealing with benefits or costs that must be discounted by the probability of their occurring before they are converted into part/whole percentages.

Table 16-1 also illustrates how one can use the percentaging approach to allocate scarce resources among various places, programs, projects, policies, persons, activities, or other units. We would allocate 72 percent of our resources to trials and 28 percent to pleas, after first giving each activity a possible minimum allocation. One could also interpret the results as meaning that the optimum mix between trials and pleas should be about 72 percent trials and 28 percent pleas. The sum downward of the weighted sums will total something other than 100 percent when noninteger weights are used or when the algebraically summed columns exceed 100 percent. In this instance, one should obtain the part/whole percentages for the last column so the allocation percentages will equal 100 percent. One cannot allocate more than 100 percent of what is available to be allocated. If all the goals had been to minimize negative ones rather than to maximize positive ones, then the weighted sums would be negative percentages. To convert them into positive percentages that amount to 100 percent, take the complement of each percentage, and then obtain the part/whole percentages of the complements.

In allocating 72 percent of the budget to trials and 28 percent to pleas, we are in effect saying that a 100 percent increase in the trials budget will generate a 72 percent increase in net satisfaction, whereas a 100 percent increase in the pleas budget will generate only a 28 percent increase in net satisfaction. This is roughly the same as saying that trials has a 0.72 elasticity coefficient and pleas has a 0.28 elasticity coefficient. These coefficients, however, are relative rather than absolute because they are interpolated to sum to 100 percent, or 1.00. Relative coefficients are fine, though; all we want to know is, relative to the total allocation-dollars available, how much should be allocated to trials and to pleas in light of their relative values. A 0.72 elasticity coefficent conforms to the reality of diminishing returns, as does any elasticity coefficient between 0 and 1.00. All part/whole percentages would have that desirable characteristic. It is meaningful to allocate in proportion to elasticity coefficients when the objects of the allocation have the same scale coefficient. Two activities, such as trials and pleas from within the same court system, would be operating on the same scale. This is in contrast to two cities, one of which may operate on a 1,000-crime scale and the other on a 100-crime scale. Under these circumstances, one might want to allocate in proportion to the product of the elasticity coefficient and the scale coefficient.

As an alternative to the percentaging approach for choosing between alternatives, one can reduce the problem shown in Table 16-1 to the question, Which is preferable, a four-point increase from 2 to 6 on a respect-for-law scale that ranges from 1 to 10, or a 90-day decrease from 120 to 30 for average case time? Such an approach of comparing increments involves conversion in the sense of subtracting 2 from 6 and 30 from 120, but the problem remains much closer to where it began than had the percentaging approach been used. This has the advantage of enabling the decision maker or decision makers to reach a decision on the basis of the basic facts, rather than on an oversimplification of the facts. The incremental calculation approach has the disadvantage of being more taxing on the decision makers. With the percentaging approach, one must merely decide whether the relative weight of respect for law is more or less than the threshold weight. Some decision makers might prefer exactness to simplicity in this context, but others might prefer to simplify the problem through percentaging analysis. The incremental calculation approach can be extended to situations involving many alternative policies and goals. In doing so, one can compare the first alternative with the second, and the winner against the third alternative. The winner of that pairing is then paired with the fourth alternative. The overall winner remains uneliminated after the series of successive paired comparisons is completed. This approach is more time-consuming and awkward than the percentaging method, particularly when multiple goals as well as many possible policies are involved.

As an alternative to the percentaging approach for allocating resources, one can do a nonlinear regression analysis between each policy and each goal using time points, cities, states, countries, or other units of analysis. One can then allocate whatever is available to be allocated in proportion to the nonlinear elasticity coefficients generated by these regression equations. This approach provides an exactness which percentages as proxies for elasticity coefficients do not provide. Regression analysis between policies and goals, however, often produces close to meaningless results because of problems of reciprocal causation, spurious causation, and multicollinearity. As a result, the magnitude and even the direction of the coefficients are often inaccurate.

The use of percentaging analysis is new in policy evaluation literature, although it has commonsense appeal. The method is especially useful when the goals are all or partly nonmonetary and when there are many goals and alternative policies. What may be needed is more systematic analysis of the implications of converting the raw scores of policies on diverse criteria into part/whole percentages. Perhaps this systematic analysis will make policy evaluation even more feasible to governmental decision makers, including those who make budget-allocation decisions.[2]

Applying Percentaging Analysis to Budget Allocation

Table 16-2 shows how the 1983 budget of the American Society for Public Administration (ASPA) might be allocated to 16 current activities if each

TABLE 16-2

Allocating the 1983 ASPA Budget in Proportion to the Attitude Scores

Rank	Current Activity	Attitude Score (Parts) (1)	Part/ Whole % (2)	% Times Budget (Optimum) (3)	Actual Budget Allocation (4)	Budget Page (5)	Actual Minus Optimum (6)
1	PA Times	1.40	14.8	$140	$123	p. 21	$−17(8)
2	PAR	1.17	12.4	117	208	19	91(2)*
3	Chapter activities	1.11	11.8	112	152	11, 13, 31	40(3)*
4	Job listings	1.00	10.6	100	60	26	−40(3)
5	Informal networking	—	—	—	—	—	—
6	Special publications	0.83	8.8	83	46	23	−37(4)
7	National conferences	0.81	8.6	81	198	15	117(1)*
8	Professional standards	0.72	7.6	72	35	16	−37(5)
9	Position taking	0.60	6.4	61	35	16	−26(7)
10	Regional conferences	0.57	6.0	57	~0	none	−57(1)
11	Training programs	0.44	4.7	45	35	16	−10(9)
12	Section activities	0.42	4.5	43	~0	13	−43(2)
13	Affirmative action	0.33	3.5	33	~0	none	−33(6)
14	Awards program	0.03	0.32	3	35	16	32(4)*
15	Study tours	neg.	0	0	~0	none	0
16	Insurance programs	neg.	0	0	20	30	20(5)*
	Totals	9.43 =whole	100% =whole	$947 =budget	$947 =budget		$0

[1]The attitude scores are translated into numbers as follows: $++ = +2$, $+ = +1$, $0 = 0$, $- = -1$, and $-- = -2$.

[2]All columns with dollars have been rounded to the nearest $1,000.

[3]Informal networking is not given a separate allocation since it is part of chapter/section activities, national/regional conferences, and PA Times/other publications.

[4]The $974,000 to be allocated comes from the $1,441,000 proposed total budget minus $494,000 in anticipated ASPA expenses that are not allocated to the 16 activities.

[5]The allocation for program development has been divided equally between the six activities of policy issues, training, professional standards, awards, promoting public administration, and promoting ASPA.

[6]The budget allocations come from the fiscal year 1983 proposed budget.

[7]The numbers to the right of column 6 show the rank order for the underfunded and the overfunded items. Asterisks appear next to the overfunded items.

activity were to receive a part of the total budget in proportion to the degree of favorable attitudes toward the activity by ASPA members. The attitude scores shown in column 1 come from averaging the responses of the 338 members of ASPA who responded to the questionnaire that was included in the September 1, 1982, issue of the *Public Administration Times*. The respondents were asked to respond to the following statement: The following activities of ASPA are important to me. They were asked to indicate a + + for agree strongly (scored +2), + for agree (scored +1), 0 for neutral (scored 0), – for disagree (scored –1), and – – for disagree strongly (scored –2).

The sum of the attitude scores in column 1 is 9.43. Column 2 shows what percentage of the whole each attitude score constitutes by calculating a part/whole percentage for each activity. According to the Approved Budget, American Society for Public Administration, 1982–1983, the proposed 1983 budget is $1,441,000. Of the total, $494,000 is for anticipated ASPA expenses that are not allocated to the 16 activities. The remaining $947,000 is to be allocated to the 16 activities. Column 3 shows how many dollars each activity would receive if the $947,000 were allocated in proportion to the attitude scores. Each amount in column 3 is calculated by multiplying $947,000 by the part/whole percentage from column 2.

Column 4 shows the actual proposed budget allocation for each of the 16 activities according to the 1983 report. Column 5 indicates the page in the report where these amounts can be found. Column 6 shows the difference between the amounts in the 1983 budget and the so-called optimum amounts if the budget were allocated in proportion to the attitude scores. The activities in column 6 marked by asterisks are overfunded in the sense that they received more than the optimum. The activities with no asterisks are underfunded, as they received less than the optimum. Column 6 also shows the rank order of the overfunded and underfunded activities.

The most underfunded activities relative to ASPA member attitudes are regional conferences, job listings, and special publications. Perhaps the national ASPA budget should be more supportive of regional conferences. Perhaps ASPA should encourage job listings by making them available without charge, or by allocating more resources to solicit job listings. Special publications perhaps deserve a larger budget allocation in view of their popularity relative to their actual budget allocation and relative to other ASPA activities. One can conduct a similar analysis for the other underfunded activities (i.e., those with a minus sign in column 6), including the professional standards, the *PA Times*, section activities, affirmative action, position taking, and training programs.

In more detailed versions of Table 16-2, we consider the attitude scores of different subgroups within ASPA, but arrive at basically the same results due to the similarity in attitudes across subgroups. We also added the criteria of direct income and expense produced by each activity. The results concerning the new optimum allocations also tend to be the same, especially if we recognize that the 16 activities are responsible for generating the dues income of ASPA largely in proportion to their attitude scores. The 16 activities may also generate volunteer labor somewhat in proportion to their attitude scores. One substantive point to note is that allocating in proportion to the attitude scores does not generally result in allocations that are drastically different from the way in which the ASPA budget is being allocated in practice. The average deviation per activity is only $45,000 on a budget of $947,000, although this figure may be considered large, given the subjectivity of what constitutes a large deviation from the optimum.

The data summarized in Table 16-2 relating ASPA member attitudes to ASPA budgeting raises questions concerning how to justify why some activities are receiving substantially larger budget allocations than their popularity might predict and why some activities are receiving substantially smaller budget allocations. The general consensus among those attending the winter 1982 meeting of the ASPA National Council was that the budgeting analysis forces one to think more clearly about the appropriateness of ASPA's current priorities and how they can be improved upon. The same kind of application of percentaging analysis to budget allocation can provide insights into numerous other areas of public-sector and not-for-profit budgeting, when criteria other than monetary profit are involved.

NOTES

1. See "Allocation Logic" in S. Nagel, *Policy Evaluation: Making Optimum Decisions* (Praeger, 1982), 230–54.
2. For more complicated variations on part/whole percentaging, see Thomas Saaty, *The Analytic Hierarchy Process: Planning, Priority Setting, Resource Allocation* (McGraw-Hill,1980); Ward Edwards and Robert Newman, *Multi-Attribute Evaluation* (Sage, 1982); Brent Wholeben, *Multiple Alternatives for Educational Evaluation and Decision-Making* (Northwest Regional Educational Laboratory, 1982); Ralph Keeney and Howard Raiffa, *Decisions with Multiple Objectives: Preferences and Value Tradeoffs* (Wiley, 1976); Allan Easton, *Complex Managerial Decisions Involving Multiple Objectives* (Wiley, 1973); John Rohrbaugh and Anne McCartt, "Decision Techtronics Group and the Use of Optimizing Analyses in New York State Resource Allocation" in S. Nagel (ed.), *Productivity and Public Policy* (Sage, 1983); and "Finding an Optimum Mix in Allocating Scarce Resources" in S. Nagel, *Policy Evaluation: Making Optimum Decisions* (Praeger, 1982), 178–254.
3. S. Nagel and Brad Malis, "Membership Survey Results," 6 *Public Administration Times* 3–4 (March 1, 1983).

QUESTIONS

---

1. If you wanted to determine which of two athletes was better in a competition including golf and bowling, how would you handle the

fact that low golf scores are desirable but low bowling scores are undesirable? Suppose John has a golf average of 80 and a bowling average of 150, and Mary has a golf average of 70 and a bowling average of 130. Who is the better combination athlete?
2. Suppose you are trying to allocate the budget of an organization in accordance with the attitude scores of the members. Suppose the organization has only two activities, internal and external. Make up some numbers for the members' attitudes toward these two activities and for the amount of money available to be allocated. Use these hypothetical numbers to show your understanding of percentaging analysis as applied to budget allocation.
3. Show that allocating a budget to trials and pleas in Table 16-1 will be influenced by, or sensitive to, whether we use part/whole, part/maximum, part/highest percentages, or some combination of the three.
4. Demonstrate that allocating a budget will be influenced by, or sensitive to, whether we invert a criterion by taking the complements of the part/whole percentages, calculating whole/part percentages, obtaining the reciprocals of the raw scores, subtracting the raw scores from the highest score, multiplying each raw score or part/whole percentage by -1, or physically reversing the scores by giving the highest alternative the lowest score and the lowest alternative the highest score.
5. How might one obtain weights for goals? How might the goals be determined? How might the alternatives be scored on the goals in terms of raw scores? How might one generate ideas for alternative policies?
6. Show how you would decide among three college courses, considering for each course the number of credits, the amount of working hours, and its usefulness in preparation for future work.

REFERENCES

Easton, Allan, *Complex Managerial Decisions Involving Multiple Objectives* (Wiley, 1973).
Edwards, Ward, and Robert Newman, *Multi-Attribute Evaluation* (Sage, 1982).
Keeney, Ralph, and Howard Raiffa, *Decisions with Multiple Objectives: Preferences and Value Tradeoffs* (Wiley, 1976).
Nagel, S., "Allocation Logic" in *Policy Evaluation: Making Optimum Decisions* (Praeger, 1982), 230–54.
Saaty, Thomas, *The Analytic Hierarchy Process: Planning, Priority Setting, Resource Allocation* (McGraw-Hill, 1980).
Wholeben, Brent, *Multiple Alternatives for Educational Evaluation and Decision-Making* (Northwest Regional Educational Laboratory, 1982).

CHAPTER 17

Interdisciplinary Methods

This chapter focuses on how perspectives from statistical analysis and the social sciences can be helpful in policy evaluation. The first half of the chapter discusses statistical analysis. The second half explores the key social sciences of psychology, political science, and economics.

Some Statistical Considerations in Policy Evaluation

Statistical analysis relates to public policy analysis in the following ways: (1) it contributes to evaluating alternative legal policies by using its input as premises in either deductive prediction or in policy optimization, and (2) a policy analysis perspective can clarify what statistical procedures should be used in order to make a statistical analysis more useful to policy makers and appliers with regard to statistical inference, prediction, and causal analysis.

This section of the chapter illustrates how each of these aspects of statistical analysis is related to public policy analysis and vice versa. The concrete illustrations include such policy problems as:

1. predicting the effects of smaller juries
2. determining an optimum percentage of defendants to hold prior to trial
3. black-white differences in sentencing
4. predicting personal injury case outcomes
5. allocating anticrime dollars across places and activities[1]

STATISTICS AS INPUTS INTO DEDUCTIVE PREDICTION AND POLICY OPTIMIZATION

Deducing Policy Effects Rather Than Inductively Observing Them. In policy analysis, it is often essential to deduce the effects of alternative legal policies before they are adopted so that postadoption inertia won't prevent an undesirable policy from being changed, and to ensure that an undesirable policy will not cause substantial harm before it can be repealed. Traditional statistical analysis evaluates alternative legal policies by: (1) comparing

355

them across places that have adopted different policies, (2) comparing places over time before and after they adopt the policies being considered, and (3) comparing an experimental group and a control group in a laboratory simulation or a contrived experiment. These methods cannot indicate the effects of the policies under consideration because of the influence of confounding variables or because an adequate study would be too expensive. Another method deduces the effects of alternative legal policies from statistically validated premises.

A good example of this method is determining the effects on conviction rates of changing from 12-person juries to 6-person juries. Inductive approaches are not as meaningful for this policy problem, as discussed in Chapter 11. Comparing the conviction rates in states that use 12-person juries with states that use 6-person juries is not adequate because differences in the conviction rates may be determined by other uncontrollable differences. In addition to differences in jury size, other differences include the characteristics of the law, the people, or the cases in the two sets of states. Comparing the same places over time before and after they shift from 12-person juries to 6-person juries does not work because the cases are not likely to be the same in the after period as they were in the before period. The cases in the after period are likely to be those in which defense attorneys are more confident of winning, and this change may lower the conviction rate. Comparing a set of 12-person juries who watch a simulated typical criminal case with a set of 6-person juries who watch the same typical criminal case does not work either because the typical criminal case is likely to result in 100 percent convictions for both sets of juries. It is, however, too . expensive to develop a whole range of simulated criminal cases, and too difficult to make that range representative of the range of real criminal cases.

If we use a deductive model to determine what the effects would be of switching from 12-person juries to 6-person juries, we should deduce our conclusions from premises that have been empirically validated, which is likely to mean validated by statistical induction. In this example, it could mean obtaining data for a large sample of 12-person jury trials to determine the percentage of cases within the sample that result in a conviction and to determine the percentage of times individual jurors vote to convict. From these two inductively validated premises and some reasonably simple deductive reasoning, one can deduce the effect of changing from 12-person juries to 6-person juries, as shown in Figure 11-1.

Other examples can be given of statistical induction providing data for deducing conclusions on matters for which we have no direct data. For example, statistical data shows there are wide variations across cities on pretrial releasing rates and narrow variations across cities on failure-to-appear rates. We can, therefore, deduce that there are probably wide variations across judges on pretrial releasing rates and narrow variations across judges on failure-to-appear rates, since the cities are like judges in this context. We also have statistical data that demonstrates correlations between political party affiliation and decisional propensities among appellate judges. Thus, we can deduce that even stronger correlations between political affiliation and decisional propensities exist among trial judges because trial judges are in a better position to inject their party-correlated values into their decisions. Trial judges: (1) do not have to write opinions justifying their decisions, as appellate judges do, (2) do not have fellow judges simultaneously deciding the same cases with them on a collegial bench as a check, and (3) usually try more subjective factual matters than the relatively more objective legal matters tried by appellate judges.[2]

Regression Equations as Inputs Into Policy Optimizing Models. The essense of a policy optimization model can be reduced to the following simple syllogism: Y is good; X causes Y; therefore adopt X. Statistical analysis can be relevant to surveying or analyzing the content of the Y goals of the public, a legislature, the framers of a constitution, or any other relevant group. An alternative is to make tentative goals and experiment with the effects of changing them once the prescriptive or optimizing conclusions are reached. Statistical analysis is especially relevant to determining the relations between alternative policies (Xs) and goals (Ys). It may involve gathering data from many places or time periods regarding how each place or time period is scored on each X and Y. This data can then be plotted as a series of data points, showing how each place or time period is geographically positioned as a Y and an X. A straight or curved line can then be fitted to the data points to minimize the sum of the distances from the points to the line. The line can also be expressed as an equation relating Y to X, called a statistical regression equation.

A good illustration of the use of regression equations as inputs into policy optimizing models is the problem of determining the optimum percent of defendants to hold in jail prior to trial. If too many defendants are held, then unduly high holding costs will be incurred with regard to jail maintenance, lost gross national product, and bitterness. If too few defendants are held in jail prior to trial, then unduly high releasing costs will be incurred with regard to rearresting those who fail to appear and the cost of crimes committed by those released.

To obtain an optimum percentage of defendants to hold, one could start by determining for each of a number of cities its holding percentage and its holding costs, and then fit a holding cost curve to this data. This kind of data was compiled for a sample of 23 American cities in 1969. The data thus generates 23 data points on a two-dimensional graph like Figure 17-1. Through the use of nonlinear regression analysis, one can fit a curve to this data similar to the total holding cost curve shown in Figure 17-1. The curve has an increasingly positive slope, because as one moves closer to holding 100 percent of the defendants, one tends to hold defendants who are not

FIGURE 17-1
The Optimum Percentage of Defendants to Hold Prior to Trial

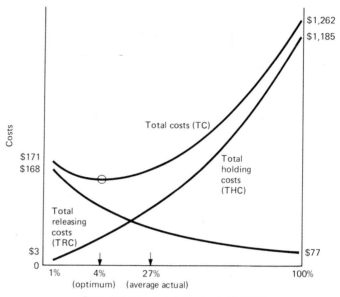

Note: $THC = \$1,185(\%H)^{1.31}$; $TRC = \$77(\%H)^{-0.17}$; $TC = THC + TRC$.

typical criminal types. These defendants incur higher holding costs with regard to lost gross national product, the bitterness owing to being acquitted or having one's case dismissed after a substantial wait in jail, and to being more costly to maintain in jail.

One could also determine for each of the cities its holding percentage and its releasing costs. Through the use of nonlinear regression analysis, one can also fit a curve to those 23 data points like the total releasing cost curve which is shown in Figure 17-1. This curve has a progressively negative slope because as less defendants are held, more recidivists and bail-jumpers are released. The next step is to compute a total cost curve by adding the holding cost curve and the releasing cost curve. Where this total cost curve bottoms out is the optimum holding percentage.

Given this data, the optimum holding policy level is 4 percent of the defendants. The average city, however, held 27 percent. Differences between the optimum and the empirical results are due to differences in goals. For example, our model emphasizes costs to society, which may not be a major concern to judges. Differences between the optimum and the empirical may also be due to differences in perceptions of the facts, despite possibly identical goals. Potentially misperceived facts include the inability to distinguish between bad and good risks.

A POLICY ANALYSIS PERSPECTIVE AS INFLUENCING
STATISTICAL PROCEDURES

The most important procedures in elementary statistics deal with: (1) determining whether a statistical relation should be considered nonchance, given the size of the relation and the size of the sample of data on which it is based, (2) determining how one can predict the position of a person, place, or thing on one variable by knowing how it is positioned on one or more other variables, and (3) determining whether a relation between two variables is a causal relation or is due to the influence of a third variable. The traditional methods for handling these procedures may be inappropriate when deciding on which governmental policies should be adopted for various social problems.

Policy Analysis and Statistical Inference. For example, a relation is traditionally attributable to chance when it can occur by chance more than 5 times out of 100. This analysis implies that it is 19 times as bad to accept a false relation (type 1 error) than it is to reject a true relation (a type 2 error). This method can work when the relation has no policy implications and the relative costs of making a type 1 error versus a type 2 error are unimportant. In policy analysis, however, these costs are important to consider.

This is well illustrated by testing the relation between black and white convicted defendants who receive jail sentences or probation. Suppose our sample includes 40 black and 50 white defendants who have been convicted of grand larceny. Sixty percent of the black defendants receive jail sentences, and 40 percent receive probation; whereas 45 percent of the white defendants receive jail sentences, and 55 percent receive probation. The relation between race and going to jail can be expressed by the 0.15 difference between the races. The statistical inference question involves determining the extent to which one could obtain a 0.15 difference with a sample size of ninety purely by chance if differences did not exist between the treatment of white and black convicted defendants. If this same difference could occur purely by chance more than 5 times out of 100, it is a chance, rather than a real or nonchance, relation.

A policy analysis approach to the statistical inference problem also involves determining the chance probability of the relation. Such an approach, however, does not automatically use a 0.05 or 0.01 chance probability threshold, above which one attributes the relation to chance and below which one does not attribute the relation to chance. A policy analysis approach determines a threshold level for each relation (or at least for the more important ones) by considering the relative costs of making a type 1 error versus a type 2 error. If it is only twice as undesirable (rather than 19 times) to falsely accuse the criminal justice system of being discriminatory than it is to falsely exonerate the criminal justice system from being discriminatory, then one would work with a 0.33 threshold rather than a 0.05 threshold.

The relative costs approach to statistical inference involves calculating $1/(X + 1)$, where X indicates the relative cost of a type 1 error to a type 2 error. Thus, if a type 1 error is 19 times as bad as a type 2 error, then the formula becomes $1/(19 + 1)$, which equals 0.05. And if a type 1 error is only twice as bad as a type 2 error, then the formula becomes $1/(2 + 1)$, which equals 0.33.

To prove the above formula, one needs some symbols for the possible costs and benefits, such as $-B$ for the type 2 error costs of accepting a false relation, $+B$ for the benefits of avoiding a type 2 error by rejecting a false relation, $-A$ for the type 1 error costs of rejecting a true relation, $+A$ for the benefits of avoiding a type 1 error by accepting a true relation, and P for the probability that the relation is true. The expected value of accepting a hypothesis is thus $(-B)(P) + (+A)(1 - P)$, which is the type 2 error costs (discounted by the probability of the costs occurring), plus the benefits from accepting the relation (discounted by the probability of the benefits occurring). The expected value of rejecting a hypothesis is $(+B)(P) + (-A)(1 - P)$, which is the benefits from rejecting the relation (discounted by the probability of the benefits occurring), plus the type 1 error costs (discounted by the probability of the costs occurring). To find the threshold probability where the two expected values are equal, we simply set these two expressions equal to each other and solve for P. The solution is $P = B/(A + B)$, which algebraically simplifies to $1/(X + 1)$, where $X = A/B$. These relations are summarized in Figure 17-2.[4]

Policy Analysis and Statistical Prediction. To illustrate statistical prediction with legal policy analysis, predict the damages likely to be awarded in personal injury cases when medical expenses are known. Suppose we have data on four personal injury cases. Damages awarded in these cases were $3,000, $3,000, $5,000, and $10,000; medical expenses were $100, $400, $300, and $600. The prediction problem involves developing a formula or decision rule for predicting damages awarded from medical expenses.

FIGURE 17-2
A Policy Analysis Approach to Determining a Threshold Probability for Accepting a Relation as Being a Nonchance Relation

Probability of the relation being true

		Relation true (P)	Relation false $(1 - P)$	Expected value (Benefits − Costs)
Alternative decisions available	Reject relation	$-B$ (type 2 error)	$+A$ (avoiding type 1 error)	$EV_R = (-B)(P) + (+A)(1 - P)$
	Accept relation	$+B$ (avoiding type 2 error)	$-A$ (type 1 error)	$EV_A = (+B)(P) + (-A)(1 - P)$

Cell entries show benefits (+'s) and costs (−'s).
Threshold level for statistical inference: $P^* = B/(A + B) = 1/(X + 1)$, where $X = A/B$.

To develop such a formula it is necessary to create a graph with damages awarded on the vertical axis and medical expenses on the horizontal axis, and then to plot a dot for each case. The first dot would be to the right of the $3,000 mark on the damages axis and above the $100 mark on the medical axis, and the same would hold for the other three dots. One would then fit a straight line to the dots so the line would be as close to the dots as possible. This line could be expressed as the equation $Y = a + b(X)$, where Y represents the predicted damages, and X represents the known medical expenses. The a represents the amount of damages where the straight line crosses the damages axis, and thus where there are zero medical expenses. The b represents the slope of the line, or how much the value of Y changes when there is a 1-unit change in X. Applying this approach yields the equation $Y = \$810 + 13(X)$. This equation indicates that if the medical expenses are zero, the predicted damages will be $810. When the medical expenses are $100, predicted damages will be $2,110.

The $810 and the 13 can be quickly determined with an electronic calculator that gives the numerical values for the Y-intercept and the slope when the 4 data points are read in. In traditional statistical prediction, which such an electronic calculator follows, the prediction line is, in effect, fitted to the dots to minimize the sum of the squared distances or deviations from the dots to the line rather than the sum of the unsquared distances. For the first case, in which the medical expenses were $100, the predicted damages would be $2,110. The actual damages, however, are $3,000. This means the deviation between actual and predicted is $890, and the squared deviation is $792,100. If the calculator had minimized the unsquared deviations, the predictive equation would have involved numbers other than $810 and 13.

Minimizing the sum of the squared deviations may be acceptable when the predictive relation lacks policy or benefit-cost implications. In policy analysis, however, this type of prediction is inapplicable. Table 17-1 clarifies why minimizing the unsquared deviations is more sensible. If a lawyer predicts the first case will yield $12 in damages and it only yields $10, then he or she will be out $2. If the second case predicts $8 in damages, and it only yields $7, then the lawyer will be out $1. The misprediction in the first case is twice as bad as the misprediction in the second case. Using the squared deviation criterion, however, the misprediction in the first case is considered

TABLE 17-1
Two Personal Injury Cases for Evaluating Alternative Prediction Criteria

Case	Predicted Damages	Actual Damages		Unsquared Deviations	Squared Deviations	
One	$12	$10		—$2 Out	$4—	
			(2 times as bad)			(4 times as bad)
Two	$ 8	$ 7		—$1 Out	$1—	

four times as bad as in the second case, since one squares the deviations between predicted and actual. A lawyer might, thus, object to a prediction method that considers the misprediction in case 1 to be four times as bad as the misprediction in case 2, rather than twice as bad. A legislator might also object to a prediction method in which the predictions are relevant to the relation between damages awarded and medical expenses as part of an analysis of a no-fault personal-injury system versus a system that bars plaintiffs from collecting damages if they are partially at fault.

If squaring the deviations is not sensible from a benefit-cost perspective, then why is it done? Primarily, calculating the "best fitting" Y-intercept and slope are easier to do when squared deviations are part of the definition of best fitting. This may be true with inexpensive electronic calculators. Data processing computers can, however, be programmed to quickly arrive at a Y-intercept and slope that satisfy a best fitting criterion expressed in terms of unsquared deviations. These computer programs should be developed to cover complicated forms of prediction, including prediction from many variables simultaneously.[5]

Policy Analysis and Statistical Causation. Traditional causal analysis in statistics and social science uses arrow or path diagrams to show how each causal factor influences an outcome and each other. For example, if the outcome is crime, the causal analysis might consider the influence of such factors as:

1. the severity of sentences
2. the probability of being apprehended
3. using poverty as an indicator of lack of opportunities
4. the quantity of people in each place for which data has been gathered
5. the number of people in the crime-prone ages between 15 and 25
6. the number and percentage of people living in metropolitan or urban areas
7. changes in some of these indicators
8. anticrime activities and expenditures

This kind of analysis yields the following equation: $Y = f(X_1, X_2, \ldots X_n)$, when crime is a function of many variables.

In policy analysis, we want to know the relation between the policy variable and crime, statistically holding other relevant variables constant even when we do not know what these other variables are or how influential each one is. We can find this relation by doing a statistical regression analysis that generates the equation, $Y = f(X, Y_{t-1})$, in which X is the policy variable and Y is crime. By having the prior year's crime as an independent variable on the right side of the equation and the subsequent year's crime as a dependent variable on the left side, we thereby statistically control for prior crime in predicting subsequent crime. Doing so indirectly controls for whatever causes prior crime, except for anticrime expenditures, because it is also an independent variable on the right side of the equation. This may not be statistically elegant since having crime on both sides of the equation approaches having a tautology. It also tells us nothing about the separate influence of all the crime-causing variables other than anticrime expenditures. This approach, however, does serve our policy analysis purpose by telling us about the relation between crime and anticrime expenditures when other crime-causing variables are statistically controlled.

Traditional causal analysis is also concerned with the concept of reciprocal causation. Such causation refers to crime's influence on positively stimulating anticrime policy through, for example, anticrime expenditures. To separate the negative from the positive influence, statistical analysis would find a variable, Z_1, that could predict anticrime expenditures, but that has no relation to crime. It would also find a variable, Z_2, that could predict crime, but that has no relation to anticrime expenditures. One can then use anticrime expenditures predicted from Z_1 to predict crime. This regression coefficient would theoretically indicate the influence of anticrime expenditures on crime without the reciprocal effect of crime on expenditures. One can also use crime predicted from Z_2 to predict anticrime expenditures. This regression coefficient would indicate crime's influence on anticrime expenditures without the reciprocal effect of expenditures on crime.

In policy analysis, however, we are interested in determining the relation between the policy variable and crime. We can achieve this by relating crime to prior anticrime dollars with the following regression equation: $Y = f(X_{t-1})$. By lagging the anticrime expenditures by about one time period, we prevent crime from influencing anticrime expenditures, since a variable cannot influence another variable at an earlier point in time. We also allow anticrime expenditures to have a better opportunity to influence results. This approach of simply lagging the policy variable is not as statistically elegant as a more multivariate approach, but it serves our policy analysis purpose.

If we join the autocorrelation variable of Y_{t-1} and the lagged policy variable of X_{t-1}, the regression analysis can generally handle both the spurious or deceiving effect of other variables and the reciprocal effect of the goal variable on the policy variable. This generates the statistical equation, $Y = f(X_{t-1}, Y_{t-1})$. We can find the nonlinear diminishing returns relation between crime and anticrime expenditures by taking the logarithm of the policy variable when doing the regression analysis. Further details on establishing these kinds of causal relations are mentioned in Chapter 13 in the section, "Simplicity in Determining Causation."[6]

SOME CONCLUSIONS ON STATISTICAL ANALYSIS AND POLICY EVALUATION

Statisticians and users of statistics should show more concern for how the statistics will be used. Causal analysis may have one meaning when it is used as part of an optimum allocation policy, and another when there is a more theoretical concern for the relative causal importance of a variety of variables. Similarly, when predicting policy-relevant outcomes, prediction analysis may be capable of talking in terms of the monetary or nonmonetary costs of mispredicting by one or more units which may be meaningless in traditional statistical prediction. In addition, statistical inference, when dealing with policy relevant relations, might benefit from considering the relative costs of type 1 errors versus type 2 errors.

Policy analysis can change the nature of statistical reasoning, and statistical reasoning can influence policy analysis. This can be applicable to statistical methods that are used to develop the input premises into deductive models designed to predetermine the effects of alternative legal policies. Intuitive premises rather than statistically validated premises might otherwise lead to meaningless conclusions. This concept can also be demonstrated with statistical methods that are used to develop optimizing models' inputs, including both surveys of values to be maximized and predictive or causal regression analyses to determine relations between alternative policies and goals.

Legal researchers have considered statistics as dry and irrelevant for analyzing the law's grand policy issues. This chapter should clarify the importance of statistics in policy prediction and optimization. On the other hand, statisticians have felt that applied research, including policy analysis research, was irrelevant for developing new statistical orientations. This chapter clarifies policy analysts' need for new high levels of statistical tools in the realms of statistical inference, prediction, and causal analysis. Interaction should be increased between legal policy people and statistical people in activities such as: (1) conferences, like the one on "Statistics in Law and Government" held in October 1979 at the University of Connecticut, (2) national meetings of political-legal and statistical associations, and (3) interdisciplinary policy studies programs, which are now developing at American universities.

Policy Evaluation:
Psychology, Politics, and Economics Combined

Policy evaluation involves a combination of policy studies and evaluation research. Both factors are concerned with having government programs work more effectively, efficiently, and equitably. Although their similarities outweigh their differences and the differences complement each other, some of these differences are important to note. Evaluation research places relatively more emphasis on:

1. psychology and sociology, rather than political science and economics
2. problems of health, education, and welfare, rather than foreign policy, civil liberties, inflation and unemployment, and economic regulation

3. the postadoption analysis of programs rather than pre-adoption
4. accepting programs, as opposed to goals, as givens
5. evaluating programs in a given place and time rather than evaluating policies that cut across places and time

Evaluation research or program evaluation is like adjudicating the guilt or innocence of a specific defendant under the legal system, whereas policy analysis sets the rules by which guilt or innocence is defined.

This part of the chapter provides three examples of program evaluation that are fully meaningful only when the perspectives of psychology, politics, and economics are combined. Our main example deals with the allocation of scarce resources; the second with poverty policy; and the third with pollution policy.[7]

AN EXAMPLE FROM APPORTIONING A BUDGET

Budget apportionment exemplifies the need to consider economics and politics simultaneously in policy analysis. For example, consider a situation in which an agency is so efficient that it reduces its costs and increases its output. Suppose, in period 1, the agency spends $5 and generates 10 benefit units. Then, in period 2, the agency spends only $3 and generates 15 benefit units. In the first period, it only had a 2-to-1 benefit/cost ratio, whereas in the second period, it had a 5-to-1 ratio. The marginal rate of return for this agency is negative since the change in output is 5 units and the change in input is -2 units, which means its slope is $5/-2$ or -2.5. The agency should not be given an incremental dollar. Its budget should be $3, instead of its previous year's budget of $5. In other words, by being so efficient, the agency in effect is penalized through a budget reduction, which may mean laying off personnel. Thus, agencies spend in a wasteful fashion whatever remains in their budgets at the end of the fiscal year, so they will not suffer a budget reduction in the following year.

The situation's political psychology or organizational behavior recognizes that punishments and rewards are not being properly administered when the marginal rate of return is used to measure growth. In theory, one could convert the agency's negative slope into a positive one by fitting a curve through the zero point, or doing a time-series analysis in which time is on the horizontal axis, and benefits and costs are on the vertical axis. This, however, would not satisfy the political realities whereby the legislature thinks that if the agency can perform so well on $3, then it shouldn't receive any more than $3, unless the agency is slated to generate more than 15 benefit units. The solution? Agencies should be empowered to use the unspent funds that they lacked time to use in the following fiscal period if they can show that it would be put to good use. These rules can simultaneously consider both the economic efficiency and the political psychology aspects of agency behavior.

Another budgeting example might show how to allocate an incremental dollar between two agencies when one operates at a high level of efficiency but shows little improvement, and the second operates at a low level of efficiency but is improving rapidly. An economics perspective would emphasize allocating the incremental dollar to the agency that is moving upward since it has a higher marginal rate of return than the high agency which showed little improvement from a previous budget increase. This solution rewards the prodigal son who shows improvement and neglects the consistently well-behaved son. The effect may be to demoralize the more efficient agency. The better solution, therefore, is to apportion the incremental dollar to both agencies. The apportionment can be determined through the use of a semilog curve fitting method that forces the returns curve through the origin in recognition of both diminishing returns and the fact that zero costs generally produce zero benefits. This method combines the marginal analysis of economics with the organizational behavior concerns of the public administration aspects of political science.[8]

AN EXAMPLE FROM POVERTY POLICY

Impressive examples of policy evaluation are the negative income tax experiments conducted in New Jersey and other states around 1970. The key policy variable was how much money welfare recipients should receive. The policy was generally expressed in terms of percentage of needs. Welfare recipients were randomly assigned to categories whereby payments were received at 50 percent, 75 percent, 100 percent, and 125 percent of needs. The key goal variable or dependent variable was ambition to find a better job. Each group was given a pretest and a posttest measuring attitudes and behavior on the ambition variable. The general theory or hypothesis was that recipients receiving only a low percentage of needs would have a low ambition level because their self-image would be low and they would be undernourished. Recipients receiving a high percentage of needs would also have a low ambition level because they would lack incentive to secure a better job. The recipients in the middle, theoretically, would have a relatively high ambition level.

Economists, concerned with the monetary aspects of the study, and psychologists, concerned with measuring ambition and the experimental methodology, were involved in the experiment. This methodology was excellent in terms of randomization, experimental controls, and pretest-posttest measurement. The results, however, were generally disappointing in that virtually no differences between any of the recipients were found in ambition levels. Perhaps, however, the right hypotheses or policy variables were not tested. If political scientists and public administrators had been more involved, they might have tested for the effects of alternative delivery systems. The main alternatives are the compulsory caseworker versus a check in the mail with no caseworker monitoring how the money is spent. A case could be made that caseworkers stimulate ambition by providing welfare recipients with useful job information and by harassment. On the other hand, one could argue that not having a caseworker stimulates ambition. Caseworkers cause recipients to be dependent upon them and thus reduce their self-esteem, which in turn, reduces ambition. One could also talk about degrees of monitoring control and argue that at low levels, ambition is down because there is no monitoring push; and at high levels, ambition is down because it becomes oppressive. Ambition would thus be at a peak between no monitoring and oppressive monitoring. The important point is that this reasoning was untested. There was inadequate concern for the political science and public administration aspects of the problem of how to set up a welfare system. With a combination of psychology, politics, and economics, the $15 million spent on the negative income tax experiments could have been more meaningfully spent.[9]

AN EXAMPLE FROM POLLUTION POLICY

Economists often suggest internalizing the external damage that polluters cause by levying a pollution tax on them. In the case of water pollution, the tax might be used to build a downstream filtration plant to clean the biodegradable pollution before it reaches a downstream drinking reservoir. Engineers would determine how much tax is needed for such a filtration plant. Each business firm along the river segment would then pay in proportion to the amount of pollution it generates. Thus, if the plant costs $2 million and firm X is responsible for 25 percent of the pollution, then it would pay $500,000 in taxes. The system provides each firm with an incentive to reduce its pollution in order to reduce its tax. The system also provides funds for cleaning up the pollution caused by those firms who find it less expensive to pay the tax than to eliminate their pollution. If all the firms eliminate their pollution, it may cost $3 million, which makes this an example of a situation in which $2 million in cure is better than $3 million in prevention. An equilibrium would theoretically result where the firms would institute as much prevention as it is economic to do, and the rest of the pollution would be cleaned up by the filtration plant.

The big economic advantage of such a system is that it places the burden of paying the pollution cost on the polluters. This, however, is also its big political disadvantage. A proposed pollution tax would stimulate numerous trade associations to lobby effectively against such a tax. These interest groups might, however, be willing to tolerate the prevailing system of regulation and litigation, which is slow and cumbersome. Much of the cost of the prevailing system is borne by the general taxpayer and those who breathe air and drink or use water. The prevailing system may not work as well as a pollution tax, but its advantage is that it is politically feasible.

Political scientists and lawyers may show more political realism than economists regarding antipollution legislation and Congress. However, they show less realism as to what is administratively possible by pushing water pollution legislation that calls for zero pollution by about 1985. The idea of zero pollution is an important political symbol, like the idea of zero deaths on the highway over Labor Day. Zero pollution, however, is likely to mean far greater costs than benefits. The optimum level of pollution recognizes that high pollution is undesirable because it can jeopardize public health in terms of waterborne and airborne diseases, as well as jeopardize businesses that require clean water and air. However, the optimum level of pollution recognizes that low pollution may be undesirable because in order to remove the last residue of pollution, the cleanup costs become so much greater. The optimum level is where the sum of the damage costs and the cleanup costs is minimized, which is likely to be at a point where pollution is neither too high nor too low.

The psychological approach to the problems of pollution is reflected in the book entitled *Environment and the Social Sciences*, published by the American Psychological Association in 1972. It emphasizes the role of psychologists in conducting experiments and developing ideas on how to convince individuals and businesses to reduce pollution and conserve energy. This perspective may overemphasize the responsibility of individuals, but the psychological theory of rewards, punishments, and incentives can apply to businesses as well.[10]

SOME CONCLUSIONS ON BEING INTERDISCIPLINARY

These examples show that many disciplines should be considered when evaluating policies, particularly psychology, politics, and economics. Other disciplines are important, such as engineering (for measuring pollution), or philosophy (for dealing with the value questions of energy equity across generations and income equity across classes). Psychology offers the experimental and quasiexperimental paradigm, plus a concern for the manipulation of rewards and punishments. Economics offers a concern for benefit-cost analysis and income minus expenses. Political science emphasizes political and administrative feasibility. Policy evaluation should combine these useful perspectives.

NOTES

1. Previous literature dealing with matters of statistics in law, criminal justice administration, and policy analysis includes Hans Baade (ed.), *Jurimetrics* (Oceana, 1963); William Fairley and Frederick Mosteller, *Statistics and Public Policy* (Addison-Wesley, 1977); Michael Finkelstein, *Quantitiative Methods in Law* (Little, Brown, 1978); S. Nagel and Marian Neef, *Legal Policy Analysis: Finding an Optimum Level or Mix* (Lexington-Heath, 1977); Glendon Schubert, *Judicial Behavior: A Reader in Theory and Research* (Rand McNally, 1964); Gresham Sykes, et al., *Law and Social Science Research: A Collection of Annotated Readings* (University of Denver College of Law, 1970); Suzette Talarico (ed.), *Criminal Justice Research: Approaches, Problems, and Policy* (Anderson, 1980).

2. For further details on deducing legal policy effects, generally from statistically or empirically validated premises, see Gary Becker and William Landes (eds.), *Essays in the Economics of Crime and Punishment* (Columbia University Press, 1974); S. Nagel (ed.), *Modeling the Criminal Justice System* (Sage, 1977); S. Nagel and Marian Neef, *Decision Theory and the Legal Process* (Lexington-Heath, 1979); Richard Posner, *Economic Analysis of Law* (Little, Brown, 1977); Gordon Tullock, *The Logic of the Law* (Basic Books, 1971). For further details deducing the effects on conviction rates of changing the size of juries, see Alan Gelfand and Herbert Solomon, "An Argument in Favor of 12-Member Juries" in S. Nagel (ed.), *Modeling the Criminal Justice System* (Sage, 1977); Bernard Grofman, "Jury Decision-Making Models and the Supreme Court," 8 *Policy Studies Journal* 749−72 (1980); S. Nagel and Marian Neef, "Deductive Modeling to Determine an Optimum Jury Size and Fraction Required to Convict," 1975 *Washington University Law Quarterly* 933−78 (1976).
3. For further details on legal policy optimization, see Haig Bohigan, *The Foundations and Mathematical Models of Operations Research with Extensions to the Criminal Justice System* (Gazette Press, 1971); Sidney Brounstein and Murray Kamrass (eds.), *Operations Research in Law Enforcement, Justice, and Societal Security* (Lexington-Heath, 1976). For further details on finding an optimum percentage of defendants to hold in jail prior to trial, see William Landes, "The Bail System: An Economic Approach," 2 *Journal of Legal Studies* 79 (1973); S. Nagel, P. Wice, and Marian Neef, *Too Much or Too Little Policy: The Example of Pretrial Release* (Sage, 1977).
4. On statistical inference, see Denton Morrison and Ramon Henkel (eds.), *The Significance Test Controversy: A Reader* (Aldine, 1974); Sidney Siegel, *Nonparametric Statistics for the Behavioral Sciences* (McGraw-Hill, 1956); Helen Walker and Joseph Lev, *Statistical Inference* (Holt, Rinehart & Winston, 1953). On deciding whether differences in the treatment of black and white convicted defendants are attributable to chance, see Jon Hagen, "Extra-Legal Attributes and Criminal Sentencing: An Assessment of a Sociological Viewpoint," 8 *Law and Society Review* 357 (1974); S. Nagel and Marian Neef, "Racial Disparities That Supposedly Do Not Exist: Some Pitfalls in Analysis of Court Records," 52 *Notre Dame Lawyer* 87−94 (1976).
5. On statistical prediction, see Allan Edwards, *An Introduction to Linear Regression and Correlation* (Freeman, 1976); Gordon Hilton, *Intermediate Politometrics* (Columbia University Press, 1976); Edward Tufte, *Data Analysis for Politics and Policy* (Prentice-Hall, 1974). On predicting the outcomes of court cases from case characteristics, see Fred Kort, "Content Analysis of Judicial Opinions and Rules of Law" in Glendon Schubert (ed.), *Judicial Decision-Making* (Free Press, 1963); S. Nagel, "Predicting Court Cases Quantitatively," 63 *Michigan Law Review* 1411−22 (1965); Sidney Ulmer, "Mathematical Models for Predicting Judicial Behavior" in James Bernd (ed.), *Mathematical Applications in Political Science* (Southern Methodist University Press, 1967).
6. On statistical causation, see Hubert Blalock, *Causal Inferences in Nonexperimental Research* (University of North Carolina Press, 1964); David Heise, *Causal Analysis* (Wiley, 1975); Hans Zeisel, *Say It With Figures* (Harper & Row, 1968). On the problem of relating crime to anticrime expenditures, see Yong Cho, *Public Policy and Urban Crime* (Ballinger, 1974); and S. Nagel, "Allocating Anti-Crime Dollars Across Places and Activities" in *Policy Evaluation: Making Optimum Decisions* (Praeger, 1982).
7. On the multidisciplinary nature of policy evaluation, see James Charlesworth (ed.), *Integration of the Social Sciences through Policy Analysis* (American Academy of Political and Social Science, 1972); Duncan MacRae, Jr., *The*

Social Function of Social Science (Yale University Press, 1976); and S. Nagel (ed.), *Policy Studies and the Social Sciences* (Transaction Books, 1979).

8. On the multidisciplinary nature of apportioning a budget, see "Budget Systems and Cost-Benefit Analysis" in John Due and Ann Friedlaender, *Government Finance: Economics of the Public Sector* (Irwin, 1973) (economics); Aaron Wildavsky, *The Politics of the Budgetary Process* (Little, Brown, 1974) (political science); "Evaluating Administration Efficiency" in Herbert Simon, Donald Smithburg, and Victor Thompson, *Public Administration* (Knopf, 1950) (psychology); and Chapter 3 in this book.

9. On the multidisciplinary nature of poverty policy, see Clair Wilcox, *Toward Social Welfare* (Irwin, 1969) (economics); Gilbert Steiner, *The State of Welfare* (Brookings, 1971) (political science); Frank Riessman, Jerome Cohen, and Arthur Pearl (eds.), *Mental Health of the Poor* (Free Press, 1964) (psychology); and Thomas Weaver (ed.); *Poverty: New Interdisciplinary Perspectives* (SRA, 1969) (general).

10. On the multidisciplinary nature of environmental policy, see Allen Kneese and Charles Schultze, *Pollution, Prices, and Public Policy* (Brookings, 1975) (economics); Walter Rosenbaum, *The Politics of Environmental Concern* (Praeger, 1977) (political science); Joachim Wohlwill and Daniel Carson (eds.), *Environment and the Social Sciences: Perspectives and Applications* (American Psychological Association, 1972) (psychology); and Peter Albertson and Margery Barnett (eds.), *Environment and Society in Transition* (New York Academy of Sciences, 1971) (general).

QUESTIONS

1. How can statistical data be used as inputs into either deductive predicting or policy optimizing?

2. In deciding whether a relation or other finding is due to chance or reality, how might a benefit-cost perspective differ from the traditional social science notion of level of statistical significance?

3. In predicting from a policy to a goal, how might a benefit-cost perspective differ from the traditional social science notion of minimizing the sum of the squared deviations in making predictions?

4. In determining causal relations between policies and goals, how can one control for spurious relations, reciprocal relations, and multicollinearity, which may be more likely to be present in policy evaluation than in ordinary social science?

5. What can political science in particular contribute to evaluating alternative public policies?

6. What can psychology and economics contribute to public policy evaluation? Use examples from budgeting, poverty, environment, and other policy fields.

7. What can other social sciences, natural sciences, and humanities contribute to the evaluation of alternative policies, particularly with regard to general contributions?

REFERENCES

MacRae, Duncan, *The Social Function of Social Science* (Yale University Press, 1976).

McCall, George, and George Weber (eds.), *Social Science and Public Policy* (Kennikat Press, 1983).

Mosteller, Frederick, and William Fairley, *Statistics and Public Policy* (Addison-Wesley, 1977).

Nagel, S. (ed.), *Policy Studies and the Social Sciences* (Transaction Books, 1979).

Talarico, Suzette (ed.), *Criminal Justice Research: Approaches, Problems, and Policy* (Anderson, 1980).

Welch, Susan, and John Comer, *Quantitative Methods for Public Administration: Techniques and Applications* (Dorsey, 1983).

PART FIVE

The Public Policy Profession

This section presents a general discussion of the following aspects of the public policy profession:

1. *Policy studies:* the study of the nature, causes, and effects of alternative public policies for achieving given goals.
2. *Ethical dilemmas:* when policy analysts are faced with decisions regarding their roles, both in the interest of societal desirability, and when someone or society may be hurt by the decisions reached.
3. *Policy evaluation:* choosing the alternative public policy that scores the highest on benefits minus costs or some other related criterion.
4. *Research utilization:* the extent to which policy evaluations are adopted by relevant government employees.

CHAPTER 18

Ethical Dilemmas in Policy Evaluation

This chapter suggests and discusses principles of ethics in policy evaluation. Ethics refers to a set of normative standards for resolving dilemmas faced by policy analysts or evaluators when they decide what role to perform in the interests of society. These standards involve policy optimizing, sensitivity analysis, partisanship, unforeseen consequences, equity, efficient research, research sharing, research validity, and handling official wrongdoing. For each dilemma, general ideas and a concrete illustrative example are discussed. The examples are often drawn from criminal justice research, but they can be borrowed from other subject matters.

The nine ethical dilemmas are in two groups. They relate to appropriate purposes, goals, and effects, and they relate to appropriate methods. Within the first group, dilemmas relate to:

1. prediction versus prediction plus prescription.
2. whether or not to work to maximize the interests of a political party or special interest group.
3. focusing on intended consequences versus all consequences.
4. efficiency versus equity as policy goals.

Within the methods group, dilemmas relate to:

5. evaluation versus evaluation plus diverse replication.
6. cost incurring versus cost saving in research.
7. whether or not to share one's raw data sets.
8. research validity versus questionable findings that are not sufficiently questioned.
9. whether or not to put people at risk in policy evaluation.[1]

Ethical Dilemmas that Relate to Appropriate Purposes, Goals, and Effects

THE OPTIMIZING DILEMMA

Policy evaluators, analysts, and researchers often present articles, reports, and findings that deal with the relations between policies and goals. Merely presenting these relations will often cause policy makers, the general public, or other researchers to jump to false conclusions regarding which policies should be adopted. To what extent is a policy evaluator obliged to clarify the relations between (1) predictive or causal findings and (2) policy decisions as to what must be done about a given problem? In other words, have policy evaluators performed their roles in a socially desirable way by abstaining from discussing the policy implications of their findings? This is the dilemma of deciding whether one should merely be concerned with prediction and causation, or whether one should also be concerned with prescription and possibly policy optimization.

More specifically, policy researchers in the criminal justice field are often interested in what variables correlate with (1) having less crime per capita across places, or (2) having reduced crime per capita over time. James Q. Wilson, for example, in the November 15, 1981, issue of the widely read magazine, *Family Weekly*, says, "Evidence on the effect of punishment suggests that certainty is more important than severity in deterring criminals." Similar statements have been made by many crime-policy researchers. Such statements imply that society should be devoting more resources to catching and convicting criminals than to imprisoning them for lengthy periods.

Suppose it is true that in a statistical analysis, crime rates can be more accurately predicted when the percentage of crimes that result in arrests or convictions is known rather than when the sentence lengths of those who are convicted are known. It does not follow that society should do more or spend more trying to catch and convict criminals and do less about length of imprisonment. Implicit or explicit statements about the relative value of increasing certainty versus increasing severity are meaningless unless the following is considered:

1. how high the probability of getting caught already is.
2. how high the severity of the penalty already is.
3. how high the benefits from crime committing are.
4. how steep the relations are among crime occurrence, certainty, severity, and crime benefits.
5. how much the monetary and other costs are for incremental increases in certainty and severity.

On the fifth matter alone, it is meaningless to draw policy conclusions from a study without considering the benefits and costs. For example, suppose a 1-unit increase in certainty produces a 10-unit decrease in crime, whereas a 1-unit increase in severity only produces a 5-unit decrease in crime. It does not, therefore, follow that we should concentrate our marginal or other resources on increasing certainty, because a 1-unit increase in certainty may cost more than twice as much as a 1-unit increase in severity. Furthermore, increasing certainty may produce undesirable side effects (however, this depends on how the increase in certainty is obtained).

The important point is that policy evaluators may be undesirably misleading people by not discussing the policy implications of their findings. This does not mean the researcher has to do an elaborate analysis of what it would cost to increase certainty and severity. However, the researcher should at least raise the issue that concentrating resources on relatively strong policies may be unwise from a benefit-cost perspective. In this particular context, the researcher might also have an obligation to note: (1) the diminishing returns of concentrating on a given policy, (2) the possibility of developing an alternative policy that was not part of the original analysis (such as reducing crime benefits), and (3) the interactive relations among policies such that certainty of being convicted means nothing if there are no substantial penalties associated with being convicted as a result of a lack of prison resources.[2]

THE PARTISAN DILEMMA

A policy evaluator may sometimes be called upon to determine the effects of alternative policies on highly partisan goals, such as maximizing the number of legislative districts dominated by either democrats or republicans. The evaluator may be asked to help prescribe a policy that will maximize the interests of some special interest group such as blacks, union members, or automobile manufacturers. Under these circumstances what should the ethical policy evaluator do, particularly in light of what is good for society?

One can argue that a policy evaluator should advise any legal group on achieving any legal purpose through legal means. Lawyers can even advise illegal groups, although they cannot ethically advise clients to act illegally. A justification for encouraging or allowing policy evaluators to give partisan advice is that if each side has good advisors, the truth and hence the best policies will emerge. This is a key argument in favor of the adversary legal system whereby lawyers go all out for each side, and a better judicial decision is thereby facilitated. Evaluators, though, are not lawyers. There are at least two differences in terms of ethics. One is that lawyers are not obligated to qualify their statements, but ethical evaluators (even when working for partisan causes) should indicate how their conclusions are dependent on their inputs. A second difference is that lawyers not only advise but also advocate. Policy analysts should mainly advise and generally leave the advocacy to others. That is especially true for argumentative public speaking, as contrasted to analysts advocating a policy in a prescriptive or optimizing mode to their clients or in the policy literature.

The redistricting field illustrates partisan dilemmas particularly well. In the 1960s when computerized redistricting was being developed, substantial conflict among the original researchers arose concerning the propriety of including political party information as input into the redistricting models. The purists opted to omit it entirely to avoid corruption of the nonpartisan evaluations. A compromise position was to input the information so the districting patterns which were outputted could show how many democrats and how many republicans would be in each district since such information is useful to policy makers and other interested persons. Another position involved programming the computer to draw district lines that would provide equal population, and also provide a percentage of districts dominated by the democrats equal to the percentage of democratic voters in the state. This could be justified as providing a form of bipartisan proportional representation. Still another position involved programming the computer to draw district lines to maximize the number of democrat-dominated districts or republican-dominated districts. This capability was justified on the grounds that by showing the democrats and the republicans how far each could go (given the constraints of nearly equal population per district and party registration figures), the redistricting evaluation system thereby facilitated moving toward a compromise between those two extreme positions.

The same capability that could maximize democrat-dominated districts could also be used to maximize black-dominated or white-dominated districts, which raises related but more complicated problems. Trying to maximize white-dominated districts may be clearly illegal, especially if it means no black representation at all. Trying to maximize black-dominated districts is not illegal, since blacks are still likely to be a minority in any state legislature. Maximizing black-dominated districts may, however, be contrary to the interests of blacks in seeking favorable state or city legislation. For example, in the state of Mississippi and the city of Chicago, blacks constitute about 40 percent of the population. They would perhaps be better off if the district lines were drawn in such a way that they would not dominate any district, but would constitute 40 percent of every district. This could be accomplished in Chicago by dividing each district into a pie slice, with the center of the pie being the heart of the black population. Blacks would then have the swing vote between the white candidates in every district, thereby guaranteeing that close to 100 percent of the elected candidates would be relatively favorable to black interests. However, this plan would likely be opposed by incumbent blacks or would-be black legislators since they tend to favor safe black-dominated districts. The policy evaluator would be facing a dilemma between the interests of the black population and the black leaders. Evaluators who work for political organizations would likely draw maps favoring the political leaders, whereas academic evaluators would draw politically unfeasible maps which favor general population categories. Party and academic evaluators, however, would be acceptably performing their roles by at least pointing out how their redistricting plans affect each of the political parties, the major ethnic groups, and the distribution of the general population among the districts.

THE UNFORESEEN CONSEQUENCES DILEMMA

Policy evaluators should foresee the important unforeseen consequences of the policies with which they are working. Failure to do so may constitute a form of negligence that would amount to evaluation malpractice. Evaluators may be covered by malpractice insurance as a matter of course to protect themselves against damages caused by their lack of foresight. It is far better to be foresightful than to be insured. Just because a consequence is unforeseen does not mean that it is unforeseeable.

The ability to foresee the effects of alternative public policies can be substantially improved if one has good predictive models of the behavior of its targeted people. For example, if one is trying to foresee the effects of alternative criminal justice policies, one had better have a model of the criminal justice system that includes plea bargaining, since it (rather than trials) is the essence of the criminal justice system. The relevance of this model to foreseeing unforeseen consequences can be illustrated by the attempt of the Vera Foundation of New York City to reduce the pretrial jail population ($-Y$) by increasing pretrial release (X_1). One might think such a goal would obviously be improved by this policy. What seems obvious, however, may not be so. By increasing pretrial release, one thereby decreases the number of defendants who are sitting in jail awaiting trial. Doing so makes them substantially less vulnerable to pleading guilty in return for the prosecutor's offer to recommend probation or a sentence equal to the time they have already served in jail awaiting trial. The detained defendants may argue that they are innocent and want a trial to prove their innocence. The prosecutor can inform the defendants that they are, indeed, entitled to a trial, but a trial will not likely be held for a few months, so they can go home if they plead guilty. This offer is difficult to refuse, especially if the defendants' witnesses are not so reliable, if they have been previously convicted and thus will not greatly further damage their résumés, and if the defendants know that upon conviction they may serve a substantial prison sentence.

If fewer defendants are in jail (X_1), fewer guilty pleas (X_2) and more trials would probably result. If there are more trials (X_3), delay in the case processing system will increase. If there is more delay in the system (X_4), the defendants sitting in jail awaiting trial will wait even longer than they were waiting before the increase in pretrial release. If the waiting time in jail increases, so too may the jail population ($+Y$) since it, like the world population, is dependent on the number of births or inputs and the length of time people live or stay in the system. If longevity rises, it may more than offset a decrease in births or inputs. The total jail population would increase even though the increased pretrial release has decreased the inputs into the jail. This could be an especially undesirable, unforeseen consequence because the policy designed to reduce the jail population actually increases it. Most unforeseen consequences involve adverse side effects, rather than adverse effects on the key goal being sought.

A dilemma occurs in the sense that the evaluator may be paralyzed out of fear of unforeseen consequences. We want evaluators to go forward and evaluate alternative public policies so our policy adoption will be more rational than it would be without policy evaluation. On the other hand, evaluators should develop contingency models showing what consequences are likely to follow the occurrence of certain contingent events. In the above example, a contingency plan could have been developed whereby prosecutors sweetened their offers of shorter sentences to those who were released, which would have held constant the number of defendants pleading guilty (X_2). If guilty pleas had still declined, the number of cases going to trial (X_3) would not have necessarily gone up if the prosecutors had been willing to dismiss more cases of low importance in the criminal justice system. If the number of trials had still increased, delay (X_4) could have remained constant by hiring more judges. If delay had still risen, the jail population could have been reduced $(-Y)$ by giving priority trials to those who were in jail well ahead of those who were out of jail. Thus, good models like those which relate to bilateral bargaining, queueing backlogs, queueing delay, and population growth can be used both for predicting consequences and also for prescribing counterpolicies.[4]

THE EQUITY DILEMMA

The equity dilemma is the often-encountered conflict in policy evaluation between the policy goals of efficiency and equity. Efficiency means choosing policies to maximize benefits minus costs. The term occasionally refers to choosing policies that will provide the highest benefit/cost ratio. The two definitions produce identical results when costs are held constant. When they are not held constant, maximizing benefits minus costs will produce policies to yield more net worth or net satisfaction. A minimum benefit level will be met and a maximum cost level will not be exceeded. There is equity when per capita equality across all groups or places is achieved with regard to either receiving benefits or paying costs. Equity may also refer to both equality of benefits per needs of the recipients, when needs differ substantially, and to equality of costs per ability to pay when this differs substantially. There are many methods to measure equity or equality. Perhaps the simplest is to determine the average deviation from the average benefit score or the average cost score. The closer the average deviation is to zero, the more equity, assuming equal needs and/or equal ability to pay.

A good illustration of the efficiency versus equity dilemma is in the area of allocating federal anticrime dollars across cities or states. If the money were to be allocated on efficiency grounds only, we could determine each city's slope or marginal rate of return between crime occurrence and anti-crime dollars by obtaining data for many previous points in time indicating how much crime occurred *(Y)* and how many anticrime dollars were spent *(X)*. This would enable us to obtain the nonlinear regression equation for each city, $Y_t = a + b_1(\log X_{t-1}) + b_2(Y_{t-1})$. The X or dollars variable is lagged one time period because it takes time for anticrime dollars to have an effect on crime, and because we want to avoid the reciprocal effect of crime on increasing anticrime dollars. The X or dollars variable is also shown as a logarithm to reflect the fact that although anticrime dollars may decrease crime, they do so at a diminishing or logarithmic rate. Crime at a prior point in time is included as a control variable to indirectly hold constant all the variables that cause crime other than anticrime dollars. Using this equation for each city, we could allocate a federal budget to the cities in accordance with their negative b_1 regression coefficients. One can prove algebraically that doing so will result in minimizing predicted crime occurrence across the cities, assuming that the regression coefficients are accurate. In other words, this allocation will provide maximum national benefits at a given budget and thus maximize efficiency.

Such an efficient allocation, however, may be quite inequitable. Perfect equity or equality would not allocate the budget across cities on a purely per capita basis. This would only equalize them on the anticrime dollar-benefits received. Some cities would be bearing higher costs than others, not just by paying more taxes per capita, but also by suffering more crime per capita. An alternative equity allocation would give each city an amount such that every city would have the same quantity of crime. Even if this were politically, economically, and algebraically possible to do, we nevertheless face a predicament among allocating on the basis of efficiency, equality of dollars, and equality of crime.

This problem could be solved by allocating in three steps as follows:

1. Give each city a minimum allocation on the basis of population in order to satisfy dollar equity.
2. Give each city whose per capita crime level exceeds a maximum threshold, an amount needed to bring it down to that maximum threshold.
3. Allocate the remainder in accordance with the regression or efficiency coefficients.

This approach may have to be considerably modified due to the inability to get meaningful negative regression coefficients. One may have to do step 2 in light of a somewhat arbitrary formula that gives extra weight to cities with a bad crime problem. Step 3 may also require a formula that allocates to the cities in accordance with subjective and objective judgments about the efficiency of the personnel, fiscal, organizational, and other managerial aspects of their police, courts, and corrections systems.

The important point is to seriously consider equity of benefits, equity of costs, and efficiency. Policy evaluators may not be obligated to find a solution that is both efficient and equitable (which may be impossible anyway). They should, however, discuss these issues explicitly in their policy evaluations. Efficiency is clearly important if policy evaluators are trying to maximize benefits minus costs. Equity is important politically because if any group or place feels its benefits are below a minimum level or its costs are above a maximum level, then the group or place may rebel in the ballot box. Equity is also important to the public image because governments are embarrassed when certain groups or places suffer to extremes. Equity can also be justified philosophically on the basis of inherent right found in the writings of Aristotle, Aquinas, Locke, Rousseau, and Marx, as well as in the basic tenets of all major religions.[5]

Ethical Dilemmas that Relate to Appropriate Methods

THE SENSITIVITY ANALYSIS DILEMMA

To what extent are policy evaluators obliged to indicate that their predictive or prescriptive conclusions would change if the data, measurement, sampling, assumptions, values, or other inputs to which the conclusions might be sensitive had changed? This is a dilemma because, on the one hand, resources for conducting elaborate research are limited, and we would not want to deter people from conducting nonelaborate research that might be useful. On the other hand, we do not want policy makers, the public, and others to conclude falsely that policy findings are more widely applicable than they might be. This dilemma, like the optimizing one, can often be resolved if researchers raise questions about the sensitivity of the findings to changes in the inputs, even if they do not test these sensitivity hypotheses.

There is no guarantee that policymakers will make use of an elaborate sensitivity analysis, but researchers will have performed their roles properly if they show how their findings would be changed if they made changes in the goals, policies available, relations, or other inputs into their analysis. For example, an elaborate analysis was done on the question of an optimum jury size that the United States Supreme Court referred to in a key case dealing with the constitutionality of alternative jury sizes. The search showed that, with a number of assumptions, the optimum jury size would be approximately seven. The Supreme Court, by way of Justice Blackmun's opinion, found that juries smaller than six were unconstitutional, but they could be smaller than 12, partly citing research on optimum jury size. This research, however, showed that an optimum jury size is dependent on: (1) the relative trade-off value, V, of convicting an innocent defendant versus not convicting a guilty defendant, (2) the percentage, P, of innocent defendants and guilty defendants who might be convicted at various jury sizes, and (3) the number of defendants, N, in jury trials who are truly innocent, and the complementary percentage of those who are truly guilty per 100 defendants. The trade-off value (between the two types of errors) that Justice Blackmun accepted was 10-to-1 (in view of its advocacy by William Blackstone, who was influential to the framers of the Constitution). This normative input was, thus, not subject to change. On the empirical input of the conviction percentages, one can show that optimum jury size is not substantially influenced by reasonable values assigned to this input. This is true partly because the average defendant is known to be convicted at a 64 percent rate, and therefore, innocent defendants are probably convicted at less than a 64 percent rate, and guilty defendants at more than a 64 percent rate. Justice Blackmun, however, ignored the conclusion's sensitivity to the third input, which is a mixture of empirical and normative elements. For the sake of discussion, it was assumed that prosecutors operate at a 95 percent confidence level in bringing defendants before jury trials (i.e., they feel 95 percent confident the defendants are guilty). If, however, one thinks prosecutors are not so careful and are operating at only a 90 percent confidence level, then much larger juries and a unanimous vote are necessary to protect the additional innocent defendants from being convicted. On the other hand, if one thinks prosecutors are especially careful and are operating at a 99 percent level, then we could have much smaller juries. Fewer innocent defendants would require protection against conviction. The correct confidence level and (more important) the correct number of truly innocent defendants who are tried per 100 defendants is impossible to determine. Thus, the bottom-line prescription is not only dependent on a highly sensitive input, but one that is also impossible to measure.

The optimum jury size between six and 12 is, thus, ultimately dependent on whether one has a liberal prodefense perception of the criminal justice system (for which 12 would be the optimum), or a conservative proprosecution perception of the criminal justice system (for which six would be optimum). Researchers have done all they can if they pointed out these sensitivity analysis matters, but they have not performed properly if these matters were ignored or neglected.[6]

THE EFFICIENT-RESEARCH DILEMMA

The efficient-research dilemma relates to conducting evaluation research in the most economical manner. Policy evaluators are ethically obliged to try to provide maximum benefits minus costs to society or their clients with regard to both their research projects and their policy recommendations. The dilemma occurs by virtue of the fact that truly efficient research may result in depriving the researcher of additional salary, released academic time, interesting travel, and data that might have future personal value. We also do not want to encourage evaluators to be unduly research-cost conscious at the expense of failing to make worthwhile expenditures. If increasing the research budget will truly benefit both the interests being served and the researcher, then there is no dilemma.

There are examples of evaluation research projects that are overly expensive relative to the insights obtained, partly because the budget was inflated in covering salaries, equipment, travel, and other items. Personnel from virtually all funding units and research units can relate many such stories. Simplicity in policy evaluation is necessary not only to save money, but also to facilitate that more policy evaluation be conducted and meaningfully communicated to policy makers. A good example of simplicity in policy evaluation is the analysis of alternative ways of providing attorneys to the poor. This problem involves three policy choices. The noncriminal legal problems of the poor can be handled mainly by volunteer attorneys, salaried government attorneys, or private attorneys who are reimbursed by the government for representing the poor. The problem involves four policy goals, namely, having a program that is (1) inexpensive, (2) visible and accessible, (3) politically feasible, and (4) likely to be staffed by reasonably aggressive lawyers who are technically competent in poverty law. On the goal of inexpensiveness, volunteer attorneys clearly score the best. Private attorneys who are reimbursed by the government are so expensive as to make that approach economically unfeasible, and thus not worth discussing further. (It was endorsed by President Reagan before he was elected as being a private marketplace solution, but rejected afterward on the grounds of expense in favor of volunteer attorneys.) Salaried government attorneys are clearly more visible and accessible than volunteer attorneys. The volunteer system, however, is much more politically feasible since it is not as likely to generate a cadre of lawyers who are as disturbing to landlords, merchants, employers, welfare bureaucrats, and local politicians as the salaried legal services program is. On the other hand, salaried government attorneys are more likely to develop specialized competence and be more willing to go to court than volunteer attorneys, who tend to be inexperienced new attorneys looking for experience.

Deciding which program is better depends on the relative weight one gives to the four goals. Conservative values are likely to weight inexpensiveness and political feasibility high. Liberal values are likely to weight visibility and accessibility and competence and aggressiveness high. With conservative value weights, the volunteer system is best. With liberal value weights, the salaried attorney system is best. This type of analysis may lead one to recommend a compromise between the two systems to obtain support from both conservatives and liberals. A compromise might involve hiring salaried government lawyers who, as part of their main functions, must coordinate the activities of volunteer lawyers within a system that requires lawyers to do some volunteering as part of their license to practice law.

This type of analysis can be done on the back of an envelope at zero cost, assuming the envelope were found in a wastebasket and the evaluator were commuting to work and thus not working on government time. The cost could be increased by doing a literature search to build on what is already known, and by interviewing people knowledgeable about alternative ways of providing legal services to the poor. The Legal Services Corporation spent over $10 million to analyze the effects of alternative delivery systems. Much of this money was spent by setting up programs that could be observed, rather than by observing already existing programs. Much of the money was also used for expensive data-gathering activities which have yet to be made accessible to other researchers. It is questionable whether the highly incremental costs over zero costs were justified by the not-so-highly incremental benefits over what is common sense to knowledgeable insiders. There is a need in policy evaluation for making more use of knowledgeable insiders. It is particularly urgent to emphasize more thought and creativity, rather than expensive data gathering, if we are going to have more efficient and useful policy research.[7]

THE RESEARCH SHARING DILEMMA

One of the most frustrating aspects of policy evaluation is not the difficulty of gathering new data, but rather the difficulty in gaining access to relevant data that has already been gathered. The research sharing dilemma is thus: an evaluation researcher is faced with the choice between withholding or sharing expensively gathered data. On the one hand, the researcher might like to keep the data to avoid embarrassing himself or herself or others, and to be able to use it for future research without others doing so. On the other hand, if we are talking about societal desirability as a dilemma-resolving criterion, then in almost all instances, the data should be shared to facilitate the development of new knowledge on which scientific research, including evaluation research, thrives.

There are many instances in which data was withheld which subsequently proved useful for secondary analysis of important policy problems. Let's take, for example, the American Bar Foundation. In 1963, data on 12,000 criminal cases randomly sampled from all 50 states was gathered at great expense by thousands of lawyers from the Foundation's county courthouses. Lee Silverstein of the American Bar Foundation coordinated the data gathering to determine the extent to which attorneys were representing criminal defendants and the effects of having an attorney. After authoring a landmark book on *Defense of the Poor in Criminal Cases in American State Courts* (Little, Brown, 1965), Lee Silverstein died. The original data and the codebooks were in the process of being discarded when they were rescued and included in the Interuniversity Consortium for Political Research at Ann Arbor, Michigan. Since then, this data set has been reused many times to test hypotheses relating to such matters as: (1) the extent to which disparities exist in the criminal justice system for various stages, crimes, and types of defendants, (2) the occurrence of delay at various stages and how delay relates to a variety of variables, and (3) various aspects of plea bargaining, pretrial release, sentencing, and jury decision making, as well as aspects of right to counsel that Lee Silverstein did not cover.

A reason often cited for withholding data is that someone in the sample might be embarrassed by its release. This can be remedied so that identifiers can be removed and the machine-readable data cannot be traced to any specific respondents or persons. One example is the Office of Economic Opportunity (OEO) Legal Services Program's data set covering about 200 variables for each of about 250 individual legal services agencies across the country. The data was originally gathered in 1970 to determine which agencies should get increased, decreased, or constant funding, and would have possibly been destroyed after serving that purpose. The data was, however, pried loose after considerable negotiation. Since then, the data has been used to test hypotheses as to what variables correlate with having high scores on a variety of ratings among legal services agencies. The data has also been used to illustrate alternative ways of allocating scarce resources across activities and places.

The most frustrating motivation for withholding data is profit-seeking. The goal is to cultivate the data in future contracts with government funding agencies. This has occurred with research institutes that have received large amounts of money from the Law Enforcement Assistance Administration (LEAA) to gather and analyze data. Their excuse for withholding data is that it is not ready for distribution, even though they have already used the data. To the credit of LEAA, much of this data has now been archived at the Interuniversity Consortium. LEAA has succeeded in prying it loose from the research institutes that were paid with tax money to gather the data, but these institutes are rather uncooperative when it comes to explaining aspects of their codes to secondary researchers. Perhaps the best way to force evaluation researchers to be ethical is to make the costs of unethical behavior substantially greater than the benefits. This may generally be the best way to encourage any kind of socially desired behavior.[8]

THE RESEARCH VALIDITY DILEMMA

Research validity refers to having conclusions that conform to empirical reality and that logically follow from meaningful premises. Policy researchers are obliged to be concerned with research validity because their conclusions will likely have societal consequences. On the other hand, policy researchers often need not be overly concerned with precise measurement because policy problems often involve determining which alternative policy is best in light of given goals. They need not determine the exact position of all the alternative policies. Guaranteeing research validity may also sometimes require extra effort and cost, which runs contrary to the cost-saving obligation of policy research. If, however, there is a conflict between research validity and cost saving, validity would probably deserve a higher priority, although this depends on how much extra validity one would obtain for the extra cost.

Empirical validity tends to depend on: (1) the representativeness of the sample of persons, places, or things on which the hypotheses arc tested, (2) the accuracy of the measurement of the characteristics or variables of these entities, and (3) the way in which this data is analyzed, particularly considering other variables that might explain the relations between the main variables. A good example to illustrate invalidity in policy relevant research might be the subject of whether black or poor defendants are treated worse than white or nonpoor defendants in the criminal justice system. On the matter of *representativeness* of the entities sampled, most of the literature on the subject tends to involve a single city at a single point in time. This will suffice for building knowledge by way of accumulating such case studies. However, individual researchers treat their case studies as being indicative of more general relations, even though many differences exist between northern and southern cities and between rival and urban areas. More important, however, most of the studies concentrate on the sentencing stage in the criminal justice process, yet they discuss racial disparities on general levels. In reality, the sentencing stage may be the least discriminatory, because by then the defendants have been filtered down to being more homogeneous. In earlier stages, issues like who gets arrested for similar crimes, who gets released on bail, who has a hired lawyer, and who has a jury trial are usually discriminatory.

Regarding *measurement*, it is common to score probation as a zero sentence on the sentencing variable, rather than have two sentencing variables, one on probation versus jail and the other on length of jail sentence. By lumping both decisions together, offsetting discriminatory patterns can disappear. This is so if whites do better on probation versus jail, possibly due to racial considerations, but blacks do better on getting shorter jail sentences, possibly by virtue of having committed less serious crimes, especially less serious larceny. On the matter of *analysis* and controlling for confounding variables, many studies attempt to control for the crime committed by looking to its average or maximum sentence. It is more meaningful to see whether the crime is against persons or property. By lumping more severe crimes together, regardless of whether they involve assault or larceny, offsetting discriminatory patterns can also disappear. This will occur if whites do better than blacks in larceny cases, which are often black-on-white; but blacks do better in assault cases, which are relatively more likely to be black-on-black.

On the matter of drawing conclusions that *logically* follow from meaningful premises, the most illogical reasoning may involve the traditional decision rule that if the differences found can be attributed to chance at more than a 0.05 probability level, then the differences will be considered chance differences rather than real differences. This 0.05 premise implies that it is

19 times as bad to falsely accuse the system of being discriminatory than it is to falsely exonerate the system as being nondiscriminatory. It is difficult to justify this 19-to-1 trade-off value in terms of the relative benefits and costs of these type 1 and type 2 errors and accuracies. Likewise, it is illogical to say that a relation of 0.10 between a dependent variable and an independent variable will not be considered substantial, since squaring this relation indicates it only explains 1 percent of the variance on the dependent variable. Such a relation may be very substantial when the 0.10 is the percentage points difference between convicted blacks receiving jail sentences (rather than probation) versus convicted whites. This is especially so if 0 percent of the whites go to jail and 10 percent of the blacks do, since this means that being black is a necessary condition for going to jail. The 0.10 difference is also especially important if 90 percent of the whites go to jail and 100 percent of the blacks do so, since this means that being black is a sufficient condition for going to jail. A 0.10 difference when jail terms are at stake can create crime-causing antisocial attitudes. Thus, it should be considered and not passed off because a nonmeaningful premise says squared regression coefficients must exceed 1 percent.

Policy evaluation is basically deductive analysis from inductively arrived-at premises. Policy analysis can be simplified to the syllogism: (1) Y is good, (2) X causes Y, and (3) therefore adopt X. Determining whether Y is good or whether X causes Y may involve: (1) surveying the values or perceptions of relevant people, (2) statistically relating Y to a higher goal, or X to Y, (3) deducing the premise from some other premises, or (4) assuming the premise is true subject to a sensitivity analysis to show how the conclusions would change for alternative premises. These methods potentially involve empirical and logical validity problems to which policy researchers must be sensitive.[9]

THE DILEMMA OF PUTTING PEOPLE AT RISK

One of the most controversial ethical issues in policy evaluation is the extent to which experiments should be conducted on people in situations where they risk being physically, mentally, or otherwise harmed. There is a dilemma in that one wants to know the effects of a proposed policy yet does not want to harm anyone who would otherwise be unharmed had it not been for the experiment. In recent years, in national policy experiments, people were randomly assigned to experimental groups and control groups. These experiments have included giving welfare recipients different amounts of aid to learn how the differences would affect their ambition to secure jobs, or giving some ex-convicts unemployment compensation and denying it to others to see how receiving it would affect their crime committing. The welfare experiment did not place people at serious risk since no one's health was jeopardized. However, the experiment may not have successfully demonstrated the effects of payment differences, given the small range of differences. Denying unemployment compensation to some ex-convicts was not a significant ethical problem because recently released convicts normally do not receive unemployment compensation.

An important criminal justice experiment that raises serious ethical problems is one which randomly assigned some juvenile delinquents to jail and some to probation. In 1966, convicted juvenile delinquents in Sacramento and Stockton were divided into three groups as follows:

1. The groups that committed minor crimes and that had minor prior records received probation.
2. The groups that committed major crimes and/or those that had major prior records received jail sentences.
3. The groups in the middle third of relatively borderline cases (in terms of their offenses and their prior records) were divided; half were randomly assigned to one-year probation terms, and half were assigned to one-year jail terms.

One year after the completion of the probation and jail terms, the crime-committing records of both groups were compared. The probation group was found to have a better postprobation record than the postjail record of the jail group. This could not be attributed to any differences in their preconviction records, since both groups had similar preconviction records. One can argue that the experiment was not unethical because those who were included could have justifiably received either probation or one-year sentences in view of their borderline characteristics. On the other hand, due process in sentencing requires more than a flip of a coin to determine who goes to jail and who does not, even if useful scientific knowledge were at stake. Subsequent to this experiment, the Supreme Court ruled that juvenile delinquents were entitled to basic due process rights (in the 1967 case of *In re Gault*), which probably would have deemed this experiment unconstitutional.

Although individuals should not be subject to risk any harm unless there is considerable offsetting justification, one should operate under the opposite presumption when the individuals are public officials. They should be protected from physical harm and from revealing irrelevant aspects of their personal lives. When, however, they have made extreme, illegal, or otherwise objectively wrong decisions, then policy researchers have an obligation to expose the wrongdoing. For example, in a proposed research project, data from approximately 10 judicial districts was to be gathered, showing for each judge the percentage of defendants released and the percentage of released defendants who appeared for trial. It was thought that judges would differ greatly on their release rates, but very slightly on their appearance rates. Some districts were to be randomly assigned to an experimental group in which rates were to be publicized among the judges, the bar, and possibly the press, and some districts were to be assigned to a control group in which the rates would not be publicized. In the after period, data was to be collected to see how the publicity affected changes in the release rates. It was anticipated that where the publicity was the strongest, the high-holding judges would be embarrassed into decreasing their holding rates in view of the extra costs they were incurring without producing and offsetting benefits. The research was subjected to considerable bureaucratic red tape because human subjects were put at risk, and the research was never funded, partly because it was considered too controversial. Thus, the dilemma of putting people at risk involves a desire to avoid harming people and a desire to validate hypotheses. Sometimes, there is also a desire to test hypotheses relevant to determining and decreasing socially undesirable behavior by public officials.[10]

CONCLUSION

Figure 18-1 summarizes the relations among the ethical dilemmas which have been discussed in this chapter. These dilemmas are arranged in two groups; one relates to ends and the other to methods. Within the ends group is a concern for purposes, goals, and effects. Purposes are divided between impact purposes and optimizing purposes. Within goals, one can contrast societal, group, and individual goals. Societal goals may involve conflicts between effectiveness, efficiency, and equity. Within effects, one can contrast foreseen and unforeseen (and possibly foreseeable) effects.

Subgroups of methods include effectiveness, efficiency, and equity of the methods used by policy evaluators, as contrasted to the effectiveness, efficiency, and equity of the policies proposed or adopted. Under effectiveness of policy research one can talk about obligations for validity and sensitivity analysis. Efficiency is divided between cost-saving and data-sharing. Under equity (or concern for fairness to human subjects), one can talk about ordinary persons to whom such an obligation is owed, or about political figures, who are more legitimately subject to risk of exposure when they do not perform their jobs well.

Reviewing the discussion of these nine ethical dilemmas, one finds three underlying factors relating to: (1) how these dilemmas differ from the ethical dilemmas in traditional social science research, (2) openness as a key element that is relevant in helping resolve the dilemmas, and (3) the need for affirmative action in acting properly when confronting the dilemmas, as contrasted to merely being open in saying what one is doing or has done.

Policy Evaluation versus Traditional Social Science

In policy evaluation, a main concern is that policies will achieve or maximize societal or group goals. In traditional social science research, there is a concern for establishing reality, particularly about predictive and causal relations, regardless of whether the findings have any policy or practical usefulness. Thus, there is generally more at stake in each of these dilemmas

FIGURE 18-1
Ethical Dilemmas in Policy Evaluation

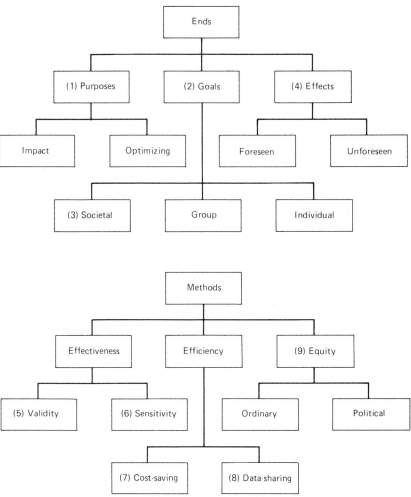

than there is in the counterpart situations. In the average social science study, one normally does not care relatively so much about the nine counterpart situations as to:

Counterpart situations that relate to purposes, goals, and effects

1. Whether an optimum relational model has been developed
2. Whether a political party or interest group uses or misuses the findings
3. Whether unanticipated relations are found when analyzing data
4. Whether one studies income equality rather than worker productivity

Counterpart situations that relate to methods

5. Whether the conclusions are sensitive to changes in the sample, measurement, or analysis
6. Whether the research costs are doubled if they are relatively small to begin with
7. Whether data is shared if it has relatively little practical value
8. Whether the research is valid if the consequences of invalidity are relatively slight

Traditional social scientists are more concerned than policy evaluators about the ninth dilemma, putting people at risk of harm. This is partly because social scientists can more often manipulate people experimentally, and because they may find it more difficult to offer a socially valuable justification for doing so. The above points are obviously generalizations and are not true in all instances since there are many social science studies that have more at stake in terms of societal importance than many policy evaluation studies do. In general, though, policy evaluators seem to need a higher sense of responsibility to perform their professional functions than ordinary social scientists, given the greater potential societal benefits and costs that are involved.[11]

OPENNESS IN RESOLVING ETHICAL DILEMMAS

Openness seems to be the key factor underlying resolution of ethical dilemmas in policy evaluation. This is similar to the blue sky laws in regulating the securities markets. Stockbrokers can legitimately sell the blue sky so long as they inform potential customers and others that this is what they are getting.[12] Likewise, policy evaluators are complying with basic ethical obligations when they make clear that they are:

Openness in relation to purposes, goals, and effects

1. Merely determining the relation between a given policy and a given goal, rather than seeking to find a policy or combination that will maximize a given goal or alternative goals
2. Working for a partisan cause or interest group, rather than giving the impression that one is performing in a nonpartisan scholarly role
3. Checking for only certain consequences so that the evaluation consumer can see which consequences have not been checked
4. Considering equity and efficiency among various available alternatives, so evaluation consumers can decide whether or not they agree

Openness in relation to methods

5. Merely drawing a conclusion on the basis of a single set of measurements, entities, assumptions, or other inputs, rather than seeking to vary these inputs to determine how such variation would affect the conclusions

6. Incurring certain itemized costs as part of the research project and offering as much justification as is reasonable
7. Making their data available for secondary analysis, as long as potential users are informed of possible defects in the data or the documentation
8. Working with certain measurements, samples, assumptions, and other evaluation inputs which allow for certain conclusions and no others
9. Openly informing people who might be part of an experiment as to what risks they are being subjected to, so they can decide whether or not to participate in it, unless important offsetting considerations are involved, such as determining or decreasing wrongdoing among public officials

AFFIRMATIVE ACTION IN RESOLVING ETHICAL DILEMMAS

Perhaps more affirmative action than openness is needed to resolve these ethical dilemmas. In the context of the blue sky laws, one might argue that stockbrokers should not be allowed to sell the blue sky, rather than merely having an ethical obligation to report that they are selling the blue sky. On the above nine dilemmas in policy analysis research, the more affirmative position might involve the following:

Affirmative action in relation to purposes, goals, and effects

1. Policy analysts should find the policy or combinations of policies to maximize a given goal or goals.
2. They should not aid groups with illegal goals, such as racist redistricting designed to decrease the influence of minority groups below a reasonably proportionate level.
3. They should check for side effects and unforeseen consequences in doing policy analysis.
4. They should be concerned with equity as a minimum constraint, and also as a constraint that is subject to a sensitivity analysis for determining how the prescriptions would differ if the equity constraints were changed.

Affirmative action in relation to methods

5. They should always do a sensitivity analysis to determine how their prescriptions might differ as a result of changing the measurement, entities, assumptions, or other inputs of their basic analysis.
6. They should try to keep research costs down.
7. They should seek to facilitate the secondary reuse of data which they have gathered.
8. They should avoid findings of questionable validity, including failure to control for alternative explanations or failure to use proper measurements, samples, and assumptions.

9. Policy analysts should not put people at risk, or else they should
be sure informed consent is involved if people are put at risk; policy
makers should be subject to exposure as wrongdoers, and their undesirable biases in decision making should be revealed.

In conclusion, policy evaluators who operate on a high level of professional responsibility should develop optimum policies and perform optimum research. Optimum policies maximize societal benefits minus societal
costs. Optimum research maximizes beneficial new knowledge minus the
costs of obtaining it. These are high and often impossible goals to achieve.
By seeking them, however, policy evaluation is likely to achieve more than it
would than with any lesser set of goals.

NOTES

1. On the ethics of policy evaluation in general, see Gordon Bermant, Herbert
Kelman, and Donald Warwick (eds.), *The Ethics of Social Intervention* (Wiley,
1978); Daniel Callahan, *The Teaching of Ethics in Higher Education* (Hastings
Center, 1982); William Dunn (ed.), *Ethics, Values, and the Practice of Policy
Analysis* (Lexington-Heath, 1982); Joel Fleishman and Bruce Payne, *Ethical
Dilemmas and the Education of Policymakers* (Hastings Center, 1980); Keith
Marvin, *Standards for Program Evaluation* (Evaluation Research Society,
1980); and John Rohr, *Ethics for Bureaucrats: An Essay on Law and Values*
(Dekker, 1978).
2. On an optimizing perspective to policy evaluation, see Duncan MacRae and
James Wilde, *Policy Analysis for Public Decisions* (Duxbury, 1979); Edith
Stokey and Richard Zeckhauser, *A Primer for Policy Analysis* (Norton, 1978);
and S. Nagel, *Policy Evaluation: Making Optimum Decisions* (Praeger, 1982).
On a relational perspective to policy evaluation, see Thomas Cook and Donald
Campbell, *Quasi-Experimentation: Design and Analysis Issues for Field Set-
tings* (Rand McNally, 1979); Laura Langbein, *Discovering Whether Programs
Work: A Guide to Statistical Methods for Program Evaluation* (Goodyear,
1980); and David Nachmias, *Public Policy Evaluation: Approaches and Methods* (St. Martin's Press, 1979). On the example of relating causal factors to crime
versus making resource-allocation recommendations, see "Tradeoffs in Crime
Reduction Among Certainty, Severity, and Crime Benefits" in S. Nagel, *Policy
Evaluation and the Legal Process* (Kennikat Press, 1984).
3. On the ethics and legality of working with political parties and interest groups,
see Daniel Gaby and Merle Treusch, *Election Campaign Handbook* (Prentice-
Hall, 1976), 289–96; and Harmon Zeigler and Michael Baer, *Lobbying: Inter-
action and Influence in American State Legislatures* (Wadsworth, 1969), 60–80.
On the example of working with political parties and interest groups in the field
of legislative redistricting, see S. Nagel, "Computers and the Law and Politics of
Redistricting," 5 *Polity* 77–93 (1971).
4. On unforeseen consequences in policy evaluation, see Sam Sieber, *Fatal
Remedies: The Ironies of Social Intervention* (Plenum, 1981); Harry Jones, *The
Efficacy of Law* (Northwestern, 1969); and Helen Ingram and Dean Mann,
Why Policies Succeed or Fail (Sage, 1980). On the example of the relation
between increasing pretrial release and thereby increasing the jail population,

see S. Nagel and Marian Neef, "Department of Unintended Consequences: Two Examples from the Legal Process," 2 *Policy Analysis* 356–60 (1976).

5. On equity as a goal in policy evaluation, see Edmund Phelps (ed.), *Economic Justice: Selected Readings* (Penguin, 1973); and John Rawls, *A Theory of Justice* (Harvard University Press, 1971). On efficiency as a goal in policy evaluation, see Roland McKean, *Efficiency in Government Through Systems Analysis* (Wiley, 1966); and Werner Hirsch, *The Economics of State and Local Government* (McGraw-Hill, 1970). On the conflict between the two, see Arthur Okun, *Equality and Efficiency: The Big Tradeoff* (Brookings, 1975). On the example of allocating anticrime dollars across places, see "Allocating Anti-crime Dollars across Places and Activities" in S. Nagel, *Policy Evaluation: Making Optimum Decisions* (Praeger, 1982).

6. On sensitivity and postoptimizing analysis, see David Anderson, Dennis Sweeney, and Thomas Williams, *An Introduction to Management Science: Quantitative Approaches to Decision-Making* (West, 1976), 143–70; Hamdy Taha, *Operations Research: An Introduction* (Macmillan, 1971), 94–109; and Harvey Wagner, *Principles of Operations Research: With Applications to Managerial Decisions* (Prentice-Hall, 1969), 129–64. On the example of the sensitivity of an optimum jury size to various inputs, see S. Nagel, "Management Science and Jury Size," 11 *Interfaces: A TIMS-ORSA Journal* 34–9 (1981).

7. On cost saving in evaluation research, see "No Money, No Time, No Technique" in James Glass and Charldean Newell, *Administrative Research Methods* (unpublished manuscript, 1982); and Rick Hesse and Gene Woolsey, *Applied Management Science: A Quick and Dirty Approach* (Science Research Associates, 1980). On the example of evaluating alternative ways of providing legal services to the poor, see S. Nagel, "How to Provide Legal Counsel for the Poor: Decision Theory" in Dorothy James (ed.), *Analyzing Poverty Policy* (Lexington-Heath, 1975); and Legal Services Corporation, *The Delivery Systems Study* (LSC, 1980).

8. On research-data sharing, see Herbert Hyman, *Secondary Analysis of Sample Surveys* (Wiley, 1972); Ralph Bisco, "Social Science Data Archives: A Review of Development," 60 *American Political Science Review* 93–109 (1966); and Inter-University Consortium for Political and Social Research, *Guide to Resources and Services* (ICPSR, 1978).

9. On research validity, see Abraham Kaplan, *The Conduct of Inquiry: Methodology for Behavioral Science* (Chandler, 1963); and Eugene Meehan, *The Theory and Method of Political Analysis* (Dorsey, 1964). On the example of research validity in the context of black-white differences in sentencing, see "The Racial Disparity That Supposedly Was Not There: Some Pitfalls to Watch for in Analyzing Court Statistics on Sentencing and Other Matters" in S. Nagel and Marian Neef, *The Legal Process: Modeling the System* (Sage, 1977).

10. On putting people at risk in social science experiments, see Federal Judicial Center, *Experimentation in the Law* (FJC, 1981); Jay Katz, *Experimentation with Human Beings* (Russell Sage Foundation, 1972); and Paul Freund (ed.), *Experimentation with Human Subjects* (Braziller, 1970). On the example of randomly assigning convicted juvenile delinquents to jail or probation, see Martin Levin, "Policy Evaluation and Recidivism," 6 *Law and Society Review* 17–46 (1971). On the example of randomly assigning judicial districts to being subjected to different kinds of publicity concerning the holding and appearance rates of individual judges, see S. Nagel, "Decision Theory and Pretrial Release Decisions" (unpublished research proposal available from author on request, 1977).

11. On ethics in general political and social science research, see "Ethical Concerns in Social Science Research" in David and Chava Nachmias, *Research Methods in the Social Sciences* (St. Martin's Press, 1981); "The Ethics of Political and Social Inquiry" in Dickinson McGaw and George Watson, *Social and Political Inquiry* (Wiley, 1976); and Nicholas Hobbs, "Ethical Issues in the Social Sciences," 5 *International Encyclopedia of the Social Sciences* 160–66 (1968).
12. On openness as a way of controlling wrongdoing in securities regulation and governmental activities, see F. B. Ashby, *Economic Effects of Blue Sky Laws* (University of Pennsylvania Press, 1926); Louis Loss, *Securities Regulation* (Little, Brown, 1951); Harold Cross, *The People's Right to Know* (Columbia University Press, 1953); and Charles Whalen, *Your Right to Know* (Random House, 1973).

QUESTIONS

1. Should policy analysts have an obligation to recommend policies that will maximize given goals, or is it enough merely to show the effects of given policies?
2. Should policy analysts carefully indicate how their recommendations or conclusions would be changed if there were changes in the goals, constraints, weights of the goals, policies considered, relations between the policies and goals, or other inputs? Explain.
3. To what extent should policy analysts participate on behalf of partisan causes or special interest groups?
4. To what extent should policy analysts be obliged to foresee what otherwise might be unforeseen consequences of alternative policies?
5. How can policy analysts take equity as well as efficiency into consideration (with equity referring to meeting minimum needs of persons, places, or groups, and efficiency referring to achieving maximum benefits minus costs)?
6. What should policy analysts' obligations be for doing research in a simple and inexpensive manner?
7. What obligations should policy analysts have to share their data and findings with other policy analysts?
8. To what extent should policy analysts be obliged to use research methods likely to produce logically and empirically valid findings?
9. What are policy analysts' obligations when, as part of a policy experiment, research involves putting people at risk of harm?

REFERENCES

Bermant, Gordon, Herbert Kelman, and Donald Warwick (eds.), *The Ethics of Social Intervention* (Wiley, 1978).
Callahan, Daniel, *The Teaching of Ethics in Higher Education* (Hastings Center, 1982).

Dunn, William (ed.), *Ethics, Values, and the Practice of Policy Analysis* (Lexington-Heath, 1982).

Fleishman, Joel, and Bruce Payne, *Ethical Dilemmas and the Education of Policy-makers* (Hastings Center, 1980).

Marvin, Keith, *Standards for Program Evaluation* (Evaluation Research Society, 1980).

McGaw, Dickinson, and George Watson, "The Ethics of Political and Social Inquiry" in *Social and Political Inquiry* (Wiley, 1976).

Nachmias, David, and Chava Nachmias, "Ethical Concerns in Social Science Research" in *Research Methods in the Social Sciences* (St. Martin's Press, 1981).

Rohr, John, *Ethics for Bureaucrats: An Essay on Law and Values* (Dekker, 1978).

CHAPTER 19

Research
Utilization

The first part of this chapter discusses the role of political scientists and political science in government. The second part discusses factors facilitating the utilization of policy evaluation research.

Political Scientists and Science in Government

As part of the development of a public policy profession with an important political and social science component, academics must become more aware of opportunities for jobs and research support that government provides and they must also become better trained and motivated to meet these opportunities. Practitioners must become more aware of what academics can contribute and also should become more oriented toward absorbing these potential contributions. Although this part of the chapter emphasizes political science, many of the principles discussed apply to other social sciences, all of which are seeking to increase their acceptability in government.

The generalizations are largely based on the *Political Science Utilization Directory*, published in 1975 by the Policy Studies Organization, which surveys members of the American Political Science Association who hold positions in government at the federal, state, and local levels. The survey asks open-ended questions concerning how political science and political scientists have been and can be used better in the government agencies for which they work. The results of the survey are published largely verbatim in the *Political Science Utilization Directory*, which is organized on an agency-by-agency basis. The most recent survey (1975) included information on 61 agencies based on 108 short essays from knowledgeable insiders. Their perceptions and insights are still quite relevant in the eighties. The Policy Studies Organization, however, is planning another survey, which will include economists, sociologists, psychologists, other social scientists, and possibly natural scientists working in government. That directory will facilitate comparisons across scholarly disciplines.

Discussing the use of political science in government is especially timely in view of the need for developing alternative careers for political science graduate students. The demand for academic positions has decreased, due largely to the plateauing population of undergraduates to be taught by political scientists. The subject is also timely due to the increase in government as a source of research funding relative to the decrease in the research budgets of universities, foundations, and individual researchers. Even during the Reagan administration, the ratio of government research funding to university and foundation research funding has been higher than in the 1960s when universities and foundations were funding much more academic research than was the government. More important than these somewhat mercenary considerations is that political and social science contribute to better governmental decision making.

PLACING POLITICAL SCIENTISTS

The Nature of Job Opportunities. Job opportunities for political scientists in government can be classified into generalist and specialist positions. Generalists can be hired without specialized knowledge of specific policies or programs, such as energy, criminal justice, housing, labor, and so on. Specialized knowledge may, however, be acquired on the job. Both generalist and specialist positions are available in legislative staffing and administrative agency positions. Legislative positions are more generalized than administrative positions. As a result, a higher percentage of legislative positions are held by people with political science graduate or undergraduate degrees than are held by people holding administrative positions. Political scientists are more likely to have generalist positions because they often lack more specialized knowledge and they gravitate toward positions that relate to policy formation rather than to implementation.

Another way to classify government job opportunities for political scientists is in terms of whether or not there is a policy and program evaluation component associated with the position. This is becoming an increasingly important part both of formal job descriptions in government and of what the jobs actually entail. The increase is due partly to evaluation requirements in appropriations and budgeting, sunset legislation, and to budget cutbacks which require evaluating alternative programs in order to decide which ones should be most reduced. Evaluation work is seldom a full-time job, but is often part of a middle-level public administration position or legislative staff position. Full-time evaluation positions have, however, been established in recent years, in virtually all the federal departments. Well-organized units are associated with the Departments of Health and Human Services, Housing and Urban Development, Defense, State, and Labor. Also within the federal executive branch are such general, cross-cutting evaluation agencies as the Office of Management and Budget and the White House Domestic Policy Staff. Within the jurisdiction of

Congress are such evaluation units as the Congressional Budget Office, Congressional Research Service, General Accounting Office, and the Office of Technology Assessment. The judicial branch has its Federal Judicial Center and the Administrative Office of the United States Courts.

Job opportunities can also be classified as federal, state, or local. Federal positions are more visible and glamorous, but state and local positions together may be more numerous. They may also grow more rapidly, especially if more authority is delegated to state and local governments, and their procedures are upgraded. Analogous to the federal evaluation units are similar agencies at the state and local level. Offices of the state auditor generals are increasingly performing evaluation functions similar to those of the General Accounting Office. State legislative reference services seek to emulate the Congressional Research Service. State legislatures often have a rules committee or other committee whose staff evaluates the impact of proposed or adopted legislation or administrative regulations. Their analysis, however, generally emphasizes the impact on the prior legal rules rather than on the state and its people.

The Skills and Training Needed. Many of the entries in the *Political Science Utilization Directory* suggest that the chances of political scientists being hired in government positions increase if applicants train to develop skills related to policy analysis and program evaluation, even in the 1980s as compared to 1960. Training in policy analysis should include foundation courses in social science research methods, especially methods that relate to questionnaires, interviewing, sampling, goal measurement, prediction, causal analysis, data processing, systematic observation, and report writing. The methodological training should also include courses in systematic decision making which are increasingly being offered in political science departments and interdisciplinary policy analysis programs. One need not be an expert at producing social science research or optimizing models, but one should at least be able to interpret such research and modeling.

Substantive training of appropriately prepared political scientists should include courses explaining how and why alternative policies are adopted and implemented. Courses that cover the basic issues and references in at least a few specific policy fields should also be included. A well-rounded education in methodology and process will provide a more concrete basis of understanding and will facilitate entry into more specialized positions. Standard courses in public administration are also advisable for political scientists who are interested in government work.

Political scientists sometimes feel inferior to economists, lawyers, or social-psychological program evaluators when applying for government jobs. They should, however, not disparage the eclectic nature of political science regarding both methods and substance. Political scientists can bridge the raw empiricism of social-psychological statistical analysis and the often unrealistic deductive models of economists. Political scientists can be particularly sensitive in their analytic work to the problems of policy adoption and implementation. Other social scientists often fail to adequately consider political and administrative feasibility. Legalistically oriented lawyers may be less in demand than in the past now that governmental problems are increasingly viewed in terms of benefits, costs, impact, and evaluation, rather than in terms of litigation, drafting, and negotiation.

Improving Relevant Political Science Training and Placement. As part of the *Political Science Utilization Directory*, political scientists in government were asked to make recommendations for improving the relevant training of political scientists. Similar questions were also asked of heads of graduate political science departments. Their responses were reported in the *Policy Studies Directory* (PSO, 1976). These recommendations emphasize the following:

1. Training in policy studies and public administration should occur at both graduate and undergraduate levels.
2. At the graduate level, students should be trained for both government work and for teaching others the knowledge and skills needed for government work.
3. The training should be interdisciplinary, although extensive course taking outside the political science department is not essential. Political scientists are capable of incorporating nonpolitical science material into their teaching.
4. The training must include a concern for both the substance of government programs and the methods for evaluating alternatives.
5. Both classroom and field experience should be provided. The field experience can include internships, working with faculty members who do consulting work, participating in realistic problem-solving simulations, and inviting more practitioner involvement in training programs to provide at least vicarious field experience.
6. The program should focus on policy formation, implementation, re-formulation, and possible termination so students can understand the total policy process.
7. Rationalist methods, which emphasize determining the relevant benefits and costs for the main alternatives, and incrementalist methods, which emphasize building on and explaining existing decisions, should be included.
8. Concern should be expressed for governmental problems at the local, state, national, and cross-national levels.
9. Students should be capable of working with given goals and also of questioning the goals themselves.
10. Research experience should be gained by developing reports, co-authoring articles, drafting seminar papers, and being required to write a thesis or extended essay at the B.A. and M.A. levels and a dissertation at the Ph.D. level.

To be fully useful, good training requires good placement procedures. Answers to the hiring questions in the *Political Science Utilization Directory* explicitly or implicitly suggest the following procedures will improve placement of political scientists in government:

1. The APSA Personnel Service could actively solicit job notices from relevant agencies which could be placed in the *APSA Personnel Newsletter*.
2. Political science graduate students can be referred to the *Public Administration Times*, a bi-weekly newspaper that contains a number of government job notices for which political scientists can qualify.
3. The APSA and/or PSO could solicit general statements from people in government agencies who are responsible for making hiring decisions, to determine their views concerning needed training and skills and appropriate procedures for making successful placements. These kinds of questions may be part of the *Social Science Utilization Directory*, which is designed to expand on the *Political Science Utilization Directory*.
4. Have more panels, workshops, symposia, and other types of sessions at APSA and regional political science meetings in which academics and practitioners can discuss and develop ideas for better placement and training.
5. Encourage members of APSA with government positions to aid in placement the way political scientists at universities are often cultivated and called upon to aid in placing graduate students from their alma maters.
6. Faculty in political science departments who are involved in placement should develop more contacts with people in government in the same way contacts are made with people at other universities to facilitate placement.
7. Ideas for placing political scientists in interest groups and research institutes are contained in the *Policy Publishers and Associations Directory* (PSO, 1980), and the *Policy Research Centers Directory* (PSO, 1978), as well as other nonacademic opportunities for political science graduate students.

GETTING POLITICAL SCIENCE USED

The Nature of the Research Uses. Political science is utilized three general ways in government. They relate to general orientation, policy decisions, and administrative decisions. On the matter of general orientation, people in government are probably substantially influenced by the governmental and social science training they received in graduate school, college, high school, and elementary school. This general background is shaped by the academic political scientists who have written textbooks for use in courses at all four levels, especially American government and, to a lesser extent, high school civics textbooks. High school materials are generally written by people with backgrounds in education rather than in political science, but they often collaborate with political scientists and even more often draw upon the literature of political scientists. Regarding adopting general policies, policy studies research, although not necessarily general social science research, may be referred to. For example, when Congress contemplates adopting a new criminal sentencing system, the hearings refer to research that has been done on discretionary sentencing versus nondiscretionary sentencing, imprisonment versus community-based corrections, imprisonment versus capital punishment, or other such issues. One can, however, argue that simply because hearings or Justice Department reports refer to such research does not mean the research will change the minds of policy makers. This would be a rare occurrence. The research probably clarifies and reinforces preconceived perceptions, values, and recommendations. For example, sentencing with less discretion for parole boards and judges is now widely accepted by policy makers. Lessened discretion was previously being advocated in criminology research to provide greater deterrence and to reduce disparities. Conservative policy makers agree with the deterrence justification and liberal policy makers argue for the disparities reduction justification. Thus, if policy research can reinforce preconceived values, it can accelerate the adoption and respectability of new public policies. Policy research that transects places and time points can also be theoretically significant in understanding the causal relations between policies and goals.

When it comes to making specific administrative decisions, neither policy studies nor social science is likely to be consulted. The relevant knowledge in these situations is factual knowledge specific to the situation and the job. If any material is likely to be consulted, it would probably be an in-house report. This report, however, could be prepared by a person with a graduate or undergraduate background in political science, public administration, or a related social science.

Getting Scholarly Researchers to Work More Usefully With Policy-Relevant Subjects. Getting political science used in government requires better communication from academics and better receptiveness from practitioners. Political science academics have been showing a substantial increase in policy studies during the 1970s. This increase seems to be due to such factors as: (1) new methodological tools and data sources for conducting more meaningful policy analysis, (2) the stimuli of social movements such as civil rights, peace, poverty, environmental protection, and sexual equality, (3) closer interdisciplinary relations, especially those facilitated by new academic programs and organizations, (4) the increasing relative attractiveness of job opportunities and grants in policy-related fields, and (5) a feeling that there has been a near saturation regarding the application of quantitative methods to non-policy-relevant topics.

As of the 1980s, there may be a retreat from controversial public policy matters among some social scientists due to their perceptions that the times have become more conservative and due to their waning enthusiasm for the public policy issues of the 1960s and the 1970s. Political scientists' concern for public policy, however, is nonideological in the sense that political scientists of a variety of ideological orientations are closely associated with policy studies. Public policy controversies do not necessarily lessen in importance, although they may change in content. There was a shift from Vietnam, civil rights, and poverty in about 1970 to inflation, energy, and productivity in about 1980, with the environment, women's rights, and Watergate in between.

Academics must learn to communicate more clearly to practitioners who may not have the time or the backgrounds to master technical presentations. Academics are increasingly writing for more popular reading as reflected in such journals as *Public Interest, Society, Social Policy*, and the *Policy Review*. They are subscribed to by practitioners in substantial numbers, as are the *Evaluation Review, Public Administration Review*, and *Foreign Affairs*, but not so much journals like *Public Policy, Policy Analysis, Policy Sciences*, or even the *Policy Studies Journal*. Some academics write for more popular, general journals like the *New Republic* and *National Review*, but this is relatively rare. Academic books are often read by practitioners after they complete their formal education. Publishers that actively seek to reach practitioners include Basic Books, Sage, Brookings, American Enterprise Institute, Urban Institute, and Lexington-Heath.

Getting Practitioners To Be More Aware of Useful Research. Formal devices to facilitate communicating the increased policy research to policy practitioners include:

1. More research projects that involve academic-practitioner collaboration
2. More research centers that can combine the creativity and broadness often associated with university research with the responsibility for meeting specifications and deadlines often associated with non-university research
3. More journals that can communicate technical findings in nontechnical language to a wider audience
4. More requirements in legislation that proposed programs be accompanied by environmental impact statements, technological assessment, and social assessment, and that ongoing programs be periodically evaluated
5. More staff personnel associated with legislatures, administrative agencies, and courts whose function is to distill and translate scholarly research to make it more usable to busy policy makers, and to more clearly inform the research community as to what is needed

These ideas can generally be found in the research suggestions in the *Political Science Utilization Directory* from practitioners, the *Policy Studies Directory* from academics, and the *Policy Research Centers Directory* from people associated with policy research centers. They also suggest the need for less formal devices, such as relevant convention panels, conferences, think tanks, visiting appointments of academics to government agencies, visiting appointments of practitioners to academic programs, inviting practitioners to participate in academic symposia, rewarding practitioners for presenting papers and publishing articles, and rewarding academics for doing consulting and other work with government agencies.

CONCLUSIONS

Political scientists are being better trained and placed in government positions, including those which involve analyzing alternative public policies and programs. As it shows more concern for specific policy problems and policy implementation to supplement its traditional emphasis on policy formation, political science is also being better used in government. There is, however, substantial room for improvement, especially since the contemporary policy orientation is so young. Much can be accomplished in both training and research, even in times of tight budgets. Training programs can be established or expanded by cross-listing faculty, courses, and students without developing new facilities, faculty lines, or fellowship money. Research projects can often be pursued without buying additional equipment, conducting expensive surveys, or obtaining released time. The general knowledge from such training and research can be relevant to being a better practitioner. The specific knowledge can also be relevant to reinforcing and accelerating the adoption and implementation of important public policies.[1]

Facilitating Policy Evaluation Research

This part of the chapter discusses 13 factors relevant to facilitating the utilization of policy evaluation research by legislative, judicial, and administrative policy makers. The term *policy evaluation research* refers to analyzing effects of alternative public policies to determine which one or combination will optimize or improve benefits or costs in achieving given goals under various constraints and conditions. *Utilization* refers to being useful or influential in the decision making of governmental policy makers from any branch or level of government.

One might distinguish between the utilization of a policy evaluation report and the adoption of a policy. Policy evaluation research could thus be classified as (1) research in which the policy recommendations were adopted versus (2) research in which the policy recommendations were rejected, regardless of whether the research was responsible. One could also classify policy evaluation research as (1) research that was read, cited, or in some way considered by the decision makers versus (2) research that, so far as is known, was not read, cited, or in some way considered by the decision makers. Thus, research could be (1) yes on both dimensions; (2) no on both dimensions; (3) yes on the adoption dimension with regard to the policy recommended, but no on having been considered in the adoption process; or (4) no on the adoption dimension, but yes on having been considered. All the case studies in the article involve policy evaluation research that was considered by the relevant decision makers. Some of the research was successful in influencing the adoption of the policies recommended, and some failed to influence the adoption of the policies recommended. The article is primarily concerned with why some research examples were relative successes and some were failures. Thirteen explanatory factors are considered relevant.

The 13 factors are grouped in terms of how they relate to: (1) opposition and support, (2) policy goals, (3) policy effects, (4) efficient cost-saving, and (5) communication methods. The meaning of these groups of factors will be clarified following discussion of the specific factors, which are further clarified by discussing at least one case study for each factor. The case studies often use examples from the criminal justice field, but through analogy, they can be applicable to any public policy subject matter. Some studies involve policy evaluation that was utilized by policy makers, and others involve policy evaluation that was ignored or explicitly rejected. Both the successes and failures help indicate the factors that make it more likely to utilize policy evaluation research.[2]

OPPOSITION AND SUPPORT

Bipartisan Support. One of the easiest ways to have a policy evaluation research project adopted is to arrange for bipartisan support, or be fortunate enough to obtain it without trying. In the criminal justice field there are at least two good examples. One relates to the pretrial release movement in the 1960s, and the other relates to the determinate sentencing movement in the 1970s. The Vera Foundation was established in New York City in the early 1960s. One of its main original purposes was to tackle the problem of overcrowded pretrial detention centers. The Foundation's research showed that pretrial release could be substantially increased without increasing the percentage of defendants who fail to appear for their court dates, provided that the pretrial release process: (1) screened defendants into good and bad risks, (2) supervised released defendants at least to the extent of having them periodically report their whereabouts to the courthouse, (3) notified released defendants shortly before their court dates as a reminder to appear in court, and/or (4) prosecuted defendants who willfully failed to appear. The general recommendations were widely adopted in numerous cities. This research helped trigger the bail reform movement which resulted in a shift from more than two-thirds of all defendants being held in jail prior to trial in the 1960s to more than two-thirds being released prior to trial in the 1970s, as a rough national average.

The Vera research involved some questionable sampling, predictive, and other procedures. Nevertheless, it is a classic in the field of criminal justice research utilization. Perhaps the main factor responsible for its success was that it struck a responsive chord among both liberals and conservatives at a time and place when pretrial detention centers were not only overcrowded, but in a state of riotous violence. Liberals endorsed the idea of increased pretrial release because (by definition in a criminal justice context) they tend to be defendant-oriented. Pretrial release is partly based on the presumption of innocence which tends to be emphasized by defendant-oriented people. Conservatives endorsed the idea of increased pretrial release because (by definition in a more general context) they tend to be oriented toward reducing domestic government expenditures. Increased pretrial release can be a big tax saver if the appearance rate can be held constant or improved through inexpensive screening, reporting, notifying, and occasional prosecuting.

In the early 1970s, Robert Martinson's extensive research showed that prison rehabilitation programs generally do not work. His work undercut a key justification for indeterminate sentences that parole boards and other corrections people used in deciding how long to keep convicted defendants in prison. Other research showed that a key factor responsible for criminals' negative attitudes toward the legal system was the indeterminacy of sentences whereby two people who committed the same crime and had the same prior record could receive very different sentences. These research projects advocated a substantial reduction in the discretion of prison authorities, parole boards, and judges for deciding the exact sentences of convicted defendants. As of the early 1970s, virtually every state allowed considerable leeway to parole boards and judges in deciding sentences. As of the early 1980s, virtually every state had decreased criminal sentencing discretion.

Like the Vera research, the Martinson research involved some questionable methods, especially in his interpretation of the findings. Nevertheless, it is also a classic in the field of criminal justice research utilization. The main factor responsible for its success may be that it struck a responsive chord between liberals and conservatives when concern for crime and the criminal justice system was at a high point. Liberals endorse the reduction of sentencing discretion because they see discretion as leading to discriminatory sentencing with unjustifiable differences across race, economic class, geography, gender, age, and other demographic categories. Conservatives endorse the reduction of sentencing discretion because they believe it leads to overly lenient sentences. Conservative legislators have often voted for lessened discretion only after they were guaranteed that the average sentence would increase through higher minimums. The important point from a research utilization perspective is that to have a high probability of extensive research utilization, one should handle a pressing problem so as to appeal favorably to both liberals and conservatives.[3]

The Need to Compromise. Securing liberal and conservative support for a policy is quite difficult since liberals and conservatives usually disagree with each other. When they are in sharp disagreement, the research that is most likely to be utilized sees something of value on each side, which can thereby facilitate compromise. A good example of this kind of policy evaluation research is the Delivery Systems Study of the Legal Services Corporation published in June 1980. The study systematically tested the effects of alternative ways of providing legal services to the poor, including variations on salaried government attorneys, reimbursed private attorneys, and organized volunteers.

During both terms of the Nixon administration, an ongoing and emotional battle erupted between liberals (who were supportive of the system of salaried government attorneys under the Legal Services Program of the Office of Economic Opportunity) and conservatives (who wanted to restore charitable legal aid, which had prevailed prior to 1965, or institute a Judicare system of reimbursed private attorneys analogous to Medicare). The Nixon administration sought to terminate the Legal Services Program partly because of a promise to Governor Reagan made during the 1972 campaign in view of Reagan's many problems with the OEO's California Rural Legal Assistance program. The program might have been terminated if Nixon had not been distracted by his Watergate problems. The matter was temporarily resolved by establishing the Legal Services Corporation as an agency independent of the regular federal departments. Part of its mandate was to conduct an extensive study of alternative systems for delivering legal services to the poor.

When Ronald Reagan became president, one of his first acts was to try to cut the Legal Services Corporation out of the federal budget. During the presidential campaign, he indicated that he favored a Judicare system which would allow poor people to enter the private marketplace to obtain legal services with government reimbursement. When he became president, he abandoned this idea as too expensive and endorsed a system of bar association volunteers similar to the disorganized and largely ineffective legal aid programs that prevailed prior to 1965. In a series of emotional budget battles, the Legal Services Corporation survived, although with a drastically reduced budget. One of the factors that enabled it to survive was the policy evaluation research embodied in the LSC Delivery Systems Study, which helped clarify how one could compromise between salaried legal services and a purely volunteer system.

A key argument in favor of salaried legal services is that they are much more visible and accessible than volunteer attorneys. The traditional volunteer system involves potential clients phoning the community fund agency for legal help. They get referred to the bar association president, who then refers them to the chairperson of the bar association legal aid committee. The chairperson refers them to somebody on the volunteer list, who then refers them to somebody in that person's law office. If the potential clients can survive this gauntlet, they may have an attorney, or at least a law student, who will provide legal help. Legal services programs, on the other hand, operate out of highly visible and accessible storefront offices. A second key argument in favor of salaried legal services is that these attorneys are more competent and aggressive because they work full time on poverty law cases. Thus, they build relevant experience, and they are not vulnerable to losing business clients as a result of aggressively representing poor people in disputes with landlords, merchants, and government officials.

The key arguments in favor of volunteer attorneys are that they are far less expensive than salaried attorneys, and they are more representative of the generally conservative bar, rather than the more liberal full-time legal services attorneys. One useful purpose that the Delivery Systems Study clarified was how one could simultaneously cull the OEO-LSC benefits of accessibility and competence, while at the same time obtain inexpensive and politically acceptable aid. These goals are possible by requiring all salaried legal services programs to devote 10 percent or more of their budgets to recruiting, training, advertising, and otherwise organizing volunteer attorneys. By having the volunteers operate out of the legal services offices, their otherwise low visibility can be overcome. By having the salaried attorneys train them and arrange for clients that fit their existing expertise, the problem of lack of competence can also be overcome. Thus, the Delivery Systems Study has been a successful example of policy evaluation research in terms of its utilization because of its sensitivity to the need to compromise and its ability to demonstrate how compromise can be meaningfully developed.[4]

No Overwhelming Interest Group Opposition. If interest group opposition is extremely strong, policy recommendations are not likely to be adopted, even if recommendations are strongly supported and they represent a compromise. A good example compares pollution tax (as a failure) to poverty law reform (as a success). In theory, the pollution tax is a meaningful way of decreasing pollution, especially water pollution. It involves determining the cost of providing an effective filtration plant for a river segment. The tax then apportions that cost among the business firms on the river in proportion to the extent to which they deposit pollutants in the river. The tax provides a meaningful incentive to the firms to reduce their pollution in the form of decreasing their tax expense and thereby increasing their profits. The tax thus internalizes the external damage which their pollution would otherwise be causing. If the business decides it is less expensive to pollute, then it pays the tax, and funds are available for cleaning the water. Either way, the environment is protected. The tax idea was developed as part of the environmental policy evaluation work of the Brookings Institution and Resources for the Future.

This kind of system is endorsed by liberals who prefer that businesses pay for pollution costs, rather than the general public, as taxpayers or as recipients of the pollution damages. The system is also endorsed by theoretical conservatives who enjoy relying on marketplace incentives, rather than regulation by government fiat, to rule their activities. The pollution tax allows choice in reducing or not reducing pollution. It also represents a compromise between a laissez-faire system of doing nothing and a socialistic system of having the government take over private business firms. In spite of the favorable policy evaluation and support, a pollution tax has never been adopted at the national, state, or city level in the United States. The explanation seems to be that opposition from businesses which prefer to have the general public pay the tax costs and the pollution costs is too strong. In other words, the economic advantage of internalizing the externalities produces an incentive to businesses and trade associations to actively lobby against anything approaching a pollution tax. The 1972 water pollution legislation specifies that the National Academy of Science shall evaluate the effectiveness of the regulatory system, but it cannot use any congressional money to study pollution taxes as an alternative.

This can be contrasted with the relative ease of changing the poverty law rules with regard to landlord-tenant relations, merchant-consumer relations, and welfare matters in the late 1960s. During that time period, numerous evaluations were made of the violations of housing codes, product repossession, and welfare procedures. These evaluations often advocated such remedies as rent withholding from unscrupulous landlords, voiding of unconscionable consumer contracts, and providing meaningful hearings to check arbitrary welfare bureaucrats. These evaluations and policy recommendations were often easily adopted in proceedings of appellate courts, legislatures, and government departments. They were not adopted with bipartisan support since they were not particularly supported by conservatives. Nor did they represent compromises. A key factor was that the opposition was generally weak, unorganized, and demoralized. When talking about air, water, noise, radiation, and solid-waste pollution, the opposition to pollution taxes consists of almost every trade association. The opposition to poverty law reform largely means slum landlords, slum merchants, welfare bureaucrats, and other such people who were considerably less capable of fighting back, especially in the late 1960s when such people were even reluctant to identify with each other.[5]

Some Interest Group Support. The absence of overwhelming interest group opposition will not, however, guarantee the adoption of policy recommendations, unless there is substantial interest group support. A good example of this is the numerous evaluations that have been made of alternative policies for decreasing illegal police searches. These evaluations (regardless of whether they have a liberal or conservative orientation) agree that excluding illegally seized evidence from the courtroom does not represent a very strong negative sanction for keeping the police in line. They also agree that unfortunately high costs will be paid for so little benefits, in terms of decreasing the likelihood of a truly guilty defendant being convicted. In addition, the evaluations advocate that suspending or dismissing the wrong-doing police would be more effective than excluding the illegally obtained evidence in achieving the goal of decreasing wrongful police behavior, while still allowing the evidence to be used to obtain needed convictions. Providing for a suspension of the guilty police officer on the first offense and a dismissal on the second offense can also be considered a compromise between providing no negative sanctions and continuing the relatively ineffective system of excluding the illegally seized evidence.

Despite all these evaluations, no state legislature has come close to adopting a system of suspensions and dismissals to enforce the prohibition against illegal searches and seizure. That is so, even though Chief Justice Burger has indicated that he would vote to no longer require the exclusionary rule for any state that adopts a meaningful system of suspensions and dismissals. The explanation for the lack of adoption seems to be that there is no substantial interest group support for such a policy. Almost no legislator is likely to run for office on a platform that strongly favors suspending and dismissing police for being overly aggressive in searching for criminal evidence. The general public is not likely to endorse this kind of legislation or legislator. Adoption has to come from a nonmajoritarian political institution such as the courts, but they have no authority to require suspensions or dismissals, as contrasted to their authority of requiring the exclusion of illegally seized evidence. The relevant administrative agencies (i.e., the police and their civil service commissions) are not likely to adopt such a rule. They view their role as being protective, not punitive toward the police. The American Civil Liberties Union (ACLU) is a relevant interest group, but it is generally only effective in the courts, and this is a legislative policy matter. Thus, the adoption of policy recommendations from evaluation research requires some interest group support and no overwhelming interest group opposition. The recommendations also benefit from bipartisan support and sensitivity to the need for compromise.[6]

POLICY GOALS

Acceptable Societal Goals. In addition to factors relating to opposition and support for explaining variations in policy evaluation utilization, one can also examine factors relating to policy goals. Some types of goals are more relevant than others to facilitating utilization. Policy recommendations will not get very far if their goals are socially unacceptable. A good example might be the study of how elected judges compare with appointed judges on deciding in favor of the liberal rather than the conservative position in economic or civil-liberties cases. In 1979, the Judiciary Committee of the Illinois General Assembly held hearings on amending the Illinois Constitution to provide for appointment of judges in place of the prevailing elected system. The results of a systematic study comparing elected and appointed judges were presented before the Committee.

A key finding was that elected judges are more liberal on economic matters than judges who are appointed to serve unexpired terms. This finding was true even when both sets of judges heard the same cases on the same state supreme courts. It also prevailed when elected democrats were compared with appointed democrats and elected republicans were compared with appointed republicans, in order to hold political party constant. The finding could be explained by noting that many elected judges have working-class backgrounds, and become judges through active party work. The appointed judges are primarily from upper-class backgrounds, and become judges through financial contributions. The study also showed that judges serving long terms before reelection or reappointment are more liberal on civil-liberties matters than judges serving short terms, probably because long-term judges are less vulnerable to public pressures.

These findings show that if one wants judges who are liberal on both economic and civil-liberties matters, then have judges who are elected for long terms. If one wants judges who are conservative on both issues, then have judges who are appointed for short terms. If one wants judges who are conservative on economic matters, but liberal on civil liberties, as advocated by libertarians such as Ayn Rand, then have judges who are appointed for long terms. Finally, if one wants judges who are liberal on economic matters but conservative on civil liberties as advocated by populists such as many AFL-CIO leaders, then have judges who are elected for short terms. These findings were presented to the members of the House Judiciary Committee. They expressed considerable interest and listened politely, but they indicated clearly they could not openly endorse one system of judicial selection over another on the basis of which system generated more liberal or conservative judges. The only socially acceptable goals related to technical competence, but the research found no differences on this dimension. This is an example of reasonably good policy-evaluation research that did not get utilized because the goals to which it related, the alternative policies, were not considered socially acceptable.

Another example of evaluation research that was reasonably well conducted, but yet rejected by the policy makers for dealing with the wrong goals, revealed that discrimination against women by juries can be reduced by having more women jurors. In the United States Supreme Court ruling which declared unconstitutional the state laws that allow women to be more easily excused from jury duty than men, the court cited none of this literature. Instead, it relied only on social science literature that showed women were underrepresented on juries relative to their proportion in the general population. The court said the equal protection clause of the Constitution is violated if women are systematically underrepresented. The implication was that it was irrelevant whether or not their increased representation would affect case outcomes. Perhaps the court deliberately avoided the goal of improving case outcomes, not because it is socially unacceptable, but because it is unacceptable to the judges in view of the problems it would raise if it were addressed. These problems include more open admission than the court might be willing to give to the idea that case outcomes can be substantially influenced by the characteristics of the decision makers.

Along related lines, the court has refused to hear cases that deal with malapportionment of judicial electoral districts. The unexpressed reason might be because the court would be forced to examine the extent to which judicial decisions are influenced by whether judges are democrats or republicans, urban or rural, or from the northern or southern parts of their states. Thus, policy evaluation research that shows the relation between alternative policies and overly controversial goals will likely be unutilized, as will policy evaluation research that relates to socially unacceptable goals.[7]

Congruence Between Societal, Group, and Individual Goals. On the matter of being oriented toward the right goals to have policy evaluation research utilized, we should note that goals can be classified as societal (both acceptable and unacceptable), group, and individual. By the word *individual*, we mean the individual policy maker, and by the word *group*, we mean political party or interest group. Policy evaluation is oriented toward societal goals. If these societal goals are congruent with group and individual goals, then the evaluation research is more likely to be adopted, or to at least be influential. If there is a conflict between these societal and individual goals, and the research is directed toward societal goals, then it is not likely to be adopted.

A good example of this is found in the legislative redistricting field. In the early 1980s, some researchers evaluated alternative redistricting plans for state legislatures, city councils, and congressional delegations. In redistricting, the societal goal is generally to provide equal population across districts and roughly proportional representation for the political parties and major ethnic groups. At the group level, political parties and ethnic groups desire to maximize their representation. Their goals may, however, conflict with the desire of incumbent legislators to remain in office. In Chicago ward redistricting, for example, various redistricting plans were developed that would provide for more nearly proportional representation of black voters by equalizing the percentage of black voters and the percentage of black members of the city council. This policy would have promoted both societal and group goals. The leading opposition came from black incumbent city council members who wanted especially safe districts that would be overwhelmingly black, even though many black votes would be wasted. The irony was that these black incumbents were advocating the same policy (although for different reasons) as the white council members who wanted to minimize black representation. The policy recommendations of the Urban League were thus defeated because they were not oriented toward individual incumbent goals, but rather toward the conflicting societal and group goals.[8]

Sensitivity to the Real Goals of the Policy Makers. Policy research is more likely to be utilized if it is directed toward acceptable societal goals and if they are congruent with the interests of incumbent policy makers. When we refer to the goals of policy makers, we should also distinguish between their expressed goals and their real goals. Their real goals may be especially relevant to research utilization.

A good example might be the work of the Federal Paperwork Commission in the 1970s. The expressed goal of the Commission was to reduce paperwork. Many consultants, including prominent social scientists, were hired to offer advice on how paperwork could be reduced. At one such conference of the Paperwork Commission, suggestions were made for applying the methods of operations research and management science to making decisions relevant to data gathering and paperwork. A model was suggested for arriving at an optimum level of paperwork by minimizing the sum of the costs of gathering the data plus the costs of not having the data available if it were not gathered. A model was particularly suggested for deciding whether or not to gather new data in light of: (1) the relative value of an error of gathering unused data versus an error of not gathering data that would be used, and (2) the probability that the data would be used.

The reaction from the administrative policy makers was the reverse of the Illinois House Judiciary Committee on the matter of elected versus appointed judges. The Judiciary Committee, in effect, said they only want to use evaluations that are directed toward the goals that they must express such as technical competence, not the goals that they were really interested in, such as, liberalism-conservatism. The staff of the Paperwork Commission said, in effect, they will only use those evaluations that were directed toward their real goal, to eliminate much government regulation. They were not interested in the goals they paid lip service to about paperwork reduction. The staff was receptive to suggestions for abolishing virtually all the data gathering of the Federal Trade Commission, the Federal Power Commission, the Interstate Commerce Commission, and the Antitrust Division of the Department of Justice. They were not as receptive to simplifying the paperwork of the Internal Revenue Service by abolishing itemized deductions in favor of the standard deduction. If the paperwork enabled business to avoid taxes or regulation, it was good paperwork, providing the paperwork did not place a burden on business. In other words, evaluation which the Paperwork Commission was most likely to utilize did not necessarily reduce paperwork or make it more rational. Instead, preferred research included research recommending the elimination of business regulatory activities under the guise of reducing paperwork.[9]

POLICY EFFECTS

No Offsetting Adverse Side Effects. Research utilization may be facilitated by recommending policies that encourage substantial political support without provoking substantial political opposition. It may also be facilitated by being directed toward achieving goals that the policy makers consider desirable. A third reason for utilization relates to the recommended policies' likely policy effects. Recommended policies are more likely to be adopted if they produce desired effects, providing there are no offsetting adverse side effects. A good example of how adverse side effects can destroy potential research utilization is in the area of developing more meaningful jury instructions.

Probably the most important and highly ambiguous jury instruction informs juries in criminal cases that they are supposed to convict only if the defendant is guilty beyond a reasonable doubt. Because of the ambiguity, some states do not tell criminal juries what standard they are to use in voting to convict or acquit. Surveys of judges show that judges consider the phrasing to correspond to a probability of guilt greater than about 0.90. No state supreme court or legislature, however, requires judges to instruct juries that they should vote to convict only if the defendant seems to be guilty with more than a 9 out of 10 probability. Evaluation research reveals that jurors interpret the verbal instruction, *beyond a reasonable doubt*, to mean something substantially less than a 0.90 probability of guilt. This research arrives at juror thresholds mainly by determining their relative weight of making an error of voting to convict an innocent defendant versus voting to acquit a guilty defendant. The same evaluation research indicates that the most meaningful instruction for getting jurors to operate above the 0.90 threshold level is to instruct them that the legal system considers an error of convicting an innocent defendant to be 10 times as bad as an error of acquitting a guilty defendant.

If evaluation research shows a considerable discrepancy between jury attitudes and the judicial meaning of *beyond a reasonable doubt*, which could be remedied by better instructions, then why are they not given? On the basis of informal discussion with judges and lawyers, the consensus seems to be that it is already difficult to convict under the present system of jury instructions. An instruction requiring guilt above a 9-out-of-10 probability, or mentioning a 10-to-1 trade-off between conviction errors and acquittal errors, is considered to increase the difficulty to convict defendants whom judges and lawyers consider guilty. The national average of convictions in criminal cases with juries is only about 60 to 70 percent, even though prosecutors carefully filter out weak cases through plea bargaining before they go to the time and expense of a jury trial. In other words, "improved" instructions would produce a desirable effect of bringing jury behavior more in conformity with the law, but they are perceived as having an offsetting adverse side effect of decreasing convictions, which is probably the key explanation for the nonutilization of this evaluation research.[10]

Reinforcing Prior Decisions. One of the best examples of research utilization by the United States Supreme Court occurred in the case of

Ballew v. *Georgia*, in which the Supreme Court made extensive use of social science research on the effects of alternative jury sizes. The key issue in the case was whether five-person juries are constitutional in light of the Sixth Amendment which provides for a right to trial by jury. The Supreme Court had previously allowed juries to deviate from the usual 12 to as low as six, but had not previously declared six to be the cutoff.

One piece of evaluation research that the Supreme Court particularly referred to involved a determination that juries of about seven persons would be optimum in terms of minimizing the weighted sum of errors of convicting the innocent plus errors of not convicting the guilty. The conviction errors were given a weight of 10 and the nonconviction errors were given a weight of 1. Calculating the conviction and acquittal errors for different jury sizes involved tentatively assuming that the probability of an innocent defendant being convicted is about 0.40 and the probability of a guilty defendant being convicted is about 0.70, since we know that the probability of an average defendant being convicted is about 0.60. Calculating the conviction and acquittal errors also involved tentatively assuming that about 5 out of 100 defendants are probably innocent and that 95 out of 100 defendants are probably guilty. This was based mainly on the idea that prosecutors operate at a 0.95 confidence level in deciding which defendants to prosecute in expensive, time consuming, and potentially embarrassing jury trials. With these normative and empirical assumptions and some simple arithmetical logic, one can deduce that seven is the optimum jury size. The bottom-line result is dependent on the 10-to-1 trade-off ratio, the probability of conviction for innocent and guilty defendants, and the number of innocent and guilty defendants per 100 jury trials.

Justice Blackmun, writing for the Supreme Court, explained most of the evaluation model. He was well qualified to do so in view of his having received a bachelor's degree in mathematics, magna cum laude from Harvard. He referred to the 10-to-1 trade-off ratio as "perhaps not an unreasonable assumption." This ratio had been advocated by William Blackstone in his *Commentaries on the Law* in 1765, which was influential to the framers of the United States Constitution. The model is not sensitive to the assumptions concerning the conviction probabilities since the 0.40 can be greatly decreased and the 0.70 can be increased without substantially affecting the figure of seven as the optimum. The model is, however, quite sensitive to the assumption about the number of innocent and guilty defendants. If one assumes a 5-to-95 split, the optimum jury size is seven. If one, however, assumes that prosecutors are not so careful in bringing defendants to jury trial and that the split is about 10 innocent to 90 guilty, then much larger juries are needed to protect those additional innocent defendants from being convicted. If one takes a more conservative proprosecution position and assumes that prosecutors are especially careful in bringing defendants to jury trial and the split is thus about 1-to-99, then much smaller juries are necessary to protect the fewer innocent defendants from being convicted. Which of these three possibilities is correct can never be known, since we have no way of knowing which defendants are truly innocent and which are truly guilty, as contrasted to knowing which are convicted and which are not convicted.

The important point from a research utilization perspective is that Justice Blackmun did not discuss the key empirical assumption of the 5-to-95 split; he only focused on the key normative assumption of the 10-to-1 trade-off. Perhaps this owes to some selective perception so he could use the evaluation research to justify prior decisions and/or preconceived notions. This is the only evaluation research that offers evidence in favor of a jury size between six and 12. Thus, the study is relevant to upholding the prior position of the Supreme Court, which ruled it was constitutional to have less than 12 jurors. The study is also relevant because it enables the Supreme Court to draw the line at about six, which is in conformity with the expressed desire of members of the Supreme Court to draw the line somewhere above one or zero jurors. In other words, an important factor in having evaluation research utilized is that it reinforces prior decisions or values, without having offsetting adverse side effects. It is a rare occurrence for a single evaluation research project to change one's preconceived notions. Evaluation researchers, however, derive satisfaction when their results are adopted, even if they only reinforce prior values, since this may accelerate the adoption of needed reforms, or may make more respectable reforms that have been recently adopted.[11]

EFFICIENT COST-SAVING

Achieving Prior Results With Less Time or Money. An important factor that can explain some research utilization is that the recommended policies are capable of achieving prior results with less time or money. Both liberals and conservatives like to save money if other factors are held constant, although their ideas about what to do with the money saved may differ. A good example of widely adopted evaluation research shows how to reduce time in processing court cases or other governmental cases without changing the quantity of cases heard, the quality of processing, or the results of the cases. Much of this research uses analogies from delay reduction models that have been successfully applied in businesses for making repairs, processing complaints, unloading ships, inspecting automobiles, and minimizing the time spent on long-distance telephone calls from the start of dialing until the party is reached. Specific examples of delay reduction methods that were suggested in evaluation research projects and have been successfully utilized in the courts include variations on optimum sequencing, critical path analysis, and manipulated work incentives.

Optimum sequencing is currently beginning to be adopted. It basically involves reordering cases away from a first-come, first-served system to one that takes shortest cases first, which reduces the average waiting time and thus the average total time. This is the courts' equivalent of an express line for small purchases in a supermarket. It is also a justification for having a small claims court. Even more time could be saved if the cases could be reordered each week by docketing the shortest cases first for trial. Nearly all court systems have computer capabilities that could reorder cases and include a maximum waiting-time constraint so that no case would be involuntarily allowed to exceed the allotted time, even if an especially long trial case were involved. Optimum sequencing may not have been more widely adopted as yet because it has not been fully evaluated. At the University of Illinois, a simulation is now working with 100,000 federal cases from 1980 to see how much time can be saved by reordering the cases on a daily, weekly, or monthly basis with 60, 120, and 180 days, and other maximum time-constraints and varying numbers of judges or processing channels.

Critical path analysis and other aspects of flow charting are now integral to judicial administration. Flow charting simply charts all the steps and paths involved in processing cases from start to finish. On each path can be noted the average amount of time consumed or other measures of central tendency or spread. One can also note the probability of moving to the next step where less than 100 percent of the cases do move to the next step. Flow charting can indicate which critical paths require special reduction. A path is critical if other parallel steps in the process must wait until it is completed. Flow charting can also be used to predict how many cases will arrive at a given step (such as being assigned to the public defender) as a result of a change in the probabilities at a prior step (such as lowering the percent detained in jail prior to trial which affects the percent of guilty pleas).

Manipulated work incentives include rewards and punishments for prosecuting attorneys to encourage them to make time-saving decisions. Rewards might include using case time as a criterion in allocating salaries. Punishments might include barring the prosecution of defendants who have been made to wait longer than a given maximum time. Many evaluation studies have focused on the potential and actual impact of such speedy trial laws. They are likely to be utilized if they can suggest time-saving incentives that do not cost much money and that do not adversely affect crime rates or conviction rates. Other examples could be given of evaluation research that becomes utilized because it suggests ways of increasing governmental productivity in terms of reducing costs while holding benefits constant, increasing benefits while holding costs constant, or (best of all) increasing benefits while reducing costs.

Examples of evaluation research could be given that do not get utilized because their costs are high and they do not produce much perceived improvement in benefits, such as higher conviction rates in criminal cases.

An example would be an evaluation that shows one can obtain (1) less convictions of defendants whose guilt would be difficult to establish if public defenders were given more resources, and (2) more convictions of defendants who receive favorable plea bargains if prosecutors were given more resources. This kind of reform would be expensive, and it would result in lowered conviction rates, since there are generally more overconvictions of weak defendants than underconvictions of strong defendants.[12]

Commercial Value in the Private Sector. A related factor relevant to facilitating the utilization of policy evaluation research is the extent to which the research might have commercial value in the private sector. A good example is the research conducted in the early 1960s on alternative ways of quantitatively analyzing Supreme Court decisions. This analysis largely began as a theoretical exercise to test alternative methods for predicting Supreme Court policies and decisions, especially for explaining variation across the decisions. Methods included statistical regression analysis, Bayesian probability analysis, and contingency-table analysis. Virtually the same methods have now been adopted by commercial looseleaf publishers for providing practicing lawyers with predictions of case outcomes in personal injury cases. The case outcomes include the probability of victory and the amount of damages awarded. This information can help practicing lawyers decide whether or not to accept a client, especially when the fee is contingent on winning, and decide whether to accept an out-of-court settlement or go to trial.

There are other examples of theoretical policy analysis which has acquired commercial value in the private sector, as contrasted to value in obtaining contracts or grants by consulting firms or academics for performing evaluations for government agencies. Analyzing alternative campaign strategies by political scientists is such an example. In the 1960s, political scientists began analyzing how political campaign budgets could best be allocated across activities and places using survey data, linear programming, and other quantitative tools. They often drew upon methods developed for marketing business products. Their analyses have contributed to the widespread use of such methods by political campaign consulting firms, which charge very substantial fees to candidates, political party organizations, and interest groups.

Not much research that evaluates, predicts, or explains alternative government policies is likely to have much transferability to business problems, as contrasted to utilization in the other direction. Businesses are, however, becoming increasingly interested in policy evaluation for use in their lobbying and other public affairs activities. As public policy analysts become more sophisticated in the use of decision-science methods, they are likely to become more innovative in improving these methods. When this occurs, some policy-analysis methodological ideas will likely be adopted by management science and operations research experts in the private sector.[13]

COMMUNICATION METHODS

Understandable Research. To facilitate research utilization, the research, or at least the policy recommendations, should be understandable to the policy makers. Policy evaluation conducted by mathematically oriented economists seeking to arrive at an optimum solution often has this shortcoming, as contrasted to psychologically oriented social scientists seeking to capture the essence of what good decision makers actually do when making decisions. A good example might be the area of allocating anticrime dollars across places or activities.

Mathematical economists' approach to this problem combines econometrics and calculus. The econometrics relates crime reduction to dollars spent in various places or on various activities. It may, for example, involve obtaining crime and expenditure data at many points in time for each place under consideration. A sophisticated time-series regression analysis would then be conducted which: (1) controls statistically for many variables that may influence both crime and anticrime expenditures and thereby interfere with relating these two variables, (2) lags the expenditures one or more years behind the crime figures to find the delayed effects of anticrime expenditures, and (3) works with the logarithms of the data to discover the nonlinear relations between crime and anticrime expenditures. The results of these regression analyses would then be inputted into calculus models. This involves setting the first derivatives of each place equal to each other in order to arrive at allocations that will equalize the nonlinear marginal rates of return across the places. Before allocating in accordance with these derivatives or nonlinear slopes, each place might be given a minimum allocation. The conclusions from such methods are difficult to understand. Moreover, the regression coefficients may be invalid because of uncontrolled spurious and reciprocal causation, complicated relations among the variables, and measurement problems likely to be present when working with multivariate analysis. Even if the regression coefficients are accurate, the allocation figures may be inaccurate because of the likelihood of clerical errors in solving so many equations simultaneously and the likelihood that computer solutions stuck at points other than the true optimum.

Psychologists and program evaluators approach this anticrime allocation problem and other allocation problems from a perspective of multiattribute utility analysis, rather than multivariate regression-calculus analysis. Attribute analysis is basically a commonsense approach that has been developed into a series of easy-to-follow steps. In the anticrime context, the steps might be:

1. Determine the characteristics or attributes that are associated with the places we would target relatively more money. These characteristics relate to either equity, whereby each place receives money in light of its needs, or to efficiency, whereby each place receives money in light

of attributes that relate to its ability to obtain a relatively high anti-crime return on the money.

2. For equity attributes, one can use population and crime occurrence for each place. This means we first decide how much of the total budget is to be allocated on the basis of equity and how much on the basis of efficiency. The total amount to be allocated on the basis of equity is then apportioned to each place in proportion to a composite score that combines population and crime occurrence, such as the product of these two numbers or another way of compositing them.

3. For efficiency attributes, one can ask knowledgeable police chiefs to score each place on police efficiency on a 0-to-100 scale or other scale. One can also ask knowledgeable court administrators to score each place on court efficiency, and knowledgeable corrections people to score each place on corrections efficiency. The total amount available for efficiency allocations can then be allocated in proportion to a composite score consisting of these three efficiency scores. A simple composite score might involve summing them if they are all on the same 0-to-100 scale, or weighting them in terms of their importance before summing.

In theory, the regression-calculus analysis approach is the best because it allocates in accordance with the marginal rates of return of each place, whereas the multiattribute approach uses efficiency attributes of the places as substitutes for marginal rates of return or nonlinear slopes. In practice, the attribute approach is more likely to be adopted because it is relatively easy to understand the procedures and the reasoning behind them, even if one does not fully agree with the subjectivity of the attributes used or how the places are sometimes scored. Federal allocations (whereby attempts to develop a systematic quantitative formula are made) are more likely to resemble understandable attribute analysis than less understandable regression-calculus analysis. When other factors are constant, the policy evaluation that is most understandable will most likely be adopted.[14]

The Policy-Making Forum. Three forums or sets of policy-making decision makers can use policy evaluation research, namely the judicial, legislative, and administrative forums. The likelihood of having policy research utilized before one of these forums depends on both the substance and the procedure associated with each forum. On the matter of substance, the appropriate forum is generally the courts if one is dealing with a matter of constitutional interpretation, judicial procedure, or common law interpretation of property, contract, tort, or personal injury rights. The appropriate forum is generally a legislative body if one is dealing with statutes, legislative procedure, or any nonconstitutional matter. Administrative agencies are especially relevant when the subject matter relates to an area that the legislative body has delegated to an administrative agency.

On the matter of procedure, the courts emphasize an adversarial procedure of direct and cross-examination at the trial-court level and debate-oriented oral argument at the appellate-court level. Lawyers are the key communicators of policy evaluation and other social science in these contexts, although policy analysts and social scientists may be called upon to testify. In the legislative realm, the appropriate procedure for communicating policy evaluation has traditionally emphasized testimony at open hearings, but there is an increasing emphasis on in-house reports from legislative agencies such as the General Accounting Office, the Congressional Budget Office, the Congressional Research Service, the Office of Technology Assessment, the congressional committee staffs, and their counterparts at state and local legislative levels. The traditional communicators have been lawyers, lobbyists, and lawyer-lobbyists, but the testimony and reports of economists and other social scientists has increased. In the administrative realm, adversarial testimony is rare except for the quasi-adjudications of independent regulatory agencies. Open hearings are not so common except for quasi-legislative rule-making proceedings. More common is the in-house staff report prepared by people who are even more likely to be economists, social scientists, and policy analysts than in the past, or those who are in the judicial or legislative realms.

Despite these differences, the similarities are more important across these policy-making forums. The list of 12 factors facilitating the utilization of policy evaluation research applies equally across all three branches of government with regard to: (1) bipartisan or bi-ideological support, (2) the need to compromise, (3) no overwhelming opposition, (4) interest group support, (5) acceptable societal goals, (6) relevance to individual goals, (7) relevance to unexpressed goals, (8) no offsetting adverse side effects, (9) reinforcement of prior decisions, (10) impact on productivity, (11) commercial value, and (12) understandable research.

One could reorganize the case studies associated with these 12 factors in terms of whether the examples involved a judicial, legislative, or administrative forum. The courts were clearly the right place to go with evaluation designed to improve pretrial release, women as jurors (although emphasizing their underrepresentation, not their differential decision making), how to instruct juries, and the effects of alternative jury sizes. Legislatures are in practical control for reducing sentencing discretion, establishing a pollution tax, setting up a system for suspending or dismissing police for making illegal searches, and proposing a constitutional amendment for electing or appointing judges. Administrative agencies are the dominant forum in reducing paperwork and in determining how legal services will be provided to the poor, although they are always subject to legislative overrruling within constitutional constraints. Some of the examples involve multiple forums such as poverty law reform mainly involving court decisions on matters of equal protection and due process, and also legislative action concerning consumer law and landlord-tenant law. Redistricting is also shared between legislatures and courts, with legislatures being given the initial redistricting work and the courts serving an oversight role. Delay reduction has involved court initiatives, but it has been partly stimulated by congressional and state-legislative speedy-trial laws. In addition to these examples of legislative-judicial control, examples of legislative-administrative control include anticrime allocation, for which Congress established a general formula which was added to by the Law Enforcement Assistance Administration.[15]

CONCLUSION: FACILITATING UTILIZATION

Figure 19-1 shows the general relations emphasized in this chapter using a stimulus-organism-response diagram. The stimulus is the evaluation research and how it is communicated. The organism, or the political system, can be divided into two parts. One part is the opposition and support, which generally refers to interest groups, political parties, and public opinion, although it can refer to groups, parties, and opinion within governmental units. The second part refers more explicitly to the governmental decision makers who can use the evaluation research. They may be legislators, judges, and/or administrators. The response relates to either the intended goals or the side effects which are not necessarily intended. The goals and effects can refer to benefits or costs. The policy evaluation is more likely to be used when: (1) it is communicated well, (2) there is low opposition and possibly high support, (3) the communication is to the appropriate government decision makers, (4) it relates to the intended goals of the decision

FIGURE 19-1
Factors Facilitating Policy Research Utilization

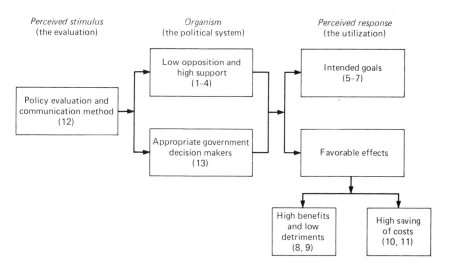

makers, and (5) it produces more benefits than costs in the eyes of the decision makers. The numbers in the diagram refer to the 13 factors discussed in the chapter.

Policy evaluation research requires an increased concern for utilization-oriented evaluation while continuing to comply with policy analysts' ethical obligations. These ethical obligations could include the following matters:

1. Policy analysts should find the policy or combination of policies to maximize a given goal or goals.
2. They should always do a sensitivity analysis to determine how their prescriptions might differ as a result of changes in measurement, entities, assumptions, or other inputs of their basic analysis.
3. They should not aid groups with illegal goals, such as racist redistricting designed to decrease the influence of minority groups below a reasonably proportionate level.
4. They should check for side effects and unforeseen consequences in conducting policy analysis.
5. They should be concerned with equity as a minimum constraint, and also as a constraint that is subject to a sensitivity analysis for determining how the prescriptions would differ if the equity constraints were changed.
6. They should try to keep research costs down.
7. They should seek to facilitate the secondary reuse of data which they have gathered.
8. They should be careful to avoid findings of questionable validity, including failure to control for alternative explanations or failure to use proper measurements, samples, and assumptions.
9. Policy analysts should be careful not to put people at risk, or else be sure informed consent is involved if this is impossible, although policy makers can and should be subject to being exposed as wrong-doers or as having undesirable biases in their decision making.[16]

Policy analysts can increase the likelihood of their evaluations being used if they emphasize a concern for validity (rather than simply writing for themselves, each other, readers who are not in a position to utilize the findings, or readers who are in a position, but are unlikely to do so because of the way the findings are presented). One can thus conclude that for policy analysts to make their findings useful, they should show or stimulate the presence of such factors in their research as: (1) bipartisan support, (2) compromise, (3) no overwhelming opposition, (4) interest group support, (5) acceptable societal goals, (6) congruence with individual goals, (7) congruence with unexpressed goals, (8) no offsetting adverse side effects, (9) reinforcement of prior decisions, (10) increased productivity, (11) possible private-sector value, (12) understandability, and (13) appropriateness of the policy-making forum.

The more these factors are emphasized, the more policy research will be utilized. Likewise, the more such research is utilized, the better off public policy will be, assuming the research is worth utilizing in terms of increasing societal benefits minus societal costs. How policy research can be more meaningful in terms of potential societal benefits and costs is the subject of other books on policy methods and substance. We hope this chapter will facilitate the actual utilization of the kind of policy evaluation research that credits the policy analysis field.[17]

NOTES

1. For further details on political scientists or political science in government, see Mary Curzan, *Careers in the Study of Political Science: A Guide for Undergraduates* (APSA, 1981); Robert Friedman, "Nonacademic Careers for Political Scientists," 10 *PS* 14–16 (1977); Erwin Hargrove, "Career Alternatives for Political Scientists" (APSA Committee on Professional Development, 1981); and "Can Political Science Develop Alternative Careers for Its Graduates?" 12 *PS* 446–50 (1979); Thomas Mann, *Career Alternatives for Political Scientists: A Guide for Faculty and Graduate Students* (APSA, 1976); Jack Walker, "Challenges of Professional Development for Political Science in the Next Decade and Beyond," 11 *PS* 484–90 (1978); and Francis Wilcox, "Some Remarks About the Relationships Between Political Science and Government Service," 11 *PS*, 332–35 (1978).

   For further details on social scientists and social science in government, see James McGregor, "Government Job-Hunting in Washington," 11 *PS*, 492–98 (1978); S. Nagel, *The Policy-Studies Handbook* (Lexington-Heath, 1980); Sharon Panian and Melvin Defleur, *Sociologists in Non-Academic Employment* (ASA, 1979); and Carol Weiss (ed.), *Using Social Research in Public Policy Making* (Lexington-Heath, 1977).

2. On research utilization in general, see Albert Cherns, *Using the Social Sciences* (Routledge & Kegan Paul, 1979); The Commission on the Social Sciences of the National Science Board, *Knowledge into Action: Improving the Nation's Use of the Social Sciences* (National Science Foundation, 1969); Irving Horowitz (ed.), *The Use and Abuse of Social Science* (Transaction Books, 1975); Irving Horowitz and James Katz, *Social Science and Public Policy in the United States* (Praeger, 1975); Charles Lindblom and David Cohen, *Usable Knowledge: Social Science and Social Problem Solving* (Yale University Press, 1979); Michael Patton, *Utilization-Focused Evaluation* (Sage, 1978); Carol Weiss (ed.), *Using Social Research in Public Policy Making* (Lexington-Heath, 1977); Carol Weiss and Michael Bucuvalas, *Social Science Research and Decision-Making* (Columbia University Press, 1980); and S. Nagel and Marian Neef (eds.), *The Political Science Utilization Directory* (PSO, 1975). The journal *Knowledge: Creation, Diffusion, and Utilization* occasionally contains articles relevant to the subject of facilitating the utilization of policy evaluation research. An example is Donna Kerr, "Knowledge Utilization: Epistemological and Political Assumptions," 2 *Knowledge: Creation, Diffusion, and Utilization* 483–502 (1981). The Nagel items cited in this chapter illustrate attempts to communicate policy evaluation research to policy makers. Some attempts were successful and others were not. One factor that facilitates eventual research utilization is a willingness to be unsuccessful, but to think positively about the value of systematic policy evaluation.

3. On pretrial release reform, see Charles Ares, Ann Rankin, and Herbert Sturz, "The Manhattan Bail Project: An Interim Report on the Use of Pre-Trial Parole," 38 *New York University Law Review* 67–95 (1963); John Goldkamp, *Two Classes of Accused: A Study of Bail and Detention in American Justice* (Ballinger, 1979); Wayne Thomas, *Bail Reform in America* (University of California Press, 1976); and S. Nagel and Marian Neef, "Bail, Not Jail, for More Defendants," 60 *Judicature* 172–78 (1976). On determinate sentencing reform, see Don Gottfredson, Leslie Wilkins, and Peter Hoffman, *Guidelines for Parole and Sentencing: A Policy Control Method* (Lexington-Heath, 1978); Robert Martinson, "What Works? Questions and Answers About Prison Reform," 35 *The Public Interest* 22–54 (1974); Richard Singer, *Just Deserts: Sentencing Based on Equality and Desert* (Ballinger, 1979); and S. Nagel, Marian Neef, and T. Weiman, "A Rational Method for Determining Prison Sentences," 61 *Judicature* 371–75 (1978).

4. On evaluating legal services for the poor, see "Representing the Poor" in Arthur Berney, et al., (eds.), *Legal Problems of the Poor: Cases and Materials* (Little, Brown, 1975), 500–88; Legal Services Corporation, *The Delivery Systems Study: A Policy Report to the Congress and the President of the United States* (LSC, 1980); "The Legal System and the Poor" in Eli Jarmel (ed.), *Legal Representation of the Poor* (Matthew Bender, 1972), 1-1 to 3-19; and S. Nagel, "Deciding How to Provide the Poor with Legal Counsel," 4 *Continuing Legal Education Review* 4–6 (September 28, 1973) and 6–7 (October 5, 1973).

5. On the evaluation and nonimplementation of the pollution tax, see William Baumol and Wallace Oates, *The Theory of Environmental Policy* (Prentice-Hall, 1975); Allen Kneese and Charles Schultze, *Pollution, Prices, and Public Policy* (Brookings, 1975); Walter Rosenbaum, *The Politics of Environmental Concern* (Praeger, 1977); and S. Nagel, "Incentives for Compliance with Environmental Law" in Lester Milbrath and Frederick Inscho (eds.), *The Politics of Environmental Policy* (Sage, 1975). On the evaluation and implementation of poverty law reform, see George Cooper et al., *Law and Poverty: Cases and Materials* (West, 1973); Joel Handler, *Social Movements and the Legal System: A Theory of Law Reform and Social Change* (Academic Press, 1978); Earl Johnson, *Justice and Reform: The Formative Years of OEO Legal Services Program* (Russell Sage Foundation, 1974); and S. Nagel, "The Poor are Getting Improved Law and Order Now," 116 *Chicago Daily Law Bulletin* 8 (12th Annual Law Day Edition, April 28, 1970).

6. On alternative methods for decreasing illegal police searches, see Chief Justice Warren Burger in *Bivens* v. *Six Unknown Named Agents of the Federal Bureau of Narcotics*, 403 U.S. 388 (1971); Jacob Landynski, *Search and Seizure and the Supreme Court: A Study in Constitutional Interpretation* (Johns Hopkins, 1966); Dallin Oaks, "Studying the Exclusionary Rule in Search and Seizure," 37 *University of Chicago Law Review* 665 (1970); Steven Schlesinger, *Exclusionary Injustice: The Problem of Illegally Obtained Evidence* (Marcel Dekker, 1977); and S. Nagel, "Testing the Effects of Excluding Illegally Seized Evidence," 1965 *Wisconsin Law Review* 283–310 (1965), cited by the Supreme Court in *United States* v. *Janis*, 428 U.S. 433 (1976).

7. On comparing elected and appointed judges, see Philip Dubois, *From Ballot to Bench: Judicial Elections and the Quest for Accountability* (University of Texas Press, 1980); Richard Watson and Randal Downing, *The Politics of the Bench and the Bar: Judicial Selection Under the Missouri Nonpartisan Court Plan* (Wiley, 1969); and S. Nagel, *Comparing Elected and Appointed Judicial Systems* (Sage, 1973). On evaluating the effects of women as jurors, see Kenneth

Davidson, Ruth Ginsburg, and Herma Kay (eds.), *Cases on Sex-Based Discrimination* (West, 1974); *Taylor v. Louisiana*, 419 U.S. 522 (1975); and S. Nagel and Lenore Weitzman, "Sex and the Unbiased Jury," 56 *Judicature* 108−11 (1972). On evaluating malapportionment in judicial electoral districts, see Robert Dixon, *Democratic Representation: Reapportionment in Law and Politics* (Oxford University Press, 1968) 559−64; *Wells v. Edwards*, 409 U.S. 1995 (1973); and S. Nagel, "Unequal Party Representation on the State Supreme Courts," 45 *Judicature* 62−5 (1961).

8. On the role of political science evaluation in redistricting, see Robert Dixon, *Democratic Representation: Reapportionment in Law and Politics* (Oxford University Press, 1968); Bernard Grofman, Arend Lijphart, Robert McKay, and Howard Scarrow (eds.), *Representation and Redistricting Issues* (Lexington-Heath, 1982); Andrea Wollock (ed.), *Reapportionment: Law and Technology* (National Conference of State Legislatures, 1980); and S. Nagel, "Computers and the Law and Politics of Redistricting," 5 *Polity* 77−93 (1972).

9. On the evaluation of alternative ideas for reducing paperwork, see Robert Fetter and Claude McMillan, *Introduction to Data Management* (Irwin, 1977); Alan Magazine and Beatrice Shields, "The Paperwork Forest: Can State and Local Government Find a Way Out?" 36 *Public Administration Review* 725−29 (1977); National Research Council, *Setting Statistical Priorities* (National Academy of Sciences, 1976); and S. Nagel, "Determining When Data is Worth Gathering," 16 *Society* 20−23 (Symposium on Paperwork Control, 1978).

10. On improving the instructions to jurors, see Bruce Sales, Amiram Elwork, and James Alfini, "Improving Comprehension for Jury Instructions" in Bruce Sales (ed.), *The Criminal Justice System* (Plenum, 1977); Rita Simon and Linda Mahan, "Quantifying Burdens of Proof: A View from the Bench, the Jury, and the Classroom," 5 *Law and Society Review* 319−30 (1971); and S. Nagel, "Bringing the Values of Jurors in Line with the Law" 63 *Judicature* 189−97 (1979).

11. Some of the research used by the Supreme Court in the jury-size cases includes Richard Lempert, "Uncovering Nondiscernible Differences in Empirical Research and the Jury-Size Cases," 73 *Michigan Law Review* 644−708 (1975); Michael Saks, *Jury Verdicts: The Role of Group Size and Social Decision Rule* (Lexington-Heath, 1977); and S. Nagel and Marian Neef, "Deductive Modeling to Determine an Optimum Jury Size and Fraction Required to Convict," 1975 *Washington University Law Quarterly* 933−79 (1976).

12. On alternative delay reduction methods, see Jan Chaiken, *Criminal Justice Models: An Overview* (Rand, 1975); Thomas Church, *Justice Delayed* (National Center for State Courts, 1978); and S. Nagel, Marian Neef, and Nancy Munshaw, "Bringing Management Science to the Courts to Reduce Delay," 62 *Judicature* 129−43 (1978). On reforming the plea bargaining system, see Arthur Rossett and Donald Cressy, *Justice by Consent: Plea Bargains in the American Courthouse* (Lippincott, 1976); *Plea Bargaining*, 13 *Law and Society Review* 189−687 (symposium issue, 1979); and S. Nagel and Marian Neef, "The Impact of Plea Bargaining on the Judicial Process," 62 *American Bar Association Journal* 1,020−22 (1976).

13. On predicting judicial decisions quantitatively for purposes of social science and law practice, see Layman Allen and Mary Caldwell, *Communication Sciences and Law: Reflections from the Jurimetrics Conference* (Bobbs-Merrill, 1965); *Evaluation Handbook* (Jury Verdict Research Co., 1960 et seq.); Colin Tapper, *Computers and the Law* (Weidenfeld & Nicolson, 1973); *Verdict Expectances* (Jury Verdict Research Co., 1960 et seq.); and S. Nagel, "Using Simple Calcula-

tions to Predict Judicial Decision," *The Practical Lawyer* 68–74 (1961). On scientific campaign allocation methods, see Robert Agranoff (ed.), *The New Style in Election Campaigns* (Holbrook Press, 1972); Robert Chartrand, *Computers and Political Campaigning* (Spartan Books, 1972); Arnold Steinberg, *Political Campaign Management: A Systems Approach* (Lexington-Heath, 1976); and "Allocating Campaign Funds" in S. Nagel, *Policy Evaluation: Making Optimum Decisions* (Praeger, 1982), 179–202. On the use of policy evaluation research in business lobbying and public affairs, see Joseph Nagel-schmidt (ed.), *The Public Affairs Handbook* (American Management Association, 1982).

14. On anticrime allocation through regression-calculus and through multiattribute analysis, see Ward Edwards and Robert Newman, *Multiattribute Evaluation* (Sage, 1982); Werner Hirsch, *The Economics of State and Local Government* (McGraw-Hill, 1970), 185–98; and "Allocating Anti-Crime Dollars Across Places and Activities," in S. Nagel, *Policy Evaluation: Making Optimum Decisions* (Praeger, 1982), 203–29.

15. On the communication of social science to judicial policy makers, see Bureau of Social Science Research, *Sources and Uses of Social and Economic Data: A Manual for Lawyers* (1973); Abraham Davis, *The United States Supreme Court and the Uses of Social Science Data* (MSS Information Corp., 1973); Harry Jones, *Law and the Social Role of Science* (Rockefeller University Press, 1966); Paul Rosen, *The Supreme Court and Social Science* (University of Illinois Press, 1972); and S. Nagel, "Law and the Social Sciences: What Can Social Science Contribute?" 51 *American Bar Association Journal* 356–58 (1965). On communicating evaluations to legislators, see Richard Brown (ed.), *The Effectiveness of Legislative Program Review* (Transaction, 1979); *Clients and Analysts: Congress*, 2 *Policy Analysis* 197–324 (Symposium Issue, 1976); Mark Chadwin (ed.), *Legislative Program Evaluation in the States: Four Case Studies* (Eagleton Institute, 1974); Leonard Saxe and Daniel Koretz (eds.), *Making Evaluation Research Useful to Congress* (Jossey-Bass, 1982); and Franklin Zweig (ed.), *Evaluation in Legislation* (Sage, 1979). On evaluating programs of administrative agencies, see Clark Abt (ed.), *The Evaluation of Social Programs* (Sage, 1976); Peter Rossi and Walter Williams, *Evaluating Social Programs: Theory, Practice and Politics* (Seminar Press, 1972); Joseph Wholey, John Scanlon, Hugh Duffy, James Fukumoto, and Leona Vogt, *Federal Evaluation Policy: Analyzing the Effects of Public Programs* (Urban Institute, 1970); and S. Nagel, "Applying a Decision-Making Perspective to the Administrative Law Process," 32 *Administrative Law Review* 107–19 (1980).

16. On the ethical obligation of policy analysts, see Joel Fleishman, Lance Liebman, and Mark Moore, *Public Duties: The Moral Obligations of Government Officials* (Harvard University Press, 1981); Joel Fleishman and Bruce Payne, *Ethical Dilemmas and the Education of Policy Makers* (Hastings Center, 1980); Keith Marvin, *Standards for Program Evaluation* (Evaluation Research Society, 1980); and Chapter 18 in this book.

17. For discussions of effective policy evaluation methods, see Duncan MacRae and James Wilde, *Policy Analysis for Public Decisions* (Duxbury, 1979); Edith Stokey and Richard Zeckhauser, *A Primer for Policy Analysis* (Norton, 1978); and S. Nagel, *Policy Evaluation: Making Optimum Decisions* (Praeger, 1982). For substantive discussions of policy evaluation, see James Anderson, David Brady, and Charles Bullock, *Public Policy and Politics in America* (Duxbury, 1978); Theodore Lowi and Alan Stone (eds.), *Nationalizing Government: Public Policies in America* (Sage, 1978); and S. Nagel (ed.), *Encyclopedia of Policy Studies* (Marcel Dekker, 1983).

QUESTIONS

1. How can the training and placement of aspiring policy analysts be improved so that they can obtain better jobs in government?
2. How can scholarly researchers be encouraged to work on policy-relevant subjects in a more useful way? How can policy practitioners be made more aware of useful studies that such researchers may be doing?
3. Give examples of policy evaluation or policies that succeeded or failed because of the presence or absence of bipartisan support, sensitivity for the need to compromise, overwhelming interest group opposition, or the lack of interest group support.
4. Give examples of policy evaluation or policies that succeeded or failed because the evaluation emphasized goals that were not socially or politically acceptable, or that were contrary to group or individual interests, or that were irrelevant to the real goals of the policy makers.
5. Give examples of policy evaluation or policies that succeeded or failed because of the presence or absence of offsetting adverse side effects as an obstacle, or the reinforcement of prior decisions as a facilitator.
6. Give examples of policy evaluation or policies that succeeded or failed because of their ability or inability to achieve prior results with less time and money, or because they had commercial value in the private sector.
7. Give examples of policy evaluation or policies that succeeded or failed because the ideas were too complicated to be well understood, or because the wrong policy-making forum was emphasized.

REFERENCES

Cherns, Albert, *Using the Social Sciences* (Routledge & Kegan Paul, 1979).
Curzan, Mary, *Careers in the Study of Political Science: A Guide for Undergraduates* (APSA, 1981).
Horowitz, Irving (ed.), *The Use and Abuse of Social Science* (Transaction Books, 1975).
Horowitz, Irving, and James Katz, *Social Science and Public Policy in the United States* (Praeger, 1975).
Koretz, Daniel, and Leonard Saxe (eds.), *Making Evaluation Research Useful to Congress* (Jossey-Bass, 1982).
Lindblom, Charles, and David Cohen, *Usable Knowledge: Social Science and Social Problem Solving* (Yale University Press, 1979).
Patton, Michael, *Utilization-Focused Evaluation* (Sage, 1978).
Rosen, Paul, *The Supreme Court and Social Science* (University of Illinois Press, 1972).
Weiss, Carol (ed.), *Using Social Research in Public Policy Making* (Lexington-Heath, 1977).

Weiss, Carol, and Michael Bucuvalas, *Social Science Research and Decision-Making* (Columbia University Press, 1980).
Wholey, Joseph, John Scanlon, Hugh Duffy, James Fukumoto, and Leona Vogt, *Federal Evaluation Policy: Analyzing the Effects of Public Programs* (Urban Institute, 1970).
Zweig, Franklin (ed.), *Evaluation in Legislation* (Sage, 1979).

GLOSSARY

The following concepts are defined in the context of public policy analysis. They are basic to understanding the discussion of the goals, means, and methods of public policy analysis, as well as the public policy profession.

allocation theory: see **optimum mix analysis**.

allowing combinations: the characteristic of a set of policy alternatives in which more than one can be chosen, but each alternative is a lump-sum alternative.

authority: persons, books, articles, or other entities that are knowledgeable about the relevant goals, policies, or relations.

basic benefit-cost analysis: see **optimum choice analysis**.

benefits: the effects (produced by alternative policies) which are considered desirable by the particular decision makers.

capitalism: private, nongovernment ownership of the major means of production, distribution, and other enterprises, with no governmental interference to equalize income or wealth.

causation: the relation between an output variable and an input variable whereby (1) the two variables move up and/or down together, (2) the input precedes the output in time, and (3) no controlling of a third variable eliminates the relation between the input and the output variables.

continuum alternatives: alternative policy choices which have inherent order and can be arranged along a continuum of possibilities, such as dollars allocated to a given policy.

costs: the effects (produced by alternative policies) which are considered undesirable by the particular decision makers.

decision theory: choosing among alternative policies in which the benefits or costs of each policy must be discounted by the probability of those benefits or costs occurring. Also called **optimum risk analysis.**

deductive analysis: drawing a conclusion from premises that are empirically validated or intuitively accepted, which generally relates to the effects of policies, although it could relate to what goals should be pursued or what policies are feasible. The basic model of recommending a policy from goals, alternative means, and relations between the goals and means is a deductive model.

democracy: a relation between a government and its people whereby governmental officeholders and policies are determined directly or indirectly by a majority

431

vote of an electorate consisting of all adults, with a provision for allowing opposition candidates and the free circulation of opposition ideas.

detriments: goals (other than monetary costs) that are to be reduced (unlike benefits), rather than increased, such as crime, pollution, illiteracy, disease, and so on.

discrete alternatives: alternative policy choices which have no inherent order and do not allow for multiples or partials on a policy, although they may allow for combinations of different policies. Also called **lump-sum or all-or-nothing alternatives**.

discretion: the extent to which decision makers are allowed to reach decisions within a range of legally permitted decisions.

effectiveness: the extent to which a policy is achieving its intended goals, or the quantity of benefits which a policy is achieving.

efficiency: the ratio of benefits achieved to costs incurred.

equality: the spread of the benefits and costs among various groups and places so they each have an equal share, which may not be equitable.

equity: the spread of the benefits and the costs among various groups or places in proportion to population, need, or other criteria of basic fairness.

ethical dilemma: a situation in which policy analysts are faced with decisions as to what they should do in performing their roles in the interest of societal desirabilty, and in which someone or society may be hurt by the decisions reached.

federalism: a relation between a national government and its provinces wherein a constitution delegates certain powers to the national government and certain powers to the provincial governments which neither can take away from the other.

freedom: mainly refers to the freedom of minority viewpoints to try to convince the majority, although the concept sometimes refers to entrepreneurial freedom to make money without necessarily considering damage to labor, the environment, consumers, or others.

goals: the objectives or criteria which a public policy is directed toward achieving.

government structures: how governments are positioned on (1) the relation between the national and state governments, (2) the relation between the legislative and executive branches of government, (3) the power of the courts to declare legislative and executive acts unconstitutional, (4) the two-party system, and (5) the democratic provision for majority rule and for minority rights to try to convert the majority.

human rights: basic principles as to freedom of speech and religion, equal treatment under the law, procedures for safeguarding the innocent from conviction or harassment, and basic economic security.

implementation: the process whereby it is attempted to convert a policy into benefits for those toward whom the policy is directed; an important issue is whether implementation should be done by the government or the private sector.

incentives: the manipulation of perceived benefits and costs to encourage socially desired behavior.

inference or inductive reasoning: the process whereby one generalizes from many specific instances to one or more characteristics or relations that cut across the instances.

initiative: situations in which people are encouraged to develop new ideas for handling social problems or consumer needs.

interdisciplinary analysis: using the methods, goals, or means that are associated with political science, economics, or sociology and psychology, or their applied counterparts of public administration, business administration, or social work and education, or occasionally other fields of knowledge.

judicial review: the power of the courts to declare legislative and administrative acts unconstitutional.

lump-sum alternatives: see **discrete alternatives**.

marginal rate of return: the number of goal achievement units that result from a 1-unit increase in a policy level or input, or the percentage of goal achievement units that result from a 1 percent increase in a policy level or input.

means: refers to public policies in the sense that they are methods toward achieving societal goals.

measurement: the positioning of a policy or a policy effect on a scale of present-absent, 0 through 100, 0 through 100 percent, -10 to $+10$, few to many, and so on.

methods: the techniques or procedures for either (1) determining the relations between policies and goals, or for (2) drawing conclusions from goals, alternative policies, and relations as to which policy or combination of policies is best under given constraints and conditions. Also refers to methods for clarifying and measuring goals and policies.

monetary: the characteristic of a policy or policy effect that is expressed in dollars or other money units.

monetize: the process whereby a nonmonetary policy or policy effect is given a value in terms of dollars or other monetary units.

mutually exclusive: the characteristic of a set of policy alternatives where only one can be chosen.

net benefits: the quantity of benefits minus costs produced by each policy.

opportunity: situations in which people can rise up to more rewarding jobs or investments of their time or resources.

optimizing: the process whereby one takes goals as givens and attempts to determine which policy or combinations of policies will maximize these goals subject to various constraints and conditions.

optimum choice analysis: choosing among alternative public policies in which each one is a discrete policy that does not allow for partial or multiple adoptions. Also called **basic benefit-cost analysis**.

optimum level analysis: choosing along a continuum of alternatives when doing too much or too little is undesirable.

optimum mix analysis or allocation theory: allocating a budget or other scarce resources among people, activities, places, or other units to maximize goal achievement subject to a budget constraint, or to minimize costs subject to a minimum satisfaction level, or to maximize benefits minus costs.

optimum risk analysis: see **decision theory**.

optimum timing: the arranging of the processing of governmental cases, applications for service, or other events to take the shortest ones first while maintaining a maximum time length on the longer ones.

percentaging analysis: handling multiple goals and multiple policies by giving each policy a part/whole percentage on each goal and then calculating a net percentage for each policy to determine: which one or combination is best, or how to allocate scarce resources among the policies.

policy evaluation: choosing among alternative public policies the one that scores the highest on benefits minus costs or some other related criterion.

policy studies: the study of the nature, causes, and effects of alternative public policies for achieving given goals.

political parties: groups of people whose purpose is to have their members elected to office, and/or their programs adopted, and who use the methods of campaigning for office for both purposes.

popular control: the substantial input into the decision making of businesses by consumers, employees, and voters.

predictability: the extent to which a policy is objectively applied so one can know in advance what the policy covers.

prediction: the process whereby one determines how many units an output variable is likely to change when there is a 1-unit change in an input variable, or the process whereby one determines how a variable is likely to score at a future point in time.

private sector: business activities and not-for-profit nongovernmental activities, although the latter activities are sometimes referred to as third-sector activities.

procedural fairness: the extent to which a policy is applied in such a way as to enable those who are deserving to defend themselves against accusations of being undeserving.

productivity: maximizing or increasing societal benefits minus societal costs, or societal benefits divided by societal costs, including nonmonetary benefits and costs.

public participation: the extent to which the majority of the affected public has a substantial impact on the policy, and the extent to which minority viewpoints are allowed to convert the majority.

public policy: governmental decisions designed to deal with various social problems such as those related to foreign policy, environmental protection, crime, unemployment, and others.

public policy analysis: determining which alternative policies, decisions, or means are best for achieving a given set of goals in light of the relations between the alternative policies and the goals.

public policy profession: the combination of individuals, training programs, research centers, associations, journals, ethical codes, job opportunities, and other institutions involved in public policy analysis.

public sector: governmental activities.

regression equation: an equation generally of the form $Y = a + bX$ which shows by b how many units Y changes for a 1-unit change in X, and which shows by a the value of Y when X is zero. Also, an equation of the form $Y = aX^b$ which shows by b the percentage change in Y for a 1 percent change in X, and which shows by a the value of Y when X is 1.

relations: the extent to which a goal is achieved or increases when a policy is adopted or is increased. Also, the extent to which any variable is present or increases when another variable is present or is increased.

reliability: the extent to which measurement of an input variable or an output variable is internally consistent across different measurement methods, measurers, or measurement periods.

research utilization: the extent to which policy evaluations are adopted by relevant people in government, or the extent to which they use policy studies to clarify or understand goals, policies, or relations between goals and policies.

sampling: analyzing the characteristics of or the relations between an input and an output variable by working with a relatively small set of persons, places, or things relative to the total quantity of the same persons, places, or things that could be analyzed.

satisficing: the process whereby one decides what minimum goal achievement would be satisfactory, and then seeks policies that will achieve this minimum goal level.

security: situations in which people have minimum anxieties about unemployment, inflation, crime, disease, war, and other occurrences that would be harmful to them economically, physically, or psychologically.

sensitivity analysis: the process whereby one varies the goals, policies, and relations between the policies and goals, or varies other inputs, and then determines how these variations affect the conclusions as to which policy or combination of policies should be adopted.

separation of powers: a relation between the legislative and executive branches of a government in which members of the legislature and the chief executive are each elected separately by the people rather than chosen by each other.

simplicity: the characteristic of policy evaluation procedures which require no calculus, preferably no algebra, possibly no arithmetic, and a minimum of expense.

socialism: government ownership of the major means of production, distribution, and other enterprises, and the equalizing of income and wealth.

sources: where the goals, policies, and relations come from, which tend to include (1) authority, (2) statistical and observational analysis, (3) deduction, and (4) sensitivity and guessing analysis.

statistical or observational analysis: analyzing specific instances to generalize about what the goals, policies, or relations might be.

threshold analysis: resolving policy evaluation problems by reducing them to questions of a form that asks whether one alternative is better than another without asking how much better or what the rank order of the policies is.

trends in policy analysis: changes over time that relate to goals, policies, methods, new professional institutions, or increased utilization.

validity: the extent to which measurement of an input variable or an output variable conforms to empirical reality. Also, whether or not a conclusion logically follows from its premises, which is logical validity as contrasted to empirical validity.

INDEX OF NAMES

442

SUBJECT INDEX

445